Today's White-Collar Crime

There are many good academic texts available on white-collar crime. However, there is no single book that serves as a single source for students interested in studying the field, both from a matter-of-fact investigative perspective, and as a decidedly academic endeavor.

This text discusses more than the basic theories and typologies of commonly encountered offenses such as fraud, forgery, embezzlement, and currency counterfeiting, to include the legalistic aspects of white-collar crime. It also provides the investigative tools and analytic techniques needed if students wish to pursue careers in the field. Because of the inextricable links between abuse-of-trust crimes such as misuse of government office, nepotism, bribery, and the realm of corporate corruption, these issues are also included in this work. The text also emphasizes the connection and coverage of white-collar crime and acts of international terrorism, in addition to the more controversial aspects of possible abuses of power within the public arena posed by the USA Patriot Act of 2001 and the asset forfeiture process.

Other unique features include a text and adapted readings format. The readings at the end of each chapter are mostly ethnographic in nature (true to the originals of the subject) and serve to capture and hold the interest of the student reader. The text provides the conceptual and theoretical frameworks to give long-term meaning to the readings. Activities and Exercises are also included in each of the ten chapters and a companion website provides additional test items and other instructor support material.

Hank J. Brightman is Associate Research Professor in the War Gaming Department of the United States Naval War College. He served as an Associate Professor and Chair of the Criminal Justice Department at Saint Peter's College from 2000–2008. He also spent 15 years in a variety of law enforcement, investigative, and intelligence analysis positions with the U.S. Department of the Interior, the United States Secret Service and the United States Navy.

Criminology and Justice Studies Series
Edited by Chester Britt, *Northeastern University*,
Shaun L. Gabbidon, *Penn State Harrisburg*, and
Nancy Rodriguez, *Arizona State University*

Criminology and Justice Studies offers works that make both intellectual and stylistic innovations in the study of crime and criminal justice. The goal of the series is to publish works that model the best scholarship and thinking in the criminology and criminal justice field today, but in a style that connects that scholarship to a wider audience including advanced undergraduates, graduate students, and the general public. The works in this series help fill the gap between academic monographs and encyclopedic textbooks by making innovative scholarship accessible to a large audience without the superficiality of many texts.

Books in the Series

Published:
Community Policing in America
Jeremy M. Wilson
Criminal Justice Theory
Edited by David E. Duffee and Edward R. Maguire
Criminological Perspectives on Race and Crime
Shaun L. Gabbidon
Race, Law and American Society: 1607 to Present
Gloria J. Browne-Marshall
Contemporary Biosocial Criminology
Edited by Anthony Walsh and Kevin M. Beaver

Forthcoming:
Not Just History: Lynching in the 21st Century
Kathryn Russell-Brown and Amanda Moras
White Collar Crime: an Opportunity Perspective
Michael Benson and Sally Simpson
White Crime in America
Shaun L. Gabbidon
Crime and the Lifecourse
Michael Benson and Alex Piquero
The New Criminal Justice
Edited by John Klofas, Natalie Kroovand Hipple, and Edmund J. McGarrell

Today's White-Collar Crime

Legal, Investigative, and Theoretical Perspectives

Hank J. Brightman
with Lindsey W. Howard

 Routledge
Taylor & Francis Group

NEW YORK AND LONDON

First published 2009
by Routledge
711 Third Avenue, New York, NY 10017

Simultaneously published in the UK
by Routledge
2 Park Square, Milton Park, Abingdon, Oxon OX14 4RN

*Routledge is an imprint of the Taylor & Francis Group,
an informa business*

© 2009 Taylor & Francis

Typeset in Sabon by
RefineCatch Limited, Bungay, Suffolk

Library of Congress Cataloging in Publication Data
A catalog record has been requested for this book

ISBN10: 0–415–99610–4 (hbk)
ISBN10: 0–415–99611–2 (pbk)
ISBN10: 0–203–88177–X (ebk)

ISBN13: 978–0–415–99610–5 (hbk)
ISBN13: 978–0–415–99611–2 (pbk)
ISBN13: 978–0–203–88177–4 (ebk)

Hank: To Sasha, for your patience with me during all of my weekend or late-night writing sessions when you would rather have been walking along the beach or sleeping. You are, and will always be, my most faithful friend.

Lindsey: To Brayden and Colby, my favorite readers and to Mr. Grubbs and his red pen. Lastly, to Dan, for just being, well, Dan.

Contents

Computers afford criminals a wide range of tools to engage in
everything from credit card fraud to blackmail and espionage.

Advanced Fee Fraud or "4–1–9" scams have been referred to
as the "national pastime of Nigeria." This article discusses
how such crimes are committed, who the victims usually
are, and why curtailing such offenses is important to
society.

Explores aspects of purchasing and contract fraud subsequent
to Hurricanes Katrina and Rita and the role of government in
combating such activities.

Examines one of the most noteworthy savings and loan scandals
of the 1980s and the controversial role that mediation played in
its outcome.

Looks beyond the consequences of President George W. Bush's
selection of Hurricane Katrina rogue Mike Brown as the head of
FEMA towards other controversial selections within his
Administration.

6 White-Collar Crime Theory: Origins and Early Developments

Examines Sutherland's quintessential general theory on why
people commit crime, Differential Association.

Understanding money laundering is critical to combating
terrorism. This article provides an excellent primer on
what money laundering is and those laws designed to
combat it.

How do employees embezzle from their businesses and why
should we care? Joseph T. Wells provides answers to both of
these important questions.

Examines the critical role that obtaining human intelligence
plays in combating terrorism.

List of Exhibits

Series Foreword

I have recently finished several years of teaching a course in white-collar crime. Although I tried several white-collar crime textbooks, I was continually disappointed by their quality. The students also seemed disappointed with the quality of what they were required to read.

Then, Dr. Brightman sent me a copy of his manuscript, and I was delighted with the freshness of his materials, his unique approach to the subject matter, and the depth of his understanding of white-collar crime. But given Hank Brightman's background, I was not surprised that he brings keener insights on white-collar crime than competing texts. His impressive background includes being an Associate Professor and Chair of the Criminal Justice department at Saint Peter's College; fifteen years in a variety of law enforcement investigative and intelligence analysis positions with the U.S. Department of the Interior, the U.S. Secret Service, the U.S. Navy; and currently, as Associate Research Professor in the War Gaming department of the U.S. Naval War College.

In addition to providing the standard sources and studies, ideological positions and disputes, theories, and typologies of white-collar crime, I am further pleased with a number of features of this book:

- The author's analysis of presidential leadership in the 20th century;
- His examination of public corruption in recent decades;
- His up-to-date information on technology and how it relates to white-collar crime;
- His matter-of-fact investigative perspective;
- His provision of investigative tools of analysis techniques that are helpful to students who are interested in pursuing careers in the field;
- His skillful connection and coverage between white-collar crime and acts of international terrorism;
- His balanced coverage of the controversial aspects of possible abuses of power within the public arena paved by the US Patriot Act of 2001 and the asset forfeiture process;

- The author's inclusion of ethnographic readings at the end of each chapter which provides a conceptual and theoretical framework to the subject under discussion.
- Professor Brightman's book is also user friendly for students, providing activities, exercises, and photographs.

In sum, this lively and readable book has marshaled an impressive array of materials which are current and are important in framing social policy in combating white-collar crime. Professor Brightman has done us all a service—those who teach no less than those who learn. This textbook is a job well done.

Clemens Bartollas
Professor of Sociology
University of Northern Iowa

Acknowledgements

No textbook ever published has been the work of just one person; but rather, such works are the result of a true team effort. In the case of this book, we are indebted to the following outstanding members of our profession:

Will Stadler—Your painstaking research and source verification were critical to ensuring the scholarly value of this text for future generations of students. We are most appreciative of your worthy efforts.

Lindsey Giselle Navarro—Your steadfast encouragement, enthusiasm, and candid feedback were invaluable to this project. Never give up on your dreams; no doubt you will accomplish them all.

Nadira Rahugnandan—the superior editing you provided on the original manuscript paved the way for a far more solid and coherent text than we could have otherwise produced.

Phil Walsky (U.S. Food & Drug Administration), Dave Torres (U.S. Secret Service) and Billy Higgins (Bureau of Industry and Security)—the contributions that you provided to the "spotlight" portions of this book help to set this text apart from other works in the field of white-collar crime.

Saint Peter's College students enrolled in Cj/So358 "Occupational & Economic Criminality" who provided feedback on the draft manuscript, especially Chris Shea, Dan Gubelli, John Rivera, Gina Cruz, and Amanda Klarmann—thank you all for sharing your thoughts on how to improve this text.

From the International Association of Law Enforcement Intelligence Analysts: Marilyn Peterson, Lisa Palmieri, Tom Nowak, and Rob Fahlman —your unrivaled knowledge of the law enforcement intelligence analysis process was critical to this project.

This work would never have come to fruition without the wisdom and kindness of three important mentors: Clem Bartollas, Frank Hagan, and Steve Rutter, all of whom would not let us give up on this book—there are no words to express our gratitude to you.

Lastly, we are also obliged to the following colleagues for their steadfast support and thoughtful recommendations for improving the text:

Saint Peter's College: Dr. Raymond Rainville, Dr. Daniel Simone Jr., Dr. Thomas Donnelly, Prof. Kari Larsen, Dr. Eugene Cornacchia, Dr. Mary Lou Yam, Dr. Fred Bonato, Dr. David Surrey, and Dr. Richard Cosgrove.

United States Naval War College: Prof. David Polatty IV, Dr. Stephen Downes-Martin, Commander David Sampson, Prof. David DellaVolpe, Dean Robert Rubel, Ensign Walter Berbrick, Ambassador Mary Ann Peters and Rear Admiral James P. "Phil" Wisecup.

Warren County College: Dr. Lisa Summins.

Seton Hall University: Dr. James Caulfield and Dr. Anthony Colella.

Southern New Hampshire University: Professor Ralph Rojas, Jr., Ms. Leah E. Capece, Esq.

Disclaimer

The views, opinions, and content expressed in this work are solely those of the author and do not represent the United States Naval War College, Department of the Navy, Department of Defense, or the United States Government.

1 Today's White-Collar Crime

Once upon a time, there was a form of crime considered so heinous and deemed so evil that simply being accused of committing it could yield banishment or capital punishment. The offense was not murder, rape, child pornography, or even terrorism. The crime was *forestalling*, and it was the biblical precursor to modern-day white-collar crimes such as fraud and price-fixing. In ancient times, forestalling, or deliberately withholding a portion of a merchant's supply of wheat, rye, or grain to inflate its value in the marketplace, could mean life or death for the working poor, and those who committed such offenses were dealt with harshly. Flash forward a millennium to September 11, 2001, when New York City Mayor Rudy Giuliani, in the wake of the destruction of the World Trade Center, immediately implemented controls to prevent local businesses from selling bottles of water for $10 to $15 each to the panicked citizens of Gotham. In doing so, he greatly curtailed price gouging and likely averted a public health crisis.

Instances of non-violent, illicit acts committed by an individual or organization for financial or other personal gain are certainly not new phenomena. Roman and Greek writings are replete with stories of fraudulent artworks and coins entering the marketplace and even the palaces of the emperors (giving birth to the Latin maxim of *caveat emptor*, meaning "let the buyer beware").

Expressions common to your parents or grandparents, such as "pig in a poke," which describes making a poor business decision, and "the cat's out of the bag," touted when a secret has been revealed, both trace their origins to the sixteenth century. During that time, when most goods and services were procured in open-air markets, consumers were urged to ensure that the livestock (e.g., lamb or calf) they purchased had not been switched with a cat or other small animal by an unscrupulous merchant prior to being wrapped in a burlap sack or bundle. In short, for as long as humanity has engaged in commerce, there have been individuals interested in obtaining more than they rightly deserve.

Yet swindling is not limited to simple merchants engaging in transactions in the marketplace. For simplicity's sake, if we examine the past 100 years, there have been numerous examples of public officials and corporate officers seeking to expand their power or prestige at the expense of others. Whether exploring the Teapot Dome Scandal of the 1920s, the production of defective military equipment during World War II, Nixon and the Watergate scandal, the savings and loan debacle of the early 1990s, or the Enron and WorldCom implosions at the start of the new millennium, public outcry has always been the same: "There ought to be a law." Of course, a myriad of laws have already been established to address white-collar crimes such as mortgage fraud and identity theft. Therefore, it is not the absence of laws, but the lack of enforcement of the various statutes, regulations, and ordinances that holistically comprise "Today's White-Collar Crime."[1]

What Is White-Collar Crime?

As an area of research, the concept of "white-collar" crime is relatively new. Unlike the study of violent crime, which is firmly routed in centuries-old classical and positivist theories of Beccaria and Lombroso, white-collar crime was not even defined until 1939. Just over 69 years ago, Professor Edwin Sutherland, Chair of the Sociology Department at Indiana University and the 29th President of the American Sociological Society, coined the now-famous term during a speech before the Society's delegates in Philadelphia. Sutherland contended that crimes were not perpetrated exclusively by the most economically disadvantaged members of society; on the contrary, he asserted that members of the privileged socioeconomic class also engaged in criminal behavior.[2] Moreover, while the types of crimes might differ from those of the lower classes (e.g., the doctor or lawyer embezzles from his firm while the street criminal engages in robbery), the primary difference between the two offenders was that the elite criminal was much less likely to be apprehended or punished due to his or her social status.[3] Needless to say, Sutherland's theory was extremely controversial, particularly since many of the academicians in the audience fancied themselves as members of the upper echelon of American society. Despite his critics, however, it must be acknowledged that Sutherland's theory of white-collar criminality served as the catalyst for an area of research that continues to this day.

In contrast to Sutherland, we, your authors, differ slightly regarding our definition of white-collar crime. While societal status may still determine access to wealth and property, the world has changed greatly since 1939. For example, the post-World War II Montgomery G.I. Bill afforded millions of veterans access to a college education. This allowed members of the lower socioeconomic classes the opportunity to expand their chances for advancement into the upper levels of society, both in the boardroom and via public office. Similarly, unfettered and inexpensive access to technology, such as personal computers and the Internet, now allow individuals to buy and sell stocks or engage in similar financial activities that were once the bastion of the Wall Street elite. Therefore, we believe that the term white-collar crime is much broader in scope, and includes virtually any non-violent act committed for financial gain, regardless of one's social status.[4] Fraud, forgery, embezzlement, counterfeiting, and misuse of public office are only a few examples of such offenses. Indeed, where does one draw the line between what was once considered a simple theft crime, such as pick-pocketing, and a 14-year-old kid engaged in an online phishing scheme to obtain credit card information?

Why Does White-Collar Crime Matter?

Despite the media sensationalism that surrounds crimes of violence such as rape, murder, assault, and robbery, it may surprise you to learn that the majority of incidents police respond to on a daily basis involve performing service calls (e.g., aiding disabled motorists, emergency medical assistance) and investigating non-violent (property) crimes such as burglary and vehicle theft.[5] According to the U.S. Department of Justice, aggregate public losses due to corporate fraud exceed the total costs suffered by individual victims of property theft. Identity theft is considered to be one of the fastest growing forms of crime in the United States today, yielding losses to individuals and businesses greater than $49 billion (USD) annually.[6] Dr. Jay Albanese, former President of the White-Collar Crime Research Consortium and author of *White-Collar Crime in America* noted:

> Little is known about the extent, seriousness, and impact of white-collar crimes on victims ... Until both the public and the government see white-collar crime as a problem of equal significance to conventional crimes, we will not achieve a comprehensive understanding of the extent of the problem.
>
> (1995, pp. 86–87)

As *New York Times* reporter Gene Racz reported in 2008, while street crimes (e.g., burglary, robbery, etc.) are estimated to inflict yearly losses of about $3.8 billion, crimes perpetrated by corporations and corrupt government officials may cost the American public ten times that amount, or approximately $500 billion per year. According to the Federal Bureau of Investigation (FBI), losses from non-health care-related insurance fraud (e.g., automobile fraud, false claims about damage to private homes and businesses, etc.) exceed approximately $80 billion annually.[7]

The Government Accountability Office (GAO) estimates that nearly 10 percent of federal funds allocated for significant domestic programs such as low income housing aid, food and medical support for children requiring such services, and educational materials are primarily lost to fraud, embezzlement, and public corruption. More than 3.4 million people are victimized each year by unscrupulous telemarketers and most of their victims represent the elderly population living on fixed incomes. As you will read later in this chapter, even in times of natural disaster, such as the 2005 Hurricane Katrina tragedy (Exhibits, 1.1, 1.2), the GAO estimates that nearly $1 billion in fraud occurred through the housing assistance scams and other false property claims made by alleged victims.[8] Lastly, a federal grand jury recently indicted three Army Reserve officers and two civilians on charges that they accepted more than $1 million in jewelry, cars, and cash in exchange for fraudulently steering contracts worth more than $8.6 million to dishonest contractors. The funds were meant to provide food, clothing, and essential services for Iraqi children. This is the fourth such case of Iraqi aid fraud in 2007 alone.

Our society bears the cost of fraud, forgery, embezzlement, and acts of official corruption by paying higher taxes, larger insurance premiums, and greater costs for basic goods and services while the working poor, children, and the elderly both here and abroad fail to receive the benefits of these

Exhibit 1.1 *Hurricane Katrina was among the worst natural disasters in American history. It also created a bureaucratic environment rife for fraud.*

Exhibit 1.2 Six Flags Amusement Park in the aftermath of Hurricane Katrina. Many of Louisiana's and Mississippi's most popular tourist attractions were devastated by this category five storm.

critical support programs. For example, the recent sub-prime mortgage fraud crisis in the United States has already cost financial institutions more than $175 billion and has placed nearly 2.4 million people—especially lower-income minorities—in jeopardy of losing their homes.

Challenges for Law Enforcement: Do You Have What It Takes to Answer the Call?

One of the most frustrating issues for law enforcement officials is the inability of the American criminal justice system to investigate, apprehend, and prosecute corporate officers or government employees who abuse their positions for personal gain. In his text entitled *Emerging Criminal Justice: Three Pillars for a Proactive Justice System* (1998), author Paul Hahn asserts that while the American criminal justice system may be well structured for combating acts of murder and mayhem, it is far less effective in the detection, apprehension, and prosecution of those who commit non-violent offenses, such as white-collar crimes.

Many of you reading this text are likely doing so because you are interested in a future career as a police officer, federal agent, district attorney, or even a state prosecutor. Indeed, you may have selected courses in criminal justice because you ultimately aspire to become a homicide detective or perhaps even the future commissioner of a major metropolitan police department. If so, you will soon realize that the river of success is best navigated not by investigating media-sensationalized crimes of passion and violence such as rape, murder, and robbery, but rather by developing investigative and analytical expertise in the more prevalent and challenging incidents of fraud, forgery, identity theft, embezzlement, counterfeiting, and corruption. Each year, the Federal Bureau of Investigation (FBI) opens more than 26,000 white-collar crime investigations. Why are these crimes so prevalent? Because as Lynne Hunt, former Section Chief for the FBI's Financial Crimes Division notes, "You hold up a bank, you get a couple thousand bucks and maybe get shot. With bank fraud, you push a couple of buttons and make a million bucks."[9] We have already mentioned that crimes such as insurance fraud, embezzlement, and abuse of public office yield annual dollar losses at least ten times higher than those resulting from street crimes. Equally importantly, they also deprive the American public—particularly our most impoverished citizens—of the full benefit of programs and services they truly need.

If this is still not enough to convince you of the importance of honing your skills in this area, consider that white-collar crimes are often committed along with violent crimes.[10] For example, a victim's credit card may be stolen during an assault, and the assailant may subsequently attempt to use this credit card to rent a car or purchase food while he or she attempts to elude authorities. In the most extreme cases, white-collar crimes such as identity theft or document fraud may be used to establish fictitious bank accounts in order to launder the proceeds of drug trafficking, or may ultimately serve as the conduit for funding acts of terror such as the horrific events of September 11, 2001. As evidence, consider that the *Al Qaeda Manual* (Exhibit 1.3) used to plan the World Trade Center and Pentagon attacks featured detailed instructions for producing forged documents and producing counterfeit currency as a means to finance their nefarious operations.[11]

What Do We Mean by "Today's White-Collar Crime?"

For serious scholars of white-collar crime, the history, definitions, theories, and typologies that encompass this field are broad and complex. However, because the purpose of this book is to introduce you to the basic concepts of white-collar criminality, we will work with a relatively simple definition. As discussed earlier in this chapter, we refer to a *white-collar crime* as a non-violent, illicit act, committed by an individual or organization for financial or other personal gain. By employing this definition, we can avoid including

Exhibit 1.3 Former Attorney General John Ashcroft displays a copy of the Al Qaeda Training Manual discovered in a raid in the United Kingdom. Among the topics included in this book are identity theft and credit card fraud.

a myriad of "street" crimes, such as robbery and extortion through violent means. This will also allow us to avoid a lengthy analysis of the differing sociological viewpoints germane to white-collar crime. First, because of the diversity of thought among leading scholars in the field as to the proximate causes of white-collar crime (e.g., socioeconomic, psychological, institutional, political, etc.), attempting to adopt a common definition of white-collar crime that satisfies sociologists, criminal justice practitioners, attorneys, and policy-makers would likely prove impossible. Second, the proactive nature of technological development and the reactive manner in which new laws are passed means that as innovative methods of committing white-collar crimes are discovered and subsequent efforts to thwart them become law, the definitive text would need to keep abreast of such changes or face obsolescence.

As you read *Today's White-Collar Crime,* you will observe that this book does more than discuss the leading theories of corporate criminality which have come to dominate this field of study. As an enhancement to theoretical examination, and in an effort to be as thorough as possible, we will also examine individual or small-scale incidents of fraud, forgery, embezzlement, and counterfeiting. We have included discussion of these offenses because, as the tragic events of 9/11 have demonstrated, investigations of seemingly petty acts of credit card fraud, identity theft, or currency counterfeiting may yield connections to larger organized groups engaged in drug trafficking, racketeering, or terrorism. The text also explores the analytical and investigative techniques presently being used within the law enforcement intelligence community to connect individual white-collar crimes to larger criminal entities. Ultimately, such analysis may help us to answer Paul Hahn's challenge posed earlier in this chapter by better investigating and prosecuting white-collar offenses and offenders (Exhibit 1.4). In doing so, this may also yield further benefits by curtailing the financial lifelines of drug cartels and terrorist cells.

Why Read This Book?

Unlike other texts devoted to the study of white-collar crime, this book is designed to elaborate beyond the theories and typologies of commonly encountered offenses such as fraud, forgery, embezzlement and currency counterfeiting. Indeed, this book will also expose you to the legal aspects of white-collar crime and present you with the investigative tools and analytical techniques necessary to pursue a career in this field. Because of the inextricable links between abuse-of-trust crimes such as misuse of

" The trouble with white collar crime is that nobody
knows what the hell it IS!"

Exhibit 1.4 One of the greatest challenges for both the public and private sectors is that white-collar crime is not readily understood.

government office, nepotism, and bribery and the realm of corporate corruption, we believe that these issues needed to be included in this work. While there are numerous excellent theoretical texts on white-collar crime, and a number of "war-story"-oriented works on the market that discuss the experiences of senior law enforcement professionals during their extensive careers, this is the first text that combines the theory and practice of white-collar crime research, investigation, and analysis with essential readings on topics ranging from mortgage fraud and cyber-crime, to government corruption and intelligence sharing.

Combining these topics with extensive experience in law enforcement and psychology, including more than fifteen years of experience in the areas of white-collar crime investigation, analysis, and behavioral assessment for the U.S. Department of the Interior, United States Secret Service, and the State of Connecticut, and by spotlighting the various law enforcement and research entities tasked with combating white-collar crime, you will be afforded the opportunity to ponder various career choices that may be available to you upon graduation. The book also features ten "thinking activity" sets intended to stimulate thought and classroom discussion in subjects ranging from media portrayals of white-collar criminals and processing search warrants, to corruption control and the analytical intelligence process.

Finally, as more than seven years have passed since the horrific events of September 11, 2001, and given the United States' significant investment in the "Global War on Terror" over the past five years, we have strived to maintain a connection between white-collar crime and acts of international terrorism. This book also explores possible abuses of power within the public arena by discussing the USA Patriot Act of 2001 and the asset forfeiture process.

After reading this text, you should be able to complete the following objectives:

1. Compare and contrast the featured readings found in each chapter with the theories and typologies of white-collar crime discussed throughout the text.
2. Define the legal elements of fraud, forgery, embezzlement, racketeering, and currency counterfeiting, as well as some of the "tools of the trade" employed by present-day forgers, counterfeiters, fraudsters, hackers, crackers, and those persons engaging in identity theft.
3. Articulate the roles and functions of various research, prosecutorial, and investigative agencies tasked with combating public corruption, waste, fraud, and abuse, identity theft, fraud, forgery, embezzlement, and counterfeiting of U.S. currency.
4. Differentiate between tactical and strategic models of intelligence, and articulate what situations dictate the use of each.

5. Discuss some of the likely trends in white-collar criminality in America in the near future, and some possible means to curtail such incidents.

Chapter Summary

Chapter 1 of this text provided you with a fundamental understanding of the origins of white-collar crime, and why it is as critically important that it be studied today as it was in the past. In addition to defining the term "white-collar crime," its links to the world's financial health, and connectivity to acts of terrorism, were also discussed.

ADAPTED READINGS

Reading 1–1: Donald Dekieffer, *Terrorists' Links to Commercial Fraud in the United States*

> *How does white-collar crime relate to the issue of terrorism? In the following article, you will have the opportunity to learn about counterfeiting, fraud, and the specific connection of these crimes to recent terrorist events.*

With the ongoing investigation of the terrorist attacks worldwide, it is gradually becoming known how these barbaric operations are being financed. What seems to be clear is that terrorists and their sympathizers have long used commercial fraud in the United States to raise funds for their activities. Although no one is sure as to the extent of these schemes, a few examples illustrate their *modus operandi*.

The 1993 World Trade Center bombing was financed, in large part, by an elaborate coupon fraud and counterfeiting conspiracy. Mahmud Abouhalima, Ibrahim Abu-Musa and Radwan Ayoub established a network of stores in New York, New Jersey and Pennsylvania, which were later identified as having associations with persons identified as the WTC bombers.

Adnand Bahour, the nephew of George Habash (leader of the Palestinian Liberation Front), set up a fraudulent coupon distribution network through his grocery stores in the Hollywood, Florida, area. Bahour was a kingpin in the national terror network creating money laundering and financing for the PLO. During the investigation and raid on the meeting hall of this network, more than 72 individuals from throughout the United States gathered in Hollywood to further their fraudulent coupon distribution network.

The Secret Service has reported that a massive credit card scam was being perpetrated by a group of Middle Easterners with affiliations to known terrorist groups. This scheme is a "Regulation Z" fraud or "Booster Check/Bust-out" scheme. The investigation revealed that a group of Middle Easterners, organized into cells located throughout the U.S., had applied for and received numerous credit cards. These cardholders systematically "boosted" the credit limits to the maximum amount available. Once they had established their portfolio of unsecured credit card debt, they submitted worthless checks as payment for these accounts in advance of purchases being made. In most cases, the checks were in amounts exceeding the cardholder's credit limits. Before the checks were returned as worthless, the cardholders purchased merchandise and obtained cash advances up to and sometimes in excess of the limits on the accounts. Losses to banks and merchants from these frauds were more than $4.5 million. Many of the fraudsters subsequently fled the country.

Several Islamic charities, which solicited funds and products from U.S. companies, are little more than fronts for terrorist organizations. Two examples of that would be the Wafa Humanitarian Organization and the Al Rashid Trust.

Numerous companies in the Middle East and elsewhere have been identified as agents for terrorists and/or states, which harbor terrorists such as Iraq and Libya. Several U.S. firms are known to have had transactions with them. For example:

- Iraqi Sanctions Regulations
- Tigris Trading, Inc., England
- Dominion International, England
- Bay Industries, Inc., California, USA
- Libyan Sanctions Regulations
- Corinthia Group Companies, Malta
- Oil Energy France, France
- Quality Shoes Company, Malta.

Further examples of activities in the U.S. to finance terrorist activities include:

- A massive cigarette smuggling ring in Detroit, smashed by the FBI, in which 19 people were arrested. The smugglers purchased large quantities of cigarettes in low-tax North Carolina and trucked them to Detroit where they were sold in Arab-owned convenience stores. The proceeds from this operation were being shipped to Hamas and other terrorist groups.
- A group of 14 Lebanese and Syrians were convicted on dozens of charges for operating a multi-state ring, which repackaged stolen and counterfeit infant formula. Much of the money acquired by this scam simply vanished, although there are some indications it was sent to the Middle East.
- Federal investigators have linked relatives and/or associates of long-time business operators in California, New York, Michigan, Illinois, Florida and Washington to bust-outs, phony checks, cigarette tax schemes, diversion

fraud, credit card fraud, counterfeit consumer products (including baby formula), insurance fraud and food stamp fraud. Investigations uncovered large amounts of cash wired from the United States to the Middle East and many of these frauds were conducted with paramilitary-like precision.

- Billions of dollars in orders for U.S. goods have been shipped to trading companies in the United Arab Emirates (UAE), especially Dubai, in the past year. More than 70 percent of all goods shipped to the UAE are subsequently exported, often to sanctioned countries such as Iraq, Iran and Afghanistan.

What Can Companies Do About This?

First, the most obvious but frequently ignored method of de-funding terrorists is to know your customer. The government regularly publishes lists of "denied parties" and updates its website, the Office of Foreign Assets Control, which can be accessed at www.treas.gov/ofac.

Second, be able to track your products. Detecting counterfeit and diverted goods is essential to knowing if you have a problem. There are several reputable companies that can help with packaging and marking technologies.

Third, after consulting your attorneys, contact law enforcement authorities such as the FBI if you suspect that you have had dealings with a suspicious individual or company.

U.S. companies can do their part to de-fund the terrorists. This is not business as usual. Being a victim of, and funding terrorists at the same time is not only naive, it can be deadly to an innocent party.

Business Check Conversions Now Allowed

Rudet Fountaini, National Sales Manager for ACM, recently informed NACM of recent changes in the management of electronic transfers of funds that allow business check conversions. These changes were implemented on September 15 by NACHA (The Electronics Payment Association): Before this recent change, Fountain said check conversions were only allowed for consumer checks.

Fountain said that one of the reasons businesses were not included in check conversions was that it was not easy to determine at the point of sale if a person writing the business check was authorized to give consent for conversion: However, the newly implemented changes mark a shift in the default position and allow for most business checks to be converted. Businesses, however, are given an opportunity to opt out of the check conversion process now that it applies to them. They can do so by either communicating verbally or by writing to a merchant; saying that they don't want to be involved in check conversion; or they can indicate on their checks that they don't participate in check conversion. To do this, Fountain said you must use business checks that contain an appropriate notation in the "auxiliary on-us field" on the far left of the business check's MICR line. This line, on the bottom of the check, typically contains such data fields as the account and check routing or transit numbers.

According to NACHA guidelines, some business checks are ineligible for conversion:

1. Business Checks that are printed on approximately eight to nine inch Check stock and use the auxiliary on-us field.
2. Checks greater than $25 000 under any circumstances.
3. Third party checks or sharedrafts.
4. Demand drafts and third party drafts that do not contain the signature of the receiver.
5. Checks provided by a credit card issuer for the purpose of accessing a credit account or checks drawn on home equity lines of credit.
6. Checks drawn on an investment company as defined in the investment Company Act of 1940,
7. Obligations of a financial institution (e.g., travelers checks, cashier's checks, official checks, money orders, etc.).
8. Checks drawn on the U.S. Treasury, a Federal Reserve Bank or a Federal Home Loan Bank.
9. Checks drawn on a state or local government that are not payable through or at a participating DFI.
10. Checks or sharedrafts payable in a medium other than United States currency.

Fountain said that ACM is considering offering services that would facilitate business-to-business check conversion made possible by this and other legislation, such as Check 21.

Source: NACM and American Check Management, January 1, 2007

Reading 1–2: Brad Heath, *Katrina Fraud Swamps System*

> *Hurricane Katrina is often considered to be among the worst natural disasters in American history. For many of us, it seems inconceivable that people would take advantage of this horrific tragedy for their own personal gain. However, as you will learn in the following article, a variety of forms of fraud proved quite problematic in the aftermath of Hurricane Katrina. As you read this article, consider the fact that white-collar crimes are acts of opportunity. Accordingly, natural disasters can readily serve as the platform for such illicit activities to occur.*

Federal agents investigating widespread fraud after the Gulf Coast hurricanes in 2005 are sifting through more than 11,000 potential cases, a backlog that could take years to resolve.

Authorities have fielded so many reports of people cheating aid programs, swindling contracts and scamming charities after the hurricanes that Homeland Security inspectors, who typically police disaster aid scams, have been "swamped," says David Dugas, the U.S. attorney in Baton Rouge.

"There's definitely a backlog," says Dugas, whose office helps coordinate an anti-fraud task force formed after the hurricanes. "Right now, that means we might not get to some cases as quickly as some people might like. If there's still a backlog in two years when we start running up against the statute of limitations, that's different."

Hurricanes Katrina and Rita triggered more than $7 billion in disaster aid to Gulf Coast households, plus billions more in government contracts and rebuilding projects. Allegations of fraud have accompanied that assistance, and prosecutors have vowed zero tolerance for people who tried to cheat the government.

About 700 people have been charged.

Most of the cases involve alleged lies to the Federal Emergency Management Agency to cash in on $2,000 payments it sent out shortly after the storms struck. In one, prosecutors charged that two roommates in Houston sent FEMA 39 claims for assistance for the two storms and lied about living in places hit by the hurricanes.

The Hurricane Katrina Fraud Task Force has referred 11,000 potential fraud cases to Homeland Security and a handful of other law enforcement agencies. Each of those was screened first to make sure there was some possibility of fraud.

Separately, the Government Accountability Office, Congress' investigative arm, identified 22,000 cases, though Dugas says many proved to be bookkeeping errors. The latest complete tally of its investigations, in September, listed more than 1,700 open criminal cases.

"It's difficult to compare those reports with other disasters, though fraud was clearly more widespread after the Gulf Coast storms," says Donna Dannels, who runs FEMA's Individual Assistance program.

When the storms hit, FEMA ignored some of its financial safeguards to get aid to victims more quickly. As a result, the GAO estimates FEMA spent $1 billion on improper disaster aid; auditors are separately reviewing storm contracts.

House Homeland Security Committee Chairman Bennie Thompson, D-Miss., says authorities should focus on those big cases first: "When the appearance is that all of your investigative might is being spent pursuing people who might have received duplicate vouchers, that's not the highest and best use of the resources of the federal government."

"Top priority usually does go to cases with the biggest dollar losses," says Marta Metelko, a spokeswoman for the Homeland Security Department's Inspector General. "It could be years before the agency's investigators can review all fraud claims," she says.

The cases include allegations of fake Social Security numbers or addresses. But authorities also have sought charges in more complex schemes. In one, the police chief in Independence, La., pleaded guilty to overbilling the government for overtime.

Other cases auditors had criticized—people spending aid money on jewelry or vacations—turned out not to be a crime, because federal law doesn't specify how the money must be spent, Dugas says.

Among the crimes authorities have pursued:

- Cheating FEMA: People who lied about where they lived to get disaster aid.
- Overbilling: Government contractors and others who overstated storm-related costs.
- Charity scams: People who posed as charity workers and kept the money.
- Social Security fraud: People who stole or made up Social Security numbers to get aid.

Source: *USA Today*, 6 July 2007

Thinking Activities

The aim of this chapter has been to provide you with an overview of what white-collar crime is, and why it is important to investigate and prosecute. In order to more fully appreciate the nature of white-collar crime, complete each of the activities listed below.

1. For three consecutive days, watch the evening news and read your local newspaper. Keep a tally of incidents of both violent and "white-collar" crime mentioned on these newscasts, and clip relevant articles from the newspaper. Do you see a trend in terms of crime reporting? In other words, do the media focus more on violent crime or white-collar crime? Why do you suspect this is the case?
2. Using one of the popular search engines found on the Internet such as Yahoo! or Google, conduct a search on the keywords "white-collar crime." Identify five websites listed in the search results. Are any specific organizations associated with these websites? Are any particular types of offenses listed more often than others?
3. Based upon Exercises 1 and 2 above, what do you think the media and the general public perceive about the nature of white-collar crime in American society? How might your perspective of these types of crimes change as a result of reading this book?

4. At this point in the course, do you feel that your skills, talents, and interests lead you towards a career in violent crime investigation, drug interdiction, or one of the forms of white-collar crime discussed in this chapter? Why do you feel this way?

2 Information Technology and White-Collar Crime

The location is a well-manicured New Jersey suburb. A well-dressed man in his late twenties sits at his solid oak computer table. The soft glow of the green-shaded brass banker's lamp casts gentle spots of light on his 24-inch color, flat-screen computer monitor. Within seconds, he has called up his secure web page via his state-of-the-art computer and cable modem. As he begins to download the 200 to 300 different credit card account numbers and cardholder names he obtained by infecting a local Internet Service Provider's server with a keystroke capture software program, he smiles. "Not bad," he mumbles to himself as he calculates the amount of money he should be able to transfer to the offshore account from which his terrorist organization routinely draws funds, "even better than last week's haul."

Shortly after the tragic events of September 11, 2001 unfolded in New York City, Washington, DC, and a rural field outside of Shanksville, Pennsylvania, our nation came together and resolved to combat terrorism at an unprecedented level. In the wake of this disaster, much of the attention of our political, law enforcement, and military leadership has focused on preventing biological/chemical warfare attacks and intercepting weapons of mass destruction that could be used against American interests both domestically and abroad. However, if there is one great weakness in America's "Global War on Terrorism," it is not our potential vulnerability at ports or border crossings, but how we protect our electronic infrastructure.

Properly executed, a simple "worm" or Trojan horse program could easily shut down the server of a major financial institution. Similarly, a denial of service attack on a Department of Defense computer system could result in failure to provide logistical support to troops headed for combat. Even simple information technology (IT) devices such as optical scanners, inkjet and laserjet printers, and laptop computers could be used to counterfeit thousands of dollars in U.S. paper currency, or produce fake drivers' licenses and other bogus forms of identification. Once manufactured and distributed, these counterfeit credentials could allow persons unauthorized access to secure facilities and therefore pose a potential threat to the general public.

Exhibit 2.1   A computer crime analyst conducts a forensic exam of a desktop computer. Analysts use special tools and techniques to uncover evidence of illegal activity on computer hard drives, CDs, DVDs, and memory devices.

Because this is a book about white-collar crime and not a treatise on global terrorism, this chapter focuses exclusively on the various tools, techniques, and methods employed by counterfeiters, credit card fraudsters, hackers, and crackers in furtherance of white-collar crimes (see Exhibit 2.1). Accordingly, this chapter will not discuss the use of information technology for purposes such as launching weapons systems or altering air traffic control patterns. However, the illicit activities discussed in this chapter (currency counterfeiting, access device fraud, and hacking and cracking secure systems for the purposes of obtaining and using financial information) could easily be applied to the funding of potential terrorists who could engage in acts of mass violence or destruction.

A Brief History of the Role of Information Technology in White-Collar Crimes

In order to more adequately comprehend what law enforcement deems "IT" or "high technology" crimes, below is a short chronology of commonly encountered "tricks-of-the-trade" from 1972 through to the present.

- In the early 1970s, "phone phreaks" used homemade devices known as "blue boxes" to dial telephone numbers anywhere in the world. "Blue boxes" emitted a high-pitched squeal that duplicated the 2600-hertz tone that controlled American Telephone & Telegraph (AT&T) switching equipment. Contemporaneously, AT&T began using computers to pinpoint "hot spots" where fraud was commonly occurring throughout their telephone network.[1]

- In the late 1970s, modems were developed for non-military use, allowing electronic data to be transmitted via commercial telephone lines. Major corporations and government agencies were among the first users to embrace this technology. Almost immediately, hackers began to emerge on the national scene.

- Because laws governing unauthorized access to computer networks were inadequate, Congress enacted the Comprehensive Crime Control Act of 1984. This Act allows the United States Secret Service and other law enforcement agencies to enforce computer trespass and credit card fraud laws. Two supplemental statutes, the Computer Fraud and Abuse Act, and Electronic Communications and Privacy Act were passed in 1986.

- The Internet emerged in the mid-1980s. Originally known as the Advanced Research Project Network (ARPANET), this network allowed the exchange of information in more than 50 countries worldwide and was used mostly by colleges and corporate research centers. By

Exhibit 2.2 How do we protect ourselves from phishing scams, identity theft, and hackers and crackers? By practicing good information security and using a bit of common sense.

1990, Arpanet had ceased to exist as a separate entity, and became absorbed into a myriad of e-mails and other networks collectively known as the Internet.[2]

- By 1994, Internet user costs had dropped dramatically, allowing non-commercial entities to go "online." Technology also improved logarithmically, allowing graphics and other files to be transmitted easily between users. Encryption and related file coding technologies allowed users to send secure information to one another, even if such transmissions were for nefarious purposes (e.g., trading of cellular telephone access codes, credit card account numbers, etc.).

- The widespread availability of "MP3s," a web-based method of distributing music via the Internet has resulted in numerous copyright infringement and piracy cases. One such example is the conviction of an Oregon college student. According to *The Chronicle of Higher Education*, Jeffrey Levy, a senior at the University of Oregon, pleaded guilty to using the campus' computer network to traffic "thousands of pirated computer programs, movies, and music recordings from a Web site to interested parties."[3]

Computer-Based Crime: A Cause for Alarm?

As a student, you probably have access to a computer at school, home, work, or perhaps at all three locations. Reflecting on your life experiences and the history of technology, have you noticed that you have more access to computers and other forms of information technology than you did just a few years ago? What about the cost of procuring technology? How much did an iPod or MP3 player cost two years ago? How much is one now?

Less than ten years ago, approximately 19 percent of computer users in the U.S. purchased goods and services over the Internet. According to the International Communications Group by 2008, the number of Americans using the Internet to purchase goods and services increased to 72 percent in 2007. Consider the following additional statistics: According to the International Communications Group:

- Each day, Dell Corporation alone sells more than $14 million in computer hardware and software.
- According to Plunkett Research Ltd., as of December 1998, there were 147 million people worldwide using the Internet. By December of 2008, this number is estimated to exceed 1.3 billion, with over 210 million in China alone.[4]

This research indicates that more people than ever will have access to information technology in the years to come. Given the relative ease with which computers and other electronic devices can be used to perpetrate white-collar crimes, professors, researchers, and law enforcement personnel must continually familiarize themselves with technological innovations and frequently monitor white-collar crime trends involving computer use.

In addition to advances in network capabilities, hardware has continued to rapidly improve since the mid-1990s. The availability of inexpensive, high-quality image scanners and color printers has led to an increase in inkjet counterfeit U.S. currency (Exhibit 2.3), credit cards, and false identification. Lastly, improved video graphics adapters (VGAs) and audio drivers have greatly enhanced images that can be transmitted via the Internet. This, in turn, has increased the demand for—and the ability to create—contraband images such as "clean" U.S. currency graphics, "sample" credit cards, and other identification documents. These items can be easily reproduced by computer users. By transferring data to an Internet Protocol (IP) address, the offender can store illicit information in a secure, off-site location thus preventing the discovery of this evidence on his or her computer's hard drive, R/W-CD ROM, DVD, or memory stick.

Exhibit 2.3 Counterfeit U.S. currency can often be difficult to detect, and often requires considerable close-up inspection.

Currency Counterfeiting: From "Raised" Notes to Inkjet Printing

It is a hot, muggy August afternoon in Compton, California. As we enter Stephanie and Randall's fifth floor apartment, we are immediately overwhelmed by the mustiness present throughout the room, and the aroma of overheated inkjet cartridges. Despite the presence of several fans rhythmically oscillating from the corners to the center of the room, Stephanie and Randall are drenched in sweat, which periodically drips on to the stack of ivory-laid papers that contain double-sided images of $20 Federal Reserve notes. "Just a few more changes using desktop publishing, and we'll be able to pass these on the street," Stephanie shouts to Randall, endeavoring to be heard over the churning of the four inkjet printers and the humming of the laptop computer attached to each.

As shown in the previous scenario, the widespread availability of low-cost information technology, particularly desktop and laptop computers, scanners, and inkjet printers has likely accelerated the act of counterfeiting U.S. currency. Yet counterfeiting is not a new problem for the United States. In fact, by the time of the Civil War's onset in 1861, nearly one-third of all currency in general circulation was estimated to be counterfeit.[5] Compounding this problem was the extensive range of bank designs—more than 1,600—used by states during the period 1793–1871, which resulted in the circulation of over 7,000 varieties of bank notes. In order to standardize currency in the United States, the Act of July 17, 1861 was passed, which allowed the U.S. Treasury Department to print and circulate Demand Notes, or "greenbacks." Shortly thereafter, in 1862, the Treasury Department was permitted to issue United States Notes, which were also known as "legal tender notes." Subsequent printing of National Bank Notes (1863–1929) and Silver Certificates (1878–1923), coupled with the Federal Reserve Act of 1913 which established the National Federal Reserve System and authorized issuance of the Federal Reserve Bank Note (FRN), further aided in defining America's national monetary instruments.[6]

Perhaps most important in the protection of United States currency was the establishment of the United States Secret Service (USSS) in 1865. Initially, Congress charged the USSS exclusively with suppressing counterfeit U.S. currency. While additional responsibilities in the areas of financial institution fraud, forgery, embezzlement, access device fraud, telecommunications fraud, computer crimes, and most notably, presidential and dignitary protection have been added to the USSS' mission, the suppression of counterfeit

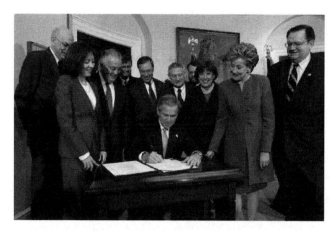

Exhibit 2.4 President George W. Bush signs H.R. 2622, the Fair and Accurate Credit Transactions Act of 2003, into law during a ceremony in the Roosevelt Room on Thursday, December 4, 2003.

U.S. currency remains a core function of its operation. Similar efforts to curtail counterfeiting across international borders were cemented at the Convention of the League of Nations on April 20, 1929. More than 104 countries and territories have ratified the 1929 Convention.

Today, the seditionist intent of the Confederacy during the Civil War to destabilize the American dollar, subsequent efforts by Adolph Hitler to produce counterfeit British £5, £10, £20, £50 notes during World War II, and the desire of extremist Middle Eastern groups to devaluate Western currency through aggressive counterfeiting of U.S. $100 FRNs during the mid-1990s have yielded less-structured, less-dogmatic—but no less significant—efforts to illegally reproduce U.S. currency. Skilled artisans such as Ivan Miassojedof and Sali Smolianoff, who painstakingly produced U.S. $100 FRNs in post-World War II Germany (c. 1945) using their own engraving plates, inks, and papers, are a far cry from the quick computer scan and inkjet printing methods of casual counterfeiters in the 1990s and today.

When it comes to the issue of manufacturing counterfeit currency (or altering genuine currency to increase its value), the laws are actually relatively simple. As described in Title 18 United States Code (USC), Section 471, currency counterfeiting allows for fines of up to $5,000, 15 years imprisonment, or both. The possession of counterfeit U.S. obligations with the intent to defraud is also punishable by a fine of up to $15,000, 15 years imprisonment, or both (18 USC 472). Similarly, "printed reproductions," such as photographs of checks, bonds, securities, or paper currency, are prohibited by 18 USC 474, and include penalties of up to $5,000, 15 years imprisonment, or both.

To illustrate the ease with which such activities can be performed, consider the following examples of currency altering and counterfeiting, ranging from the least technologically advanced (i.e., *raised notes*) to the most skill-intensive (*offset printing*):

- One method of altering genuine U.S. currency is to glue a piece of a higher denomination bill to the corner of a bill of lower denomination. By fanning several of these notes together with just the corners exposed, the notes can be passed at a bar, nightclub, or other location where currency is usually exchanged quickly without thorough inspection. This type of activity is known as passing a *raised note*.
- Black-and-white, monochromatic, or color copiers can be used to produce high-quality reproductions of genuine U.S. currency. The higher the image quality, the more likely that the validity of the note will not be questioned. In many cases, black-and-white copies of genuine FRNs are hand-colored by the suspect or another party involved in the offense.
- Much like the "Stephanie and Randall" scenario presented earlier in this chapter, simply by using an inkjet printer (i.e., a computer peripheral printer that uses water-soluble ink), the suspect can produce a high-quality counterfeit note when the printer is connected to a desktop or laptop computer and image scanner. This form of counterfeit currency is referred to by the United States Secret Service as a "P-note." Many U.S. currency images are also available through illicit Internet web pages, thus allowing the user to avoid purchasing a scanner altogether. Armed with an inexpensive graphic editing software program, the suspect can further alter or enhance the counterfeit note, thus improving the odds that it will be successfully passed.
- In large-scale, organized counterfeiting operations, an offset printing press may be purchased. Through a combination of homemade engraved plates, blank die stamps, collotype, or silk screening, the printers attempt to create the impression of "relief" that is found only in genuine U.S. paper currency produced at the Treasury's Bureau of Printing and Engraving.
- A wide range of papers are used to simulate the unique feel and texture of genuine U.S. currency. Ivory-laid, medium stock paper is frequently used. In some cases, suspects attempt to "draw" fibers of various colors into the paper prior to printing, in an effort to replicate the fibers found in genuine U.S. notes. Either prior to or after printing, false watermarks and security threads are copied into the counterfeit note, thus creating

the appearance that the note is genuine. Lastly, black and green glitter may be used to simulate the color-shifting ink found in authentic U.S. paper currency.

As described later in this chapter, many U.S.-based counterfeiting activities are not intended to destabilize the American economy, but rather stem from a desire on the part of the offender to obtain goods and services for personal use.[7] Organized, capital-intensive operations which require equipment such as offset printing presses have given way to the "casual counterfeiter" who produces $100–$200 in total in counterfeit $20 FRNs for immediate, personal gain. Such trends become evident when publicly available data relating to the U.S. Secret Service's suppression of counterfeiting "plants" (i.e., equipment set up for the purpose of creating counterfeit U.S. currency) are examined.

For example, in 1995, there were approximately 29 plant suppressions for inkjet printer/computer set-ups. By comparison, about 321 of these types of plants were destroyed by the U.S. Secret Service in 1997. While the destruction of "P-note"-producing plants increased, the number of offset plants decreased, from 60 seized and destroyed in 1995, to 23 in 1997. Lastly, by 1998, 43 percent of the counterfeit currency seized in the United States had been produced on inkjet printers—an increase of 8500 percent![8]

It is important to remember that currency is not the only item counterfeited by white-collar criminals. In fact, there has been a rapid increase in the counterfeiting of software and information technology equipment from the late 1990s through the early twenty-first century. In 1999 alone, U.S.-based firm Lucent Technologies uncovered more than 43 reels of counterfeit SYSTIMAX Power Sum 1061 copper cable, and 130 cases of counterfeit SYSTIMAX products in various retail outlets within the Republic of China.[9] On October 25, 2000, Adaptec Inc., an electronic information storage provider located in Milpitas, California, seized more than US$1 million in counterfeit software and peripherals from six American companies.[10] Similarly, Microsoft Corporation, the largest provider of computer operating systems in the world, seized more than US$1 million worth of counterfeit software from two Georgia businesses that were allegedly distributing unauthorized versions of Windows 98 and Office 2000 Professional Edition.[11] U.S. law allows for penalties of up to US$2 million and ten years imprisonment for each incident of breach of trademark and copyright infringement.

Hacking and Cracking

There are a variety of websites and computer applications available which afford prospective thieves the opportunity to engage in white-collar crimes.

For example, armed with readily available public domain software programs such as *CreditMaster, Credit Wizard, Axgene,* or *CardPro,* virtually anyone can generate fraudulent credit card numbers using only a simple personal computer. Credit card numbers are based on an algorithm utilized by the credit card manufacturers at the time of card issuance. After obtaining these numbers, they can be entered into a "war dialer"—a simple program that allows the credit card numbers to be entered into an automated long-distance calling system. If the call goes through, the suspect can record the card number, and then use this information to purchase a variety of goods and services via the Internet. In some cases, he or she may also sell the computer-generated card numbers to other parties, so that they can also acquire goods and services.

In addition to credit card number generators, numerous websites, such as "Wall's Hacker and Cracker Links"[12] are available via the Internet for the prospective white-collar criminal. The above-mentioned site lists approximately 2,000 software applications and tools that are available free of charge to the general public. Programs range from "touch-tone dialer for bank services," to applications to "credit card copier schematics."

Hacking is defined as accessing a restricted system through an exposed security flaw. For example, individuals can run a subroutine or script to divert resources away from a security scheme. Another tactic is a denial of service (DoS) attack which fools the host computer with a null password string or an invalid operation code. This allows a hacker with basic programming skills to gain unauthorized access to a wide range of commercial websites, government systems, and personal electronic mail networks. Worms and Trojan horses allow the target computer to "think" it is executing a simple program when it is in fact performing an additional task. For example, the application "Back Orifice," which was widely distributed in 1998 by the "Cult of the Dead Cow Hacker Club," allowed potential attackers to receive copies of all of the keystrokes entered on a target's computer.[13] Periodically, the infected computer would e-mail all of the keystrokes entered into memory to a secure file transfer protocol (ftp) web page belonging to the suspects. They would then be able to record system passwords, credit card numbers, and other personal information entered into the victim's computer for their own financial gain.

By comparison, *cracking* refers to utilizing system access codes (e.g., username/passwords, account numbers/PINs) to gain unauthorized entry to an access device. These codes or passwords may be obtained through social engineering such as "schmoozing" a co-worker to get their username and password, or sending someone a bogus electronic mail message that claims to be from an Internet Service Provider, bank, or Web merchant and requests personal access information. For example, many users of the popular online electronic payment service PayPal—which is linked to the eBay auction

Website—recently received an electronic mail message stating that there was a problem with their accounts. Recipients were asked to provide their PayPal account information, credit card number, and account number using a form in the body of the e-mail message. This technique, known as *phishing*, allowed several crackers to purchase goods and services from eBay prior to the hoax being detected.

Another form of cracking is referred to as "dumpster diving," which means simply sifting through a home or business trash receptacle or dumpster in hopes of finding discarded—but valid—user names, passwords, or access codes that may prove fruitful for the cyber-criminal.[14] Many offenders employ combinations of hacking, cracking, and phishing methodologies in their endeavors.

Information technology infrastructure damage caused by hackers and crackers has reached staggering levels in just the past few years. For example, recent viruses including worms (the most powerful and destructive form of virus) have resulted in events such as the "Code Red" attack in 2001, which impacted more than 30,000 computers worldwide in just fourteen hours. Such crimes are not restricted to just U.S.-based websites. According to a recent press release of the Indian Government in New Delhi, 612 websites were defaced in March 2008 compared with to 214 websites the previous month with no end in sight.[15] Allen *et al.* (2000, p. 24) have prophetically noted: "as the Internet and other national information infra-structures become larger, more complex, and more interdependent, the frequency and severity of unauthorized intrusions will escalate." As we move towards more centralized information systems, such as those proposed by the Defense Department's Information Awareness Office for combating terrorism, savvy hackers and crackers could gain access to an individual's sensitive medical, financial, employment, and public records through a single server, thus creating the possibility for widespread incidents of identity theft.

Identity Theft: The Future is Now

As we discussed in Chapter 1 of this book, identity theft (sometimes also referred to as identity takeover) is considered to be America's fastest growing consumer crime, affecting the lives of more than eight million people during the first quarter of 2008 alone—an increase of more than 50 percent from 2003.[16] According to the National White-Collar Crime Research Center (NW3C), the costs associated with identity theft are rising so rapidly—both in terms of total dollar loss and the emotional toll it takes on its victims—that it is becoming increasingly difficult to quantify. For example, in 2002, identity theft accounted for more than $343 million in losses, compared with $160 million the year before, and the average victim spent more than 28 months fighting to restore his or her credit (NW3C, 2003). In just one case five years ago, more than 30,000 victims were defrauded of $2.7 million in a scam in which the suspects, Linus Baptiste and Hakeem Mohammed of the New York Metropolitan Area, stole personal information during their employment at a data management and storage company affiliated with the major credit reporting bureaus.[17] Similarly, 2007's TJX data theft case placed more than 47.5 million people who shopped at T.J. Maxx and Marshalls at risk for possible identity theft.[18]

Law enforcement officials continue to see an influx of altered and counterfeit forms of *source* documents. Source documents, sometimes referred to as *foundation* records, are used to establish a person's identity for the purpose of establishing credit, making financial transactions at a bank, or gaining access to areas or information not generally available to the public. Examples of source documents include birth certificates, social security cards, drivers' licenses, vehicle registrations and titles, high school and college transcripts, tax records and business forms. Scores of identification websites exist from which both genuine and counterfeit source documents may be purchased for a nominal fee and downloaded from the web to the forger's desktop computer or laptop. Using a variety of inexpensive desktop publishing software (or counterfeit or pirated copies of genuine software), the forger is able to construct an alternate identity that can be used to obtain genuine credit cards in the name of the fictitious party, cash counterfeit checks, and conduct other illicit transactions. Legitimate check printing programs, such as the commercially available Versa Check mentioned earlier in this book, can be used to produce authentic-looking checks for fictitious persons or businesses.

Genuine checks from a business or an individual can be captured electronically using an optical scanner. Later, the payee name, dollar amount, authorized signature of the approving official (referred to as the *maker*) or endorsement can be altered using desktop publishing software, and the document can be printed on commercial check stock, which is readily available at most office and stationery stores. The forged or counterfeited foundation records are then used to obtain credit cards, secure mortgages, and purchase automobiles or other luxury items. In some cases, the forger will secretly obtain personal identifying information from an unsuspecting person, construct an altered or counterfeit source document, and use this information to purchase goods and services in the name of the victim. These types of offenses, referred to as *identity takeover* or *identity fraud*, are becoming increasingly common to the United States and other industrialized nations.[19]

It is important to note that identity theft need not be an IT-based crime. Through *social engineering*, a suspect can simply misrepresent oneself over the telephone as a representative of a credit card bureau, financial institution, law enforcement agency, or business for the purpose of obtaining a legitimate cardholder's name, card number, PIN, or other personal information in order to fraudulently use this information. The would-be offenders can also intercept a pre-approved credit card offer or loan application through the mail, and change the address to which the card or loan disbursement check should be sent. One of the most common and basic forms of perpetrating identity theft is through *dumpster diving*, which was discussed earlier in this chapter. Unfortunately, many people do not properly shred discarded mail that has been sent to them. Often, these mailings, such as utility bills and insurance statements, contain sensitive personal information that can be used by fraudsters as a source document to obtain genuine identification. Alternatively, the white-collar criminal could simply complete the application for a pre-approved credit card or loan, giving an alternate address.

As you will learn from your reading in this chapter on Nigerian advance-fee fraud, identity theft has taken on an increasingly global dimension. When the oil industry in Nigeria began to collapse in the 1980s, highly-educated engineers, lawyers, and doctors endeavored to find other ways to survive. Technology yielded a relatively easy way for Nigerians to perpetrate "get rich quick" schemes on unsuspecting Westerners. Indeed, as Insa Nolte of the University of Birmingham's African Studies Department recently commented, "The availability of e-mail helped to transform a local form of fraud into one of Nigeria's most important export industries."[20]

The success of the Nigerians in harnessing technology to more efficiently engage in white-collar crimes serves as a harbinger for others who would seek to use computer hardware and software to commit acts of identity theft, credit card fraud, and currency counterfeiting. Without question, there is an inextricable link between the availability of inexpensive, sophisticated information technology and the prevalence of white-collar crime in the twenty-first century.

Chapter Summary

Chapter 2 provided you with insight into the range of white-collar crimes that often involve the use of information technology. A history of information technology-based crimes was presented, as was information on commonly encountered offenses such as fraud, forgery, currency counterfeiting, and identity theft. As illustrated by these various techniques, credit and debit card fraud, like currency counterfeiting, can be accomplished in many different ways. Indeed, the scope and complexity of the offense is limited only by the suspect's imagination and level of access to technology.

ADAPTED READINGS

Reading 2–1: Amber Ennis, *A Look at Crime in the Age of Technology*

Many of us could not consider life without computers. Indeed, they make our lives easier in a variety of ways. However, as the following article will demonstrate, the rapid infusion of information technology into our society is not without its unintended consequences.

Considering the overwhelming influx of new technology around every corner, it is no surprise that computer-related fraud is becoming more and more commonplace. In fact, modern technology, while offering instant information and communication for many, has given criminals a new avenue to carry out carefully meditated crimes. The advances of digital technology offer a sense of security for criminals attempting to maintain anonymity in cyberspace. Whether a false security or not, these technologically savvy criminals are using computers for a variety of crimes.

Although web-based applications such as eBay and online banking are designed to make consumers' lives easier, oftentimes, there are kinks in the system that foster fraud. In February of 2004, 19-year-old Cole Bartiromo pled guilty to multiple counts of fraud involving an eBay scheme (Yang, 2004). Bartiromo, along with two others, was offering various items for sale on the auction site; on receiving payment from the winning buyers, he never sent the purchases. Additionally, he was charged with bank fraud for attempting to persuade a bank employee to wire $400,000 to an offshore account. Bartiromo also planned to have the eBay checks cashed and wired to the account.

While Bartiromo's actions were relatively low-key, corporate computer crime can happen on a much larger scale, resulting in multi-million dollar payoffs. Dr. David L. Carter, professor at Michigan State University's School of Criminal Justice, outlines four types of computer crime in his article "Computer Crime Categories: How Techno-criminals Operate" (Carter, 1995). Carter describes the first type as "crime in which the computer is the target." This type of crime includes "such offenses as theft of intellectual property, theft of marketing information (e.g., customer lists, pricing data, or marketing plans), or blackmail based on information gained from computerized files (e.g., medical information, personal history, or sexual preference)" (ibid.). Criminals who commit this type of computer crime are using the computer to obtain knowledge or to damage programs. According to Carter, this is relatively easy for a professional to do, as most operating systems offer ways to bypass security features.

In 2003, Roman Meydbray, a former manager at Creative Explosions, Inc., a software development firm, used his knowledge of information systems to break into his old firm's email system and damage the server. Meydbray "deleted an e-mail server domain, accessed the e-mail account belonging to the president of Creative Explosions, and made configuration changes to the mail servers that caused e-mails to be rejected" (Computer Crime Research Center [CCRC], 2005). Meydbray's computer was seized during the investigation, and he later pled guilty to one count of unlawful access to stored communications and one count of unauthorized access to a computer and recklessly causing damage (ibid.).

Carter's second type of computer crime uses the computer as the "instrumentality of the crime" (Carter, 1995). Some examples include "fraudulent use of automated teller machine (ATM) cards and accounts; theft of money from accrual, conversion, or transfer accounts; and credit card fraud" (Carter, 1995), among others. Crimes in this category are committed by infiltrating and manipulating computers to assist in the crime. Since these types of crimes are generally more public, they require a careful knowledge of the surrounding surveillance as well as the manipulation of the machines. These types of crimes are risky; they can, however, result in a high payout if carried out.

The work of the "ATM gang" in 2001 accomplished just that. The group purchased 50 ATM machines, set them up in several states, and linked the machines to national banking services in order to steal victims' account information as they were withdrawing money (NBC News, 2003). After the victims had withdrawn cash, the gang would take the account information to legitimate ATM machines and perform the fraudulent transactions. Nearly 21,000 bank accounts were affected, resulting in a payout of $4 million for the criminals. Two were charged in the heist, yet the "alleged mastermind" fled to Europe and was never apprehended.

The third type of computer crime in Carter's hierarchy involves computers being incidental to other crimes (Carter, 1995). In this type of crime, the computer is not directly involved, but is related to another crime. Carter observes that in these cases, the computer is not necessary; the computer, however, allows the crime to be carried out more quickly and anonymously than without the aid of the computer. In most situations, the data is stored electronically and is used as evidence once recovered.

During a routine methamphetamine drug bust in northern New Mexico in late 2006, police found additional evidence incriminating three people at Royal Crest mobile home park. Authorities found and confiscated 3 USB port memory sticks containing classified information from Los Alamos National Laboratory (Associated Press, 2006). It was later found that an employee of Los Alamos who was connected with one of the drug dealers retrieved the information. Authorities did not release much information concerning the contents of the memory sticks except that "they appeared to contain classified material and were stored on a computer file" (ibid.).

The last of Carter's four types of computer crime is crime associated with the prevalence of computers. These crimes are not necessarily new, but they have been generated in such ways that they are seen as updated versions of traditional crimes. Some examples are "software piracy/counterfeiting, copyright violation of computer programs, counterfeit equipment, black market computer equipment and programs, and theft of technological equipment" (Carter, 1995). With the growing expense of up-to-date software, more copyright laws are being heavily publicized to combat increasing piracy crimes. Still, this type of crime can be found in numerous locations worldwide, and is perhaps the most performed type of computer crime.

In 2005, Maksym Vysochanskyy of the Ukraine pled guilty to charges of criminal copyright infringement and trafficking. Vysochanskyy reproduced illegal copies of software such as that by Adobe, Microsoft, and others and then sold them via eBay and personal websites (Sonderby, 2005). He used several online aliases to disguise his identity and set up various email accounts by which to communicate with potential buyers. Vysochanskyy's case was one of the first intellectual property cases to involve extradition.

There are obvious downsides to living in the computerized twenty-first century, as evidenced by these cases. However, as with anything, we must expect the evil to be let in with the good. There is no disputing the fact that computers are a necessary part of our daily lives, so no quick fixes are probable. Soon digital forensics experts may have the knowledge and capabilities to more effectively combat the problems associated with the age of technology. Until then, we can only use our resources to take preventative measures and inform others about the threat of computer crime,

References

The Associated Press. (2006, October 25). New details emerge in Los Alamos case. CBS News. Retrieved August 30, 2007, from http://www.cbsnews.com/stories/2006/10/24/national/main2122004.shtml

Carter, D. L. (1995, July). Computer crime categories: How techno-criminals operate. Retrieved August 26, 2007, from http://nsi.org/Library/Compsec/crimecom.html

Computer Crime Research Center. (2005, July 11). Computer crime case: Former manager pleads guilty. Retrieved August 26, 2007, from http://www.crime-research.org/news/21.07.2005/1375/

NBC News. (2003, December 11). ATM fraud: Banking on your money. Retrieved August 29, 2007, from http://www.msnbc.msn.com/id/3607110/

Sonderby, C. P. (2005, November 29). Guilty plea in international software piracy and financial crime prosecution: Case involves extradition for intellectual property crimes. U.S. Department of Justice. Retrieved August 29, 2007, from http://www.usdoj.gov/criminal/cybercrime/vysochanskyyPlea.htm

Yang, D. W. (2004, March 1). Mission Viejo teen guilty in Internet auction fraud; defendant also admits $400,000 bank fraud. U.S. Department of Justice. Retrieved August 26, 2007, from http://www.cybercrime.gov/bartiromoPlea.htm

Source: *Forensic Examiner*, © 2007, American College of Forensic Examiners

Reading 2–2: Peter Carbonara, *The Scam that Will Not Die*

Many of the readers of this text may have received unsolicited e-mails informing them of large lottery winnings or too-good-to-be-true business ventures. Hopefully, your first reaction was simply to delete these e-mails and not to respond to them. However, have you ever wondered the origin of such schemes? The aim of this article is to familiarize you with the ever-increasing world of advance fee fraud scams.

Imagine turning on your computer and finding an e-mail like this:

CONFIDENTIAL: Dear Sir, Good day and compliments. This letter will definitely come to you as a huge surprise, but I implore you to take the time to go through it carefully as the decision you make will go off a long way to determine the future and continued existence of the entire members of my family. Pease allow me to introduce myself. My name is Dr. (Mrs.) Mariam Abacha, the wife of the late head of state and commander in chief of the armed forces of the federal republic of Nigeria who died on the 8th of June 1998. My ordeal started immediately after my husband's death on the morning of June 8th, 1998, and the subsequent take-over of government by the last administration. The present democratic government is determined to portray all the good work of my late husband in a bad light and have gone as far as confiscating all my late husband's assets, properties, freezing our accounts both within and outside Nigeria. My late husband had/has eighty million USD ($80,000,000.00) specially preserved and well packed in trunk boxes of which only my husband and I knew about. It is packed in such a way to forestall just anybody having access to it. It is this sum that I seek your assistance to get out of Nigeria as soon as possible before the present civilian government finds out about it and confiscate it just like they have done to all our assets. I implore you to please give consideration to my predicament and help a widow in need. May Allah show you mercy as you do so. Yours faithfully, Dr. (Mrs.) Mariam Abacha (M.O.N)

What Dr. (Mrs.) Abacha is saying here is that she's so desperate for help moving this $80 million that she has been reduced to sending plaintive e-mail messages to regular people she doesn't know in America. Most sane people, upon seeing that sort of thing in their inboxes, realize the letter isn't really from Mrs. Abacha, assume that it's a scam or a joke and simply hit delete.

Others, however, take the bait. They respond, tentatively at first, but also with a furtive glimmer of hope or greed or anxiety that can be used to turn even a levelheaded citizen into a gold-plated sucker. E-mail exchanges and phone calls follow. Over time, bit by bit, the proposition starts to seem real: Help move the money and get a cut of that $80 mil.

Eventually the mark finds himself talking to a very intelligent and persuasive person with an African accent who has been designated to act for Mrs. Abacha. The African will describe several trunks packed with $100 bills, all of which have been dyed black or stamped with red to prevent them from being stolen. He'll produce official-looking documents concerning the money. He'll even produce a few genuine bills and clean them with a mystery solvent. It will be explained that transporting, storing, insuring and cleaning the rest will require money—maybe $50,000—in exchange for which Mrs. Abacha's agent will offer a hefty slice of the $80 million. Convinced by the cleaned bills that he's seen with his own eyes, the mark will raise the money (maybe enlisting friends and family to help), deliver it and wait for the payoff.

But there will be delays. More money may be required to pay an export duty or to bribe Nigerian customs officials. Then even that won't be enough. More will be needed. And then more again. Eventually Mrs. Abacha's representative will disappear. Eventually the mark will realize he's been had.

Second Only to "Herbal Viagra"

This kind of advance-fee scam—or 419 scam, for the section of the Nigerian penal code that covers it—has been a thriving enterprise for at least 20 years. It is, by some estimates, the second-largest industry in Nigeria, after oil.

Only a tiny fraction of the people who receive an advance-fee pitch fall for it, of course. But if you increase the number of appeals—and, thanks to the Internet, they are increasing at an alarming rate—the number of suckers grows proportionately.

In addition, there's reason to believe that fraction has been growing as well: Scams of all kinds flourish when times are good and the stock market is hot, conditions that until recently prevailed here in the U.S. According to the U.S. Secret Service, which polices such scams in this country and recently opened a branch office in Lagos, Nigeria, to fight them, West African advance-fee scams have cost Americans $100 million over the past three years.

How did Nigeria become such a prolific source of those swindles? Having been on the receiving end of generations of colonial rule, the populace of Nigeria (and neighbors like Ghana and the Ivory Coast) is generally well educated, English-speaking and very poor. After gaining its independence in 1960, Nigeria suffered decades of freewheeling official corruption, exacerbated by religious and ethnic strife and greased by money from the country's oil and mineral resources. U.S. law enforcement authorities say Nigerian president Olusegun Obasanjo appears serious about cleaning things up, but the task is huge and the progress, by all accounts, glacial. In its most recent Corruption Perceptions Index, the nonprofit monitoring group Transparency International ranked Nigeria second only to Bangladesh in crookedness.

In short, Nigeria—Africa's fastest-growing country—has become a place where even honest people learn to game the system just to survive. And in that environment, it's only logical that the real crooks would be very good at what they do. It's also logical that this talent would busy itself fleecing the English-speaking world's largest pool of wealth. Bruce Townsend, chief of the Secret Service's financial crimes division, says West African gangs are well organized and have diversified into things like bank fraud, identity theft and drug dealing.

Their sophistication naturally extends to technology, so the once laborious business of trolling for suckers is now done easily, quickly and anonymously via bulk e-mail and fax. "It's very easy," a spokesman for Nigeria's antifraud agencies told the newspaper *Newswatch*. Would-be scammers merely walk into one of the country's many Internet cafes and set up an online account. "All it costs," he added, "is a few hundred naira." The equivalent, that is, of about three U.S. dollars. The Washington, D.C.-based National Consumer League says that West African advance-fee fraud is now the third biggest consumer come-on on the Internet. According to anti-spam software maker Brightmail, the only kind of junk e-mail more common are pitches for "herbal Viagra."

That some Americans will fall for almost any well-packaged financial scheme, no matter how insane, has long been understood by both freelance con artists and their Wall Street cousins. But a handful of Americans have lost more than money to Nigerian scams, usually when they've been convinced to go to Africa or Europe, where they're more vulnerable. Last August, Kenyan police rescued three kidnapped Americans who'd been lured to Nairobi by a Nigerian gang. A year earlier, Jerry Stratton, a Florida plumbing contractor who'd been bilked of about $67,000, went to London deluded into thinking he could recover his money from the West African "businessmen" with whom he'd been dealing. Ultimately, Stratton killed himself in his hotel room, leaving a note. "If anything happens to me," it read, "look for three people. They are Nigerians. They are responsible."

"Going Shopping" with Buzz Siler

On paper, advance-fee come-ons seem so preposterous that it's hard to see how anyone could fall for them. Swindling, though, is a kind of theater, and a gifted performer can make even the most tired script come to life. The best Nigerian con artists are experienced, sophisticated and quick to adapt to changing circumstances and exploit newly glimpsed weaknesses. (Recent waves of e-mail have incorporated post-9/11 angles, in some instances, invoking the fortune of a rich Nigerian, killed in the attacks, who left no heirs.)

A rare glimpse into such artistry comes to us via Lawrence "Buzz" Siler. A Portland, OR, inventor who runs a company that makes money pouches and other security gadgets for banks, Siler got a fax from the ubiquitous Mrs. Abacha, describing $25.6 million she wanted invested on her behalf in the U.S., in the autumn of 2000. "Obviously somebody offering you $25 million is pretty ridiculous, so I wrote back just to see where it was all going," Siler says. He also called the FBI, which put him in touch with the Secret Service, which in turn enlisted him as an undercover agent.

Soon Siler was getting a steady stream of pitches from several would-be scammers, among them one Victor Okiti, a Nigerian who, it turned out, had twice entered this country under a false identity. Siler says the tenacity and professionalism of the various con men who contacted him were impressive. Like all adept salesmen, they tailored their spiel to the mood of their target. When Siler seemed to respond to the soft sell, they'd sweet-talk him. Once, when he balked at putting down a $25,000 advance fee, Okiti berated him about all the people who'd taken risks on his behalf. Siler spoke to Okiti and others innumerable times over a period of months. Bit by bit, he says, the deals that at first seemed so phony almost started to seem real. "There was a very thin line that I could have stepped over to start believing these guys," he says.

While continuing to string along Okiti, Siler met with two other teams of scammers in Atlanta hotel rooms, each time bringing along money provided by the Secret Service and a female agent posing as his girlfriend. Once each transaction was done, Siler was to say a prearranged code phrase and a group of armed agents would burst in from the adjoining room and make arrests. (The busts didn't go off without a hitch: During one of the two Atlanta stings, Siler had to say—then shout—the code words "go shopping" three times before the agents heard him.)

Then last summer Siler met Victor Okiti in a Houston hotel room. Okiti showed him a trunk of $100 bills, each stamped with "UN"—meaning, he was told, unnegotiable. Naturally, they would need to be cleaned. Secret Service agents videotaped the meeting via hidden camera and arrested Okiti. Last August he pleaded guilty to wire fraud and counterfeiting and is now serving an 18-month federal sentence.

A Philadelphia Story

Many con men have mastered the technical aspects of their craft: careful preparation, meticulous documentation, back-up stories and the like. Perhaps what distinguishes the true artists among them is an ability to turn their dupes into quasi-accomplices. Astonishingly often, the swindle-ee actually expedites his own fleecing through a kind of temporary insanity, a willingness—or desperation—to suspend disbelief and prolong the possibility of getting rich quick. The most interesting (not to mention, weirdest) example of this phenomenon may be the advance-fee fraud case of Edward Mezvinsky, a 64-year-old former Democratic Congressman from Iowa.

A onetime liberal folk hero who, as a member of the House Judiciary Committee, voted to impeach President Nixon in 1974, Mezvinsky later served as President Carter's representative to the UN Commission on Human Rights, before setting himself up as a Philadelphia-based lawyer and self-described international businessman. He is scheduled to go on trial in Philadelphia this fall to face a 66-count federal indictment accusing him of stealing some $10.4 million. The list of alleged victims includes not only numerous banks and business associates, but also several long-time friends and his mother-in-law. His wife Marjorie Margolies-Mezvinsky, also a former member of Congress, was thought to have a bright future in national Democratic politics until her husband's fall.

Some of the frauds Mezvinsky is accused of were fairly simple affairs with no connection—directly, anyway—to West African cons. But he was also involved —sometimes as scammer and sometimes as sucker—in several deals that come straight out of the Nigerian playbook. Starting in the early 1990s, Mezvinsky found himself being tapped repeatedly by a parade of West Africans. According to Robert Zauzmer, the assistant U.S. attorney prosecuting the case, a "sort of mailing list of potential victims" appears to circulate along the Nigerian grapevine. (This explains why Buzz Siler got so many pitches—and why he was able to help bust three separate groups of scammers.) Mezvinsky must have been a con artist's dream: an apparently upstanding American politician who's financially ambitious and has access to wealthy friends and banks only too happy to lend him money.

Most significantly, however, it appears Mezvinsky believed, or wanted to believe, their increasingly crazy pitches. (He declined to be interviewed for this article.) Of the approximately $13.3 million that flowed through Mezvinsky's bank accounts between 1995 and 2000—most of it, says Zauzmer, the product of fraud or embezzlement—about $2.6 million went to con men, a portion of which turned up in bank accounts in New York City and Boston that federal investigators believe were controlled by West African swindlers.

Starting in the late 1980s, according to Zauzmer, Mezvinsky got involved in a series of shady dealings. He began scamming a long list of victims, many of them friends, promising big returns from West African oil or investment schemes.

Starting in late 1996, Mezvinsky solicited $365,000 from a Maryland urologist. A year later he got $1 million from a certified financial planner in Florida. Between January 1998 and January 1999, he received $1.2 million from an Italian businessman. In 1999 he got yet another $1 million from a retired Pennsylvania business executive and $500,000 from a Virginia investor. Each got a different story, but the general pitch was that if they would give Mezvinsky their money—which he promised to hold in trust at a U.S. bank, risk-free—he would guarantee a hefty and quick profit.

But even as Mezvinsky was scamming people, he was letting himself get scammed by West Africans—apparently hoping that the big score would help him pay off the large debts he was accumulating.

The whole thing crashed to earth when David Sonders, the Virginia investor, sued. Soon after, in January 2000, Mezvinsky and his wife declared bankruptcy. The filing shows debts in excess of $7 million, much of it unsecured personal loans from friends and business associates, including $25,000 lent in 1999 by Bernard Nussbaum, a prominent New York City attorney and President

Clinton's first White House counsel. (Nussbaum declined to discuss the matter.) Mezvinsky's wife pulled out of the race for the Democratic nomination to one of Pennsylvania's U.S. Senate seats.

Amazingly, even all that public humiliation wasn't enough to scare him away from African hustlers. Just six months later—by which time FBI agents were looking into his affairs—Mezvinsky convinced Robert Farrell, a Maryland friend and business associate, to fly to Chicago to scope out a deal for him. Farrell says he was met at Chicago's Midway Airport by a man with an African accent and a gun who drove him to a self-storage facility near the University of Chicago. There he was shown a wooden chest supposedly containing—what else?—$81 million in $100 bills, dyed black. At a nearby motel, a second African, a "Mr. Timothy" produced a vial of liquid, poured it into a bucket of water and soaked some of the bills. They were rinsed and dried and given to Farrell, who was driven back to the airport with bills in hand. Farrell says he doesn't know if the deal proceeded further.

Meanwhile, Mezvinsky—was confined to his home by a federal judge and ordered to wear an electronic monitoring bracelet—and mounted an unorthodox defense. His lawyers argued that any responsibility he may have had was diminished by a combination of manic depression and Lariam, an antimalarial drug that is, in fact, known to cause unpleasant temporary psychological effects in some people. (Mezvinsky also sued Hoffman-LaRoche, the maker of the drug, and the doctor who had prescribed it, a long-time friend.)

Mezvinsky was found guilty, and has since been sentenced to an 80-month prison term. He'll be 71 before he's eligible for parole; although he's in jail—the Africans who defrauded him are not. No doubt they're as far away from Philadelphia as they can get, whoever they are. Which in one respect makes the whole Mezvinsky fiasco, for all of its convolutions, a typical Nigerian advance-fee swindle. The mark has been fleeced, his money has vanished, and no one knows who or where the scammers are.

Do the Hustle

Merely reading Jay Robert Nash's out-of-print 1976 compendium of scam artistry, *Hustlers and Con Men*, leaves many solid citizens feeling duped. (For a similar experience, check out Joseph Wells' *Frankensteins of Fraud*, currently available at www.cfenet.com.) Here are some of the most notorious members of Nash's gallery, plus a couple of other scams that arguably belong in the pantheon:

- Cassie Chadwick: Claiming to be the illegitimate daughter of steel magnate Andrew Carnegie, won the confidence of the Cleveland banking community, which "loaned" her anywhere from $500,000 to $1 million between 1897 and 1904.
- Charles Ponzi: The father of the modern pyramid scheme, pulled in $20

million in 1920 by promising investors a 100 percent return on international postal coupons in 90 days. Like all perpetrators of his eponymous scam, Ponzi paid off old investors with new investors' money.

- Oscar Hartzell: Between 1922 and 1935, some 75,000 Midwesterners advanced him funds on the claim that he'd been put in control of the mythical fortune of Sir Francis Drake.
- Victor "The Count" Lustig: In the early 1920s posed as a French official and sold the Eiffel Tower as scrap metal for an estimated $50,000. When out of embarrassment, the scam wasn't reported, Lustig sold the tower again—this time for an estimated $75,000.
- Phillip Musica: As CEO of drug company McKesson & Robbins, sent the reputable corporation into ruin in 1938 by duping auditors with phantom drug inventories. Musica, who went by the alias F. Donald Coster at the time, reportedly bought his way into the company with bootlegging profits.
- Alvin Clarence Thomas: A consummate hustler who faked clumsiness on Texas golf courses during the 1930s and 1940s, and then took his marks for all they were worth. Also known as "Titanic" Thompson—he may have survived the sinking—he reportedly earned $250,000 a year on the links.
- Florida land scams: Forty years after the 1920s Florida land boom, Northerners were still being duped into buying swampland by slogans like "$10 down and $10 a month." Most of the lots proved unreachable by car, and drainage was usually forbidden by law.
- Robert Vesco: Accused of embezzling $224 million from the Investors Overseas Service mutual fund, fled U.S. in 1972 when a $250,000 donation to the Nixon campaign fund didn't get him off. Later as a fugitive in Cuba, he marketed and sold a bogus AIDS and cancer drug called TX.

Source: *Business Credit*, © 2003, National Association of Credit Management

Thinking Activities

1. After reading "The Scam that Will Not Die," can you think of any circumstances in which engaging in such forms of illicit behavior would be considered acceptable? In other words, if you were faced with a similar situation, would you engage in such activities?
2. If you have not taken Sociology or Criminology, use the Internet to query "Merton's Strain Theory." How might this theory apply to the Nigerian advance fee fraud scam?
3. Based on the information presented in this chapter, and your own research and personal reflection, think about ways in which you might be vulnerable to identity theft and credit card fraud. What actions might you take to protect yourself and your privacy?
4. To illustrate how ingrained into American culture computers and

other high-tech gadgets have become, attempt to spend 24 hours "unplugged." During this period, you may not surf the World Wide Web, check e-mail, use your cellular telephone or pager, turn on a computer, listen to or view DVDs, watch television or videos, or listen to an iPod, MP3 player, or the radio. Record your feelings and insights gained during your "unplugged" experience.

5. Conduct an informal survey of your family and friends to determine what level of access to information technology they have available to them. Based on these forms of technology, which kinds of white-collar crimes might be occurring in your area?

6. Do you or any of your friends possess altered or fraudulent identification? If yes, for what purpose? Do you believe that it is wrong to use a fake driver's license to purchase alcohol or to get into a nightclub? Why or why not?

7. What are the differences between hacking and cracking? Is there a difference between the way such offenses are portrayed in movies and television and reality? Discuss some of these differences with your classmates.

8. Do you believe that enough emphasis is placed on the ethical use of technology in American society? Why or why not?

3 The Corporate–State Corruption Connection

Can It Be Stopped?

In business for less than eight years, the corporate officers of Cyberfauxes technologies have a serious problem. When their company was added to the NASDAQ exchange a year ago, the initial public offering (IPO) price for their stock was nearly $125 per share. Yet, despite having several former senior executive service advisors from the previous presidential administration on its board, the company's "vision" failed to translate into a viable software product with the sales to match.

Desperate to keep the price of the stock up, the CEO and President of Cyberfauxes conspire with an "independent" auditing firm to produce a third-quarter earnings report that indicates inflated sales revenues and non-existent record profits. The stock price rises accordingly and the corporate officers—and several government officials who also have ties to the prior presidential administration—take advantage of this situation by selling off their shares at the inflated price. Only later do the general shareholders and the lower-level employees, who had invested much of their pension earnings in stock options, realize that the report has been falsified and that the company's stock is essentially worthless. Cyberfauxes files for bankruptcy, leaving the lower-level employees of the company and the American public to suffer the consequences.

In Chapter 1 of this text, we mentioned that white-collar crime is defined as a non-violent, illicit act committed by an individual or organization for financial or other personal gain. It is important to note that personal gain is not always financial; rather, it may include power, recognition, or even our more base instincts such as sexuality—all of which are embraced as symbols of status and prestige in our collective culture. Accordingly, the following section of this chapter will provide the reader with examples of public officials who have allowed their desires for wealth, power, and carnal satisfaction to usurp their obligations to the public trust.

The Honorable Thomas E. White: Modern-Day Horatio Alger or Opportunist?

Upon inspecting the credentials of The Honorable Thomas E. White, one cannot help but be impressed by a man who appears to epitomize the American dream. The son of a bus driver and raised in the inner city of Detroit, Mr. White earned an appointment to the United States Military Academy at West Point. He subsequently served as a commissioned Army officer from 1967 through 1990, rising to the rank of Brigadier General. His impressive military career included two combat tours in Vietnam, Director of the Armor/Anti-Armor Special Task Force, Executive Assistant to the Chairman of the Joint Chiefs of Staff, advanced learning in the area of operations research at the Naval Postgraduate School, and subsequent training at the United States Army War College. Upon retiring from the Army in July of 1990, Mr. White accepted a position as the Vice Chairman of Enron Energy Services. At an annual salary of more than $5.5 million (USD), he also served on Enron's Executive Committee and was Chairman and Chief Executive Officer for Enron Operations Corporation.

Similar to Mr. White, Enron was considered by many in the corporate world to be business' personification of the rags-to-riches success story. Founded in 1985, the Houston-based company was admired on Wall Street as a technological innovator. Enron developed an expertise in purchasing electricity wholesale from the power generators and subsequently selling it to consumers for a profit. Much of Enron's initial success can be attributed to the dynamic and charismatic founder, the late Kenneth Lay. Lay parlayed a small natural gas merger between his own Houston Natural Gas and the Internorth pipeline company of Nebraska into a global energy commodities broker. At the height of its success, Enron traded an average of $2.7 billion worth of contracts a day online[1] and bought and sold more than 1,500 commodities such as natural gas, refined petroleum products, electric power, coal, steel, telecommunications bandwidth, data storage, pulp and paper products, lumber, and oil.[2]

Thus the relationship between Mr. White and Enron appeared to be an almost perfect, Horatio Alger-like, union blending the individual and the organization. This image was further enhanced when Mr. White left the successful corporation to become the 18th Secretary of the Army on May 31, 2001.

Less than six months later, Enron had filed for bankruptcy amidst a sea of controversy that it had misrepresented its real value by overstating profits by nearly $600 million and hiding debts of more than $500 million through a series of intricate business partnerships and questionable accounting practices. During this time, Enron's senior management officials received warning to sell their stock; however, the lower level employees and millions

Exhibit 3.1 Former Enron CEO Ken Lay addresses the media next to his wife Linda after being found guilty on all counts at the Bob Casey U.S. Courthouse in Houston, Texas, May 25, 2006. The collapse of Enron had serious financial consequences for the stock and retirement portfolios of millions of Americans.

of Americans, who invested their pension funds in this corporation, never received notification. Worth more than $80 per share in early 2001, at the time of this book's publication, Enron's stock is worth less than $1 per share, and will likely have a devastating economic impact on the pension-investment portfolios of America's present and future retirees.

One of those who did not lose his life's savings was Army Secretary White, who made approximately $12 million on the sale of his more than 400,000 shares of Enron stock[3]—the last of which was sold on October 30, 2001, just 33 days before the corporation filed for Chapter 11 Bankruptcy protection. He confirmed holding more than 20 meetings and telephone conversations with employees and officers of Enron prior to the December bankruptcy filing.

Mr. White, who held the most Enron stock of the fifteen appointees within the Bush administration who were also shareholders, has also become embroiled in several other issues involving alleged abuse of trust. One such example occurred in early March 2002, when Army Secretary White was

Exhibit 3.2 William Donaldson, chairman of the Securities and Exchange Commission, testifies on September 9, 2003 before the Senate Banking, Housing and Urban Affairs Committee about the progress of restoring investor confidence in the wake of accounting scandals at places like Enron, Arthur Andersen and World Com.

authorized use of a military jet for an official meeting in Seattle, Washington. Accompanying him was his wife, Susan. However, instead of simply returning to Washington, D.C. after the Seattle meeting, Mr. White ordered that the aircraft be flown to Colorado, so that he and his wife could close on the sale of their three-story home in Aspen, a prominent resort community. Mr. White's alleged personal use of a military aircraft, vehicle, or other government equipment could be deemed as a violation of both a 1997 Department of Defense Directive and overarching requirements which call for suspension of the employee for a minimum of 30 days, or termination for a second offense. Secretary White resigned his position on April 25, 2003.

Mr. White is certainly not alone in being subjected to public scrutiny and government investigation for his possible foreknowledge of the collapse of Enron. Indeed, there are numerous public officials whose connections to Enron were called into question. Consider the following examples:

Exhibit 3.3 Former Enron CEO Jeff Skilling outside the Bob Casey U.S. Courthouse with his attorney Daniel Petrocelli after the end of his fraud and conspiracy trial on May 25, 2006 in Houston, Texas. After 16 weeks of testimony and six days of deliberation, the jury found Skilling guilty on 19 of 28 counts.

- Karl Rove, the top campaign fundraiser for President Bush who left the White House for private life, allegedly organized a lucrative Enron consulting contract for campaign strategist Ralph Reed, rather than paying him from campaign funds.[4]
- During the period 1989–2001, Enron contributed over $1.1 million to republican, democrat, and independent elected officials in the U.S. House and Senate. Of these contributions, approximately 67 percent were allocated to Republican politicians.[5]
- The Enron Corporation, and the employees who worked for it, comprised the single largest contributing group to George W. Bush's gubernatorial and presidential campaigns.[6]
- The late Kenneth Lay, who was informally referred to as "Kenny Boy"

by both former President George Herbert Walker Bush and current President George W. Bush, was considered to be a close friend of the family. In 1993, he provided key cabinet officials in the former Bush White House (e.g., James Baker and Robert Mosbacher) with jobs at Enron.[7]

- Mr. Lay aided current President Bush's transition team in the selection of candidates for key positions in the Federal Energy Regulatory Commission.[8]
- Former White House Economic Advisor Lawrence Lindsey, Former Treasury Secretary Paul O'Neill, and Commerce Secretary Don Evans all have ties to Enron and CEO Kenneth Lay. Immediately before Enron collapsed, Lay placed calls to Treasury Secretary O'Neill and Commerce Secretary Evans.[9]

Of course, the Enron debacle is not the first case in U.S. history where allegations of collusion between the private sector and government officials have surfaced. Indeed, as we will discuss later in this chapter, one need only examine the Teapot Dome Scandal of the 1920s and the dubious relationships between oil field operators Harry Sinclair and Edward Doheny, Senator-turned-Interior Secretary Albert B. Fall, Secretary of the Navy Edwin N. Denby, and Attorney General Harry M. Daugherty, and the similarities will become evident.

Moreover, Army Secretary White is not the first government official to be accused of misusing government equipment such as an aircraft or vehicle. For example, John Sununu, former Chief of Staff in the George H.W. Bush Administration, took dozens of trips in military aircraft in less then two years. Dubbed "Air Sununu" by the press, destinations included golf outings and trips to the dentist.[10] He also allegedly used a White House limousine to travel to a stamp auction. Under considerable pressure from pundits not just within the Democratic Party, but also in the Bush Administration, Mr. Sununu resigned on December 3, 1991.

If All Politics are Local: Can the Same Can Be Said for Abuse of Office Crimes?

In connecting the events of the past with those of the present, it becomes apparent that government corruption, or at least detection and reporting of such offenses, appears to be cyclical. However, such corruption is not confined to the boundaries of the District of Columbia, but rather pervades all forms of federal, state, county, and local government. Below are examples of other abuse-of-trust offenses involving public officials at these various levels of administration.

- Jane Swift, the Acting Governor of Massachusetts opted not to run as the Republican Party candidate for the 2002 Governor's race in large part due to public outrage over her using a State Police helicopter to fly from the Statehouse in Boston to her home in North Adams for the 2001 Thanksgiving holiday. Previously, she was fined $1,250 by the state Ethics commission for using state employees to baby-sit her daughter.[11]

- During the period March 1999 through April 2000, eight Pennsylvania lawmakers were investigated, charged, or convicted of engaging in acts of perjury, graft, and influence peddling. Of these eight officials, one resigned and four opted not to seek re-election.[12]

- A massive investigation of corruption in San Bernardino County (California) resulted in multiple federal grand jury indictments against five public officials and two private businessmen for allegedly partaking in a bribery scheme. The scam allegedly involved a complex conspiracy in which the officials would receive kickbacks in exchange for approving contracts to construct billboards at the intersections of Interstates 10 and 215 in the City of Colton. Those indicted include San Bernardino County Supervisor Gerald Eaves, Orange County businessman W. Shepardson McCook, Abe Beltran and Donald Sanders, the latter two of whom served as members of the Colton City Council. James Hlawek, the Chief Administrative Officer for San Bernadino County, and Allan Steward, a Laguna Beach commercial real estate developer, were also charged.[13]

- Former North Bergen (New Jersey) official Joseph Auriemma was indicted on May 6, 2002, by a federal grand jury on six counts including extortion, corrupt persuasion, witness tampering, and several counts of mail fraud. Auriemma allegedly accepted more than $35,000 in cash and complementary construction and renovation work (e.g., an upgraded bathroom, new roof, new furnace and air conditioning system, etc.) on his homes located in Bloomfield and Wildwood, New Jersey. The indictment asserts that from 1995 to 2001, Auriemma improperly awarded a municipal contractor more than $2.5 million in township contracts.[14]

- Former Hudson County (New Jersey) Executive Robert "Bob" Janiszewski went from being considered among New Jersey's most lasting political personalities to a principal target of a federal corruption sting. After agreeing to serve as a cooperating witness for the U.S. Government in its case against several politicians in Hudson County accused of accepting kickbacks and bribes, Janiszewski resigned his post as Hudson County Democratic Chairman and County Executive and literally vanished from sight. After working at a village ski shop in Upstate New York, he was arrested and is currently serving a 41-month prison term in Pennsylvania.[15]

- On February 16, 2000, George Knapp, the former second-in-command of the Town of Poughkeepsie (New York) water department, signed a plea agreement on the charge of conspiracy to commit mail fraud. His guilty plea came one day after former Town Attorney Frank Redl agreed to a deal with prosecutors to plead guilty to conspiracy to obstruct justice. Just two days later, Dutchess County GOP Chairman William Paroli, Sr. agreed to a plea deal on one count of conspiracy to commit extortion. All of these men were allegedly involved in a multi-year scheme to extort prospective contractors who desired to do business in the Town of Poughkeepsie.[16]

In each of the above-mentioned cases, officials allegedly misused the trust that the public had placed in them for their own personal gain. As you can see, some of the common elements of these cases are improperly derived proceeds, receiving services without providing compensation, and misuse of government equipment. Moreover, all of the incidents described in this section exhibit the seven behavioral characteristics researched by scholar Susan Shapiro in her typology of abuse-of-trust crimes, namely "lying, misrepresentation, stealing, misappropriation, self-dealing, corruption, and role conflict."[17]

Marty Barnes: A Case Study in Egoism and Egregious Behavior

An additional personality trait inherent in many of the individuals who engage in such acts appears to be egoism. Perhaps the best illustration of this characteristic is Paterson (New Jersey) Mayor Marty Barnes. Barnes was named in a 40-count grand jury indictment in early 2002 for allegedly accepting lavish gifts from city contractors.[18] Among those items or benefits he allegedly received were vacations to a castle in England with his spouse and to Aruba, Rio, and the Kentucky Derby with (contractor-supplied) girlfriends. He also allegedly received complementary designer suits, new furniture, various private-sector jobs for friends and associates, and construction of a lavish swimming pool at his home—complete with a Polynesian-style waterfall. Barnes pleaded guilty on July 1, 2002 to charges of mail fraud, filing false income tax returns, and lying on ethics disclosure statements. In April 2003, he was sentenced to 37 months in prison.

The brazen manner in which Barnes would flaunt his bon vivant lifestyle appears similar to the 1992 case involving former Bureau of Land Management (BLM) Deputy Director Eugene "Dean" Stepanek. Mr. Stepanek retired from the Bureau of Land Management in 1992 while facing dual Office of the Inspector General and Justice Department investigations regarding the alleged misuse of government funds spent traveling to Russia to visit his lover. The Russian woman subsequently flew to Colorado where she remained for a month, and Deputy Chief Stepanek used BLM funds to finance his three separate trips from Washington, D.C. to Fort Collins to visit her. Mr. Stepanek paid restitution to the government in the amount of $7,000, although he subsequently claimed that he was forced to retire by upper-level officials in the George H.W. Bush Administration. An administrative law judge dismissed his case.

Teapot Dome and Enron: Back to the Future?

Long before the controversies of the Enron stock implosion, previous presidential administrations faced difficult questions regarding their relationships with the energy sector—particularly the petroleum industry. A well-known example is the Teapot Dome Scandal of the 1920s. In 1921, Albert B. Fall, President Warren Harding's Secretary of the Interior, successfully lobbied Secretary of the Navy Edwin Denby to turn over control of the nation's government-owned oil reserves to him. In exchange for $400,000 in personal compensation, Fall quietly established leases with the Mammoth Oil Company owned by Harry Sinclair and Edward Doheny's Pan American Petroleum Company.[19] Shortly thereafter, Secretary of the Interior Fall's lavish lifestyle came under public scrutiny. A subsequent investigation yielded lawsuits against the Government for illegally obtained contracts. In 1927, the Supreme Court ruled that the oil leases had been obtained by means of corruption and therefore rendered the Elk Hills and Teapot Dome leases invalid in February 1927 and October 1927, respectively. Management of the oil reserves was again returned to the Department of the Navy. In 1929, Albert Fall was found guilty of bribery and sentenced to one year in prison and a $100,000 fine.[20] Harry Sinclair received a short jail sentence for contempt of court and obstruction of justice. Edward Doheny was acquitted of bribery charges in 1930.

Links between Texas oil barons and the Office of the Chief Executive are also clearly evident when one examines the substantial campaign contributions made to both Republican and Democratic candidates alike, from Lyndon B. Johnson to Richard Nixon and George H.W. Bush to George W. Bush. For example, consider the case of Jack E. McGregor, a former executive of the Carey Energy Corporation and the former Marine Corps commanding officer of Billy Carter, the brother of former President Jimmy Carter.

In late April of 1979, nearing the end of the Carter Presidency, Billy Carter met with McGregor in Washington, D.C. regarding a get-rich-quick oil supply scheme that he had devised. McGregor suggested that the brother of the President meet with Charter Crude Oil, a subsidiary of the Charter

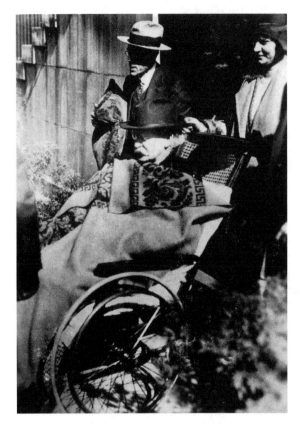

Exhibit 3.4 Warren G. Harding, the 29th President of the United States, presided over one of the most corrupt administrations in history. Among the scandals he faced during his tenure were Teapot Dome, allegations of kickbacks and bribes in the wake of prohibition, and an extra-marital affair involving his fathering of an illegitimate child.

Company, which had recently purchased Carey Energy Corporation. Billy met with officials at Charter Crude Oil, and proffered a deal in which he would attempt to persuade the Libyans to double their crude oil production from approximately 100,000 to 200,000 barrels per day. In exchange for this increase in production, Billy would receive 55 cents compensation for each barrel over 100,000 that he was able to convince the Libyans to produce, thus grossing him about $20 million a year. Unfortunately for Billy, the Libyans never increased production; instead, they cut their crude supply in half.

Jack McGregor also has ties to George H.W. and George W. Bush. All three men went to Yale, and are members of the University's prestigious baseball "Bulldog Club." McGregor is also tied to Raymond K. Mason, Sr.,

Exhibit 3.5 The Teapot Dome oil scandal was among the most well-known public corruption issues of the twentieth century. Secretary of the Interior Albert B. Fall spent time in prison for bribery, while Secretary of the Navy Edwin N. Denby was forced to resign.

the former Chairman and Chief Executive Officer of Carey Energy's parent company, Charter Company. Mason later served as Chairman, Chief Executive Officer, and controlling shareholder of American Banks of Florida (1978–98), and as Director of Tesoro Petroleum Corporation, in which he held more than 20,000 shares according to his Tax Year 1999 Form 144 Filings. On March 8, 2001, President Bush appointed Tesoro Petroleum Director Sean O'Keefe as the new Deputy Director of the Office of Management and Budget. O'Keefe was subsequently nominated by President Bush to serve as the Administrator for the National Aeronautics and Space Administration (NASA). O'Keefe's nomination was confirmed by the Senate on December 21, 2001. Conspicuously absent from all of the White House press materials on O'Keefe was his service in the energy sector.

Similarly, Neil Bush, the brother of President George W. Bush, was also actively involved in JNB International, an inexperienced oil and gas exploration company which was awarded presidential concessions in Argentina. When JNB was absorbed into several other petroleum companies, Neil Bush was hired as a consultant at another Argentinean oil and gas exploration company, Plains Resources. According to a 1992 *New York Times* article,

Bush was hired by the firm because of his family's close relationship with Carlos Menem, who at the time was the President of Argentina, while George H.W. Bush was in the White House.[21]

Lastly, President George W. Bush served on the Board of Directors of Harken Energy and was permitted to purchase company stock at a 40 percent discount, which is not an uncommon opportunity given to senior officials in many businesses. However, in 1990, President Bush failed to file a timely disclosure pertaining to the sale of $826,560 worth of Harken stock—just one week before the stock slid into a six-month decline that resulted in a loss of more than 60 percent of its prior value. Shortly thereafter, Harken also improperly restated its earnings to the Securities and Exchange Commission, prompting *U.S. News and World Report* to remark in a 1992 article that Harken Energy was "characterized by a pattern of financial deal making so burdened with debt and tangled stock swaps that its largest creditors threatened to shut down the company."[22] When questioned by reporters about Harken's improper financial reporting to federal regulators (just weeks after the Enron and WorldCom stories had begun to intensify), President Bush shrugged and simply replied, "In the corporate world, sometimes things aren't exactly black and white when it comes to accounting procedures."

Accordingly, from Teapot Dome to Enron, the relationships between energy companies and the Office of the Chief Executive raise serious questions as to the ability of the government to effectively carry out its responsibilities without undue influence or conflict of interest. This issue will be further addressed in the final chapter of this text.

Nepotism: Personal Connections Over Professional Qualifications?

In 1967, Congress enacted the Anti-Nepotism Act, at least in part to address the concerns that lawmakers had regarding the close relationship between President John F. Kennedy, and his brother, Robert, whom the president had nominated for Attorney General in 1961 and who subsequently received Congressional approval to occupy this post. The law was written to prohibit relatives of high-level government officials from being appointed, employed, promoted, or advanced in the federal service.

One of the loopholes apparent in this act is that it does not apply to persons who held public positions prior to marriage. For example, a U.S. Representative or Senator who marries his or her aide can allow this person to continue working in the same capacity, provided the person held the job before their marriage. Moreover, the president reserves the right to appoint any private citizen to a commission or research panel, such as former President Clinton's assignment of then First Lady-turned-Senator Hillary Rodham Clinton to the Task Force on National Health Care Reform in 1993. Although Mrs. Clinton served as the leader of this committee, its members were not designated as government employees, nor did they have any supervisory or policy-making authority. Had former President Clinton appointed his wife to a competitive appointment or excepted service position within the executive branch (or otherwise influenced her selection), he would have violated the Nepotism regulations found at Title 5 United States Code, Section 3110.

Moreover, if Mrs. Clinton had performed the duties of what would normally be considered a government position without compensation, such actions would have violated the Anti-Deficiency Act, which prohibits such "voluntary services . . . except for emergencies involving the safety of human life or the protection of property"[23] for a period of time not to exceed one month, with an additional second month extension possible if the emergency persists.

Who is considered a relative according to the nepotism regulations in federal hiring? A list of persons who would be covered by this section of federal law is shown in Exhibit 3.6.

Given the fact that many of you may aspire to careers in federal law enforcement, it is important to know that Federal nepotism regulations do not prohibit relatives of those currently employed in federal service from obtaining government jobs. For example, assume that you have a brother employed by the government, and there is a position in his agency for which you wish to apply. If you are eligible for a position in the competitive service, apply for the position in the same manner as any other candidate, are found eligible for hire, and are not given any preference for selection because your brother works for the agency, then you can indeed be selected for the position. The intent of the law is to prohibit promotion or advancement of relatives because of non-merit factors at the expense of other qualified candidates or employees in the federal work force. This law covers all members of the Executive Branch (including the President, Vice President, Cabinet Officers and Department Heads) as well as many Legislative Branch and Judicial Branch positions.

Father♦Mother♦Son♦Daughter♦Brother♦Sister♦Uncle
♦Aunt♦First Cousin♦Nephew♦Niece♦Husband ♦Wife
Father-in-law♦Mother-in-law♦Son-in-law♦Daughter-in-law
♦Brother-in-law♦Sister-in-law♦ Stepfather♦ Stepmother♦
Stepsister♦half brother♦half sister

Exhibit 3.6 Persons covered under nepotism regulations for federal employment.

While there are some circumstances that allow for the emergency hiring of relatives during a national emergency or natural disaster (similar to the previously-discussed Anti-Deficiency Act), in most cases, failure to adhere to the nepotism regulations will nullify an improper appointment, and may require that the U.S. Department of the Treasury be reimbursed by the former selectee for any salary he or she has received.

Issues of nepotism are sometimes interlaced with other offenses such as waste, fraud, and abuse, and even national security. For example, in February of 2002, an investigation was conducted into possible operations security (OPSEC) violations committed by U.S. Army General Tommy Franks, former Commander in Chief of the United States Central Command. According to eyewitness testimony, General Franks allegedly allowed his wife Cathy to attend classified briefings, gave her a military bodyguard to whom she was not entitled, and may not have properly reimbursed the government for all of her travel when she accompanied him on official trips.

Misuse of Government Equipment and Supplies

As of April 2002, there were more than 2.5 million government credit cards in circulation.[24] These cards allow public employees to purchase a variety of goods and services for official use in a timely and efficient manner. Although the majority of federal employees who use these cards adhere to government procurement regulations, there are those who violate the public trust by using them for personal gain. Consider the following examples of credit card misuse cited in former Office of Management and Budget (OMB) Director Mitchell E. Daniels' April 18, 2002, memorandum to the heads of federal government departments and agencies:[25]

- Working together in a conspiracy to defraud the United States, an employee and his supervisor used their government credit cards to purchase scanners, printers, personal digital assistants (PDAs), cellular telephone accessories, and digital cameras for their own use. Both employees resigned instead of facing criminal charges.
- An employee prepared fictitious invoices using the names of legitimate companies with whom the government did business to hide $14,000 in unauthorized, personal purchases.
- In an effort to enjoy an enhanced lifestyle that included frequent air travel and dining at fancy restaurants, an employee charged over $12,000 in personal expenses to his government credit card.

At one federal agency alone, the OMB estimates that government employees spent more than $4 million in unauthorized "transactions . . . such as . . . [purchases made at] jewelry stores, [and] antique shops."[26] In one of the most noteworthy cases in recent history, three clerical employees assigned to the Central Intelligence Agency in Langley, Virginia, illegally intercepted the government credit card numbers of 108 undercover field operatives located around the globe, and used this information to obtain cash advances and to purchase satellite dishes, widescreen televisions, car tires, compact disc players, and NBA tickets. By the time they were apprehended, these three employees had spent more than $160,000 in taxpayer money on the above-mentioned luxury items and also compromised the safety and security of these 108 CIA employees and their families.

Misuse of government credit cards is only one area of concern for federal managers. Unauthorized use of government office equipment such as personal computers, related equipment and software, Internet services, email, library resources, telephones, fax machines, photocopiers, and office supplies is a growing problem for the public sector. In particular, sending or receiving sexually explicit materials, loading government-licensed software on to personal computer systems, and engaging in side businesses during government work time have become especially problematic. In a similar fashion, the misuse of telephone functions, such as long distance services and toll calls (e.g., adult entertainment services, psychic hotlines and horoscopes, etc.) from federal telephones costs U.S. taxpayers millions—if not billions—of dollars each fiscal year. Even when employees are apprehended for misusing government office equipment, supplies, or services, the penalties rarely exact more punishment than suspension or termination. In fact, one of the only official use offenses carrying clear and specific penalties is the willful misuse of a government vehicle (31 USC 1344–49).

The actions of Army Secretary Hon. Thomas E. White and former White House Chief of Staff John Sununu discussed earlier in this chapter clearly demonstrate the use of passenger motor vehicles or aircraft for purposes other than official government missions (i.e., flying to Aspen on a military jet to close on the sale of a home and attending a stamp auction, respectively). In the case of Kimm v. Dept. of Treasury, the Merit Systems Protection Board (MSPB) found that "persons not deemed essential" to the government's mission, such as friends, spouses, and other family members should normally not be permitted transport in government-owned or operated conveyances. The bottom line is that if the use of the government vessel, aircraft, or motor vehicle is wholly unrelated to the purpose for which it has been authorized, such activities would be considered willful misuse. Accordingly, punishment under this statute carries a mandatory 30-day suspension without pay.

Bribery

Of all of the offenses described in this chapter thus far (i.e., betraying the public trust, nepotism, and misuse of government equipment), none exacts more outrage from the American public than bribery (18 USC 201). White-collar crime scholar Jay Albanese defines bribery as "the voluntary giving or receiving of anything of value in corrupt payment for an official act, with the intent to influence the action of a public official."[27] The Office of the Inspector General's case files contain a myriad of incidents in which employees have accepted bribes or attempted to solicit prospective vendors in exchange for lucrative government contracts. One typical example is as follows:

> In one large scam, a General Services Administration motor transportation officer who supervised operations of a regional government fleet of cars worked with an automotive repair inspector in a three-part scheme: (1) the vendor, a car-repair company, submitted inflated claims to the GSA officer, who approved them, then took cash for the difference between the inflated claim and true cost; (2) they solicited cash that was intended for two holiday parties for GSA employees, but instead kept the money; (3) they took cash sporadically along with free service for their own cars. The GSA transportation officer took $1,350 along with free service. The inspector also gave the vendors confidential bidding information for which he received $18,850 and free service.

The temptations available to both civil service employees and elected officials willing to select vendors for public projects without fair competition are considerable. In 2005, former California Congressman Randy "Duke" Cunningham, who held seats on both the House Intelligence Committee and Appropriations Subcommittee, pled guilty to accepting more than $2.4 million in bribes from Mitchell Wade, a defense contractor. He is currently serving an eight-year prison term. In a related story, Kyle "Dusty" Foggo, the third highest-ranking officer in the Central Intelligence Agency, quit his post in May 2006 after allegations of additional payoffs to Representative Cunningham surfaced. In 2007, Mr. Foggo was indicted on eleven counts of conspiracy, wire fraud, money laundering, and depriving taxpayers of honest services as a result of the "Duke" Cunningham corruption probe.

On February 2, 1980, Congressman Frank Thompson, a New Jersey Democrat, was arrested in a FBI undercover operation known as "Abscam" for receiving $45,000 in cash in exchange for aiding phony Arab sheiks in their efforts to obtain a gaming license to open a casino in Atlantic City.[28] Thompson received a sentence of three years in federal prison. Also criminally implicated in the Abscam case was South Philadelphia Democratic Congressman Michael Myers, who received a two-year prison sentence and whose behavior was deemed so egregious that he was expelled from Congress—the first such expulsion since the Civil War. Apparently, Myers was dissatisfied with the $15,000 bribe that the undercover agents offered him in exchange for special favors, and was recorded by surveillance video cameras uttering the now famous phrase "money talks, bull walks."[29]

More recently, the U.S. House of Representatives expelled Ohio Congressman James Trafficant for his conviction on bribery, fraud, and tax evasion charges, as well as being found guilty of nine Congressional ethics violations connected to these acts. The colorful Congressman responded by saying that he was the victim of a government conspiracy, and quipped, "I am proud to be an American. I hate the government, but I love America."[30]

Protecting Technology from the Corporate–State Corruption Paradigm

The Bureau of Industry and Security

One of the most important questions that you might have is who prevents corrupt practices from being committed between foreign governments and U.S. corporations? Alternatively, who ensures that foreign leaders attempting to entice U.S.-based corporations into providing sensitive information technology equipment, biological agents, or other products to their nations are apprehended? To combat such practices, Congress enacted three laws, namely the Trading With the Enemy Act of 1917 (P.L. 65–91), the Foreign Corrupt Practices Act of 1977 (15 USC 78), and the Export Administration Act (50 USC 2410). Of these three laws, the most aggressively and successfully enforced has been the latter, which falls under the jurisdiction of the U.S. Department of Bureau of Industry and Security (BIS). BIS Special Agents are responsible for ensuring that sensitive electronic equipment, military hardware, biological products, and radiological materials are not exported to countries with which the U.S. currently maintains an embargo (Iraq, North Korea, and Cuba) or that might utilize these items in a manner contrary to national security (e.g., Libya, Iran, Sudan, and Syria). Many BIS investigations have resulted in criminal penalties against major corporations in the computer, chemical manufacturing, and petroleum industries. Special agents of the BIS also investigate sales of chemical and biological weapons and conduct educational seminars for business executives in an effort to aid the industry in complying with federal export regulations. For additional information on the roles and responsibilities of the Bureau of Industry and Security, refer to its website located at URL: http://www.bis.doc.gov/about/index.htm

Chapter Summary

Chapter 3 of this book examines the sometimes dubious relationships between major corporations and government policymakers. Specific cases where public officials allegedly betrayed the public trust were presented, as well as salient discussion of commonly-encountered offenses such as nepotism and misuse of government equipment were presented. Lastly, the act of bribery was briefly discussed, along with some examples of modern-day offenders.

ADAPTED READINGS

Reading 3–1: Charlie Cray, *Disaster Profiteering: The Flood of Crony Contracting Following Hurricane Katrina*

> *In Reading 1–2, we examined some of the fraud that occurred in the wake of hurricanes Katrina and Rita. However, such acts are not confined simply to individuals misrepresenting themselves to obtain government benefits. Rather, as you will learn in the ensuing article, the entire process of procuring goods and services for a community in need can be rife with fraudulent activities such as improper contracting and procurement.*

After Hurricane Katrina came ashore, President Bush promised relief for those in the Gulf region affected by the storm. But the relief he has been most generous in delivering has been to contractors.

That at least is the view of a growing number of government watchdogs and congressional critics, who say a series of exemptions to competitive bidding and other procurement requirements adopted by the Federal Emergency Management Agency (FEMA) and the Army Corps of Engineers has effectively turned the Gulf region reconstruction and cleanup contracts into a feeding frenzy for "disaster profiteers"—a network of crony contractors for whom the $200 billion cleanup and reconstruction promises to be a significant windfall.

They say FEMA's no-bid and limited-bid contracts are of such magnitude that they will give prime contractors an advantage that will last far beyond the initial emergency phase, and put local contractors at a distinct disadvantage.

By the end of September, there were ominous signs that the same pattern of "fundamentally flawed contracting strategies" described by congressional investigators as the cause of the epidemic of waste and corruption witnessed in Iraq was beginning to repeat itself in Louisiana and Mississippi. Many of the same companies involved in Iraq—Fluor, Beehtel, CH2M Hill and Halliburton—are now poised to clean up at home.

And some in Congress seem only too willing to provide them a helping hand. In late September, for example, Senator Mel Martinez, R-Florida, reserved a room on Capitol Hill for a "Katrina Reconstruction Summit" co-sponsored by Halliburton.

Contracting Out Contracting Out

"You are likely to see the equivalent of war profiteering—disaster profiteering," says Danielle Brian, director of the Project on Government Oversight, which is monitoring the contracts.

But the contractors say the critics are off base. Randal Perkins, the founder of Florida-based Ashbritt, which has received one of the largest cleanup contracts for debris removal in Mississippi, says no one from his company attended Martinez's summit. While he and his wife have donated $10,000 to Martinez's Senate campaign fund since 2000, he says anyone who knows how the disaster contracting game works knows that the contracts are secured long before the storms hit shore and have nothing to do with lobbying on the Hill or campaign contributions.

"We have more pre-positioned contracts than any other company in the country because we are the best in the business," Perkins says. "I'd ask the people who are complaining—where they were five years ago when these contracts were bid nationally?"

Ashbritt's contract was, in fact, awarded through a competitive process involving 22 bidders.

Yet government watchdogs maintain that there's much more to the game than pure merit-based competition. Companies like Ashbritt are able to anticipate potentially lucrative opportunities because they have hired former FEMA and Corps officials who can guide them through the process.

Ashbritt has come a long way since 1992, when it received its first subcontract from Brown & Root (a Halliburton subsidiary) after Hurricane Andrew. The company also employs top lobbyists including former Representative James A. Hayes, D. Louisiana, and Mississippi Governor Haley Barbour's former firm, Barbour Griffith and Rogers, which helped Ashbritt get work after the 2004 Florida hurricanes.

Perkins says it would be "naive" to expect businesses to restrain themselves from hiring lobbyists who can help them navigate the maze of bureaucracy in Washington.

"We hired [former Army Corps of Engineers Director] Mike Parker to work with us on this Corps project . . . We're dealing with contracting specialists. We're dealing with both the civilian and military sides of the Corps. We're dealing with the Defense Contract Audit Agency, small and minority business specialists. There are a lot of legal and protocol issues that we have to deal with. So I went out and found the best person available. . . . We play by the rules, and if you stay above-board, those are the parameters. If it's okay for state and local governments to hire lobbyists in Washington, why isn't it okay for private industry?"

Yet small business groups complain that the pre-existing contracts put companies like Ashbritt at a distinct advantage over local businesses hardest hit by the hurricane, many of whom are eager to get a piece of the action. The Army Corps of Engineers reported receiving over 6,300 phone calls within two weeks after Katrina landed, many from local and regional contractors who have complained that their calls were ignored. The Corps responded that its web site clearly directs inquiries to the prime contractors, but many local businesses had their Internet access knocked out by the storm and say the prime contractors have been slow to return their calls.

Small business owners also say that by turning the contracting process over to prime contractors like Ashbritt, the Corps and FEMA have effectively privatized the enforcement of federal Acquisition Regulations and disaster relief laws such as the Stafford Act, which require contracting officials to prioritize local businesses and give 5 percent of contracts to minority owned businesses. As a result, they have not been surprised by early reports which suggest that over 90 percent of the $2 billion in initial contracts was awarded to companies based outside of the three primary affected states, and that minority businesses received just 1.5 percent of the first $1.6 billion.

Many local businesses have turned to their elected officials for help. At a congressional hearing in early November, Representative Charles Pickering, R. Mississippi, complained about the lack of contracting work going to local companies in his state, noting only 5.6 percent of Army Corps contracts for work in Mississippi—where Ashbritt is the prime contractor—had gone to Mississippi companies.

"When you have a hurricane of that magnitude that devastates the coastal community of two states, it's very difficult at the inception to get local contractors going." Perkins responds. "We've got a recovery operation that we have to mobilize 24 hours before the storm comes to shore. So at first you have to use contractors from outside the region. Then, as the recovery moves forward, you start supplementing contractors from other areas with local and statewide contractors."

"We now have three offices open in the impacted area where we talk to subcontractors," Perkins adds. "And we've gone out of our way to help smaller subcontractors by waiving some of the more stringent [Army Corps] insurance requirements by taking out umbrella policies that smaller contractors can use who can't afford to meet the requirements. I maintain that we've done a good job putting money back into Mississippi contractors."

Outsourcing Relief

There is little disagreement, even among FEMA's supporters, that the agency is still reeling from public criticism of its response to Katrina and additional responsibilities created by Hurricanes Rita and Wilma, and in its presem form is virtually incapable of managing and overseeing contracts expected to cost $200 billion.

Although apologists say FEMA cannot be expected to maintain the kind of large bureaucracy necessary to handle a sudden emergency on a full time basis, the agency is supposed to be prepared for disasters, and intense hurricanes are likely to occur on a regular basis for the foreseable future, thanks to the combination of naturally occurring 25-year cycles for hurricanes and the human made problem of global warming. Complicating matters is FEMA's shift in priorities from disaster relief to counterterrorism in recent years, and the gutting of the agency's acquisition workforce under the guise of "acquisition reform"—an attempt to streamline federal procurement processes that affected most federal contracting bureaucracies in the 1990s.

As a result, FEMA has farmed out much of the procurement management process to companies like Acquisition Solutions and is using existing contracting vehicles negotiated by other agencies.

Where some see this as a formula for flexibility, others see the lack of a strong coordinating authority in the government as a formula for chaos, waste and fraud.

Just weeks after Katrina hit, congressional watchdogs began to question FEMA's decision to pay Carnival Cruise Lines up to $236 million to house 7,000 people in three cruise liners, especially when the government of Greece was ready to provide two ships for free. A Senate Federal Financial Management Subcommittee's investigation into the six-month contract found that taxpayers will end up paying four times the amount, per person, that vacation cruise passengers would pay, although Carnival's overhead costs are far lower than during normal cruises.

"Finding out after the fact that we're spending taxpayer money on no-bid contracts and sweetheart deals for cruise lines is no way to run a recovery effort," Senator Tom Coburn, R. Oklahoma, complained. Coburn and Senator Barack Obama, D. Illinois, have pressed Homeland Security Secretary Michael Chertoff for an explanation and introduced a bill that would create a Chief Financial Officer (CFO) to oversee all expenditures associated with the Hurricane Katrina relief and reconstruction effort.

"It should be remembered that the federal government sought us out," Terry Thornton, a Carnival vice president says. Although "the urgency of the situation demanded fast action," Thornton says the contracts were competitively bid, and that the Military Sealift Command, a branch of the Navy, asked 75 vessel owners to submit bids.

Setting Aside the Set-Aside Rules

Apart from rushing into questionable contracts during the immediate emergency, critics say the Bush administration also used the initial emergency as cover for a series of waivers and exemptions from federal contracting regulations that have made it much more difficult for those whose businesses and jobs were blown away to get in on the action.

One of the first such waivers was a directive that lifted the limit for small federal credit card purchases requiring cost comparisons from $2,500 to $250,000, and raised the threshold for subcontracts having to meet competitive bidding requirements to $10 million.

"This new exception raises serious concerns that the same problems that dogged U.S. contracting in Iraq—failures in competition, failures in transparency, and failures in integrity—will arise in the hurricane relief effort," Christopher Yukins, associate professor of government contracting law at George Washington University Law School concluded at one of the first congressional hearings on the reconstruction.

The directive was rescinded and the $2,500 cap restored in early October.

Another waiver that was immediately criticized as unnecessary and unfair to workers was a Department of Labor decision to waive requirements established under the Davis Bacon Act a New Deal-era law that requires contractors to pay their employees a regional prevailing wage for similar work and provide payroll reports to federal overseers.

"Absent a wage floor and reporting, the door is open to fraud of various kinds," says James Hale, vice president and regional manager of the Laborers International Union. "One can't determine if a contractor is utilizing ghost employees."

The policy was finally reversed in late October, but only after moderate Republicans in the House of Representatives began to pressure the White House and a subcontractor hired by Halliburton was caught using 100 undocumented immigrants to replace union electricians working on a Louisiana Navy base.

"It is a downright shame that any contractor would use this tragedy as an opportunity to line his pockets by breaking the law and hiring a low skilled, low-wage and undocumented work force," Senator Mary Landrien, D. Louisiana, suggested. "The federal government must ensure that every company, no matter how big, follows the Law and provides Gulf Coast residents with the jobs they deserve."

Although Halliburton denies any connection, critics note that company subcontractors are also using loss wage workers from outside the region to cut the costs of its troop support work in Iraq. Retired U.S. Navy Admiral David Nash, the former head of the U.S. Program Management Office in Baghdad, was hired to head up the government contracting group of BE&K ... the Halliburton subcontractor caught using undocumented workers.

Although these may be simply coincidental connections, many in Congress are concerned that the epidemic of fraud and other abuses witnessed in Iraq could be repeated at home. Nineteen members of the congressional Progressive Caucus have demanded that the Bush administration suspend Halliburton from any Katrina related contracts based upon unresolved criminal investigations related to its prior work in Iraq.

"The aftermath of Hurricane Katrina demonstrated the tragic consequences of having an administration where cronyism trumps competence," says Caucus co chair Rep. Barbara Lee. D.California. "The fact that the President would cut wages for impacted workers, while handing out millions in no-bid contracts to well connected firms is a perfect snapshot to this administration's priorities."

Although the Bush administration has not responded to the Caucus's call to suspend Halliburton, the administration's defenders maintain that criticism of Halliburton is partisan-driven and stems from the company's association with Vice President Dick Cheney, the former CEO of Halliburton.

Yet there are other factors to consider, including the Army Corps' unusually cozy relationship with the company. Right before Katrina hit, the Corps demoted its top civilian contracting expert. Bunnatine Greenhouse, who testified to Congress that "the abuse related to contracts awarded to Halliburton represents the most blatant and improper contract abuse I have ever witnessed during the course of my professional career."

Meanwhile, the administration's chief of procurement policy, David Safavian was himself indicted in September while he was working on the Katrina contracts, for obstructing an ongoing investigation into the activities of disgraced Republican lobbyist Jack Abramoff.

At a time when scandals, indictments and charges of cronyism are beginning to pile up on the Bush White House's doorstep, it is perhaps no surprise that the administration would avoid establishing tough suspension and debarment standards that might punish their cronies.

Other companies with dubious backgrounds, besides Halliburton, have benefited from the administration's policy. Consider Circle B Enterprises, which received a $287.5 million FEMA contract to supply temporary housing. The company's president, Lackte G Williams, formerly ran a Georgia company called Sweetwater Homes Inc. that residents say constructed shoddy houses. Sweetwater went out of business in 2001. When Williams applied for a building license from the state again in 2003, the state refused to grant it until he fixed old warranty claims. FEMA officials defend Circle B Enterprises based on work it did in Florida after the 2004 hurricanes.

Another apparently shady beneficiary of law standards for contractors is Texas-based Goldstar FMS, which was hired as a subcontractor by Henderson Consulting, through whom it provided 45 ambulances at $800 a day Goldstar was raided by the FBI in association with a Medicaid fraud investigation earlier this year.

FEMA officials say they use the General Services Administration's suspension and debarment list to screen companies applying for all federal contracts, as well as FEMA's own database. But these background checks are rarely comprehensive enough to include disputes with the IRS or other parts of the government, and fail to block contractors that are still under criminal investigation for problems experienced in Iraq, including Halliburton.

In an effort to demand greater accountability and transparency, Senator

Frank Lautenberg, D. New Jersey, has proposed that the government establish a database of all contractors' compliance histories. The Senate passed a similar proposal in a 2006 defense appropriations bill.

In addition to placing inspectors on the ground and improving cross-agency coordination, critics say that federal contracting agencies need to improve the transparency of the process and not leave that up to the contractors, especially when it comes to revealing the identities of subcontractors and the terms under which they are carrying out the actual work.

"We're not restricted [from posting subcontracts]," Ashbritt's Perkins says. "We submit all our contracting data to the Army Corps on a weekly basis and that's all available from them if they so choose."

The layering of contracts in Iraq was a major impediment to auditors and investigators attempting to protect taxpayers from fraud. And as the Halliburton case suggests the lack of transparency in subcontracting, combined with the various procurement waivers, has also made it more difficult to assess how much the impacted communities have benefited, and what abuses have occurred.

"No one knows what the state of subcontracting in the region is," says James Hale of the Laborers' International Union.

"The vast majority of workers are being paid below a livable wage. However, no one seems to know what contractors are being reimbursed for labor costs. On cost-plus contracts, subcontractor reimbursement rates are whatever the prime [contractor] determines and actual rates of pay are unknown. In fixed bid [contracts], actual reimbursement rates are unknown and subcontractor rates are both unknown and subject to great fluctuation. There is simply no ability to ascertain or monitor the contractor/subcontractor relationships. This is an open invitation for exploitation, fraud and abuse."

Betting on the Weather

As global warming intensifies, the damage from future hurricanes will increase. And with federal agencies increasingly relying upon private contractors to manage the fallout, the new disaster profiteers will face unprecedented opportunities

"Our company will look at government forecasts on this kind of spending," says Randy Perkins, whose company has been transformed from an obscure Florida subcontractor after Hurricane Andrew into one of the major players in the emerging disaster industry.

After beating out the competition, like so many contractors, Ashbritt's ability to maintain its advantage in the future will continue to depend upon its ability to anticipate opportunities and develop a cozy relationship with the Army Corps of Engineers and other government bureaucracies.

"We look at opportunities that are 12, 14 months away with various agencies. We'll look and search and try to find something that best suits our capabilities.

There's nothing wrong with us asking to meet with an agency beforehand. It happens every day in Washington."

Source: *Multinational Monitor,* © 2005

Reading 3–2: Charlie Cray, *Meet the War Profiteers*

> *The very notion that some corporations and members of our society could endeavor to personally benefit from war seems strange. Yet, the United States has a rich history of "war profiteering," to the extent that former President Harry Truman is often remembered for his aggressive pursuit of those who would place our nation's soldiers, sailors, airmen, and marines in harm's way in order to personally prosper. As you will learn in the following article, unfortunately, what was true during World War I and World War II remains the same today.*

Forty-five dollar cases of soda; $85,000 trucks, in need of minor repairs, torched and abandoned; tens of millions of dollars in gasoline surcharges; thousands of meals prepared but never served to the troops, while Third World nationals, paid a pittance by their subcontractors get fed spoiled leftovers; contaminated water served to the troops. These are among the many abuses committed by Halliburton/KBR and its subsidiaries in Iraq, brought to light by a relative handful of whistleblowers and government officials.

Halliburton has been the biggest contractor in Iraq, receiving some $20 billion from both its oil and troop logistics contracts, but it is not alone. The Iraq war is the most privatized war in U.S. history, and many corporations have gotten fat feeding off the public trough.

Stuart Brandes, author of *Warhogs*, a history of war profiteering in the United States, suggests that all wars introduce new meaning to the term "war profiteer."

- In the Revolutionary War, officers of the Continental Army were convicted of defrauding troops of their pay, embezzlement and misappropriating government property.
- During the Civil War, stories about the adulteration of supplies made "shoddy" a dirty word, leading Congress to pass the Frauds Act of 1863—the legacy of which survives in the False Claims Act.
- Anticipating the country's entry into World War I, Congress made the deliberate inflation of prices ("profiteering") during wartime a crime. By then it was clear that war profiteering not only harmed taxpayers, but also undermined the military's own mission.
- During World War II, Senator Harry Truman held hundreds of hearings on the issue, saving taxpayers an estimated $15 billion (in 1940s dollars).

As Edwin Sutherland suggested in his 1948 book *White Collar Crime*, the first comprehensive look at corporate crime, industry regulations for most of the major war-related industries "were made chiefly by representatives of the large industries and in their favor." The result was after-tax profits of 100 percent and higher in the steel, meat and chemicals sectors. Despite their considerable influence over war-time standards, many large corporations were charged with violating price regulations, restraint of trade in war-related materials and tax evasion, according to Sutherland. Some (such as RCA) were accused of treason for passing technological secrets (in this case, related to radar) to the enemy (the Department of Justice dropped the issue when the chief of the Signal Corps, who pushed for the prosecution, went on to work for RCA).

The historical record throughout these wars, and others, suggests that the definition of "war profiteering" is—perhaps out of necessity due to ever-evolving corporate perfidy—"disturbingly imprecise," as Brandes puts it.

Without a strict definition, it's impossible to objectively determine who might be the worst war profiteer in the Iraq war, and the broader "war on terror." But there is no shortage of bad actors. Here, presented alphabetically, is a list of 10 of the worst war profiteers not named Halliburton.

Aegis Defense Services

The General Accountability Office (GAO) estimates that there are about 48,000 private security and military contractors (PMCs) in Iraq. Industry analysts expect it will be a $200 billion-a-year global business by 2010.

This increased use of contractors is creating a novel set of battlefield problems. As the GAO puts it, because PMCs fall outside the chain of command, as well as the Code of Military Justice, they "continue to enter the battle space without coordinating with the U.S. military, putting both the military and security providers at a greater risk for injury."

George Washington University Professor Deborah Avant, an expert on the industry, says while some established PMCs may act very professionally, companies like Aegis—a UK firm whose founder and CEO Tim Spicer was implicated for breaking an arms embargo in Sierra Leone—give the entire industry a black eye and reputation for being "mercenaries."

In March, the *Charlotte News-Observer* reported that security contractors in Iraq regularly reported shooting into civilian cars. The newspaper's report was based on documents provided by the military in response to a Freedom of Information Act request; the military redacted names from the released documents.

Like the abuses at Abu Ghraib, the problem was largely ignored until a "trophy video" of security guards firing with automatic rifles at civilian cars was posted on a web site linked to Aegis.

The Army's Criminal Investigation Division determined that no charges would be filed against Aegis or its employees. One reason: President Bush signed Executive Order 13303 in 2003, granting the contractors immunity from prosecution in Iraq's courts. Some experts on the industry believe private military contractors were immune from military prosecution until late 2006, when Congress passed legislation bringing PMCs under the Uniform Code of Military Justice, although others say that prior legislation already provided for such prosecution.

Aegis officials say an independent review board investigation of the "trophy video" found that

> the films were recorded during Aegis' legitimate operations in support of the Multi-National Force Iraq and the incidents recorded were within the Rules for the Use of Force. There was no evidence of any civilian casualties as a result of the incidents and the images published were all taken out of context and were therefore highly misleading in what they represented.

"It is regrettable that the actions of one Aegis contractor, who has been the subject of separate court action in the UK, brought into question the high standards of behavior achieved by our team in Iraq," Spicer says. "Aegis is a prime contractor to the U.S. Government with an exemplary record of performance."

BearingPoint—Economic Hit Men

BearingPoint was brought into Iraq under a $240 million U.S. Agency for International Development (AID) sole-source contract to "facilitate Iraq's economic recovery"—to take charge of writing its business law, set up its tax collection system and trade and customs rules, close down the oil-for-food program (the main source of food for 60 percent of the population), and plan the privatization of key state-owned industries, among other things.

BearingPoint later received a contract to facilitate "private-sector involvement in strategic sectors." The company was reportedly "assigned" by the U.S. government to help the Iraqi Oil Ministry draft a new oil law. Iraqis have ultimately had less influence over the drafting of their own economic laws than the technocrats at the CPA, U.S. MD and BearingPoint, a situation many believe violates international law on the duty of occupiers.

A leaked memo written on March 26, 2003, by Lord Goldsmith, the British Attorney General, apparently warned British Prime Minister Tony Blair that "the imposition of major structural economic reforms would not be authorized by international law." On the U.S. side, General Jay Garner, the first CPA head, says he was sacked a month into the job because he had called for swift and free elections, rejecting proposals to impose a privatization program first.

BearingPoint actually helped MD write the specifications for the contract to design Iraq's "competitive private sector"—the contract that BearingPoint then went on to administer.

"Economic reform work is part of a public-sector division that is Bearing-Point's most successful unit and has buoyed the company in recent years," according to the *Washington Post*. "The 550 people working in economic reconstruction have often spent years in government jobs or working with organizations like the World Bank."

Bechtel: Precast Profits

The San Francisco-based construction and engineering giant received one of the largest no-bid contracts—worth $2.4 billion—to help coordinate and rebuild a large part of Iraq's infrastructure, including electric power systems, roads, railroad systems, municipal water and sanitation services, government buildings, irrigation systems, and a port. But the company has been criticized for everything from shoddy school repairs to failing to finish a large hospital on time and within budget.

Although U.S. AID chief Andrew Natsios originally promised a Middle Eastern Marshall Plan, Iraq reconstruction is now widely acknowledged to have been a total failure.

Natsios should have known that all would not go smoothly with Bechtel in the lead: Prior to joining the Bush administration, he was chief executive of the Massachusetts Turnpike Authority, where he oversaw the Big Dig—a major highway tunnel project—as the cost exploded from $2.6 billion to $14.6 billion under Bechtel's lead.

In July, Stuart Bowen, the Special Inspector General for Iraq Reconstruction (SIGIR), released an audit of the Basra Children's Hospital Project, a favorite project of Laura Bush's, which was $70 million to $90 million over budget, and a year-and-a-half behind schedule. Bechtel's contract to coordinate the project was immediately canceled.

In November [2007] the company announced it was leaving Iraq, having completed most of the rest of its contract obligations. By almost any standard, the results were terrible. After over three years of work, the country was generating less electricity than it was before the war, potable water hookups were delivered to just over half of the number of people anticipated, and sewage services had also not met the anticipated goal, according to SIGIR.

CACI, Titan and the Outsourcing of Intelligence

In early 2005, CIA officials admitted that at least 50 percent of its estimated $40 billion budget that year would go to private contractors.

Years before the war on terror began, Pentagon officials began to raise serious national security concerns about the outsourcing of intelligence and related work considered to be an inherent function of government. A December 2000 Army intelligence memo uncovered by the Center for Public Integrity warned explicitly against the use of contractors for sensitive intelligence work.

"At the tactical level," the memo explained, "the intelligence function under the operational control of the Army performed by military in the operating forces is an inherently governmental function barred from private sector performance."

That was no longer the Pentagon view by the time of the Iraqi invasion, as private firms gained huge intelligence responsibilities in Iraq.

Leading contractors CACI and Titan surpassed the worst fears of privatization opponents. The firms were centrally involved in the abuses at Abu Ghraib. CACI provided a total of 36 interrogators, including up to 10 at Abu Ghraib at any one time, according to the company. Titan personnel provided translation services.

Neither CACI nor its employees have yet been charged with a crime. Company officials claim their employees were never involved in the most egregious acts at the prison. Critics, however, cite a leaked report from Army investigator Major General Antonio Taguba that implicates CACI employee Stephen Stefanowicz in the abuse of prisoners. They say the contractors have so far escaped punishment only because of the lack of any system of accountability.

CACI denies the findings of the Taguba report, asserting in a briefing paper titled "Truth and Error in the Media Portrayal of CACI in Iraq" that "All of Maj. Gen. Taguba's allegations regarding this employee remain unsupported based on all of the evidence made available to date." The company adds that other investigations have not supported Taguba's findings.

Since the war on terror began, just one civilian, CIA contract interrogator David A. Passaro, has been indicted and convicted, for felony assault associated with interrogation tactics.

The Center for Constitutional Rights (CCR) in New York has helped some of the detainees at Abu Ghraib file civil lawsuits in the U.S. against CACI and Titan and their employees.

"We believe that CACI and Titan engaged in a conspiracy to torture and abuse detainees, and did so to make more money," says Susan Burke, an attorney hired by CCR, whose lawsuit has survived various motions to dismiss and is proceeding into discovery before a federal district court. Whatever the outcome of that and related cases, it's already clear that the publicity generated by the cases have had an effect: CACI announced last September that it would no longer do interrogation work in Iraq. (CACI's CEO says its interrogation work was only one percent of the company's business.)

Despite Titan's other problems (in early 2005, it pleaded guilty to three felony international bribery charges and agreed to pay a record $28.5 million Foreign Corrupt Practices Act penalty), its contract with the Army has been extended numerous times, and is currently worth over $1 billion.

Chevron, Exxonmobil and the Other Petro-Imperialists

Despite all the talk about civil war and chaos, just four years into the occupation, the oil giants' takeover of Iraq's oil is nearly complete. The process has involved an evolving series of deft legal maneuvers and appointments, starting with Paul Bremer's CPA orders, and provisions inserted into the new Iraqi constitution that open the doors to foreign investors. Key will be whether the petro-imperialists can convince the Iraqi parliament to pass a new petroleum law to facilitate foreign control, as now appears virtually certain.

The oil industry giants have kept a relatively low profile throughout the process, lending just a few senior statesmen to the CPA, including Philip Carroll (Shell U.S., Fluor) and Rob McKee (ConocoPhillips and Halliburton). In addition, the CPA's liaison to the fledgling Iraqi Oil Ministry, a highly sensitive position, was filled by Chevron-Texaco Vice President Norm Szydlowski.

Greg Muttitt of the UK non-profit Platform says Chevron, Shell and ConocoPhillips are among the most interested in Iraq of all the major oil companies.

Companies such as Shell and Chevron have signed agreements with the Iraqi government, and begun to train Iraqi staff and conduct studies. These have given the companies vital access to Oil Ministry officials, as well as geological data, which would give them an advantage in bidding for future contracts, although Iraqi Oil Minister Hussain al-Shahristani said in August that the final competition will be wide open.

A key milestone in the privatization process occurred in September 2004, when U.S.-appointed Interim Prime Minister Ayad Allawi preempted Iraq's January 2005 elections (and the subsequent drafting of the Constitution) by writing guidelines which were intended to form the basis of a new petroleum law. His policy would have effectively excluded the government from any future involvement in oil production, while promising to privatize the Iraqi National Oil Company. Although Allawi is no longer in power, his plans heavily influenced future thinking on oil policy.

The plans for a new Iraq petroleum law were made public at a press conference in Washington D.C. by Adel Agbdul Mahdi, formerly the finance minister and now a Deputy President of Iraq.

A key provision in the new law is a commitment to using Production Sharing Agreements (PSAs), which will lock the government into a long-term commitment (up to 50 years) to sharing oil revenues, and restrict its right to introduce any new laws that might affect the companies' profitability. Muttitt says they are designed to favor private companies at the expense of exporting governments, which is why none of the top oil-producing countries in the Middle East use PSAs.

Under Iraq's forthcoming petroleum law, all new fields and some existing fields are likely to be opened up to private companies through the use of PSAs. Since less than 20 of Iraq's 80 known oil fields have already been developed, if Iraq's government commits to signing the PSAs, it could cost the country up to nearly $200 billion in lost revenues, according to Muttitt.

The Baker-Hamilton Commission lent further support for this agenda, emphasizing the need for privatization and foreign control of Iraqi oil resources.

Thus, despite the common perception that the war has been a total failure, for those who initiated it, the ultimate prize may still be within reach.

The Coalition Provisional Authority: The Lords of War

The Coalition Provisional Authority (CPA) was the temporary governing authority set up by the United States to rule Iraq at the start of the U.S. occupation. It disbanded on June 28, 2004, after the transfer of sovereignty to the new Iraqi government. Virtually every aspect of the CPA's performance is now viewed as defined by incompetence.

But problems at the CPA extend far beyond mere questions of competence. In at least a couple of respects, the CPA itself can be accused of war profiteering.

The most obvious form of that occurred in the southern province of Al-Hillah, where U.S. contracting officials conspired to rig more than $8 million worth of construction and services contracts. A CPA former comptroller, Robert Stein, pleaded guilty in February 2006 to bribery, money laundering, conspiracy and using government money to purchase an array of high-powered rifles and grenade launchers. Stein admitted that, in exchange for payments and other favors, he steered business to companies owned by his co-conspirator, Philip Bloom. In April, Bloom admitted to plying CPA personnel for favors with jewelry, first-class plane tickets and sexual favors from women he employed at a villa in Baghdad. Bloom faces as long as 40 years in prison and nearly $8 million in penalties.

Other CPA officials charged for their involvement in the scam include Lt. Col. Michael Wheeler, who smuggled $100,000 of stolen money into the United States, and Lt. Col. Debra Harrison, who used still more money to buy a Cadillac and build a hot tub at her house back in New Jersey.

At the end of July, Inspector General Bowen, whose office uncovered the seam, reported that 82 preliminary and criminal investigations were still open, involving a variety of crimes, including bribery/kickbacks (21), theft/larceny (19), contract fraud (17), falsified billing, embezzlement and other alleged crimes. Twenty-five of those cases have been referred to the Department of Justice, including 15 that stem from the Bloom/Stein conspiracy.

"Most current investigations directly or indirectly involve allegations against a U.S. government official or military officer," Bowen reported to Congress.

The environment created by the CPA "positively encouraged corruption," says Alan Grayson, a Florida-based attorney who has represented a number of whistleblowers now trying to expose the fraud.

At the CPA's headquarters inside the Green Zone, for example, inexperienced political appointees were seen tossing bricks of $100 bills around like footballs. Other news reports suggested one contractor had been paid $100,000 to refurbish an Olympic swimming pool, and that a military assistant had gambled away as much as $60,000 while accompanying the Iraqi Olympic team to the Philippines.

"In the early days, there was no record keeping. They were flushed with money and seized assets. People just didn't follow established procedures," said Charles Krohn, a former CPA official. "You were dealing with inexperienced people who didn't understand that there's always a day of reckoning."

According to Representative Henry Waxman, D-California, "The CPA's entire accounting system consisted of just one contractor maintaining Excel spreadsheets. That's one person for $20 billion." The flagrant frittering away of Iraqi funds reached a crescendo right before the CPA pulled up stakes and went home. In the final weeks before it turned control of the country over to Iraq's interim government, the CPA went on an extraordinary spending spree—even flying in two planes stuffed with $4 billion worth of cash loaded onto pallets during the last week alone.

Custer Battles

In March 2006, Custer Battles became the first Iraq occupation contractor to be found guilty of defrauding the U.S. government. The jury in the case found the company and its top executives guilty on a total of 37 charges of fraud, ordering them to pay more than $10 million in damages for, among other things, using fake invoices and sham companies incorporated offshore to bill U.S. taxpayers.

In August, the judge in the case dismissed the charges, ruling that since the CPA was not technically part of the U.S. government, there was no basis for claiming the United States was defrauded.

According to Custer Battles' attorney Robert Rhoad, the company's two owners—Mike Battles and Scott Battles—were "ecstatic" about the decision.

"As we have said all along, the evidence at trial showed that Custer Battles performed the [contracted-for services] on time, on budget, and to the satisfaction of the Coalition Provisional Authority," David Douglass, trial counsel for Custer Battles, stated. "There simply was no evidence of fraud or an intent to defraud the CPA nor were any false claims submitted to the United States."

But the judge stated in his ruling that that the company had submitted "false and fraudulently inflated invoices."

He allowed the jury's verdict to stand against the company (but not its owners) for retaliating against the whistleblowers who originally brought the case under the False Claims Act, which allows citizens to initiate a private right of action to recover money on taxpayers' behalf.

Among the evidence presented in court: documents which revealed that Custer Battles had marked up invoices for food (a $33,000 order billed at $432,000), electricity ($400,000 for $74,000 worth) and other equipment by huge margins.

During the trial, retired Brigadier General Hugh Tant III testified that the fraud "was probably the worst I've ever seen in my 30 years in the Army." Tant reported that when he originally confronted company co-founder Mike Battles about the fact that 34 of 36 trucks supplied by the firm didn't work, Battles responded: "You asked for trucks and we complied with our contract and it is immaterial whether the trucks were operational."

With Stuart Bowen's office estimating that there is a backlog of some 70 fraud cases pending against various contractors, critics say the Department of Justice has been dragging its feet and should create a special task force devoted to the problem, like it did when the accounting fraud at Enron spread like an epidemic to other companies. "I hope this administration is not in denial, but that may be the case," says James Moorman, an expert in False Claims Act cases with the group Taxpayers Against Fraud.

Normally, the government makes a decision to join or not join a case within 60 days, but many of the Iraq False Claims Act cases have been delayed for two years and more—an unprecedented duration. Cases filed under the False Claims act are sealed and prevented from moving forward until the government decides whether or not it will join the case, which means that the defendants can't even be publicly identified, making it impossible for federal contracting officers to suspend alleged fraudsters from any new contracts. (In May, the U.S. Air Force barred Custer Battles from any new contracts until March 2009.)

General Dynamics

General Dynamics' has received the most direct benefit from the Iraq war of all the large defense contractors, according to a July 2006 report in the *Washington Post*. "The combat-systems business . . . it's a cash cow for them," one industry analyst told the *Post*.

The company's profits have tripled since 9/11. Among those who can take credit is David K. Heebner, a former top aide to Army Chief of Staff Eric Shinseki who was hired by General Dynamics in 1999. The company won a $4 billion contract to produce Stryker armored vehicles a year later, 1,658 of which have been delivered to the Army since the Iraq invasion began.

"It's clear that the Army was leaning toward handing a multi-billion dollar contract to General Dynamics at the very time Heebner may have been in negotiations with the company for a high-paying executive position," says Jeffrey St. Clair, author of *Grand Theft Pentagon*. By March 2006, Heebner reported owning 33,500 shares in the company, which were worth well over $4 million. He also reported 21,050 options.

Not everyone in the military has been happy with the Stryker contract. A former Pentagon analyst describes the 8-wheeled vehicle as "riding in a dune buggy armored in tinfoil," i.e. particularly vulnerable to the Iraqi insurgents' favorite weapons, rocket-propelled grenades and improvised explosive devices.

The GAO has also found other problems, including serious maintenance requirements and deficiencies in the training provided to soldiers for its use.

Meanwhile, the company has added former Attorney General John Ashcroft to its stable of high-powered lobbyists. Also working the account are Juleanna Glover Weiss, Vice President Dick Cheney's former press secretary, Lori Day Sharp, who worked under Ashcroft at the Justice Department, and Willie Gaynor, a former Commerce Department official who was worked for the 2004 Bush/Cheney re-election campaign.

Nour USA Ltd.

Incorporated shortly after the war began, Nour has received contracts worth up to a total of $400 million, including a contract to provide security for Iraq's oil infrastructure.

Nour's founder, Abul Huda Farouki, a resident of Northern Virginia, is closely tied to Ahmed Chalabi, the formerly favorite Iraqi exile of the Bush administration neoconservatives who provided misleading information about WMDs.

Given his background and numerous ties to Nour and a network of other companies, including Erinys (bankrolled by Nour and tied to Chalabi through his nephew, the company's attorney), many Iraqis are skeptical about Chalabi's denial of reports that he received a $2 million finder's fee for helping Nour obtain an $80 million pipeline security contract. One company consultant who didn't deny getting paid to help out is William Cohen, the former defense secretary under President Clinton.

Other bidders on the contract, including Dyncorp, point out that Nour had no prior related experience and that its bid on the oil security contract was too low to be credible. The company reportedly recruits from Chalabi's former militia, a charge the company has denied.

Nour contends on its website that:

> The collaborating entities that formed Nour have almost a century of successful corporate history in performing contracts and making investments throughout the Middle East, particularly under difficult circumstances. Their operations have been defined by their application of Western management techniques and economic principles tempered by local customs and conditions and needs of local personnel.

The company did not respond to a request for comment for this story.

James Woolsey

Former CIA director James Woolsey was an outspoken proponent of regime change in Iraq, even before 9/11. And since the Iraq war began, he and his wife Suzanne have done pretty well. Woolsey is a vice president at Booz Allen Hamilton, a contractor called "the shadow intelligence community" by one former CIA deputy director.

In addition to serving on the board of Fluor, one of the largest Iraq reconstruction contractors, Suzanne Woolsey also works as a trustee at the Institute for Defense Analysis, a nonprofit corporation paid to do analytical and strategic research for top Pentagon officials.

For Mr. Woolsey, the war was the ultimate pay-off for years of anti-Saddam advocacy. In addition to being a member of the neoconservative cabal known as the Project for a New American Century (PNAC), he was also appointed by

Douglas Feith and Donald Rumsfeld to the Bush administration's Defense Policy Board, as well as advisory boards for the Navy and CIA.

Woolsey was also a member of the Committee for the Liberation of Iraq (CLI), a private group founded to build support for the war in 2002 by former Lockheed Martin vice president Robert Jackson, another PNAC member who also wrote the Republican Party foreign policy platform in 2000.

Woolsey and the CLI lobbied members of Congress to pass the Iraq Liberation Act (ILA), which allocated nearly $100 million to Ahmed Chalabi's Iraq National Congress INC, for whom Woolsey was a paid adviser. Right after 9/11, Woolsey went off to Europe, returning with an unnamed source's dubious claim that he had observed a meeting between Mohammed Atta, the lead 9/11 skyjacker, and an Iraqi agent in Prague.

As soon as the occupation began, Woolsey turned his attention to helping businesses get in on the action, becoming a featured speaker at related contractor and investor gatherings.

In addition to working for Booz Allen, he is a principal in the Paladin Capital Group, a Carlyle-like investment strategies firm, and has connections to Global Options, a risk management consulting firm headed by Neil Livingstone, with whom Woolsey serves on the Defense Policy Board.

Besides Woolsey and Livingstone, seven other members of the 30-member Defense Policy Board selected by Douglas Feith and Donald Rumsfeld have stood to benefit financially from the war, according to the Center for Public Integrity.

Source: *Multinational Monitor*, © 2006, Essential Information, Inc.

Thinking Activities

1. Much of the discussion in this chapter focused on the relationship between large corporations—especially the energy sector and America's government officials. Using the Internet, research the backgrounds of your state's U.S. congressional leaders. What occupation or firm were they employed in prior to entering public service?

2. In his analysis of the Bill Clinton–Monica Lewinsky affair, Author Gary Potter comments:

   > the greatest contradiction in this scandal may be that it served as a gigantic distraction from actually doing some thing to help the 80 percent of the population who do not own the nation's wealth ... [or] give great amounts of money to political campaigns, and whose welfare is greatly threatened by political inaction
   >
   > (Potter, 2002, pp. 145–146)

Based on what you've read in this chapter, and through conducting additional research via the World Wide Web, how would you rate the severity of "Monicagate" compared with other incidents in U.S. history such as the Teapot Dome Scandal?

3. Scholar Susan Shapiro has identified seven characteristics of abuse-of-trust offenders including "lying, misrepresentation, stealing, misappropriation, self-dealing, corruption, and role conflict" (Schlegel and Weisburd, 1994, p. 45). After reviewing this chapter's selected readings on corruption in Congress and war and disaster profiteering, which of Shapiro's seven characteristics might apply to the individuals discussed in each of these case studies?

4. Have you, or any one you know, ever been turned down for a job or promotion only to learn later that the person selected had a special connection to the selecting official? What were the circumstances surrounding this event? In contrast, have you ever used a personal relationship to obtain a job or promotion? If so, do you feel this was appropriate? Why or why not?

5. Are there any circumstances in which you feel it is appropriate to use government equipment for personal use (e.g., surfing the Internet, burning CDs, photocopying homework assignments)? What is your position on bringing pens, highlighters, Post-it notes and other office supplies purchased by your employer to school for class work?

4 The Origins of Public Corruption Control in the United States, 1883–1969

As a student of criminal justice or criminology, you may have asked yourself, "what causes people to break the rules?" More specifically, you may question why those members of society who have taken an oath to uphold the United States Constitution, the laws of their state, or to serve and protect others would be willing to exchange these solemn vows for their own personal gain. Perhaps you are more cynical, and think that it is simply human nature for people to lie, cheat, or steal from others. You may be familiar with Lord John Dalberg-Acton's famous statement from 1870 that "power tends to corrupt, and absolute power corrupts absolutely. Great men are almost always bad men." Yet did you know that despite Lord Acton's worthy admonishment, he actually supported the Confederacy during the Civil War? The bottom line is that when we explore governmental structures, systems, processes, and people, the line between right and wrong becomes ambiguous. Inasmuch as democratic societies have a rich history of striving to "do well" for their citizenry, there are also equal measures of wrongdoing. Moreover, the history of corruption within countries that cling to the tenets of democratic Republicanism is somewhat cyclical, and the history of the United States provides a myriad of examples of how corruption follows regular patterns over time.

The purpose of this chapter is to examine these patterns by exploring three of the four periods of corruption control within the United States: specifically, the Anti-Patronage, Progressive, and Scientific Administration movements. Through analysis of America's efforts to combat corruption from the 1880s through 1969, this chapter will lay the foundation for Chapter 5's meaningful study of more modern efforts to control corruption, collectively referred to as the Pantopic (or all-seeing) period (1970 to present).

Democracy and Corruption

The Greek philosopher Plato (427–347 BCE) believed that democracies were the fairest of all forms of a constitutional government. However, as discussed in length in his classic work *The Republic*, Plato further believed that a government ruled by the people would ultimately break down because jealousy over one another's respective functions within the society, and improper decision-making by an uneducated public, would yield chaos, subsequently giving way to a desire for order and stability achievable only through despotism.[1] Similarly, the Roman historian Polybius (c. 200–118 BCE) noted that the "desire for luxury, bribery for the sake of political power, and the substitution of eagerness for wealth . . ." in lieu of wise governance, results in corruption.[2] Such corruption ultimately transforms a democratic society into a form of mobocracy.

Both Plato and Polybius viewed corruption as inevitable in nearly every form of constitutional government: monarchy would give way to tyranny, aristocracy would yield oligarchy, and democracy would ultimately self-destruct into mob rule. Polybius produced a number of important writings pertaining to mixed constitutional forms of governance in an effort to curtail corruption. In fact, history scholar Marshall Davies Lloyd, in his paper entitled "Polybius and the Founding Fathers: The Separation of Powers" (1998), goes so far as to attribute America's system of checks and balances (i.e., the Executive, Legislative, and Judicial branches) to Polybius' writings.[3] It is important to note that both Plato and Polybius believed that there is a cyclical pattern to power. Societies move from monarchy to aristocracy, from aristocracy to democracy, and inevitably return to monarchy. Alternatively, in their corrupted forms, societies transition from tyranny to oligarchy, from oligarchy to mob-rule, and ultimately return to tyranny. Plato and Polybius espouse a certain order to life, and corruption is merely an accepted part of it.

The beliefs of these ancient Greek and Roman scholars are comparable to the values shared in many other cultures. For example, bribery has long since been accepted in India as a way of life. For example, in April 2002, a law enforcement officer in Punjab sought to secure a government position for his daughter—hoping that placing her in this job would give him access to increased levels of graft. He attempted to coax the officials who recorded the entrance exam scores into raising her final grade by providing them with a $100,000 bribe. Unfortunately (for the police officer and his daughter), he attempted to pay the exam administrators with counterfeit currency and was subsequently arrested.[4]

Another example of bribery can be found in Mexico, where the public frequently provides government officials with *mordida*—which literally translates into English as "the bite," but more accurately refers to a bribe. During her several years traveling throughout Mexico, author Christina Johns observed the following: "Want your tourist card stamped? You pay the mordida. Want the dates on your tourist card extended? You pay the mordida. Want your car registered? You pay the mordida."[5] Johns goes so far as to posit that the Mexicans cannot understand all of the controversy surrounding Watergate. She notes, "We were in Mexico at the time [1974] and Mexican friends and colleagues would ask me: What is everybody so upset about? What do they think politicians do but lie and steal and cheat and break the law? That's why they become politicians—so they can break the law."[6] Even in the United States, the "honest graft" era of Boss Tweed and Tammany Hall—in which $75 million to $200 million was swindled from New York City between 1865 and 1871, or the mayoralty of Boston's James Michael Curley, who was able to build a 17-room home complete with a mahogany stairway and crystal chandelier on a small public servant's salary, are remembered to this day with a form of renegade reverence.[7]

Attorney W. Michael Kramer presents a more dire correlation, theorizing that "corrupt officials burden developing countries with unfinished projects and crushing debt—conditions that lead to economic decline and international terrorism."[8] Such predictions appear to be holding true for the Iraqi reconstruction, where the Government Accountability Office (GAO) estimates that billions of dollars are being diverted annually to corrupt members of parliament, their families, and insurgent groups with whom they have formed alliances.[9]

We also recently learned of the indictment of former FBI agent John J. Connelly. Connelly, while assigned to the Organized Crime Squad in the Boston Field Office of the Federal Bureau of Investigation, provided information and assistance to James "Whitey" Bulger, Stephen "The Rifleman" Flemmi, and other members of their Winter Hill Gang. In exchange, the federal agent received cash, jewelry, and expensive cases of wine. As detailed in the gripping book *Black Mass*, the disappearance of Whitey Bulger—the reputed racketeering, drug trafficking, and extortion crime boss inextricably linked to the New England mafia and to the deaths of three confidential informants critical to the prosecution of organized crime groups in Massachusetts, Rhode Island, and New Hampshire—is directly attributable to FBI Agent Connelly's corrupt activities, and collusion on the part of his supervisor, John Morris.[10]

Complicating matters is the fact that there is no distinct, legal definition of the word corruption, nor "does it appear in the criminal code."[11] For simplicity's sake, this chapter uses Joseph T. Wells' definition, which states that, "the fraudster wrongfully uses his influence in a business transaction to procure some benefit for himself or another person contrary to his duty to his employer or the rights of another."[12] While reading this section of the text, we would encourage you to remember another quotation often attributed to Plato: "Nothing is incorruptible, except for personal character that will not be corrupted."[13] Government structures and systems engineered to combat waste, fraud, and abuse may or may

Exhibit 4.1 James Joseph "Whitey" Bulger, Jr. is a fugitive wanted for racketeering, murder, conspiracy to commit murder, extortion, conspiracy to commit extortion, money laundering, conspiracy to commit money laundering and narcotics distribution fugitive. He is also the alleged leader of the Winter Hill Gang, an Irish-American crime family based in the Boston, Massachusetts area.

not yield positive results. However, if you are able to routinely assess your own perspective on corruption, you will be in a much better position to avoid some of the misdeeds of public officials that we discussed in Chapter 3 of this book.

Corruption Control: A Call to Action

Offenses such as bribery, receiving kickbacks, or exerting undue influence over others have likely existed throughout recorded history. Such acts are not exclusive to Europe, Asia, and the developing nations of the world. More than 100 years ago, many activists within the United States, particularly those who had been previously involved with the abolitionist movement of the Civil War Era, began to call for the reformation of government policies and procedures in the areas of public employment, code enforcement, and education. Joseph Rue's "comparative study of spelling performance by 33,000 students in 1897"[14] was at least in part an effort to assess the effectiveness of those employed as public school teachers. The ranks of the public service, including those persons employed in education, engineering, law enforcement, and public health, were rife with employees lacking legitimate qualifications or simply functioning as a conduit for graft. Thus was born what authors Frank Anechairico and James B. Jacobs refer to as the "antipatronage vision"[15] of corruption control. Through the development of a merit-based civil service system, the reformers hoped to curtail the "spoils" system that had become pervasive in public employee hiring, particularly at the local level.

For example, prior to the passage of the Federal Civil Service Act of 1883, it was not uncommon for city jobs to be awarded in exchange for cash, gifts, or services at the ward or district level. New York's subsequent implementation of a civil service program—the first such system in the nation—was designed to provide a mechanism through which "comparative merit or achievement . . . [would govern] . . . each individual's selection and progress in the service, and in which the conditions and rewards of performance contribute to the competency and continuity of the service."[16] Such a system was also desirable because many of those persons employed as safety monitors for food products and medicines had failed to adequately protect public health. Upton Sinclair, an author and social activist, wrote his text *The Jungle* (1906) about pervasive abuses in the meat processing industry. Among Sinclair's startling revelations was his observation that many of the meat packing facilities located in and around the Chicago stockyards allowed rodent droppings, animal hair, insects, and decaying and diseased meat to be included in processed products such as sausage and cold cuts. He also documented other severe health and safety issues such as employees routinely being injured during the meat packing process, and the subsequent inclusion of human bodily fluids and tissue into meat foodstuffs.[17]

Thus evolving from the anti-patronage movement was the establishment of a "progressive vision" of corruption control within the United States. Spanning from approximately 1900 to 1933, the focus of the progressive movement was to separate public administration from party politics,[18] and protect the masses from corporate abuses through ensuring public trust in those acting in positions of power. To quote former President Theodore Roosevelt in his 1910 speech entitled "The New Nationalism":

> One of the fundamental necessities in a representative government such as ours is to make certain that the men to whom the people delegate their power shall serve the people by whom they are elected, and not the special interests. We believe that every national officer, elected or appointed, should be forbidden to perform any service or receive any compensation, directly or indirectly, from interstate corporations; and a similar provision could not fail to be useful within the states.[19]

During Roosevelt's tenure as President of the United States, he strived to eliminate the spoils system that had become pervasive in public office and reintroduce competition into the marketplace. In 1903, he tasked Congress with the formation of a Department of Commerce and Labor and a Bureau of Corporations authorized to investigate business combinations and to warn them against practices harmful to the public. In 1906, in response to Sinclair's concerns about the safety of America's meat supply documented in *The Jungle*, issues pertaining to the quality of drugs being manufactured, and the highly exaggerated claims proffered by the producers of health tonics, salves, and potions, Congress enacted The Pure Food and Drug Act.[20] Among the key provisions of the Act are the following:

- Any meat products to be sold in interstate commerce must be inspected by federal regulators.
- An agency was established to evaluate the health and safety of food-stuffs and medical products (known today as the Food and Drug Administration (FDA)).
- Specific drugs and chemical compounds were made available by prescription only. Any new drugs would require extensive testing and analysis by the FDA prior to being approved for public use. Lastly, addictive drugs must be labeled as habit-forming.

Roosevelt's enforcement of the Sherman Anti-Trust Act against the major railroad operators, United States Steel Corporation and Standard Oil Company, yielded victories for the American public both in terms of value and choice of services. Roosevelt left his successor, William Howard Taft, with a legacy of corruption control. He warned, "We can as little afford to tolerate a dishonest man in the public service as a coward in the army . . . the corruptionist in public life, whether he be bribe-giver or bribe-taker, strikes at the heart of the commonwealth."[21] During the period 1909–13, the Taft Administration continued to strive for reduced corporate influence in government and fair market competition by filing more than 80 antitrust actions. Most notably, in 1911, American tobacco was deemed to be a monopoly. Later that same year, the court ruled that John D. Rockefeller's Standard Oil should be broken up into 33 companies.

Immediately following Taft, Woodrow Wilson continued the fight to curtail the linkages between private entities and government policies. Wilson, in his acceptance speech for the Democratic nomination for President on July 7, 1912, stated that "Big business is not dangerous because it is big, but because its business is an unwholesome inflation created by privileges and exemptions which it ought not to enjoy."[22] Among Wilson's greatest successes was the passage of the Federal Trade Commission Act of September 26, 1914. The Act established an organization (the Federal Trade Commission) comprised of five commissioners—not more than three of whom could be from the same political party. The terms of office for each commissioner were also staggered, thus reducing the likelihood of widespread political influence. Most importantly, commissioners were prohibited from being involved in any other corporation or business. The United States' subsequent foray into World War I presented Wilson with new challenges, such as curtailing corruption in the wartime economy. For example, war profiteers, such as the fictional character in Jules Romain's *Verdun*, manufactured substandard boots for the troops. In an effort to combat such corruption, Wilson enlisted Herbert Hoover to manage the Food Administration, an agency responsible for ensuring that the allies abroad received adequate provisions. The Food Administration also prevented rationing and the formation of a black-market economy in the United States.

Unfortunately, the advances in corruption control during the administrations of Presidents Roosevelt, Taft, and Wilson came to a near grinding halt during the sordid term of Warren G. Harding (1921–23) and the tepid tenure of Calvin "Silent Cal" Coolidge (1923–29). Harding, an ardent supporter of big business, is frequently mentioned in discussions regarding the Teapot Dome Scandal, which was described in Chapter 3 of this book. His campaign promise of "less government in business and more business in government,"[23] coupled with his entourage referred to as the Ohio gang— many of whom were later charged with defrauding the government, and some of whom went to jail—did not reflect positively on his presidency. Moreover, Harding was implicated in two sex scandals.[24] The first involved Carrie Phillips, a German sympathizer during World War I, who tried to blackmail Harding and was paid hush money by the Republican Party. The second involved Nan Britton, an attractive blonde 30 years Harding's junior, who alleged that they had conceived an illegitimate child together in a closet of the U.S. Senate prior to Harding's run for the presidency in 1920. Succeeding Harding, President Calvin Coolidge was forced to carry the political baggage of scandals that rocked the former Office of the Chief Executive.

When he finally managed to shed some of the stigma of the Harding Administration, Coolidge's efforts at policymaking were heavily geared towards the reduction of taxes and empowerment of business. A man of few words, Coolidge's motto was, "I have noticed that nothing I have never said ever did me any harm."[25] Another tenet attributable to Coolidge was, "the business of America is business"—although historians dispute whether he actually ever uttered this phrase. What is not in dispute is that Coolidge did little to curtail the questionable practices of American businesses.

Perhaps the only bright spot in the Coolidge Administration was the tenure of Charles Gates Dawes as Vice President from 1925–29. Dawes had previously served as a successful attorney, businessman, banker, campaign organizer for the McKinley Presidential Campaign of 1895, Comptroller of the Currency, and Brigadier General during World War I. He was the co-recipient of the Nobel Peace Prize in 1925 for his Dawes Plan, which established a system for Germany to make reparations to the allied nations of Europe, while at the same time restoring Germany's economy and rebuilding its physical infrastructure.[26] From 1929 to 1932, he served as the U.S. Ambassador to Great Britain, and would have led the American delegation to the World Disarmament Conference in Geneva, Switzerland were he not urged by President Hoover to serve as the recently-established Chairman of the Reconstruction Finance Corporation (RFC). For several months, Dawes worked tirelessly to provide loans to those establishments that, as Hoover stated in a 1932 press statement, "protect the credit structure of the Nation whose collapse would mean the complete disaster to . . . the great fiduciary institutions, savings banks, insurance companies, building and loan associations. That is, the whole people."[27] Perhaps the best example of the sheer honesty and integrity that guided Dawes was his resignation from the RFC in June 1932. In dire need of a $90 million RFC loan for his Central Republic Bank of Chicago, Dawes believed that remaining a member of the Corporation would have been a conflict of interest.

Dawes was a strong advocate of reform. His appointment as the first Director of the Bureau of the Budget in 1921 resulted in the reduction of the national debt by $1 billion and a balanced budget by 1922.[28] In 1926, Dawes sought a special investigation into the growing problem of organized crime and the government's inability to counter it effectively. In concert with President Coolidge, he also formed a "special tax intelligence unit" in 1928. Lastly, Dawes is widely credited with conceptualizing the tax evasion investigative strategy that ultimately netted gangster Al Capone an 11-year prison term beginning in 1931. After serving eight years in federal prisons, and with his health deteriorating from syphilis, Capone was released in 1939, eight years before his death.

Despite the efforts of reformers such as Charles Dawes, the majority of Coolidge appointees did little to bridge the gap between corporate wealth and government corruption. In 1927, Eleanor Roosevelt described President Coolidge as a man "who apparently has no dreams, who glories in shrewd politics and firmly believes that the economy is in some way a kind of spiritual triumph."[29] During his tenure, the gap between the wealthy and poor continued to widen (e.g., it was estimated that the average U.S. family needed approximately $2,000 of annual income to survive in the 1920s, yet 60 percent of all American families earned less than this amount). Over-production of foodstuffs and commodities, over-expansion of credit and soaring levels of personal and corporate debt, coupled with Coolidge's "say nothing" approach to governance, ultimately led to an economy on the verge of collapse. Opting not to run for re-election in 1928, Coolidge bestowed upon Herbert Hoover an unenviable place in American history—

the opportunity to largely serve as the fall guy for the stock market crash of October 1929, and the worldwide Great Depression swirling around it.

This is unfortunate because Hoover made several lasting and important contributions to corruption control. For example, as previously noted, Hoover served as the Food Administrator during World War I, and strove to curtail fraud and abuse in the distribution of foodstuffs both within the United States and on the Front. He also served admirably as Harding's Secretary of Commerce, and was responsible for "transforming the department into a service organization. His work was guided by efficiency, standardization and the elimination of waste,"[30]—tenets that would be further expanded upon through the bureaucratization and scientific administration approaches of Franklin Roosevelt and his successors. Hoover was also aware of the risky practices of commercial lending institutions such as speculating in the stock market with their depositors' funds. He called for an investigation of the banking industry, and tighter regulations on how funds could be invested.

Hoover created the Reconstruction Finance Corporation (RFC)—chaired by Charles Dawes, which loaned monies to a variety of businesses and allowed for government scrutiny of the recipients. He reorganized the formerly corrupt Bureau of Investigation in 1924 into what ultimately evolved into the Federal Bureau of Investigation (1935) under the direction of

Exhibit 4.2 Herbert Hoover, the 31st President of the United States, had held office for just eight months when the stock market crashed, ushering in the Great Depression.

J. Edgar Hoover (no relation). Lastly, President Hoover's establishment of the U.S. Bureau of Prisons helped to professionalize corrections-oriented occupations, ensure humane treatment of offenders, and curtail corruption in America's justice system.[31] Unfortunately, faced with unemployment of more than 12 million Americans, 20,000 bankrupt companies, more than 1,600 banks out of business, and one in twenty farmers losing his or her land, Hoover left office with one of the lowest approval ratings since Andrew Johnson's impeachment by the House of Representatives in 1868.[32]

Roots of the "Scientific Era" of Corruption Control

Franklin D. Roosevelt's election as President of the United States in 1933 ushered in dramatic changes in the way in which government operated—differences that can still be felt to this day vis-à-vis the social reform policies emanating from his "New Deal" programs (1933–38). Faced with record levels of unemployment (by 1933, there were more than 13,000,000 people out of work in the United States—an unemployment rate of more than 23 percent), the lowest homebuilding levels in U.S. history, farm foreclosure rates of 25 percent, and more than a 29 percent drop in the Gross National Product since 1929, Roosevelt knew that the United States' economy could only recover through cooperative partnerships between the public and private sectors.[33]

Unlike the staunchly pro-business policies of the Harding and Coolidge Administrations, or the more laissez-faire approach touted by his predecessor, President Hoover, Roosevelt enacted an unprecedented program of government–industry cooperation. Through the National Recovery Act, Home Owners' Loan Corporation, Public Works Administration, Federal Deposit Insurance Corporation, and Federal Securities Act, Roosevelt ensured that the U.S. Government would play a role in regulating and monitoring key elements of the private sector for many years to come.

Of equal importance was the passage of the Wagner Act (officially referred to as the National Labor Relations Act of 1935), which allowed employees the right to participate in collective bargaining and brought the federal government into the labor-management dispute process through the establishment of a National Labor Relations Board. The enactment of the Fair Labor Standards Act in 1938 set a national minimum wage, restricted the number of hours children could work, protected them from hazardous conditions, set the standard work week at 40 hours, and prohibited deductions from employee wages for uniforms, tools, etc., if such deductions lowered the worker's salary below the minimum wage.[34]

Yet Roosevelt was much less a Progressive than his fifth cousin and former President, Theodore Roosevelt. Franklin Roosevelt saw his mandate within

Exhibit 4.3 *In an effort to combat the Great Depression, President Franklin D. Roosevelt enacted a variety of "New Deal" programs, including the Works Progress Administration, which at its height employed more than 3.4 million Americans on a variety of public projects such as building roads, bridges, and parks.*

the New Deal "to energize private enterprise." His foray into the private sector through legislation created a host of federal agencies, each with its own specific regulatory authority. Roosevelt's organizational policies were consistent with the socio-scientific research of the World War II era.[35] Max Weber's comprehensive theory of bureaucratization (originally released in 1922) provided some of the underpinnings for the form of ministerial bureaucracy that was widely successful during Hitler's National Socialist Era (1933–45), and also proved effective in blending capitalism and social policy under Roosevelt. Roosevelt successfully utilized social programs in a manner that undercut the grassroots efforts of the Communist Party of America. Robert Dreyfus, in his review of *It Didn't Happen Here: Why Socialism Failed in the United States*,[36] notes Roosevelt's brilliance

> [in] seducing labor leaders—including many of the more militant leaders of the brand-new Congress of Industrial Organizations (CIO)—and scrambling to co-opt socialists by propounding left-sounding programs, FDR prevented organized labor from linking up with the Socialist and

Communist parties in the early 1930s. By 1936 the Socialist Party was all but dead, and the Communist Party was one of Roosevelt's loudest supporters.[37]

President Roosevelt also supported passage of the 1939 Hatch Act (also referred to as the Clean Politics Act), which prohibited federal civil service employees from taking an active part in political parties and campaigns. While on its surface the Act appeared progressive (in fact, elements of it were based on provisions written into the original Civil Service Act of 1883), the law actually prohibited membership in certain political entities—such as the Communist Party.

Roosevelt's expansion and restructuring of the Executive Branch during the New Deal, coupled with the infusion of presidential activism, created a tone that would remain part of American politics through the administrations of Truman, Eisenhower, Kennedy, and Johnson. In their text *In the Web of Politics: Three Decades of the U.S. Federal Executive* (2000), authors Joel Aberbach and Bert Rockman note, "the New Deal coalition and its ideas outlasted the New Deal itself. The burden of proof for nearly two generations was generally on why government should not do something rather than why it should."[38] This sentiment applied not only to the formation of proposals that could prove critical to the American people, but also to the measurements that would be used to assess the effectiveness and efficiency of these programs.

The Scientific Administration Model: Systematic Evaluation

The World War II era in American society produced a host of technological innovations. From radar systems and microwave ovens, to viable commercial aircraft (e.g., the DC-3) and the Frisbee, there was a mood in America that nearly all of our problems could be resolved through science. Such beliefs became even more pronounced with the advent of computer systems and the atomic bomb. Weber recognized this trend at its onset, prophesizing,

> It is apparent that today we are proceeding towards an evolution which resembles (the ancient kingdom of Egypt) in every detail, except that it is built on other foundations, on technically more perfect, more rationalized, and therefore much more mechanized foundations.[39]

The merger of Weber's bureaucratization theory with the organizational research of Leonard White at the University of Chicago and Frank Goodnow of Columbia University, as well as the public administration research into external control conducted by Luther Gulick and experimental designs used by leading engineers and mathematicians of the 1930s and 1940s, resulted in the development of a corruption control system which espoused that "the correct deployment of administrative authority, coupled with comprehensive monitoring and evaluation, would prevent corruption or quickly bring it to light."[40]

It is important to note that the haste in which much of the scientific administration research conducted within America's leading colleges and universities found its way into governmental systems was the result of the intermeshed relationship which existed between academe and the military-industrial complex at the close of the Second World War. Much of this nexus can be attributed to Vannevar Bush, who went from being a Professor of Physics and Dean of the Engineering School and Vice President at the Massachusetts Institute of Technology (1923–38) to Director of the U.S. Office of Scientific Research and Development (1941–1945) and President of the Carnegie Foundation (1939–1955). He also personally supervised the Manhattan Project, which led to the successful deployment of atomic weapons on Hiroshima and Nagasaki on August 6 and 9, 1945, respectively. Ultimately, Dr. Bush proposed a National Research Foundation, a concept that eventually became the National Science Foundation, still in existence today.[41]

Vannevar Bush built a conduit that reaped tremendous research benefits for the military by establishing a federal funding base at public and private institutions. Monies were also funneled into quasi-corporate think tanks (e.g., Rockefeller, Carnegie), thereby strengthening the relationship between the military and the private sector. This funding produced models such as *game theory* and the concept of *Nash's equilibrium* at the RAND Corporation in 1950, for which Dr. John Nash ultimately won the Nobel Prize in 1994.

While I have devoted much of my own research agenda to the development of game theory models (designed to examine corruption in military and law enforcement systems), it is beyond the scope of this short book to discuss the intricacies of *game theory*, equilibria, or economic modeling. However, the following example should provide a relatively simple illustration of the application of a scientific model to corruption control.

A Scientific Model at Work: The "Beautiful Minds" of Co-Conspirators

Lori is a career criminal with a penchant for hacking into federal law enforcement agencies' computer networks, extracting sensitive case files, contacting the persons named in the files, and offering—for a substantial fee—to erase these files from each respective agency's database. In contrast,

Lisa is a career intelligence analyst with the National Infrastructure Protection Center (NIPC), specializing in technology threat assessment and detection of unauthorized system users. On the surface, it would seem that if each of them acts in her own best interest, they cancel each other out. In other words, if Lori hacks into the system and Lisa detects her presence, Lisa simply denies her access to the system. This is referred to as a zero sum game in game theory because the payoff is equal for both players.

However, if we explore this game scenario further, acting in their own best interests, what happens if Lisa fails to detect Lori's unauthorized access due to lack of skill or laziness? Lori benefits financially and Lisa probably gets fired. Or, what happens if Lori doesn't bother to hack into the system in the first place (e.g., she is too tired or lazy)? While Lori would not benefit financially, Lisa would still benefit less because, if no incidents of attack or vulnerabilities are perceived to exist against her agency's information system, why should the agency expend funds to employ her? Lori maintains the status quo, and Lisa risks being fired.

Now let's apply a simple version of Nash's equilibrium to this scenario. Lisa, cognizant that she may lose her position if there are no attacks against her agency's information systems, and Lori, realizing that her life will be considerably richer from a financial perspective if she hacks into the agency's database, come to an arrangement in which Lori will attempt to gain access to Lisa's agency network four times in the month of December. They agree that three of these attempts will be unsuccessful (i.e., Lori will be denied access to the system, and Lisa will be able to mention in her monthly status report that she staved off three hacker attacks on the agency's system). For the fourth attempt, Lori easily enters the system using an official username and remote password that Lisa has created for her. Lori downloads the sensitive information she needs, offers to erase the appropriate files for her client, and collects her sizable fee, which she splits with Lisa.

Nash's equilibrium mathematically demonstrates that if all players choose their responses by also considering what is best for the other members of the group, the highest overall payoff is obtained. In other words, both Lori and Lisa benefit most from engaging in the conspiracy.

Marjit and Shi (1998) reach similar conclusions in their game theory and equilibrium research into corruption control, noting that, "even when the announced penalty for the crime is very high . . . controlling crime becomes difficult because the probability of detection can be affected by the effort of a corrupt official."[42]

Nash's theory is also wholly consistent with research into computer and Internet-related crimes.

According to InterGov, an international organization that works with police agencies to combat cybercrime, insiders commit about 80 percent

Scenario	Value to Lori	Value to Lisa	EVENT TOTAL
Lori Attacks System/Lisa Detects Intrusion (Zero Sum Game)	-10	+10	0
Lori Attacks System/Lisa Fails to Detect Intrusion	+10	-20	-10
Lori Doesn't Attack/Lisa could be fired for lack of attacks to System	0	-10	-10
Lori and Lisa Conspire	+10	+10	+20
TOTALS	**+10**	**-10**	**0**

Exhibit 4.4 Payoff values for simple form game between Lori and Lisa.

of all computer and Internet–related crime . . . [In addition] insider attacks are more of a threat because they are better conceived, due mostly to direct system access and knowledge of a system's architecture.[43]

Given the high dollar value in the underworld that is placed on law enforcement-sensitive information, agencies must remain steadfast in their efforts to recruit employees, who—in the words of the U.S. Secret Service— are *worthy of trust and confidence*, and must be aware of the important role that scientific models such as Nash's Equilibrium can play in formulating effective corruption control policies.

Thus, the scientific administration model would argue that it is Lisa's position, not Lori's, which must be engineered so as to prevent corrupt practices from occurring. This might be accomplished by preventing Lisa from creating new user passwords, splitting network access and network monitoring functions between two separate departments, etc.

Challenges of the Scientific Administration Model

As America moved from the Roosevelt Era of the 1930s and 1940s into the more technologically-advanced era of the 1950s and the 1960s and America's fascination with the "space race" escalated, so too did the belief that social problems could be solved through scientific solutions. The Johnson Administration's "War on Poverty" portion of the Great Society vision was in many respects a space-engineering extension of Roosevelt's New Deal. The "War on Poverty" created large-scale public programs in "federal health, housing, employment, services integration, community planning, urban renewal, welfare, family programs."[44] Along with these new programs came congressional mandates to evaluate the efficacy of appropriated expenditures. The U.S. General Accounting Office (now referred to as the

Government Accountability Office) had previously focused predominantly on comprehensive accounting. However, it saw its role expanded to include more analytical and investigative activities. The Johnson Administration also made extensive use of academicians in a variety of evaluative roles. Author Michael Patton refers to this period as the birth of "program evaluation as a distinct field" (1996, p. 11). While the focus of these assessments stretched far beyond issues of corruption and into programmatic areas, they served as precursors to the form of corruption control that has been in place in American society since the early days of the Nixon Administration.

Our next chapter will explore the role of the Nixon Presidency would play in both combating and engaging in acts of corruption; as well the legacy this administration would play in shaping future corruption control strategies.

Chapter Summary

Chapter 4 provided you with a brief history of corruption control in the United States. Special emphasis was placed on the Anti-Patronage movement (1870–1900), Progressive period (1900–1933), and Scientific Administration (1933–1969) models of combating corruption in American government. This chapter also discussed various tools such as Nash Equilibrium that can be used to identify opportunities for conspiracy between would-be offenders and corrupt public officials.

ADAPTED READINGS

Reading 4–1: *Elizabeth Kolbert,* FELLOWship of the Ring

> *New York City in the twenty-first century is quite different than 120 years ago, when graft and corruption ruled the day. In order to fully understand how far we have come, the following article discusses what conditions were like for those doing business in New York City during the Tweed era of the 1870s. As you review this article, consider the challenges you would have faced obtaining basic government services during that period; or—worse yet—how difficult is would have been to pursue your chosen career as a police officer, criminal investigator, or prosecutor.*

On December 12, 1870, the *New York Sun*, a newspaper that had been hostile to Boss Tweed, suddenly proposed that a monument be raised in his honor.

Whether the suggestion represented a change of heart or was just a joke—the paper recommended that Tweed be cast in a nautical pose, repairing the lines on his steam yacht in the midst of a hurricane—is difficult to say. In any case, Tammany Hall embraced the *Sun*'s idea. The Tweed Testimonial Association was formed, and a circular was printed—at public expense—to solicit donations for the erection of a statue of Tweed "in consideration of his services to the Commonwealth of New York."

Tweed was at that point at the height of his power, and few were the projects that he didn't have a hand in. It was Tweed who pushed through the bill that legalized millions of dollars' worth of watered Erie Railroad stock, and also Tweed who arranged for the Albany legislature to incorporate the Metropolitan Museum of Art. Among the many posts he held simultaneously were that of New York state senator, head of the city's Department of Public Works, president of the County Board of Supervisors, and Grand Sachem of Tammany Hall. Not surprisingly, the Testimonial Association made rapid headway, collecting nearly eight thousand dollars by the middle of March. Meanwhile, unsolicited suggestions for the design of the monument poured in. The Herald recommended that the Boss be rendered in Indian garb, the city charter in one hand and a peace pipe in the other. The virulently anti-Tammany *Times* proposed that the statue of George Washington in Union Square Park be taken down and replaced by one of Tweed, to illustrate the progress of history. Finally, Tweed himself graciously refused the honor. "Statues are not erected to living men, but to those who have ended their careers," he wrote. "I claim to be a live man, and hope (Divine Providence permitting) to survive in all my vigor, politically and physically, some years to come." The *Sun* printed Tweed's demurral under the headline "A GREAT MAN'S MODESTY," with the subhead "The Hon. William M. Tweed declines the *Sun*'s Statue—characteristic letter from the great New York philanthropist—he thinks that virtue should be its own reward."

In the end, of course, Tweed still got his monument, albeit an unintended one. Situated on Chambers Street, just behind City Hall, the building that started out as the New York County Courthouse but eventually became known as the Tweed Courthouse features a neoclassical facade, a five-story Romanesque Revival rotunda, and thirty courtrooms, the most ornate of which are resplendent with granite columns and polychrome brick. It is among the most sumptuous public buildings in the city and, on a constant dollar basis, without question the most expensive. The final bill for its construction, which stretched over twenty years, exceeded fifteen million dollars—more than four times the cost of the Houses of Parliament, as outraged observers pointed out, and twice what the United States had recently paid to purchase Alaska.

Sometime in the next few days, painters and floor-layers will put the final touches on the job of restoring the Tweed, a monumental undertaking in itself. The project, begun in 1999, involved, on any given day, more than two hundred construction workers, along with brass smiths in India, tile-makers in England, foundrymen in Alabama, and stonecutters in Georgia, and it proceeded at a near-record pace. Perhaps inevitably, given the building's history, the success of the project has been glossed not just in architectural terms but in moral ones as well. Speaking at the courthouse back in December, Mayor Rudy Giuliani boasted that the restoration would "purify the building and remove the stench of Boss Tweed and corruption." As is so often the case with such high-minded enterprises, however, the real lesson has proved less edifying. Completed at a cost of nearly ninety million dollars, the Tweed restoration is shaping up into a second municipal debacle—one that, although quite different from the first, is not quite different enough.

William Marcy Tweed, who was not actually named William Marcy Tweed, was born on April 3, 1823, in lower Manhattan. In all likelihood, his middle initial stood for his mother's maiden name, Magear, and Marcy was another joke perpetrated by the newspapers. (In the eighteen-thirties, William L. Marcy served three terms as governor of New York, and is credited with adapting to political use the motto "To the victor belongs the spoils.") A contemporary of Tweed's described him as a good-looking young man, "with dark brown hair and clear, gritty eyes"; however, photographs show that by middle age he was bald and stout. In the famous Thomas Nast cartoons, he is inevitably pictured bursting out of his waistcoat—at his heaviest, Tweed weighed close to three hundred pounds—with a huge diamond glittering on his shirtfront.

Both in his strengths and in his limitations, Tweed was a quintessential Tammany man—or, at least, what we have come to consider one. He was not particularly eloquent—"I can't talk, and I know it," he once said—or even clever, and his early years were devoted to a series of ventures that mostly ended badly. For a while, Tweed worked with his father-in-law manufacturing brushes, before following his father into chair-making. He was active as a volunteer fireman, and in 1850 ran—and lost—his first campaign, for assistant alderman. Two years later, he was elected to Congress, where he served, without distinction, as a member of the Committee on Invalid Pensions. He passed no legislation, made one speech, and according to one of his biographers, Leo Hershkowitz, the author of "Tweed's New York," was not renominated. In 1861, his chair business failed. Filing for bankruptcy, Tweed offered the following list of his worldly assets: "Three Hats, Two Caps, Two Thick Overcoats, One Thin Overcoat, Three Pair Pants, Six Vests, Two Dress Coats, One Business Coat, Three Pair Boots, Two Pair Shoes, Ten Pair Socks, Thirty Collars, Twelve Linen Shirts, Twelve Cotton Shirts, Ten Handkerchiefs."

Tweed's one substantial talent seems to have been a grasp of city politics, which is to say, of human frailty. In 1863, he was appointed deputy street commissioner, and as another of his biographers, Alexander B. Callow, Jr., points out in "The Tweed Ring," over the next four years he proceeded to quadruple the department's payroll. In 1864, he bought a controlling interest in a printing company, which quickly became the city's supplier of vouchers and stationery. As a member of the Board of Supervisors, Tweed organized his first ring, which took a neat fifteen per cent off the top of every city contract. (A "ring," in the words of one of Tweed's henchmen, was "a collection of men united for some common object.") Five years after declaring bankruptcy, he owned a brownstone in Manhattan and a home in Greenwich, Connecticut. In 1871, when his daughter Mary Amelia got married, the *Sun* reported that the scene in Tweed's Fifth Avenue mansion was so splendid that it "beggared description." The *Herald* estimated the value of the wedding gifts at seven hundred thousand dollars—roughly ten million dollars in today's money.

As an exercise in graft, the courthouse has been described as Tweed's masterwork, and the brazenness of the self-dealing is almost unimaginable today, Enron notwithstanding. The original, fairly modest appropriation stipulated that the entire courthouse, construction of which began in 1861, should cost no more than two hundred and fifty thousand dollars, including all its furnishings. But Tweed convinced his colleagues on the Board of Supervisors that this was too niggardly. First, they added a million dollars to the project, then an additional eight hundred thousand, and so on. It is estimated that less than twenty-five per cent of expenditures went toward actual construction. A carpenter named George Miller, also known as Lucky, was paid three hundred and sixty thousand dollars for one month's work. Andrew Garvey, a plasterer, received five hundred thousand dollars for a year's work, and then a million dollars to repair that work. (He became known as the Prince of Plasterers.) For three tables and forty chairs, the city paid nearly a hundred and eighty thousand dollars; for "brooms, etc.," forty-one thousand dollars. One check, in the amount of sixty-four thousand dollars, was made out simply to "T.C. Cash." The marble for the building was quarried near Tuckahoe, New York, until Tweed and his cronies acquired a quarry in western Massachusetts.

Five years into the project, after millions had been disbursed with little to show for it, a group of outraged citizens demanded an inquiry, and the Special Committee to Investigate the Courthouse was formed. It acted quickly, and found no justification for concern, even as it ran up a bill of more than eighteen thousand dollars for twelve days' work. Nearly half that amount went to Tweed's printing company, which published the committee's official report.

Jack Waite is the architect who oversaw the Tweed's restoration, and on a spectacular spring morning not long ago I arranged to meet him on the courthouse's front steps, which lead up to three sets of giant walnut doors. As I waited, people kept coming up to me and asking when the building would be open. I told them I had no idea.

The courthouse is now strictly off limits, closed to the general public, to the press, and even, in the company of a reporter, to its architect. Waite arrived, and the best we could do was take a walk around the outside. "If there's one building that really encapsulates the history of New York during the second half of the nineteenth century, when the city became the capital of the world, it's this one," he told me. "Tweed liked fine things." As we circled the block, Waite pointed out how the original ruddy-hued marble from Tuckahoe had weathered and could be distinguished from the paler, Massachusetts stones.

Thanks to its associations, the Tweed was neglected and unloved almost from the moment it was completed. For half a century, it served as a county court; then it was converted into a city court and then a family court. Eventually, many of its soaring chambers were partitioned into offices for use by second-tier city agencies. The building's polychrome brick was painted gray, its entry foyer walled off to make space for rest rooms, and its intricately molded cast-iron steps encased in concrete. In 1974, a task force appointed by Mayor Abe Beame described the Tweed as "one million cubic feet of unusable space" and recommended that it be demolished. Architecturally speaking, neglect may have been the best thing for the building. "It's all intact, because everyone was afraid to spend any money on it," Waite observed.

When the city began work on the renovation, it had only the sketchiest idea of what the building might be used for. This was either idealism or folly, or both. There was still no firm plan midway through the project, even after *Newsday*, invoking Tweed, reported on how much the work was costing. Finally, the Giuliani administration hired an architectural consultant to study the matter, at a cost of a hundred and fifty thousand dollars. The consultant considered everything from high-end condos to a boutique hotel before concluding that only a museum made sense for the building, both because of its splendor and because so much public money was going into restoring it. Not long afterward, Giuliani offered the Tweed to the Museum of the City of New York.

The museum's board of directors was attracted by the idea of being given, gratis, a fine new home for its collections of antique toys and silverware. But it turned out that the board didn't want quite the same building that the city was working on. The Tweed has enormous windows, which the city had had refurbished at a substantial cost; from the museum's perspective, these windows let in too much light. A ventilation system for a restaurant had been installed on the east side of the building, but the museum's consultants wanted to put the restaurant on the west side. Even as the city was ordering high-tech glass panels for the doors etched with beavers and Indian braves, the museum's architects were drawing up plans to have the doorways modified. The Giuliani administration agreed to a second round of renovations—much of it aimed at undoing the work of the first—and, what's more, agreed to foot half the bill. The remodelling was expected to take two years and to cost more than forty million dollars.

Mayor Michael Bloomberg held his inaugural party in the Tweed, but he made it clear early on that he was not entirely happy with the deal Giuliani had struck. His objections—at least the ones that he voiced—ranged from the effects of the museum's move on its current uptown neighbors to technical concerns about the Tweed's landmark status. Then suddenly, in March, while talking to a group of schoolchildren from Staten Island, he scuttled the museum plan in favor of a brand-new one that seemed entirely of his own devising. Instead of bestowing the building on the Museum of the City of New York, or any other museum, he announced his intention to turn it back into city offices. He said he wanted to move several hundred of the city's school administrators into the top floors of the Tweed and turn the ground level into a demonstration school. The justification he offered for the move was that, since the courthouse is so close to City Hall, it would show his commitment to education. "Symbolism is important," he told the children.

Even many members of Bloomberg's own staff seemed taken aback, and reaction to the plan in the rest of the city ran from outrage to disbelief. "Ludicrous" was the assessment of John Dyson, the former deputy mayor who had overseen the renovation. One city official covered his face with his hands when I asked about Bloomberg's idea. "I can't even talk about it," he said. "My feelings are too strong."

The nature of municipal government is such that it is possible that Bloomberg will have his way, but unlikely. Location aside, there is nothing about the Tweed that suits it to the use the Mayor has in mind. To accommodate a school full of children, not to mention hundreds of bureaucrats, much of the renovation would have to be gutted, again at considerable expense. In the meantime, the courthouse just sits there—magnificent, but empty—guarded at a cost of fifteen thousand dollars a month.

Ultimately, Tweed's masterwork proved to be his undoing. On July 22, 1871, the *Times* ran a front-page story headlined "THE SECRET ACCOUNTS," with the subhead "Proofs of Undoubted Frauds Brought to Light." In it, the paper provided what it claimed was incontrovertible evidence of the Boss's swindles. (One of the *Times'* sources is believed to have been a young man named James O'Brien, who worked his way into the Tweed ring's favor by serving as a trustee of the Tweed Testimonial Association.) In the weeks that followed, one account after another related in monstrous detail—$404,347.72 spent on safes, $565,713.34 on carpets—the extent of the thievery. An often repeated story from the period is that one of Tweed's cronies, Richard (Slippery Dick) Connolly, the city comptroller, tried to buy the *Times* off—in one version offering five hundred thousand dollars, in another five million. "I don't think that the devil will ever make a higher bid for me," the paper's publisher, George Jones, is said to have replied. That November, Tweed still managed to get reelected to the State Senate, but in December he was indicted.

From that point on, Tweed suffered a rapid, if colorful, descent. The first of his trials, which took place in his own, half-finished courthouse, ended in a hung jury, amid rumors, never substantiated, that the jurors had been bribed. At his second trial, Tweed was convicted on two hundred and four counts of auditing failures. (Before heading off to a cell in the Tombs, he is reported to have had dinner sent over from Delmonico's.) Tweed appealed his sentence, and nineteen months later he was released, only to be hastily rearrested on different charges. Bail was set at three million dollars, a sum that even Tweed's friends couldn't muster. His incarceration was lightened, in the quaint fashion of the time, by frequent trips home for dinner. On one such jaunt, Tweed went upstairs and never came back down. Six months later, he was sighted in Cuba. A few months after that, he was arrested in Spain, where he was discovered posing as a seaman. Tweed had supposedly been recognized on the basis of a Thomas Nast cartoon.

Initially, Tweed's ruin was heralded as a victory for the cause of reform.

Among the celebratory verses written at the time was a poem, "The House That Tweed Built," which cheerfully proclaimed:

> Let us hope, The Boss and his gang will have plenty, of rope,
> Till they swing,
> The whole Ring,
> To Sing-Sing.

Samuel Tilden, a lawyer who took much of the credit for pursuing Tweed, became, on the basis of that pursuit, governor of New York, and almost, in an Al Gore sort of way, President of the United States.

But the reformers' achievement soon proved to be a hollow one. The Tweed ring had been a huge operation, involving, among many others, the mayor, "Elegant" Oakey Hall; the president of the Department of Public Parks, Peter (Brains) Sweeny; and Slippery Dick Connolly. Some of the members fled after the ring was exposed, some made partial restitution, and many more continued on in government service. When Tweed, suffering from heart trouble and diabetes, finally realized that there was no other hope, he approached the state attorney general, offering to provide a full account of his misdeeds, and to hand over all his property, in return for his release. Tweed wrote out his confession, even providing checks from various associates as evidence, only to have the attorney general reject the offer. The problem was not, as Alexander B. Callow, Jr., points out, that Tweed had provided too little evidence but that he had provided too much. Implicated in his various schemes was half of official New York. "Could even Mr. Tilden afford to have Tweed's story told?" the *Times* wondered.

Tweed spent the last months of his life in the Ludlow Street jail, on the Lower East Side, which he had, in his official capacity, also helped to build, in a room where he kept a piano and a servant. Ill and disheartened, he was down to a hundred and sixty pounds. On April 12, 1878, his daughter came to visit and stepped out to fetch her father some ice cream. Tweed died while she was gone. He was fifty-five. His last words are reported to have been "I hope they will be satisfied, now they have got me."

Source: *The New Yorker*, © 2002, The Condé Nast Publications Inc.

Reading 4–2: David Witwer, *The Scandal of George Scalise: A Case Study in the Rise of Labor Racketeering in the 1930s*

Despite the corruption control reforms made in the post-Boss Tweed era, scandal continued to plague America, especially in the labor relations arena. This article will expose you to the challenges faced by America's unions in their struggle to combat corruption from within; as well as allow you to more fully understand the origins of corruption within unions and broader organized crime entities.

It started with a single column. In January 1940, the columnist, Westbrook Pegler exposed the criminal past and organized crime connections of George Scalise, the President of the Building Service Employees International Union (BSEIU).(1) A previously obscure figure, now pushed into the spotlight by Pegler's columns, Scalise became the central player in a scandal that tarnished the newly reborn labor movement. At first, his claims of innocence and devotion to the union cause appeared to protect him from Pegler's revelations. But within a few months the situation changed drastically. In April 1940, newspaper headlines across the country announced Scalise's arrest by New York County District Attorney, Thomas E. Dewey, proclaiming the indictment of a rapacious union leader. The *Chicago Tribune's* headline, for instance, read, "Indict Scalise, Union Czar, in Extortion Case." Dewey's prosecutors explained that Scalise had used his control over the union to shake down employers, taking over $100,000 in the last three years. Pilloried by the press, ousted from his union position, Scalise claimed that he had been "Peglerized."(2) By that October, Scalise had been convicted in a New York State court, and sentenced to serve 10 to 20 years in prison.(3)

Scalise's sudden fall from power caused an embarrassing scandal for the labor movement, one that in subsequent decades would be followed and then overshadowed by other corruption scandals, culminating in the case of Jimmy Hoffa and the Teamsters. Like Hoffa's, Scalise's notoriety stemmed partly from the allegations of corruption and partly from his connections with organized crime. Pegler used Scalise's case to call for new restrictions on labor unions, but also to highlight the growing problem of organized crime's influence in the union movement, a phenomenon seen at the time as a recent development.(4) While Pegler did more to assert these connections than to explain them, Scalise's union career does provide a case study on how organized crime came to play an increasing role in organized labor during the 1930s. Not the stereotypical thug, but instead a smooth, well-connected operator, Scalise's rise in the BSEIU failed to generate alarm within the American Federation of Labor (API). Yet, his career was solidly based on his ties to organized crime. Moreover, he came out of a segment of the union movement marked by collusive agreements that often exploited the membership. Scalise benefited from the growing power organized crime had gained over vulnerable union leaders in the late 1920s and early 1930s. And finally, once in power, he demonstrated the myriad of ways that corruption could be made a profitable enterprise by unscrupulous leaders willing to sacrifice the needs of their membership.

Such a case study fills a gap in the existing historical literature. While popular accounts of the rise of labor racketeering in the 1930s abound, much of this material amounts to sensational journalism, or it reflects the anti-union bias of particular authors.(5) While these accounts all agree that organized crime came to play a growing role in the affairs of certain unions in the 1930s, they have little to say about how or why that happened.(6) The most comprehensive study on the subject of union corruption, John Hutchinson's, *The Imperfect Union* (1970), asserts that in the 1930s organized crime groups began a systematic effort to become involved in labor racketeering. "They succeeded," he wrote, "in the years following Repeal [of Prohibition] in achieving an unparalleled influence in labor-management relations."(7) Hutchinson blames a number of factors for the growing role of organized crime, including government corruption, "the tolerant ethics of the time," and emphasizes the "quiescence" of union leaders.(8) Yet, instead of pursuing the issue of causation, his book consists more of a series of quick vignettes of labor scandals in that era. He does not provide in-depth information on the kinds of relationships that emerged between individual union leaders and organized crime, nor does he explain the functions of the various corrupt arrangements.(9) He has even less to say about the role of the employers or the complaints of the union membership. In the three decades since Hutchinson's work appeared, little more has been written on this subject. The most recent generation of labor historians have ignored the subject of union corruption.

The Scalise case provides an opportunity to fill in this missing piece of the story. His case offers a rich source of first-hand information partly because of the investigative records left behind by the New York County District Attorney's Office, Those records are supplemented by the testimony of Scalise's co-conspirators, who became witnesses for the prosecution at his trial in 1940. Finally, the previously overlooked testimony of Roger Touhy, a gang leader in Chicago and a rival of Al Capone, provides another important piece of this history. The combination of these sources affords an in-depth history of how organized crime groups worked methodically to corrupt national union leaders in the l930s and in so doing undercut the only recently won gains of union members. This history also challenges the typical depiction of employers as simple victims of labor racketeering. In reality, businessmen's role in these schemes ranged across a spectrum, with some paying extortion out of fear for their vulnerable enterprises. Other employers, however, used arrangements with organized crime and corrupt union officials to serve their needs, controlling competition and hedging their bets against a rising wave of labor militancy in the 1930s. News accounts, like much of the scholarship that has followed, had little to say about the complicity of these employers. Instead the media emphasized the nefarious role of union leaders, whose misdeeds—in these accounts—justified objections to the growing role of organized labor.

The Exposé

In 1940, Pegler was one of the nation's most popular daily columnists. His column, entitled "Fair Enough," appeared six days a week in 132 newspapers across the country.(10) Writing this column since 1933, he covered a wide range of subjects, often giving them a distinctive, wryly humorous twist. On January 3, 1938, for instance, his entire column consisted of the same sentence repeated 50 times, the hard lesson learned from a New Year's Day hangover, "I must not mix champagne, whisky and gin."(11) But he was perhaps best known for a vituperative style, which he wielded on occasion like a nasty weapon, delivering vicious insults and making insinuations, but staying just within the margins of slander and libel laws. Profiling him in 1940, the *Saturday Evening Post*, explained that he appealed to readers, who "get a vicarious satisfaction out of his persistent swats at the objects of his displeasure. Thousands of others who find that they usually disagree with him, read his column as a kind of tonic for their adrenal glands. He infuriates them and they enjoy it." (12)

Over the course of the 1930s, his politics had drifted steadily to the right. Although he voted for Franklin Delano Roosevelt in 1932 and 1936, in the years that followed he became a strident critic of the New Deal. Similarly, his views on organized labor grew increasingly negative in these years and by 1939 he began to write on the problem of union corruption. In November that year, in his daily column, he broke the story that Willie Bioff, the West Coast Representative of the International Alliance of Theater and Stagehand Employees (IATSE), had been convicted years before on a pandering charge, but had never served out his sentence. Over the next few months, Pegler regularly returned to the story, mocking Bioff's attempts to excuse his actions, and chiding law enforcement officials to do their duty and force Bioff to finish serving his sentence.

From the start, Pegler's coverage of union corruption focused on what he viewed as the irresponsible power of union leaders and it formed part of a more general conservative counter-attack on the New Deal. The columnist charged that the Wagner Act (1935), which granted unions legal protections, gave too much power to union leaders. In August 1939, just a few months before breaking his story on Bioff, Pegler warned, ". . . organized labor is assuming the powers of government without the responsibility of government, and with business in shackles that is a lopsided arrangement which cannot continue indefinitely." Highlighting the criminal misdeeds of individual union leaders bolstered his argument about the dangers presented by a growing labor movement. Such stories fed, what Pegler declared was a growing public reaction "against extortion, mob violence, racketeering . . ., and the establishment of an irresponsible invisible government in the hands of union leaders." (13)

Pegler and other conservatives had come to see attacks on union leaders as a way to undercut popular support for the New Deal. An important proponent of this tactic was Roy Howard, who ran the Scripps-Howard newspaper chain, where Pegler was based, and who played an influential role in Republican politics. (14) Howard wrote one of his editors in early 1940 that the Wagner Act, and its effects, should constitute the central issue in the coming presidential campaign. "I think the Wagner Act furnishes as good a stage and as good a setting as we could expect to find for this fight." In another letter, Howard asserted, "a tidal wave of popular disgust with and opposition to the arrogance of union labor leadership is building up." Referring to his favorite Presidential candidate, Wendell Willkie, Howard claimed that, "If Willkie could be made to see it [the importance of this growing hostility], and could get his political surfboard up on the crest of that wave, it would I am certain carry him on a long and successful ride." (15)

Howard and Pegler's role in the media put them in a position to promote this issue. Their motives, in turn, influenced the nature of their news coverage. The public outrage, which they hoped to encourage, fed on a particular depiction of union corruption, one that emphasized the role of union leaders and as a matter of course minimized the part played by employers. This pattern fit comfortably within a larger trend of negative news coverage of unions that reflected the consanguinity of interests and outlook between publishers and other employers. William J. Puette, referred to this norm in his book, *Through Jaundiced Eyes: How the Media View Organized Labor* (1992). Puette wrote, "The image of labor unions projected in the press, as in other media, is one of corruption, greed, self-interest, and power."(16) Stories on corruption tend to emphasize the activities of union leaders and not their counterparts in business.

It was in that larger political context, that on January 19, 1940, Pegler's column took the form of an open letter to William Green, the President of the American Federation of Labor (AFL). Pegler wrote, "I am going to tell you today that the head of one of your big international unions was sentenced to Atlanta Penitentiary for four years and six months for white slavery . . . The man I mean is George Scalese [*sic*], a Brooklyn racketeer who has become president of the Building Service Employees International Union. Scalese is a criminal of the vilest type that it is possible to imagine and a member of an old mob in Brooklyn." Pegler asserted that Scalise had worked as a bodyguard for Frankie Uale, alias Yale, a notorious gangster murdered in 1928, allegedly on the orders of Al Capone. "Since the repeal of Prohibition," Pegler wrote, "he and other hoodlums of the same type in Brooklyn and New York have gone into the labor movement." The column went on to provide details of the crime for which Scalise had been convicted. Back in 1913, a federal court found that, "He [Scalise] and another hoodlum named Joe Alfano, alias Fox, transported a girl from Brooklyn to Boonton, N.J., to work her as a prostitute for their profit." Both men received stiff sentences because the crime was deemed "unusually vicious." According to Pegler, the federal judge in the case, "In his charge to the jury, spoke of the details of the case as 'nauseating' and told the jurymen that they were to disregard evidence that the girl was beaten, seduced and persuaded to live with your distinguished colleague in the labor movement on false promises of marriage. Scalese wasn't on trial for those amiable little acts of rudeness." Noting that he had heard that Scalise had applied for a presidential pardon, Pegler insinuated that Green might have signed on to support the application. "You wouldn't happen to know anything about that [application for a Presidential pardon], would you, Mr. Green. Of course it is ironic that a man who can't hold public office or even vote, who lost his citizenship for a rotten crime, should be eligible to and hold the presidency of a big union."(17)

It was a startling revelation, but at first Scalise seemed to hold his own against the onslaught. He called a meeting of the executive board of BSEIU, presenting them with both his written defense against Pegler's charges and the offer to resign should they find it necessary. While not denying the conviction,

Scalise emphasized how long ago the crime had occurred and asserted that in the years since he been an upstanding citizen, and a devoted labor leader. He reviewed his career since 1917, when he had gotten out of prison. He had, he explained, worked at a variety of jobs "very often of the most menial kind." By 1929 he found work at a garage in Brooklyn, where, he wrote, "I washed, serviced and cleaned automobiles." There he became involved in the labor movement, "to try and improve my lot and that of my fellow workers." He helped to organize Teamsters Local 272, and then served as an officer of the local. It was from that position that he was brought into BSEIU in 1933, and four years later he won election as President of the national union. Working to build BSEIU had brought him enemies and those enemies, he implied, were behind Pegler's exposé. Scalise made one theme central to his defense. "I have paid my debt to society for the act I committed as a youth. Is it the American way to brand a person forever, even though person has been punished and has learned a sufficient lesson to lead an honorable life?"(18)

For BSEIU's Executive Board, the answer to that question was a resounding, no. Claiming they had "been fairly deluged with resolutions, telegrams, and letters from the Local Unions affiliated with our International Union, affirming and reaffirming their faith and confidence in our General President, George Scalise," the Board refused to accept his resignation. Instead they issued a unanimous resolution stating their continued confidence in his leadership.(19)

Scalise had sent a similar written defense to key leaders in the AFL, and once again he followed up by making a personal appearance, this time before the AFL's executive board.(20) Like their counterparts in BSELU, the AFL leaders found Scalise's defense convincing. Writing privately to Scalise, Joseph A. Padway, the AFL's General Counsel, reassured him that Pegler's exposé of his "boyish indiscretion" had done him little harm. "In the few comments I have heard around here, not a single derogatory statement was made about you, but everyone damns and curses a writer who will resurrect an act of a young lad, which has long since been forgotten."(21) At a press conference in early February, the AFL's President Green responded to questions about Scalise by saying that he had had a long talk with the embattled BSEIU President. According to Green, Scalise "challenges any one to attack his record since he committed the crime for which he was convicted when he was 18 years of age." Green asserted that it was not fair to continue to punish a man for a crime committed so long ago. "I don't think a man should be hounded to the end of his life for a crime committed as a youth and for which he had paid the penalty." The AFL president even acknowledged that he supported Scalise's application for a Presidential pardon. "All I can say is that as far as I know, and I have known him only since 1937, Mr. Scalise has gone straight, that his conduct has been satisfactory, that he has been punished enough and that as a matter of simple justice, he having paid a penalty twenty-seven years ago, his civil rights should be restored."(22)

This decision to support Scalise in the end damaged the reputation of Green and the AFL's entire leadership. They left themselves vulnerable to the charges of complicity that were made when the true nature of Scalise's union activities were revealed. Since Green and other AFL leaders were not political novices the question arises of why they took the risk and staked their reputations on Scalise's good character.

There were reasons for the AFL leaders to discount Pegler's attack. As Scalise claimed, his criminal record showed only that one arrest and that one conviction.(23) For "a criminal of the vilest type that it is possible to imagine," as Pegler had described him, Scalise did not have much of a rap sheet. On the other hand, the AFL leaders must have weighed Pegler's animus against organized labor, including the columnist's tendency to lump broad categories of union leadership under the label racketeer. He displayed that tendency once again, a couple of weeks after his exposure of Scalise, before the AFL's leadership had made a public pronouncement on the BSEIU president. On February 1, 1940, Pegler explained in his column that he disagreed with those who argued that, while there might be a few bad apples, the AFL was generally an honest organization. "From that opinion," Pegler wrote, "I have to dissent to the extreme of saying that, in my opinion, the American Federation of Labor is rotten with extortion and racketeering."(24) Six days later he used the words "criminal scum" to refer to the AFL's top officials, deftly insinuating that the organization's entire leadership fit such a label.(25) If Pegler saw just another racketeer, union officials, on the other hand, would have noticed that the Building Service Union apparently had flourished under Scalise's leadership. It was while he was serving as the BSEIU's East Coast Representative that the union had made its big organizing breakthrough in New York City, and those gains continued once he became the national president. From 1934 to 1940, the union's membership in that city had risen from 1500 to 30,000.(26)

Then too, apparently Scalise could be very convincing. By all accounts he was a pleasant, even a charming man, who did not fit the part of a menacing gangster. The press referred to him as a dapper dresser, and press photos show him invariably smiling, wearing tasteful formal attire.(27) In one photo he was proudly standing behind a seated Mayor Fiorello LaGuardia during a set of collective bargaining negotiations; not publicity shy, he offers the camera a friendly look.(28) He was married, with a teenaged daughter, and lived in a modest house in Brooklyn, near his parents whom he helped to support.(29) As his long-term secretary, Anna Kimmel, put it, "Mr. Scalise always treated everyone nicely, including myself."(30) Internal union correspondence reveals a man comfortable committing his thoughts to writing, who also displayed a sure grasp of the bureaucratic intricacies of his organization.(31) He cultivated his contacts in the AFL, presenting influential people, like the General Counsel Padway, with generous Christmas gifts.(32) This was a man who sought respectability, so much so that he had worked to gather influential supporters for a presidential pardon that would restore the civil rights he lost because of his one criminal conviction, twenty-seven years earlier.

Scalise's Union Career

And yet, unfortunately for Green and the AFL, Scalise had not led a life of selfless devotion to the cause of labor since his earlier "boyish indiscretion." Instead, he was a professional fixer, and he had made his way in a part of the labor movement where arrangements and side deals, backed up with the threat of violence, offered businessmen stability and security for a price. This was a kind of marginal sphere in the world of organized labor, largely unwritten about by labor historians, but still a significant part of the union movement in New York and other cities in the 1920s and 1930s.(33) Here organized labor gained a firm foothold through collusive arrangements that benefited employers, but often sacrificed the interests of the workers. Thanks to his ties with organized crime, Scalise emerged out of this murky field to assume the presidency of BSEIU in 1937. He won election to that office in return for an agreement to share the unions revenue with the successor to Al Capone's gang in Chicago. Meanwhile, in New York, he used his office to subvert the union's recent gains among Manhattan's building workers.

The specific nature of Scalise's ties to organized crime—whether he was an associate or a member of the Mafia—remain unknown, but clearly he was connected. His most important relationship was with Anthony Carfano, also known as Little Augie Pisano, or sometimes just "the Kid." Allegedly a capo, or captain, in what became known as Genovese Crime Family, Carfano ran a crew in Brooklyn. In the early days of Prohibition, Carfano had accompanied his fellow Brooklyn crime figure Al Capone to Chicago and spent some years there working in Capone's organization. Back in Brooklyn, he had a reputation for toughness, but he also maintained a much less flamboyant appearance than his old associate Capone. Carfano dressed conservatively, and as the *New York Times* put it, "in appearance, resembled a business executive." He apparently cultivated that image, making his headquarters in a downtown Brooklyn office building. Politically connected, he was the son-in-law of John De Salvio, better known as Jimmy Kelly, the Democratic Party leader for Greenwich Village.(34)

Describing his relationship with Carfano, Scalise once explained it this way, "We're partners." Carfano got half of everything that Scalise received.(35) In return, Carfano provided Scalise with influential backing and a range of connections. With Carfano to vouch for him, Scalise maintained contacts with a number of other prominent criminal figures. He had close contacts with Louis "Lepke" Buchalter, whose Jewish gang was involved in a number of labor racketeering schemes and dominated the Garment District. He allegedly also had ties with Joey Amberg, a leading figure in the Brooklyn gang scene, who was later pushed aside by the Jewish-Italian organized crime group dubbed by the press, Murder Inc.(36) These were relationships that Scalise could draw upon to serve his needs. A police wiretap on Scalise's office in 1934, picked him up using Carfano's contacts to arrange for James Plumeri, a Lucchese Crime Family member, to damage some trucks in lower Manhattan, apparently as part of Scalise's efforts to organize Teamsters Local 272. According to the police report, Carfano told Scalise, "that job was made this morning on those trucks," and now Scalise should get together some money "for the boys."(37)

These connections, and his personal style, apparently made him a skilled fixer. While this might not be an expertise commonly put on résumés, it was for that time and place a valuable asset. In the world of illegal arrangements—such as offering or accepting bribes, or making collusive agreements to limit competition—participants risk legal and financial repercussions if one party to the deal proves untrustworthy. Moreover, should the deal go sour, the individuals involved cannot seek legal remedies. It takes a particular type of person to instill trust, and also to offer the needed assurances that the agreed upon conditions of the deal will be met. A fixer does not necessarily have to be personally a tough guy, but he must have access to the kind of extra-legal force that all parties know can be called upon should circumstances warrant it. Scalise was both well connected and charming, and the police wiretap on his office in 1934 revealed a range of people calling on him to broker their illegal arrangements. For instance, in April 1934, Louis Block, later an official in the Butchers Union, called Scalise to ask him to use his contacts at the Brooklyn District Attorney's Office to fix the case of his brother, Max Block, who was facing trial on a murder charge. What precise action Scalise took remains unclear, but a year later court records showed that a Brooklyn judge directed a verdict of not guilty in Max Block's case.(38) Scalise evidently was practiced at making such arrangements. Four days before Block's phone call, the wiretap recorded Scalise explaining to a Jimmy Sabella, that "it would cost five bills to get a case thrown out in the Coney Island Magistrate's Court."(39)

Scalise's activities do not fit the standard, cinematic depiction of organized crime, but they exemplify a mainstay of what groups like the Italian American Mafia actually do. Crimes of violence, such as extortion and robbery, and vice activities, tend to garner a great deal of attention in most popular accounts of the Mafia. But in these endeavors organized criminal groups have little advantage over more temporary bands of criminals, who may have a greater willingness to engage in violence or better access to illegal goods and services. As brokers of illegal arrangements, however, organized criminal groups do enjoy real advantages. Their relative longevity, the geographic reach of their contacts, and their ability to adjudicate potential disputes, all enhance their ability to serve as a kind of dependable brokerage service in a wide array of settings.(40) Labor racketeering exemplified just such an opportunity, and in the 1930s organized crime figures like Scalise moved into this area.

It was as a broker, not as an aggrieved worker, that Scalise came to play a role in the labor movement. Louis Marcus, a labor lawyer who became a close associate of Scalise, testified that in 1929 Scalise asked his help in setting up a Brooklyn branch of Teamsters Local 272, a union of parking garage workers. This marked Scalise's first involvement in organized labor. According to Marcus, Scalise told him he would get the local's charter from "the Dutchman," a reference to the gangster Arthur Flegenheimer, also known as Dutch Schultz, who controlled Local 272's Manhattan office. Over the next couple of years Marcus did the legal work as Scalise built up the Brooklyn branch of Local 272, setting its offices up in the same downtown office building where Carfano made his headquarters.(41)

Unions of parking garage employees attracted gangsters, because organization could most quickly be achieved through selective acts of violence. Damage to cars parked in non-union garages—ice pick punctures to the tires or slashed upholstery—could quickly force an employer to sign his employees into the union. And union organization in turn provided a cover for corralling the businessmen into an employers' organization, whose dues could be tapped by organized crime. In spite of the use of force against employers in such an organizing campaign, this was not a case of out and out extortion; employers enjoyed some real benefits. This kind of collusive arrangement between a union and an employers' organization offered parking garage owners a way to manage competition. Employers' associations could set uniform rates and limit the entrance of new competitors. For the average union member, on the other hand, such a union often brought little change except the addition of regular dues deducted from their pay. Indeed the way the union was built made such conditions likely. As union organizers, Scalise, and others of his type, went into the labor movement to make money; they came from outside the ranks of the workers in the industry, with whom they did not really identify. Nor did they depend upon those workers to organize the union through mass picketing and long strikes. Instead they used selective acts of violence committed by a few individuals, probably with links to organized crime. Free from having to depend on a mobilized, united membership, the Union's leadership could safely ignore the members' needs, or sacrifice them to the interests of the employers. As a result, as unskilled workers scattered across a wide area and laboring in small shops, garage employees, and others caught in similar situations, had little knowledge of their union, and often no say in its affairs.(42)

Police reports indicate that in the early 1930s, Scalise worked closely with Louis Levine, a parking garage owner, to build up the Kings County Garage Association, at the same time as Local 272 steadily enrolled the borough's garage employees. This two-fold organizing campaign was marked by occasional reports of violence and property destruction.(43) Levine's participation suggests the benefits that at least some employers saw in this type of collusive organization. Comments from the newly enrolled union membership, however, indicate that they failed to enjoy similar gains. When prosecutors spoke with William Davis, a rank and file member of the local, they noted, "Davis has indicated that the union rate of wages is considerably lower than that paid to a non-union man."(44) Another member, writing to the AFL, and referring to Local 272, complained, "This is a racket all over." He described an organization where members were enrolled without their knowledge by employers, who simply began deducting the men's dues, and never informed them about what constituted the union scale. Members had no say in the affairs of their union;

according to the letter, "this bunch of racketeers . . . run this Union, just as they please."(45)

The organization of garage workers in Brooklyn stemmed not from any emerging worker militancy, but rather from an effort to control competition among employers. In this way, Scalise's history draws attention to another aspect of the important workplace changes of the Great Depression. The standard explanation of union growth in the 1930s highlights the workers' quest for stability in response to the sweeping economic uncertainties they faced.(46) A parallel quest on the part of many small employers, however, also played a role, as bosses were willing to help corral their workers into organizations they believed could bring market stability.(47) While genuine union organizers used this opportunity to achieve significant gains for workers, Scalise, and others like him, responded in a more straightforward, entrepreneurial fashion. The needs of employers and the more hospitable organizing environment of the 1930s offered a chance to make money.

Like a businessman seeking new opportunities for growth, Scalise pursued a range of ventures within organized labor. According to the labor lawyer, Marcus, in 1930, a year after he began working on Teamsters Local 272, Scalise hired him to set up a beauticians' local in Brooklyn, on the understanding that in this operation Scalise would be partners with the gangster Joey Amberg. A couple of years later, he told Marcus he was going to acquire the charter for a non-kosher butchers local union, explaining that this venture would be a shared undertaking with Carfano, who would help finance it.(48) The collusive nature of this enterprise became clear a couple of weeks later, when Scalise asked Marcus to form an association of Italian-American butchers, an employers' association to go along with the new union.(49) In 1931, Scalise helped set up another associate, Isidore "Izzy" Schwartz, in a bakery drivers' local. When that venture failed, Scalise arranged for Schwartz to get a charter for a window cleaners local from the Building Service Employees International Union (BSEIU). Union pickets then worked to support a strong employers' association among Brooklyn's window cleaners. The association policed the industry, forbidding contractors from taking any members' customers and imposing a regular schedule of dues payments.(50)

Scalise was a professional fixer, who had come to see the business possibilities of organizing unions in order to build collusive arrangements in certain industries. The potential for profit in such arrangements and his organized crime connections brought him into the labor movement. That same combination also led him into the Building Service Employees' union.

BSEIU and Organized Crime

It was through Schwartz and the window cleaning business that Scalise began his rise in the Building Service Union. In his efforts to get Schwartz a charter for a window washers union from BSEIU, Scalise had turned to his Mafia sponsor, Carfano, asking him to use his influence. The national headquarters of BSEIU was located in Chicago, and it turned out that Carfano's old ties to the Capone gang proved useful in gaining the union charter. Schwartz later testified that Scalise explained, "he had to get a hold of Augie [Carfano] to get some connections out there [in Chicago], to get this through."(51) In the years that followed, Scalise drew on those same ties, first to gain an official position in the Building Service Union, and then to quickly move up the ranks to president.

Carfano's influence with BSEIU stemmed from the role that the successor to the Capone organization, the Chicago Mafia, often referred to as the Outfit, had come to play in the affairs of the union. The Outfit had acquired its role through the vulnerability of BSEIU's top leadership in Chicago, who sought to lead a union in a hostile and insecure environment.

BSEIU had been originally organized in the 1910s in Chicago, first as a local of flat janitors (i.e. janitors working in residential buildings). Led by William F. Quesse, the union conducted a fiercely fought organizing campaign marked by violent incidents committed by both sides. In 1921, the union's top leadership, ten officers including Quesse, were indicted in Chicago on a range of charges including extortion and conspiracy to blow up buildings. Historian John B. Jencz has recently traced how employers' organizations, promoting an anti-union campaign, played a pivotal role in this prosecution. Convicted on the broadest of the conspiracy charges, the leadership of BSEIU was sentenced to one to five years in state prison. It was only the union's strong political ties to Chicago's Mayor William "Big Bill" Thompson that protected the organization from destruction at the hands of this employer offensive, and eventually, in 1924, won the union's leaders a pardon from the governor.(52)

A few years later, the union faced attack from a different direction. This time Capone's gang, the Outfit, sought control of the organization, essentially seeking to tap into the national body's treasury. Given the links between Mayor Thompson's administration and this same gang, BSEIU leaders could expect little help from their political allies this time around.(53)

The precise details of what occurred remain unknown, but conflicting, partial accounts do provide the broad outlines. In the late 1920s and early 1930s, Roger Touhy was a bootlegger based in Chicago's northwest suburbs. According to him, one of Capone's associates, Marcus "Studdy" Looney, met with Touhy and his brother in 1929 to discuss a plan to strong arm a number of unions in the city. Looney brought with him a list of unions with the amounts held in their treasuries. As Touhy tells it, he and his brother chose not to participate, and in the months that followed a number of old-time leaders from the Teamsters, the Painters Union, and the Building Service Employees' Union came to him for protection from Capone's people. Touhy referred specifically to Jerry Horan, who was then the President of the BSEIU, as one of the leaders of this faction of unionists who moved up to the northwest suburbs seeking protection from Capone.(54)

This account can be partially corroborated. In the Teamsters Union, one of the other organizations mentioned by Looney, the national president, Daniel Tobin began to receive death threats in early 1930 from individuals in Chicago.

Minutes of meetings from the Teamsters' executive board in that period referred to the situation.(55) "One of the Vice-Presidents called attention of the Board to the situation in Chicago where certain undesirables were endeavoring to break into our local union."(56) Writing a letter in March 1932, Tobin described how many unions by that time had been taken over. "Conditions in the Labor Movement among unions in Chicago are not good and the strong arm element seems to be getting control of many unions, consequently the need for all of us being extremely careful."(57) Another source of corroboration comes from union leaders who faced similar threats a few years later. Mart Taylor, who led a Chicago local of elevator operators, described being given a stark choice in early 1936: put one of the Outfit's people on the union payroll and agree to cooperate, or be killed.(58) In the Chicago Bartenders Union, George B. McLane, testified before a grand jury that he was given a similar choice in 1935.(59) There is little reason to think that the technique had differed significantly six years earlier. Further corroboration comes from the fact that a number of prominent labor leaders were killed in Chicago in the early to mid-1930s.(60) Although none of the murderers was ever arrested, and officially the cases remained unsolved, the deaths were generally credited to the Chicago Outfit, which the victims were believed to have resisted. The ineffectiveness of law enforcement in these cases demonstrated the dilemma faced by those local union officials, who might have wanted to resist. They would receive no meaningful protection from the authorities. Indeed the authorities, such as they were, seemed to be working with the Outfit.

According to Touhy, the union officials, who had originally come to him for protection, eventually came to terms with Capone's organization. Touhy claimed that BSEIU President Horan had been deeply affected by the killing of his brother-in-law, William J. Rooney, who was gunned down in front of his home in March 1931. An influential figure in both Building Service Union and the Sheet Metal Workers, Rooney had helped make Horan president of BSEIU.(61) After a couple of years of seeking shelter with Touhy up in the northwest suburbs, Horan had had enough of resistance and all that it implied. Touhy recalled, "He [Horan] was even afraid of the men who were supposed to be his bodyguards." In April 1933, according to Touhy, Horan and Art Wallace, a leader in the Painters Union, came to him and said they were going to give up the fight. Horan then went to a meeting that the Chief Investigator for the Cook County prosecutor's office, Daniel Gilbert, had arranged with Ted Newberry, one of the leading figures in the Outfit. With Gilbert officiating, Horan agreed to turn over control of his union. After that, Touhy explained, the Building Service Union president took instructions from Murray Humphreys, the Outfit's specialist in union matters.(62)

A bootlegger, a rival of Capone, and himself the target of allegations that he strong armed union officials, Touhy's account should be read with a healthy amount of skepticism.(63) But it generally squares with the commentaries provided by other sources and it helps explain how the Outfit came to wield influence over the Building Service Union.(64) By 1934, when Willie Bioff, then a low level official in the Chicago Stage Hands Union, met with Outfit leaders, they referred to Horan and the Building Service Employees as one of the leaders and one of unions that they controlled.(65)

The process by which the Outfit gained control of BSEIU and other unions during this period challenges the standard explanation of union corruption. Hutchinson, in his comprehensive book on the subject, *The Imperfect Union* (1970), argued that although other factors played a role, corrupt unions became corrupt because of the weak morals of their leaders. Those leaders succumbed to temptation, in turn, because the philosophy of business union-ism (the emphasis on simple bread and butter goals) provided little incentive to take the moral high road. As Hutchinson saw it, "in the presence of tempta-tion or error the so-called business unionists could have used a stronger creed."(66) But in Chicago, and presumably elsewhere as well, temptation had little to do with how organized crime gained influence over unions in this period. Instead, vulnerable union officials succumbed to threats and terror. They did so while trying to operate in a hostile atmosphere, where the state, in the form of a corrupt local government, offered them no protection. The list of dead union officials in Chicago highlights the degree to which the Outfit, and other similar organized crime groups, could make good on their threats. In such an environment, the decision of a union leader like Horan appears as less an example of moral susceptibility and more the rational response of someone stuck in a bad spot.

Having spent time in Capone's organization in the early 1920s, Carfano, Scalise's Mafia sponsor, apparently still had strong ties to the Chicago Outfit and he used those connections to benefit Scalise. In 1932, Carfano helped Scalise get a charter for a local union of window washers. Scalise put his long-term associate, Izzy Schwartz in charge of the local. Two years later, when the BSEIU's representative in New York City retired, Scalise asked Carfano to help him get the job. According to Schwartz, Scalise told him, "that he would get in touch with Augie [Carfano] and let Augie go to work out there [in Chicago] and see what he can do for him." A couple of months later, BSEIU's President Horan appointed Scalise to be the union's Eastern Representative. Scalise explained to Schwartz that a deal had been arranged with the Chicago mob for Carfano and Scalise to get fifty percent of the union's proceeds from any newly organized members in the East. They would be operating the BSEIU in the East on a commission basis.(67)

In April 1937, Scalise got word that President Horan was ill, and thought to be on his deathbed. Schwartz later testified that talking with Scalise about it, he raised the possibility of Scalise becoming the next president. "Well, we laughed at it—he laughed at it for a moment and then he thought of the possibilities about it there, he would try for it; so he called Augie then. For his part, Carfano agreed to help, but he was not hopeful. After hanging up the phone, Scalise told Schwartz, "that Augie told him 'O.K.' he will see what he can do, but not to bank on it."(68)

In the end, Scalise became the top candidate because of the political problems that beset the candidate originally sponsored by the Outfit, Thomas Burke. Burke had gained power in a Chicago local after the murder of its previous leader, Louis Alterie, apparently by the Outfit. Burke's ties to the Outfit were a matter of common knowledge within the union and so several of the BSEIU board members, who would be the ones voting to pick Horan's replacement, viewed him with distaste. Then too another candidate from Chicago, William McFetridge, had greater seniority within the union, and he threatened to divide the vote of the Chicago officers. Scalise became a compromise candidate. Since his ties to organized crime were not well known, he did not raise the same objections as had Burke. An outsider, he offered a face-saving alternative to the Chicago officers, and in the end he won the presidency by a unanimous vote of the board.(69)

The Outfit had come to see the value of someone like Scalise, who had strong ties to organized crime, but still maintained a respectable image within the labor movement. Such individuals became front men as the Outfit moved to gain control of national unions. George Browne played a similar role in the Outfit's successful effort in 1934 to gain control of the national office of the Stage Hands Union. Willie Bioff, a close associate of Browne, later testified that the Outfit's leaders told him in 1934, "They said they could use a man like him [Browne], he has a nice clean background, and they need a front man like him, it is very important to them."(70)

As the front man for the Outfit, and the partner of Carfano, Scalise worked out arrangements to siphon money out of the BSEIU treasury. Scalise received an official salary of $1,000 a month and he arranged to give half of that to the Outfit. At the same time, he worked with the union's secretary-treasurer to drain money out of the union through fake expense vouchers. Poring over these vouchers in 1940, Dewey's investigators charged that from 1937 to 1940, Scalise took $60,087, an amount that came close to doubling his official salary for those years. At the same time, they found evidence that other fake expense vouchers were being used to send the Outfit about $3,000 every month. All told, during the roughly two and a half years of his presidency, prosecutors estimated that Scalise helped the Outfit take about $100,000 out of the BSEIU treasury. In this activity he seemed to play the part of the accomplice, not the instigator. Helping to loot the union had been part of the deal Scalise had made in order to be come president of the union. His actual authority in the organization was limited to the East Coast, with occasional disputes emerging with the Outfit over what was included in that area.(71)

Scalise in New York: The Many Profitable Avenues of Labor Corruption

If for much of the country, he was the president of the union in name only, in New York City Scalise's power was far more real. There he benefited from a successful organizing campaign that had dramatically expanded the membership of the BSEIU in the Manhattan's residential and office buildings, and in the city's hotels. He used the union's growth to enrich himself in a number of ways, essentially accepting money in return for subverting the newly won gains of the city's building employees. In return for payments from employers, he transformed elements of BSEIU into a kind of variation on the company union, which the Wagner Act recently had made illegal. Thus he offered employers a way to cope with the unfamiliar landscape of the New Deal.

With a skeletal organization in New York, the BSEIU had been attempting to organize in the city since the mid-1920s. Success finally came in the fall of 1934, when—with the support of unionized garment workers—local BSEIU organizers won a strike in the city's Garment District. Spurred on by that success, the union went on to enjoy gains in Manhattan's office buildings and apartment houses. In 1937, a breakthrough came in the hotel industry, where the newly formed New York Hotel Trades Council oversaw agreements between hotel owners and the BSEIU. Within a few years, the previously unorganized building workers of New York became one of the largest segments of the national union. From 1934 to 1940, the union's membership in New York City rose from 1200 to over 30,000, while the national union's membership that year stood at 60,000 total. During those same years, Local 32B, which stood at the center of this organizing campaign, mushroomed from 300 members to 14,000. By 1940, Local 32B was by far the largest BSEIU local in the country.(72)

Scalise played no significant role in these organizing campaigns, except to profit from them. The various accounts of organizers all agree that in 1934 Horan imposed Scalise upon them and at first they saw very little of him. He did not attend pre-strike rallies or regular union meetings. Local union officials organized the members and won the strikes without his assistance.(73)

But then, once these locals began to grow, Scalise asserted himself. In Local 32B, Scalise used his influence as a national union officer to gain control over the local and then to begin to drain money out of it. He pressured the local to appoint one of his friends, David Sullivan, to an official post in the local and then backed Sullivan's steady movement up the ranks. Sullivan became the head of the local in 1938, following an election in which another officer in the local later testified both he and Sullivan stuffed the ballot box to rig the vote. As Sullivan's power grew, other officers within the local were intimidated and compromised. James Bambrick had been one of the leading forces behind Local 32B's growth, and had viewed Scalise's influence in the organization with suspicion. One day in 1937, Scalise informed him that a professional killer from Chicago was in the city with orders to kill Bambrick. To save his life, Bambrick arranged to draw $10,000 out of Local 32B's funds and hand it over to Scalise. Apparently having accomplished his goal, Scalise returned $2500 of the money to Bambrick, explaining that that was the local leader's share. According to later testimony, Scalise used his influence over Local 32B to pull money out of the local in a variety of ways. As was the case with the national union, false expense vouchers covered embezzlement from the local's funds. Service providers doing business with the local, such as the union's accountant and a physician doing work for the local's health plan, paid kickbacks that went to

Scalise. Local officials were pressured to accept payoffs from businessmen and then to share the proceeds with Sullivan, who in all likelihood passed some of the money along to Scalise. In this way, Scalise corrupted a local whose growth initially had promised to bring real benefits to the city's building employees.(74)

He corrupted a dynamic growing local, but Scalise also made money by setting up other locals, whose main purpose from the start would be to siphon off money from workers. In April 1938, Scalise set up a charter for Local 94, the Bowling and Billiard Academy Employees Union. The officers he installed to run the new union were operatives for a Tammany Hall political boss, Jimmy Hines, and their chief asset apparently was their experience in stuffing ballot boxes. Scalise arranged for the local to sign a contract with the Bowling Alley Proprietors Association, which granted the union a closed shop and mandated that members' dues be deducted automatically from their paychecks. New York's pin boys suddenly found themselves members of Local 94, and discovered that they now must pay a $5 initiation fee and $2 monthly dues. Since they made only 6 cents a game, these payments to the union constituted a significant financial obligation. Nor could they see any tangible benefits brought by this newly imposed union membership. As one wrote to the District Attorney's office, "The boys in general are opposed to such a union because it offers nothing in return for the $2.00 per month and the academy owners are all inclined to pay the present scale of 6 cents [per] single and 3 cents [per] double [i.e. when two pin boys were working one lane] without such a union which is without a doubt a 'PACKET.' " Nor did the members have any real voice in their union. At the local's first election, Scalise's appointees marked 400 ballots for themselves, thus overwhelming the 300 votes cast by actual members of the local.(75) In effect, Local 94 was a sham local, never intended to better the lives of its members; it simply conspired with the employers to impose a new tax on workers laboring in the industry. This tax became yet another way for Scalise to profit from his position in the BSEIU.

For employers, these kinds of arrangements with Scalise offered a pre-emptive strike against the possibility of a more militant union entering their workplace.(76) The changed legal and political atmosphere of the New Deal had undercut previous methods of blocking union organization, including seeking injunctions and forming company unions. However, by allowing Scalise to set up operations—such as Local 94—employers dodged these newly erected legal protections. Scalise provided them with a new kind of company union, one for which the employer suffered no legal liability. Better yet, the workers, not the employer, paid for the cost of this service, in the form of membership dues payments that Scalise or his surrogates then siphoned out of the union funds.

These schemes received relatively little attention when Scalise's indictment was announced in April 1940. Instead the District Attorney's Office and the newspapers focused on allegations that Scalise had extorted vast sums of money from New York's employers. The front page headline in the *New York Times* read, "Scalise, Union Head, Seized in $100,000 Extortion Plot." (77) Other reports referred to this amount as a "$100,000 levy" that Scalise had exacted from employers over a period of three years. The story from the Associated Press included in its lead a reference to "Scalise's alleged tribute-fixing activities." (78) In this way, the press coverage painted these employers as victims, forced to pay money out of fear for the safety of their businesses, but the reality was a much less black and white.

Employers who pay money to union officials do so for a variety of reasons, but for prosecutors those payments fall into one of two categories, either bribery or extortion. The difference lies in the motivation of the employer when he makes the payment. If the employer makes the payment in hopes of encouraging the union official to betray his responsibilities to his membership, then the money is deemed a bribe, and the employer is as culpable as the union official. But, if the employer pays because of threats made by the union official, then the employer is a victim of extortion. The gray area in all of this is what constitutes a threat on the part of the union official and what actually motivates the employer to make a payment. In describing the extortion charges against Scalise in 1940, Dewey's prosecutors explained that employers had paid after Scalise threatened to call strikes, made excessive wage demands, or threatened to unionize nonunion operations. (79) But, even an honest union official, attempting to represent his membership and build the organization, must threaten employers with strikes and attempt to unionize non-union businesses. Similarly the difference between reasonable and excessive wage demands often depends on whether one is the employer or the employee, as anyone familiar with collective bargaining negotiations knows. The employer's motives in making a payment, on the other hand, may be a mix of fear and avarice. He pays money and thus keeps his labor force non-union or moderates the union's demands. He would not have made the payment without concern about the effect that unionization would have on his business, but given the benefit he derives from the payment it is hard to see him as purely a victim.

This blurry line between extortion and bribery may have led Dewey's office to pursue a different tack when they brought Scalise to trial. In press conferences at the time of Scalise's arrest, on April 22, Dewey and his aides referred to the grand jury testimony of employers who had been victims of extortion. But by late May, as investigators working their way through the union's financial records found growing evidence of Scalise's malfeasance, Dewey's office submitted a second indictment, charging larceny and forgery. In the end, the charges from the second indictment were the only ones that Dewey's office brought to trial. (80)

Had the District Attorney gone forward with the extortion case, the result would have been a double standard of justice. A subsequent prosecution, involving Frank Gold, an official in BSEIU's Local 32B, demonstrated how charging a union official with extortion could give employers a free pass. At his trial in 1941, prosecutors charged that Gold had extorted money from various midtown building management firms. As the *New York Times* explained, "The prosecution contended that Gold between 1937 and 1939 used his influence in the union as a club to enforce payments to him under threat of 'trouble' with Local 32B." On the stand, employers testified to making payments that ranged between $400 and $1500 to Gold and in return getting favorable union contracts. Taking the stand in his own defense, Gold at first described these payments as gifts pushed on him by the employers, and he claimed the money had not influenced him in his duties as a union official. During his cross-examination by the prosecution, however, Gold retreated a bit, and admitted he had been influenced. In gaining that admission, however, the prosecutor himself slipped into depicting these payments as bribes. In one exchange, the prosecutor asked, "Were you influenced to such an extent that, in 1938 and 1939, you were willing to 'sell' your workers in your council district?" Gold still claimed, "That was not my intention." To which the prosecutor returned, "Did you sell them out?" And, Gold at last admitted, "The way you put it, I guess I did." A sales transaction requires a buyer, and by using this kind of language the prosecutor acknowledged the benefits that the employers sought to gain. In the end Gold was convicted of extortion, but the transactions he took part in look a lot more like bribery. None of the employers, who had received favorable union contracts, suffered any legal repercussions.(81)

Seen from the union membership's point of view, the employers were not the victims in these conspiracies, instead they were the real winners. Among the companies listed in the extortion indictment filed against Scalise by the District Attorney's Office was the Handiman Company, a janitorial contractor who testified to making a payment of $11,750. Dewey's aides described this as one of the payments made out of fear. In this case, Scalise allegedly used his control of BSEIU Local 32J to pressure Handiman and other cleaning contractors into giving him money. However, an employee of the company, writing to the District Attorney's Office, put forward a different scenario. According to this employee, the company bought off the union in order to take shameless advantage of its workers. While the union's contract limited the cleaning women to six hours of work a night, they were routinely forced to stay much longer. "Some of them start at 7 PM and have so much to do they cannot finish until 4 in the morning." Although Handiman was supposed to pay for holidays, it did not. The company deducted money from the employees' wages for damages and other purposes without explanation or justification. The letter closed with the straightforward conclusion about the contractor's relationship with the union, "And also he is a partner to 32J union." Similarly, Dewey's indictment listed the National House Cleaning Company as another victim of Scalise's extortion. But, according to a letter from one of the company's employees, the business was doing quite well indeed. National had forced all of its workers to join Local 32J, deducted their dues every month, and yet continued to pay substandard wages. "Some people do not get 10 cents per hour if you checked the times they worked." If someone was being victimized, it was not the National House Cleaning Company. As this employee put it, "Now as far as the union goes it is nothing but a racket—and I also think that the contractor is in with the union."(82)

Conclusion

Taken as an example of the problem of union corruption, Scalise's case offers a few useful lessons. His early career in organized labor highlights the problematic world of the collusive unions. Especially in fields where mass picketing was not necessary to achieve organization, and where unskilled workers labored in small numbers at widely scattered worksites, an exploitative union like Teamsters Local 272 could emerge. Scalise, and others like him, are better seen as union entrepreneurs, eager to profit on the most minimal level of organization, pitching the union as a tool to help the employers. Scalise's rise in the Building Service Union also demonstrates the growing role of organized crime in this period. Because of the vulnerability of union leaders, especially in locales such as Chicago, several national unions in this period were forced to make accommodations. According to court testimony, it was during this time that the Chicago Outfit gained control over the BSEIU, the International Alliance of Theater and Stage Employees' Union, the Laborers', and the Laundry Workers Union. The Outfit sought to install front men, like Scalise, who had clean records, but who would work with the group to drain money from the union's treasury. A similar process of intimidation enmeshed many local leaders in relationships with organized crime. On a more individual level, the ever industrious Scalise demonstrated the myriad of ways that a corrupt official could milk money out of the union. Finally, the employers, who were usually depicted as the most prominent victims of these activities, often better fit the role of active co-conspirators.

The true victims were the union members, many of whom became deeply disillusioned with the organizations they were forced to join. One BSEIU member in New York wrote to Westbrook Pegler in 1942, explaining how five years earlier she and the other cleaning women at the hotel where she worked were forced to join the union. They paid $2 a month in dues, which she considered a hefty amount. "We were getting only $13—a week." And in return, she and the other members got nothing. "Well, anyway this Schwartz-Scalise gang didn't better our conditions [on the] contrary we were more slaved than before we had no increase in our wages, no vacations, but more work as they laid off people."(83) Pegler tapped into that disillusionment, drawing on the problem of union corruption to build a general condemnation of organized labor, and the New Deal in general. Stories on corrupt union leaders provided a rallying point around which to build public hostility. The early decision of the AFL to support Scalise would prove fateful, as his scandal helped to undercut the legitimacy of unions.

Notes

(1) *Chicago Tribune*, April 27, 1940, in Thomas E. Dewey Scrapbooks [Microfilm Edition], v. 3–4, roll 2, University of Rochester, Rochester, New York, (hereafter Dewey Scrapbooks).

(2) Quoted headline is from, *Chicago Tribune*, April 27, 1940, examples of the general newspaper coverage containing both the District Attorney's explanation of the charges and the term "Peglerized," see also: Citizen-zen-C ushing, [Cushing, Oklahoma] April 22,1940; *Philadelphia Record*, April 28, 1940; *Los Angeles News*, April 22, 1940; in Thomas E. Dewey Scrapbooks [Microfilm Edition], v. 3–4, roll 2, University of Rochester, Rochester, New York, (hereafter Dewey Scrapbooks). *Time Magazine*, May 6, 1940, pp. 20–21.

(3) *New York Times*, October 8, 1940, p. 1.

(4) Pegler for instance carefully linked Scalise to a well-known Brooklyn racketeer, Frank Yale. "Since the repeal of Prohibition, he [Yale] and other hoodlums of the same type in Brooklyn and New York have gone into the labor movement." Westbrook Pegler, "Fair Enough," January 19, 1940, Box 120, (James) Westbrook Pegler Papers, Herbert Hoover Presidential Library, West Branch, Iowa.

(5) Contemporary accounts of the growing problem of organized crime involvement in labor unions and the phenomenon of labor racketeering include: Fred D. Pasley, *Muscling in* (New York, 1931); Harold Seidman, *Labor Czars: A History of Labor Racketeering* (New York, 1938); Frank Dalton O'Sullivan, *Enemies of Industry* (Chicago, 1933); Gordon L. Hostetter and Thomas Quinn Beesley, *It's a Racket* (Chicago, 1929); Edward Dean Sullivan, *This Labor Union Racket* (New York, 1936); Walter Chambers, *Labor Unions and the Public* (New York, 1936): Malcolm Johnson, *Crime on the Labor Front* (New York, 1950).

(6) In his popular history of the Teamsters Union, journalist Steven Brill focused on the 1930s as the pivotal decade, when organized crime gained a hold on that union. "It was during these hard, violent times that many of the big-city Teamsters locals and joint councils made their first alliances with local gangsters." Using more dramatic language, but offering no further specifics the President's Commission on Organized Crime similarly described the 1930s as the crucial decade. Stephen Fox, on the other hand, does offer an explanation. He cites the role of the depression and the end of prohibition. The Depression, he argues, made businesses and employees more pliant and Prohibition's repeal motivated gangsters to find a new source of income. Drawing on secondary sources, however, Fox supplies little in the way direct evidence, nor does he provide a description of how organized crime groups expanded their influence. Steven Drill, *The Teamsters* (New York, 1978), p. 360; President's Commission on Organized Crime, *The Edge: Organized Crime, Business, and Labor Unions* (Washington, D.C., 1986), p. 4; Stephen Fox, *Blood and*

Power: Organized Crime in Twentieth Century America (New York, 1989), pp. 174–79.

(7) John Hutchinson, *The Imperfect Union: A History of Corruption in American Trade Unions* (New York, 1970), p. 68.

(8) Ibid., p. 117.

(9) Two more theoretical studies of union corruption do address the nature of the corrupt arrangements that emerged, but these authors base their functional explanations of corruption on broad overviews and do little to trace the process the historical change in particular unions that resulted in a growing role for organized crime. See: Philip Taft, *Corruption and Racketeering in the Labor Movement* (Ithaca, New York, 1958); and Daniel Bell, *The End of Ideology: On the Exhaustion of Political Ideas in the Fifties* (Glencoe, Illinois, 1960).

(10) Jack Alexander, "He's Against," *The Saturday Evening Post*, v. 213, (September 14, 1940), p. 10.

(11) "Fair Enough," January 3, 1939, Box 119, Pegler Papers.

(12) Jack Alexander, "He's Against," *The Saturday Evening Post*, v. 213, (September 14, 1940), p. 10.

(13) Westbrook Pegler, "Fair Enough," August 15, 1939, Box 119, Pegler Papers.

(14) *New York Times*, November 21, 1964, p. 29.

(15) Roy W. Howard to G.B. Parker, April 12, 1940, Executive Correspondence, City File Washington, D.C., George B. Parker Folder, Box 169; Roy W. Howard to O.B. Parker, October 26, 1941, Executive Correspondence, City File Washington, D.C., George B. Parker Folder, Box 180, Roy W. Howard Papers, Library of Congress, Washington, D.C.

(16) William J. Puette, *Through Jaundiced Eyes: How the Media View Organized Labor* (Ithaca, New York, 1992), p. 59.

(17) Westbrook Pegler, "Fair Enough," January 19, 1940, Box 120 Pegler Papers.

(18) *New York Times*, January 28, 1940, p. 29; "A Frank Statement from George Scalisse," The Building Service Employee, v. 1, no. 4 (May 1940), pp. 6–7.

(19) *New York Times*, January 28, 1940, p. 29; "A Frank Statement from George Scalise."

(20) Minutes of the Meeting of the Executive Council, American Federation of Labor, Hotel Everglades, Miami, Florida, January 29–February 9, 1940, pp. 67–73, George Meany Memorial Archives, AFL-CIO, Silver Spring, Maryland.

(21) Joseph A. Padway to George Scalise, January 21, 1940, enclosed with Beth Pitt to Westbrook Pegler, June 18, 1944, Box 82, Folder: Building Service Employees International Union, 1944, Box 82, Pegler Papers.

(22) *New York Times*, February 10, 1940, p. 16.

(23) Criminal Record, Police Department, City of New York, George Scalise, May 24, 1940, Box 2566, Papers of the New York County District Attorney's Office, New York City Municipal Archives, New York, New York, (hereafter NYDA Papers).

(24) Westbrook Pegler, "Fair Enough," February 1, 1940, Box 120, Pegler Papers.

(25) Westbrook Pegler, "Fair Enough," February 6, 1940, Box 120, Pegler Papers.

(26) Record on Appeal, People of the State of New York Against George Scalise, (1940) Appellant Division, First Department, v. 7991, pp. 232–33.

(27) "Racketeer Scalise," *Time*, v. 35, (May 6, 1940), pp. 20–21; *Chicago Tribune*, April 27, 1940, Dewey Scrapbook, v. 3–4, roll 2.

(28) "Columnist Pegler Puts the Finger of the Law on a New York Union Leader," *Life*, v. 8, (May 6, 1940), p. 35.

(29) Memorandum to Chief Investigator, from Thomas M. Fay, Jr., May 3, 1940, Box 2566, Papers of the New York County District Attorney's Office, New York City Municipal Archives, New York, New York, (hereafter NYDA Papers); "A Frank Statement from George Scalise."

(30) Record on Appeal, People of the State of New York Against George Scalise, (1940) Appellant Division, First Department, v. 7991, p. 310

(31) George Scalise to Jerry Horan, July 29, 1935; George Scalise to Charles Hardy, August 19, 1938; Paul B. David to George Scalise, August 22, 1938; George Scalise to Charles Hardy, August 29, 1938, all in Box 2567, NYDA Papers.

(32) George Scalise to Paul David, December 27, 1938, Box 2567, NYDA Papers.

(33) Exceptions include: Andrew Wender Cohen, "The Struggle for Order: Law, Labor, and Resistance to the Corporate Ideal in Chicago, 1900–1940," (Dissertation, University of Chicago, 1999); John B. Jentz, "Unions, Cartels, and the Political Economy of the American Cities: the Chicago Flat Janitors' Union in the Progressive Era and 1920s," *Studies in American Political Development*, v. 14 (Spring 2000), pp. 51–71; Colin Gordon, "The Lost City of Solidarity: Metropolitan Unionism in Historical Perspective," *Politics and Society*, v. 27 (1999), pp. 564–68, 573; Barbara Wayne Newell, *Chicago and the Labor Movement: Metropolitan Unionism in the 1930s* (Urbana, Illinois, 1961), pp. 209–25.

(34) People v. Scalise, p. 1005; *New York Times*, October 8, 1940, p. 1; September 26, 1959, p. 1; September 27, 1959, p. 1; October 7, 1959, p. 37; Peter Maas, The Valachi Papers, (New York, 1986; reprint, New York, 1968), pp. 124 & 203.

(35) People v. Scalise, p. 1005, 1030.

(36) *New York Times*, October 8, 1940, p.1; Memo to Mr. Dreiband from A. Robertson, June 14, 1940, Box 2566, NYDA Papers; Alan Block, *East Side-West Side: Organizing Crime in New York*, 1930–1950 (New Brunswick, New Jersey, 1983), pp. 225–6; James J. Bambrick, *The Building Service Story* (New York, 1948), pp. 20–21.

(37) John F. O'Connell to Mr. Dreiband, June 14, 1940, Box 2566, NYDA Papers.

(38) Memo to Alex Dreiband from J. Barst, June 18, 1940, Box 2566, NYDA Papers.

(39) Memo to Alex Dreiband from J. Barst, June 19, 1940, Box 2566, NYDA Papers.

(40) Peter Reuter, Jonathan Rubinstein, and Simon Wynn, *Racketeering in Legitimate Industries: Two Case Studies* (Washington, D.C., 1983), pp. 12–14; Peter Reuter, *Disorganized Crime: The Economics of the Visible Hand* (Cambridge, Massachusetts, 1983), pp. 150–73; Howard Abadinsky, *Organized Crime* (Chicago, 1994), pp. 294–99; New York State Organized Crime Task Force, *Corruption and Racketeering in the New York City Construction Industry* (New York, 1990), pp. 75–79.

(41) Statement of Louis Marcus to Alfred J. Scotti, June 6, 1940, Box 2566, NYDA Papers.

(42) Thomas Hughes to J.L. Devring, November 10, 1919, and J.L. Devring to Thomas L. Hughes, November 14, 1919, both in Box 24, Series I, International Brotherhood of Teamsters, Chauffeurs, and Warehousemen Papers, State Historical Society of Wisconsin, Madison, Wisconsin, (hereafter IBT Papers); Fred D. Pasley, *Muscling In* (New York, 1931), pp. 19–23; writing about such organizations, Pegler notes that they were "known as an ice-pick or razor blade union because it was noticed that the tires of cars which were parked in non-union garages came down of ice pick punctures in their tires and of razor slashes in their upholstery." Westbrook Pegler, "Fair Enough," April 29, 1940, Box 120, Pegler Papers.

(43) In 1940, Dewey's staff gathered together police and prosecutor's reports made in 1932–33 on Local 272 and its activities. These reports are gathered together and annotated, in the following investigative memorandum: Memo to Mr. Gurfein from Mr. Mertens, April 30, 1940, Box 2566, NYDA Papers.

(44) Ibid.

(45) Signed, "8,000 Members" to President Green, A.F. of L., July 22, 1935, Reel 37, American Federation of Labor Records: The William Green Era, Microfilm Edition, Reel 37.

(46) Robert Zieger, *American Workers, American Unions* (Baltimore, 1994, 2nd edition), pp. 27–291; Melvyn Dubofsky, "Not so 'Turbulent Years': A New Look at the 1930s," Charles Stephenson, ed. *Life and Labor: Dimensions of American Working Class History* (Albany, New York, 1986), pp. 205–223; David Brody, *Workers in Industrial America: Essays on the Twentieth Century Struggle* (New York, 1980), pp. 102–103.

(47) Colin Gordon, *New Deals: Business, Labor and Politics in America, 1920–1935* (New York, 1994), pp. 87–127; Barbara Wayne Newell, *Chicago and the Labor Movement: Metropolitan Unionism in the 1930s* (Urbana, Illinois, 1961), pp. 209–25; Donald Garnel, *The Rise of Teamster Power in the West* (Los Angeles, 1972), pp. 68–73; Irving Bernstein, *Turbulent Years: A History of the American Worker, 1933–1941* (Boston, 1970), pp. 84–89.

(48) Statement of Louis Marcus to Alfred J. Scotti.

(49) People v. Scalise, p. 448.

(50) People v. Scalise, pp. 992–1001; Statement by Sol Berkowitz, September 20, 1935, Box 2569, NYDA Papers.

(51) People v. Scalise, p. 996.

(52) John B. Jentz, "Unions, Cartels, and the Political Economy of American Cities: The Chicago Flat Janitors' Union in the Progressive Era and the 1920s," *Studies in American Political Development*, v. 14 (Spring 2000), pp.51–71. See also, John B. Jentz, "Citizenship, Self-Respect, and Political Power: Chicago's Flat Janitors Trailblaze the Service Employees International Union, 1912–1921," *Labor's Heritage*, v. 9, no. 1 (Summer 1997), pp. 4–23.

(53) Douglas Bukowski, *Big Bill Thompson, Chicago, and the Politics of Image* (Chicago, 1998), pp. 186–87, 222–23; Roger Biles, *Big City Boss in Depression and War: Mayor Edward J. Kelly of Chicago* (DeKalb, Illinois, 1984), p. 103.

(54) Roger Touhy with Ray Brennan, *The Stolen Years* (Cleveland, 1959), pp. 83–86,

(55) Daniel Tobin to Michael Casey, February 20, 1930; Daniel Tobin to Michael Casey, February 21, 1930; Daniel Tobin to Michael Casey, February 28, 1930, all in Box 16, Series I, Teamster Papers.

(56) Minutes of General Executive Board Meeting, January 15, 1930, in Twelfth Convention, International Brotherhood of Teamsters, Chauffeurs, Stablemen and Helpers of America, Held in the City of Cincinnati, Ohio, Commencing September 8, 1930, Reports of Officers, p. 149.

(57) Daniel Tobin to Michael Casey, March 29, 1932, Box 16, Series I, Teamster Papers.

(58) *Chicago Tribune*, March 23, 1943, p. 2.

(59) *Chicago Tribune*, March 24, 1943, p. 2.

(60) Among the Teamsters this list would include: Ely H. Orr, Secretary-Treasurer of Local 706, Chicago Newspaper Drivers, shot to death by men firing from a passing automobile, July 25, 1931; Timothy Lynch, head of a suburban Chicago Teamsters local, murdered by men waiting in the bushes outside his house, on November 9, 1931; Patrick Berrell, a Vice President of the International Brotherhood of Teamsters, the union's top representative in Chicago, gunned down, July 21, 1932 in the parking lot of a Wisconsin roadhouse; Michael J. Calvin, leader of an independent Teamster union in Chicago, killed by shots fired from a passing automobile, November 23, 1936; *Chicago Tribune*, July 26, 1931, p. 1; November 10, 1931, p. 1; July 22, 1932, p. 1; November 24, 1936.

The list in other unions would include: William Rooney, a leader in the Sheetmetal Workers union and also in the Chicago Flat Janitors, killed March 19, 1931; Louis Alterie, leader of the Chicago Office, Theater, and Amusement Janitors' Union, shot to death as he left his home in the morning, July 18, 1935; Thomas Maloy, killed by shots fired from a passing automobile, February 4, 1935; Dennis Zeigler, leader of a local of Operating Engineers, shot while walking to his home, February 24, 1933; *Chicago Tribune*, March 20, 1931, p. 5; February 5, 1935, p. 1, July 19, 1935, p. 1; March 26, 1943.

(61) *Chicago Tribune*, March 20, 1931, p. 5; March 21, 1931, p. 2; *Chicago American*, March 8, 1950, p.1; March 11, 1950, p. 1.

(62) Testimony of Roger Touhy, Transcript of Proceedings, pp. 271–2, in United States of America, ex rel, Roger Touhy vs. Joseph E. Ragen, U.S. District Court, Northern District of Illinois, 48 C 448, Box No. 1500, National Archives, Chicago, Illinois.

(63) Memorandum for Mr. Clegg, March 22, 1934; M.H. Purvis to Director, Division of Investigation, March 23, 1934, Section 1, FBI Files, 7-HQ-759, Box 92, RG 65, National Archives, College Park, Maryland.

(64) News reports of Scalise's sentencing hearing refer to a probation report that reviewed the history of how Jerry Horan was forced by the Chicago "Syndicate" to take orders from them sometime in 1931 or 1932, and in this way the group acquired control over the BSEIU. This report was not included in the official trial transcript. *New York Times*, October 8, 1940, p. 1.

(65) Trial Transcript, U.S. v. Louis Campagna, *et al.*, U.S. Court of Appeals for the Second Circuit, Case No. 19456, p. 141, Box 5808, Record Group 276, National Archives, New York, New York.

(66) Hutchison, *Imperfect Union*, p. 372.

(67) People v. Scalise, pp. 994–1005.

(68) People v. Scalise, pp. 1010–12.

(69) People v. Scalise, pp. 1013–1022; *Chicago Tribune*, April 28, 1940, clipping in Dewey Scrapbook, v. 3–4, Roll 2, Dewey Papers; "Nelson Named in Inquiry on Scalise Union," *Chicago Tribune*, n.d., Folder: BSEIU 1935–1940, Box 82, Pegler Papers.

(70) U.S. v. Campagna, p. 141.

(71) People v. Scalise, pp. 177–80, 1027–9, 1031–4, 1162–4, 2373–8, 2590–1; *New York Journal-American*, September 27, 1945, clipping in Folder: BSEIU 1945–47, Box 82, Pegler Papers; *Chicago American*, May 5, 1940; *Chicago Tribune*, May 4, 1940, both in Dewey Scrapbook, v. 3–4, Roll 2, Dewey Papers.

(72) People v. Scalise, pp. 232–3, 1308, 1352–3; Bambrick, Building Service Story, pp. 2–4, 7–19, 22–28, 37–40, Edward B. Bell to Westbrook Pegler, March 6, 1942, Folder: BSEIU, 1941–43, Box 82, Pegler Papers.

(73) *New York Times*, October 8, 1940, p.1; Memorandum, A. Robertson to Mr. Gurfein, May 22, 1940, Box 2566, NYDA Papers; Bambrick, Building Service Story, p. 13.

(74) Bambrick, Building Service Story, pp. 29 & 42; *New York Times*, April 14, 1944, p. 21; August 23, 1944, p. 20; August 29, 1944, p. 19; *Chicago Tribune*, April 27, 1940, Dewey Scrapbook, v.3–4, Roll 2; *New York Journal American*, September 27, 1945, news clipping, Folder: BSEIU, 1945–47,

Box 82, Pegler Papers; Memo on Local 32B and David Sullivan, undated, unsigned, Folder BSEIU, undated, Box 82, Pegler Papers.

(75)   Memorandum entitled, "Bowling and Billiard Academy Employees Union Local 94, B.S.E.I.U.," no date, no author, Box 2566, NYDA Papers.

(76)   An example of the way of some employers in New York's hotel industry turned to Scalise to avoid the possibility of a more militant form of labor union is described in Edward B. Bell to Westbrook Pegler, March 6, 1942, Folder Building Service Employees International Union, 1941–43, Box 82, Pegler Papers.

(77)   *New York Times*, April 22, 1940, p. 1.

(78)   *Chicago Tribune*, April 22, 1940; *Chicago American*, April 22, 1940, both in Dewey Scrapbook, v. 3–4, Roll 2.

(79)   *New York Times*, April 22, 1940, p. 1.

(80)   *New York Times*, May 30, 1940, p. 19; October 8, 1940, p. 1.

(81)   *New York Times*, February 19, 1941, p. 22; February 22, 1941, p. 32; February 26, 1941, p. 23.

(82)   *New York Times*, April 27, 1940, p. 1; Anonymous to Mr. Dewey, March 17, 1940; One of the National Help to District Attorney, March 5, 1940, both in Box 2566, NYDA Papers.

(83)   Marie H. to Westbrook Pegler, January 29, 1942, Folder: BSEIU 1935–1940, Box 82, Pegler Papers.

Source: *Journal of Social History*, © 2003

Thinking Activities

1. Do you believe that persons should be selected for public positions based solely on their merits (e.g., grades in school, test scores, experience, etc.) or are their other factors that should be considered? Have you ever lost a job to someone else even though you felt you were better qualified or more deserving? How did you handle this situation? In contrast, if you had a politically connected relative or senior public official in your family, would you use your link to this person to help you secure a public position? Why or why not?

2. Rent any of the following films from your local DVD store: *All the King's Men, Mr. Smith Goes to Washington, The Last Hurrah, The Untouchables,* or *Hoffa.* What *specific* aspects of corruption are present in the film, and what approaches do law enforcement or the government use to combat them?

3. The Nash Equilibrium example involving Lori and Lisa included earlier in this chapter presents a model for examining when corruption may occur between two parties. What other scenarios or situations could you apply this model to? How could your insights into this area prove useful in conducting white-collar crime investigations?

4. Based upon your understanding of the anti-patronage, progressive, and scientific administration models of corruption control presented in this chapter, which of these approaches, if any, do you believe proved most effective in combating corruption within the United States? Explain your thinking.

5 The "Modern Era" of Public Corruption Control

The 1970s Through Today

> I want to say this to the television audience. I made my mistakes, but in all of my years of public life, I have never profited, never profited from public service. I have earned every cent. And in all of my years of public life, I have never obstructed justice. And I think, too, that I can say that in my years of public life, that I welcome this kind of examination because people have got to know whether or not their President's a crook. Well, I'm not a crook. I've earned everything I've got.
>
> (Former President Richard M. Nixon, November 17, 1973)

On the surface, the 37th President of the United States, Richard Milhous Nixon, seemed to have it all. A former naval officer, congressman, and Vice President under Dwight D. Eisenhower, he had accomplished much during his presidency, including expanding relations with the People's Republic of China, negotiating an end of U.S. involvement in Vietnam, and strengthening environmental regulations and worker safety laws. He enjoyed a 51 percent approval rating through June 1973, and was generally regarded by the American people as hard-working and honest. Indeed, his reputation as a thrifty man, dating back to his famous "Checkers" speech of 1952 (in which he refuted claims that he had received $18,000 from his political supporters), was further strengthened by his tenacity in detecting what he believed to be excesses in government funding for public programs. How then did President Nixon transform from a well-regarded champion of eschewing excesses in federal funding to the man often regarded as the most corrupt president in American history? This chapter will strive to answer this question. Perhaps more importantly, we will explore the role that the Nixon Administration's misdeeds played in shaping corruption control policies, many of which are still in effect today.

Nixon: From Corruption Controller to Investigative Target

From his earliest days in office, President Richard Nixon sought to dismantle Lyndon B. Johnson's Great Society vision, particularly the War on Poverty programs, which had flourished since their inception in 1964. There were three primary reasons for Nixon's aversion to the Johnson Era programs. First, Nixon's election victory over Democratic candidate Hubert Humphrey was in large part assured by conservative voters—especially those who feared a breakdown in American society subsequent to the Detroit riots of 1967. Second, he wished to create the appearance that he was fiscally austere by cutting approximately $4 billion from the 1969 budget; in reality, however, Nixon actually increased spending and the federal deficit each year during his tenure in office. Third, and most important for the purposes of this chapter, Nixon believed that Great Society programs such as Medicaid, enacted in 1965 to provide health care to America's neediest members, and Medicare, a 1965 amendment to the Social Security Act designed to provide health services to this nation's elderly, were rife with fiscal mismanagement, waste, and fraud.

There were certainly a myriad of healthcare fraud and abuse cases to validate Nixon's assertions. For example, in 1973, Pulitzer Prize-winning reporter William Sherman authored a 12-part series on what he referred to as "Medicaid mills" operating in the New York City area.[1] The online publication *Free Market Medicine* (2000) provides dentist Dr. Marvin J. Schissel's account of the "Medicaid mills" environment operating within his profession. He writes:

> Although hasty, shoddy work that brings in more money under the unit-fee system is the most common abuse of the Medicaid program, there are certain other abuses that may seem even more distasteful: unnecessary procedures, claiming previous work as one's own, asking payment for work that was not done, prescribing high-profit work in place of more-needed, low profit work, and completely falsifying claim forms.[2]

Similarly, practices such as rendering fraudulent diagnoses, unbundling—breaking out a series of services provided to a patient thus yielding a higher per-item fee, upcoding (i.e., using billing codes that provide higher payment rates than the codes for service s actually furnished to patients), and billing for services not rendered (i.e., submitting false claims) were also pervasive in the Medicare system.[3]

Yet troubles related to the social programs emanating from the War on Poverty were only some of the fraud and corruption issues that the Nixon Administration sought to correct. Abuses in employee labor—particularly in high-risk industries such as chemical manufacturing, electroplating, ship-building, and construction—led to enactment of the Occupational Safety and Health Act of 1970 and its regulatory arm, the Occupational Safety and Health Administration (OSHA). Improper disposal and discharges of industrial waste resulted in passage of the National Environmental Policy Act (1970), Clean Air Act (1970), and Clean Water Act.

The Nixon Administration also engaged in some high profile anti-trust actions, including *Ford Motor Company v. U.S.* (405 U.S. 596) in 1972 and *U.S. v. Falstaff Brewing Company*, which, at the time, was the fourth largest brewery in America (410 U.S. 526). He also endorsed restrictions for television and radio advertisements promoting cigarette use (1969) and supported requirements for cigarette health warnings in print media (1972).

Ironically, the ultimate cause of Nixon's failure as president was probably his obsession with control. While he successfully enacted a host of laws and regulations aimed at monitoring the health, safety, and fiscal performance of corporations and the Executive Branch agencies under his authority, his Administration ". . . sought, with little subtlety, to circumvent legislative constraint."[4]

For example, Nixon was unhappy with the non-partisan, civil service orientation of the Bureau of the Budget—an agency that had been specifically designed to serve as a resource available to the Chief Executive. In 1970, he restructured this organization into the Office of Management and Budget (OMB). In doing so, Nixon dramatically altered the orientation of the Bureau of the Budget from the non-partisan support organization envisioned by former Director Charles Gates Dawes into a tool used by the president to monitor agencies and senior cabinet officials in the Executive Branch.[5] By keeping the executive agencies under constant observation, controlling their access to funding, and having the ability to conduct functional investigations via the OMB, Nixon's management of the executive office was not unlike the relationship between jailer and prisoner, and is referred to as an all encompassing perspective.

The All Encompassing Vision of Corruption Control

The *panopticon* prison was conceptualized by English Philosopher Jeremy Bentham around 1791 to ensure correctional staff maintained a 360-degree view of the inmates at all times.[6] Those incarcerated, however, could not see the observers and were subject to monitoring at all times. Similarly, the all encompassing vision of corruption control argues that left unchecked, public officials will engage in corrupt practices such as fraud, bribery, extortion, and other abuses of power.[7] You will recall that the Scientific Administration model of corruption control, employed by presidents from Franklin

D. Roosevelt to Lyndon B. Johnson, used structural design and engineering as its overarching method for eliminating the concentration of power in any one location. In contrast, the all encompassing vision, which has existed since early into the Nixon Administration, does not concern itself with the design of corruption control systems, but rather relies on "a comprehensive system of administrative/criminal laws . . . enforced by law enforcement agencies using a full array of investigative tools, including covert operations."[8]

It is also noteworthy that at approximately the same time the Nixon Administration was strengthening worker protections through the newly-established Occupational Safety and Health Administration, reducing corporate pollution through the Clean Air Act and Clean Water Act, and engaging in major anti-trust actions against the Ford Motor Company, Falstaff Brewing, and the tobacco companies, the Office of the Chief Executive was also apparently engaging in illegal activities internationally and domestically. During the period 1969 through 1970, Nixon stated emphatically that the United States was respecting the neutrality of Cambodia with regard to its position on the Vietnam conflict. In reality, Nixon had ordered covert bombings of Cambodian areas in which he claimed "so-called enemy sanctuaries" existed.[9] American troops also assisted South Vietnamese forces in the invasion of Laos in 1971 and secretly participated in the Chilean insurrection.

Domestically, Nixon masked his desire for a centralized, tightly controlled Executive Branch through a program that he dubbed the "Quality of Life Review" (QLR). Using his newly reorganized Office of Management and Budget—a hybrid of the former Bureau of the Budget, Nixon was initially successful in preventing agency heads from leaking information on the Administration's plans under threat of a QLR review. He had hoped to make extensive and powerful consolidations of federal law enforcement, investigative, and intelligence functions by restructuring and expanding the Bureau of Narcotics and Dangerous Drugs and the Office of National Narcotics Intelligence. He was also interested in limiting the investigative authority of the Federal Bureau of Investigation in matters pertaining to the Office of the Chief Executive.

In addition to orchestrating secret military actions in Cambodia, Laos, and Chile, Nixon attempted to subvert the American political system through illegal intelligence gathering activities at DNC Headquarters. He also sought to centralize the Executive Branch's police powers, and prevent full disclosure of the White House's plans by intimidating upper-level Executive Branch members to remain silent or face "Quality of Life Review" of their respective agencies. Ironically, the June 17, 1972 Democratic National Committee (DNC) Headquarters break-in perpetrated by members of Nixon's Committee to Reelect the President (CREEP) actually resulted in a broadening of the FBI's powers to investigate misconduct on the part of

Exhibit 5.1   Richard Nixon, the 37th President of the United States, delivers the "V" sign upon his final departure from the White House on August 9, 1974. Nixon resigned in the wake of possible impeachment during the Watergate Scandal.

senior elected officials (including the president), and led to enacting the Independent Counsel Act in 1978.[10]

Following his resignation of the Presidency on August 9, 1974, Nixon was disbarred from the New York State Bar in 1976 and subsequently resigned from the State Bar of California.

Some scholars have argued that President Gerald R. Ford's granting of a full pardon to former President Nixon in August of 1974, less than one month after Ford assumed office, was a form of Nash equilibrium (corruption between the President and Former Vice-President); however, there is little evidence to support this. Indeed, Ford also pardoned World War II radio propagandist "Tokyo Rose" in 1977 but few would suggest that he was secretly supporting the resurrection of the Empire of Japan. Nevertheless,

Ford's pardon of Nixon was likely a major factor in his 1976 election loss to Jimmy Carter.

Jimmy Carter: The First All Encompassing President

Without question, no president in U.S. history has done more to foster and expand the all encompassing vision of corruption control than James Earl Carter, Jr. A former naval officer and agricultural businessman, Carter served as the Governor of Georgia from 1971–75. During his tenure as Governor, Carter implemented a financial management system referred to as "Zero-based budgeting," designed to require state program managers to justify all monies that would be expended on public projects. Interestingly, a similar financial system was implemented during his term as president, but it met with such resistance from both Executive Branch managers and Congress that it was ultimately abandoned.[11] He also enacted Georgia's first "sunshine" law, which allowed the public to participate in a variety of government meetings, particularly when policy issues were to be discussed.

Carter's most pronounced reforms in public administration occurred in 1978, while he served as the 39th President of the United States. He advocated passage of the 1978 Civil Service Reform Act, which served a dual role by

> enhanc[ing] the responsiveness of the higher civil service by allowing individuals to be transferred to other jobs . . . to broaden their perspectives or to make better use of their talents . . . [and] to provide incentives for recalcitrant or difficult individuals to leave the civil service.[12]

The Civil Service Reform Act (CSRA) of 1978 also established a new tier of federal employees, referred to as the "Senior Executive Service," designed to hold top Executive Branch agency managers and administrators "accountable for individual and organizational performance."[13] Lastly, comparable to civil service reforms enacted during the Franklin D. Roosevelt Administration, the CSRA of 1978 reinforced federal employee rights to collective bargaining and union representation, while specifically denying them the right to strike.

The Inspector General Program

Carter's belief in the all encompassing vision of corruption control (i.e., left unchecked, government officials would engage in corrupt and illegal activities) led to the passage of the Inspector General Act of 1978.[14] Inspector Generals (IGs) are non-partisan, independent managers who examine

Exhibit 5.2   The Office of the Inspector General is responsible for investigating possible waste, fraud, and abuse in Federal programs. This important executive branch agency enforces a variety of criminal statutes and regulations.

programs in which federal monies have been expended. Specifically, IGs are concerned with issues of waste, fraud, and abuse. Cabinet-level IGs are nominated by the president with the advice and consent of the U.S. Senate. Inspector Generals can also be appointed to serve at individual agencies within the Executive Branch. The head of the respective agency can make such appointments. Cabinet-level IGs can only be removed by the President of the United States. An agency head can remove Inspector Generals serving at the individual agency level. Specific elements of the Inspector Generals' mission are as follows:[15]

- Conduct independent and objective audits, investigations, and inspections.
- Prevent and detect waste, fraud, and abuse.
- Promote economy, effectiveness, and efficiency.
- Review pending legislation and regulation.
- Keep the agency head and Congress fully and currently informed.

IG findings can be used in criminal prosecutions of corrupt officials, to assist agency heads or cabinet-level officials in determining if disciplinary action is warranted against employees, and to aid Congress in determining future funding requirements for Executive Branch programs based on their effectiveness and efficiency. In order to enhance the likelihood that incidents of waste, fraud, and abuse will be reported to IG Offices, both the 1978 Civil Service Reform Act and the Inspector General Act include whistleblower protection provisions for those employees who report illicit activities. Whistleblower protections for federal workers and government contractors were enhanced in 1989 and 1994, when the definition of reportable activities was broadened, and remedies for reprisal against whistleblowers were increased.

The Office of the Special Counsel (OSC), also an "independent federal investigative and prosecutorial agency,"[16] further protects workers from reprisal if they have reported acts of waste, fraud, and abuse or raised alleged violations of the Hatch Act. One of the most important facets of the Inspector General Act is that its authority applies not only to federal agencies, but also to a myriad of programs funded with federal monies. Accordingly, state and municipal projects funded through government grants have seen the influence of Carter's policies vis-à-vis audits and investigations conducted by the federal Inspectors General, largely in the areas of housing, health and human services, education, and environmental protection.

Taking their cue from the federal government, state and local governments followed, and began forming their own internal investigative units in the late 1970s. Corruption control further developed through the use of forensic accounting and fraud detection techniques, as well as covert and overt surveillance. Another method of corruption control involves comprehensive undercover operations, such as the New York City Department of Investigation (DOI)'s integrity test program, in which "DOI agents posing as contractors offered bribes to city inspectors to overlook violations or to expedite code approvals.[17] By the mid-1980s, these types of activities were commonplace in cities such as New York and Philadelphia. Similar functions were added in other major metropolitan areas (e.g., Los Angeles, Chicago) in the 1990s.

In addition to external IGs, many agencies also incorporated inspection offices into their respective organizations. Unlike the independent inspectors general, the inspection offices serve as a first line of defense for official review of incidents or procedures. An historical example is the United States Secret Service. Prior to the passage of the Homeland Security Act of 2002, this agency was subject to investigation by any of the Treasury Department's six major offices in Houston, Chicago, San Francisco, Miami, Philadelphia, and Los Angeles, as well as inspections emanating from OIG headquarters in Washington, D.C. Moreover, at least once every three years, each field office of the U.S. Secret Service was subject to a comprehensive inspection, covering topics such as program operations, adherence to established policy, employee satisfaction, and customer feedback. Inspectors focused on evidence management, compliance with equipment use policies, and allocation of office resources. By effectively utilizing its own internal inspection program, the Secret Service detected possible deficiencies in its standard operating procedures or policies, thus pre-empting possible large-scale findings that could result from an OIG investigation or audit. However, the status of this inspection program is unknown since the integration of the U.S. Secret Service into the Department of Homeland Security in early 2003.

When compared with the prior Nixon Administration and later Reagan years, the Carter Administration remained remarkably unsoiled by corruption encompassing the majority of the period 1970–90. From 1978–79, FBI undercover agents participated in Operation ABSCAM—an acronym for the fictitious *Abdul Enterprises, Ltd.* Agents and FBI informants posed as sheiks from the fabricated business entity, and offered members of Congress bribes in exchange for political favors. All of the transactions were recorded on videotape. The result of this investigation was the indictment and conviction of eight persons, including a U.S. Senator and four U.S. Congressmen on charges of conspiracy and bribery.[18]

Carter's most noteworthy brush with scandal broke during the presidential campaign in 1980. The incident involved his brother, Billy, who received $220,000 in interest-free "loans" from the Libyan government, in exchange for "waging a controversial goodwill campaign . . . on their behalf."[19] The actual level of foreknowledge on the part of the Carter Administration remains unclear to this day. However, it appears that senior-level officials—including former President Carter—were aware of ties between Billy Carter and Libyan diplomat Gibril Shollouf as early as the summer of 1978. Moreover, in January of 1979, President Carter's mother, Lillian, and Billy hosted a "lavish reception at the Atlanta Hilton" for more than 24 Libyan dignitaries.[20] While Republican leaders in Congress were quick to attach the name "Billygate" to the event, and called for a committee to investigate the matter, congressional action did not follow. Instead, the Grand Old Party endeavored to make it a significant campaign issue in the 1980 presidential election, and it likely contributed to Carter's defeat in his bid for reelection.

It is worth noting that Republican members of Congress said little about the relationship between the petroleum companies and Billy Carter—a subject that will be further discussed later in this book. Similarly, the deafening silence on the part of Republicans during the 2000 election race with respect to Neil Bush, George W. Bush's younger brother who, during the Reagan-Bush era, was inextricably linked to the Silverado Savings and Loan scandal which cost U.S. taxpayers more than $1 billion, suggests a partisan double standard exists when examining the role of siblings engaged in corrupt practices.

While President Carter strived to make lasting and significant contributions to the all encompassing vision of corruption control in the United States, many of the policies and programs he enacted were subsequently reversed or altered during the Reagan and George H.W. Bush Administrations (1981–93).

The Reagan–Bush I Years: The Doldrums of Corruption Control

In the slightly more than 100 years that America has wrestled with various corruption control strategies (i.e., anti-patronage, progressive, scientific administration, all encompassing vision), no period lacked efforts to curtail such acts as the twelve years that Ronald Reagan and George Herbert Walker Bush served as Chief Executives of the United States. Whereas Calvin Coolidge had at least shown the foresight to appoint Charles Gates Dawes as Vice President, the Reagan and Bush Administrations were rife with scandals, and correspondingly deficient in their efforts to combat them. Summarizing the research of Shelley Ross (1988) in their text *White-collar Deviance* (1999), authors David R. Simon and Frank E. Hagan conclude the following about the Reagan years: "Between 1980–88 over 200 Reaganites came under either ethical or criminal investigation, the greatest number of scandals in any Administration in American history."[21] Rosoff, Pontell, and Tillman (2006) keenly observe that "one of President Carter's *last* official acts was the issuance of an executive order toughening the notification requirements for companies wishing to export products whose use is restricted in the United States. One of President Reagan's *first* official acts was the immediate revocation of the month-old Carter order."[22] From Iran-Contra to Wedtech, to the collapse of the Bank of Credit and Commerce International (BCCI), and the Savings and Loan scandals, neither Ronald Reagan nor George H.W. Bush effectively developed any significant corruption control policies.

To its credit, Congress *did* enact legislation designed to protect communities from manufacturer's releasing of toxic chemicals (e.g., Superfund Amendments & Reauthorization Act of 1986) and prevent government entities from improperly disposing of hazardous wastes (e.g., Resource Conservation & Recovery Act, Federal Facilities Compliance Act of 1992), although neither president actively supported these pieces of legislation. Perhaps the most important law passed during the Reagan Era was the *1986 False Claims Act Amendments*. Originally enacted during the Civil War to prevent fraudsters from misrepresenting sawdust as gunpowder, the Act provides generous financial incentives for those reporting incidents of misrepresentation to the government[23] More recently, in an effort to reduce

Medicare and Medicaid costs due to billing fraud, both private citizens and the government are now authorized to sue individuals or organizations that they strongly believe are submitting false claims to the government. By applying the *Qui Tam provisions* of the False Claims Act, the person who reports the offense (i.e., the whistleblower) can receive as much as three times the amount of damages suffered by the government, as well as a civil penalty ranging from a minimum of $5,500 to a maximum of $11,000 for each claim.[24]

Like Nixon, Reagan used the Office of Management and Budget (OMB) as both carrot and stick to reward loyal administrators with substantial budgets, and punish those who disagreed with his policies by requiring that their agencies perform comprehensive cost-benefit analyses and functional program reviews to the satisfaction of the OMB.[25] He was also able to employ the Senior Executive Service provisions of the 1978 Civil Service Reform Act (CSRA) to fill posts at the sub-cabinet level with sycophants committed to the values of conservatism[26]—the classic example being former Secretary of the Interior James G. Watt. Later in 1981, Reagan used Carter's CSRA again to fire striking members of the Professional Air Traffic Controllers Organization (PATCO). According to Ronald Kramer's research into the 1986 Space Shuttle *Challenger* explosion, at least some of the responsibility for this tragic event may have been the result of Reagan's transformation of NASA from an agency grounded in "sober and rational assessment"[27] to a business venture in which the agency would strive to launch commercial satellites as a normal and routine practice. Federal spending grew dramatically during Reagan's tenure, particularly in the area of national defense. Strikingly similar to Nixon was the Reagan Administration's engagement in covert operations, predominantly in Latin America (Nicaragua, Honduras, and El Salvador), Grenada, Libya, Ethiopia, Chad, and Afghanistan as opposed to Southeast Asia. In many ways, the George H.W. Bush Administration was more ambivalent than the Reagan White House. George Herbert Walker Bush complained publicly about being chided for lacking what he referred to as "that vision thing." However, as will be discussed later in this book, he had the self-preservationist instinct to pardon several principal players involved in the Iran-Contra scandal.[28] President Bush showed tremendous leadership during the first Gulf War. However, his inner circle's desire to manage the nation without the involvement of Congress created a situation which, after the war concluded, immediately set his Administration at odds with both the House and the Senate.[29]

Lacking a clear domestic agenda, Bush was faced with responding to difficult questions regarding the overt and covert roles of the U.S. with respect to democratizing Latin America, linkages between the petroleum industry and the development of national energy policy, effective environmental strategies in light of catastrophic releases such as the *Exxon Valdez* oil spill, and the viability of continuing the "War on Drugs." These issues presented significant challenges, but were not the only topics requiring resolution. In fact, a soft but steady rumbling of questions began to emerge about Bush's three sons. John Ellis "Jeb" Bush (who would later become Governor of Florida) had defaulted on a $4.6 million loan from the Broward Savings and Loan, and both of his business partners had been involved in other savings and loan misuse schemes.[30] President Bush's other son Neil, Director of the disastrous Silverado Savings & Loan, made a series of bad loans in excess of $100 million to two of his business partners.[31] Ultimately, the Denver-based business failed, and the fallout cost U.S. taxpayers more than $1.3 billion. Lastly, in 1984, George W. Bush had managed to merge his failed Arbusto Limited with the Spectrum 7 Energy Corporation. Ultimately, the company was blended into Harken Energy Corporation in 1986, and George W. Bush was given 212,000 shares of stock and a directorship with the Dallas-based corporation. George W. Bush cashed out his stock at a 250 percent profit just weeks before severe corporate losses were announced.[32] Moreover, he submitted several late filings to the Securities and Exchange Commission (more than eight months had elapsed since the transactions occurred)— alleging that the originals must have been lost in the mail or by the SEC. Additional discussion on George W. Bush and his relationship with the energy companies follows later in this book.

The combination of a weak domestic agenda, poor record on protecting the environment, lack of fiscal acumen, and little long-term vision likely contributed to George Herbert Walker Bush's loss of the presidential election to William Jefferson Clinton in 1992. Along with Bush's departure from the White House, the stagnant pool of corruption control policy that had collected during the Reagan-Bush years again began to percolate.

Clinton, Reinventing Government, and the Future of Corruption Control

It is likely that some readers of this text equate corruption with President Clinton. After all, there was, in order of public sentiment, the Monica Lewinsky "scandal," Whitewater, Travelgate, Johnny Chung and the Democratic National Committee donations, the Lincoln Bedroom debacle, and the appointment of his wife, Hillary Rodham Clinton, as Health Care Czar. In reality, however, for all of the millions of dollars spent investigating these incidents, little actually came of them. Bill Clinton did indeed perjure himself, for which he was ultimately fined and disbarred in Arkansas. He did engage in "sexual relations" with Ms. Lewinsky, although he was not intimate with a German sympathizer during wartime, nor did he sire a child in the Senate cloakroom as former President Warren G. Harding allegedly had. Independent Counsel Robert Ray found insufficient evidence existed to support allegations that Mrs. Clinton had acted improperly by firing seven White House employees. Similarly, her participation in the Health Care Reform Working Group did not constitute nepotism on the part President Clinton, and it now appears that the impetus behind the Whitewater investigation was not the pursuit of the public interest, but rather may have been timed to give former President Bush a ratings boost as the 1992 presidential election approached.

Ironically, perhaps the most important—and least investigated—of the Clinton incidents involved "illegal campaign contributions . . . and the possible give-away of classified material to the Chinese Army (again, for campaign contributions)."[33] Given the prevalence of questionable campaign funds in major federal elections, neither party chose to examine this issue too extensively.

In many ways, Clinton's presidency was a hybrid, combining Johnson's social activism, Carter's program review techniques, and Truman's fiscal restraint. "Reinventing government," later referred to as the National Performance Review (NPR), was undertaken with the stated purpose of "cutting red tape, putting customers first, empowering employees to get results, and cutting back to basics."[34] Elements of the NPR are similar to the Progressive vision of corruption control: hire good people, give them the flexibility to perform their jobs effectively in the best interest of their customers, and reward them based on merit.[35] However, Clinton also imposed a all encompassing style of corruption control during his eight-year presidency, by strengthening protections for Inspectors General from administrative allegations (Executive Order 12993 of March 21, 1996), and allowing the Office of Special Counsel greater investigative authority (e.g., permitting the OSC to investigate whistleblower complaints filed by Federal Aviation Agency personnel and extending whistleblower authority to military personnel).[36]

Through the NPR, former President Clinton reduced scientific administration-era elements of corruption control by eliminating bureaucratic management systems that had been in place since the Presidency of Franklin D. Roosevelt. Lastly, the Clinton Administration aggressively employed anti-patronage techniques by encouraging IGs and other investigative agencies to utilize the False Claims Act in order to deter persons and organizations from engaging in future acts of Medicare and Medicaid fraud.

While some of Clinton's ideas may have resulted in streamlining government operations (e.g., eliminating red tape), such reforms may also have had adverse effects by eliminating crucial checks and balances in government purchasing prevalent in the scientific administration era. Similarly, NPR's objective of eliminating 272,900 federal jobs likely impacted the

Executive Branch's ability to monitor contractors and detect fraud in government programs. Fewer employees yield less people available to report incidents of waste, fraud, and abuse. In their final analysis of Clinton's National Performance Review, authors Joel Aberbach and Bert Rockman conclude

> A true reinvention of U.S. government along the lines of the NPR would necessitate curtailing powerful political influences at work within the federal government's administrative apparatus . . . [the consequences of which] . . . would include at least a partial eclipse of both congressional and presidential authority and enhancement of bureaucratic power.[37]

Is such a revision in the best interest of the United States? Eerily, with respect to law enforcement and investigation, it appears that America is moving somewhat closer to a centralized form of government based on the provisions of the *USA Patriot Act of 2001*[38] and other recently enacted legislation.

The G.W. Bush Administration's Strategy for Corruption Control

It is still too early to accurately calculate for posterity which corruption control strategy the George W. Bush White House will have ultimately utilized during its eight year tenure. However, while we might have originally speculated that he is supportive of the all encompassing vision of corruption control based on his steadfast support of strict penalties for corporate fraudsters, President Bush quietly repealed the majority of tough corporate penalties found in his Security and Exchange Commission reform during the summer of 2002. Further evidence that he is perhaps less all encompassing than his image would suggest is manifest in his repeated assertions that the now five-year old Department of Homeland Security should not include whistleblower protection provisions for its workers. Moreover, he cannot be regarded as overly progressive, in that since 2001 he has lobbied for—and succeeded in—reducing the number of career civil service positions in federal government, arguing instead for excepted service jobs which enumerate far fewer rights and protections than those found in the 1978 Civil Service Reform Act.

Incidents of alleged corruption have also proved to be a challenge for the Bush White House. Vice President Cheney's Chief of Staff, I. Lewis "Scooter" Libby, was convicted in 2006 for disclosing the identity of former Central Intelligence Agency Operative Valerie Plame Wilson and sentenced to 30 months in prison. His sentence was later commuted by President Bush. Another key official, Larry Franklin of the Department of

Defense, pled guilty in 2006 for disseminating classified information to a foreign government. Republican lobbyist Jack Abramoff, who was highly regarded by President Bush himself, is currently serving a six-year prison sentence for providing lavish gifts to members of Congress (including former Ohio Republican Congressman Bob Ney, also currently in prison). Another Bush Administration official, top-ranking procurement officer David Safavian, is currently serving an 18-month sentence for engaging unethical dealings with Abramoff.

President Bush experienced early successes in combating corruption, including signing into law HR 2356, the "Bipartisan Campaign Reform Act of 2002."[39] However, by the time of the 2006 national elections, 42 percent of voters polled by Gallup stated that government corruption and the lack of ethics among elected officials were of greater concern than the threat of further acts of terrorism reaching America's shores.

Chapter Summary

The primary focus of this chapter was on the all encompassing vision of corruption control embarked upon during the Presidency of Richard M. Nixon. The chapter also discussed the corruption control approach of the administrations from Jimmy Carter to Bill Clinton, which appeared to include elements of all encompassing, scientific administration, and progressive forms of corruption control. The specific approach that the George W. Bush Administration has opted to employ will only be defined with the passing of time.

The Food and Drug Administration's Office of Criminal Investigations

One of the predominant goals of corruption control within the United States is to prevent wayward government officials from allowing unsafe foods or drugs to enter the marketplace. In 1992, in an effort to protect the public from consuming tainted goods, purchasing outdated or repackaged pharmaceuticals, or accepting false claims regarding the efficacy of "cure all" pills and potions, former Food and Drug Administration (FDA) Commissioner David Kessler established the Office of Criminal Investigations (OCI) within this agency. In addition to investigating counterfeit pharmaceuticals and cosmetics, thwarting the distribution of off-spec or spoiled foodstuffs such as baby formula and seafood, and curtailing black market or "backdoor" drug sales,

FDA's OCI also serves as the lead agency for investigating major incidents of alleged product tampering. For example, in June 1993, the news media received hundreds of reports almost simultaneously across the United States from "concerned citizens" stating that they had found used syringes and other foreign objects in cans of Pepsi Cola and other soft drinks. OCI responded immediately, and determined that the reports were a hoax intended to discredit the major cola beverage manufacturers. Sixty people were subsequently arrested, and a situation that could have provoked a national panic and yielded economic ruin for Pepsi was averted. OCI also maintains an Office of Internal Affairs (OIA) responsible for probing alleged FDA employee misconduct and other sensitive matters. The unit's investigators, many of whom previously served as agents with the U.S. Secret Service, Federal Bureau of Investigation, Drug Enforcement Administration, and U.S. Customs Service, possess a variety of special skills such as computer forensics, polygraphy, and technical surveillance operations. In addition to its headquarters in Rockville, Maryland, the Office of Criminal Investigations maintains approximately twenty-one field offices, resident offices, and domiciles in locations ranging from Los Angeles, California and Atlanta, Georgia to Jersey City, New Jersey and San Juan, Puerto Rico.

ADAPTED READINGS

Reading 5–1: Dennis F. Thompson, *Mediated Corruption: The Case of the Keating Five*

What causes public officials to engage in acts of corruption? While this chapter has endeavored to address corruption control from a historical perspective, it is equally important to look at why senior government officials would engage in such behaviors. Are there specific conditions to lead to such activities? In the following article, you will have the opportunity to explore the concept of "mediated corruption," and the now infamous Keating Five who serve as a case study for misuse of office.

The case of the "Keating Five"—featuring five prominent U.S. Senators and Charles Keating, Jr., a savings-and-loan financier who contributed to their campaigns—has "come to symbolize public distrust of elected officials" and has reinforced the widespread view that many members of Congress and the institution itself are corrupt.(1) The nine months of investigation and seven weeks of hearings conducted by the Senate Ethics Committee that concluded in January 1992 revealed an underside of our system of representation to a depth and in a detail rarely seen before.

The broad shape of this underside is familiar enough: politicians take money from contributors to get elected, then do favors for them. But the deeper significance, theoretical and practical, is to be found in the details and in the relation of those details to principles of democratic representation. Although the case reveals a darker side of our politics, we can still try to recognize degrees of darkness. We should aim for a kind of moral chiaroscuro. More generally, the case can help us better understand a form of political corruption that is becoming increasingly common but has not received the attention it deserves from political scientists or political theorists.

This form of corruption involves the use of public office for private purposes in a manner that subverts the democratic process. It may be called mediated corruption because the corrupt acts are mediated by the political process. The public official's contribution to the corruption is filtered through various practices that are otherwise legitimate and may even be duties of office. As a result, both the official and citizens are less likely to recognize that the official has done anything wrong or that any serious harm has been done.

Mediated corruption is still a form of corruption. It includes the three main elements of the general concept of corruption: a public official gains, a private citizen receives a benefit, and the connection between the gain and the benefit is improper.(2) But mediated corruption differs from conventional corruption with respect to each of these three elements: (a) the gain that the politician receives is political, not personal and is not illegitimate in itself, as in conventional corruption; (b) how the public official provides the benefit is improper, not necessarily the benefit itself, or the fact that the particular citizen receives the benefit; (c) the connection between the gain and the benefit is improper because it damages the democratic process, not because the public official provides the benefit with a corrupt motive. In each of these elements, the concept of mediated corruption links the acts of individual officials to qualities of the democratic process. In this way, the concept provides a partial synthesis of conventional corruption (familiar in contemporary political science) and systematic corruption (found in traditional political theory).

To show the value of the concept of mediated corruption, I criticize two interpretations of the Keating Five case that assume a conventional concept of corruption. A concept of mediated corruption, I suggest, provides a better characterization of this case and, by implication, of the many similar cases that have occurred and are likely to occur. The characterization is intended to identify more coherently the aspects of actions and practices that we regard, or should regard, as wrong. The concept of mediated corruption helps bring our considered judgments about corruption in particular cases into "reflective equilibrium" with our moral and political principles.(3)

What the Keating Five Gave and What They Got

A brief summary of the events in this case will set the stage for examining the competing interpretations.(4) The senators who are forever joined together by the name the Keating Five had never worked together as a group before, and will (it is safe to assume) never work together again. Four are Democrats—Dennis DeConcini (Arizona), Alan Cranston (California), John Glenn (Ohio), and Donald Riegle (Michigan)—and one is a Republican, John McCain (Arizona).

They were brought together by Charles Keating, Jr., now in prison in California, convicted on charges of fraud and racketeering. As chairman of a home construction company in Phoenix, he bought Lincoln Savings and Loan in California in 1984 and began to shift its assets from home loans to high-risk projects, violating a wide variety of state and federal regulations in the process. In 1989, Lincoln collapsed, wiping out the savings of twenty-three thousand (mostly elderly) uninsured customers and costing taxpayers over two billion dollars. It was the biggest failure in what came to be the most costly financial scandal in American history. Lincoln came to symbolize the savings-and-loan crisis.

But to many in the financial community during the years before the collapse, Keating was a model of the financial entrepreneur that the Republican administration wished to encourage through its policy of deregulation. His most visible political lobbying was directed against the new rule prohibiting direct investment by savings-and-loans, which many legitimate financial institutions and many members of Congress also opposed. His most prominent and persistent target was Edwin Gray, the head of the three-member bank board that regulated the industry, himself a controversial figure.

The fateful meeting that would forever link the Keating Five took place on April 2, 1987, in the early evening in DeConcini's office. The senators asked Gray why the investigation of Lincoln and their "friend" Keating was taking so long. Gray said later that he was intimidated by this "show of force." Toward the end of the meeting, he suggested that the senators talk directly to the San Francisco examiners who were handling the Lincoln case. And so they did, a week later, in what was to become the most scrutinized meeting in the hearings. The senators told the examiners that they believed that the government was harassing a constituent. After the regulators reported that they were about to make a "criminal referral" against Lincoln, the senators seemed to back off.

After that meeting, McCain, Riegle, and Glenn had no further dealings of significance with Keating. Glenn arranged a lunch for Keating and House Speaker Jim Wright the following January, but the committee concluded that although this showed "poor judgment," Glenn's actions were not "improper" (U.S. Senate 1991b, 18). McCain had already broken off relations with Keating, who had called him a "wimp" for refusing to put pressure on the bank board. Cranston and DeConcini continued to act on Keating's behalf.

The Keating Five, particularly DeConcini and Cranston, certainly provided this constituent with good service. Since an act of corruption typically involves an exchange of some kind, we have to ask, What did the Senators get in return? The answer is $1.3 million, all within legal limits.(5) But this figure and this fact, handy for headline writers, obscure some important details (especially the timing and uses of the funds) that should affect our assessment of corruption.

In February 1991, the Ethics Committee rebuked four of the Senators—DeConcini and Riegle more severely, McCain and Glenn less so—and said that further action was warranted only against Cranston. Then in November, after much behind-the-scenes political negotiation, the committee reported to the full Senate that Cranston had "violated established norms of behavior in the Senate." To avoid a stronger resolution by the committee (which would have required a Senate vote), Cranston formally accepted the reprimand. In a dramatic speech on the floor, he also claimed that he had done nothing worse than had most of his colleagues in the Senate.

Competition or Corruption?

Cranston's own defense exemplifies, in a cynical form, one of the two standard interpretations of the conduct of the Keating Five. This interpretation holds that the conduct was part of a normal competitive process, in which all politicians are encouraged by the political system to solicit support and bestow favors in order to win elections. We may call this the competitive politics theory.(6) On this view, most politicians are not corrupt, nor is the system—even if some citizens like Keating happen to have corrupt designs. The quest for campaign contributions and the provision of service to influential contributors are necessary features of a healthy competitive politics.

The second interpretation also holds that what the Keating Five did is not significantly different from what other members have done but concludes that it is corrupt. On this view (call it the pervasive corruption theory), most politicians are corrupt or (more sympathetically) are forced by the system to act in corrupt ways even if they begin with honest intentions.(7) This interpretation is naturally more popular among the press, the public, and academics than it is among politicians. It is consistent with the views both of those who urge radical reforms in the political system (e.g., abolishing campaign contributions completely) and of those who believe that corruption is unavoidable in government (and either accept it or advocate reducing the scope of government).

These two common interpretations seem to be different. Indeed, they seem to be opposites, since one finds corruption where the other does not. But on closer inspection, their concepts of corruption turn out to be fundamentally similar. We can begin to see the similarity in the fact that they both conclude that the conduct of the Keating Five is not morally distinguishable from that of most other politicians.(8) On both accounts, the Keating Five were simply intervening with administrators on behalf of a campaign contributor, a common practice. The competitive politics theory accepts the practice, the pervasive corruption theory condemns it. But on neither theory do the details of the case (e.g., what kind of intervention) make any difference in the moral assessment.

The reason that both theories take this view is that they agree in their fundamental assumptions. The analysis that follows focuses on three of these assumptions (each corresponding to an element in the general concept of corruption) and argues that each is mistaken. Understanding why they are mistaken points toward the need for a concept of mediated corruption.

First, both interpretations assume that corruption requires that the public official receive a personal gain, either directly or indirectly in the form of an advantage that is not distinguished from personal gain. They disagree about whether a campaign contribution should count as personal gain in the required sense, but they agree that some such gain or its moral equivalent is necessary. The image of the self-serving politician acting on base motives contrary to the public interest supplies much of the force of the moralistic reactions to corruption, both the defensiveness of the competitive politics view, and the censoriousness of the pervasive corruption view. This is also the image that most public officials themselves evidently have of the corrupt official: the more personal and the larger the payoff and the less the favor seems part of the job, the more likely is the conduct to be regarded as corrupt (Peters and Welch 1978, 980–81). Second, both interpretations assume that corruption requires that the citizen receive a benefit that is not deserved or be threatened with not receiving one that is deserved. More generally, the justice of the constituent's claim is the only aspect of the benefit that is relevant to the determination of corruption. Third, both interpretations assume that corruption requires a corrupt motive. The personal or political gain and the citizen's benefit are connected in the mind of the public official. The official knowingly acts for the contributor in exchange for gain to himself or herself.

Personal Gain: The Ambiguity of Self-Interest

Is personal gain by an official a necessary element of corruption? Only one of the Keating Five—McCain—ever received anything from Keating for his own personal use, and he (along with Glenn) is generally considered to have been the least guilty of the group. (The McCain family took some vacation trips to Keating's Bahamas home in the early 1980s, for which McCain eventually paid when notified by the company in 1989.) If personal gain is an element of the corruption in the Keating Five case, it must be found in the campaign contributions. Should campaign contributions count as the personal gain that the conventional concept of corruption requires?

This case suggests a negative answer. Cranston received no personal financial benefit, yet his conduct was reasonably regarded as the most flagrant of the Five; he was the only one ultimately reprimanded by the Senate. Most of the $850,000 Keating gave to Cranston went to voter registration groups, which had public-spirited names such as Center for the Participation in Democracy and had the purpose of trying to increase turnout in several different states. One of Cranston's main defenses was that he did not gain personally from these contributions.

But one might say that he did gain politically, or at least he thought he would.(9) Why not count this political advantage as the element of personal gain? This is a tempting move and is commonly made, but it should be avoided. It is a mistake to try to force contributions into the category of personal gain. Doing so obscures a moral difference between personal and political gain. These should be distinguished even if one insists on treating both as forms of self-interest. "Personal gain" refers to goods that are usable generally in pursuit of one's own interest (including that of one's family) and are not necessary by-products of political activity. "Political gain" (which may also be a kind of self-interest) involves goods that are usable primarily in the political process, and are necessary by-products of this process.

The distinction is important because in our political system (and any democracy based on elections) the pursuit of political profit is a necessary element in the structure of incentives in a way that the pursuit of personal profit is not.(10) Our system depends on politicians' seeking political advantage: we count on their wanting to be elected or reelected. Among the advantages that they must seek are campaign contributions. If political gain were part of what makes a contribution corrupt, it would also discredit many other kinds of political support, such as organizational efforts on behalf of a candidate, on which a robust democratic politics depends. This is part of the truth in the competitive politics theory.

Some political scientists would offer a more sophisticated rationale for regarding contributions as just another form of personal gain. They would begin with the methodological assumption that politicians act only on self-interest, seeking to maximize their chances of reelection or in other ways to advance their careers. They could then argue that contributions, to the extent that they help achieve these goals, constitute personal gain no less than other goods that further the self-interest of politicians. The trouble with this expansive concept of personal gain is that it does not help identify which contributions should be permitted and which should not. As far as the personal gain is concerned, all contributions are created equal: they are either all proper or all corrupt. If self-interest is viewed favorably (as in some competitive politics theories), the expansive concept would not require that any contributions be prohibited, even those involving what would normally be considered bribery or extortion. If self-interest is viewed unfavorably (as in some pervasive corruption theories), the concept would imply that no contribution should be permitted, even those serving what would normally be regarded as the public interest. In either case, the self-interest assumption does not itself supply any way to distinguish legitimate from illegitimate pursuit of personal gain.

Neither could we get much help with this difficulty from a more refined model based on principal-agent theory, which is sometimes used to analyze corruption.(11) On this model, the politician acts as an agent for constituents, the principals. Because of the costs of monitoring and other factors, the principals cannot reliably control the agent's actions. In the absence of other constraints, the resulting "slack" allows the agent to act on his or her own interest contrary to that of the principals. The model could help us see that corruption may be partly the result of the structure of incentives in the system: agent-principal slack creates moral hazards that permit corruption. But the model is neutral between proper and improper behavior. It is applicable to corrupt principals and agents as to honest ones. It could treat the Keating Five as agents of Keating in carrying out corrupt purposes. It does not explain why we should have a system that allows some kinds of incentives (contributions) and not other kinds (bribes). It might be said, of course, that taking bribes has more socially harmful consequences than accepting campaign contributions. But if this is the claim, then what is wrong is no longer the personal gain, but a certain kind of personal gain; and it is wrong not because it is a personal gain at all but because of its effects on the system.

If the presence of personal gain is not necessary to make a contribution corrupt, neither is its absence sufficient to make a contribution correct. Consider this hypothetical example. Suppose that after meeting with Mother Theresa (which in fact he did), Keating decides in a fit of saintly fervor that a portion of his campaign contributions and those of others he solicits for the Keating Five should go secretly to a government trust fund to support new programs to help the poor. Suppose, further, that the Keating Five, respecting this act of charity by a constituent, work together behind the scenes to establish the Mother Theresa Fund for this purpose. (To add a further touch of irony, let the fund be administered, at Keating's request, by Ed Gray.) None of the senators would have gained personally, and a good cause would have been served.(12) Would there be any grounds for concern about corruption?

There surely would be some. Keating would have managed to promote a private project with the aid of public officials but without the warrant of the democratic process. The cause, however noble, was not one that citizens or their representatives had chosen through legitimate procedures. Acting on principle for higher causes can be no less corrupting—and may be even more dangerous—than acting for personal gain because the perpetrators are more likely to be able to enlist others in their schemes. Oliver North would have not been able to mobilize so much support for his projects in the Iran-Contra affair had he been acting mainly for personal gain.

Official Favors: The Perils of Constituent Service

Consider now the second element of corruption, the official favors that the senators provided. The Keating Five claimed that there was nothing improper about the help they gave Keating. The benefits that Keating received were all provided in the name of "constituent service," a normal practice in a political system where representatives have to compete for the support of voters and campaign contributors.

The senators—and even the Ethics Committee at times—seemed to assume that if what a member does is constituent service and breaks no law, it is never improper. If the conduct does not involve bribery, extortion, or an illegal campaign contribution, it is not only acceptable but admirable.(13) This is the competitive politics theory in its purest form. But as the hearings progressed, some of the senators came to accept a slightly more moderate view. In effect, they allowed that otherwise proper constituent service could become improper if it were provided unfairly. It would be wrong (and perhaps evidence of corruption) if it were provided only to big contributors.(14) The senators seemed to accept as a reasonable test the question, Does the member typically intervene in this way for other constituents?

DeConcini made it a major part of his defense to show that he responded to virtually any constituent who asked for help. (He brandished a list of 75,000 constituents who could be called to testify, though to everyone's relief he settled for inviting only three—a social worker for Hispanics, a drug-busting sheriff, and a handicapped veteran.)(15) Despite these heroic efforts, the answer to the question in this case is still probably negative: what the Keating Five provided was not typical constituent service. Five senators meeting in private with regulators on a specific case is unusual. During the hearings, no one could cite a sufficiently close precedent.(16)

But even if we were to accept that the senators would do for other constituents what they did for Keating, we should still be concerned about another feature of this case, what may be called "the problem of too many representatives." Only DeConcini and McCain could claim Keating as a constituent in the conventional (electoral) sense. The other three count as his representatives mainly by virtue of his business interests in their states.(17) It is true that business interests, like other interests, may deserve representation; and geographical districts need not define the limits of representation, even of constituency service. However, we may reasonably criticize multiple representation if, in practice (as this case suggests), the extra representatives tend to go disproportionately to those with greater financial resources. That this tendency is undesirable is part of the truth in the pervasive corruption theory. A fair system of democratic representation does not grant more representatives to some citizens just because they have more financial resources.

So far, these criticisms could be consistent with the concept of conventional corruption, which assesses the benefit only in relation to the justice of the constituent's claims. Mediated corruption goes further and considers the effects on the policymaking process—most importantly, the foreseeable reactions of other officials (in this case, the regulators, staff, and other members). Instead of asking whether a member would provide this benefit equally for any constituent, mediated corruption asks whether the benefit should be provided in this way at all.

Unmentioned in the Constitution, unimagined by the founders, and until recently unanalyzed by journalists, constituent service has become a major part of the job of most members of Congress (Cain, Ferejohn, and Fiorina 1987,

50–76; and Fenno 1978, 101). It serves some valuable functions, the most important of which, perhaps, is to provide a check on abuse of power by executive agencies in individual cases—in effect, fulfilling the role played by an ombudsman in some other political systems.(18) If administrators are "harassing a constituent," as some of the senators said they suspected in this case, members may be obligated to intervene not only to protect the constituent but also to correct administrative procedures.

Yet, as recent scholarship has emphasized, constituent service is not a wholly beneficial practice even when legitimately performed (Cain, Ferejohn, and Fiorina 1987, 197–229). Even if the casework done by each individual member is perfectly proper, the collective consequences may not be so beneficial for the system as a whole. One danger is that as constituent service becomes such a prominent part of the job, legislative duties suffer. Voters tend to pay more attention to personalized service than to legislative records, and political responsibility for these records withers. Another danger is that by concentrating on righting wrongs against individual citizens, constituent service can favor particular remedies over general reforms. Ad hoc and local solutions do not necessarily produce changes in procedures or policies that benefit the public as a whole. Yet another danger is that to the extent that incumbents gain electoral advantage through constituent service, new members who might bring fresh policy views or offer new criticisms of government performance are less likely to make their way into the legislature.

Once we accept that constituent service, quite independently of campaign contributions, is a mixed democratic blessing, we can see that to justify any act of constituent service, it is not sufficient to point to the benefit to particular constituents or even to the value of the practice for the system in general. Standards to assess constituent service are best derived from principles of legislative ethics, which identify the general characteristics that a system of representation should have in order to provide conditions for making morally justifiable decisions (Thompson 1987, chap. 4). Three principles—generality, autonomy, and publicity—yield three sets of standards.

Standards of generality require that legislative actions be justifiable in terms that apply to all citizens equally. These standards refer most directly to legislation itself, where they favor actions that provide public goods for a broad class of citizens over those that confer private advantage on individual citizens. They also have institutional implications, one of the most important of which is the separation of powers, a chief purpose of which is to maintain the appropriate level of generality by assigning to branches other than the legislative the role of applying the laws. Legislative actions that are appropriate in the process of making laws may not always be appropriate in the process of administering them. Some of the most important standards of legislative ethics, therefore, in various ways prescribe that any legislative intervention should be appropriate to the administrative proceeding in question.

In the Keating case, the senators evidently did not recognize any difference between what would be an appropriate intervention in rule-making proceedings and what would be appropriate in quasi-adjudicatory proceedings (which the Lincoln case resembled). In the latter kind of proceeding, there is generally more procedural protection for constituents and less legitimate scope for disputes about policy.(19) Some political bargaining, of course, is necessary in the administrative process; but at least some of the senators in this case went beyond what we might call the "normal range" of acceptable political pressure. They did more than make status inquiries (which are perfectly proper). To the regulators, their conduct looked more like a threat (specifically, a threat to oppose a pending bill to fund the savings-and-loan bailouts, which was generally believed to be urgently needed).

Standards of autonomy prescribe that representatives act on relevant reasons (Thompson 1987, 111–14). They require that any intervention be appropriate to the substantive merits of the constituent's case. Such standards would not prohibit members from acting aggressively on behalf of constituents, but they would clearly direct members to consider the substance of constituents' claims in deciding whether and how to intervene. Members may have a duty to support meritorious claims; but they should not press claims that they have, or should have, reason to believe are without merit. Furthermore, the higher the stakes, the greater the responsibility to investigate the merits of a claim. More generally, simply pressing claims without any regard to their merits is to promote a policymaking process moved more by considerations of power than of purpose.(20)

Many members may not recognize an ethical problem in intervention, because they take their roles to be like a lawyer's, whose duty is assumed to be to press a client's case without regard to merits. They may consider the only alternative to be to play a judge's role, which would allow no scope for partiality toward their constituents. But the role of the representative differs from both, permitting members to give special consideration to their own constituents provided that they take into account the effect on other citizens and on the public generally.

Keating's case, it is now known (and could have been known then) lacked merit. Glenn and McCain made some effort to find out about the case before they went to the meetings with Gray and the regulators. Giving the senators the benefit of the doubt, we might say that under the pressures of time they took all the steps one could reasonably expect before they intervened with the regulators. The senators did, after all, have some evidence at the time (a letter from Alan Greenspan and a statement from the firm of Arthur Young) that appeared to lend credibility to Keating's complaints. But once the senators heard about the regulators' intention to make a criminal referral, they had adequate notice that his claims were questionable. Although criminal referrals are not unusual and are not clear evidence of wrongdoing, a conscientious senator (indeed, even a prudent one) would have looked more closely into the merits of Keating's case before continuing to assist him. The only two who continued to press his case, DeConcini and Cranston, did not. This is partly why their conduct could be criticized more severely, as the special counsel (and, less clearly, the Ethics Committee) suggested.

Standards of publicity require that an intervention take place in ways that could be justified publicly. It is, of course, neither practical nor desirable that all interventions be formally on the record and made public at the time. But the intervention should not be so clandestine that the member and the agency cannot be held accountable should the action later be called into question.(21) This is why some members put in writing their inquiries to administrative agencies and keep a record of other similar contacts.

The interventions for Keating, though not strictly secret, fell short of meeting the publicity principle. The pattern of the interventions—after-hours meetings, the absence of aides, early morning phone calls to regulators at home, the vagueness of records (except for the famous "transcript" of the April 9 meeting)—made it difficult to reconstruct the events. They create a reasonable suspicion that the discussions were never intended to be accessible for public review.

The constituent service that the senators provided Keating, as measured by these standards, did not serve the democratic process well. To this extent—and in varying degrees in the case of each senator—the benefits that Keating received qualify as improperly provided; they count as the second element of mediated corruption. With the concept of mediated corruption, then, we can criticize some forms of constituent service for contributors without rejecting all forms as does the pervasive theory, or accepting all forms as does competitive theory.

Corrupt Connections: The Significance of Mixed Motives

In any form of corruption, there must be an improper connection between the benefit granted and the gain received. Otherwise, there would be only simple bias or simple malfeasance. With conventional corruption, we look for the link in the guilty mind of the public official—a corrupt motive. But the question immediately arises, How can we distinguish corrupt motives from other kinds? We have already seen that personal gain is neither a necessary nor a sufficient condition, nor is the impropriety of the benefit. Therefore, the corruption has to be found partly in the nature of the exchange. The difficulty is that corrupt exchanges do not seem obviously different from many of the other kinds of deals that go on in politics—exchanges of support of various kinds, without which political life could not go on at all. Politics is replete with quid pro quos: you vote for my bill, and I'll support yours; you raise funds for my primary campaign, and I'll endorse you in the next election. What is so corrupt about the exchange of campaign contributions for constituent service? Without an answer to this question, we would be forced either to brand nearly all ordinary politics as corrupt or to excuse much political corruption as just ordinary politics.

The competitive politics theory, fearing a purification of the process that might enervate political life, attempts to contain the concept of corruption. It insists on narrow criteria for what counts as a corrupt link. The connection between the contribution and the service must be close in two senses: proximate in time and explicit in word or deed. In the case of several of the Keating Five, the connection between the contributions and the service were, by these standards, close. The connection was especially close in the case of Cranston, one reason that the committee singled him out for special criticism. He solicited contributions from Keating while he was also working to help Lincoln with its problems. His chief fundraiser combined discussions about regulations and contributions. Favors and contributions were also linked in memos and informal comments. He made the connection explicit in a memorable line delivered at a dinner at the Belair Hotel, where he "came up and patted Mr. Keating on the back and said, 'Ah, the mutual aid society'."(22)

The committee found the contributions and services to be "substantially linked" through an "impermissible pattern of conduct," but they stopped short of finding "corrupt intent" (U.S. Senate 1991b, 36). Why did the committee decline to find corruption here? The connection, it would seem, could hardly be closer. For that matter, we might also ask why the committee did not find the pattern impermissible in the case of Riegle and DeConcini. Part of the answer probably is that "corrupt intent" is the language of the bribery statutes, and the committee did not dare suggest that campaign contributions could be bribes. The line between contributions and bribes must be kept bright.

But is the line so bright? "Almost a hair's line difference" separates bribes and contributions, Russell Long once testified (Noonan 1984, 801). Courts have not been able to provide a principled way of distinguishing the two.(23) There is, furthermore, no good reason to believe that connections between contributions and benefits that are proximate and explicit are any more corrupt than connections that are indirect and implicit. The former may be only the more detectable—not necessarily the more deliberate or damaging—form of corruption.

Are we driven, then, to accept the conclusion of the pervasive corruption theory on this point, that virtually all contributions are corrupt? This theory is right to insist that corruption should be viewed in the context of the political system, that it can work through patterns of conduct, institutional routines, and informal norms. But the theory does not encourage the kinds of distinctions that seem necessary in the kind of politics we actually have and are likely to have in the foreseeable future. It treats, for example, the explicit, proximate bribe the same as the routine thousand-dollar campaign contribution to one's longtime party favorite.

Both the competitive politics and pervasive corruption theories assume the criterion of the corrupt connection to be the actual motives of the citizens and politicians. This assumption is mistaken, because it ignores an important structural feature of representative government. Any electorally based representative system permits—indeed, requires—representatives to act on mixed motives. They act for the benefit of particular constituents, for the good of the whole district or state, for the good of the nation, and for their own interest in reelection or future political ambitions. Some of these motives may be more admirable than others; but none is illegitimate in itself, and all are necessary in some measure in our system.

Under the circumstances of mixed motives, it is hard enough for any official, however conscientious, to separate proper from improper motives and, more generally, to find the right balance of motives in making any particular decision (see Douglas 1952, 44, 85–92). It is harder still for citizens—even well-informed and nonpartisan ones—to judge at a distance whether the official has really found that balance. Therefore, in the design of a representative system or in the practice of judging representatives, we cannot in general count on being able to evaluate motives in individual cases.

What we need, instead, is a standard that assesses an individual official's action in the context of the system as whole. The standard should identify systematic tendencies that we know from past experience are likely to lead to corruption. It would then refer to the motives on which any official in the circumstances may be presumed to act, instead of the motives on which this official actually acts. It is just this kind of logic that underlies the so-called appearance standard, at least when properly interpreted.

In a plethora of codes, rules, and statutes that regulate the ethics of government, public officials are now enjoined to avoid the appearance of impropriety (U.S. Senate 1991b, Additional Views, 14–16). The term appearance is unfortunate, however, as it encourages misinterpretations of the standard.(24) The mere appearance of an ethical wrong is contrasted with a real wrong, and the violation of the appearance standard is taken to be a minor, lesser offense, a sort of pale reflection of the real offense. The standard then comes to be regarded as merely prudential, a piece of political advice, which, if not followed, is seen as grounds for a charge of mistaken judgment, rather than an ethical wrong. Notice that the Ethics Committee found that DeConcini and Riegle, whom they charged with creating an appearance of impropriety, showed only "insensitivity and poor judgment" (U.S. Senate 1991b, 17, 19).

Properly interpreted, the appearance standard identifies a distinct wrong, quite independent of—and potentially no less serious than—the wrong of which it is an appearance. It would be better called a "tendency" standard, since it presumes that under certain conditions, the connection between a contribution and a benefit tends to be improper. The standard seeks, first, to reduce the occasions on which the connection is improper in the conventional sense. These are the occasions on which the provision of the benefit is actually motivated primarily by the contribution. But the second, more distinctive, aim of the standard is to decrease the occasions on which the connection is reasonably perceived to be improper. This perception is grounded on our general knowledge of the conditions that tend to produce actual improper connections, but the wrong is based on a different kind of moral failure. When an official accepts large contributions from interested individuals under certain conditions, whether or not the official's judgment is actually influenced, citizens are morally justified in believing the official's judgment has been so influenced and acting on that belief themselves. The official is guilty of failing to take into account the reasonable reactions of citizens.(25)

The justification for this kind of standard should be distinguished from the type of argument (common in discussions of rule utilitarianism) that justifies particular acts by appeals to general rules or policies. In the rule utilitarian argument, an overly broad rule is justified by showing that the costs of deciding each case are greater than the costs of wrongly deciding some cases. The argument for the appearance standard differs in two respects. First, it counts as a cost not simply the risk that a case might be wrongly decided but also the likelihood that the public will perceive the case to have been wrongly decided. Public confidence could be undermined, and misconduct by others encouraged, even if a case were rightly decided but not so perceived. Second, the rationale for the appearance standard rests in part on a publicity principle, which holds that the reasons on which public officials may be assumed to act should be accessible to citizens. Appearances, then, are in these ways valuable beyond their role as evidence for corrupt motives.

Because appearances are often the only window that citizens have on official conduct, rejecting the appearance standard is tantamount to denying democratic accountability. This was dramatically demonstrated in the objections frequently raised during the hearings by several of the senators and their attorneys. Cranston, most notably, kept objecting to the idea that his conduct should be judged by how it appears to a reasonable person. That is a "mythical person," he said. The only real person who can judge is the senator himself. "You were not there. I was there. And I know that what I knew at the time . . . convinced me that my actions were appropriate" (U.S. Senate 1991a, pt. 1, November 16, 1990, pp. 121–22).

The appearance standard, however, does not itself identify the kinds of conditions that would warrant a conclusion of mediated corruption but only points in the right direction—away from actual motives to presumed motives and objective intentions and thereby to the tendencies or conditions that create corrupt connections in democratic systems. We still need some basis on which to distinguish corrupt from noncorrupt contributions.

We can begin to see the basis for such a distinction in the common reaction that there was something peculiar about Keating's lavishing support on senators whose political views he so strongly opposed. Cranston and Keating were an odd couple: an arch-conservative Arizona businessman devoted to the free market and opposed to pornography and abortion teamed up with one of the leading liberals in the Senate, a former candidate for president who had called for a nuclear freeze and higher social spending. The two differed even on government policy toward the financial services industry.

This ideological incongruence is significant not because it exposes cynical or self-interested motives but because it reveals apolitical practices. Specifically, it identifies a type of contribution that serves no public political function. A contribution given without regard to the political positions of the candidate only incidentally provides political support. Its aim is primarily to influence the candidate when in office. In its pure form, it has no function other than to translate the desires of a contributor directly into governmental action. In effect, it short-circuits the democratic process. Contrast this kind of contribution with one given to support a candidate with whom one shares a general political orientation or agrees on issues that one thinks salient.(26) A contribution of this kind directly serves a political function: its aim is to help a candidate get elected, and it works through the political process.(27) Rather than bypassing the process, the contribution animates it.

Neither the pervasive corruption nor the competitive politics view can easily distinguish these types of contributions (though the competitive politics view could recognize an analogous distinction between contributions that further the competitive process and those that do not). The basis of the distinction is the principle that citizens should influence their representatives—and representatives should influence policy—only in ways that can be contested through public discussion in a democratic political process. This principle is consistent with a wide range of conceptions of representation. The problem with the first kind of contribution, the Keating type, is not that it makes a representative an agent of individual constituents but that it makes the representative an apolitical agent. The objection is not only that the contributions come with strings attached but also (even more insidiously) that the strings have no political substance.(28)

Ideological incongruence, which is common enough in current campaign finance (as big contributors hedge their electoral bets), is not itself a necessary or sufficient condition of corruption. Neither does its absence make an otherwise questionable practice acceptable. However, its presence is a strong indication in any particular case that corruption may also be present. More generally, the concept points toward a comprehensive criterion for identifying corrupt connections.

The connection between contributions and benefits is corrupt ff it bypasses the democratic process. The corruption here is twofold. It consists, first, in the actual and presumed tendency of certain kinds of contributions to influence the actions of representatives without regard to the substantive merits of issues. This is the corruption of the representative's judgment. The corruption also shows itself in broader effects on the democratic process, namely, in the actual and presumed tendency to undermine substantive political competition and deliberation. This is the corruption of the representative system.

There are, of course, many different ways in which contributions might be regarded as undermining the democratic process; and which ways we build into the concept of corruption will depend on what conceptions of democracy we accept. The principles of legislative ethics invoked earlier to assess forms of constituency service could be used again here to generate some criteria for identifying corrupt connections. We could then hold that a connection is more likely to be corrupt, (a) the more particular the aim of the contributor, (b) the less closely the contribution is connected to the merits of conduct it is intended to influence, and (c) the less accessible the exchange is to publicity. Each of these criteria would have to be specified more fully and translated into enforceable standards before we could conclude that we have a satisfactory test for the corrupt connection in mediated corruption.(29) But it should already be clear that the criteria presuppose an approach that makes the relationship to democratic processes more fundamental than do conventional approaches to corruption.

Conclusion

Mediated corruption is not new, but it is newly prospering. It thrives in the world of large, multinational financial institutions that increasingly interact, in closed and complex ways, with governments. Many of the major governmental scandals in recent years have involved a large measure of mediated corruption—the affairs of Iran-Contra, Housing and Urban Development (under Samuel Pierce), the Bank of Credit and Commerce International, and the Banca Nazionale del Lavoro's Atlanta branch, among others. Where private greed mixes easily with the public good, where the difference between serving citizens and serving supporters blurs, where secret funds lubricate the schemes of public officials, there mediated corruption is likely to flourish.

We can better understand the cunning ways of this growing form of corruption if we keep in mind its distinctive characteristics. The concept of mediated corruption serves this purpose. Each of its three elements, it has been argued here, differs from those of conventional corruption, the kind assumed by the competitive politics and pervasive corruption theories.

First, in mediated corruption a public official typically receives a political gain. But, as the pervasive corruption mistakenly denies and the competitive politics theory rightly implies, there is nothing wrong with this gain itself. Mediated corruption, furthermore, does not require that the public official personally gain or otherwise serve his (narrow) self-interest, as conventional corruption typically assumes. The gain contributes to mediated corruption insofar as it damages the democratic process—for example, by influencing a representative to serve private purposes without regard to their substantive merits.

Second, the public official provides a benefit, typically as an intermediary attempting to influence other officials to serve a constituent's private ends.(30) Contrary to both the competitive politics and the pervasive corruption views, the benefit itself may be deserved and may even be something that the official would provide for any constituent. But if the way in which the official provides the benefit damages the democratic process, it still counts as a contribution to the corruption. The way in which the member presses the constituent's claim, not simply the justice of the claim, is relevant to the assessment of the corruption.

Third, the connection between the gain and the benefit is corrupt if it would lead a reasonable citizen to believe that an exchange has taken place that damages the democratic process in specified ways (typically in ways that bypass the process). Mediated corruption thus adds an appearance standard to the corrupt-motive test of conventional corruption. It goes further, and, like the pervasive corruption theory, relates the corruption in any particular case to corruption of the system as a whole. But the standards for determining whether the connection is corrupt are more fine-grained than that theory allows. They permit some connections that might otherwise seem corrupt (e.g., money is not necessarily corrupting) and condemn some connections that otherwise seem legitimate (money can be corrupting independently of the inequalities it perpetuates). The standards ultimately depend on what kind of democratic process we wish to maintain.

The concept of mediated corruption is consistent with a wide range of theories of democracy but is probably best justified from the perspective of a theory that prescribes that officials act on considerations of moral principle, rather than only on calculations of political power. This is sometimes called the deliberative conception of democracy (see Cohen 1989, 17–34; Larmore 1987, esp. 59–66; Manin 1987).(31) As we have seen, mediated corruption characteristically attempts to translate private interest directly into public policy, bypassing the democratic processes of political discussion and competition. It thereby blocks our considering the moral reasons for and against a policy. Mediated corruption also prevents deliberately adopting a policy even without considering moral reasons: it precludes deliberation about whether to deliberate.

If we accept the concept of mediated corruption (as a supplement to the concept of conventional corruption), at least three implications follow. First, cases like the Keating Five would look different in the future. It would be easier to justify making finer distinctions of kind and degree in judging misconduct. The kind of conduct in which McCain and Glenn engaged, for example, would be more clearly distinguishable from that of the other three; and the kind of conduct in which all five engaged would be more clearly set apart from that of most other senators. More generally, we would hear less talk of motives (whether honest or rationalized), fewer appeals to constituent service as if it excused all sins, and fewer attacks on the appearance standard. We would see more concern about the mixing of private profit and public service, more attention to the merits of constituents' claims, and more worry about the effects of practices of individual representatives on the broader process of democratic representation. This shift of attention from the individual to the system (or, more precisely, to the effects of individual behavior on the system) would require not only new ways of thinking but also new standards of ethics.

The practical change most emphasized by the committee and most often mentioned by observers is campaign finance reform. Reducing the importance of money in campaigns (and politics more generally) is certainly desirable and could be seen as one of the implications of the concept of mediated corruption. But since the dominating role of money in politics is objectionable from the perspective of many different theories, it is worth emphasizing an implication that points toward a different dimension of reform. The concept of mediated corruption helps bring out the fact that money is not the only important source of corruption. Some of the kinds of misconduct to which mediated corruption calls attention depend less on money than do the kinds condemned by conventional corruption. As far as public officials are concerned, mediated corruption works its wiles less through greed than through ambition and even a misplaced sense of duty. Even some quite radical campaign finance reforms would not completely eliminate some forms of mediated corruption. Recall that political action committees, the *bête noire* of many progressive reformers, played almost no role in the case of the Keating Five.

A second implication of adopting the concept of mediated corruption concerns the process by which charges of unethical conduct should be heard and decided. In the Keating Five case, the process was directed by the Ethics Committee of the Senate. Legislatures have traditionally insisted on exclusive authority to discipline their own members, and the ethics committees of both houses have in the past managed to bring some tough judgments against some of their colleagues. But these have almost always been in flagrant cases of wrongdoing, closer to clear violations of rules that resembled the criminal law. It is difficult enough for colleagues who have worked together for years and may have to work together again to bring themselves to judge one another harshly in these cases. It may be almost impossible in cases involving mediated corruption. The less the charge is like conventional corruption, the harder it is to reach a severe judgment. The member implicated in mediated corruption, showing no obvious signs of a guilty mind or especially selfish motives, is often seen as simply doing his job. Under such circumstances, the sympathy of one's colleagues is maximized, their capacity for objectivity, minimized.

Furthermore, the legislature is, in a sense, also judging itself—specifically, its own practices and procedures, through which the corruption is mediated. In these circumstances, we might reasonably wonder whether anybody, including a legislative body, should be a judge in its own case. The clear implication of these considerations, suggested in part by the concept of mediated corruption, is that we should consider establishing an outside body to judge cases of ethics violations. To overcome possible constitutional objections, Congress could ultimately control the body; but it should be established in a way that would have at least the independence and respect of an institution like the Congressional Budget Office.

The third implication is methodological in character and is perhaps the most significant for the study of corruption and democracy. The concept of mediated corruption has the potential to integrate the very different approaches to corruption that prevail in political theory and in social science. The difference was strikingly illustrated some years ago when the *American Political Science Review* published a pair of articles on corruption, one by a political theorist and one by two political scientists (Dobel 1978; Peters and Welch 1978). The editor perhaps intended to take a step toward unifying the discipline by putting the articles together in the same section. Yet the articles had little in common except the common word corruption in their titles; the authors might as well have been writing about different subjects.

The political theorist faithfully followed his tradition, invoking Machiavelli, Rousseau, Montesquieu, and Madison (among others), and presented corruption as a characteristic of a political system as whole. He saw it as a sickness of the body politic, a turning away from civic virtue toward private interests. It may afflict individual citizens and their rulers, but it can only be fully understood from the perspective of the whole society.(32) The political scientists described corruption in terms of transactions between individuals. The transactions, of course, take place within a system; and the system may be called corrupt when its structures and incentives encourage corruption. But the basic unit of analysis remains an exchange between individual officials and individual citizens.

Mediated corruption holds the promise of putting back together the structuralist and the individualist conceptions of corruption that these intellectual traditions have split apart. The integrating instrument, it has been suggested here, is the idea of the democratic process. With mediated corruption, we cannot decide whether corruption exists, let alone how serious it is, without paying attention to its effects on the democratic process and therefore without making moral judgments about the kind of democratic process we wish to encourage. The concept of mediated corruption permits a conclusion that corruption is pervasive and the system needs radical reform; but the grounds of the conclusion, as well as the nature of the reform, would be guided by a conception of the democratic process. Mediated corruption also supports judgments about individuals competing within the existing system; these, too, are to be shaped by a view of the democratic process. We cannot assess either patterns of systematic corruption or instances of individual corruption without presupposing a theory of democracy.

Because the concept of mediated corruption is theory-dependent in this way, we should not suppose that we can understand corruption without making value judgments about politics. In this respect, those social scientists who try to justify corruption in some societies as necessary to achieve certain political values (such as efficiency or social integration) are right about the structure of the argument required to assess corruption.(33) Whether certain kinds of conduct should count as corrupt depends in part on its net effects on the political system as a whole. However, in making their calculations, these social scientists tend to give too much weight to outcome values relative to process values, a mistake that the approach of mediated corruption avoids.

The social scientists who find corruption functional also tend to assume that their methods are objective and realistic while the methods of those who criticize corruption are subjective and moralistic. But even if we were to accept certain kinds of corruption as functional, we would still be making a moral judgment. As this search for the meaning of corruption in the case of the Keating Five should make clear, on the subject of corruption, we are all moralists. The only question is what kind of moralists we want to be. Unlike the

Keating Five, their apologists, and even most of their critics, we should try to be democratic moralists.

Notes

(1) Berke 1991. Although other factors no doubt contributed to the low public regard for Congress in this period, the percentage of respondents who rated the honesty and ethical standards of senators "very high" or "high" declined by five points between 1990 and 1991; and the rating of Congress itself fell to an all-time low (Hugick 1991; Hugick and Hueber 1991). Other surveys found that a majority of respondents believed that at least half of the members of Congress are "corrupt" and that the institution itself is "corrupt" (CBS News/*New York Times* 1991; NBC News/*Wall Street Journal* 1992). The latter survey found that of the "scandals and controversies that have taken place during the past few years in Washington," the handling of problems with the savings-and-loan industry "most bothered" more respondents than any other.

(2) This general concept is meant to be consistent with a wide variety of definitions in the social science literature. However, further specification of the concept beyond this level of generality remains controversial (mostly with regard to what should count as "improper"). (It should be noted that in some forms of conventional corruption, the "public official" and "private citizen" may be the same person.) For a review of various approaches, see Heidenheimer, Johnston, and LeVine 1989, 7–14; Peters and Welch 1978, 974–78.

(3) The most influential explanation of reflective equilibrium is Rawls 1971, 48–51. A more recent systematic account is Richardson 1990.

(4) No one is likely to mistake this summary for authoritative history. It is intended to serve only as a simplified reminder of some of the highlights of the case. The summary (as well as subsequent comments about the case) relies primarily on the evidence presented during the hearings and in the reports of the special counsel and the Ethics Committee. See U.S. Senate 1991a, 1991b. Two readable accounts of the affair, including some useful background material, are Adams 1990, pt. 4; Pizzo *et al.* 1989, 263–97.

(5) Keating acted often as a broker for others, sometimes as a "bundler," taking "the separate individual contributions and bundling them together, . . . claiming credit for the harvest" (Sorauf 1992, 54). This is yet another way in which the corruption in this case could be regarded as mediated.

(6) Examples of this interpretation typical of many public comments on the affair are Yoder 1991 and testimony by Senator Daniel Inouye (U.S. Senate 1991a, pt. 3, December 3, 1990, pp. 2–50). Similar views can also be found in court opinions and in more general discussions of campaign reform (e.g., McCormick v. U.S. 1991, 1825; Gottlieb 1989). The

competitive politics view is also consistent with a number of well-known analyses of corruption (e.g., Banfield 1975; Wilson 1974, 29–38). Although the view might be supported by various democratic theories, the version of pluralist theory (sometimes called the competitive theory of democracy) is its most natural ally. The classic statements are those of Schumpeter (1962) and Downs (1957).

(7) Typical examples of this interpretation from public comment on the case are Abramson and Rogers 1991, Etzioni 1990/91, and Wilkinson 1991. Also see the affidavit of Senator Ernest Hollings (U.S. Senate 1991a, Exhibits of Senator DeConcini, 493–95). In the literature on campaign reform and political corruption more generally, the interpretation would find support in several different analyses (e.g., Etzioni 1984; Lowenstein 1985, 826–28; Lowenstein 1989, 301–35; Noonan 1984, 621–51). For discussions of democratic theory that could be used to support this view, see Cohen and Rogers 1983; Dahl 1989, chap.9; Lindblom 1977, pt. 5.

(8) This conclusion is evidently widely accepted by the public. Asked in an NBC/*Wall Street Journal* poll whether they thought that the ethical violations of which the Keating Five were accused are "typical" of the behavior of Senators and members of Congress, 71% of the respondents agreed that they were; 19% disagreed.

(9) The conventional wisdom that higher turnout helps the Democrats has been challenged. See DeNardo 1980; Tucker, Vedlitz, and DeNardo 1986.

(10) Compare Madison's observation in Federalist 51: "Ambition must be made to counteract ambition . . . This policy of supplying, by opposite and rival interests, the defect of better motives, might be traced through the whole system of human affairs" (Hamilton, Madison, and Jay 1961, 349).

(11) A pioneering work that exemplifies both the strengths and weaknesses of this approach is Rose-Ackerman 1978, 6–10.

(12) A variation on this hypothetical example actually took place. According to the testimony of James Grogan, a Keating aide, Senator DeConcini's wife at times solicited contributions from Keating for her favorite charities in the community (U.S. Senate 1991a, pt. 4, December 14, 1990, pp. 248–49).

(13) U.S. Senate 1991b, 14–16; idem 1991a, pt. 1, November 16, 1990, pp. 126–32 and November 19, 1990, pp. 91–92.

(14) U.S. Senate 1991a, pt. 1, November 16, 1990, p. 111 and November 19, 1990, p. 23.

(15) Ibid., pt. 4, December 10, 1990, pp. 58–94.

(16) Lobbying the Defense Department to support Apache helicopters, asking the Customs Service for an exception to trade restrictions, questioning the Justice Department about a potential indictment of a shipyard company (U.S. Senate 1991a, pt. 1, November 19, 1990, pp. 14–17; idem, pt. 4, December 10, 1990, pp. 9–12; idem, pt. 6, January 10, 1991, pp. 137–40)—these examples and all of the others paraded before the committee lacked some critical feature of the Keating case. None involved pressure on independent regulators to give special treatment to a particular

company in a quasi-adjudicatory process; and in none did the intervention continue after the member could reasonably have been expected to know that company's intentions were questionable, if not illegal.

(17) Admittedly, the three senators not from Arizona could claim that they were acting for the constituents in their own states who would benefit from Keating's businesses. But this ceases to be constituent service and should, like legislative activity, be evaluated from a broader perspective that takes into account all of a representative's constituents. From this perspective, the benefits that these senators were providing to some of their constituents arguably did not serve most others well, specifically taxpayers and depositors.

(18) Relying on constituents to call attention to administrative abuses (what has been called "fire alarm" oversight) is said to be more common and more efficient than direct and continuous monitoring by Congress, called "police patrol" oversight (McCubbins and Schwartz 1984). But on the limitations of this and other forms of retrospective monitoring, see McCubbins, Noll, and Weingast 1987.

(19) Cf. Kappel 1989; Rosenberg 1990.

(20) Consider the standards practiced in Cranston's office, as described in the testimony of his aide, Carolyn Jordan: "Unless you have a complete kook, . . . the number one rule of this game is you never kiss a constituent off. That's the rule in our office. And you never tell them, no, unless they're asking you to do something that is just so far from the beaten path" (U.S. Senate 1991b, *Additional Views*, 84).

(21) Many of the opinions in the line of cases interpreting the Administrative Procedures Act (*Pillsbury* and its progeny) are especially critical of secret congressional interventions, even when the courts do not invalidate the agency results. See Kappel 1989, 144–47.

(22) U.S. Senate 1991a, pt. 4, December 14, 1990, p. 178.

(23) Generally, see Lowenstein 1985, 808–9, esp. n. 86–87; Noonan 1984, 621–51, 687–90, 696–97. See also the opinions of Justices Brennan and White in *U.S.* v. *Brewster* 1977, 558. In the most recent case dealing with public corruption, the best that the Supreme Court could do to justify sustaining a narrow standard (requiring explicit promises) was to say that a broader standard would "open to prosecution . . . conduct that in a very real sense is unavoidable so long as election campaigns are financed by private contributions or expenditures, as they have been from the beginning of the nation" (*McCormick* v. *U.S.* 1991, 1816).

(24) The small academic literature on the subject has tended to be critical of the standard (Morgan 1992; Roberts 1985, 177–89; but see also Kappel 1989, 154–71). A helpful (and rare) discussion of the appearance standard by a contemporary philosopher is Driver 1992.

(25) The potential effect on the conduct of others is the principal reason that Thomist ethics has traditionally treated appearing to do wrong under certain conditions as a distinct wrong. The wrong is called "giving

scandal" and is defined as providing the "occasion for another's fall." It is considered a sin if one's otherwise permissible action is of the kind that is in itself conducive to sin, and it remains sinful whether or not one intends it to have any effect on others (Aquinas 1972, vol. 35, 109–37).

(26) Some further specification of what should count as a general political orientation or a salient issue may be necessary in some circumstances, but it should be clear that agreement on the value of constituent service itself (the principle on which Keating and the Keating Five evidently most strongly agreed) is not sufficient. Constituent service, as has been suggested, may itself undermine the democratic process. Furthermore, in this case it seems plausible to conclude on the basis of his actions that Keating was less interested in constituent service justified as a general practice for all citizens than in the specific services provided for one constituent.

(27) Lowenstein proposes a similar distinction between contributions "intended to influence official conduct and accepted with the knowledge that they are so intended" and those "intended solely to help the candidate get elected" (1985, 847). The distinction drawn in the text differs in at least two respects: (1) it takes the function, rather than actual intentions, as the criterion; and (2) it treats elections as only one of the relevant parts of the political process. Noonan also distinguishes contributions from bribes (1984, 696–97); but the two characteristics he regards as critical—size and secrecy—are better interpreted as indicators of the more basic distinction made in the text. If a contribution is small relative not to the total contributions but to other contributions a candidate receives and if it is public (or if the pattern of which it is a part is made public), then the contribution could be more plausibly seen as support for the candidate, rather than an attempt to influence official conduct.

(28) This may be part of the rationale underlying the recent Supreme Court decision upholding a law that places limits on the ability of corporations to make independent expenditures on behalf of political candidates (*Austin v. Michigan Chamber of Commerce* 1990). Wealth accumulated by a corporation has "little or no correlation to the public's support for the corporation's political ideas" and therefore has "corrosive and distorting" effects on the political process (p. 1397). The idea is presumably that though the corporation is using the money to express substantive political views, the corporation's ability to do so does not derive from any substantive political support; its economic success ought not be translated so directly into political influence. See also Taylor 1991 and, more generally, Stark 1992.

(29) An example of such a standard—already followed by some members—would be a rule requiring separation of the fund-raising from other functions in the offices of members (see U.S. Senate 1991b, *Additional Views*, 102).

(30) A public official may act more directly than did the senators in this case.

For example, when inserting a tax break for a particular company or individual in legislation, a member is more plausibly regarded as the direct agent than is the Internal Revenue Service. However, the corruption may still count as largely mediated because the other elements of corruption (the gain and the gain-benefit connection) continue to be mediated through the political process.

(31) For a valuable analysis of the relation of deliberation specifically to problems of political finance, see Beitz 1989, 192–213.

(32) Montesquieu, who among traditional political theorists most explicitly discusses corruption in branches of government, writes that a state will "perish when its legislative power becomes more corrupt than its executive" (1949–51, vol. 2, p. 407). More generally, see his "Corruption of Principle in the Three Governments" (vol. 2, 349–66).

(33) For criticisms and further citations to the "functionalist" literature, see Rose-Ackerman 1978, 88–92; cf. Friedrich 1972, pt. 3.

References

Abramson, Jill, and David Rogers. 1991. "The Keating 535: Five Are on the Grill, but Other Lawmakers Help Big Donors, Too." *Wall Street Journal*, January 10.

Adams, James Ring. 1990. *The Big Fix: Inside the S&L Scandal*. New York: Wiley.

Aquinas, Thomas. 1972. *Summa Theologiae*. New York: McGraw-Hill.

Austin v. Michigan Chamber of Commerce. 1990. 110 S. Ct. 1391.

Banfield, Edward C. 1975. "Corruption as a Feature of Governmental Organization." *Journal of Law and Economics* 18:587–605.

Beitz, Charles. 1989. *Political Equality*. Princeton: Princeton University Press.

Berke, Richard L. 1991. "Cranston Rebuked by Ethics Panel." *New York Times*, November 21.

Cain, Bruce, John Ferejohn, and Morris Fiorina. 1987. *The Personal Vote: Constituency Service and Electoral Independence*. Cambridge: Harvard University Press.

CBS News/*New York Times*. 1991. Telephone interview, National sample of 1280 adults, October 5–7. (Roper Center for Public Opinion Research, University of Connecticut).

Cohen, Joshua. 1989. "Deliberation and Democratic Legitimacy." In *The Good Polity*, ed. Alan Hamlin and Philip Pettit. Oxford: Basil Blackwell.

Cohen, Joshua, and Joel Rogers. 1983. *On Democracy*. New York: Penguin.

Dahl, Robert A. 1989. *Democracy and Its Critics*. New Haven: Yale University Press.

DeNardo, James. 1980. "Turnout and the Vote: The Joke's on the Democrats." *American Political Science Review* 74:406–20.

Dobel, J. Patrick. 1978. "The Corruption of a State." *American Political Science Review* 72:958–73.

Douglas, Paul. 1952. *Ethics in Government*. Cambridge: Harvard University Press.

Downs, Anthony. 1957. *An Economic Theory of Democracy*. New York: Harper.

Driver, Julia. 1992. "Caesar's Wife: On the Moral Significance of Appearing Good." *Journal of Philosophy* 89:331–43.

Etzioni, Amitai. 1984. *Capital Corruption*. New York: Harcourt Brace Jovanovich.

Etzioni, Amitai. 1990/91. "The Keating Six?" *Responsive Community* 1:6–9.

Fenno, Richard. 1978. *Home Style: House Members in Their Districts.* Boston: Little, Brown.

Friedrich, Carl J. 1972. *The Pathology of Politics.* New York: Harper & Row.

Gottlieb, Stephen. 1989. "The Dilemma of Election Campaign Finance Reform." *Hofstra Law Review* 18:213–300.

Hamilton, Alexander, James Madison, and John Jay. 1961. *The Federalist Papers.* Ed. Jacob E. Cooke. Middletown, CT: Wesleyan University Press.

Heidenheimer, Arnold, Michael Johnston, and Victor T. LeVine, eds. 1989. *Political Corruption: A Handbook.* 2d ed. New Brunswick: Transaction.

Hugick, Larry. 1991. "Majority Disapproves of Congress." *Gallup Poll Monthly,* August, pp. 45–46.

Hugick, Larry, and Graham Hueber. 1991. "Pharmacists and Clergy Rate Highest for Honesty and Ethics." *Gallup Poll Monthly,* May, pp. 29–31.

Kappel, Brett G. 1989. "Judicial Restrictions on Improper Congressional Influence in Administrative Decision-Making: A Defense of the *Pillsbury* Doctrine." *Journal of Law and Politics* 6:135–71.

Larmore, Charles. 1987. *Patterns of Moral Complexity.* Cambridge: Cambridge University Press.

Lindblom, Charles. 1977. *Politics and Markets.* New York: Basic Books.

Lowenstein, Daniel H. 1985. "Political Bribery and the Intermediate Theory of Politics." *University of California, Los Angeles Law Review* 32:784–851.

Lowenstein, Daniel H. 1989. "On Campaign Finance Reform: The Root of All Evil Is Deeply Rooted." *Hofstra Law Review* 18:301–67.

McCormick v. U.S. 1991. 111 S.Ct. 1807.

McCubbins, Mathew D., Roger Noll, and Barry R. Weingast. 1987. "Administrative Procedures as Instruments of Political Control." *Journal of Law, Economics, and Organization* 3:243–77.

McCubbins, Mathew D., and Thomas Schwartz. 1984. "Congressional Oversight Overlooked: Police Patrols Versus Fire Alarms." *American Journal of Political Science* 28:165–79.

Manin, Bernard. 1987. "On Legitimacy and Political Deliberation." *Political Theory* 15:338–68.

Montesquieu, Baron de. 1949–51. *De l'esprit des lois.* In *Montesquieu: Oeuvres Complètes,* ed. Roger Caillois. Paris: Gallimard.

Morgan, Peter W. 1992. "The Appearance of Propriety: Ethics Reform and the Blifil Paradoxes." *Stanford Law Review* 44:593–621.

NBC News/*Wall Street Journal.* 1990. Telephone Interview, National sample of 1002 registered voters, December 8–11. (Roper Center for Public Opinion Research, University of Connecticut).

NBC News/*Wall Street Journal.* 1992. Telephone interview, National sample of 1001 registered voters, April 11–14. (Roper Center for Public Opinion Research, University of Connecticut).

Noonan, John T., Jr. 1984. *Bribes.* Berkeley: University of California Press.

Peters, John G., and Susan Welch. 1978. "Political Corruption in America: A Search for Definitions and a Theory." *American Political Science Review* 78:974–84.

Pizzo, Stephen, Mary Fricker, and Paul Moulo. 1989. *Inside Job: The Looting of America's Savings and Loans.* New York: McGraw-Hill.

Rawls, John. 1971. *A Theory of Justice.* Cambridge: Harvard University Press.

Richardson, Henry S. 1990. "Specifying Norms as a Way To Resolve Concrete Ethical Problems." *Philosophy and Public Affairs* 19:279–310.

Roberts, Robert N. 1985. "Lord, Protect Me from the Appearance of Wrongdoing." In *Public Personnel Policy*, ed. David H. Rosenbloom. Port Washington, N.Y.: Associated Faculty.

Rose-Ackerman, Susan. 1978. *Corruption: A Study in Political Economy*. New York: Academic.

Rosenberg, Morton, and Jack Maskell. 1990. "Congressional Intervention in the Administrative Process: Legal and Ethical Considerations." Washington: Congressional Research Service Report. 1–78.

Schumpeter, Joseph. 1962. *Capitalism, Socialism, and Democracy*. 3d ed. New York: Harper.

Sorauf, Frank J. 1992. *Inside Campaign Finance: Myths and Realities*. New Haven: Yale University Press.

Stark, Andrew. 1992. "Corporate Electoral Activity, Constitutional Discourse, and Conceptions of the Individual." *American Political Science Review* 86:626–37.

Taylor, Samuel M. 1991. "*Austin v. Michigan Chamber of Commerce*: Addressing a 'New Corruption' in Campaign Financing." *North Carolina Law Review* 69:1060–79.

Thompson, Dennis F. 1987. *Political Ethics and Public Office*. Cambridge: Harvard University Press.

Tucker, Harvey J., Arnold Vedlitz, and James DeNardo. 1986. "Controversy: Does Heavy Turnout Help Democrats in Presidential Elections?" *American Political Science Review* 80:1292–1304.

U.S. Senate. Select Committee on Ethics. 1991a. *Preliminary Inquiry into Allegations Regarding Senators Cranston, DeConcini, Glenn, McCain, and Riegle, and Lincoln Savings and Loan*. 101st Congress, 2d sess., 15 Nov. 1990–16 Jan. 1991.

U.S. Senate, Select Committee on Ethics. 1991b. *Investigation of Senator Alan Cranston Together with Additional Views*. 102d Congress, 1st sess., 20 Nov. 1991.

U.S. v. Brewster. 1977. 408 U.S. 521.

Wilkinson, Francis. 1991. "Rules of the Game: The Senate's Money Politics." *Rolling Stone*, August 8.

Wilson, James Q. 1974. "Corruption Is Not Always Scandalous." In *Theft of the City*, ed. John A. Gardiner and David J. Olson. Bloomington: Indiana University Press.

Yoder, Edwin M., Jr. 1991. "The Keating Five: Was It All in a Day's Work?" *Washington Post*, January 18.

Source: *American Political Science Review*, © 1993, American Political Science Association.

Reading 5–2: Karen Tumulty, Mark Thompson and Mike Allen, *How Many More Mike Browns Are Out There?*

It is often stated that the President of the United States is only as effective as the cabinet they lead. Accordingly, in the case of President George W. Bush, several of his former picks for senior executive posts have raised concerns about his efficacy in office. The following article highlights several of President Bush's selections for top officers within his Administration, including the now infamous Michael Brown (Brown served as Director of the Federal Emergency Management Agency during the Hurricane Katrina disaster). As you read this article, consider how and why each of these individuals was selected for their respective post, and how this relates to the broader issue of public corruption addressed within this chapter.

In presidential politics, the victor always gets the spoils, and chief among them is the vast warren of offices that make up the federal bureaucracy. Historically, the U.S. public has never paid much attention to the people the President chooses to sit behind those thousands of desks. A benign cronyism is more or less presumed, with old friends and big donors getting comfortable positions and impressive titles, and with few real consequences for the nation.

But then came Michael Brown. When President Bush's former point man on disasters was discovered to have more expertise about the rules of Arabian horse competition than about the management of a catastrophe, it was a reminder that the competence of government officials who are not household names can have a life or death impact. The Brown debacle has raised pointed questions about whether political connections, not qualifications, have helped an unusually high number of Bush appointees land vitally important jobs in the Federal Government.

The Bush Administration didn't invent cronyism; John F. Kennedy turned the Justice Department over to his brother, while Bill Clinton gave his most ambitious domestic policy initiative to his wife. Jimmy Carter made his old friend Bert Lance his budget director, only to see him hauled in front of the Senate to answer questions on his past banking practices in Georgia, and George H.W. Bush deposited so many friends at the Commerce Department that the agency was known internally as "Bush Gardens." The difference is that this Bush Administration had a plan from day one for remaking the bureaucracy, and has done so with greater success.

As far back as the Florida recount, soon-to-be Vice President Dick Cheney was poring over organizational charts of the government with an eye toward stocking it with people sympathetic to the incoming Administration. Clay Johnson III, Bush's former Yale roommate and the Administration's chief architect of personnel, recalls preparing for the inner circle's first trip from Austin, Texas, to Washington: "We were standing there getting ready to get on a plane, looking at each other like: Can you believe what we're getting ready to do?"

The Office of Personnel Management's Plum Book, published at the start of each presidential Administration, shows that there are more than 3,000 positions a President can fill without consideration for civil service rules. And Bush has gone further than most Presidents to put political stalwarts in some of the most important government jobs you've never heard of, and to give them genuine power over the bureaucracy. "These folks are really good at using the instruments of government to promote the President's political agenda," says Paul Light, a professor of public service at New York University and a well-known expert on the machinery of government. "And I think that takes you well into the gray zone where few Presidents have dared to go in the past. It's the coordination and centralization that's important here."

The White House makes no apologies for organizing government in a way that makes it easier to carry out Bush's agenda. Johnson says the centralization is "very intentional, and it starts with the people you pick . . . They're there to implement the President's priorities." Johnson asserts that appointees are chosen on merit, with political credentials used only as a tie breaker between qualified people. "Everybody knows somebody," he says. "Were they appointed because they knew somebody? No. What we focused on is: Does the government work, and can it be caused to work better and more responsibly? . . . We want the programs to work." But across the government, some experienced civil servants say they are being shut out of the decision making at their agencies. "It depresses people, right down to the level of a clerk-typist," says Leo Bosner, head of the Federal Emergency Management Agency's (FEMA's) largest union. "The senior to mid-level managers have really been pushed into a corner career-wise."

Some of the appointments are raising serious concerns in the agencies themselves and on Capitol Hill about the competence and independence of agencies that the country relies on to keep us safe, healthy and secure. Internal e-mail messages obtained by TIME show that scientists' drug-safety decisions at the Food and Drug Administration (FDA) are being second-guessed by a 33-year-old doctor turned stock picker. At the Office of Management and Budget, an ex-lobbyist with minimal purchasing experience oversaw $300 billion in spending, until his arrest last week. At the Department of Homeland Security, an agency the Administration initially resisted, a well-connected White House aide with minimal experience is poised to take over what many consider the single most crucial post in ensuring that terrorists do not enter the country again. And who is acting as watchdog at every federal agency? A corps of inspectors general who may be increasingly chosen more for their political credentials than their investigative ones.

Nowhere in the federal bureaucracy is it more important to insulate government experts from the influences of politics and special interests than at the Food and Drug Administration, the agency charged with assuring the safety of everything from new vaccines and dietary supplements to animal feed and hair dye. That is why many within the department, as well as in the broader scientific community, were startled when, in July, Scott Gottlieb was named deputy commissioner for medical and scientific affairs, one of three deputies in the agency's second-ranked post at FDA.

His official FDA biography notes that Gottlieb, 33, who got his medical degree at Mount Sinai School of Medicine, did a previous stint providing policy advice at the agency, as well as at the Centers for Medicare and Medicaid Services, and was a fellow at the American Enterprise Institute, a conservative think tank. What the bio omits is that his most recent job was as editor of a popular Wall Street newsletter, the Forbes/Gottlieb Medical Technology Investor, in which he offered such tips as "Three Biotech Stocks to Buy Now." In declaring Gottlieb a "noted authority" who had written more than 300 policy and medical articles, the biography neglects the fact that many of those articles criticized the FDA for being too slow to approve new drugs and too quick to issue warning letters when it suspects ones already on the market might be unsafe. FDA Commissioner Lester Crawford, who resigned suddenly and without explanation last Friday, wrote in response to e-mailed questions that Gottlieb is "talented and smart, and I am delighted to have been able to recruit him back to the agency to help me fulfill our public-health goals." But others, including Jimmy Carter—era FDA Commissioner Donald Kennedy, a former Stanford University president and now executive editor-in-chief of the journal Science, say Gottlieb breaks the mold of appointees at that level who are generally career FDA scientists or experts well known in their field. "The appointment comes out of nowhere. I've never seen anything like that," says Kennedy.

Gottlieb's financial ties to the drug industry were at one time quite extensive. Upon taking his new job, he recused himself for up to a year from any deliberations involving nine companies that are regulated by the FDA and "where a reasonable person would question my impartiality in the matter." Among them are Eli Lilly, Roche and Proctor & Gamble, according to his Aug. 5 "Disqualification Statement Regarding Former Clients," a copy of which was obtained by TIME. Gottlieb, though, insists that his role at the agency is limited to shaping broad policies, such as improving communication between the FDA, doctors and patients, and developing a strategy for dealing with pandemics of such diseases as flu, West Nile virus and SARS.

Would he ever be involved in determining whether an individual drug should be on the market? "Of course not," Gottlieb told *TIME*. "Not only wouldn't I be involved in that . . . But I would not be in a situation where I would be adjudicating the scientific or medical expertise of the [FDA] on a review matter. That's not my role. It's not my expertise. We defer to the career staff to make scientific and medical decisions."

Behind the scenes, however, Gottlieb has shown an interest in precisely those kinds of deliberations. One instance took place on Sept. 15, when the FDA decided to stop the trial of a drug for multiple sclerosis during which three people had developed an unusual disorder in which their bodies eliminated their blood platelets and one died of intra-cerebral bleeding as a result. In an e-mail obtained by *TIME*, Gottlieb speculated that the complication might have been the result of the disease and not the drug. "Just seems like an overreaction to place a clinical hold" on the trial, he wrote. An FDA scientist rejected his analysis and replied that the complication "seems very clearly a drug-related event." Two days prior, when word broke that the FDA had sent a "non-approvable" letter to Pfizer Inc., formally rejecting its Oporia drug for osteoporosis, senior officials at the FDA's Center for Drug Evaluation and Research received copies of an e-mail from Gottlieb expressing his surprise that what he thought would be a routine approval had been turned down. Gottlieb asked for an explanation.

Gottlieb defends his e-mails, which were circulated widely at the FDA. "Part of my job is to ask questions both so I understand how the agency works, and how it reaches its decisions," he told *TIME*. However, a scientist at the agency said they "really confirmed people's worst fears that he was only going to be happy if we were acting in a way that would make the pharmaceutical industry happy."

The Oporia decision gave Pfizer plenty of reason to be unhappy: the drug had been expected to produce $1 billion a year in sales for the company. Pfizer's stock fell 1.4% the day the rejection was announced. The FDA has not revealed why it rejected the drug, and Pfizer has said it is "considering various courses of action" that might resuscitate its application for approval.

Health experts note that Gottlieb's appointment comes at a time of increased tension between the agency and drug companies, which are concerned that new drugs will have a more difficult time making it onto the market in the wake of the type of safety problems that persuaded Merck to pull its best-selling painkiller Vioxx from the market last year. The agency's independence has also come under question, most recently with its decision last month to prevent the emergency contraceptive known as Plan B from being sold over the counter, after an FDA advisory panel recommended it could be. That Gottlieb sits at the second tier of the agency, critics say, sends anything but a reassuring signal.

David Safavian didn't have much hands-on experience in government contracting when the Bush Administration tapped him in 2003 to be its chief procurement officer. A law-school internship helping the Pentagon buy helicopters was about the extent of it. Yet as administrator of the Office of Federal Procurement Policy, Safavian, 38, was placed in charge of the $300 billion the government spends each year on everything from paper clips to nuclear submarines, as well as the $62 billion already earmarked for Hurricane Katrina recovery efforts. It was his job to ensure that the government got the most for its money and that competition for federal contracts—among companies as well as between government workers and private contractors—was fair. It was his job until he resigned on Sept. 16 and was subsequently arrested and charged with lying and obstructing a criminal investigation into Republican lobbyist Jack Abramoff's dealings with the Federal Government.

Safavian spent the bulk of his pregovernment career as a lobbyist, and his nomination to a top oversight position stunned the tightly knit federal procurement community. A dozen procurement experts interviewed by TIME said he was the most unqualified person to hold the job since its creation in 1974. Most of those who held the post before Safavian were well-versed in the arcane world of federal contracts. "Safavian is a good example of a person who had great party credentials but no substantive credentials," says Danielle Brian, executive director of the Project on Government Oversight, a nonprofit

Washington watchdog group. "It's one of the most powerful positions in terms of impacting what the government does, and the kind of job—like FEMA director—that needs to be filled by a professional." Nevertheless, Safavian's April 2004 confirmation hearing before the Senate Governmental Affairs Committee (attended by only five of the panel's 17 members) lasted just 67 minutes, and not a single question was asked about his qualifications.

The committee did hold up Safavian's confirmation for a year, in part because of concerns about work his lobbying firm, Janus-Merritt Strategies, had done that he was required to divulge to the panel but failed to. The firm's filings showed that it represented two men suspected of links to terrorism (Safavian said one of the men was "erroneously listed," and the other's omission was an "inadvertent error") as well as two suspect African regimes. Ultimately, the committee and the full Senate unanimously approved Safavian for the post.

His political clout, federal procurement experts say privately, came from his late-1990s lobbying partnership with Grover Norquist, now head of Americans for Tax Reform and a close ally of the Bush Administration. Norquist is an antitax advocate who once famously declared that his goal was to shrink the Federal Government so he could "drag it into the bathroom and drown it in the bathtub." As the U.S. procurement czar, Safavian was pushing in that direction by seeking to shift government work to private contractors, contending it was cheaper. Federal procurement insiders say his relationship with Norquist gave Safavian the edge in snaring the procurement post. But Norquist has "no memory" of urging the Administration to put Safavian in the post, says an associate speaking on Norquist's behalf. A White House official said Norquist "didn't influence the decision." Clay Johnson, who was designated by the White House to answer all of *TIME*'s questions about administration staffing issues and who oversaw the procurement post, says Safavian was "by far the most qualified person" for the job. Perhaps it also didn't hurt that Safavian's wife Jennifer works as a lawyer for the House Government Reform Committee, which oversees federal contracting.

In addition, Safavian had worked at a law firm in the mid-'90s with Jack Abramoff, one of the capital's highest-paid lobbyists, a top G.O.P. fund raiser and a close friend of House majority leader Tom DeLay. Abramoff was indicted last month on unrelated fraud and conspiracy charges. In 2002, Abramoff invited Safavian on a weeklong golf outing to Scotland's famed St. Andrews course (as Abramoff had done with DeLay in 2000). Seven months after the trip, an anonymous call to a government hotline said lobbyists had picked up the tab for the jaunt. That wasn't true; Safavian paid $3,100 for the trip. But the government alleges that he lied when he repeatedly told investigators that Abramoff had no business dealings with the General Services Administration, where Safavian worked at the time. Prosecutors alleged last week, however, that Safavian worked closely with Abramoff—identified only as "Lobbyist A" in the criminal complaint against Safavian—to give Abramoff an inside track in his efforts to acquire control of two pieces of federal property in the

Washington area. Safavian, who is free without bail, declined to be interviewed for this story. His attorney, Barbara Van Gelder, said the government is trying to pressure her client to help in its probe of Abramoff. "This is a creative use of the criminal code to secure his cooperation," she said.

Three days after the Sept. 12 resignation of FEMA's Michael Brown, Julie Myers, the Bush Administration's nominee to head Immigration and Customs Enforcement (ICE) came before the Senate Homeland Security and Governmental Affairs Committee. The session did not go well. "I think we ought to have a meeting with [Homeland Security Secretary] Mike Chertoff," Ohio Republican George Voinovich told Myers. "I'd really like to have him spend some time with us, telling us personally why he thinks you're qualified for the job. Because based on the resume, I don't think you are."

Immigration and Customs Enforcement is one of 22 agencies operating under the umbrella of the Department of Homeland Security, but its function goes to the heart of why the department was created: to prevent terrorists from slipping into the U.S. If that weren't enough, the head of ICE must also contend with money launderers, drug smugglers, illegal-arms merchants and the vast responsibility that comes with managing 20,000 government employees and a $4 billion budget. Expectations were high that whoever was appointed to fill the job would be, in the words of Michael Greenberger, head of the University of Maryland's Center for Health and Homeland Security, "a very high-powered, well-recognized intelligence manager."

Instead the Administration nominated Myers, 36, currently a special assistant handling personnel issues for Bush. She has experience in law-enforcement management, including jobs in the White House and the Commerce, Justice and Treasury departments, but she barely meets the five-year minimum required by law. Her most significant responsibility has been as Assistant Secretary for Export Enforcement at the Commerce Department, where, she told Senators, she supervised 170 employees and a $25 million budget.

Myers may appear short on qualifications, but she has plenty of connections. She worked briefly for Chertoff as his chief of staff at the Justice Department's criminal division, and two days after her hearing, she married Chertoff's current chief of staff, John Wood. Her uncle is Air Force General Richard Myers, the outgoing Chairman of the Joint Chiefs of Staff. Julie Myers was on her honeymoon last week and was unavailable to comment on the questions about her qualifications raised by the Senate. A representative referred *TIME* to people who had worked with her, one of whom was Stuart Levey, the Treasury Department's Under Secretary for Terrorism and Financial Crime. "She was great, and she impressed everyone around her in all these jobs," he said. "She's very efficient, and she's assertive and strong and smart, and I think she's wonderful."

To critics, Myers' appointment is a symptom of deeper ills in the Homeland Security Department, a huge new bureaucracy that the Bush Administration resisted creating. Among those problems, they say, is a tendency on the part of the Administration's political appointees to discard in-house expertise, particularly when it could lead to additional government regulation of industry. For instance, when Congress passed the intelligence reform bill last year, it gave the Transportation Security Administration (TSA) a deadline of April 1, 2005, to come up with plans to assess the threat to various forms of shipping and transportation—including rail, mass transit, highways and pipelines—and make specific proposals for strengthening security. Two former high-ranking Homeland Security officials tell TIME that the plans were nearly complete and had been put into thick binders in early April for final review when Deputy Secretary Michael Jackson abruptly reassigned that responsibility to the agency's policy shop. Jackson was worried that presenting Congress with such detailed proposals would only invite it to return later and demand to know why Homeland Security had not carried them out. "If we put this out there, this is what we're going to be held to," says one of the two officials, characterizing Jackson's stance. Nearly six months after Congress's deadline, in the wake of the summer's subway bombings in London, TSA spokeswoman Amy Von Walter says the agency is in the process of declassifying the document and expects to post a short summary on its website soon.

In the meantime, Myers' nomination could be in trouble. Voinovich says his concerns were satisfied after a 35-minute call with Chertoff, in which the Homeland Security Secretary argued forcefully on Myers' behalf. But other senators are raising questions, and Democrats have seized on Myers' appointment as an example of the Bush Administration's preference for political allies over experience.

The Post-Watergate law creating the position of inspector general (IG) states that the federal watchdogs must be hired "without regard to political affiliation," on the basis of their ability in such disciplines as accounting, auditing and investigating. It may not sound like the most exciting job, but the 57 inspectors general in the Federal Government can be the last line of defense against fraud and abuse. Because their primary duty is to ask nosy questions, their independence is crucial.

But critics say some of the Bush IGs have been too cozy with the Administration. "The IGs have become more political over the years, and it seems to have accelerated," said A. Ernest Fitzgerald, who has been battling the Defense Department since his 1969 discovery of $2 billion in cost overruns on a cargo plane, and who, at 79, still works as a civilian Air Force manager. A study by Representative Henry Waxman of California, the top Democrat on the House Government Reform Committee, found that more than 60% of the IGs nominated by the Bush Administration had political experience and less than 20% had auditing experience—almost the obverse of those measures during the Clinton Administration. About half the current IGs are holdovers from Clinton.

Johnson says political connections may be a thumb on the scale between two candidates with equal credentials, but rarely are they the overriding factor in a personnel decision. Speaking of all such appointments, not just the IGs, he said, "I am aware of one or two situations where politics carried the day and the person was not in the job a year later."

Still, several of the President's IGs fit comfortably into the friends-and-family category. Until recently, the most famous Bush inspector general was Janet Rehnquist, a daughter of the late Chief Justice. Rehnquist had been a lawyer for the Senate Permanent Subcommittee on Investigations and worked in the counsel's office during George H.W. Bush's presidency before becoming an IG at the Department of Health and Human Services. In that sense, she was qualified for the job. But a scathing report by the Government Accountability Office asserted that she had "created the perception that she lacked appropriate independence in certain situations" and had "compromised her ability to serve as an effective leader." Rehnquist also faced questions about travel that included sightseeing and free time, her decision to delay an audit of the Florida pension system at the request of the President's brother, Governor Jeb Bush of Florida, and the unauthorized gun she kept in her office. She resigned in June 2003 ahead of the report.

Three weeks ago, however, Joseph Schmitz supplanted Rehnquist as the most notorious Bush IG. Schmitz, who worked as an aide to former Reagan Administration Attorney General Ed Meese and whose father John was a Republican Congressman from Orange County, Calif., quit his post at the Pentagon following complaints from Senate Finance Committee chairman Charles Grassley, Republican of Iowa. In particular, Grassley questioned Schmitz's acceptance of a trip to South Korea, paid for in part by a former lobbying client, according to Senate staff members and public lobbying records, and Schmitz's use of eight tickets to a Washington Nationals baseball game. But those issues aren't the ones that led to questions about his independence from the White House. Those concerns came to light after Schmitz chose to show the White House his department's final report on a multiyear investigation into the Air Force's plan to lease air-refueling tankers from Boeing for much more than it would have cost to buy them. After two weeks of talks with the Administration, Schmitz agreed to black out the names of senior White House officials who appeared to have played a role in pushing and approving what turned out to be a controversial procurement arrangement. Schmitz ultimately sent the report to Capitol Hill, but Senators are irked that they have not yet received an original, unredacted copy.

Congressional aides said they are still scratching their heads about how Schmitz got his job. He now works for the parent company of Blackwater USA, a military contractor that, in his old job, he might have been responsible for investigating.

WHO IS SHE? JULIE MYERS A 1994 graduate of Cornell Law school, Myers, 36, has held a variety of posts in the Bush Administration, including Deputy Assistant Treasury Secretary in charge of money laundering and financial crimes. She barely has the five years of experience in law-enforcement management required by law to head this agency.

WHOM DOES SHE KNOW? *Myers' husband is Homeland Security Secretary Michael Chertoff's chief of staff *She is the niece of Richard Myers, Chairman of the Joint Chiefs of Staff *She was part of Ken Starr's team

WHAT WOULD SHE DO? As head of Immigration and Customs Enforcement (ICE), Myers would be charged with keeping terrorists from crossing the border and would report directly to Chertoff.

* ICE has 20,000 employees and a budget of roughly $4 Billion. Myers previously managed 170 people and $25 million annually.
* HER NOMINATION appears on track, although a Senate committee questioned her qualifications.

WHO IS HE? DAVID SAFAVIAN The former lobbyist also worked as a congressional aide and for the General Services Administration before Bush picked him to oversee all federal procurement. An Iranian American, Safavian has served on the board of the Islamic Institute and has lobbied on its behalf.

WHOM DOES HE KNOW? *White House ally and tax-cut advocate Grover Norquist is a former lobbying partner *Representative Tom Davis employs Safavian's wife and is leading a probe of the response to Katrina

WHAT DID HE DO? As chief procurement officer, Safavian oversaw $300 billion in federal money and an additional $62 billion approved for Hurricane Katrina relief.

* PROCUREMENT EXPERTS were dismayed by his inexperience and eagerness to hand out large contracts to the private sector.
* TWO WEEKS AGO, Safavian resigned and was then arrested for allegedly lying to government investigators about his dealings with lobbyist Jack Abramoff.

WHO IS HE? SCOTT GOTTLIEB A 33-year-old doctor, Gottlieb handicapped health stocks and blogged as fdainsider.com before returning to the Food and Drug Administration in July. In the past, he has been a fierce critic of the agency he now helps run, complaining that it is too slow to approve new medicines and too quick to issue warnings about drugs on the market.

WHOM DOES HE KNOW? As a fellow at the conservative American Enterprise Institute, Gottlieb befriended future FDA chief Mark McLellan, left, brother of White House spokesman Scott McLellan

WHAT DOES HE DO? As deputy commissioner for medical and scientific affairs, Gottlieb crafts broad policies, such as designing ways to improve doctor–patient communication.

* INTERNAL FDA E-MAILS show Gottlieb has second-guessed agency scientists on drug-safety questions at least twice in his first weeks on the job.
* HIS APPOINTMENT comes at a time of growing concern over the safety of drugs and the independence of the Federal Government's most important consumer-protection agency.

> THE PEOPLE IN CHARGE ARE POLITICAL AND INEXPERIENCED ... THEIR WATCHDOGS ARE ALSO POLITICAL AND INEXPERIENCED.
>
> REP. HENRY WAXMAN

> I AM AWARE OF ... SITUATIONS WHERE POLITICS CARRIED THE DAY AND THE PERSON WAS NOT IN THE JOB A YEAR LATER.
>
> CLAY JOHNSON III

Source: *Time Magazine* © 2005 Time Inc.

Thinking Activities

1. Imagine that you have the ability to travel through time, up to and including returning to the year 1900. If you were looking to make the greatest impact on corruption control, in which presidential administration would you wish to serve? Why?
2. Using the World Wide Web, go to URL: http://www.ignet.gov and select an Inspector General office that interests you. Research the role and function of this OIG. Would you consider working for this agency? In what capacity would you wish to serve (e.g., criminal investigator, auditor, program analyst, etc.)?
3. Rent any of the following films from your local DVD store: *All the President's Men, Nixon, Wag the Dog,* or *War, Inc.* While watching the movie, consider the prevailing issues of corruption, as well as what investigative techniques or policies would prove most successful in combating these forms of corruption.

6 White-Collar Crime Theory
Origins and Early Developments

Introduction

As you read the first five chapters of this text, you may have been surprised that we have focused thus far on the practices and processes of combating white-collar crime, rather than the theories and typologies of white-collar criminality. Indeed, from the basics of currency counterfeiting and identity theft, to personal dishonesty and corruption control, this book has not yet examined the more academic aspects of the study of white-collar crime.

However, such understanding is critical to a course in white-collar crime or corruption, whether your interests sway you towards a career in law enforcement, or your desire is to conduct scholarly research in a specific area such as elite deviance or individual motivations for engaging in acts of fraud, forgery, embezzlement, identity theft, or currency counterfeiting.

The aim of this chapter is to provide you with a basic understanding of the early white-collar crime theories and theorists. Accordingly, we begin with a discussion of various typologies that pertain to white-collar crimes throughout history. Immediately following, you will be exposed to various positivist perspectives of white-collar criminality, ranging from Robert K. Merton's (1938) social strain theory[1] and Edwin Sutherland's complementary theories of differential association[2] (1947) and (1949) white-collar criminality,[3] to the subsequent research of Donald Cressey[4] and Marshall Clinard.[5] Lastly, the concluding section of this chapter sets the stage for understanding research conducted over the past 30 years by Herbert Edelhertz,[6] M.D. Ermann and R.J. Lundman,[7] Diane Vaughan,[8] Frank Hagan,[9] and David Simon[10] that will be explored in Chapter 7 of this text book.

White-Collar Crimes throughout History

Many modern criminologists attribute the origins of the study of white-collar criminality to Sutherland's address before the American Sociological

Society in Philadelphia in December of 1939.[11] However, historical evidence of the public's intolerance for consumption-oriented offenses dates back to the time of the Old Testament, circa 930 BCE.[12] As we noted in the Chapter 1 of this book, Proverbs (11:26) admonishes, "People curse the man who hoards grain, but blessing crowns him who is willing to sell" (New International Version). Roger Magnuson notes that since the New Testament period (c. 7 CE), societies have held contempt for those individuals who consume the greatest share of goods and services.[13] Such distrust of those who would seek to excessively consume goods has permeated nearly all of recorded history. Accordingly, the offense of over-consumption—or more accurately, consumption only by a select few while goods and services are withheld from the general populace—has been part of Western criminal law for more than 500 years. You may recall that the English monarchical term for these activities was *forestalling* (i.e., deliberately withholding goods or services from the marketplace to increase demand and inflate prices). Such actions were the predecessors of modern-day statutes such as the Sherman Antitrust Act[14] and the Robinson-Patman Act, designed to protect consumers from monopolies and price gouging). From Immanuel Kant to Karl Marx, philosophers have intensely debated the relationship between one's level of consumption, and his or her culpability and punishment for excessive use of resources.

The quality of the goods and services to be consumed by the populace has also been of great concern throughout history. In Chapter 1, we provided you with the origins of terms such as "pig in a poke," and "the cat's out of the bag". However, as we previously discussed at the onset of this text, long before consumers were being cheated in the marketplaces of medieval England, Roman artisans often copied Greek sculptures. Counterfeit coins have been found dating back to the reign of King Gyges of Lydia around 648 BCE. Often, these copies were passed to unsuspecting merchants or buyers who assumed that they were genuine. In addition to artwork and currency, items with real value, such as deeds to property or identity documents, were also often copied or reproduced. The word originally used to describe these acts accordingly was termed *forgery*—which stems from the French word *forger*, meaning to make or fabricate. The Western legal tradition refers to such misrepresentations as *fraud*, or *theft by deception* (see Chapter 8). Fraudulent coins have been uncovered in the collections of French art patrons dating back to the thirteenth and fourteenth centuries. Well-respected Italian artists including Giovanni Cavino and Pirro Ligorio were considered experts in the forging of coins during the sixteenth century. More recently, by the time of the American Civil War in 1861, nearly one-third of the currency and treasury obligations in general circulation was counterfeit.

Should We Simply Call it "Greedy" Crime? A Look at Conspicuous Consumption and Strain Theory

If you asked your friends why some people are inclined to engage in acts of white-collar criminality while others are not, they would probably respond in one word: greed. Connecting crime to greed is certainly not a new concept, as evidenced by the previous discussion to the Biblical and British monarchial notion of forestalling. Moreover, greed and corruption are frequently associated, as explored in Chapters 3 through 5 of this book.

Some scholars relate the concept of personal greed to the broader social construct of materialism or consumerism.[15] One such theorist was Thorstein Veblen (1857–1929). Veblen served as a professor of political economics at several colleges including the University of Chicago, Stanford, and the University of Missouri. He was also a teacher of prominent criminologist Edwin Sutherland, as will be discussed later in this chapter. Veblen's most widely read work, *The Theory of the Leisure Class*, first published in 1899,

Exhibit 6.1 Thorstein Veblen, a prominent scholar and author of the Theory of the Leisure Class *was an important role model for Edwin Sutherland, the father of the Theory of White-Collar Criminality. Veblen's concept of "conspicuous consumption" and the "status treadmill" were instrumental in the social crime theories during the period from the 1930s through the 1960s.*

was a scholarly and satirical examination of the American and Western European class systems. However, it is not his examination of social class, but rather his insights into the spending and purchasing patterns of the middle and upper strata of society (Veblen, [1912] 1994, pp. 43–62) that provide us with a fundamental understanding of the economic concept of *consumerism*. Specifically, Veblen notes that

> throughout the entire evolution of conspicuous expenditure, whether of goods or of services or human life, runs the obvious implication that in order to effectually mend the consumer's good fame it must be an expenditure of superfluities. In order to be reputable it must be wasteful. No merit would accrue from the consumption of the base necessities of life.[16]

Similarly, Robert K. Merton's (1910–2003) Theory of Social Strain (1938) concludes that strain (also known as *anomie*) is "a form of social chaos, due to the imbalance between the approved goals of society and the legitimate means of attaining them."[17] Merton categorized his theory into five "reactions" to the gap between goals and means.[18] These five reactions are: *conformity, innovation, ritualism, retreatism,* and *rebellion.* According

Exhibit 6.2　Robert K. Merton and his Theory of Social Anomie (1938) formed the foundation for many future scholars in their quest to understand why people engage in illegal acts such as fraud, forgery, and embezzlement.

to Merton's theory, most people *conform* to societal goals, and use legitimate means to achieve them (e.g., obtaining an education, working hard, etc.). However, some people, while accepting societal goals, reject legitimate means of obtaining them and turn to *innovation*, such as deviant or illicit means.[19] *Ritualism* refers to the belief that one will never actually be able to meet the goals set by society, but he or she will continue to embrace legitimate means in their daily lives (e.g., hard work and adherence to social norms.[20] Those persons who engage in *retreatism* reject both the goals set forth by society and the institutionalized means to achieve them. Lastly, *rebellion* refers to replacing the existing social order with a new socio-economic structure.

Both Veblen and Merton bridge the gap between the positivist and social constructionist perspectives of greed, noting that it is the response behavior of the individual functioning within his or her own group that is of importance. Merton attests that the status-based rationale for consumerism does "not fully account for the prevailing patterns of consumption."[21] In other words, there must be some *positivist* element that motivates people from all walks of life to want more tangible goods and services, even if obtaining such items can only be done through illegitimate means. It is the research of Edwin Sutherland that explores this topic.

Sutherland, Differential Association and White-Collar Crime

As a former student of Veblen, Sutherland's initial efforts differ somewhat from his teacher's economic concept of *consumerism*. While Sutherland was interested in issues of social class and the nature of capitalist societies, his work focused less on social class than either Veblen or Merton, and instead forged new directions in the positivist perspective with his publication of the Theory of Differential Association in 1947. Summarized by West (1967) in his book *The Young Offender*, Sutherland's theory of differential association essentially states "young people develop into criminals by learning wrongful ways from bad companions, and by seeing powerful and successful adults breaking the law."[22] This theory was groundbreaking at the time of its presentation, because many criminologists had only recently progressed from the concept of the *physical* "bad seed" (i.e., certain individuals were predisposed to commit crimes based on intrinsic, biological factors as noted in the works of late nineteenth-century researchers such as Enrico Ferri and Raffaele Garafolo), to the *psychological* "bad seed" (e.g., Freudian theories of psychoanalysis.[23] Indeed, much of the research conducted prior to Merton and Sutherland had collectively been termed "a turgid mass of stale metaphysics, dark sayings, random historical illusions, and mawkish [*sic*] ethical raptures."[24] Initially published in his text *Criminology* in 1934, Sutherland further refined his theory in 1939, and ultimately expanded it into a nine-point statement in 1947. These nine points are as follows:

1. Criminal behavior is learned.
2. Criminal behavior is learned in interaction with other persons in a process of communication.
3. The principal part of criminal behavior occurs within personal intimate groups.
4. Learning includes the techniques of the crime and the specific motives, drives, and rationalizations.
5. The group's definitions and perceptions of legal codes influence the individuals' adherence to, or violation of these codes.
6. Delinquency occurs when attitudes and justifications for violating these legal codes outweigh adherence to them.
7. Differential association may vary in frequency, duration, priority, and intensity.
8. The process of learning criminal behavior involves all of the mechanisms that are employed in any other form of learning.
9. Criminal behavior is not explained simply by one's needs and values since non-criminal behavior is also an expression of these same needs and values.[25]

At this point in the chapter, you might wonder how Sutherland made the leap from thinking that criminal behavior is learned (differential association) to his later theory of white-collar criminality. In reality, the two theories are connected.

If criminal behavior is learned, and this learning takes place within intimate personal groups (differential association), wouldn't the wealthiest members of society be just as likely to learn about illicit activity as those persons at the lowest rung of the socioeconomic ladder? It was Sutherland's contention that white-collar crime was no less than an epidemic in American society, fueled by an unholy alliance between businesses and politicians.[26] He noted, "Persons of the upper socioeconomic class engage in much criminal behavior and this criminal behavior differs from the criminal behavior of the lower socioeconomic class,"[27] predominantly due to variations in the judicial or administrative treatment of white-collar offenders versus street offenders. Sutherland believed that the act of simply conducting business-as-usual could itself be construed as a corrupt practice. He further asserted that prosecution of white-collar offenders was rare, because of their power and positions in American society, as well as a perceived apathy on the part of the American public with respect to the commission of acts of embezzlement and other financial crimes. This notion of unequal treatment of offenders due to their socioeconomic status developed into a separate area of study in the 1960s and 1970s, and continues to remain controversial today.

Despite his comments on unequal treatment of offenders due to social class, Sutherland's theory was *not* a social constructionist theory because of its inextricable links to his earlier theory of differential association. Similarly, Merton and Richard Cloward and Lloyd Ohlin's (1960) version of strain theory held that the frustrated goal of obtaining wealth leads to strain;[28] therefore, strain is not exclusive to a specific social class. Each of these theories is also consistent with scholar Stanton Wheeler's later research, which found that normally, the utility (i.e., usefulness of a product) increases nearly logarithmically with consumption because buyers reach a point at which they derive little or any additional benefit from a product. This is referred to as the point of diminishing returns. Yet within American society, Wheeler found that consumers at a variety of levels of the socioeconomic status spectrum never experience a point of diminishing return (i.e., as consumption increases, utility also increases). Their motivation is not necessarily one of greed, "but rather fear of falling, of losing what they have worked so hard to gain."[29]

In short, referring to your friends' earlier comments that white-collar crime is essentially all about greed, this contention is only partly correct. White-collar crime is also about losing status—both for ourselves and our families. But what if we don't consider ourselves greedy? What if those practices that we engage in to protect our status are not even illegal? Is it still necessary to revise our existing economic system to make it fairer for everyone?

Tappan's Response to Sutherland

It might surprise you to learn that despite the strife caused in the 1930s by massive unemployment, food shortages, and political unrest, many Americans, including some at the lowest socioeconomic level, were not in favor of reexamining America's capitalistic nature, perhaps because of the commonality of their shared culture and well-established identity.[30] Moreover, for those members of the elite class who led privileged lives free from the hardships faced by the working poor and underclass, the thought of change was not comforting.[31]

Sutherland's assertion that crime was rampant within—but not exclusive to—the highest social stratum was deemed personally offensive to many of this group's members. Paul Tappan, an attorney and sociologist critical of Sutherland's theory, quipped that suspicions over the manner in which professionals conducted their business had reached the point at which one person might ask another, "What crooked practices are found in your occupation?" at a dinner party or cocktail reception.[32]

As an attorney, Tappan believed that one should not be labeled as a criminal (even as a "white-collar" criminal) without being afforded proper criminal procedure, resulting in a conviction in a court of law. He also felt that in order to be a criminal, one must think of oneself as a criminal. Central to Tappan's argument was his contention that there were a variety of business practices that might be ethically questionable, but were not illegal. For example, is a businesswoman a criminal if she, out of greed, business acumen, or competitive motivations, breaches a trust with her customers, keeps wages down, or undercuts the prices of her fellow merchants?[33] In response, Sutherland commented that just because an offender is not prosecuted does not mean that a crime has not taken place. Moreover, very few offenders actually consider their actions to be "criminal," especially those who, as Steven Messner and Richard Rosenfeld in their theory of *institutional anomie*[34] noted, might justify their participation in financial crimes because of inequities within America's economic "system."[35] Michael Benson's (1990) study of labeling and stigmatization of white-collar criminal offenders[36] further supports this argument by concluding that even those persons who have been apprehended, tried, and convicted for financially-driven crimes rarely feel contrite for their actions; but rather, the institutional "shaming" of such persons "provokes anger and resentment as offenders attempt to maintain a morally acceptable view of self."[37]

White-Collar Criminality: Motivations and Offender Rationalization

Thus far, this chapter has explored the history of white-collar crimes dating back to 930 BCE with an emphasis on forestalling, forgery, and theft by deception. The techniques employed in the commission of many modern-day equivalent offenses were discussed in Chapter 2 of this book, and the laws and statutes themselves will be explained in Chapter 8. You have also been provided with an overview of Veblen's concept of *consumerism*, Merton's *social strain* theory, and Sutherland's theories of *differential association* and *white-collar criminality*, respectively. There have been some common themes throughout this brief discussion, such as the relationship between social learning, behavioral response, and the desire for goods and services even at the wealthiest levels of American society. What has not been discussed is *why* people commit white-collar crimes. Researcher Donald Cressey believed that there are clear-cut motivations for those who would engage in such activities, and that this behavior is situational.

Cressey initially served as one of Edwin Sutherland's research assistants.

However, he strived to clarify the technical elements of Sutherland's theories, particularly his theory of *differential association*. In 1953, Cressey published a study entitled *Other People's Money*,[38] which examined the characteristics of embezzlers serving sentences in federal penitentiaries. Essentially, he concluded that three circumstances needed to exist if an act of embezzlement was to occur.[39] First, the offender must be in a situation that could not be corrected through conventional means such as borrowing money from friends, relatives, a financial institution, or selling items with collateral value. Second, the offender must have the knowledge, skills, and ability to commit the act. For example, if he or she wished to transfer funds from a bank's central server to an offshore account in the Cayman Islands, the offender would need requisite access codes, a terminal and modem capable of performing the transaction, and proficiency in the use of the various software applications involved in the transfer of funds from the bank's system to a remote account. Lastly, Cressey believed that the offender must create a "suitable rationalization to 'adjust' the contradiction between their actions and the normative standards of society."[40] Rationalization may extend beyond acts of embezzlement. For example, Joseph T. Wells (1992) contends "antitrust violators usually maintain they are seeking to stabilize an out-of-control price situation when they conspire to fix prices."[41] Similarly, Neal Shover (1998) notes that one's propensity to engage in an act of white-collar criminality may stem from a personal or external pressure to be successful.[42]

In addition to Cressey's research into the motivating factors for committing acts of embezzlement, noted scholars including Marshall Clinard[43], Frank Hartung,[44] Ernest Burgess,[45] Donald Newman,[46] and Richard Quinney[47] examined issues of white-collar criminality from both positivist and social-constructionist perspectives. For example, Clinard's study of World War II-era black marketeers questioned whether wartime activities such as buying and selling restricted or rationed goods could really be considered "white-collar" crimes. He found specific characteristics for those persons engaged in selling on the Black Market. These traits included "egocentricity, emotional insecurity, and feelings of personal inadequacy."[48] Hartung's examination of the meat industry during this same period wrestled with the question of criminality, and, in what appears to be shades of Tappan, drew Burgess' response that "persons violating regulatory laws, such as black marketers, could not be regarded as criminals because they did not so view themselves and were not so viewed by the public."[49]

Donald Newman[50] and Richard Quinney[51] further expanded upon the technical definition of white-collar criminality by asserting that the context (i.e., the offender's occupation) is central to the discussion of whether or not a white-collar crime has occurred. Quinney believed that the definition of white-collar crime was flawed, and he preferred to examine such offenses through "the dichotomy of corporate and occupational crime."[52] Regardless of each of these scholars' specific definitions of white-collar criminality, it is undeniable that each played a vital role in the ultimate integration of the term "white-collar crime" into the average American's vocabulary.

Blacklisting and the Doldrums of White-Collar Crime Research

Unfortunately, the momentum of Sutherland, Cressey, *et al.* that had erupted during the late 1940s and early 1950s was all but halted by the early 1960s. The rise of McCarthyism prompted many criminologists to explore other areas of criminal research that were not as markedly tied to the capitalist system, such as juvenile delinquency and gang violence.[53] Academicians feared being labeled as "communists" and losing critical research funding (and perhaps even their livelihoods). While events such as the Vietnam Conflict, the Black Power movement, and Watergate served to reawaken research interests in topics related to social and economic inequality,[54] we would argue that, with few exceptions, the research base for post-McCarthy era white-collar crime scholarship has proved far less controversial than the uproar caused by Sutherland in his 1939 speech before the American Sociological Society.

It is our belief that the modern era in white-collar crime research has shifted from efforts to generalize characteristics of the offender to exploring the outcomes of committing such acts. Interestingly, Robert K. Merton accurately predicted this trend more than 40 years ago.[55]

Feminist Theory and the Role of Women in White-Collar Crime

As mentioned earlier in this chapter, Marshall Clinard's (1952) study of the characteristics of black marketeers[56] and Donald Cressey's (1953) research into the motivations and rationalizations of embezzlers[57] were important milestones in helping us to understand the characteristics of white-collar criminals. However, since their work in the late 1940s and early 1950s, very little academic research has been produced that focuses on the *positivist* perspective of fraud, forgery, embezzlement, counterfeiting, and the operation of illegal markets. Many academicians have instead opted to focus on grouping white-collar crimes into the broad categories of occupational crime and corporate (or organizational) crime. However, there are a small number of researchers who remain committed to connecting the "microlevels" and "macrolevels" of behavior and societal influences as

David Friedrichs refers to them.[58] Such is the case with the study of white-collar crime within the larger arena of feministic theory.

Meda Chesney-Lind, one of the preeminent scholars in the social constructionist field of critical-feminist theory, has devoted considerable time and effort studying trends in both violent and non-violent crimes committed by women. Her findings suggest that Freda Adler's "liberation hypothesis," (1975) which posited that as women moved into more prominent socio-economic roles of American society and assumed more "traditionally male" positions, their participation in criminal activity would also increase, has not proven accurate.[59] Rather, Chesney-Lind's research suggests that no dramatic increase in violent or non-violent crime among women during the period has occurred in the past twenty years.[60] While embezzlement increased by 40.8 percent from 1990–2000, dollar amounts among women's cases were relatively low when compared with their male counterparts. This research is also supported by Kathleen Daly's (1989) study pertaining to the role of gender in white-collar crimes such as embezzlement, postal fraud, credit fraud, and false claims.[61] Important among her findings was the fact that women in the study were more prone to commit offenses individually, as opposed to male offenders, who worked in groups.[62]

Ngaire Naffine attributes much of the increase in arrest rates for non-violent, female offenders to increased prosecution of petty offenses such as shoplifting, check forgery, etc. Her analysis did not find any correlation between increased numbers of women serving in middle and upper-level management positions and overall increases in white-collar crime incident rates.[63] Lastly, Dorothy Zietz came to similar conclusions in her examination of convicted female offenders at the California Institution for Women.[64]

Such findings are important because they challenge both Adler's liberation hypothesis and America's patriarchal system, which assert that as more women rise through the corporate ranks and/or secure positions of higher public trust, their propensity to commit white-collar crimes will also increase[65] (Chapman, 1980).

While not specifically focused on white-collar criminality, we believe that Meda Chesney-Lind's efforts to explore the characteristics of female offenders within the patriarchal boundaries of American society are closer to Sutherland and Cressey's initial research intentions than perhaps any other theorist of the modern era.

Chapter Summary

Sutherland's theory of white-collar criminality remains among the most important contributions to the areas of sociological and criminological study of the past 100 years. Sutherland's companion theory of *differential association* (i.e., criminal behavior is learned within intimate groups) fostered tremendous research into criminal learning theories, with regard to delinquent juveniles and organized criminal entities. However, it would be irresponsible to suggest that there are not flaws. As author Jay Albanese notes in his text *White Collar Crime in America* (1995), "What Sutherland's theory shortchanges is individual volition. Even in the face of pressure, a person must *decide* to go along the easiest route or to make his or her own path."[66] Yet the economic emphasis of Sutherland's theories, coupled with Merton's *social strain* and Cressey's research into *offender motivation and rationalization* celebrate a form of positivist research not frequently encountered since the conclusion of the McCarthy era. Before moving on to the thinking questions at the conclusion of this chapter, take a few minutes to familiarize yourself with the summary in Exhibit 6.3. Be sure that you understand the basic elements of each theory, and can compare and contrast them.

ADAPTED READINGS

Reading 6–1: B. McCarthy, *The Attitudes and Actions of Others: Tutelage and Sutherland's Theory of Differential Association*

> *As we discussed earlier in this chapter, the research of Edwin Sutherland and his contemporaries into white-collar criminality remains among the most important contributions to twentieth-century criminology. However, it is Sutherland's other theory, differential association that actually served to dramatically broaden the research agenda in areas ranging from juvenile delinquency to employment-based crime. The following article goes into greater depth on differential association, and its impact upon the field.*

Contemporary studies of Sutherland's differential association theory argue that people learn about crime predominantly or exclusively through exposure to attitudes and motives that legitimize such behaviours. I suggest that Sutherland's writings demonstrate an equal concern with more direct exposure to crime; that is, with tutelage in criminal methods. I test this interpretation with models of drug selling and theft among a sample of homeless youths. In both cases, models that include deviant associations, attitudes, and desires improve with the addition of a measure of tutelage. Disregarding the role of

Theorist	Year	Classification	Theory or typology
Veblen	1899	Positivist due to Veblen's extensive discussion of the individual's motivations for engaging in social climbing; although elements could be considered Social Constructionist based on their connection to Marx's theory of fetishization	*Conspicuous Consumption*: People are more interested in *appearing* wealthy (i.e., obtaining prestige symbols) than in generating real wealth
Merton	1938	Positivist because it focuses mostly on the response on the part of the individual in selecting legitimate or illegitimate means to meet approved social norms (further emphasized by Cloward and Ohlin in 1960)	*Social Strain*: There is a gap between societal expectations and one's ability to meet them. To bridge this gap, one will engage in either legitimate or illegitimate means.
Sutherland	1947/1949	Differential Association is Positivist, although there are quasi-Social Constructionist elements to his Theory of White-Collar Crime such as his discussion of Capitalistic society and its role in white-collar crime and the disproportionate adjudication of offense-type and offender based on his or her social class	*Differential Association/ White-Collar Crime*: Criminal behavior is learned from bad associates in personal intimate groups. Members of the upper-most socioeconomic group also engage in criminal activity and it differs from the forms engaged in by the lower classes. Adjudication is based on social class
Tappan	1947	Combination of Social Constructionist and Positivist because his theory requires that society first enact criminal laws and that the would-be offender recognize his or her behavior as criminal in nature (also see Benson's labeling and stigmatization of white-collar offenders (1990) and Messner and Rosenfeld's institutional anomie (1994))	*Response to Sutherland*: White-Collar Crime is not a crime unless an act has been codified as a crime, one believes they have committed a crime, and they actually got caught
Clinard	1952	Positivist because it focuses on the individual actor and the relationship between their inner conflicts and personal emotional characteristics	*Characteristics of "Black Marketeers"*: Individuals who managed the underground economy during World War II tended to have similar characteristics such as egocentricity, emotional insecurity, and feelings of personal in adequacy.
Cressey	1953	Positivist: Cressey's Theory focused specifically on the characteristics of embezzlers and not on the societal labeling or stigmatization	*Embezzlement*: People engage in acts of embezzlement if they have financial needs that cannot be otherwise met legitimately; have the knowledge, skills, and abilities to commit the act; and have rationalized that it is acceptable to carry out such acts.

Exhibit 6.3 Positivist and social constructionist perspectives on white-collar crime.

tutelage may, therefore, mis-specify the differential association process and encourage misinterpretations of findings that correspond with Sutherland's theory.

In recent years, tests of differential association have characteristically employed one of two interpretations of Sutherland's theory. One approach constructs Sutherland's theory as exclusively one of attitude transference; that is, people acquire definitions legitimizing crime through contact with offenders who communicate attitudes and motives that condone criminal or deviant activities (e.g. Warr and Stafford 1991; Warr 1993). Thus, over-exposure to these "symbolic elements," particularly through associations with deviant peers, leads to a criminal outlook and subsequent involvement in crime. Using a less restrictive approach, a second interpretation affirms the primacy of symbolic elements while suggesting that Sutherland's theory also indicates an aware-ness of others' activities as a means for learning criminal techniques. However, proponents of this perspective argue that such exposure is of minimal import-ance and therefore can be omitted readily from models of differential associ-ation (e.g. Matsueda 1982; Tittle *et al.* 1986; Jackson *et al.* 1986; Matsueda and Heimer 1987).(1)

Despite individual differences in these two approaches, both conclude that the acquisition of symbolic elements—be it attitudes, motives, or drives (or some combination thereof)—is the key intervening factor between deviant associations and crime in Sutherland's theory.(2) I suggest that the body of Sutherland's writings reveal a different approach. These works suggest that both skills and symbolic elements are central to the differential association process, and together intervene between deviant associations and crime. I test this interpretation of Sutherland's theory in models of drug selling and theft among homeless youths. Before describing this analysis, I first summarize the prevailing approach to differential association and then outline the alternative interpretation that I then explore.(3)

Behaviour and Attitudes in Differential Association

In a recent test of differential association theory, Warr and Stafford (1991; see also Warr 1993) exemplify the first interpretation described above; that is, one that concentrates exclusively on attitudes. According to Warr and Stafford, Sutherland's theory is an attitude formation theory that focuses on the influ-ence of peers' views but neglects their behaviour. Thus, they maintain that the distinguishing feature of Sutherland's theory is "its insistence that attitude transference is the mechanism by which delinquency is socially transmitted" (1991: 853).

Warr and Stafford test this approach with data from a nationally representa-tive, five-year panel study of youths in the United States (the National Youth Survey). In their analysis, they include measures of the respondent's and peers' attitudes toward three deviant activities (class-room cheating, petty theft (<$5), and marijuana use), as well as reports of peers' involvement in these behaviours. For each activity, Warr and Stafford find that peers' "deviant" attitudes and behaviour influence the respondent's delinquency indirectly through their encouragement of the respondent's deviant views. However, peers' deviant behaviour also has a strong direct effect on respondents' delinquent activities. According to Warr and Stafford this direct effect is inconsistent with Sutherland's theory, because, in their view, the theory of differential association focuses on "what peers think" not "what peers do".

Jackson *et al.* (1986) and Tittle *et al.* (1986) present a second interpretation of differential association. They argue that associations with deviants foster attitudes, motives, and drives that support criminal acts and provide exposure to techniques suitable for criminal activities. However, they do not include a measure of access to criminal techniques in their analyses. Instead, they argue that omitting this variable is not a "serious" deficiency (Tittle *et al.* 1986: 412) because "Sutherland himself recognized that knowledge of criminal techniques is usually not an important variable (Jackson *et al.* 1986: 342).

Tittle *et al.* and Jackson *et al.* test their model of differential association with data from people aged 15 and older living in the United States (i.e. in Iowa, New Jersey, and Oregon). They estimate models of predictions of future involvement in six activities: assault, tax cheating, minor and serious theft, gambling, and marijuana use. In testing their explication, Tittle *et al.* and Jackson *et al.* find that associating with criminals (i.e. having friends who have been arrested) fosters motives for several types of crime (e.g. minor theft and drug use) which in turn increases a willingness to consider offending at some future date. Thus, they conclude that effects of associations on crime are realized only through motives.

Matsueda (1982) and Matsueda and Heimer (1987) adopt a similar approach. Using data from the 1965 Richmond, California Youth Project (see Hirschi 1969), both studies estimate models of juvenile delinquency that include measures of the number of friends arrested and deviant attitudes;(4) yet they exclude items that measure direct exposure to criminal behaviour. As anticipated, Matsueda finds that, in full models, only deviant attitudes have a direct effect on delinquency; Matsueda and Heimer obtain similar results. However, in models that control for race Matsueda and Heimer report that the number of delinquent friends has a significant effect on delinquency, independent of attitudes. They conclude that this direct effect of friends' behaviour provides "negative evidence for differential association" (1987: 831).

The approach used in Matsueda's (1982) and Matsueda and Heimer's (1987) articles reflects a position later articulated by Matsueda (1988: 281). According to Matsueda, although the process of differential association involves learning both definitions and techniques for committing crimes, the former are decidedly more important and should account for any effect of the latter. Thus, Matsueda's approach suggests that deviant attitudes are sufficient for specifying the process by which exposure to criminal behaviour patterns encourages crime.

Notwithstanding their individual idiosyncrasies, the two approaches described above agree that the key variables in Sutherland's theory are exposure to, and acquisition of, symbolic elements that legitimize criminal acts. Both dismiss the role of more direct contact with crime and deny that tutelage in such behaviours is a fundamental part of differential association. Indeed, they argue that evidence of the direct effect of exposure to others' offending calls into question the differential association process. This interpretation reflects a dramatic separation of the key elements of Sutherland's theory.

Although differential association was originally seen as the pre-eminent sociological theory of its time, these contemporary approaches view it through a lens that narrowly focuses on the psychological experiences of attitude transference. At the same time this viewpoint obscures the more social elements of interactions with deviant others—instruction in techniques of offending in tutelage relationships. In essence, this lens elevates attitudes at the expense of actions.(5)

Alternatively, I argue that Sutherland's theory explicitly recognizes the direct exposure of others' criminal behaviour and testifies to the centrality of this contact as a source for learning the skills required by certain offences. This position is reflected not only in Sutherland's exposition of differential association, but appears in all of his major works. For example, in his discussion of the various propositions that comprise differential association (e.g. his discussion of propositions one through three and six) Sutherland repeatedly commented on the role of others as a source for acquiring knowledge of criminal techniques. He recognized that one learns definitions that support offending through a process that involves both verbal communication and the "communication of gestures" (Sutherland 1947: 6). The fourth proposition of differential association captures both of these sources of criminal definitions. According to this proposition:

> When criminal behaviour is learned, the learning includes (a) techniques of committing the crime, which are sometimes complicated, sometimes very simple; (b) the specific direction of motives, drives, rationalizations, and attitudes. (1947: 6)

Sutherland's notes on the origins of differential association affirm the importance of criminal contact as a means for learning how to offend. According to Sutherland, his work on professional theft provided the key insights into differential association; he commented that: "(t)here I seemed to see in magnified form the process that occurs in all crime" (1942: 17). Sutherland (1937) concluded that professional theft requires personal training by those adept in this crime; thus, he noted that selection and tutelage are the most important elements in this process (Sutherland 1937: 211–13). As part of this tutelage, neophytes acquire knowledge of theft by "apprenticeship methods" and receive "verbal instructions" about how to commit thefts, as well as actual assistance in the commission of crimes (1937: 213).

Recognizing that tutelage was not unique to this type of crime, Sutherland described the importance of instruction in the genesis of several offences, including shoplifting. He stated that a person may become acquainted with, and attracted to a professional shoplifter, and "learn from him the techniques, values, and codes of shoplifting, and under this tutelage become a professional shoplifter" (1939: 5). Similarly, in his classic study on white-collar crime, Sutherland (1983: 224) demonstrated that offenders frequently acquired their expertise from co-workers:

> he learns from those who have the same rank as his own how they make a success. He learns specific techniques of violating the law, together with definitions of situations in which those techniques may be used.

Sutherland (1939: 213–14) also argued that other, less highly specialized crimes, such as juvenile shoplifting and auto theft, require specific skills. Thus, he concluded that although one does not necessarily need tutelage to commit all offences, "[m]ost crimes, however, require *training*" (1947: 213, emphasis added).

The above suggests that contemporary interpretations of differential association have erred in focusing exclusively on symbolic elements while ignoring the effects of exposure to, and acquisition of, criminal skills. This oversight is significant for several reasons. First, the neglect of criminal skills encourages interpretations of differential association inconsistent with Sutherland's thesis. Secondly, it promotes the use of models that mis-specify the differential association process. Third, it leads to the rejection of findings consistent with Sutherland's theory. For example, contrary to Sutherland's position as outlined above, Warr and Stafford (1991) claim that a direct effect of peers' behaviour on one's criminality is inconsistent with Sutherland's theory. Likewise, Matsueda and Heimer (1987: 83 1) conclude that their significant main effect of delinquent friends on respondents' delinquency conflicts with Sutherland's theory. However, failing to include exposure to, or acquisition of criminal skills, makes it impossible to determine if this variable intervenes in the relationship between associations and crime; if this is the case, including skills may transform an unsupportive main effect into a supportive indirect one.

To address the concerns I raise, subsequent research must use more theoretically compelling models of differential association. Although Sutherland noted that most crimes require some training, he did not distinguish offences that are most amenable to tutelage from those that do not require it. As a step in this direction, I explore two types of crime that may be enhanced by training: theft and drug selling among homeless youths. Data from homeless adolescents are particularly well suited to test Sutherland's thesis because of this group's extensive exposure to the crimes that often characterize street life. Moreover, the adversity of street life (e.g. hunger, lack of shelter, and unemployment) often places these youths in a "crisis" situation; a condition that Sutherland (1937: 212) noted often encourages association with criminals and exposure to potential tutelage relationships.

Data, Measures, and Methods

The data used in this analysis were collected in Toronto in 1987–88. At that time, social service workers estimated that between 10,000 and 15,000 adolescents lived on the streets and shelters in Toronto. I used a purposive sampling strategy to contact these youths and over a one-year period collected data from 390 homeless adolescents. As part of my sampling strategy I approached adolescents in several social service agencies (six public shelters and three counselling agencies), as well as those I met in several "street" locales (e.g. downtown parks, shopping malls, train stations, and other sites popular for pan-handling and sleeping). Potential respondents answered several screening questions (e.g. about age and familiarity with street topics) and a reading assessment test before completing an anonymous self-report survey.

Demographic data from the sample indicate that approximately two thirds of the sample were male and one third were female. At the time of the study, 20 per cent of respondents were 16 years of age or younger, 21 per cent were 17, 23 per cent were 18, and 36 per cent were 19 years old. Sixty-two per cent were sleeping in a shelter, 12 per cent were residing temporarily with friends or relatives, 23 per cent were "living on the street" and 3 per cent were housed in public hotels or in an unspecified location. Overall, these youths report greater involvement in crime than is usually recorded in self-report studies; however, their participation and involvement in crime are significantly greater after they leave home (see McCarthy and Hagan 1991).

My analysis focuses on relationships between crime and three concepts central to differential association: deviant associations, symbolic elements that support offending, and tutelage in criminal activities. I explore the effects of these variables on two types of crime: drug selling and theft since leaving home. I use two items to measure drug trafficking: the frequency of selling marijuana (and other cannabis products) and the frequency of selling hallucinogenics, cocaine, and heroin. My measure of theft incorporates several activities: motor vehicle theft; stealing from a vehicle; break, enter, and theft; shoplifting something valued at $50 or more; possession of stolen property; and theft of goods valued at $50 or more. I use the natural-logs of all items to correct for skewness.

I use two variables to capture various dimensions of deviant associations. According to Sutherland, the differential association process is influenced by frequency, priority, duration, and intensity. However, most data do not allow for an easy demarcation of these dimensions. Thus, the two measures used in this study both involve the frequency of exposure to deviant associations; however, the first variable also captures elements of priority, whereas the second measure may reflect intensity.

The first variable, deviant associations at home, reflects the proportion of the respondent's friends who were arrested and who sold drugs while the respondent lived at home. The second variable, deviant associations on the street, replicates these measures but is based on information on friendships started since leaving home. These relationships may be more "intense" because street youths experience greater social isolation upon leaving home (e.g. separation from family and friends at home); moreover, they depend on street friends for several types of support.

Both variables use the proportion of deviant friends rather than the more commonly used absolute number; this approach resonates more strongly with Sutherland's emphasis on the ratio of associations. Ideally the variables would have also included a measure of the number of friends who participated in theft, but this information was not available.(6)

I measure symbolic elements that support law violations with two variables: deviant attitudes and deviant desires. The former uses Likert scale answers to three questions about the law and illegal acts. The first measure asks whether it should be legal to use drugs; the second item inquires about whether it is ever right to damage, destroy, or take others' property; and the third measure queries respondents' positions on breaking the law in general. Unfortunately, direct measures of deviant desires were not collected in this study; instead, I use two items as proxies. These Likert-scale items asked respondents about their affinity for danger and taking chances, two characteristics often associated with criminal or deviant activities (see Hagan 1990).

I use six questions to measure tutelage; these are crime-specific and focus on criminal instruction offered by tutors. I measure tutelage in drug selling with respondents' accounts of offers to help sell, actual assistance in selling, and reported sources of information about drug trafficking as a way of making money. I use three parallel questions for tutelage in theft. In each case, I created an ordinal scale that reflects the amount of exposure to tutelage. For example, the question about offers to help sell drugs has the following five response categories: (a) not approached about selling drugs; (b) received offers from friends whom the respondent believed were not actively involved in trafficking; (c) approached by friends or adults assumed to be actively involved in selling; (d) received solicitations from both non-selling and selling friends; (e) propositioned by both friends and adults involved in drug trafficking (parallel codings are used for the remaining indicators; see Table 1).

In addition to these variables, I also control for the effects of four additional correlates of crime: age, gender, family relationships, and school experiences. The first two of these are self-explanatory; the third combines commonly used indicators of parental attachment (Hirschi 1969) or relational and instrumental control (Hagan 1990) in a scale measure of family relationships, and the fourth, school experiences, adds measures of involvement in school activities (homework), commitment (grades), and trouble with teachers (see Hirschi 1969).

Although the independent variables used in this analysis are conceptually distinct, it is plausible that they are highly correlated. However, collinearity diagnostics suggest that associations among the independent variables do not

Table 1. Descriptive Statistics for All Indicators (n = 390)

	χ	sd	a^a
Age	17.597	1.457	
Gender[b]	0.667	0.472	
Family relationships			0.720
Did your mother know who you were with when you were out at night?[c]	1.133	0.877	
Did your father know who you were with when you were out at night?[c]	0.923	0.808	
Did your mother know where you were when you were out at night?[c]	1.279	0.888	
Did your father know where you were when you were out at night?[c]	1.018	0.868	
Would you like to be the kind of person your your mother was?[d]	0.649	0.834	
Would you like to be the kind of person your your father was?[d]	0.705	0.847	
Did you talk about your thoughts and feelings with your mother?[c]	0.915	0.873	
Did you talk about your thoughts and feelings with your father?[c]	0.659	0.785	
School experiences			0.546
How often did you do homework/projects after school?[c]	1.703	1.329	
How often did you have troubles with teachers?[c]	1.903	1.267	
What was your average grade in your last year of school?[f]	3.215	0.077	
Deviant associations at home			0.446
How many of your home friends had been arrested?[g]	3.633	3.284	
How many of your home friends sell drugs?[g]	2.031	2.672	
Deviant associations on the street			0.476
How many of your street friends have been arrested?[g]	5.138	3.723	
How many of your street friends sell drugs?[g]	2.431	2.907	
Deviant attitudes			0.594
It is right to break the law.[h]	2.054	1.031	
It is not always wrong to damage, destroy or take other's property.[i]	2.274	1.156	
People should have the legal right to take the drugs they want.[i]	3.105	1.371	
Deviant desires			0.609
The things I like to do best are dangerous.[i]	2.942	1.181	
I like to take chances.[i]	3.518	1.119	
Tutelage in theft			0.681
Has anyone offered to help you steal?[j]	0.841	1.061	
Did anyone help you steal?[k]	0.738	1.077	
How did you find out that you could make money stealing?[l]	0.787	1.358	

Tutelage in drug selling		0.753
Has anyone offered to help you sell drugs?[j]	0.854	1.164
Did anyone help you sell drugs?[k]	0.505	0.995
How did you find out that you could make money selling drugs?[l]	0.564	1.154
Theft		0.774
Age		
Theft over $50[m]	1.014	1.507
Break and enter[m]	0.518	1.082
Shoplifting over $50[m]	0.683	1.277
Possession of stolen property[m]	0.610	1.173
Theft from an automobile[m]	0.609	1.234
Theft of an automobile[m]	0.291	0.758
Drug selling		0.776
Selling marijuana[m]	1.342	1.757
Selling other drugs[m]	0.884	1.529

[a] Cronbach's α and Pearson correlation coefficient for variables with only two indicators.
[b] 0 = Female, 1 = Male.
[c] 0 = Never, 1 = Sometimes, 2 = Usually, 3 = Always.
[d] 0 = Not at, 1 = In some ways, 2 = In most ways, 3 = In every way.
[e] 0 = Always, 1 = Often, 2 = Sometimes, 3 = Rarely, 4 = Never.
[f] 0 = 0 to 40, 1 = 41 to 50, 2 = 51 to 60, 3 = 61 to 70, 4 = 71 to 80, 5 = Over 80.
[g] 0 = 0, 1 = 1% to 10% . . . 10 = 91% to 100%.
[h] 0 = Never, 1 = In a few cases, 2 = Sometimes, 3 = Often, 4 = In most cases.
[i] 0 = Strongly disagree, 1 = Disagree, 2 = Undecided, 3 = Agree, 4 = Strongly agree.
[j] 0 = No offers, 1 = Offers from friends not known to be involved, 2 = Offers from involved friends or adults, 3 = Offers from uninvolved and involved friends, 4 = Offers from involved friends and adults.
[k] As above except with "Help" replacing "Offers" and non-offenders coded as zero.
[l] As above except "Talked with" replaces "Offers from" and those who reported knowing from other experiences coded as zero.
[m] 0 through 99, natural log used in analysis.

appear to be a problem; only two correlations are greater than 0.350 (i.e. between deviant attitudes and desires at 0.435, and between deviant associations at home and since leaving home at 0.403). As well, variable tolerance scores are all above 0.7 and reciprocal variance inflation factors are all below 1.5.(7)

In this analysis I use two series of OLS equations (reduced form and full) to estimate models of drug selling and theft.(8) The first equation in each series includes the effects of the four control variables. In subsequent equations I introduce deviant associations before leaving home (equation 2), associations on the street (equation 3), deviant attitudes and desires (equation 4), and lastly, tutelage (equation 5). Given the focus of this paper, I report only the direct effects of these variables on crime; however, regression analyses of the indirect relationships confirm that deviant associations at home and on the street are strongly related to all three intervening variables.

My discussion centres on those effects that are statistically significant and how the introduction of additional variables influences the size and significance of these effects. Some critics suggest that tests of statistical inference are inappropriate when data are collected from non-probability sampling designs such as purposive sampling. However, this assertion ignores the underlying assumption that in addition to random-sampling, such tests also assume that the probability of non-response is known and minimal. Yet, as noted by most sampling experts (e.g. Cochran 1963; Kish 1965; Sudman 1976), nonresponse error in probability sampling is often so serious as to make ordinary sampling error minor in comparison. According to Henkel (1976: 78–80), inferences from such samples are "nonsensical" and "cannot be made on any statistical ground". Rather than rejecting techniques of statistical inference for all but randomly collected data with perfect response rates, I assume that these techniques can be used with less perfect data (data with non-response or from non-probability designs) but I acknowledge that caution must be used in generalizing from these studies. Thus, I follow Mohr (1990) and use these tests as indicators of the strength of a relationship and to assess the likelihood that an effect of a certain size occurred as the result of random forces alone. As Mohr notes, the tests help to assess "whether or not a certain relationship or other quantity is worth further thought—whether it might repay additional research effort" (1990: 8).

Results

As anticipated, the results of equation I for drug selling (see Table 2) indicate that gender, family relationships, and school experiences significantly influence the frequency of this type of crime. Equations 2 and 3 reveal that drug selling also increases with deviant associations both before and since leaving home (β = 0.310, $p < 0.01$ and $\beta = 0.218$, $p < 0.01$); moreover, although controlling for street friendships reduces somewhat the direct effect of associations from home, the latter remains sizeable and significant ($\beta = 0.226$, $p < 0.01$).

According to equation 4, deviant attitudes and desires also have strong direct effects on drug trafficking ($\beta = 0.184$, $P = 0.246$, $p < 0.01$); as well, they reduce the direct effect of associations before and since leaving home (see equation 4). However, adding these variables does not eliminate the direct effect of home and street associations; instead, both variables retain their sizeable and significant effects ($\beta = 0.146$, $p < 0.01$ and $\beta = 0.144$, $p < 0.01$).

The effects of home and street associations change more dramatically with the introduction of tutelage in drug selling in equation 5; both are substantially reduced in size, the effect of street friendships becomes non-significant and the effect of associations at home moves close to non-significance ($p = 0.091$, $t = 2.03$).(9) Moreover, the effect of tutelage surpasses those of all other independent variables ($\beta = 0.377$), $p < 0.01$) and improves the model's adjusted [R^2] by almost 40 per cent (i.e. from 29 per cent to 41 per cent).

The equations for theft provide comparable results. The direct effects of associations (at home and on the street) on theft are sizeable and significant in

Table 2. Regression Coefficients for OLS Models of Drug Selling and Theft (n = 390)

Variable name	Equation 1			Equation 2			Equation 3			Equation 4			Equation 5		
	b	se	β	b	se	β	b	se	β	b	se	β	b	se	β
Drug selling															
Age	0.220	0.114	0.103	0.178	0.109	0.083	0.167	0.107	0.079	0.294**	0.101	0.138	0.275**	0.092	0.129
Gender	0.760*	0.355	0.116	0.718*	0.337	0.109	0.783*	0.331	0.119	0.220	0.318	0.033	0.372	0.291	0.057
Family Rel	-0.106**	0.039	-0.134	-0.090*	0.037	-0.114	-0.080*	0.037	-0.102	-0.038	0.05	-0.048	-0.024	0.032	-0.030
School Exp	-0.139**	0.052	-0.134	-0.082	0.051	-0.079	-0.071	0.050	-0.068	-0.046	0.047	-0.044	-0.045	0.043	-0.046
Home Assoc	—	—	—	0.190**	0.029	0.310	0.138**	0.031	0.226	0.089**	0.030	0.146	0.056*	0.028	0.091
Street Assoc	—	—	—	—	—	—	0.118**	0.027	0.218	0.078**	0.026	0.144	0.031	0.024	0.056
Dev Attitudes	—	—	—	—	—	—	—	—	—	0.215**	0.060	0.184	0.192**	0.055	0.165
Dev Desires	—	—	—	—	—	—	—	—	—	0.371**	0.073	0.246	0.299**	0.067	0.199
Tutelage	—	—	—	—	—	—	—	—	—	—	—	—	0.431**	0.049	0.377
Constant	-0.422	1.922		-1.243	1.831		-1.852	1.795		-7.606	1.846		-7.105	1.683	
Adjusted R²	0.063			0.154			0.191			0.292			0.412		
Theft															
Age	0.286	0.194	0.078	0.229	0.187	0.062	0.216*	0.184	0.059	0.422*	0.176	0.115	0.405*	0.171	0.110
Gender	2.294**	0.604	0.202	2.233**	0.582	0.210	2.320**	0.573	0.203	1.325*	0.558	0.116	1.465**	0.543	0.129
Family Rel	-0.249**	0.066	-0.183	-0.225**	0.064	-0.165	-0.207**	0.063	-0.153	-0.126*	0.061	-0.092	-0.112	0.059	-0.082
School Exp	-0.223*	0.089	-0.125	-0.142	0.087	-0.079	-0.124	0.085	-0.069	-0.073	0.082	-0.042	-0.076	0.079	-0.042
Home Assoc	—	—	—	0.271	0.050	0.256	0.193**	0.053	0.182	0.108*	0.052	0.102	0.073	0.051	0.069
Street Assoc	—	—	—	—	—	—	0.183**	0.047	0.193	0.120**	0.045	0.127	0.071	0.045	0.075
Dev Attitudes	—	—	—	—	—	—	—	—	—	0.495**	0.104	0.247	0.475**	0.101	0.236
Dev Desires	—	—	—	—	—	—	—	—	—	0.436**	0.127	0.167	0.360**	0.125	0.139
Tutelage	—	—	—	—	—	—	—	—	—	—	—	—	0.435**	0.090	0.221
Constant	0.501	3.252		-0.714	3.146		-1.735	3.101		-11.180	3.220		10.677	3.131	
Adjusted R²	0.105			0.166			0.196			0.289			0.326		

* p < 0.05, ** p < 0.01.

equations 2, 3, and 4; however, both are diminished substantially and reduced to non-significance with the introduction of tutelage in equation 5. Moreover, tutelage has a large effect on theft ($\beta = 0.221$, $p < 0.01$) and increases the model's adjusted R^2 by just over 10 per cent (i.e. from 29 per cent to 33 per cent).

Overall, these findings provide considerable support for introducing tutelage to improve models of differential association. Additional analyses reported elsewhere (McCarthy and Hagan 1995) demonstrate that the effects of tutelage are also apparent in covariance structural equation models of drug selling, theft, and prostitution, and that these effects remain when controls are introduced for past criminal activity, time at risk, and situational adversity (i.e. hunger and lack of shelter). As well, the effects of tutelage are not altered in models that introduce data on at-home youths to correct for any sample-selection bias that arises from using data on homeless adolescents. Together, these results provide considerable support for Sutherland's thesis.

Discussion

At one time, Edwin Sutherland was one of the most revered figures in the history of sociological criminology; yet the theory of differential association that Sutherland regarded as his central contribution (Cohen *et al.* 1956) is currently severely criticized and of uncertain influence (e.g. see Kornhauser 1978; Hirschi 1969; Hirschi and Gottfredson 1979). In a 1988 review of the "current state of differential association theory" Matsueda (1988: 277) argues that although Sutherland's theory was instrumental in bringing sociology to the forefront of criminology, by the 1980s it had fallen from grace and was supplanted by social control or integrated theories. This conclusion is supported by Stitt and Giacopassi's (1992) finding that in 28 volumes of *Criminology* (1963–91), only 11 of 215 empirically-based articles (just over 5 per cent) focus on differential association theory.

Clearly, studies by Matsueda (1982), Matsueda and Heimer (1987), Tittle *et al.* (1986), and Jackson *et al.* (1986) have helped to rescue differential association theory from potential empirical oblivion. In the years preceding these studies, tests supporting differential association were notably absent from major sociological and criminological journals. None the less, recent studies' exclusive focus on deviant attitudes and motives has contributed to the current confusion about the educational importance of others' behaviours. This confusion is most evident in the limited interpretation of Sutherland's theory as one of attitudes, not actions, and in tests of differential association that ignore measures of tutelage.

Alternatively, I argue that the body of Sutherland's work underscores the centrality of others as a source for acquiring criminal skills. In his writings on professional thieves, white-collar offenders, juvenile theft, and other crimes, Sutherland consistently returned to the role of tutelage. The models estimated in this article affirm that, for homeless youths, tutelage is an integral part of the process of learning theft and drug selling.

Although the data used in this article are from a sub-group of the adolescent population, and one that is disproportionately involved in crime (McCarthy and Hagan 1991), other studies suggest that tutelage is not specific to any one group. Both classic and contemporary ethnographies (e.g. Thrasher 1927; Sullivan 1989; Padilla 1992) describe the role of mentors and tutors in the transmission of criminal skills, as does a recent study on high-school students (Bruinsma 1992). These studies affirm that, regardless of the population studied, tutelage in criminal techniques is an important element of much offending. Thus, subsequent tests of differential association would be enhanced by including measures of tutelage. These investigations should improve our ability to specify the crimes most amenable to criminal training and locate where tutelage occurs with the greatest frequency and the most success. This approach would bring us closer to the sociological criminology originally envisioned by Sutherland.

Notes

(1) Broader-based studies that test for effects specified by several theories also use these interpretations (e.g. Elliott *et al.* 1985; Thornberry *et al.* 1994).

(2) As Matsueda (1988: 280) notes, the theory also contains assumptions about normative conflict and differential social organization; however, these refer to societal processes that are beyond this paper's focus on processes that operate at the individual level (Cressey 1960).

(3) Although there are a number of revisions of Sutherland's theory (e.g. Cloward and Ohlin 1960; Glaser 1956; Burgess and Akers 1966), as well as theories that integrate Sutherland's ideas (e.g. Elliott *et al.* 1985; Thornberry *et al.* 1994), I concentrate exclusively on differential association. I prefer Sutherland's focus on teachers who provide criminal instruction to theories that place more emphasis on interested students who actively pursue knowledge through modelling and imitation (e.g. Akers 1985).

(4) In their studies Matsueda (1982) and Matsueda and Heimer (1987) refer to their measure as "deviant definitions," however, I argue that such measures may be better indicators of attitudes.

(5) These researchers are not the first to neglect Sutherland's focus on learning methods of offending from other's criminal behaviour. In response to criticisms of differential association, Donald Cressey (1960) notes that the second most common oversight concerning Sutherland's theory is a disregard of Sutherland's emphasis that exposure to patterns of criminal behaviour is more important than an awareness of others' criminal attitudes.

(6) A number of studies (see Agnew 1991) suggest that peer associations

interact with other dimensions of peer relationships (e.g. attachment, time spent together, and peer pressure). I combined associations since leaving home with indicators of attachment (looking after friends or being looked after) and support (extent of help given to and received from friends); however, neither of the interaction terms had significant effects in the models discussed below so they were not included in the final analysis.

(7) Bivariate correlations between the independent and dependent variables also suggest that they are not measuring the same phenomenon. The smallest coefficient is 0.291 (between associations and theft), the largest is 0.589 (desires and drug selling), and all but one are lower than 0.5.

(8) The models used in this analysis are recursive. Although Thornberry *et al.*'s (1994) recent analysis of longitudinal data suggests that although many of these effects are probably non-recursive (e.g. beliefs at time one may encourage crime at time two, which entrenches beliefs at time three) the cross-sectional nature of these data do not allow for an adequate test of such effects. Although longitudinal data are preferred I was unable to locate any that collected measures of tutelage.

(9) The significance of this effect suggests that tutelage from friends from several sites (e.g. at home or in gangs) may be important for specific crimes.

References

Agnew, R. (1991), "The Interactive Effects of Peer Delinquency", *Criminology*, 29: 47–72.

Akers, R. (1985), *Deviant Behavior: A Social Learning Approach*, 3rd edn. Belmont, CA: Wadsworth.

Bruinsma, G. (1992), "Differential Association Theory Reconsidered: An Extension and Its Empirical Test", *Journal of Quantitative Criminology*, 8: 29–49.

Burgess, R., and Akers, R. (1966), "A Differential Association-reinforcement Theory of Criminal Behavior", *Social Problems*, 14: 128–47.

Cloward R., and Ohlin, L. (1960), *Delinquency and Opportunity: A Theory of Delinquent Gangs*. Glencoe, IL: Free Press.

Cochran, W. (1963), *Sampling Techniques*. New York: John Wiley and Sons.

Cohen, A., Lindesmith, A., and Schuessler, K. (1956), *The Sutherland Papers*. Bloomington: Indiana University Press.

Cressey, D. (1960), "Epidemiology and Individual Conduct: A Case from Criminology", *Pacific Sociological Review*, 3: 47–58.

Elliott, D., Huizinga, D., and Agfton, S. (1985), *Delinquency and Drug Use*. Beverly Hills, CA: Sage.

Glaser, D. (1956), "Criminality Theories and Behavioral Images", *American Journal of Sociology*, 61: 433–44.

Hagan, J. (1990), *Structural Criminology*. New Brunswick, NJ: Rutgers University Press.

Henkel, R. (1976), *Tests of Significance*. Beverly Hills: Sage.

Hirschi, T. (1969), *Causes of Delinquency*. Berkeley: Free Press.

Hirschi, T. and Gottfredson, M. (1979), "Introduction: The Sutherland Tradition", in T. Hirschi and M. Gottfredson, eds., *Understanding Crime-current Theory and Research*. Beverly Hills: Sage.

Jackson, E., Tittle, C., and Burke, M-J. (1986), "Offense-specific Models of the Differential Association Process", *Social Problems*, 33: 335–56.

Kish, L. (1965), *Survey Sampling*. New York: John Wiley and Sons.

Kornhauser, R. (1978), *Social Sources of Delinquency*. Chicago: University of Chicago Press.

Matsueda, R. (1982), "Testing Control Theory and Differential Association: A Causal Modelling Approach", *American Sociological Review*, 47: 489–504.

—— (1988), "The Current State of Differential Association Theory", *Crime and Delinquency*, 34: 277–306.

Matsueda, R., and Heimer, K. (1987), "Race, Family Structure, and Delinquency: A Test of Differential Association and Social Control Theories", *American Sociological Review*, 52: 826–40.

McCarthy, B., and Hagan, J. (1991), "Homelessness: A Criminogenic Situation?", *British Journal of Criminology* 31: 39 3–410.

—— (1995), "Getting into Crime: The Structure and Process of Criminal Embeddedness", *Social Science Research*, 24: 63–95.

Mohr, L. (1990), *Understanding Significance Testing*. Newbury Park: Sage.

Padilla, F. (1992), *The Gang as an American Enterprise*. New Brunswick, Nj: Rutgers University Press.

Stitt, B. G., and Giacopassi, D. (1992), "Trends in the Connectivity of Theory and Research in Criminology", *The Criminologist*, 17: 1–6.

Sullivan, M. (1989), *Getting Paid: Youth Crime and Work in the Inner City*. Ithaca: Cornell University Press.

Sudman, S. (1976), *Applied Sampling*. New York: Academic Press.

Sutherland, E. (1937), *The Professional Thief—By a Professional Thief*, annotated and interpreted by Edwin Sutherland. Chicago: University of Chicago Press.

—— (1939), *Principles of Criminology*, 3rd edn. Philadelphia: J. B. Lippincott.

—— (1947), *Principles of Criminology*, 4th edn. Philadelphia: J. B. Lippincott.

—— (1956), "Development of the Theory", (orig. 1942), in A. Cohen, A. Lindesmith, and K. Schuessler, eds., *The Sutherland Papers*. Bloomington: Indiana University Press.

—— (1983), *White Collar Crime—The Uncut Version* (orig. 1949). New Haven: Yale University Press.

Thornberry, T., Lizotte, A., Krohn, M., Farnworth, M., and Jang, S.-J. (1994), "Delinquent Peers, Beliefs, And Delinquent Behavior: A Longitudinal Test of Interactional Theory", *Criminology*, 32: 47–83.

Thrasher, F. (1927), *The Gang—A Study of 1,313 Gangs in Chicago*, 2nd edn. Chicago: University of Chicago Press.

Tittle, C., Burke, M-J., and Jackson, E. (1986), "Modeling Sutherland's Theory of Differential Association: Toward an Empirical Clarification", *Social Forces*, 405–33.

Warr, M. (1993), "Age, Peers, and Delinquency", *Criminology*, 31: 17–40.

Warr, M., and Stafford, M. (1991), "The Influence of Delinquent Peers: What They Think or What They Do?", *Criminology*, 29: 851–66.

Source: *British Journal of Criminology*, 36(1) (1996): 135–47, © Institute for the Study and Treatment of Delinquency 1996

Reading 6–2: Neil Steinberg, *Running After the Joneses*

> *In his classic text,* The Theory of the Leisure Class, *sociologist Thorstein Veblen explores the reasons why those living in Western cultures feel it is more important to appear wealthy than to actually be financial secure. In this article, author Neil Steinberg explores this phenomenon using his own life as an example. As you enjoy this reading, consider what you would do if you were in the author's situation.*

The neighbors threw a party Saturday night. My wife made her mango chutney dip and set it on a glass plate with crackers. Then we trooped over to join other neighbors who were drinking red wine out of delicate glasses, digging into various cheeses and admiring the candles floating in bowls.

Nothing about the party wasn't fun. They had archery in back for the kids. A raffle to benefit leukemia research. Chips and salsa, fancy cookies and Mexican spiced coffee. The host even tapped me to sneak out and smoke a cigar under the starlight.

Yet I came home troubled, burdened, worried about something that I had difficulty even expressing to my wife. Their furniture, it was so . . . so . . . nice. The sofa, with its thick embroidered upholstery, shot through with gold thread, that looks as if it came from a medieval French tapestry. The writing desk. The little cabinet.

So nice, and so much of it: chairs and love seats and sofas and ottomans and God knows what else. Our furniture, which had been so new when we bought it, suddenly looked threadbare and tattered and completely unacceptable.

"We need new furniture," I informed my wife, gravely.

Call it envy. Call it competitiveness. Call it a desire to meet community standards. But the need to keep up with the Joneses both spurs our personal working lives and drives our national economy, and most of us don't realize it.

Your immediate reaction might be denial. Keeping up with the neighbors? Such a lumpen worry. Not an emotion worthy of an independent-minded go-getter like you. No way.

But do you mow your lawn? Paint your house? Clean it? Are your bookshelves made of cinder block? The need to keep up is woven so deeply into our culture it can be hard to recognize. How many automobile commercials have you seen where the new car is proudly unveiled in the driveway to the eye-popping wonder of the hapless next-door neighbor, who glances back at his own jalopy, sitting in his driveway, with mingled remorse and shame?

On the surface, this is completely irrational. Who cares whether your neighbor—someone you might not even like—admires your car or not? You sure didn't sound out his wishes before you bought it. "Hey, Hank, I'm thinking about a Land Rover—that OK with you?"

So obviously you aren't buying the car to win his approval. Or are you? Could you really be standing in the showroom, deciding what your neighbor will envy most, and not even know it?

Many economists would say yes. Why else would anyone buy a $50,000 Lexus instead of a $5,000 used Pontiac? They will both get you where you're going. New leather smells nice, but the purely rational person would take a deep whiff in the showroom, then go buy the Pontiac and pocket the extra 45 grand for a rainy day. Something complex is at work here.

But what? The question has fascinated economists for more than 100 years. In his seminal masterpiece, *The Theory of the Leisure Class*, Thorstein Veblen first outlined how humans express their superiority through displays of wealth, famously dubbing the process "conspicuous consumption." He said we don't even have to know our neighbors to sculpt our lives to meet their approval.

"One's neighbors, mechanically speaking, often are socially not one's neighbors, or even acquaintances," he writes. "And still their transient good opinion has a high degree of utility."

So much so that we prefer to buy things rather than save money or enjoy free time. We earn more money than our parents—the average household income, in real dollars, has doubled since 1960. There is no law that this windfall has to be spent on fancy sofas and new kitchens. People could have chosen to work less—a person earning $500,000 a year could, in theory, decide to live frugally, work for a year, and then spend the next five years pursuing modest leisure activities, studying Irish literature or climbing mountains or whatever dreams dwell in the smithy of our souls.

And the rare individualist will indeed take a sabbatical, will put a hot career on hold to raise a child or build a log cabin. But most people with jobs don't. They worry about harming their careers, and leisure loses out to material goods. Thus we work away our lives, in a steady escalation, a suburban arms race where the stakes steadily spiral up over the years. We can see this choice most plainly in the size of new houses. Half a century ago, the average new house was just about 1,000 square feet. In 1970 it was 1,500 square feet. Today it's 2,400.

During the same time, the American family shrank, on average, by half a person, from 3.7 to 3.2, so we have fewer people in bigger houses.

Many of us can see this in operation if we look at our own lives. I grew up in a family of five in a three-bedroom ranch house in Berea, Ohio. My brother and I shared a bedroom for our entire childhood. There were two bathrooms, one with a tub, one with a shower.

Today, my family of four lives in a five-bedroom Queen Anne house with three bathrooms, and we sometimes feel deprived—my neighbors' new homes are larger and more splendid. When we remodeled our kitchen, I splurged on a $2,500 Wolf industrial stove—I liked the big red knobs—and felt rich until the guy across the street pulled down his entire house and built a new house with a kitchen three times the size of ours, with a Wolf that was twice as big and cost $9,000 and has eight burners. Perhaps for those days when he's boiling an ox.

I don't think he actually dusted his hands together and thought, "That'll show Steinberg" after he signed the credit card slip and bought the Wolf. I'm sure if you asked him, he'll scoff, "That guy? The guy who rakes his own leaves! No way!"

No, in fact, I'm sure the logic is that he has the money. He's building a new house anyway. Why not? The logic marches you toward the biggest stove you can buy. You want a big kitchen for the big parties you're going to throw for your big circle of big friends. And a big kitchen needs a big stove.

The stove's practical utility is limited—the truth is, most of the time it sits there, just like my stove, and the pot of tea boils just the same as mine or yours. Rather, the eight-burner stove is a display, one we can trace directly back to the eight-branched elk horns worn by the best hunter in a tribe of Cro-Magnons 20,000 years ago.

Or by the elk itself, for that matter. All animals are hierarchical. The best hunter gets the best part of the catch. How does one prove he's the best, the strongest? Well, there are combats with rivals, but those are taxing and take away from energy needed for the hunt. Far better to establish one's superiority through display—the loud roar, the big mane, the curling tusk.

The eight-burner stove.

Surely we aren't just elk with industrial stoves—don't humans, with our complex brains, bring anything more to the party? Or is keeping up with the Joneses (a phrase, by the way, that dates back to a World War I-era newspaper cartoon of that name, where an immigrant family struggled to impress their well-heeled neighbors, the Joneses, who, delightfully, were never actually seen in the strip) merely the human version of a peacock spreading its tail?

We push beyond just playing our socio-biological role when we at least become aware of the process, and either join in or do not join in as a conscious decision. It can take courage—or obliviousness—to break the mold. Men wore business suits to work for 100 years, conforming to one another in style, trying to outdo each other in fit and costliness.

And then a scruffy group of computer nerds became so obsessed with writing program code that they forgot to dress, went to work in cargo shorts and Hawaiian shirts, and became millionaires anyway. Now suits are the exception, a shift that the elk will never make.

We can demur, if we choose. I did not, for instance, run out and put $10,000 worth of furniture on the credit card, much as I would have liked to. Instead, I shopped around, realized how much this stuff costs, and tamped down the desire, soberly recognizing that the party had done its job. Throwing the party was my host's way of saying, "Hey, I've got floating candles to burn and expensive bottles of Fat Tire beer and $5 cigars to give away!"

Not that any of this was conscious—my neighbor was not trying to scare off potential rivals while wooing the ladies on the block by displaying the glory of his furniture. He's a nice guy. His entire goal, I know, was to give his friends a good time while raising a little money to fight leukemia.

But it is good to make the effort to grasp the subtext. The lawn grows, and when we get off the couch with a grunt to go mow it, it might help to realize we are also preserving our place in the social order. I told my wife that the money from this Forbes piece would go toward a new sofa. Sure, the old one is still functional. But we have 40,000 years of human social history to think about. Cultural norms are not to be pooh-poohed. Values must be respected or you run the risk of being ostracized.

Viewed that way, acquiring fancy new stuff can almost be seen as a duty, an act of altruism, a way of respecting social forces far greater than ourselves. Assuming, of course, you have the money to spend.

Source: Forbes Online (http://www.forbes.com/2008/05/08/keeping-up-joneses-ent-competition08-cx-ns_0508steinberg_print.html)

Thinking Activities

This chapter presented you with the framework for understanding the connections between social learning and one's propensity to engage in white-collar criminal acts. In order to enhance your understanding of social strain and differential association, answer each of the following questions. After you have collected your answers, discuss them in small groups with other members of your class. Are there similarities and differences in your responses? Be prepared to share your findings with the larger class and your instructor.

1. Ask your parents or grandparents to provide you with a brief history summarizing your family's arrival upon the North American continent. How did your family come to reside where they live today? What were the occupations of your grandparents? Do they differ from the positions held by your parents?

2. Have you seen a change in your family's socioeconomic status from the time of your grandparents? What, if any, are the differences between your grandparents' and parents' levels of education and your own? If you are the first generation in your family to attend college, do you consider this to be an opportunity or a burden? Why?

3. Name a particular skill that you have acquired. Were you taught this skill? If so, who taught it to you? Have you taught this skill to anyone else?

4. Are there any circumstances in which you believe it is acceptable to engage in an act of white-collar crime (e.g., embezzlement)? For example, what if someone in your family needed a major operation, and the only way you could afford to pay for it would be to steal the money from your job? What rationalization would you make to justify participating in such an act?

5. What are some of the reasons that you decided to obtain a college degree or further your education? Do you believe that there is a set amount of money that will make you "happy"? Or, like Stanton Wheeler, do you believe that even the wealthiest Americans no longer reach a point of diminishing returns with respect to the products they consume?

7 Organizational Crime and Corporate Criminal Liabilities

The year is 1990, and America has just endured one of its worst fiscal crises in over 60 years. In order to foster competition, the U.S. government had previously encouraged its citizens to frequent their local small-scale lending institutions, known as "savings and loans," or "S&Ls." In large numbers, individuals and small businesses used these S&Ls for everything from obtaining mortgages and securing car loans to establishing business lines of credit. For more than ten years, small lending institutions essentially had unrestricted management of their investment portfolios. During that time, these banks provided real estate and commercial loans to those organizations and individuals they deemed worthy. As you will learn at the close of this chapter, the result was that savings and loan corporations were assuming far more risk than could reasonably be considered prudent. In addition to substantial investments in "junk" bonds and risky stocks, many of the senior officers of these institutions were using the funds entrusted to them for personal "loans," purchasing luxury items such as multi-million dollar yachts and extravagant art collections. At the conclusion of the crisis, nearly $500 billion in taxpayer funds had been spent in an effort to stop the financial damage caused by the savings and loan crisis.

In a similar manner, the Enron Corporation debacle caused economic devastation to its shareholders, resulting in the significant reduction and, in some cases, absolute depletion of pension monies for both individual account holders and many county public organizations.

In order to understand the incidents leading to Enron's demise, it is important to comprehend a brief history of the company. In 1985, two energy trading companies, Houston Natural Gas and InterNorth merged into a new corporation known as Enron. On the surface, the new publicly-traded company appeared to perform quite well. In addition to the many individual investors who purchased shares of this energy trading corporation, a substantial number of pension funds and other public interests invested in Enron stock. The company was thriving, and because its earnings frequently surpassed market estimates, investors' confidence—and savings—continued to flourish.

However, in reality, all was not well. Enron's leaders hid the company's losses in order to preserve and maintain investor confidence. Additionally, in the summer of 2001, many of Enron's senior leadership quietly sold their own shares, fully anticipating that the company would go bankrupt. On October 16, 2001, Enron reported a loss of $638 million in their third quarter, which reduced the value of the company by $1.2 billon.[1] In December of 2001, Enron declared bankruptcy. The price of this once-fêted stock dropped from $90.00 per share to 50 cents per share. In addition to the 4,000 employees of Enron who lost their jobs, millions of Americans—individual investors and pension funds alike—lost huge portions of their retirement savings that had been invested in this now worthless company.[2]

Whether the case is the S&L debacle of the 1980s–1990s or the Enron scandal of just eight years ago, how and why do corporate executives engage in such behaviors? Is there a reason why fraud and other illegal behaviors occur within large organizations? Lastly, are such incidents restricted to the private sector or are public and not-for-profit organizations also susceptible to these misdeeds? The aim of this chapter is to explore several of the most widely known organizational and corporate typologies of crime. Specifically, we will examine how and why white-collar crime flourishes within organizations and corporations, with special emphasis on the private sector.

The "Democracy" of White-Collar Crime

In 1970, Herbert Edelhertz, former chief of the fraud section of the United States Department of Justice remarked "white collar crime is democratic . . . It can be committed by a bank teller, or the head of his institution."[3] His subsequent categorizations of offense types presented his effort to separate *occupational* crimes (i.e., acts committed because of one's position) from *corporate* crimes, such as engaging in loan fraud to favor the company's business position. Specifically, Edelhertz divides white-collar offenses into the following four distinct areas:[4]

1. Crimes by individuals on an individual or ad hoc basis.
2. Crimes committed in the course of one's occupation by operating inside a business or governmental organization in violation of loyalty or public trust.
3. Crimes incidental to and in furtherance of business operations, but not the central purpose of the organization.
4. White-collar crime as a business, or as the central activity.

Edelhertz' research led to the Justice Department's present-day definition of a white-collar crime as "those classes of non-violent illegal activities which traditionally involve . . . deceit, deception, concealment . . . breach of trust, subterfuge, or illegal circumvention."[5] This approach of categorizing fraud, forgery, and embezzlement as either the misdeeds of individuals within a group, or the broader purpose of an organization, blends nicely with Simon and Hagan's (1999) concept of organizational deviance (i.e., "acts of immense physical, financial, and moral harm committed by wealthy and powerful corporations."[6] The study of organizational deviance has become a major theme in white-collar crime research since the 1970s, and demonstrates a marked departure from the strain, learning, and motivation-rationalization research conducted in the late 1930s through early 1950s by Merton, Sutherland, and Cressey that we explored in the previous chapter.

Corporate Crime and Changes in the Research Agenda

Along with the categorization of occupational crime and organizational crime, much of the academic literature over the past 35 years examined ethnographies and historical analyses of corporate wrongdoing. Scholar Gilbert Geis' commentary on antitrust violations by senior executives at General Electric and the Westinghouse Electric Corporation provides insight into the "willful and blatant nature" of corporate crime in the late 1950s and early 1960s.[7] Additionally, Susan Shapiro's analysis of "Zoogate," a situation in which the Houston Zoo advertised live cobras but actually displayed rubber models, since live cobras could not survive in the harsh lighting conditions necessary for the exhibit,[8] serves as an excellent example of organizational fraud. Shapiro goes further in terms of classification than many of her contemporaries, noting that the term white-collar crime should only be used to describe abuse-of-trust crimes which require persons to "manipulate norms of disclosure, disinterestedness, and role competence."[9]

If we assume there is a distinct difference between occupational and corporate crime, it is interesting to note that much of our academic research efforts since the 1970s have ignored the former and focused on the latter. Quoting David Maurer in his text *Crime as Work*, author Peter Letkemann notes "actually, we know little about crime as a way of life; in fact, we have more data on the behavior pattern of almost any obscure primitive tribe than we have on these problem areas within our own culture."[10] Why has so little research been conducted on the characteristics of workers who engage in acts of fraud, forgery, embezzlement, counterfeiting and information technology-based crimes? One answer could be that criminologists have often strived to develop universal theories of criminality. In other words, why should we choose to solely study white-collar offender behavior when an all-encompassing explanation for violent and non-violent behavior might be within reach? Alternatively, perhaps academicians have chosen to focus on the characteristics of violent offenders, possibly believing that such research will prove more valuable to society than profiling white-collar criminals. For example, the 1997 edition of Douglas *et al.*'s *Crime Classification Manual* focuses *exclusively* on classifying offenders engaged in acts of homicide, arson, rape, and sexual assault.[11] White-collar forms of behavior such as fraud, forgery, embezzlement, and counterfeiting are not mentioned.

This is also true when we explore practitioner-based analysis. The United States Secret Service recently expanded upon its *Exceptional Case Study Project* (ECSP).[12] The ECSP was initially designed to develop a profile for assassins, attackers, and near-lethal approaches of public officials. However, it now includes characterizations of those persons involved in acts of domestic violence, stalking, and school-based violence. While the agency has diligently developed profiles for violent offenders, it has not conducted similar research on offenders engaged in financial crimes, which are at the heart of the Secret Service's original mission of 1865. Ironically, the *Al Qaeda Training Manual* specifically instructs its operatives on how to produce fake currency and fraudulent financial documents.[13] Is it possible that if the Secret Service chose to focus its efforts in this area, such research could ultimately aid in the identification of terrorist cells and networks connected through illegal wire transfers, credit card fraud, and identity theft?

The Shift Towards Organizational Crime Research

To paraphrase Gary Green in his text *Occupational Crime* (1990), the reason the field of criminology no longer enjoys a research emphasis that focuses on the individual occupational offender and his or her motivations and behaviors may also relate to the issue of enforcement.[14] In other words, it makes more sense for regulatory agencies to assess the culture and structure of an organization with respect to its susceptibility to fraud than to pursue individual suspects, which not only requires intensive research, but also is time-consuming.[15] Taking a somewhat different approach than Herbert Edelhertz, Green essentially divides occupational criminality into four categories: *organizational* occupational crime (e.g., crimes against consumers, workers, and the environment); *state authority* occupational crime, such as genocide and torture, police brutality, civil rights violations and bribe-taking (i.e., acts that Shapiro (1990) would collectively refer to as abuse-of-trust crimes); *professional* occupational crime including those occurring in the medical, psychological, and legal professions; and *individual* occupational crime (e.g., employee theft, consumer fraud, personal income tax evasion, and securities violations).[16]

However, Green's categorization of white-collar offenses is similar to Edelhertz' 1970 typology in that it implies there is an aspect of democracy in the commission of acts of white-collar criminality. Put more succinctly by Kip Schlegel and David Weisburd: "white-collar crime is nothing more than another form of lawbreaking—like rape, vandalism, and simple assault —and readily can be incorporated into an explanatory framework that accounts for the causes of all criminal behavior."[17] Green's focus on offense types—and the broader issue of organizational crime—is a trend that has become popular in the white-collar crime research of the past three and a half decades.

CSI and Organizational Crime

Hit television shows such as *CSI* focus on the use of forensic techniques to solve murders, rapes, and other *mala in se* offenses. Perhaps it will surprise you to know that white-collar crime researchers have applied their own form of forensic analysis to our field for nearly thirty years. For example, consider David Ermann and Richard Lundman's (1978) theory of organizational crime.[18] An extension of Clinard and Quinney's (1973) theory which divided white-collar crime into two types: occupational and corporate,[19] Ermann and Lundman (1978) suggested that there are three major aspects of organizational crime, specifically (1) conflict between organizational goals; (2) organizational environment; and (3) internal culture and structure.[20] According to this typology, it is essential that companies have realistic mission statements and strong internal controls. Moreover, the organization must avoid relying on the individual employee's personal ethics to curtail criminal activity in the workplace.

Similarly, Kip Schlegel and David Weisburd's analysis of organizational crime (1992, Chapter 2), emphasizes the important function that a well-defined, realistic mission statement performs within an organization. The mission statement must express shared values strictly upheld and enforced by management. Accordingly, Wells notes "behaviorists generally conclude that one of the single most important factors influencing group behavior is the attitude of management"[21] Accompanying a strong mission statement supported by management should be strong internal controls. It is important to understand that these recommendations apply not only to Fortune 500 corporations, but to other institutions as well.

Now, using our CSI forensics-style skills, let's consider the case of Indiana University, and its well-known former Basketball Coach "Bobby" Knight.

Indiana University and the Bobby Knight Debacle: A Case Study in Organizational Crime?

Exhibit 7.1　Bobby Knight, one of the most successful coaches in NCAA basketball history, was a legend during his tenure at Indiana University. He is also well known for his allegedly explosive temper and on-court outbursts.

Few coaches in the history of NCAA athletics have proven as controversial as Bobby Knight. In his 29 years coaching the varsity basketball team at Indiana University (IU), his Hoosiers earned three national championships and amassed 763 victories. Yet throughout his career, Coach Knight also developed a reputation as being highly temperamental, and is considered relentless in his pursuit of winning.

Beginning in 1975, when he allegedly assaulted a sports reporter in the team's locker room, to a 1979 conviction for striking a Puerto Rican police officer during a warm-up session at the Pan American Games, and throughout a series of on-court outbursts in the 1980s in which he turned over benches, threw folding chairs, and shouted expletives at competing coaches and referees, Coach Knight maintained the support of Indiana University's President and Board of Trustees.

As evidence, consider the 1998 letter written by IU President Myles Brand and Chairman of the Board of Trustees John Walda to members of the media defending Knight's visceral style of coaching. Brand and Walda asserted that the media was biased in its relentless coverage of Knight's on- and off-court behavior (e.g., reporting Knight's alleged racist comments in a Moore County (Indiana) diner that resulted in a physical altercation between Knight and a customer).

Ultimately, it would take several more incidents to force IU President Brand to fire Mr. Knight. One of these situations involved the alleged choking of former player Neil Reed, for which Knight was fined $30,000 and suspended for three games. Another was the alleged arm-twisting of—and accompanying deluge of expletives toward—IU freshman Kent Harvey, which was prompted by Harvey supposedly asking the Coach, "Hey, Knight! What's up?" In defense of his reaction, Coach Knight maintains that the student should have referred to him as "Mr. Knight," and not by his last name.

Was Coach Knight's alleged misconduct simply grounded in his obsession to win at all costs? Or was there something more—a tacit understanding between Indiana University officials and alumni that as long as Knight and his Hoosiers continued to flourish, Knight's personal issues would be ignored?

Returning to the research by Ermann and Lundman (1978), if we examine the three major aspects of organizational crime (conflict between organizational goals, organizational environment, and internal culture and structure), it seems readily apparent that Indiana University's organizational goal was to win basketball games, thus drawing alumni support and improve the financial position of the college. Yet the organizational environment was rife with tensions—not just between Coach Knight and his players, but also among faculty members who repeatedly demanded Knight's resignation due to his alleged abuse of student athletes. Contributing to the hostile environment was the enigmatic response of the President and the Board of Trustees, who considered Knight's program an alumni support windfall for the university. Lastly, despite his propensity towards violence and aggression, the internal culture of IU supported Coach Knight even after his termination. This is evidenced by the death threats against IU freshman Kent Harvey and the four other witnesses who reported the incident to campus police, as well as the burning of Harvey's effigy on the IU campus during an organized march of thousands of students from Assembly Hall to President Brand's residence.

While the case of Coach Knight is not a severe example of organizational crime—especially when compared with a large business entity such as Enron or WorldCom—it does possess the two requisite elements of organizational crime: (1) an environment willing to tolerate his improper behavior (provided the Hoosiers continued to win games); and (2) a culture apathetic to issues of student athlete abuse and hostile to the reporting of such incidents. Ultimately, were it not for the incorporation of internal controls (such as IU's "zero tolerance" policy on abusive behavior towards students established in 2000), Coach Knight would have continued to rely on his own personal ethics for guidance, beliefs that are clearly inconsistent with the National Collegiate Athletic Association's policy statement on the purpose of post-secondary sports.

Ten Steps to Reduce Organizational Crime

In 1980, Marshall Clinard and Peter Yeager published their study of America's top Fortune 500 companies.[22] Based upon their analysis, these top 500 companies possessed an average of 2.7 violations (such as securities and exchange fraud) per organization, with nearly 60 percent of the companies averaging 4.4 violations or more.[23,24] They suggested ten steps to curtail corporate crime, which included the following:[25]

1. Strengthening consent agreements and decrees . . . to provide substantial remedies for violations and to include systematic follow-ups.
2. Increases in fine ceilings, with fines to be assessed according to the nature of the violation and in proportion to the company's annual sales.
3. Stiff criminal penalties for violations of health and safety or environmental regulations that "recklessly endanger" the public or employees.
4. Stronger statutes to prohibit companies that previously had violated federal laws from receiving federal contracts.
5. Mandatory publicity for corporate civil and criminal violations.
6. More extensive use of imprisonment with longer sentences. Community service in place of incarceration should be prohibited by law, except for unusual circumstances.
7. Convicted corporate offenders should be prevented from being indemnified by their companies.
8. Management officials convicted of criminally violating corporate

responsibilities should be prohibited for three years from assuming similar management positions in their company or others.

9. Directors would be liable, but not criminally, for being derelict in their duty to prevent illegal corporate actions.
10. A new commercial-bribery statute should be enacted to help prosecute corporate executives who receive kickbacks from their customers or suppliers.

Unfortunately, despite the tremendous scope of research conducted by Clinard and Yeager, it took more than twenty years before the bulk of their recommendations were considered by the Securities and Exchange Commission—America's corporate watchdog. After the collapse of Enron in 2001 and WorldCom in 2002, former SEC Chairman Harvey Pitt (with the full support of President George W. Bush) vowed to establish stringent new rules aligned with many of the ten recommendations found in Clinard and Yeager's study. However, as we discussed in Chapter 5 of this book, during the summer of 2002, President Bush quietly repealed many of these new sanctions and programs. In our opinion, among the most damaging of the sanctions that President Bush repealed was the elimination of a strategic enforcement unit designed to seek out and eliminate corrupt business practices in America's largest corporations. Why would Bush repeal these standards after creating a public outcry that rigorous new procedures were needed to protect the interests of individual investors and the American economy? The answer may be found in David Simon's Theory of Elite Deviance.

Elite Organizational Deviance and Corporate America: Environmental Examples

David R. Simon's concept of *elite organizational deviance* conjures up images of legendary sociologist C. Wright Mills passionately composing his famous work about America's major corporate executives, celebrities, military leaders, and politicians entitled *The Power Elite*.[26] Indeed, Simon often cites Mills in his (1996) book *Elite Deviance*[27] and his subsequent work, co-authored with Frank E. Hagan, entitled *White-Collar Deviance*[28] (1999). Both texts emphasize Simon's theory that crime and deviance are societally patterned (2002). According to Simon, one area of criminality overlooked by modern-day academicians is the analysis of patterns of illegal activity that exist at the core of large-scale corporate, industrial society[29] (1996). Simon contends that major corporations have enormous "behind-the-scenes" influence in our political system, which he refers to as "the invisible government."[30] Much of this influence is actually legal, and is the result of lobbying efforts, soft-money campaign contributions, and similar financial incentives.

For example, consider the fate of the public hazardous waste site clean-up program known as the "Superfund." Due to aggressive lobbying from Chemical Manufacturers of America, a major White House campaign contributor, the President did not push for reauthorization of the "Superfund" provisions of the Comprehensive Environmental Response, Compensation, and Liability Act of 1980[31] (CERCLA) or the Superfund Amendments and Reauthorization Act of 1986[32] (SARA). These laws required major chemical corporations to allocate funds for the remediation of America's most contaminated waste sites, many of which were abandoned by defunct businesses. Since 2004, all of the money for waste site clean-up has come from taxpayers. This shift has dramatically realigned the purpose of the program, which was originally designed to ensure that polluters pay the costs of clean-up.

Additional aspects of corporate wrong-doing within the environmental arena are commonplace. One such case is Polychlorinated Biphenyl (PCB) contamination. Initially discovered in 1865 and later synthesized in 1881, Polychlorinated Biphenyl (PCB) is a lubricating and cooling fluid comprised of 209 chlorinated compounds commonly referred to as *congeners*. The substance was widely used in electrical transformers, lighting ballasts, and industrial machinery from 1927 through 1977. Adverse health effects posed by PCBs were first documented in 1933 when nearly 96 percent of the workers at the Swann Chemical Company contracted skin lesions, blackheads, and other forms of chemical acne. Other symptoms of exposure included loss of appetite, lack of energy, and sexual dysfunction. Later exposure by workers at the Halowax Corporation in 1936 resulted in severe liver damage. By 1965, the Monsanto Corporation had determined that dioxin, a contaminant frequently found in PCBs, was capable of causing cancer.

Large quantities of PCBs were released into the environment from the early 1920s through the late 1970s in the course of product manufacturing and through accidental leaks, spills, and industrial fires. Once discharged, PCBs did not easily break down in soil or water, and traveled great distances via the air and underground rivers. As the contaminants affixed themselves to organisms, birds, reptiles, and mammals would consume the contaminants which increased in toxicity as they moved up the food chain—a process referred to as *bioaccumulation*. Ultimately, humans began consuming these highly concentrated forms of PCBs and dioxins through contaminated sport fish (e.g., lake trout, bass, etc.), as well as through beef and dairy cattle that had been exposed to PCBs through feed and grazing pastures. Infants born of women who had consumed large quantities of contaminated fish and dairy exhibited behavioral problems such as a deficiency in motor skills and short-term memory loss.

In a 1968 case involving the residents of Kyushu, Japan, more than 1,000 people became ill after eating Yusho—a rice-bran oil that was contaminated with PCBs. More than 50 deaths were attributed to this poisoning, and two out of twelve children were stillborn. By 1970, the Monsanto Corporation and Campbell's Soup had begun destroying pigs and chickens who had been feeding in areas where high levels of PCBs-in-soil were detected. The Agency for Toxic Substances and Disease Registry (ATSDR) and state and local public health agencies began alerting the public to the hazards posed by ingesting foodstuffs contaminated with PCBs.

In 1974, Congress passed the Safe Drinking Water Act in an effort to curtail ingestion of toxic substances, including PCBs. The United States Environmental Protection Agency (EPA) subsequently banned the use of PCBs in most industrial applications in 1979. However, substantial quantities of PCBs from used electrical equipment, faulty transformers, old lighting ballasts, and non-ferrous wiring and insulation that had been disposed of in landfills continued to yield in excess of 74,000 pounds of PCBs during the six-year period from 1987 to 1993. Residual waste found at uncontrolled or abandoned hazardous waste sites continue to account for the majority of releases of PCBs into the environment.

While a myriad of cases involving the disposal of PCBs occurred from the early 1930s through late 1970s, perhaps no single corporation is more associated with the discharge of PCBs than General Electric (GE). GE's production of electrical transformers and capacitors from the 1940s through the 1970s resulted in the substantial release of PCBs into major waterways such as the Hudson (New York) and Housatonic (Massachusetts) rivers. The Hudson River PCB plume spans nearly 200 miles, with an estimated 1.3 million pounds of contaminant alleged to have been released during the thirty years that plants operated in Hudson Falls and Fort Edward. Most of the contaminants settled on the river's bottom, which adversely affected both aquatic life and the $40 million per year commercial and recreational fishing industries along the Hudson. As part of a consent agreement between the United States Department of Justice, U.S. Environmental Protection Agency, and General Electric, GE has agreed to pay $78 million to the EPA as compensation for commercial response activities. General Electric also began a major Hudson River dredging project in 2007. Similarly, approximately 550 feet of sediment and 170 feet of soil located in and adjacent to the Housatonic River in Pittsfield, Massachusetts, were excavated in the 1990s as part of an agreement between GE and the EPA. General Electric also was held responsible for the removal of contaminated fill that it had given to the Town of Pittsfield for use as cover in playgrounds and residential neighborhoods. Some of this fill tested as high as 40,000 parts per million (PPM), well in excess of the EPA's legal safety standard of 2 PPM.

Much of the controversy surrounding General Electric's handling of the PCB contamination incidents in New York's Hudson Valley and Pittsfield, Massachusetts stems from its efforts to downplay the product's risk to human health and the environment. As early as the 1930s, workers at General Electric, as well as some of their clientele, were complaining of chemical acne after being exposed to PCBs. In 1937, production managers at GE's Wireworks factory in York, Pennsylvania began meeting with upper-level executives to discuss the outbreak of skin lesions and discomfort being experienced by employees at the facility. GE conducted confidential studies on the effects of PCB-in-oil exposure in 1938 and 1947, and found that exposure to these substances could damage target organs such as the liver and kidneys.

Yet GE's most hotly debated action was the release of a 1999 internal research study that purportedly showed little correlation between exposure to PCBs and mortality. The study was touted by major industries such as Fox Valley paper as evidence that the PCB scare had been overblown by the media and environmental watchdog organizations. However, it was later discovered that General Electric had not employed scientific rigor in their research, and the results were severely flawed. For example, the GE study had examined only airborne exposure to PCBs, not the more common routes of exposure: ingestion and absorption. The researchers had also pre-selected study participants—many of whom had worked for General Electric for less than a year. Lastly, the study failed to address those who had contracted—but not yet died from cancer (i.e., it was a snapshot as opposed to a longitudinal study).

The behavior by the manufacturers of PCBs, who ultimately did abandon their use though only after a period of intense public pressure and ensuing governmental regulation, is indicative of the challenges posed by attempting to impose standards upon Simon's "invisible government." Other examples include public safety abuses in the meat processing industry, cover-ups and conspiracies in the tobacco trade,[33] and Pharma Fraud, which will be discussed later in this chapter.

Curtailing Corporate Crime: A Self-Regulating Approach

If David Simon is correct that government cannot be trusted to monitor the private sector, what other alternative approaches should be considered? One of the most interesting proposals for curtailing corporate crime is suggested by John Braithwaite, who recommends that the government compel each company to establish rules for itself or its employees, unique to their particular circumstances.[34] Random federal audits would then be performed to monitor compliance.[35] David Friedrichs notes that there are benefits to this

Exhibit 7.2 The illicit disposal of hazardous waste poses serious risks for human health and the environment. Some corporations illegally dispose of toxic substances in order to reduce operating costs or increase their profit margin.

approach because "government does not even begin to have either the resources or the expertise to police or regulate fully all the activities of corporations, retail businesses, professionals, and legitimate white collar and blue collar entrepreneurs."[36]

While self-regulating, imposing international standards, and providing limited government oversight may prove appropriate for some portions of the private sector, applying the peer review and censure approach to professional organizations has not proven successful. For example, Gary Green notes, "of the approximately 320,000 physicians in the United States in the early 1970s . . . only seventy-two licenses were revoked each year."[37] Similarly, the American Bar Association (ABA) rarely recommends to state bar associations that attorneys be disbarred. Friedrichs notes that on aver-age, only a small number of lawyers are removed from the legal profession by the American Bar Association each year.[38]

In perhaps the most extreme example of the challenge of private sector self-policing, some members of Congress, representatives of the media, and outside researchers have suggested that the aircraft hijackings of September 11, 2001 were the result of inadequate security on the part of the major air carriers who provided their own security at the terminals and gates. Despite being required to comply with stringent guidelines established by the Federal Aviation Administration, the airlines were often found to be in violation of security regulations. It is still too early to tell whether the shift from privat-ization to federalization of airport security in 2002 will actually result in marked improvements in airport security, or if the American people would be better served adopting the industry models suggested by Braithwaite and Friedrichs.

However, regardless of the mechanisms employed to reduce organiza-tional crime, nearly all of the academic literature in our field suggests that employees should not be left to rely on their own personal ethics to decide what constitutes proper and improper behavior.[39]

Sarbanes-Oxley: Antidote or Catalyst to Corporate Criminal Liability?

If the consensus among academicians is that organizations should not have the power to self-regulate their behaviors, one of the most powerful legislative tools to shape corporate action should be the Sarbanes-Oxley Act of 2002. Named for Senator Paul Sarbanes, a long-serving former Senator (D-Maryland) and Representative Michael Oxley, a former Republican from Ohio, the Sarbanes-Oxley Act, also known as "SOX" is designed to combat fraud in public companies. SOX consists of eleven titles or sections designed to strengthen investor confidence in public corporations, and pre-vent failings of large organizations such as Enron and WorldCom. The law also provides a number of tools for auditors which can prove valu-able in assessing the overall health of the public corporation. These tools include regulatory checklists, compliance software, communication and collaboration software, and technical assistance databases. One of the major emphases of Sarbanes-Oxley is that public corporations use a consist-ent, document management and workflow approach to doing business. Towards this end, three types of software—data mining, file retrieval, and pattern recognition can play a valuable role in ensuring compliance with the Act.[40]

Of the 11 titles which comprise SOX, there are five sections that are particularly noteworthy with respect to combating fraud within public corporations. These are as follows:

- *Section 302—Corporate Responsibility for Financial Reports*: In the past, major officers of corporations would often plead ignorance to understanding the intricacies of the financial statements they were signing. This was frequently used as a defense when a company was suspected of engaging in fraudulent record-keeping. SOX now requires that corporate officers responsible for signing financial reports attest that they have fully reviewed the report, and that they are aware of the financial condition of their organization. Moreover, the report now requires that officers identify any internal deficiencies that could affect reporting or record-keeping, and that such evaluations have occurred within ninety days of the certification of the report.

- *Section 401—Disclosures in Periodic Reports*: Common financial statements such as off-balance sheet liabilities, obligations, or transactions must now be accurately presented in the company's financial report. In the past, companies would often record transactions in places other than their primary ledger which prevented them from being subjected to auditor scrutiny. "Off-the-books" transactions prevented auditors from accurately evaluating the financial health of an organization, sometimes giving shareholders a false sense of security in a corporation that was otherwise in fiscal crisis. Section 401 of Sarbanes-Oxley further charges the Commission responsible for overseeing the Act with frequently evaluating generally accepted accounting principals and other approaches that could result in portraying a less-than-accurate picture of a corporations fiscal well-being.

- *Section 404—Enhanced Financial Disclosures*: As we discussed earlier in this chapter, one of the greatest indicators of fraud within an organization is a lack of a common definition what should be deemed appropriate and inappropriate behaviors. Left to their own devices, employees and the corporations whom they serve sometimes branch out in different directions in terms of practices and approaches to doing business, some of which may lead to fraudulent activities. In order to prevent such occurrences, SOX requires that corporations possess a defined internal structure for financial reporting. In addition to maintaining such a structure, the organization must report on how effective their controls are with respect to reporting their financial status. Lastly, in order to prevent endless falsely positive self-reporting of their internal controls, the registered accounting firm responsible for reviewing the corporation must also attest to and report on the efficacy of the internal structure and control procedures that they use.

- *Section 409—Real Time Issuer Disclosures*: In the past, public corporations were not legally required to immediately report substantial changes in their financial condition such as a major financial loss or impending bankruptcy. Sometimes, this allowed senior corporate officers to quietly sell off their shares of the company before "the bottom dropped out" some months later. Indeed, the individual shareholder's only indication that something might be wrong with regards to the fiscal health of a corporation might be at the issuance of a quarterly report—far too late to protect one's assets. Accordingly, Section 409 of Sarbanes-Oxley now requires that corporations immediately disclose to the public any urgent "material changes in their financial condition of operations." One of the other important changes promulgated in this section of the Act is the requirement that public corporations provide information on the status of the company through clear and understandable language, supported by graphical representations of their fiscal well-being over time. For example, many companies now include trend-line charts in their prospectuses, so that the public will have a better understanding of how that corporation in performing in both the short and long term.

- *Section 802—Criminal Penalties for Altering Documents*: In Chapter 5 of this text, we discussed the panoptic vision of public corruption control. Specifically, that left unchecked, government employees would engage in corrupt practices. Thus, it could be argued that what is true for public employees is also true for publicly-held corporations. While sections 302, 401, 404, and 409 of SOX discuss the means by which companies must now report their fiscal status and the internal controls that must be put in place to accomplish this, Section 302 is really the weight behind the Act. Specifically, this section of Sarbanes-Oxley imposes penalties of up to 20 years imprisonment for "altering, destroying, mutilating, concealing ... [and] falsifying [financial] records." However, the Act goes further, by not only imposing these penalties upon the senior officers of these corporations, but also on external accountants responsible for maintaining these records The act requires that audit and financial review records be maintained for a period of five years. Failure on the part of the accountant to maintain such records is punishable by up to 10 years imprisonment.

You may be asking yourself whether Sarbanes-Oxley will ultimately prove valuable in combating white-collar crime. In reality, the answer to that question is unclear. For example, in fiscal year 2003, there were over 199 financial fraud and reporting cases under SOX, resulting in 32 companies being suspended from trading. During this same period, the assets of 36 individuals and companies were frozen, and the government sought to prohibit

110 executives from serving in publicly-traded companies. However, at the time of the development of this textbook, we are unaware of any cases in which anyone has been criminally sentenced for violating Sarbanes-Oxley. In other words, while there have been some efforts to rein in corporations who are not accurately reporting their financial condition, there does not appear to be a significant enforcement effort to bring the CEOs and CFOs of major corporations who violate the Act to justice. Edwin Sutherland's assessment of the swift punishment of those who engage in crime in the streets, compared with the lack of prosecution of "crime in the suites" appears as germane today as it was in 1939.

The Case of Big Pharma: Should We Consider a Sarbanes-Oxley Approach?

January 23, 2001: The U.S. Department of Justice announces that the Bayer Corporation has agreed to pay a total of $14 million to the federal government and 45 states, in an effort to settle a major case in which the pharmaceutical manufacturer had deliberately inflated the price of medications to increase their profits. Bayer further agrees to government monitoring for a period of five years.

If this were an isolated case of misconduct on the part of a drug manufacturer, we might simply be inclined to dismiss this as a simple case of corporate wrongdoing. However, in July 2008, Bristol-Myers Squibb, a major pharmaceutical corporation, agreed to pay $40 million to 43 states for a variety of alleged, illicit activities ranging from providing kickbacks and "improper inducements" to wholesalers[41]—actions not unlike the Bayer case of seven years earlier. In another 2001 high-profile case, Columbia/HCA Healthcare Corporation paid $881 million in response to allegations that it had submitted fraudulent reports on the cost of its products and had paid kickbacks to doctors for product referrals.

Increasingly, the government has focused its investigative efforts on the pharmaceutical industry, particularly in the areas of pharmaceutical pricing, and Medicare/Medicaid reimbursement. For example, the Office of the Inspector General's 2006 Work Plan focuses heavily on investigating and targeting for prosecution pharmaceutical companies engaged in over-billing for prescriptions under part D of Medicare[42] Part D of Medicare is the low-cost prescription drug benefit now provided to more than 40 million Americans at a taxpayer cost of more than $30 billion annually. It is not surprising wonder that pharmaceutical or "pharma" fraud has become an avenue rife for fraud. According to the World Trade Organization's 2005 Report, pharmaceutical products now account for 3 percent of all global trade. Moreover, Medicaid (the government's program for low income and disabled Americans) now covers nearly one-in-six Americans (i.e., about 53 million people). Spending on Medicaid has doubled in the past ten years[43] In a 2003 lawsuit filed by the State of California against big pharma companies Abbot and Wyeth, it was alleged that the state's Med-Cal prescription drug program had been overcharged by nearly 900 percent.[44]

Much like the period before Sarbanes-Oxley, when corporations were afforded wide latitude in the manner in which they reported profits and losses, major pharmaceutical manufactures are essentially "on their honor" to report the prices of their drugs. Not surprisingly, given this freedom in reporting, drug makers often publish one price for their drugs, but charge their customers (such as hospitals, pharmacists, etc.) a much lower price. Customers subsequently request reimbursement from Medicaid at the higher price published by the drug makers, and pocket the difference. In the 2001 Bayer case, this was referred to as "marketing the spread"[45] of course, the greater the spread, the larger the profits for the pharmaceutical companies and those who distribute their products.

As the price of these drugs increases, the burden for the government's Medicaid and Medicare Part D plan to keep up with the rising costs of these prescriptions becomes heavier, with taxpayers shouldering the bulk of the debt. For example, in the State of Texas alone between 1994 and 2003, the state budget grew 65 percent while Medicaid spending grew by 90 percent.[46]

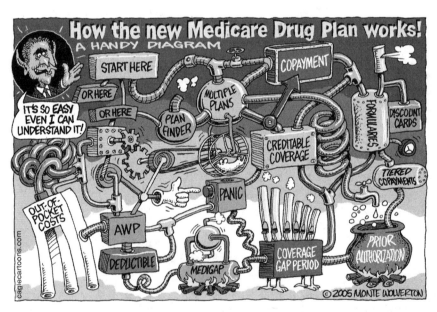

Exhibit 7.3 As Monte Wolverton depicts in this cartoon, understanding the Medicare prescription drug program is confusing at best, and presents many opportunities for Pharma fraud.

If the self-reporting of drug prices approach has failed, is the solution to adopt a Sarbanes-Oxleyesque approach in which strict controls for setting and broadcasting drug costs should be implemented? Specifically, should a section 802 provision affording criminal penalties be implemented? As the ensuing section of this chapter will discuss, employing a panoptic, individual-offender based approach to combating fraud and other organizational misdeeds may not the best solution to the challenges posed by corporate crime.

White-Collar Crime: Other Perspectives

One of the themes of the current and previous chapters of this text is the change in the research agenda from the pre-McCarthy era emphasis on common characteristics of would-be offenders to the categorization of occupational and corporate crimes since the early 1970s. However, there are a handful of academicians committed to examining white-collar criminality by studying the influence and interplay between individual offenders and their complex societies. In addition to Edleherz, Green, Yeager and Simon, criminologist John Braithwaite's proposition that "powerlessness and poverty increase the chances that needs are so little satisfied that crime is an irresistible temptation to actors alienated from the social order, that punishment is noncredible to actors who have nothing to lose" is an excellent example of the latter,[47] Braithwaite asserts that criminal acts are provoked by ". . . the humiliation of the offender and the offender's perceived right to humiliate the victim."[48] In exploring humiliation further, he identifies six forms of societies in which such behavior is culturally accepted or institutionally encouraged. These include *inegalitarian* societies, *racist* societies, *patriarchal* societies, *ageist* societies, *totalitarian* societies, and *retributive* societies.[49] It is important for you to note that these categories are *not* mutually exclusive. For example, American society could be collectively typified as racist, due to its historically segregationist policies such as the Jim Crow laws; patriarchal, because of the lack of equal pay and opportunity to excel for women in the workplace; and ageist, based on the general disregard for the wisdom and experience of senior members of our society, as well as its quest for eternal youth. Some Middle Eastern countries may exhibit elements of an all-powerful political tribunal (totalitarianism), lack of social and reproductive rights for women (patriarchy), and employ an "eye-for-an-eye" approach to equal justice (retribution).

While Braithwaite attributes much of violent criminal behavior to the humiliation posed by inegalitarian, racist, patriarchal, ageist, totalitarian, and retributive societies, he does see some value in humiliating or shaming white-collar offenders. Specifically, his theory notes that

> [for] individuals and corporations alike, shaming from without (e.g., by state agencies) and from within (e.g., by corporate colleagues) is a normative form of social control that has the potential to be far more effective than other forms of social control (especially coercive ones).[50]

David Friedrichs' analysis of Braithwaite's theory stresses that the value of social humiliation lies in the reintegration of the individual (or corporation) into society, rather than the stigmatization of the offender from society. The term used to describe such behavior is *reintegrative shaming*. These findings are consistent with Michael Benson's study on the emotional aspects of white-collar offenders, which suggests that "to be convicted of a crime makes one a criminal and *nothing but* a criminal." Like Braithwaite, Benson asserts that "by this stigmatization, society rejects offenders, making them outsiders . . . rather than making offenders feel repentant, it provokes anger and resentment as offenders attempt to maintain a morally acceptable view of self."[51]

Also consistent with Braithwaite and Benson on the role of humiliation in social integration is the research of Gregory Grose and W. Byron Groves[52] (1988). As described in David Greenberg's *Crime and Capitalism: Readings in Marxist Criminology* (1993), their theory draws heavily on portions of Karl Marx's writings on basic human needs, noting "the need to be recognized may be universal . . . [however,] social arrangements can frustrate it by denying to individuals or groups the opportunity to make a contribution to the achievement of a collective goal and to be valued for that contribution."[53] In language comparable to Robert Merton's 1938 strain theory,[54] Grose and Groves indicate that if one lacks legitimate methods to achieve this recognition, he or she may resort to illicit means to obtain it.[55]

Researcher David M. Gordon has a slightly different perspective on the disparity between workers and managers, including the specific role that crime plays within American society. Gordon reflects, "I've been unable to escape the mounting suspicion that those countries with the top-heaviest systems of labor control [such as the United States] are also those who lock up the highest proportion of their population."[56] In other words, there is a relationship between control in corporate America and management of the general society through incarceration. Low-level workers are expected to do as they are told, not just in the factory, but also within the confines of the criminal justice system in order to avoid negative consequences.

One of the best ways to keep workers "in line" is through the implementation of standards that ensure employee loyalty. Scholar Diane Vaughan has extensively studied the methods used by major corporations and other large organizations, and has identified six key elements that can be utilized to ensure employee loyalty. These are as follows:[57]

1. Recruit individuals similar to those already employed within the organization.
2. Reward those who put the needs of the company before themselves (e.g., raises, bonuses, etc.).
3. Provide long-term incentive packages such as profit sharing, retirement and pension plans that reward longevity in service.
4. Provide social and recreational activities for employees that foster organizational membership
5. Isolate employees from the outside community by requiring them to work long hours and transfer to other duty stations frequently
6. Create positions that are so technically specialized that it would be difficult for the employee to transfer to a position in another company.

Vaughn's research into corporate loyalty is typified in the 2000 film entitled *Boiler Room* (2000) starring Giovanni Ribisi as Seth Davis—a 19-year-old, fast-talking, high-pressure stockbroker. In this film, it is the character's fear of losing his material possessions, coupled with an organization that has successfully managed to integrate the six elements necessary to ensure employee loyalty, which keeps him from going "legitimate."

Bridging the Gap Between Theory and Practice: Spotlight on the National White Collar Crime Center (NW3C)

For more than twenty years, the National White Collar Crime Center (NW3C) has provided high-quality research and technical support to various federal, state, and local law enforcement agencies engaged in the fight against fraud, forgery, embezzlement, and other economic crimes. Because the NW3C has no investigative authority of its own, many premier regulatory and intelligence agencies feel comfortable employing the various resources available through the Center without fear that their cases will be "stolen away" after arrests have been made. For example, in 2001, the Federal Bureau of Investigation (FBI), in partnership with NW3C, completed a year-long case code-named "Operation Cyber Loss." The Internet Fraud Complaint Center (IFCC), located at the NW3C, served as the catalyst for this joint enforcement action. As a result of this major effort, nearly 90 people and organizations were charged with offenses ranging from non-delivery of merchandise and online marketing scams to bank fraud and credit card fraud. The FBI estimates that more than 75,000 people are victimized via the Internet each year, with aggregate losses of more than $300 million.[58]

In addition to supporting law enforcement and investigative agencies, the NW3C also houses the White Collar Crime Research Consortium (WCCRC). The WCCRC consists of professors, researchers, and criminal justice practitioners engaged in the study of occupational and economic crimes. Both the NW3C and the WCCRC frequently sponsor training programs and produce scholarly literature for both law enforcement official use and to promote public awareness of white-collar crime.

For further information, see http://www.nw3c.org

Chapter Summary

Generally speaking, the original agenda offered by Sutherland and his contemporaries can be viewed collectively as an effort to examine individual motivations for engaging in acts of white-collar criminality. As we discussed in the previous chapter, scholars such as Donald Cressey and Marshall Clinard explored not simply issues of social class, but rather the specific characteristics of such offenders, including their motivations and rationalizations for committing these acts. In sharp contrast, the period of academic research from approximately 1970 to present has been marked by a strong desire to divide behavior into two distinct groups: *occupational crime* and *corporate* (or *organizational*) *crime*. Rather than focus on the characteristics of the individual offender, analysis of organizational structure and the environment in which businesses compete have become popular areas of study; particularly with respect to the commission of fraudulent activities in corporations, public institutions, and professional organizations of various shapes, sizes, and structures (e.g., Edelhertz, Green, *et al*).

In our opinion, we believe that the vision shared by Sutherland and Cressey during the first three decades of white-collar crime research, as well as the efforts over the past 40 years to examine corporate crime and understand illicit organizational activities, are equally important to the field. Accordingly, given the small amount of data that scholars have collected in the area of white-collar criminality during the past nearly seventy years (at least when compared with other aspects of criminology such as research into violent behavior), we must strive to meet David Friedrich's challenge of identifying and connecting "macrolevel" and "microlevel" research within the discipline.

ADAPTED READINGS

Reading 7–1: Davita Silfen Glasberg and Dan Skidmore, *The Dialectics of White-Collar Crime: The Anatomy of the Savings and Loan Crisis and the Case of Silverado Banking, Savings and Loan Association*

> *Earlier in this chapter, we mentioned the serious harm caused to both the American and global economy by the savings and loan crisis of the 1980s. What were the root causes of this disaster and how does it connect to the larger issues of organizational and corporate crime discussed in this chapter?*

The savings and loan bailout stands out as the first time in U.S. history that Congress agreed to bail out an entire industry as opposed to a single corporation. It is by far the most expensive bailout to which Congress has ever agreed, and the first time a bailout has been underwritten with a blank check rather than a specified dollar amount. It is costing the United States taxpayers $200 billion and counting to bail out the S&L industry from the crisis of the 1980s (Bradsher, 1994; see also Bater, 1994). Estimates are that the savings and loan bailout will total more than $500 billion over the next forty years (with some experts insisting that the cost may total more than $1 trillion over the next thirty years; Hays & Hornik, 1990, p. 50). The sticker shock of that cost tends to invite simplified analyses of the cause of the crisis. Two competing perspectives prevail: on one hand are stories of individual fraud and greed that dominate the popular press; on the other are arguments focusing on organizational factors that differentiate white-collar crime from other crimes, an analysis that tends to receive favor in sociological studies of the crisis.

Fraud remains an intriguing focus of media examinations of the S&L crisis. The popular press continues to emphasize fraud as the major culprit in the S&L crisis. In 1991 alone, the FBI budgeted more than $125 million to pursue cases of fraud in the industry (U.S. Congress: Senate, 1992, p. 45), resulting in 6,405 indictments for bank-related crimes; 96.5 percent of the resolved cases resulted in convictions of S&L violators by the end of 1995, with more than three-quarters of those convicted going to prison (Singletary, 1995, p. A10; U.S. Department of Justice, 1992, p. 66).

Many scholars (cf. Barth, 1991; Barth, Batholomew, & Labich, 1989) counter that fraud accounted for very little of the dollar value lost in the crisis. Although half of the insolvent thrifts have been found to involve elements of fraud in 1988 (Barth, 1991), observers have estimated that fraud accounts for as little as 3 percent of the cost of the bailout (cf. Barth, 1991, p. 44; Ely, 1990). Others offered a more conservative estimate of 10 percent (Barth, Bartholomew, & Labich, 1989).

On the other hand, Calavita and Pontell (1990, 1991, 1993, 1997) note that the measures used by observers like Ely and Barth *et al.* were seriously flawed and grossly underestimated the amount of fraud involved in the crisis. They argue instead that deregulation, coupled with the banks' structural role as trustees of other people's money, facilitated what they termed "collective embezzlement" in the industry as standard operating procedure. Under bank deregulation, there were far fewer field supervisors and auditors, and consequently much less oversight of the financial status and practices of the savings and loans. In the absence of adequate and regular oversight, fraud became not only possible but standard operating procedure. Deregulation of banking (both de facto with early, unofficial relaxations of regulations, and later, de jure in formal legislation) created conditions that made regular fraudulent practices the norm (see also Zimring & Hawkins, 1993). Thus, even in some fraud-based analyses, deregulation emerges as a critical factor in the savings and loan industry's crisis.

This brief introduction to the debate concerning the nature of the S&L crisis points to theoretical difficulties with the very conceptualization of white-collar occupational and organizational crime. Conceptualizations of white-collar crime have been preoccupied typically with identifying the unique characteristics that differentiate it from other crimes, "rather [than] to search for interactions along different dimensions and between multiple components that make up crime and societal reaction to crime" (Schlegel & Weisburd, 1993, p. 4). That is, sociological analyses of white-collar crimes such as those behaviors found in the S&L crisis focus on the common static elements that make white-collar crime distinctive. A more fruitful pursuit may be to examine white-collar crime as interactive or as a dialectic process.

A second theoretical issue implied by the dominant analyses of the S&L crisis is the distinction between occupational and organizational crime. Although inquiries often blend these two aspects of white-collar crime, they are frequently conceptualized as having important dimensional differences. Occupational crime is commonly defined as illegal activities engaged in by individuals against the organization for their own gain in the course of their occupational duties (Clinard & Quinney, 1973; Coleman, 1985; Hagan, 1985; Sutherland, 1949). Analyses of the individuals who have perpetrated fraud against the thrift institutions imply the problem to be greedy individuals who need to be removed from the institutions to solve the problem. In contrast, organizational crime is defined as illegal behavior "committed by executives and managers acting as representatives of their institutions on behalf of those institutions" (Calavita & Pontell, 1994, p. 300; see also Hagan, 1985; Schrager & Short, 1978; Wheeler & Rothman, 1982).

The definition of organizational crime implies a focus on the internal structure of the organization itself, as if the organization exists independently of external forces that might create relations, processes, and structures within organizations. Analyses of the S&L crisis based on this perspective imply the crisis of the S&L industry to be an incredible coincidence of many individual thrifts adopting similar standard operating procedures. Here, the individual thrifts need only to restructure to correct the crisis. The problem with this analysis is that it does not explain why so many thrift institutions would suffer crises at the same time: what common factor, external to individual S&L institutions, might explain the phenomenon? This perspective suggests that the problem might be the very structure of the industry, suggesting that the industry needs to be reorganized. We suggest that the S&L crisis may represent a combination of both occupational and organizational crime: the structure of the financial industry in general and the thrift industry in particular operated in an environment created by deregulation that became fertile ground for behaviors that benefited the organizations and individuals to the detriment of the organizations. This dialectical process may also be more fruitfully under-stood in the context of an ongoing state project of economic intervention in which contradictory policy and implementation forces and relationships oper-ate to produce unintended consequences (Glasberg & Skidmore, 1997a, 1997b; Skidmore & Glasberg, 1996).

Our analysis points to an intersection of the literature on occupational and organizational crime with the literature on the state. Indeed, Calavita and Pon-tell (1994) for example, advocated the incorporation of the state as a factor in the explanation of organizational cranes like those characterizing the S&L debacle. However, they focused on factors that affected inconsistent state enforcement or regulations and prosecution of violators, implying that organ-izational crime may be facilitated by a failure to enforce existing restrictions against deviant or criminal behavior. However, an analysis of the provisions of bank deregulation in 1982 suggests that the state may also play a more direct role in generating crimes by creating legislatively the very conditions that enable them to occur.

Such an approach has been used to powerful effect in Vaughan's (1996) analysis of the 1986 shuttle *Challenger* disaster. She found that the tragedy of the *Challenger*'s explosion was not so much the result of individual hubris and organizational wrongdoing, but more the result of the intersection of the vari-ous levels of organizational culture within NASA, the national organizational environment of competitive production and scarce resources among con-tractors, and organizational uncertainty produced by layers of secrecy within NASA and between NASA and its civilian contractors. Vaughan's analysis points to a useful application for understanding the S&L crisis: we would do well to look beyond individual greed and fraud and internal cultures within the S&L industry to contradictory environments created within and between the industry and its operational context of the political economy. Such an analytical agenda suggests the need to explore the relationship between state policy and its implementation within the industry and the decision-making processes of individual firms and their executives.

Theories of the state that conventionally frame policy analyses are limited in this endeavor, however. State theorists' agenda generally focuses more on pol-icy making than on policy implementation and its consequences, whether intended by the policy or not. For example, capitalist state structuralists

(Jessop, 1990; Vallochi, 1989) and business dominance theorists (Akard, 1992; Burris, 1992; Domhoff, 1990, 1991; Useem, 1984) emphasize largely the role of the state in reinforcing and subsidizing capital accumulation interests through the development and implementation of policy. Business dominance theorists argue that capital accumulation interests actively manipulate the decision making process to address their needs. In contrast, capitalist state structuralists insist that such manipulation is unnecessary: the state produces policies that give advantage to capitalists because it has no other option; to ignore such interests is to court economic disaster and thus political legitimacy crises. State-centered theorists argue that the state remains independent of influence by such interests and produces policies based on its own agenda contoured by past legislative precedents, political and party needs, and state managers' interests in expanding their administrative domain and autonomy (see, e.g., Amenta & Parikh, 1991; Amenta & Skocpol, 1988; Hooks, 1990, 1993; Skocpol, 1988, 1992).

These theories may be useful in explaining deregulation legislation as either an attempt by the state to reinforce finance capital accumulation interests in the industry, or a way to resolve an economic crisis that had potential for undermining the state. However, these theories are limited in explaining the impact of that legislation on the industry because they do not focus on the effects policy may have on corporate behavior. Yet it would be useful to engage an analysis of the role of the state policy of deregulation in facilitating the corporate crimes punctuating the S&L industry crisis. How did the provisions of deregulation affect behavior within the thrifts industry in general and within individual thrift institutions? A dialectic perspective is more useful as a dynamic framework for examining the resonance between legislation and the unintended outcomes of its implementation. That is, deregulation legislation did not appear to be pursued by the industry in order to facilitate the looting of the thrift institutions, as business dominance theorists might argue. It did not appear to be the state's agenda to facilitate such behavior; indeed, the state's agenda seems to argue against supporting behavior that would cost it billions of dollars in deposit insurance payouts and other bailout costs. A dialectic perspective, on the other hand, suggests that deregulation was initially passed as part of a larger state project of economic intervention that created contradictorily the conditions enabling organizational strategies and crimes benefitting both individual executives and the thrift institutions while costing the state a great deal of money (Glasberg & Skidmore, 1997a, 1997b; Skidmore & Glasberg, 1996).

One limitation of state theory, then, is its focus on de jure policy creation rather than de facto policy implementation and the outcomes and behaviors it might produce. In the instance of the savings and loan industry's crisis we are confronted with a case in which state policy contained defeating incentives and produced unintended consequences (i.e., the industry's deepening crisis). This critique of state theory points to an avenue for expanding an understanding of organizational and occupational crimes. That is, do such behaviors represent individual or organizational deviance? Or are they the result of a dialectical process among the state, the economy, the industry, and individuals, such that the behaviors are enabled by external incentives or permissions contained in state policy, even if those incentives contradict other state policies identifying such behaviors as unethical or criminal?

To better evaluate the relationship between the state and the organizational crimes in the S&L crisis, it is useful to analyze the development of the industry, and then examine the effects of deregulation through analyses of case studies of failed thrift institutions. How did the S&L industry develop in the first place, and what was its purpose? How did it later get into such severe difficulties? What role did individual greed and fraud play in the deepening crisis, and what role did bank deregulation, which was supposed to alleviate the industry's crisis, play?

I The S&L Industry as a State Project

The savings and loan industry's existence can be understood as an out-growth of the larger welfare state regime's project of economic intervention: it was initially created as part of the United States' economic recovery efforts following the Great Depression of the 1930s. Large commercial banks had abandoned housing lending in favor of more lucrative corporate and state lending, or had charged interest rates that made home mortgages inaccessible to Americans on a moderate income. Congress facilitated the creation of "thrift" depository institutions (S&L banks and mutual savings banks) to fill this void. The S&L branch of the banking industry was created to supply affordable mortgages to working-class families, so that the American Dream of home ownership would not slip beyond their grasp. To ensure an ongoing commitment to the home mortgage market, thrifts were prohibited by law from offering high interest rates on deposits and from investing in speculative instruments like real estate, stocks, and development projects—strategies that commercial banks were permitted to adopt (U.S. Congress: House, 1989a). This regulation of banking created a structure of institutional distinctions within the industry: commercial banks were allowed to invest in a broad variety of instruments (including corporate, governmental, and mortgage lending; stocks and bonds investments; and real estate speculation), to charge market-based interest on loans, and to pay competitive interest rates on deposits. S&L institutions, on the other hand, operated within restrictions not placed on the commercial banks, including a narrow definition of their business activities to home mortgages offered at lower interest rates and for longer maturities than commercial banks; prohibitions against paying out high interest rates on deposits; and restrictions against investing in high-yield but risky investment instruments like real estate speculation and junk bonds.

Up until the late 1970's, S&Ls prospered under these regulations securing low-cost, long-term residential mortgages as their industry niche. What happened to undermine an industry that had a clearly defined market with little competition, and which had performed well for almost sixty years?

The legacy of the state project set the stage for the crisis. Formal laws and regulations creating the S&L industry were intended to separate the markets of S&L and commercial banks, so as to reduce or eliminate destructive competition or unfair advantage to the larger commercial banks that would be detrimental to working class and middle class potential home buyers. But those same laws and regulations neglected to take into account the fact that depositors may choose which of these institutions provided a better return on their deposits. In a larger sense, then, commercial banks and savings and loans did compete unequally in the single market for depositors, if not in the same market for investments. This meant that the regulations had in fact created structural hindrances for S&L institutions so that the thrifts could not compete effectively with commercial banks or roll with the punches in the economy. For example, the "Q differential," or "regulation Q," enacted in 1966, established interest rate ceilings for the entire banking industry and created an interest-rate differential between commercial banks and S&Ls. This differential—one-"Q"uarter of 1 percent on 30-month and 6-month small-saver certificates—allowed thrifts to compete with commercial banks by offering a slightly higher return on savings; this provided thrifts the capital they needed to fulfill their mortgage mission.

Contradictorily, regulation Q (a form of state economic intervention designed to preserve the integrity of the banking industry) in some sense precipitated the S&L crisis (Barth, 1991). In the late 1970's, nondepository financial corporations such as Merrill Lynch and retailers like Sears began offering investment products at "market rates"—rates higher than the rate-controlled depository institutions were allowed to offer. As savers became increasingly sophisticated about the effects of inflation on their savings, passbook accounts became less desirable. Small depositors, the primary source of thrifts' capital, withdrew their savings to invest in higher-rate instruments such as the money market mutual funds offered by nondepository financial institutions. According to Edwin Brooks, then president of the U.S. League of Savings Associations (the "US League," a S&L trade group), in the first four months of 1980 S&Ls acquired net new savings of $587 million and closed mortgage loans of $18.4 billion representing a 93% decline in savings and a 35% decline in mortgages from the same period the previous year (U.S. Congress: House, 1980, pp. 24, 25). Thus, despite the Q differential, by the end of the 1970s deposits, and therefore mortgage money, began to dry up. According to Paul Volcker, then chair of the Federal Reserve, in 1976 thrifts provided almost 65% of all residential mortgage money. By 1979, this amount had fallen to 37% and the estimated annualized rate based on lending for the first half of 1980 was 16.4% (U.S. Congress: House, 1980, p. 49).

As a result of decades of mortgage lending, the asset side of S&L's ledgers were burdened with long-term mortgages slowly being repaid at rates as low as 6 percent or 7 percent. To offset these old investments, rates on new mortgages climbed as high as 16 percent. On the liability side, competition with nondepository financial institutions for deposits created losses as interest rates paid on deposits surpassed those received from loans (U.S. Congress: House, 1981a, p. 46; see also Barth, 1991). The shortage of deposits, combined with high mortgage interest rates, meant that money for housing was effectively unavailable. Indicative of the historical relation between the state and the banking industry, federal legislators were concerned that the destruction of the thrifts meant "destroying the last vestige of a specialized mortgage finance supplier" (U.S. Congress: House, 1981, p. 2). Moreover, because housing is associated with a number of industries (such as building materials, major appliances, and textiles) the absence of mortgage monies aggravated the larger downturn in the U.S. economy. Thus, the state's attempt to stabilize the economy through bank regulation set the stage contradictorily for instability in the $&L industry and in the larger economy.

II Deregulation: Institutional Shifts in the State Project

In the early 1980s, industry trade groups argued that the thrift industry's role as a provider of affordable mortgages, in accordance with its Congressional mandate, produced the thrift's decline—not poor management (no one as yet raised the spectre of fraud). A majority of legislators concurred, arguing that the policies constituting the Congressional mandate of the 1930s were anachronisms given the economic troubles of the 1970s; the crisis required a shift in the structure of the relation between the state and the banking industry. This deregulatory shift would relax interest rate limits and remove restrictions on the intermingling of commercial banking, home banking, real estate, and securities investing (U.S. Congress: House, 1981a). The legislature's endorsement of this analysis of the crisis exonerated banking management from the S&L crisis.

Instead, Congress assumed the industry's crisis to be rooted in the structure of banking, and established the Depository Institutions Deregulation Committee (DIDC). The DIDC's charge was to free thrifts from rate regulations that diminished their competitiveness with nondepository financial organizations. Its first action, then, was to eliminate interest rate regulation in an effort to avoid the competitive advantage regulation Q gave S&Ls (U.S. Congress: House, 1980).

In addition to legislative shifts in the relation between the state and the banking industry, the deregulatory state project also involved de facto shifts in regulatory policy. Prior to formal deregulation, restrictions on the relations between thrifts, commercial banks, nondepository financials, and bank holding companies were subverted with the regulators' permission. Citicorp's purchase of Fidelity, a California S&L, is one example of a formerly prohibited activity receiving regulatory authorization. Deregulation provided de jure approval to de facto regulatory policy.

Yet, even with passage of the Garn-St. Germain Act formally deregulating banks, the industry remained troubled. This is because the Garn-St. Germain Act contained incentives for investment behaviors within the industry that defeated the intent of the legislation. For example, unlike the Depression-era Glass-Steagall Act that established the FDIC and limited the securities activities of depository institutions, the 1982 net-worth guarantee allowed S&Ls to become involved in speculative, high-risk investments while simultaneously positioning the state to bail out the industry (National Commission on Financial Institution Reform, Recovery, and Enforcement, 1993). Moreover, the existence of federal deposit insurance subsidized the increasing risks associated with the casino-like atmosphere of a deregulated industry and encouraged fraud: because all deposits were insured up to $100,000 per account, fraudulent thrifts could offer some of the highest interest rates to attract a steady input of deposits while reassuring customers of the security of their money. Thus, thrift institutions could engage in high-stakes speculative investments and unorthodox bookkeeping with impunity because the costs of such ventures would be underwritten by the federal government. Thus, a combination of federal policies created a ripe environment for fraud, abuse, and organizational crime.

According to a range of Congressional witnesses and a Congressional National Commission on the Financial Institutions Reform, Recovery, and Enforcement Act (FIRREA), the post-deregulation banking industry crisis was rooted in the regulatory shifts that modified the state-industry relation (see U.S. Congress: House, 1989a, 1989b, 1989c). Deregulation blurred the lines between banks and thrifts and between depository and nondepository financial institutions, lifted restrictions on loan and deposit interest rates, removed the prohibition against interest payments on demand deposits (checking accounts), and permitted depository institutions to become involved in public revenue bonds and a wider variety of consumer and commercial loans. Deregulation, ostensibly designed to relieve the late '70s–early '80s S&L crisis, opened the industry to formerly state-proscribed market practices. Unprecedented, high interest rates on deposits, imprudent real-estate speculation, and participation in the junk-bond market—all departures from thrifts' home mortgage niche—were state sanctioned. According to the National Commission: "[g]overnment policies made the system vulnerable to corruption. [F]raud was not the cause of the debacle" (National Commission on Financial Institution Reform, Recovery, and Enforcement, 1993, p. 8).

How, specifically, did deregulatory policy and the contradictory forces it unleashed in the industry interact dialectically with the economy, the industry, and the individuals within the industry to shape corporate and executive criminal behavior? Let us examine one case study of an S&L crisis to explore the role of state projects and state policy in the dialectical processes creating organizational crimes in the industry.

III Silverado Bank: Deregulation and Unreal Estate Speculation

Silverado banking, savings and loan association (hereafter referred to as Silverado Bank) began in 1956 as Mile High Savings and Loan Association, a bank chartered by the State of Colorado. It was a typically unnoteworthy savings and loan, solid but unimpressive in its growth as a home mortgage lender until the mid-1980s, when it became Silverado Bank and began showing explosive growth in assets and investments. Yet, only two years after posting significant growth, Silverado collapsed, and by the end of 1988 Federal regulators closed the bank. How did such an impressive success story turn so quickly into a disaster?

Silverado's story includes many of the elements found in other S&L stories: power, intrigue, murky business ethics, legal gray areas, and the fall of the rich and famous (all of which we will get to shortly). But the story of Silverado Bank also highlights another important factor in the S&L crisis: wild real estate speculation by erstwhile stodgy but solvent S&L institutions, facilitated by deregulation. This case highlights the intersection of organizational crime and occupational crimes with state policy as the enabling structural environment.

In the early 1980s Silverado Bank, like many S&L institutions, sought to close the gap between older, low-interest mortgage payments coming in and high interest payments of deposits going out by taking advantage of the more relaxed environment created by deregulation. Colorado's economy was booming, primarily due to the oil industry, and real estate development projects grew rapidly. Deregulation now allowed S&L institutions like Silverado to enter real estate speculation and commercial development projects that were previously inaccessible to them. Silverado entered that market aggressively; indeed, by the mid-1980s Silverado had shifted its focus from a single-family home mortgage lender to a "complex financial institution specializing in commercial real estate lending" (U.S. Congress: House, 1990a, p. 249). By 1986, $1.1 billion in commercial real estate construction loans, "the riskiest types of loans an S&L could make," accounted for 85 percent of Silverado's loan portfolio (U.S. Congress: House, 1990a, p. 68). The initial profits from Silverado's activities in these investments were considerable: its total assets grew 347 percent between 1980 and 1983, when its total assets were $370 million; it continued to show phenomenal growth until 1987, when its total assets were over $2.2 billion. Its annual asset growth rates were equally outstanding: 1984 alone posted an asset growth rate of 157 percent (U.S. Congress: House, 1990a, p. 120, 248–49, 1990b, p. 158). Such figures would be the envy of any business.

But this incredible balloon began to quickly lose air. Although Colorado's economy continued to boom while other state economies were in recession, that charmed existence did not last. Both the state and the economy collided to affect Silverado's strategy of real estate speculation. First, the state once again intervened in the general economy (not just in the structure of the banking industry) as part of its continuing state project in the mid-1980s, when Federal Reserve Board Chairman Paul A. Volcker allowed the interest rate to free float. This served to undermine the real estate speculation investments that thrifts like Silverado sought to resolve its cash flow crisis. In addition, the oil industry bust (caused by sharply declining prices) caught up with Colorado in the late 1980s, and consequently, as it did in states like Texas and California, the real estate market imploded. Banks like Silverado that were overexposed in real estate speculation and commercial development projects found themselves getting sucked under in the vortex of delinquencies and foreclosures, which skyrocketed in 1987 and 1988. Audited financial statements for the bank showed Silverado had a $200 million insolvency (U.S. Congress: House, 1990a, p. 67, 1990b). Rather than acknowledge the problem and get out of real estate as quickly as they could, Silverado's management developed a scheme for creating the image of a still-healthy and growing institution that complied with federal solvency standards. Enter the "quid pro quo" program.

Under the quid pro quo program, Silverado would arrange a deal with borrowers that the bank would provide the loans the borrowers requested plus a premium on the loan, which the borrower agreed to use to purchase stock in Silverado Financial Corporation, the holding company that owned Silverado (U.S. Congress: House, 1990a, 1990b, p. 162–63). This arrangement created the appearance of increasing Silverado's capital structure. Two major auditing firms, Ernst & Whitney, and later Coopers & Lybrand, concluded that, "Silverado directly and indirectly provided the funds for its own capital infusions contrary to applicable regulations" (U.S. Congress: House, 1990a, p. 121). Coopers & Lybrand specifically noted that these transactions did not constitute an actual contribution of new capital to the bank at all (U.S. Congress: House, 1990a, p. 257).

Coupled with Silverado's aggressive venture into real estate development projects was Silverado's foray into a new and complex investment tool: residual interests in real estate mortgage investment conduits (REMICs). REMICs are pooled mortgages that are sold to investors. The pool contains a hierarchy of tranches, with each tranch containing its own risk level and relative yield: high-risk tranches offered high yields. Silverado invested in the "residual" tranches—those that remained when all other tranches had been sold. These residual tranches were the highest-risk tranches in the pool, offering the highest return on investment—often as high as 18 percent return when Silverado purchased them. Like junk bonds, these high-risk tranches offered an attractive potential to earn vast amounts of money to help close the gap between high interest deposit payouts and low interest mortgage receipts. But, like junk bonds, the risk was great for a huge loss. The risk associated with the residual tranch of REMICs is that their yield is highly sensitive to the difference between the effective interest rates on the pooled mortgages and the international interest rate established by the London InterBank Offering Rate (LIBOR). A large increase in LIBOR "could wipe out most of the value of the residuals" (U.S.

Congress: House, 1990a, p. 263). A steady LIBOR could produce a very nice return to Silverado.

Despite the risks associated with investing in the residual tranches, Silverado could not resist the potential high yield, and invested heavily. By the end of 1987 the bank had invested $500 million in REMIC residuals. At first the investment seemed like a shrewd investment indeed: LIBOR had dropped from 8 percent in the first quarter of 1986 to almost 5 percent by the end of that year; the following year LIBOR remained fairly stable into the first quarter of 1988. But after that first quarter LIBOR began to rise sharply, from slightly more than 6 percent in late 1987 to 9.5 percent in 1989 (U.S. Congress: House, 1990a, p. 263). The results were catastrophic for Silverado: the rise in LIBOR effectively wiped out their investments.

Silverado clearly needed to take fairly drastic measures to recapitalize, or at least to reshuffle their ledger so as to appear solvent. In addition to the creative financing of the quid pro quo program, Silverado used some creative accounting procedures. Although its growth in the mid-1980s was explosive, its growth in 1986 was healthy but smaller compared to the earlier years. The bank sought to protect itself from the enormous risks the earlier loans posed by forming a "pool" of these existing loans in 1986; they then sold discounted junior interests in the pool to outside investors while retaining senior interest itself. Holders of senior interest received preferential payments of interest and principal on the loans in the pool before the holders of junior interests. Much like junk bonds, the appeal to purchasers of junior interests in the pool was the potential for high yield; the risk was that in the event of default on a loan in the pool, the holders of junior interests would be the first in line to lose their investment (U.S. Congress: House, 1990a, p. 257, 1990b, p. 164).

In his testimony before Congress, Brian C. McCormally, District Counsel for the Office of Thrift Supervision in Topeka, Kansas, pointed to the organizational or corporate crime inherent in these investments, complaining that the primary purpose of the loan pools was to "circumvent the appropriate recognition of loan losses and to manipulate the institution's balance sheet" (U.S. Congress: House, 1990a, p. 13). That is, with loans pooled into one large entity, losses of one loan may be balanced out by healthier loans in the pool, thereby creating the image of a healthier bank than is the case. That practice of pooling loans helped Silverado to stall off federal regulators from noticing that the bank was actually in serious trouble.

In addition to the questionable practice of pooling loans, Silverado Bank approved several loans that raised questions of conflicts of interest, particularly between board member Neil Bush and two borrowers who also happened to be his business partners (U.S. Congress: House, 1990b. pp. 165–67). Bill Walters, often referred to as the Donald Trump of Denver, was one of the most powerful developers of both commercial and residential property in that city, and a substantial borrower at Silverado even before Neil Bush joined the bank's board. Walters was also a limited partner in Bush's JNB Exploration Company, with a 6.25 percent interest. That interest was based on Walters' January 1983 investment of $150,000 in JNB. Bush insisted he had no involvement in day-to-day decision making in the firm. Walters also owned the bank that loaned JNB $1.75 million in 1983.

Testimony before Congress revealed that Bush had introduced or voted to approve $106 million in loans to Walters. Rep. Frank Annunzio of Illinois noted that Walters' complex relationship with Bush produced a powerful conflict of interest, in that Walters was both a partner and a stockholder in JNB, as well as a major lender to the firm; that power of pursestrings would surely influence Bush to be favorably disposed toward loans Walters requested of Silverado (U.S. Congress: House, 1990a, p.106). Grumbled Annunzio, "what makes matters worse is that all of the loans are in default and the taxpayers stand to lose every cent of the money" (U.S. Congress: House, 1990a, p. 103).

A year and a half after Walters' investment in JNB, Ken Good also became a partner with Bush in JNB Exploration Company, with a 25 percent interest. He contributed $10,000 to JNB for his interest. For his part, Bush invested a mere $100 to capitalize JNB, but he insisted that his investment was more substantially in sweat: he contributed his expertise in generating the deals for JNB (U.S. Congress: House, 1990a, pp. 98–103).

In 1986 the partnership between Good and Bush was restructured, wherein Good retained an option to invest another $3 million in the firm. By then, Good "personally and through various entities owned and held a 33.75 percent interest in JNB, and was both a general and limited partner of JNB" (U.S. Congress: House, 1990a, p. 103). Bush maintained that Good, like Walters, was not a principal in JNB; Good was simply a funding partner and not involved in decision making at the firm. It was not until this restructuring of their partnership in 1986 that Bush finally began to feel uncomfortable with the conflicts of interest their partnership posed, and agreed to abstain from participating in decisions at Silverado involving loans to Good. Prior to this, Bush had maintained that because neither Walters nor Good participated in day-to-day decision making at JNB, there was no legal conflict of interest posed when loans for either man came before Silverado's board. Indeed, Both Walters and Good received unanimous approval by Silverado's board for loans.

Like Walters, Good had provided Bush with loans that raised questions of conflicts of interest for Bush as a board member at Silverado making decisions concerning loans for Good. In 1984, Good loaned Bush $100,000 for a commodities deal, over which Good maintained 100 percent control and full discretion for investing the money in a high-risk pool. The loan was to be repaid only if the investment succeeded. It is unclear why Good did not simply invest the money himself instead of investing it in the name of Neil Bush. But by 1990, with the investment unsuccessful, Good forgave the loan. Even Bush admitted that this arrangement sounded "a little fishy" (U.S. Congress: House, 1990a, p. 107).

Throughout the Congressional hearings, Bush maintained that there were no legal conflicts of interest, that what may have appeared to be conflicts of interest were more a reflection of life in a relatively small town:

In a small town case where there is one banker and one lender and there are like 10 directors, like in our situation, and everybody is intertwined and there is a relationship, how can you preclude loans to be made which, you know, like a doctor in the community or the bank, the guy down the street that does the construction work on homes. It just doesn't make sense. (U.S. Congress: House, 1990a, p. 117)

Bush argued that because Bill Walters was the preeminent developer in Denver, it would not make sense to preclude making loans to him: if Silverado wanted to embark on an aggressive program of making real estate development loans, they would surely have to make some to Walters. Bush repeatedly argued that no fraud had taken place.

However, Federal regulators rejected Bush's characterization, citing his relationship with Good and Walters as a conflict of interest. But they imposed the mildest possible penalty against Bush in what amounted to a "cease and desist" order that he not engage in such activities in the future (Tolchin, 1991, p. D2). They did not bar him from ever again participating in the S&L industry. Five other individuals, including Michael Wise, James Metz, Richard Vandapool, and Robert Murray were barred from future participation in the banking business. They agreed to accept that penalty; Bush refused to agree to the order, threatening a long, expensive, and protracted set of law suits (U.S. Congress: House, 1990b, p. 5). The U.S. government backed away from the threatened struggle, and instead imposed the mildest of sanctions against the son of the President of the United States.

Observers of corporate structures and processes generally agree that the first line of defense against management excesses and abuses is an active, "alert and involved" board of directors who "collectively are charged with providing wise counsel, setting prudent policies, and ensuring the implementation of such policies" (U.S. Congress: House, 1990a, p. 11). This is particularly so when a corporation adopts an aggressive, speculative, or unusual philosophy regarding its conduct of business. The second line of defense is the independent accounting auditors, who make annual reports concerning the health and well being of the firm. Where was Silverado's board when decisions were being made about questionable loans and about unusual programs such as the quid pro quo program. And where was the bank's independent auditor?

Silverado's board apparently supported these corporate violations in its unusually high level of consensus: there was unanimous agreement of virtually every decision made by the board. Like many other failed S&L institutions, Silverado's directors offered little if any critical challenges to management. And contrary to senior managers' insistance that unanimous decisions reflect consensus building, internal documents from the bank indicate processes of groupthink at work. For example, Florian Barth, a director on Silverado's board, complained in a letter to Chairman of the Board Michael Wise that the outside directors were simply rubber stamps controlled by James Metz, director and majority stockholder, and Wise (U.S. Congress: House, 1990b, p. 109). Brian C.

McCormally, District Counsel from the Office of Thrift Supervision in Topeka, Kansas, testified to Congress that one director "admitted to leaning over to officers who attended board meetings and asking, 'Is this loan OK to approve?'" (U.S. Congress: House, 1990a, pp. 11–12).

Neil Bush was actively recruited to serve on the bank's board by board president Michael Wise. In a July 15, 1985 letter to board members, Wise notes that he has been negotiating with Bush, then only 30 years old, to join the board. It is unclear just what qualifications young Neil Bush might have had to serve on the bank's board, other than his role as head of JNB Explorations, an oil exploration firm. Such a qualification is weak at best: one could perhaps argue that his role at JNB makes him appropriate to serve on the board of a bank that invests in oil projects; but the fact is that the vast majority of Silverado's lending portfolio was in real estate, not oil exploration. More notably, Wise makes a point of emphasizing the fact that Neil is the son of the Vice President of the United States. Nowhere in the letter does Wise give any details about Bush's unique qualifications or contributions that would make him an asset to the board. That he does, however, remind the board of his political pedigree suggests that Wise was looking for someone with an image of powerful connections who would not be likely to know much about banking to launch a challenge to senior management's lending decisions brought to the board.

Much energy in Congressional hearings was devoted to the role that Neil Bush and his connection to the White House might have played in contributing to federal regulators' loose rein on Silverado and their slow pace in finally closing the bank. And indeed, although "everyone was in agreement in 1988 that the institution was dead," it remained open and operating; and when the Colorado Savings and Loan Commissioner attempted in October 1988 to enforce the order to Silverado to raise $62 million or face closure, the Federal Savings and Loan Insurance Corporation in Washington quickly requested a two-month delay. Notably, it was not until the day after the national election (when Neil's father George was elected President of the United States) that Kermit Mowbry, president of the Federal Home Loan Bank of Topeka, formally recommended that Silverado be placed into receivership (U.S. Congress: House, 1990b, p. 3). That delay has never been adequately explained; the timing, however, on placing the bank on which the President's son is a board member, into receivership is striking. It seemed that Bush was at least initially carefully selected by Wise for his inexperience in banking and thus his naive complicity with the board's groupthink, and his credentials as the son of the Vice President to attract new investors.

And where was the bank's independent auditor during all this? Ernst & Whitney acted as Silverado's independent auditor from 1977 until 1985, when Silverado fired them. The bank originally stated that it had fired the accounting firm to avoid the appearance of conflicts of interest. Congressional investigations found that Silverado's chief financial officer, Robert M. Lewis, who was hired by Silverado in 1984, was also a partner of Ernst & Whitney. This could call into question just how independent the audit of the bank could be, and thus Silverado argued, they fired Ernst & Whitney. Later, Silverado's officers insisted they fired the accounting firm because of substantial overcharges for the audits. However, investigations revealed that Ernst & Whitney was increasingly concerned about the thrift's practices. The accounting firm produced a scathing critique of the bank's business practices in 1985, including its quid pro quo program and its lending pools, and gave the bank a qualified report. Silverado felt the accounting firm was too strict in its application of accounting principles to the bank's "cutting edge" transactions, and fired the firm (U.S. Congress: House, 1990a, pp. 13–14).

Ironically, they hired another Big 8 accounting firm, Coopers & Lybrand, who came to many of the same conclusions Ernst & Whitney had: Silverado was engaged in practices that did not conform to generally accepted accounting procedures (GAAP), and therefore received a qualified financial statement from the auditors in 1987 (U.S. Congress: House, 1990a, pp. 236273). The apparent attempts by Silverado Bank to generate legitimation of its "cooked" books by the independent auditor had failed; the auditors' qualified report became the first loud thunderclap of the destructive storm to quickly rage about Silverado.

Silverado's house of cards quickly collapsed from there. They could no longer shuffle assets and liabilities to cover their disastrous investments. Finally, in December 1988 Federal regulators closed the insolvent Silverado Banking, Savings and Loan Association of Denver. Its desperate attempts to recapitalize and to cover its condition long enough to buy time to do so earned it the dubious nickname of Desparado Bank (Purdy, 1990, p. A21).

The big question, of course, is how could the bank have managed to engage in such outrageous unorthodox accounting practices and high-flying gambling in their investment strategies for so long before someone noticed? Why weren't they stopped sooner—before it ended up costing taxpayers money? The answer, for Silverado's own case and for the S&L crisis in general, lay in the processes of deregulation and its implementation. Under deregulation, there were fewer field supervisors and inspectors than when the thrifts were more tightly regulated. Mowbry acknowledged in testimony before Congress that a lack of resources at his regulatory oversight office, particularly too few examiners, was a factor in the demise of Silverado (U.S. Congress: House, 1990b, pp. 22, 37). He complained that deregulation had opened all sorts of new and complex investment and banking opportunities for thrifts without the labor power necessary to oversee operations; and repeated requests to the Office of Management and Budget to secure more examiners were turned down (U.S. Congress: House, 1990b, p. 38). Indeed, Rep. Mary Rose Oakar of Ohio noted that her Congressional subcommittee on Federal employee compensation found that 88,000 Federal employees, including many from supervisory offices of banking institutions, had been transferred to Pentagon activities, thereby robbing the banks' oversight and regulatory offices of personnel to adequately examine banks like Silverado (U.S. Congress: House, 1990b, p. 38).

The upshot here was that Silverado was not thoroughly examined for a period of about three years, from 1983 until December 1986, when a six-month examination "presented a devastatingly clear picture of Silverado's deteriorating financial condition, apparent conflicts of interest, and unsafe and unsound practices" (U.S. Congress: House, 1990a, pp. 39–40). At that point, regulators placed Silverado under receivership, but it was obviously too late. Silverado's gamble of shifting its business emphasis from low-interest single home mortgages to commercial real estate development speculation, REMIC residual investments, and sleight-of-hand accounting practices as strategies to close the cash gaps created by low-interest mortgage incomes and high-interest payments on deposits had so severely undermined the bank that it could not recover.

Like other S&L cases, Silverado clearly had its share of fraudulent, unorthodox, and excessive management decisions, questions of unethical conduct and conflicts of interest, and a board of directors that did not perform its job of critically evaluating and perhaps challenging senior management's decisions. In addition were its business decisions facilitated by contradictory policies under deregulation: a shift from the thrift's more traditional low-interest home mortgage business that produced relatively meager profits to the much riskier but potentially high-yielding business of commercial real estate development speculation, and investments in REMIC residuals. Both of these investment gambles cost Silverado its existence when the real estate market collapsed and LIBOR rose sharply. And the lack of complete regulatory oversight for over three years allowed the gambler to continue to pour good money after bad in a desperate attempt to recover the losses. When pressed by Congress to identify what he would have done differently if given the chance to avoid the $1 billion loss Silverado would cost taxpayers, Bush admitted, "I wouldn't have allowed for that high a concentration of commercial real estate" (U.S. Congress: House, 1990a, p. 132).

IV Discussion

Our application of a dialectical approach to the analysis of the S&L crisis suggests an interactive process between contradictory policies in the state project of economic intervention and corporate strategies to resolve those contradictions, producing unintended consequences of widespread individual and organizational white-collar crime.

This suggests an intersection between the literature on occupational and organizational crime with the literature on the state. Although state theories typically focus on the generation of policies that reinforce capital accumulation interests, they commonly do not analyze the effects such policies may have on corporate behavior that can damage capital accumulation processes. Some observers have called for an incorporation of state theory into analyses of factors affecting differential enforcement of regulations against corporate offenders. They did not acknowledge that some state policy may contain contradictory incentives for corporate and executive behaviors as standard operating procedures that essentially defeat the intent of the policy.

Our analysis illustrates how the Garn-St. Germain Act of 1982 deregulating the banking industry created the structural environment of contradictory forces facilitating organizational crimes in the S&L institutions. For example, deregulation allowed S&L institutions to offer higher interest rates on deposits than in the past in order to compete with those offered by commercial banks so the thrifts could attract more business. This seriously reduced their cash flow because low interest mortgage payments trickled into the thrifts slower than high interest payments on deposits flowed out, eroding their cash flow and making them vulnerable to insolvency.

Deregulation also enabled the thrifts to venture into riskier nontraditional investments such as real estate speculation, development projects, and junk bonds. Some thrifts shifted their emphasis in lending away from low-interest home mortgages and decidedly toward these riskier investments. When the volatile real estate markets collapsed, those thrifts heavily exposed in such high-risk ventures found themselves running huge deficits and becoming insolvent.

Finally, deregulation of the industry meant that there were fewer field supervisors and bank examiners to oversee the thrifts' activities. This lack of supervision facilitated fraud, overextension, and lack of prudence in investments, as well as possible criminal behavior on the part of some thrift executives. In addition, the combination of policies of deregulation and deposit insurance programs encouraged unprecedented high interest rates on deposits, wildly risky real estate speculation, and participation in the junk bond market, all of which departed from the thrifts' traditional home mortgage business, and much of which was characterized by corporate fraud and manipulation as standard operating procedure justified by deregulation legislation. What is crucial here is the structural role that state policy played in generating these behaviors: such offenses were not the result of corporations and their executives circumventing regulations or violating strict prohibitions against their activities. Rather, these cases of corporate violations of the public trust were engendered by the structures of the state's own policies of deregulation and deposit insurance.

The case of Silverado Banking, Savings and Loan Association illustrates how deregulation exacerbated the thrift industry's problems rather than liberated it to compete more effectively in the economy. The state project of economic intervention involving bank deregulation as a remedy to the thrift industry's capital accumulation crisis of the late 1970s and early 1980s became an important force in the dialectical process facilitating a devastating crisis in the industry. A lax regulatory environment in which there was little or no oversight of thrifts' activities encouraged highly risky speculative investments that were previously forbidden for thrifts and that left them vulnerable to abrupt market shifts in the real estate markets and manipulations in the junk bond markets.

Our analysis suggests that the S&L crisis was not simply the result of a lack of oversight that enabled collective embezzlement by dismantling the restraints to greedy and criminal individuals' behavior. It was more the result of informal and formal deregulation that relaxed or eliminated investment and payout guidelines and restrictions, often situating thrift institutions in a context of contradictory forces. At the same time, deregulation also unleashed as acceptable previously prohibited high-risk strategies for resolving the cash-flow crisis created by those contradictory forces. Thus, the savings and loan industry's crisis was not just a case of individual greed and fraud or an industry-wide culture of collective embezzlement, but rather the unintended consequence of the dialectics of deregulation and regulation as a state project.

V Conclusion

Our analytical focus here on one case study is not intended as a contradiction of our emphasis on the industry and its place in the larger political economy as opposed to individual organizations or individuals within organizations. Rather, we offer this case as a vehicle for unraveling the relationships and processes that similarly affected other thrifts. The case traces and highlights the ways in which state policy shaped organizational and individual (particularly executive) behaviors. The case illustrates the intersection of both occupational and organizational crimes as enabled by the state project of deregulation. The individual and corporate behaviors that are often the focus of analyses of the S&L crisis occurred in an industrial context of contradictory conditions of low income from low-interest mortgages and high payouts of deposit account interest. This industrial context and the individual and corporate behaviors and strategies to resolve the contradiction were facilitated by the policies in the state project of economic intervention, particularly deregulation, that enabled S&L institutions to enter risky investments like real estate speculation without careful oversight.

We emphasize here that our analysis is not specifically about the uniqueness of the case of Silverado or its individual executives, regardless of how these may indeed set that thrift apart from most other S&L institutions (for example, few if any had directors that were as politically connected as Neil Bush). We offer the case of Silverado Bank as an illustration of the dialectic relationship between the S&L industry and its larger political and economic context, and how embeddedness of the industry in that context created the conditions that fostered the industry's crisis.

References

Akard, Patrick J. 1992. "Corporate mobilization and political power: The transformation of US economic policy in the 1970s." *American Sociological Review* 57: 597–615.

Amenta, Edwin & Sunita Parikh. 1991. "Comment: Capitalists did not want the Social Security Act: A critique of the 'capitalist dominance' thesis." *American Sociological Review* 56: 124–29.

Amenta, Edwin, & Theda Skocpol. 1988. "Redefining the New Deal: World War II and the development of social provision in the US." In Margaret Weir, Ann Shola Orloff, & Theda Skocpol (Eds.), *The politics of social policy in the United States* (pp. 81122). Princeton, NJ: Princeton University Press.

Barth, James R. 1991. *The great savings and loan debacle.* Washington, DC: The American Enterprise Institute Press.

Barth, James R., Philip F. Bartholomew, & Carol J. Labich. 1989. "Moral hazard and the thrift crisis: An analysis of 1988 resolutions." Research Paper No. 160. Bank Structure and Competition. (Office of Policy and Economic Research, Home Loan Bank Board, Washington, D.C.)

Bater, Jeff. 1994. "Greenspan: Banking system recovers." *United Press International,* September 22.

Bradsher, Keith. 1994. "S&Ls see new threat, this time from banks." *New York Times,* October 20, p. D6.

Burris, Val. 1992. "Elite policy-planning networks in the United States." *Research in Politics and Society* 4: 111–34.

Calavita, Kitty & Henry N. Pontell. 1990. " 'Heads I win, tails you lose': Deregulation, crime, and crisis in the savings and loan industry." *Crime and Delinquency* 36(3): 309–41.

———. 1991. " 'Other People's Money' revisited: embezzlement in the savings and loan insurance industries." *Social Problems* 38(1): 94–112.

———. 1993, "The savings and loan industry." In Michael Tonry & Albert J. Reiss (Eds.), *Beyond the law: Crimes in complex organizations* (pp. 203–45). Chicago: The University of Chicago Press.

———. 1994. "The state and white-collar crime: Saving the savings and loans." *Law and Society Review* 28(2): 297–324.

———. 1997. *Big money crime: Fraud and politics in the savings and loan crisis.* Berkeley: University of California Press.

Clinard, Marshall B. & Richard Quinney (Eds.). 1973. *Criminal behavior systems: A typology.* (2nd ed.). New York: Holt, Rinehart & Winston.

Coleman, James W. 1985. *The criminal elite: The sociology of white-collar crime.* New York: St. Martin's Press.

Domhoff, G. William. 1990. *The power elite and the state: How policy is made in America.* New York: Aldine de Gruyter.

———. 1991b. "Class, power, and parties during the New Deal: A critique of Skocpol's theory of state autonomy." *Berkeley Journal of Sociology* 36: 1–49.

Glasberg, Davita Silfen & Dan Skidmore. 1997a. "The dialectics of state economic intervention: Bank deregulation and the savings and loan bailout." *The Sociological Quarterly* 38(1): 67–93.

———. 1997b. *Corporate welfare policy and the welfare state: Bank deregulations and the savings and loan bailout.* New York: Aldine de Gruyter.

Hagan, John. 1985. *Modern criminology: Crime, criminal behavior, and its control.* New York: McGraw-Hill, Inc.

Hays, Gorey & Richard Hornik. 1990. "No end in sight: Politicians huff blame as the $500 billion S&L crisis races out of control." *Time,* August 13: 50–52.

Hooks, Gregory. 1990. "The rise of the Pentagon and US state building: The defense program as industrial policy." *American Journal of Sociology* 96: 358–404.

——. 1993. "The weakness of strong theories: The U.S. state's dominance of the World War II investment process." *American Sociological Review* 58: 37–53.

Jessop, Bob 1990. *State Theory: Putting the Capitalist State in its place*. Pennsylvania State University Press.

National Commission on Financial Institution Reform, Recovery, and Enforcement. 1993. *Origins and Causes of the S&L Debacle: A Blueprint for Reform*. Washington DC: Government Printing Office.

Purdy, Penelope. 1990. "A bank they called 'Desperado.' " *New York Times*, July 17: A21.

Schlegel, Kip & David Weisburd. 1993. "White-collar crime: The parallax view." In Kip Schlegel & David Weisburd (Eds.), *White-collar crime reconsidered* (pp. 327). Boston: Northeastern University Press.

Schrager, Laura Shill & James F. Short, Jr. 1978. "Toward a sociology of organizational crime." *Social Problems* 25(4): 407–19.

Singletary, Michael. 1995. "Justice Department hails prosecutions at banks, S&Ls." *Washington Post*, November, 1995: A10.

Skidmore, Dan & Davita Silfen Glasberg. 1996. "State theory and corporate welfare: The crisis and bailout of the savings and loan industry from a contingency perspective." *Political Power and Social Theory* 9: 149–91.

Skocpol, Theda. 1988. "The limits of the New Deal system and the roots of the contemporary welfare dilemmas." In Margaret Weir, Ann Shola Orloff, & Theda Skocpol (Eds.), *The politics of social policy in the United States* (pp. 293–311). Princeton, NJ: Princeton University Press.

——. 1992. *Protecting soldiers and mothers: The political origins of social policy in the United States*. Cambridge, MA: Harvard University Press.

Sutherland, Edwin H. 1949. *White-collar crime*. New York: Dryden.

Tolchin, Martin. 1991. "Mildest possible penalty is imposed on Neil Bush." *New York Times*. April 19: D2.

U.S. Congress: House. 19080. *Oversight Hearings on Depository Institutions Deregulation Committee. Committee on Banking, Finance, and Urban Affairs, Subcommittee on Financial Institutions, Supervision, Regulation, and Insurance*. 96th Congress, 2nd session. Washington, DC: Government Publications Office.

——. 1981. *Conduct of Monetary Policy. Committee on Banking, Finance, and Urban Affairs*. 96th Congress, 2nd session. Washington, DC: Government Publications Office.

——. 1989a. *The Other Side of the Savings and Loan Industry. Committee on Banking, Finance, and Urban Affairs, Subcommittee on Financial Institutions Supervision, Regulation and Insurance*. 101st Congress, 1st session. Washington, DC: Government Printing Office.

——. 1989b. *Financial Institutions Reform, Recovery, and Enforcement Act of 1989, pts. 1 and 2. Committee on Banking, Finance, and Urban Affairs, Subcommittee on Financial Institutions Supervision, Regulation and Insurance*. 101st Congress, 1st session. Washington, DC: Government Publications Office.

——. 1989c. *Administration Plan to Resolve the Savings and Loan Crisis. Committee on Banking, Finance, and Urban Affairs*. 101st Congress, 1st session. Washington, DC: Government Publications Office.

——. 1990a. *Silverado Banking, Savings and Loan Association, Part I. Committee on Banking, Finance, and Urban Affairs*. 101st Congress, 2nd session. Washington, DC: Government Publications Office.

—— . 1990b. *Silverado Banking, Savings and Loan Association, Part II. Committee on Banking, Finance, and Urban Affairs. 101st Congress,* 2nd session. Washington, DC: Government Publications Office.

U.S. Congress: Senate. 1992. *Efforts to Combat Criminal Financial Institution Fraud. Committee on Banking, Housing, and Urban Affairs, Subcommittee on Consumer and Regulatory Affairs. 102nd Congress,* 2nd session. Washington, DC: US Government Publications Office.

U.S. Department of Justice. 1992. *Attacking Financial Institution Fraud, Fiscal Year 1992 Second Quarterly Report.* Washington, DC: U.S. Department of Justice.

Useem, Michael. 1984. *The inner circle.* New York: Oxford University Press.

Vallochi, Steven. 1989. "The relative autonomy of the state and the origins of British welfare policy." *Sociological Forum* 4: 349–65.

Vaughan, Diane. 1996. *The Challenger Launch Decision Risky: Technology, Culture, and Deviance at NASA.* Chicago: University of Chicago Press.

Wheeler, Stanton and Mitchell Lewis Rothman. 1982. "The organization as weapon in white-collar crime." *Michigan Law Review* 80(7): 1403–26.

Zimring, Franklin E. and Gordon Hawkins. 1993. "Crime, justice, and the savings and loan crisis." In Michael J. Tonry & Albert J. Reiss (Eds.), *Beyond the law: Crime in complex organizations* (pp. 247–92). Chicago: The University of Chicago Press.

Source: *The American Journal of Economics and Sociology,* © 1998.

Reading 7–2: Dell P. Champlin and Janet T. Knoedler, *Corporations, Workers, and the Public Interest*

> *David Simon's analysis of "the invisible government" in his theory of elite deviance raises serious questions regarding the role that corporations play in our daily lives. As this chapter has discussed, if these entities are not capable of policing themselves, and our politicians are increasingly less willing to enact broad-sweeping legislation such as Sarbanes-Oxley, what will the landscape of public sector/private sector look like in the years to come?*

The corporate scandals of the past year have raised profound questions regarding corporations and the public interest. As Thorstein Veblen observed, in a society dominated by pecuniary interests corporations are presumed to be operating in the public interest unless proven otherwise (1988). However, accounting records rigged to inflate profits, insider deals to promote stock sales, and excessive executive compensation in companies in or near bankruptcy are actions that cannot be construed as being in the public interest by anyone's standard. In his classic article on corporate responsibility, Milton Friedman opposed enforcing standards of socially responsible behavior on corporations because it would constitute "doing good with someone else's money" (1970). According to Friedman, businesses have a fiduciary responsibility to their stockholders to maximize profits. Seen in that context, the actions of corporations such as Enron, WorldCom, Tyco, and others disclosed over this past year are noteworthy not because they represent cases of corporate misdeeds but because they violate even the most minimal standard of responsible behavior—the protection of stockholder interests.

In this paper, we examine the role of the legal system in erasing the "public interest" from official corporate duties and in relieving corporations of any responsibility to their own workers. In the first section we discuss the importance of the public interest in the early history of corporation law. We then examine the question that preoccupied John R. Commons and other progressives in the early twentieth century, namely, what is the public interest duty of corporations and government in regard to labor? More specifically, we ask, just who is included in the public interest? Recent corporate scandals have included actions that were clearly harmful to workers, including layoffs, reductions in wages and benefits, and the collapse of retirement savings held in 401(k) plans invested in worthless corporate stock. However, it is primarily activities in the latter category that have been regarded as being outside of socially accepted business practices. In other words, it is not harm to workers as employees that has provoked the outrage but, rather, harm to workers as investors. We argue in this paper that the disparate treatment of workers in regard to the public interest has its roots in the nineteenth and early years of the twentieth centuries.(1)

Corporations and the Public Interest

Unlike modern interpreters of his ideas, Adam Smith was not an ardent proponent of corporations. Given the great legal privileges extended to the joint stock companies of his day, Smith argued that the corporate form was, at best, suited only to such industries as banking, insurance, canal transportation, and public utilities and, at worst, intended to suppress competition (Smith 1937; Baldwin 1987; Korten 1995). Smith's view became the accepted view in the early United States: business enterprises could not incorporate without receiving a special charter from their state legislatures. Moreover, the public interest had to be given explicit attention: during the late eighteenth and first half of the nineteenth century, state legislatures typically held to the view that the corporate form "should not be resorted to unless the public interest was involved" (Evans 1941, 21).

Under that standard, relatively few charters were granted, with the charters typically listing the public benefits to result from the activities of a given corporation. Moreover, the corporations that received charters were kept on a tight leash: corporate charters were limited in duration, often with automatic sunset dates of twenty-five or fifty years; all investors had equal voting rights and in some cases were required to be local residents; corporations were not permitted to own other businesses; and corporations were restricted to engaging in the business activities specifically authorized in their charters (Hightower 1997; Korten 1995). Corporations that failed to serve the public interest in the view of state legislatures could be, and often were, dissolved (ibid.). As Adolf Berle and Gardiner Means explained, in the negotiation between a group of proponents for the charter and a legislative body, the proponents "were required to justify every clause of it to outsiders; they were thus checked at every point and the resulting document had some semblance of having been examined with a view to protecting all of the interests involved" (1991, 127).

Business enterprise began to chafe at these carefully constructed restrictions on incorporation and corporate activities by the middle of the eighteenth century. The weakening of the earlier system of special charters by the states began with the "disarray" in the United States after the Civil War, which industrial capitalists exploited to their economic advantage. The noted reporter on the robber barons, Matthew Josephson, described how "the halls of legislation were transformed into a mart where the price of votes was haggled over, and laws, made to order, were bought and sold" (quoted in Korten 1995, 58).(2) As corporate concentration became a feature of the post-bellum U.S. economy, the earlier restrictions were loosened by permitting more discretion in "what economic pursuits corporations could follow and what were the responsibilities of company officers and boards of directors" (Nader 2000, 101). By the end of the nineteenth century, the instrument of corporate charters was transformed from a check on the activities of corporations into a device for raising revenues for the various states (Baldwin 1987), who competed with each other to pass less and less restrictive general incorporation laws. As Jim Hightower explained, "today the corporate chartering process is so perfunctory it can be handled by a phone call" (1997, 33).

This race to the bottom was led by New Jersey and Delaware, which weakened the rights of citizens while giving corporations the right to "operate in any fashion not explicitly prohibited by law" (Korten 1995, 58). In the words of Ralph Nader, "[T]he Delaware corporation syndrome . . . represented a major victory for corporate power in America. No longer would the corporate charter constitute even a pretense of being a corporate governance mechanism providing accountability to the shareholders and other affected corporate constituencies . . . By conscious lobbying, corporations turned restrictive charter laws into instruments for further concentration of power in the hands of management. A constitutional structure for accountability rights by people inside as well as outside the corporate structure passed into history" (2000, 102). The earlier expectation—that the quid pro quo for a corporate charter was a specific obligation by business enterprise to serve the public interest—also became a historical artifact.

Free Labor and the Public Interest

Corporations also gained a virtual free hand over workers during this same period. Early institutionalists recognized that the status of labor in the United States was primarily a product of the legal system. Edwin Witte, a prominent labor economist of the 1930s and 1940s, summarized the institutionalist view: "[G]overnment is the rule maker and the umpire in the American system of free enterprise. Property, contract, bankruptcy—in fact, all existing economic institutions—are defined by law" (1957, 6). According to John Dennis Chasse, Richard Ely and the other "new economists" writing in the late nineteenth century believed that "the root of the labor problem" lay in the legal form of the wage contract and the type of freedom enforced by the courts (1991, 803). Building on this insight, we argue that the wage contract and the laissez-faire interpretation of freedom supported by the courts also determined the place of labor in the public interest. Specifically, we argue that the public interest came to be de fined in a way that was often antithetical to the interests of workers or even excluded them altogether.

In the twentieth century, the "labor problem" was usually viewed as the "wage problem." (3) However, institutional labor economists such as Ely and Commons used the term "labor problems" to refer to a whole host of difficulties that plagued workers in the late nineteenth century such as long hours, industrial accidents, and working conditions as well as low incomes (Barbash 1976; Chasse 1991). Primary among these "problems" was the labor contract itself. These early institutionalists recognized that while price is important, it is equally important to clarify just what is being exchanged. The prevailing view is that the wage bargain consists of the sale of a commodity called "labor" for a mutually agreed upon price. For institutionalists, the wage bargain is an institution that developed historically and culturally, and what is being exchanged is not a commodity but a set of rights (Commons 1909–10). Thus, understanding the wage bargain as an institution rather than as a commodity exchange is crucial for understanding the relative status of workers and corporations. We argue that the applicability of the concept of the public interest to labor is derived from the way the wage contract developed as an institution and how it was codified in labor law.

Barbara Fried (2001) stated that the "essential question for progressive reformers" was "how to dismantle the constitutional laissez-faire," which consisted of two main aspects: (a) protection of private property from government interference and (b) protection of individual freedom as embodied in freedom of contract. These two ideas shaped court philosophy from the mid-1880s until the late 1930s. This same period coincides with the rise of the factory system and the vast expansion of industrial wage labor. Thus, it is not surprising that constitutional laissez-faire strongly influenced the institutional development of the wage contract.

While economic freedom in the late nineteenth century was strongly associated with the political doctrine of laissez-faire, in antebellum America the meaning of economic freedom as it applied to labor was strongly conditioned by the institution of slavery (Roediger 1991; Bridges 1986). According to Charles McCurdy (1984), wage slavery and its antithesis, free labor, were important concepts in distinguishing the social and economic system of the North from that of the South. Historian Eric Foner wrote that Northerners considered those "who worked at the will and profit of others" to be slaves (quoted in McCurdy 1984, 27), and this category included slaves, indentured servants, and those who worked for hire. In contrast, free labor referred to those who owned the product of their labor (McCurdy 1984). The dichotomy between wage slavery and free labor allowed individual workers to distance themselves from any association with slavery (McCurdy 1984; Laurie 1989). However, the free labor-wage slavery distinction later proved to be incompatible with the laissez-faire interpretation of economic freedom, Laissez-faire is based on "freedom from coercion" and on private property rights. Both principles were not applicable to the early meanings of "free labor" and "wage slavery," and the definitions of these terms subsequently changed to conform more closely to the prevailing economic philosophy of the courts.(4)

In the early nineteenth century, "free labor" meant lack of dependence on another for one's livelihood. This independence was assured by ownership of land that allowed the production of one's subsistence or by the ability to sell the fruits of one's labor in the market. Both types of economic arrangements characterized the household economy of the eighteenth century and early craft labor (Laurie 1989). Laissez-faire relies on the traditional economic liberal emphasis on freedom from constraint. How does this work for "free labor"? The "lack of coercion" that defined "free labor" in antebellum America came primarily from but two sources: the institution of slavery and the condition of poverty. After the Civil War, the coercive force of slavery lessened as an issue for "free labor." However, the coercive force of poverty increased in the late nineteenth century along with the growing industrialization of the U.S. economy. The early institutionalists, reformers in the progressive era, and Marxists saw coercion coming from a private sector that presented limited choices to individual workers (Fried 2001; Wunderlin 1992; Friedman 1998). Polanyi (1957) put it bluntly as the choice to "work, starve, or go to the workhouse."

In contrast, economic liberalism does not recognize poverty or economic privation as a source of coercion. For economic liberals, the presumption is that because a private transaction is voluntary, it is therefore free of coercion, That is, the wage contract is "free" in the laissez-faire sense if there is no government interference, regardless of the actual terms agreed to by the parties involved. Institutionalists like Commons and Robert Hale disagreed and argued that the coercive power of the state not only was felt in government action but permeated the private sector as well. That is, coercion in the private sector derives from power that has been delegated to it by the state through the laws of property and contract (Fried 2001). The notion that coercive force comes from many sources is also central to the writings of Commons. In his 1931 article, he defined an institution as "collective action in control, liberation and expansion of individual action," and said that all "collective actions establish re lations of rights, duties" and working rules (Commons 1931). According to Chasse, Commons defined a "right as the power to command state officials to enforce one's will on others. This makes the state a party to every transaction" (Chasse 1986, 767).

As discussed above, the laissez-faire interpretation of economic freedom fundamentally transformed the concept of "free labor" and strongly influenced the development 'of the wage contract. The ideal of economic independence contained in the term "free labor" was replaced by the ideal of laissez-faire, which serves the public interest by promoting economic efficiency and mutually beneficial outcomes. However, as institurionalists and progressives were at pains to point out, the proponents of laissez-faire in the labor market overlooked the problem of property rights. That is, just how does the notion of private property apply to labor?

The term "free labor" originally meant those who "owned their own toil" (McCurdy 1984, 27). However, according to Commons, with the rise of the factory system, workers lost these ownership rights to the banker capitalists (Gruchy 1947). As a consequence, the term "free labor" lost its original meaning. Freedom for workers in regard to the labor contract was reduced to only one dimension of economic liberalism-freedom from coercion by government. Workers were "free" to enter into a labor contract-free from interference (or protection) by government. However, this so-called freedom was essentially meaningless without the associated rights of property.

Working for a wage means that the ownership rights to one's labor belong to the employer. Thus, "owning one's own toil" no longer meant owning the right to the product but ownership of an abstraction called labor. This abstraction is treated as if it were a simple commodity in economic theory, but it is an uneasy fit. As Jennings (2003) pointed out, it is often unclear just what this commodity is that is being sold in neoclassical labor markets. Employers hire workers, but workers sell time, and the wage is based on the value of effort. Polanyi (1957), of course, called labor a fictitious commodity. More important for our discussion here, ownership of this commodity conveys no rights. As institutionalists such as J. M. Clark, Hale, and Commons pointed out, property rights as defined by the court essentially mean the right to expected future earnings (Commons 1924). For a wageworker, there are no expected earnings from labor outside of the workplace. When the labor contract is signed, no "property" is actually transferred. The loss of property rights in any meaningful sense means that the utilitarian definition of an economy serving the public interest which depends on both economic liberty and property simply does not apply to labor.

Between the 1880s and the 1930s, the courts consistently supported the concept of "freedom of contract," which often denied to workers additional rights they may have gained through political action. The laissez-faire concept of "freedom of contract" was initially applied to labor in an 1886 decision by the Pennsylvania Supreme Court overturning a law against paying wages in scrip (Fried 2001). Decisions by other courts continued to promote the notion of a "constitutional doctrine of liberty of contact culminating in the 1905 Lochner v. New York decision by the Supreme Court (Fried 2001, 32). This decision declared unconstitutional a New York state law setting maximum hours for bakers. Other decisions overturned state minimum wage laws and laws protecting union membership and organizing (McCurdy 1983).

Protective labor legislation was passed during this period. Indeed, the success of legislation protecting some workers and the failure of other reform efforts illustrates the peculiar status of workers in relation to the concept of public interest. Protective labor legislation was justified on the basis of public health. That is, it was deemed to be in the public interest to protect women not because they were workers but because they represented motherhood. Similarly, maximum hour laws for railroad workers were upheld because the public might be affected. In general, laws designed to protect workers from conditions injurious to their health were overturned unless some connection to public health could be established. And it was clear that the "public" in public health did not include workers themselves (McCurdy 1983).

According to Bruce Kaufman (1997), institutionalists saw the fundamental problem for labor as inequality of bargaining power. Ely, Commons, and others believed competition between employers coupled with weak bargaining power by workers led to a "race to the bottom" in terms of wages and working conditions. Commons asserted that "instead of promoting a harmony of interests, competition with unequal bargaining power degenerates into a cutthroat struggle of 'survival of the fittest' in which more liberal, progressive employers are forced to lower labor standards to the level of their most grasping level" (quoted in Kaufman 1997, 31). Inequality of bargaining power was also a primary concern of Karl Marx, and this issue continues to figure prominently in economic policy debates today. However, prior to the 1930s this inequality was considered less important than the doctrine of freedom of contract. For example, in the Lochner v. New York decision, the Supreme Court based its rejection of the maximum hours law on the notion that the only issue was bargaining power (McCurdy 1983).

According to McCurdy, "Five Lochner judges said that the bakeshop law was not a police regulation because the proffered health rationale was so unreasonable that it must be a "mere pretense" for something else. For the majority, the only plausible explanation for the statute was that it had been enacted to improve the bargaining position of the baker-workers union" (1983, 25). That is, the Supreme Court specifically discarded inequality in bargaining power between employer and employees as a legitimate issue of public policy.

In the Adair and Coppae decisions, which overturned state laws protecting employees' right to union membership, the Court also specifically recognized the inequality of bargaining power between workers and employers (McCurdy 1983). The Court argued that this inequality was "the inevitable outcome of the free operation of any scheme of liberty and property interests" (Fried 2001). That is, it was argued that the Court could not redress inequality of bargaining power without interfering with private property rights (Fried 2001). The 1935 passage of the Wagner Act brought to an end the freedom of contract doctrine at least as it applied to labor agreements with unions. Outside of the union context, however, freedom of contract survived in weakened form until only recently in the philosophy of employment-at-will. Even without the claim of constitutionality that gave so much power to the doctrine of freedom of contract, the notion of "employment at will" still held sway over workers' rights until the 1970s and 1980s. In some states, laws now protect workers in a number of areas such as unjust dismissal, worker health and safety, and worker privacy (Bellam 2000).(5)

Conclusion

In *Social Control of Business*, Clark argued that economic theories and legal doctrines based on a concept of individualism were inapplicable in an age of corporations and trade unions (1969, 29). Nonetheless, that individualism seems to have mistakenly informed our legal framework, which in turn has lavished privileges and freedoms upon corporations in the hope that they would see fit to serve the community by providing jobs, output, and dividends. At the same time, the legal framework granting the full rights of property to corporations tilted against the worker. Events of the past year suggest that many in corporate America no longer feel a responsibility to endow even incidental benefits to the communities they presumably serve. Because the privileged position of corporations and the limited protections for workers are merely legal constructs and not natural states, we argue that sensible public policy could reverse these tendencies and restore the responsibilities that corporations once bore for the public interest.

Notes

(1) We rely on this definition of the public interest that we developed in an earlier paper: "[E]conomic welfare in the public interest turns on the notion of sufficient output for the entire community and on an adequate portion of that output distributed to each member of the community" (Champlin and Knoedler 2002, 878).

(2) Naomi Lamoreaux observed that by the end of the nineteenth century states were relatively powerless over the corporations that were seeking an end to the restrictions they faced under the old corporate chartering system due to the ease with which nationally based firms could shift their operations out of the states (1985). In that context, it may nor have been a race to the bottom between the states but an "auction" hosted by the large national corporations for the right to issue their charters.

(3) For example, the most frequently analyzed of any labor policy is the minimum wage (Waltman 2000). Even when the issue appears to be wider in scope, the main focus typically remains on the wage. For example, during the 1980s an intense debate erupted over whether newly created jobs were good jobs or bad ones. In most cases, a good job was simply defined as one with a decent wage (Champlin 1995).

(4) Lawrence Glickman (1997) linked the change in the meaning of wage slavery to the rise of consumerism in the early twentieth century. Although he

made an interesting and valid point, the issue of consumerism is beyond the scope of the current discussion.

(5) Katherine Stone (1992) argued that these laws expanding individual worker rights have actually worked to undermine unions due to the Preemption Doctrine of Section 301 of the Labor Relations Management Act. This provision forces a union member to follow arbitration procedures to settle grievances. Thus, a union member cannot take violations of state laws to court but rather only to private arbitration hearings. In essence, union members have fewer rights than non-union employees when it comes to enforcement of state labor laws.

References

Baldwin, William. *Market Power, Competition, and Antitrust Policy*. Homewood, Ill.: Irwin, 1987.

Barbash, Jack. "The Legal Foundations of Capitalism and the Labor Problem." *Journal of Economic Issues* 10, no. 4 (December 1976).

Bellam, Deborah A. "Employment-at-Will: The Impending Death of a Doctrine." *American Business Law Journal* 37, no. 4 (2000): 653–87.

Berle, Adolf A., and Gardiner C. Means. *The Modem Corporation and Private Property*. New Brunswick, N.J.: Transaction Publishers, 1991.

Bridges, Amy. "Becoming American: The Working Classes in the United States before the Civil War." In *Working Class Formation: Nineteenth-Century Patterns in Western Europe and the United States*, edited by Ira Katznelson and Aristide R. Zolberg. Princeton, N.J.: Princeton University Press, 1986.

Champlin, Dell. "Understanding Job Quality in an Era of Structural Change: What Can Economics Learn from Industrial Relations?" *Journal of Economic Issues* 29, no. 3 (September 1995).

Champlin, Dell P., and Janet T. Knoedler. "Wages in the Public Interest: Insights from Thorstein Veblen and J. M. Clark." *Journal of Economic Issues* 36, no. 4 (December 2002): 877–91.

Chasse, John Dennis. "John Commons and the Democratic Stare." *Journal of Economic Issues* 20, no. 3 (September 1986): 759–84.

——— . The American Association for Labor Legislation: "An Episode in Institutionalist Policy Analysis." *Journal of Economics Issues* 25, no. 3 (September 1991): 799–828.

Clark, John Maurice. *Social Control of Business*. New York: Augustus M. Kelley, 1969.

Commons, John R. "American Shoemakers, 1648–1895: A Sketch of Industrial Evolution." *Quarterly Journal of Economies* 24 (November 1909–10): 39–84.

——— . *Legal Foundations of Capitalism*. New York: Macmillan, Co., 1924.

——— . "Institutional Economics." *American Economic Review* 21(1931): 648–57.

——— . Quoted in Bruce E. Kaufman, *Government Regulation of the Employment Relationship Madison*, Wis.: Industrial Relations Research Association, 1997.

Evans, George Herberton, Jr. *Business Incorporations in the United Stares, 1800–1943*. National Bureau of Economic Research, 1941.

Fried, Barbara H. *The Progressive Aasault on Laissez Faire: Robert Hale and the First Law and Economics Movement*. Cambridge, Mass.: Harvard University Press, 2001.

Friedman, Gerald. *State-Making and Labor Movements: France and the United States, 1876–1914.* Ithaca, N.Y.: Cornell University Press, 1998.

Friedman, Milton. "The Social Responsibility of Business Is to Increase Its Profits." *New York Times Magazine,* September 13, 1970.

Glickman, Lawrence B. *A Living Wage: American Workers and the Making of Consumer Society.* Ithaca, N.Y.: Cornell University Press, 1997.

Gruchy, Allan G. *Modern Economic Thought: The American Contribution.* New York: Prentice-Hall, Inc., 1947.

Hightower, Jim, *There's Nothing in the Middle of the Road but Yellow Stripes and Dead Armadillos.* New York: HarperCollins, 1997.

Jennings, Ann. "Dead Metaphors and Living Wages: On the Role of Measurement and Logic in Economic Debates." In *The Institutionalist Tradition in Labor Economics,* edited by Dell Champlin and Janet Knoedler. Forthcoming 2003.

Kaufman, Bruce E. "Labor Markets and Employment Regulation: The View of the 'Old' Institutionalists." In *Government Regulation of the Employment Relationship,* edited by Bruce E. Kaufman. Madison, Wis.: Industrial Relations Research Association, 1997.

Korten, David. *When Corporations Rule the World.* West Hartford, Conn.: Kumarian Press, Inc., 1995.

Lamoreaux, Naomi. *The Great Merger Movement in American Business, 1895–1904.* Cambridge: Cambridge University Press, 1985.

Laurie, Bruce. *Artisans into Workers: Labor in Nineteenth Century America.* New York: Noonday, 1989, 3–14.

McCurdy, Charles. "The Roots of 'Liberty of Contract' Reconsidered: Major Premises in the Law of Employment, 1867–1937." *Yearbook 1984.* Washington, D.C.: Supreme Court Historical Society, 1984.

Nader, Ralph. "Corporate Power in America." In *The Ralph Nader Reader,* edited by Ralph Nader and Barbara Ehrenreich. New York: Seven Stories Press, 2000.

Polanyi, Karl. *The Great Transformation.* Boston, Mass.: Beacon Press, 1957.

Roediger, David R. *The Wages of Whiteness.* London: Verso 1991.

Smith, Adam. *The Wealth of Nations.* New York: Modern Library, 1937.

Stone, Katherine. "The Legacy of Industrial Pluralism: The Tension between Individual Employment Rights and the New Deal Collective Bargaining System." *University of Chicago Law Review* (spring 1992).

Veblen, Thorstein B. *Theory of Business Enterprise.* New Brunswick, N.J.: Transaction Publishers, 1988.

Waltman, Jerold. *The Politics of the Minimum Wage.* Urbana, Ill.: University of Illinois Press, 2000.

Witte, Edwin E. "Economics and Public Policy." *American Economic Review* 47, no. 1 (March 1957): 1–21.

Wunderlin, Clarence. *Visions of the New Industrial Order: Social Science and Labor Theory in America's Progressive Era.* New York: Columbia University Press, 1992.

Source: *Journal of Economic Issues,* © 2003 Association of Evolutionary Economics.

Thinking Activities

This activity set will help you to focus your own thoughts in this area, and assist you in applying the theories you've learned in this chapter to future investigative work in the field. Be prepared to share your findings with other students in small or large groups, and with your instructor.

1. Rent and watch the DVDs *Wall Street* (1987) and *Boiler Room* (2000).

   • Based on your analysis of both films, do you observe similarities (i.e., common characteristics) between the leading characters, stockbroker Bud Fox in *Wall Street* and stockbroker Seth Davis in *Boiler Room*?

   • Describe the organizational environment of Bud Fox's trading firm and the one in which Seth Davis is employed. How are they similar? Are there any differences between the two? In each film, do you believe there was a conflict between the firm's mission and existing laws and regulations on stock and securities trading? How did each company employ incentives and rewards to keep their employees committed to their jobs?

   • In both films, do you believe that the main characters were given a concrete, explicit company policy on ethical standards, or did their personal values guide their decisions?

   • Did the other characters in each film play a role in influencing the behavior of the main character (e.g., Gordon Gekko in *Wall Street*, Chris and Greg in *Boiler Room*)?

2. Using the Internet, find the websites of two organizations. The first organization should be a major corporation. The second should be either a federal, state, or local agency. Explore both of these two websites thoroughly, and print them out. Answer the following questions:

   • What is the mission of the corporation or agency? Is it clearly defined or ambiguous? Does the agency have a clearly defined structure?

   • Do you see any potential conflicts between the corporation or agency's mission and the actual activities each performs on a daily basis?

   • Approximately how many employees does the company or agency employ? Does it use specific incentives to ensure employee loyalty? Compare each organization's benefits package with the strategies discussed by researcher Diane Vaughan earlier in the chapter.

- Do you think that either of these organizations might have a problem with fraud and other white-collar offenses? Would criminal acts committed at each entity be more properly classified as individual or organizational?
- Apply Gary Green's four categories of occupational crime to the two websites. Which of these four categories might apply to each?
- How might you apply Marshall Clinard and Peter Yeager's ten recommendations for reducing corporate crime to these organizations?
- Do you believe that possible fraud or other abuses within each organization might be tied to larger societal issues? Why or why not?

8 White-Collar Crime
A Legalistic Perspective

Throughout the first seven chapters of this book, you have been exposed to a variety of theories and typologies relevant to the study of white-collar crime. However, to fully appreciate the scope and complexity of white-collar crime within the United States, this chapter will provide you with a basic understanding of commonly encountered white-collar crimes from a legalistic perspective, beyond the rudimentary discussion of Sarbanes-Oxley Act discussed in the previous chapter. You may notice that this portion of the text is a bit longer than those you have examined thus far. We do not apologize for this. Rather, We believe that as future investigators, special agents, or prosecutors, understanding the key elements of commonly encountered white-collar crime statutes will prove critical to your success in this field.

Examples of criminal statutes that will be discussed include conspiracy, mail fraud, wire fraud, extortion through interstate commerce, access device fraud, embezzlement, check forgery and fraud, false entries and statements, and money laundering. In addition, this chapter will also briefly discuss asset forfeiture from a procedural standpoint (i.e., how federal, state, and local governments seize the property of businesses and private citizens), as well as the extent to which seizing such assets determines suspect target selection and overall investigative priorities. While such decisions may not seem germane to the law enforcement officer working in the field, asset forfeiture plays a crucial role in the strategic decision-making process at the most senior levels of criminal justice agencies. Indeed, as budgets decrease and the level of both personnel and equipment stagnates, the role of asset forfeiture becomes far more critical to state and local law enforcement agencies than one might expect.

The Development of White-Collar Criminal Law

One of the biggest mistakes that a prospective white-collar criminal investigator can make is to create a false dichotomy between the behavioral aspects of offenders and the legal elements of specific offenses. Laws are not written by themselves; on the contrary, they are crafted by people inextricably linked to the societies in which they reside. Much like waves in the ocean, laws are constantly changing. Just as the cyclical phases of the moon affect the tides, so too do differing perspectives of acceptable social norms influence criminal laws. Nowhere is this statement more accurate than in defining white-collar crime. For example, many activities that were accepted in Sutherland's era as simply conducting business are today deemed illegal.

Throughout the history of Western civilization, various acts have been considered *mala in se* (i.e., evil in themselves). Crimes such as murder, rape, arson, assault, and robbery have nearly always produced social condemnation, often expressed through long-term incapacitation or the imposition of a death sentence. In contrast, acts prohibited by statute or regulation, but not deemed evil themselves (i.e., *mala prohibita* offenses), frequently resulted in subjecting the offender to public humiliation, short-term deprivation of freedom, or surrendering wealth to the state or community. From a historical perspective, some white-collar offenses such as *forestalling* were punishable as far back in history as the reign of Henry II circa 1216–72. The pain incurred by offenders who committed acts of white-collar criminality often coincided with the belief of scholars-of-the-day that such transgressions were *mala prohibita*, not *mala in se*. In his text *Controversies in White-Collar Crime* (2002), author Gary W. Potter notes,

> Some confusion over the issue of criminality emanates from the more polite names we give to white-collar robbery. But politeness aside, we may rest assured that price-fixing; fraud; restraint of trade; false advertising and environmental pollution are every bit as criminal as the FBI's index crimes.[1]

Moreover, while the majority of offenses discussed in this text (i.e., fraud, forgery, embezzlement, currency counterfeiting, identity theft, and abuse of public trust crimes) are classified federally as *felonies*—in other words, punishable by a minimum sentence of a year plus a day in prison (as opposed to a *misdemeanor* which is punishable by up to and including one year incarceration), those persons convicted of committing white-collar crimes are far more likely to receive probation or community service than persons adjudicated for crimes such as murder, rape, and assault.[2]

Differing Burdens of Proof: White-Collar Criminal and Civil Cases

As you may recall from your introductory courses in criminal justice, criminal cases require the establishment of proof *beyond a reasonable doubt* that the defendant committed the act with which he or she has been charged. Comparatively, civil cases require only that it is more probable than not (i.e., *preponderance of the evidence*) that the defendant named in the action was responsible for events unfolding in the manner that they did. The burden of proof in a criminal trial is far greater than that of a civil matter because the defendant risks not only losing financial assets, but may actually be deprived of personal freedom, the right to vote, and other entitlements. In some cases, a defendant may be found not guilty in a criminal trial and subsequently deemed liable or negligent in a civil case (e.g., O.J. Simpson was found not guilty in the murder of Nicole Brown Simpson, but was found negligent in preventing her death).

Removed from criminal and civil proceedings is the process of asset forfeiture. As we will discuss later in this chapter, asset forfeiture refers to the seizure of property or possessions (e.g., cash, securities, real estate, motor vehicles, computers, etc.), belonging to an individual or business. Forfeiture actions may be conducted judicially or administratively. Items that are eligible for forfeiture are often items that were used as part of the crime (*instrumentalities*)—such as a desktop computer, optical scanner, or inkjet printer used to produce counterfeit currency—or the proceeds of an illegal act (i.e., *ill-gotten gains*). Examples of proceeds include, but are no by means limited to, cash, jewelry, electronic equipment, boats, etc.

Despite the frustrations that investigators experience when their cases are diverted from criminal prosecution to civil court or when they are painstakingly completing the necessary procedures to initiate forfeiture proceedings, the importance of detailed work in white-collar crime cases cannot be overstated. As you learned in the first chapter of this book, the successful identification of a suspect in a murder case may hinge upon an incident involving the fraudulent use of a victim's credit card. Similarly, identifying and prosecuting members of terrorist cells engaged in heinous acts such as the September 11, 2001 attacks on New York City and Washington, D.C. would not have been possible without asset tracing and money laundering analyses (see Chapter 9).

Underpinnings of the American Legal System: The Need for Training and Education

Newly-hired law enforcement personnel will quickly learn that investigations are driven by paperwork. From subpoenas and warrants to affidavits and

courtroom transcripts, the criminal justice system is rife with documentation—and for good reason. You may recall from your earlier courses in
criminal justice that the American judicial system is predicated upon a
concept of English law known as *due process*. Due process stems from King
John's *Magna Carta* enacted in 1215. The Magna Carta requires that the
government follow a rule of law that is consistently applied to all citizens.[3]
In America, laws are essentially derived from three sources: (1) the English
Common-law, (2) our Declaration of Independence (which asserts our rights
to life, liberty, and the pursuit of happiness), and (3) our own Federal
Constitution. The latter specifies certain other rights we have as U.S. citizens, and emphasizes the uniform application of law to all of the members
of our society. In order to protect Americans from political harassment, false
arrest, and imprisonment, in 1789, Congress enacted ten amendments to the
U.S. Constitution, collectively referred to as the *Bill of Rights*.

In total, "of the 23 specific rights guaranteed in these amendments, 12
have a direct bearing on criminal procedure, and of these, the Fourth, Fifth,
and Sixth, Amendments are the most relevant for law enforcement."[4] Rights
such as those described in the First Amendment (i.e., assurance of the right
to freedom of speech (particularly political speech) and expression, freedom
of the press, and prohibition against the establishment of a state religion),
the Second Amendment (i.e., right to keep and bear arms and maintain
a standing militia), and the Third Amendment (prohibition against the
stationing of soldiers in private homes) are also important to maintaining
a free and open society. However, the application of law to white-collar
crime investigations generally falls within the confines of three other
amendments—freedom against unreasonable search and seizure (Fourth
Amendment), the right against self-incrimination and assurance of due process of law (Fifth Amendment), and the right to legal counsel and a speedy
trial (Sixth Amendment).

Whereas local uniformed police are often subjected to civilian complaints
for excessive use of force or garnering a suspect's confession under duress,
white-collar crime investigators are less likely to face criminal proceedings
or civil lawsuits for such allegations. They are, however, more likely to be
accused of offenses such as violating a suspect's constitutional right to
search and seizure or engaging in an unlawful arrest. To counter such claims,
many law enforcement agents tasked with investigating white-collar crimes
such as fraud, forgery, and embezzlement are now required to undergo
extensive coursework at the academy level addressing the preparation of
and guidelines for search and seizure warrants, civil and criminal forfeiture
procedures, searches incidental to arrest, chain of custody logs, and evidence
management policies.

Although their importance cannot be refuted, training on these police
academy topics has traditionally been marginal compared to physical

conditioning, defensive tactics, and firearms training. Rather, it was assumed that special agents and criminal investigators would learn the legal and procedural aspects of their profession "on the job," often through the passage of wisdom from senior agents to new trainees. Yet as the ranks of "senior" investigators shrink due to attrition, early retirement buyouts, and organizational downsizing, institutional memory for search, seizure, and arrest policies that are consistent with the Fourth, Fifth, and Sixth Amendments also fades.

Less than six years ago, approximately 30 percent of the 1.6 million federal career workers were eligible to retire and an additional 20 percent qualified for an early retirement. It is estimated that nearly 50 percent of the senior executives in federal service (i.e., those who set policy and guidelines for law enforcement and regulatory agencies such as the U.S. Secret Service, Federal Bureau of Investigation, and Securities and Exchange Commission) could retire before 2010. Thus, the need for future investigators to understand the underpinnings of U.S. Constitutional law prior to entering on duty cannot be overstated. Lastly, the importance of properly completing the paperwork that supports these Constitutional rights is essential to protecting the American due process, and those sworn to uphold it.

Search and Arrest Warrants: The Workhorses of White-Collar Crime Investigations

Once you become an investigator or special agent assigned to work white-collar crime cases, you will quickly learn that your agency has developed detailed reporting procedures. You will be required to complete specific forms connected to the incidents that you will be investigating. Whether completing inventory control and counterfeit currency specimen forms for the U.S. Secret Service (SSF-1544s and SSF-1604s), interview/witness statements for the Federal Bureau of Investigation (Form 302), or implied consent statute forms for the Department of Defense (referred to as a "FM 113s"), it is absolutely essential that you prepare requisite paperwork as accurately and completely as possible. Failure to do so may result in tainting evidence which will render it inadmissible at trial. When evidence such as a witness statement, criminal confession, CD-ROM containing financial information, or Inkjet printer used to create counterfeit currency is illegally obtained (i.e., seized in violation of the Fourth or Fifth Amendments), it is considered to be a *fruit of a poisonous tree*—meaning not just that particular piece of evidence, but any subsequent statements, documents, or physical evidence that stems from the original illicitly obtained evidence are also inadmissible.[5] The court case frequently cited as an illustration of this legal precept (commonly referred to as the *exclusionary rule*) is the 1963 case of *Wong Sun v. United States*.[6]

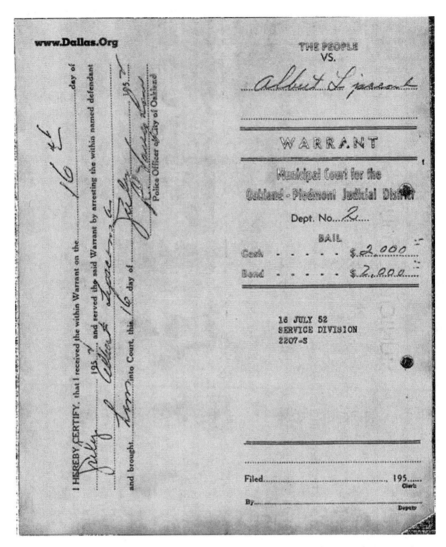

Exhibit 8.1 Arrest warrants such as the one shown here are often issued after a search and seizure warrant has already produced evidence of a crime.

In addition to possible evidentiary issues, illegally obtained information or property may result in criminal charges being filed against the agent or investigator, civil penalties, or disciplinary action such as suspension or removal from office. Moreover, if ill-gotten data is entered into an agency's central information system—such as the U.S. Secret Service's Master Central Index (MCI) or Treasury Enforcement Communications System (TECS-II)—efforts to conduct accurate intelligence analysis in the future may be compromised.

While specific forms and reporting procedures vary from agency to agency, there are two documents that nearly always contain similar information due to the constitutional requirements established in the Fourth Amendment: the search warrant application and the arrest warrant application. One of the main tenets of the U.S. Constitution is that personal property or liberty should not be taken from anyone without due process of law. The Fourth Amendment specifically states that

> The right of the people to be secure in their persons, houses, papers, and effects, against unreasonable searches and seizures, shall not be violated, and no warrants shall issue, but upon probable cause, supported by oath or affirmation, and particularly describing the place to be searched, and the persons or things to be seized.[7]

Accordingly, if you, as an investigator, seek to gather evidence of a white-collar offense such as fraud, forgery, embezzlement, bribery, or counterfeiting, you must have more than mere suspicion that a crime has occurred and that evidence of that crime is housed at a specific location. If you believe that the area where the evidence is present would normally afford someone a *reasonable expectation of privacy* (e.g., a house, apartment, cabin cruiser, or recreational vehicle), you cannot normally search the premises unless a valid search warrant supported by probable cause and issued by the court has been obtained (exceptions to the warrant requirements will be discussed later in this chapter).

As stated in the 1959 U.S. Supreme Court decision in *Draper v. United States*,[8] "probable cause exists where an officer of reasonable caution believes that an offense is being or is about to be committed, based on objective facts and circumstances."[9] Warrant applications are often prepared by the investigator or agent, or in some cases, by a prosecutor, assistant district attorney, or assistant U.S. attorney. Although these applications vary slightly from jurisdiction to jurisdiction, they all contain essentially the same information, including the following:

1. Normally, search warrant applications must be submitted in writing. In rare circumstances, such as a situation occurring in the middle of the night when evidence might be destroyed if the officer waits until regular court hours, a warrant application may be made telephonically. However, a formal written application must still be completed as soon as possible.
2. The application must provide the exact name of the location to be searched, or the names of any persons to be searched, and specifically describe the property sought.
3. The warrant application must provide the specific facts that lead the

investigator to have probable cause that a crime has been committed (e.g., witness statement, confidential informant, etc.) and cite the specific regulation or statute that has allegedly been violated.

4. The anticipated date that the search is to occur and the agency that will be serving the warrant must be provided. Normally, a warrant must be executed within ten calendar days from the date of issuance. Only a sworn law enforcement officer such as a federal agent, criminal investigator, county sheriff, or local police officer can serve the warrant.

5. An oath or affirmation on the part of the investigator or other law enforcement official requesting the warrant must be included in the application.

As a white-collar crime investigator, your application should include *only* those items that you believe are strictly related to the specific crime or crimes which you are investigating. For example, if you were conducting a search of a residence for credit card fraud, you might wish to list genuine and counterfeit credit cards, charge slips, magnetic card readers, embossing equipment, genuine and fictitious identity cards, cancelled credit card draft checks, personal bank account summaries and credit card payment statements in your warrant application. Do *not* include phrases such as "all electronics and appliances located in the area where credit card manufacturing equipment may be found" in your application unless you are prepared to spend hours— or perhaps days—inventorying and securing items such as toasters, blenders, and clock radios! While you may find items that have been purchased with the proceeds of credit card fraud (e.g., computer equipment, and stereo systems), the process for seizing and forfeiting these items is very different than the procedure used in the search warrant application, and will be discussed later in this chapter. The most important questions that you, the white-collar crime investigator, should ask yourself during the warrant application process are, "what specific materials or equipment might have been used to commit this crime?" and "what documents or other evidence support my theory?"

After filing the application, a judge will review the information contained in the your request to ensure that it is not overly broad, does not lack probable cause, or is not otherwise invalid. Provided that the application meets all of the above-mentioned criteria, the judge will issue a signed warrant which you, as a sworn law enforcement officer, will then execute. Most federal and state guidelines require that those executing the warrant adhere to the *knock and announce rule*[10] which requires that officers knock, wait a reasonable time, and announce their authority and purpose. If not admitted, the officers may then forcibly enter the premises. In unusual circumstances, a "no-knock" warrant may be issued, which specifically allows law enforcement officers to enter without first announcing their intentions. As you will learn in Chapter 9, these warrants are generally only issued when *tactical intelligence* strongly suggests that announcing the officers' intentions might result in their immediate and serious bodily harm.

Upon entering the premises, you or your fellow officers should present the owner/occupant with a copy of the signed warrant. Subsequently, all evidence discovered during the search process will be cataloged in a document known as a chain-of-custody sheet or inventory control form, and secured at an off-site location. Agency guidelines will dictate who is responsible for inventorying and securing evidence, thus minimizing the possibility that evidence tampering or lost property will become an issue in impending criminal proceedings. Lastly, you or one of your fellow officers or agents should return the warrant to the judge who originally issued it, along with a comprehensive listing of those items that were seized.

Exceptions to the Search/Seizure Warrant Requirement

It will probably not surprise you to learn that exceptions exist to the Fourth Amendment's search and seizure provisions. Examples in which a warrant may not be required include—but are not limited to—the following:[11]

- Provided the investigator is not trespassing, any contraband item (e.g., counterfeit currency, sawed-off shotgun, marijuana, etc.) that is located in plain view may be seized.
- As upheld by the 1925 U.S. Supreme Court decision in *Carroll v. United States*[12] (also sometimes referred to as the *Carroll Doctrine* or the *Mobility Doctrine*), an automobile may be searched without warrant when an officer or investigator has probable cause to believe that fruits or instruments of a crime might be located inside. Such searches are deemed reasonable by the court because a motor vehicle can easily be moved, which could result in the loss of evidence. In 1982, in the *United States v. Ross* ruling, the Supreme Court expanded search boundaries to include closed containers located inside a vehicle.
- When a suspect consents to a search of any location in which they have a *reasonable expectation to privacy*, the investigator may conduct a search without first obtaining a warrant (*Schneckloth v. Bustamonte*, 1973[13]). However, the suspect reserves the right to end the search at any time unless contraband or evidence of a crime is found during the consented portion of the search.
- As established in *Chimel v. California*[14] (1969) and *United States v. Robinson* (1973), investigators, agents, and other law enforcement personnel may conduct warrantless searches of the area in immediate proximity to a suspect during his or her arrest. The primary reason for

such searches is to protect the officer or agent from weapons, although any evidence obtained in the "sit and reach" area of a suspect during a lawful arrest may be presented in a criminal proceeding. The general rule is that the arresting officers or agents may search the area within an "arm's length" or "lunging distance" between the suspect and the officers. If the arrest occurs inside a dwelling, building, or other structure, the officers may search adjacent rooms, closets, etc. for other people that might attempt to interfere with the arrest or injure the law enforcement officers in the performance of their duties. However, drawers, cabinets, and other areas where a person could not reasonably be expected to hide cannot be searched without a warrant.

- When evidence of a crime is furnished by a third party to a police officer, investigator, or other law enforcement official, and the third party was not directed to obtain this information at the request of the officer (i.e., acting as a government agent), then the evidence is admissible in court even if it was obtained illegally. This ruling is found in the U.S. Supreme Court's 1921 decision in *Burdeau v. McDowell*.[15]

- The case of *California v. Greenwood*[16] (1988) established that property is considered abandoned when a person throws a bag in a public trash receptacle and walks away from it. Subsequently, the bag can be searched without obtaining a search warrant. Federal agents often refer to searching for evidence in large trash receptacles as *dumpster diving*.

- Property being impounded by a law enforcement agency can be searched to ensure that the inventory is accurate and complete. For example, if an unregistered, uninsured automobile is towed and secured at a police impound lot, officers would conduct a complete inventory of the vehicle to ensure that its contents are properly recorded.

- Lastly, when *exigent* circumstances exist, such as an immediate threat to public safety, the survival of the police officer, or even a border crossing, searches may be conducted without benefit of a warrant.

While at first glance it may appear that there are numerous exceptions to the Fourth Amendment, courts have very little tolerance for white-collar crime investigators who "bend the rules" to conduct warrantless searches. You are strongly encouraged to consider the warning of former Assistant U.S. Attorney Andrew Grosso, who notes, "investigators should not avoid securing warrants in white-collar crime cases merely because the process to obtain them appears difficult and time consuming."[17]

One of the greatest distinctions between local uniformed police officers and federal and state white-collar crime investigators involves the use of arrest warrants. In daily police work, law enforcement officers often catch suspects "in the act." For example, if a man is running down the street clutching a purse that he just stole from a bystander and the police officer observes this event, the officer can apprehend the suspect without a warrant. Other examples where law enforcement officials might act similarly include offenses such as assault, drunk driving, possession of narcotics, soliciting prostitution, trespassing, etc.

In your case, as a special agent assigned to white-collar crime investigations, arrests are normally the result of days, weeks, or months of tedious investigative work such as surveillance, monitoring telephone conversations, and analysis of financial transactions. It is quite rare that you will simply stumble upon a credit card fraud ring or a group engaged in mortgage loan fraud. White-collar crime investigators are normally not chasing down suspects who have produced massive amounts of counterfeit currency in "hot pursuit;" but rather, you will have built a solid case prior to making an arrest. Therefore, when an arrest is not made as a result of your immediate observation, an exigent situation does not exist, and the arrest is to be made in a private residence, a warrant is required.

Arrest Warrants

The Fourth Amendment to the U.S. Constitution asserts that American citizens should not be deprived of their personal property or liberty except when probable cause exists. Similarly, an arrest warrant requires that a written application be made to the court; that the agent, investigator, prosecutor or assistant U.S. attorney cite the specific offense that the government believes the suspect has violated; that the date and location where the warrant is issued be supplied; that the conditions for release (e.g., bail or discounted cash surety) of the arrestee be articulated; and that the judge or other authorized judicial official such as the clerk of the court sign the warrant.

A copy of the arrest warrant will be provided to the arrestee, and the warrant will subsequently be returned to the court without reasonable delay. For purposes of efficiency, the search warrant and arrest warrant are often submitted, issued, and executed together. After the arrest has been made, the prosecutor, district attorney's office, or assistant U.S attorney will complete one of three types of charging documents. These are as follows:

- When the offense involves a misdemeanor or regulatory offense, a *complaint* may be issued. Given that most white-collar crimes are felonies (i.e., punishable by a minimum of one year plus one day imprisonment), complaints are not often completed for these offenses and are not used in the federal system.
- An *information* outlines the formal charge or charges, the law or laws that have been violated, and the evidence to support the charge or

charges. A prosecutor or assistant U.S. attorney usually files the *infor-mation* at the preliminary hearing or arraignment.

• Lastly, a felony charge must be presented before a grand jury—a group of 16 to 23 sworn jurors who meet secretly either biweekly or monthly. Provided that 12 or more of the members of the grand jury agree that there is sufficient evidence to link the suspect to the offense, they will issue an *indictment* or *true bill*. Grand juries possess tremendous power because they can subpoena witnesses and evidence and require a defendant to testify without his or her attorney present. Rather than be *indicted*, a defendant can waive his or her right to a grand jury, and instead opt for the prosecution (e.g., the assistant U.S. attorney) to file an *information*.

Other Important Paperwork for the White-Collar Crime Investigator

As you learned earlier in this chapter, each agency has its own unique report-ing requirements that must be strictly adhered to by you, the investigator, assigned to white-collar criminal cases. However, nearly all enforcement entities will use some form of written narrative or incident report in order to record the significant facts of the case or document the procedures employed by investigators. Chain-of-custody and inventory control logs are necessary to ensure that evidence is not compromised prior to trial and that contra-band items are properly discarded after judicial proceedings have concluded. In some cases, you may also prepare a document known as a *Subpoena duces tecum*[18] (SDT) in order to gather information not usually made available to the general public. For example, a U.S. Secret Service agent investigating the exchange of stolen credit card numbers via the Internet might prepare a SDT for an Internet Service Provider, requesting the actual name of the e-mail account holder, as well as his or her address and tele-phone number. FBI agents examining possible financial institution fraud might serve a subpoena on a bank, requiring copies of a specific customer's checking account transactions during a six-month period. A subpoena can also be used to compel a witness to appear in court. In all cases, a subpoena application is made to the court using a procedure similar to the one used to obtaining a search or arrest warrant. Upon signature by the judge or clerk of the court, the subpoena can be served either personally or via U.S. Mail. In both cases, an *affidavit of service* is required, to ensure that the subpoena was indeed served on the individual or institution named in the application.

In addition to narrative reports, warrants, subpoenas, and evidence forms, law enforcement agencies have strict requirements for documenting inter-views with witnesses and suspects. One of the key provisions of the Bill of

Rights is protection against self-incrimination, as described in the Fifth Amendment to the U.S. Constitution. In 1966, the U.S. Supreme Court strengthened a suspect's protection from self-incrimination in its interpretation of *Miranda v. Arizona*.[19] Central to the Court's position was that custodial interrogation of a suspect could not occur unless the suspect was informed of his or her right against self-incrimination (i.e., "anything you say can and will be used against you,") and, as asserted in the Sixth Amendment, that legal counsel would be appointed for a suspect who could not afford such representation. Lastly, the ruling required that suspects be made aware that they were not required to answer any questions prior to consulting with their attorneys. While there are limited exceptions to *Miranda*, such as a suspect spontaneously blurting out a murder confession in the back of the squad car on the way to the police station, or exigent circumstances that might result in serious harm to the public if a suspect were not interrogated (e.g., "where in the school did you plant the bomb?") such cases are uncommon, and are rarely applicable to white-collar offenses. Accordingly, most investigative agencies require that suspects and witnesses sign a *Waiver of Miranda Rights form* prior to questioning, and/or require that those being interviewed indicate in their written statements that they have been advised of their rights and are making statements voluntarily, without any form of duress or coercion.

It is important to note that both the Fifth Amendment and the *Miranda Warnings* are designed to protect American citizens from self-incrimination, and to ensure that a suspect's Sixth Amendment right to legal counsel is not violated.[20] Therefore, prior to questioning a suspect or witness, you should ensure that a subject fully understands his or her rights. In some cases, this could mean articulating these rights in Spanish, Arabic, or another foreign language (even in Sign Language or Braille).

Questioning juveniles presents additional challenges. The federal system is not equipped to handle persons under the age of 18 (i.e., there are no separate facilities or correctional standards for them). Accordingly, federal law enforcement officials will normally refer a case involving a juvenile to a state or local law enforcement jurisdiction for questioning and prosecution.

By adhering to the search and seizure, arrest, and interviewing and interrogation policies of their agencies, white-collar crime investigators can dramatically reduce the risk that their department's cases will be "thrown out" at trial. Equally importantly, following procedures as meticulously as possible may prevent investigators from encountering disciplinary actions, civil, or criminal sanctions for violating a suspect's constitutional rights.

White-Collar Criminal Statutes: A Primer

Depending on the agency to which you, as an investigator or agent, are assigned, you will be provided with a summary of the specific laws and regulations specific to your jurisdiction. In order to restrict police powers, nearly all of the law enforcement agencies at the federal or state executive branch level have a limited scope of authority with respect to what they can actually enforce. The exception to this rule is the United States Marshals Service, whose central role in nearly every federal law enforcement initiative provides them with tremendous authority and jurisdiction.

For example, the United States Secret Service is tasked with presidential protection duties and the investigation of financial crimes such as counterfeiting of U.S. currency and obligations (U.S. Treasury checks, savings bonds, etc.), access device fraud, and computer crimes. The Office of the Inspector General for the U.S. Department of Education examines waste, fraud, and abuse in federal student financial aid and grant programs. By limiting an agency's enforcement capabilities to specific regulations and sections of the United States Code (USC), the U.S. Congress provides a check on the powers of the executive branch of the United States government. What remains to be seen, however, is what effect the *USA Patriot Act of 2001* (HR 3162), passed in the aftermath of the September 11, 2001 tragedy, will have on the possible centralization of law enforcement powers.[21]

The 2001 Patriot Act afforded federal law enforcement agencies broad authority for intelligence gathering and information sharing, provided such activities are related to the investigation and suppression of terrorism. The surveillance and information sharing components of the Patriot Act were further expanded in 2006. Regardless of how much latitude the *USA Patriot Act* may provide agencies assigned to terrorism cases, departments conducting white-collar crime investigations will likely still only retain organization-specific authority to investigate acts of fraud, forgery, embezzlement, money laundering, counterfeiting of U.S. currency, etc. Accordingly, this portion of the chapter will provide you with a fundamental understanding of major federal criminal statutes commonly cited by special agents and law enforcement personnel assigned to white-collar crime cases.

Conspiracy

Found at Title 18, Section 371 of the United States Code, scholar and noted author Jay Albanese refers to conspiracy as "the characteristic white-collar crime."[22] Conspiracy is commonly referred to as an *inchoate* offense, meaning that the intended illegal act, or legal act to be carried out through illegal means, does not need to be completed for the crime of conspiracy to have been committed. For conspiracy to occur, there must be two or more persons who scheme to commit an offense against the United States or its respective agencies. One or more of the persons involved must commit an *overt act* in furtherance of the conspiracy. Consider the following example:

Kat, a junior at Biggstown College, works part-time as a customer service representative at a local bank. After arriving late for work one day, Kat's boss lectures her on the importance of punctuality, which results in a heated exchange between them. Kat is fired on the spot. Later that day, in the apartment of Kat's boyfriend Toby, the two devise a scheme to hack into the bank's central computer, and using Kat's customer service security code, transfer $50,000 from a wealthy customer's account to Toby's. However, in order for the plan to work, Kat will need a laptop computer and modem. Toby walks down the hall to his friend Tom's apartment, and asks to borrow his laptop for a few hours (Toby does not explain to Tom why he needs the computer). Toby returns to his own apartment, hands the laptop to Kat, and she begins dialing into the bank's mainframe computer. Whether Kat actually succeeds in illegally transferring the funds is irrelevant, because as soon as Toby borrowed the laptop from Tom, the first overt act in furtherance of the conspiracy was committed. If convicted, Kat and Toby could face prison sentences of up to five years each, individual fines of up to $10,000, or both. Because Tom was unaware of the conspiracy, he could not be charged. However, if Kat or Toby "let him in on the scheme" after they had committed it, Tom could be charged as an *Accessory After the Fact* pursuant to 18 USC 3. If convicted, he could receive half of the maximum sentence provided in the statute.

While conspiracy is one of the most frequently used offenses by prosecutors, it is sometimes improperly used as a means to coerce the defendant into accepting a lesser plea. Because conspiracy is considered to be an inchoate offense, many people mistakenly believe that this lessens the burden of proof for the prosecution. Nothing could be further from the truth.

Mail Fraud

One of the most commonly used statutes in the prosecution of persons who commit white-collar crimes is *Mail Fraud*. Often times, the U.S. Attorney's Office or Prosecutor will use the mail fraud charge as a means to reach a plea agreement with a defendant. Found in Title 18 of the United States Code, Section 1341, the elements of mail fraud are:[23]

1. Intent to defraud or obtain money or property under fictitious or fraudulent pretenses, or supplying a counterfeit coin, security or other item for the above-stated purpose;
2. Placement of the item in a U.S. postal mail box or facility—which now also includes private mailing services such as Federal Express, United Parcel Service, DHL, Airborne Express, etc.;

3. Routing of the item through the U.S. Mail (or other delivery service described in element number 2);
4. Intentional delivery to an intended person.

The following is a hypothetical example of mail fraud.

Vinnie and Jayne purchase a direct mailing list from the American Society for the Prevention of Cruelty to Animals (ASPCA) for approximately 500 people who live in their area and recently adopted stray dogs and cats from the local animal shelter. Unbeknownst to the ASCPA, Vinnie and Jayne draft a letter on bogus ASPCA letterhead informing the parties who recently adopted from the local shelter that they can receive five years of unlimited veterinary care if they send a certified check or money order payable to "Vinnie and Jayne's Pet Health Services" (located at Vinnie's home address) within the next ten days. Neither Vinnie nor Jayne has any actual veterinary training, nor do they intend to provide such services. It is not necessary for a potential victim to send a check or money order to Vinnie and Jayne in order to establish grounds for a conviction. Moreover, although this is a federal crime, mail does not need to travel between states in order for mail fraud to have been committed. If convicted, Vinnie and Jayne could receive fines of up to $1,000 for each offense, be imprisoned for up to five years per offense, or both. This means that if Vinnie and Jayne mailed out 500 bogus letters, they could receive the maximum fine and prison term for *each* letter they sent.

Wire Fraud

As with most forms of fraud, wire fraud[24] (18 USC 1343) involves the common element of intent to defraud for the purpose of obtaining money or property through false or fictitious means. Wire fraud requires the transmission of any image, writings, sign, signal, or sound via television, telephone, radio, cable, or other form of telecommunications in interstate or foreign commerce. Prosecutors often use the charge of wire fraud as a "catch all" for computer crimes, because as soon as you sign on to the Internet, you have most likely linked to a network or server located in a different state and have thus engaged in interstate commerce. Again, the intended purpose of the fraudster is to dupe people out of their money or property. An example of wire fraud is as follows:

The marketing and promotions director of WZXCLM 109.5 FM, the tri-state area's major pop radio station, announces a contest in which the first 25 listeners who come to the radio station and donate their watches to "Timepieces for the Needy" will be entered in a contest to win an all-expense paid trip to London for New Year's Eve. The radio station collects the watches and distributes them to members of the staff as performance incentives. The marketing and promotions director then draws a fictitious winner in the contest, thus ensuring that no one will actually be sent to England. If convicted, the director of WZXCLM could face a fine of up to $1,000, five years imprisonment, or both.

Access Device Fraud

Found in Title 18 of the United States Code, Section 1029,[25] access device fraud is becoming increasingly popular with juveniles both within the U.S. and abroad. It is defined as the *knowing and intentional defrauding of another by use of a card, plate, code, account number, electronic serial number, mobile identification number, personal identification number, or other telecommunications service, equipment, or instrument identifier.*

Much of the increase in access device fraud is due to the proliferation of low-security, Internet-based companies accepting credit cards for payment, increases in bank-issued debit/check cards linked to the MasterCard or Visa networks, and the widespread availability of inexpensive, miniature "skimming" devices capable of storing large amounts of credit card data into memory. Also troubling is that many of the point-of-sale (PoS) magnetic card-reading terminals, which were previously located behind the cashier's booth at most stores, are now located directly in front of the customer. This allows a thief to easily swipe another person's credit card without the cashier connecting the card to the customer.

While there are currently no provisions in the federal law for juveniles engaged in these activities, penalties for adults committing acts of access device fraud range from a year's imprisonment for unauthorized use of a credit card/personal account number to ten years plus substantial fines for using or trafficking in hardware or software designed to provide unauthorized access to telecommunications services.

One example of a commonly encountered violation under this statute includes trafficking in illegal magnetic card readers and skimming devices in order to steal legitimate credit card information from customers or clients. A more sophisticated scenario would involve producing fraudulent credit cards using a plastic embosser (to generate the raised card numbers), a magnetic card reader/decoder to replicate the magnetic stripe, an Inkjet or LaserJet printer to recreate the graphic design of the card, and downloading unauthorized valid credit card numbers via the World Wide Web using a keystroke capture program or fictitious website.

Another statute related to access device fraud is 18 USC 1030,[26] "Fraud and Related Activity in Connection with the Use of Computers." Activities such as hacking a protected computer system (such as a U.S. Government owned or operated website), knowingly sending viruses, e-mail bombs, or other applications capable of damaging hardware, software, or stored data, and trafficking in passwords or access codes for protected websites and governmental, corporate, and educational institution computer systems are prohibited by this statute. Penalties vary from substantial fines and/or up to ten years imprisonment.

Embezzlement

In his 1996 book entitled *Trusted Criminals*, author David Friedrichs refers to embezzlement as a form of employee theft.[27] Much like Donald Cressey observed in his research, Friedrichs discovered that employees who commit such offenses, particularly when dollar amounts of such thefts are small, tend to rationalize theft as long-term, zero-interest loans or as fringe benefits for being overworked and underpaid. In short, these employees feel they are simply leveling the playing field between higher paid managers and themselves. Friedrichs further notes that while employee theft crimes such as embezzlement can occur at any level within an organization, from a part-time shipping clerk to a senior executive, "higher-level employees are best positioned to steal from a company on the largest scale, and by some estimates, executives and managers are responsible for the largest proportion of losses businesses suffer at the hands of their employees."[28]

Strictly speaking, embezzlement is a form of *larceny*. However, larceny involves the actual or constructive taking and carrying away the property of another without consent and against the will of the owner, and with the intent to permanently deprive the owner of the property. In contrast, the federal charge of *Theft, Embezzlement or Misapplication by Bank Officer or Employee* (18 USC 656 et seq.), adds the specific requirements that the offender must be connected to a federal reserve bank, its agents, or must be an employee of the receiver, and have been granted the authority to care for or manage such funds.

Consider the following example.

Simone is a full-time website designer in the online banking section of MegaBank Financial Services—a federally insured financial institution in accordance with the requirements of the Federal Deposit Insurance Corporation. Among Simone's assigned duties are the development of new web pages for the Bank's consumer savings section and recording account numbers and personal identification numbers (PINs) for online customer access into the system. During a six-month period, Simone enters approximately 6,400 account numbers and PINs into MegaBank's central section. She randomly selects twenty new accounts each day, charges each of these accounts a bogus $2.50 "service processing fee," and transfers the money from this fictitious fee into her personal savings account at the bank. At the end of this six-month period, Simone has amassed about $6,000 in her personal checking account ($50/day × 5 days per week = $250 for approximately 24 weeks = $6,000.00). While the daily, weekly, and monthly theft resulting from Simone's illegal activities does not exceed the $1,000 threshold needed for the full sentence of 30 years, $1 million fine, or both, the *total* dollar value of her embezzlement ($6,000) over this six-month period would make her eligible for the maximum sentence. Alternatively, she could face the lesser sentence of up to a year's imprisonment, a fine, or both. The suspect in this case could also be charged with access device fraud (18 USC 1029) because specific account numbers, PINs, and/or passwords were utilized as part of the crime.

Check Fraud and Forgery

White-collar crimes involving financial instruments can take many forms, from forging payee signatures on payment vouchers to producing counterfeit checks using an Inkjet or LaserJet printer, genuine check stock security paper, and a commercial software application such as VersaCheck. VersaCheck has been on the market since mid-1996, selling hundreds of thousands of copies since its creation. While the program is designed for small businesses to manage their check writing functions, the use of VersaCheck and similar software applications for illicit purposes has continued to rise, particularly among young people. For example, on August 29, 2000, 19-year-old Terrance Christian of Fort Meyers, Florida, downloaded a copy of a check manufacturing software application via the World Wide Web (using a computer at his local public library). He subsequently printed bogus checks on the library's printer, and was able to cash approximately $1,000 in checks at an area food market before being arrested.

Another case from the year 2000 comes from the *Detroit Free Press*. In this case, the alleged suspect was Timothy M. Evans, also 19 years of age, and a former student at the Auburn Hills campus of Oakland University (OU) in Michigan. The OU Police Department alleged that Evans used his job in the financial aid office of the University to obtain student names, addresses, social security numbers, and related personal information.

Using false identification documents, he subsequently established checking accounts in the names of these students, and drafted checks to himself for about $4,000, which he then deposited into his personal bank account. Activities such as the forging or attempted passing of counterfeit personal or corporate checks are generally prosecuted via the *Bank Fraud* statute found at18 USC 1344,[29] which makes it a felony to knowingly negotiate or attempt to negotiate a false or altered check at a federally chartered financial institution. Violation of this section of the United States Code is punishable by fines of up to $10,000, five years imprisonment, or both.

It should be noted that attempted forgery of U.S. treasury checks (e.g., tax refunds, social security checks, etc.) and other governmental obligations would be prosecuted under the provisions of 18 USC 510,[30] and offenders may be sentenced to substantial fines and/or up to ten years imprisonment.

False Statements and Entries

In addition to *conspiracy* and *mail fraud*, the use of *the false statements and entries* provisions of 18 USC 1001[31] can serve as a highly valuable tool for white-collar crime investigators. The statute applies to nearly all federal documents such as government employment applications, student loan requests, federal income tax forms, government housing assistance programs, U.S. passport applications, federal mortgage assistance, proposals for government grants and contracts, criminal and civil investigation forms used by federal law enforcement agencies, and U.S. court documents. False statements and entries are often "stacked" on top of other possible offenses with which a suspect could be charged, thus eliciting cooperation from an otherwise hostile party. Consider the following example, which is based on a case that I was actually involved with as the senior law enforcement specialist.

An asbestos mitigation contractor frequently uses non-certified employees, who do not have proper health and safety training, to conduct asbestos removal. The contractor decides to bid on a project at a National Park Service site. The government requires that the project employees maintain training and certification in proper asbestos remediation techniques. The contractor submits his project proposal to the National Park Service, and includes phony asbestos mitigation training certificates for his employees. He also offers to charge far less than the market rate for the project (he can only do this because he is actually using untrained employees which cost him far less money). Upon further investigation, the National Park Service determines that the proposed employees for the project are not actually trained, and that fraudulent certifications were included with the bid proposal. The contractor could be charged with both mail fraud (18 USC 1341) and false statements and entries (18 USC 1001) because the information contained in his bid package was in itself materially false or fictitious. Those found in violation of 18 USC 1001 can be fined, imprisoned for up to 5 years, or both.

Money Laundering

At no time in American history has the concept of *money laundering* become so pronounced. After the terrorist attacks on New York City and Washington, DC, on September 11, 2001, President George W. Bush vowed in a speech to the American public to "direct every resource at his command—every means of diplomacy, every tool of intelligence, every financial influence and every necessary weapon of war—to the disruption and defeat of the global terrorist network."[32] Among the key provisions of his strategy was to identify and immobilize the flow of monies derived from illicit activities such as drug trafficking and weapons sales, which are often used to execute terrorist acts around the world.

Unfortunately, determining which funds are the result of ill-gotten gains and those obtained through legitimate business ventures is extremely difficult—particularly when legitimate assets are blended with illegitimate operations. One of the great challenges that the United States faces in implementing this approach is that, according to Senator Carl Levin (speaking on September 26, 2001 before the Senate Committee on Banking, Housing, and Urban Affairs on Banking and Money Laundering), "unlike drug and organized crime operations, terrorist acts sometimes do not generate illegal proceeds that have to be laundered. Terrorists use financial networks to collect funds from both legitimate and illegitimate sources and make them available to carry out terrorist acts."[33]

For example, nineteen of the terrorists identified by the FBI as part of the September 11, 2001 tragedy used a combination of cash, checks, ATM transactions, wire transfers, and credit cards to fund their travel and other expenses. Such dealings are no more illegal than using a credit card to purchase airline tickets via the World Wide Web (although other would-be hijackers did engage in identify theft, which would render some of these funds as ill-gotten gains). Generally, efforts to track such transactions from a money laundering perspective in an attempt to thwart terrorist attacks are, to quote Brandeis University Economics Professor Jane Hughes, "about as debilitating to the bad guys as a stubbed toe."[34]

Technically, money laundering *is* a violation of Title 18, United States Code, Section 1956,[35] punishable by up to twenty years imprisonment, fines of $500,000 or greater (up to twice the value of the property involved), or both. However, one of the most important aspects of this statute is that for money laundering to occur, there must first be a *specified unlawful activity* (SUA) through which "dirty" assets were obtained. For example, if an organized crime group committed mail fraud (18 USC 1341), and then attempted to legitimize the funds that they had derived from this unlawful act in an effort to evade taxes or circumvent the financial institution reporting requirements for cash deposits or withdrawals in excess of $10,000, they have committed both the *SUA* (mail fraud) and money laundering. Simply converting cash derived from legitimate business operations to assets such as jewelry, yachts, and luxury automobiles is *not* considered money laundering. There must be a *SUA* for 18 USC 1956 to be chargeable.

As we will discuss in Chapter 9, investigators and analysts use a variety of techniques in an effort to detect laundering of illegally obtained assets. Intelligence research specialists often look for patterns in transactions (e.g., a series of large deposits at the beginning of the month and smaller deposits at the end of the month), infusions of large sums of money into a non-cash business, purchases of real estate properties for quick resale, substantial wire transfers to and from overseas financial institutions, and significant financial interests in foreign owned or operated businesses.

President Bush's post-9/11 call-to-action against money laundering has raised eyebrows among both conservatives and liberals alike. For example, many of the assets used to fund the activities of terrorist groups are derived from a mixture of legitimate sources (such as oil production, construction projects, etc.) and covert illicit activities such as drug dealing. Moreover, the blending of such assets makes it nearly impossible to determine what has been legally obtained, and what assets have come from ill-gotten gains.

The Challenge of Proving Money Laundering

In 1979, while running his first business, Arbusto Energy, George W. Bush received approximately $50,000 from James Bath—a longtime family friend. In exchange for these funds, Bath received 5 percent of the holdings in the Arbusto Company.[36] According to investigative journalist Wayne Madsen, Bath is reported to have had significant ties to both the bin Laden family and the now-defunct Bank of Commerce and Credit International (BCCI), the financial institution of choice for drug dealers, illegal arms dealers, and others seeking to launder money during the late 1970s and 1980s.[37] BCCI also held CIA-funds used for trafficking weapons to the Afghani rebels during their war against the Soviets in the 1980s.

Arbusto later developed into Harken Energy Corporation, and in 1987, Saudi Sheik Abdullah Taha Bakhsh purchased a 17.6 percent stake in the company. Sheik Bakhsh's business partner in this venture was Khalid Bin Mahfouz—a major shareholder in BCCI who is also believed to have contributed large sums of money to Osama bin Laden and the Al Qaeda terror network. While we are by no means suggesting that President Bush was aware of the nefarious activities of Mr. Bath, Mr. Bakhsh, or Mr. Mahfouz, this example simply illustrates the difficulty that the law enforcement and intelligence community encounters when attempting to separate legitimate from illegitimate proceeds when investigating money laundering allegations.

Close-knit cultures such as those often found in the Middle East and Asia avoid employing traditional banking protocols such as executing wire transfers and establishing foreign accounts. Rather, the U.S. Department of State notes the prevalence of *hawala* (or *hundi*) as a preferred method for conducting financial transactions. Hawala bankers or operators, referred to as *hawaladars*, use their connections to facilitate money movement worldwide. Hawala transfers take place with little if, any, paper trail; and when records are kept, they are usually kept in code. The essential element of hawala transactions is trust between the operator and customer. In those nations where banking institutions are considered unreliable at best (or corrupt at worse), hawala have existed for thousands of years and will likely continue to do so—regardless of any prohibitions that might be imposed against their use by the United States in its war on terrorism.

Lastly, there is an inherent legal tension between investigating and seizing the assets of those persons and organizations suspected of engaging in money laundering as a means of furthering terrorist acts around the world, and the Fourth Amendment protection to be secure in one's person, papers, and property. Lawrence Lindsey, Chairman of President Bush's National Economic Counsel noted in a 1999 presentation on the subject of money laundering that

> there is no question the threats posed by international terrorists and drug cartels are a serious threat to our national security and our individual liberty . . . [but] . . . money laundering enforcement practices are the kind of blanket search that the writers of the Constitution sought to prohibit. We have overstepped the bounds of balance and reason.[38]

The ensuing section of this chapter will specifically address the appropriateness of seizing assets of those suspected of white-collar crimes and money laundering.

Asset Forfeiture: Boon to Law Enforcement or Fourth Amendment Nightmare?

One of the most controversial actions being undertaken by federal, state, and local governments is the process of asset forfeiture and equitable sharing. Historically, governments have seized property for thousands of years, often without just cause. It can be argued that the due process movement—beginning with the enactment of the *Magna Carta* in 1215, continuing through the passage of the U.S. Constitution in 1787 and the Fourth Amendment to the Bill of Rights in 1789—was designed to protect citizens' rights in matters of property seizure. In fact, forfeiture had only been used twice in the history of the United States prior to the latter part of the twentieth century. Congress first allowed the homes of Confederate soldiers to be seized during the Civil War in 1862, and in 1970, allowed limited seizure of marine vessels, aircraft, and other conveyances when drug trafficking and/or organized criminal enterprises were suspected.

In our opinion, the passage of the Comprehensive Crime Control Act (CCCA) in 1984 appears somewhat inconsistent with this legal tradition. One of the main functions of the CCCA was to establish a comprehensive asset forfeiture program at the federal level. The purpose of asset forfeiture is to assist police in enforcing the law, improve their capabilities through enhanced revenue, and expand cooperation between agencies.

Pursuant to the CCCA, certain federal agencies have the authority to seize assets that are derived from criminal activities, such as fraud and forgery. Specific statutes also allow law enforcement agencies to seize property used in the commission of a crime (e.g., confiscating a computer, scanner, and printer used to produce counterfeit U.S. paper currency). Various laws have provisions for asset forfeiture, such as the Racketeer Influenced and Corrupt Organizations Act of 1970[39] (18 USC 1963), which allows for the seizure of assets obtained through money laundering; confiscation of equipment and materials involved in the production of child pornography or obtained through as a result of selling such items (18 USC 2253 *et seq.*), forfeiture of vehicles used to smuggle illegal aliens (8 USC 1324(b)), and lawful taking of counterfeit currency manufacturing equipment (18 USC 492). However, the authority and procedures for seizing assets and initiating forfeiture procedures are generally found in just three places: civil judicial forfeiture (18 USC 981), criminal forfeiture (18 USC 982) and administrative forfeiture through U.S. Justice Department-approved regulations established at the agency level and authorized in 19 USC 1607. A summary of each of these three common forms of forfeiture actions are provided below:

Civil Judicial Forfeiture

This form of lawful government acquisition results when the proceeds of crimes such as *false statements and entries* (18 USC 1001), *counterfeiting of U.S. currency* (18 USC 472), *access device fraud* (18 USC 1029), *fraud in connection with computers* (18 USC 1030), *mail fraud* (18 USC 1341), *wire fraud* (18 USC 1343), or *money laundering* (18 USC 1956) have been discovered. Proceeds include, but are not limited to, cash, jewelry, electronics, vehicles, real estate, stocks, bonds, and other items of value. Civil judicial forfeiture is referred to as an *in rem* action, meaning that the property serves as its own defendant. In other words, a human suspect does not need to be charged or convicted for the property to be forfeited.

Criminal Forfeiture

Used by the government to lawfully obtain assets that result from criminal acts such as those listed under civil judicial forfeiture, 18 USC 982 requires that the specific items to be seized are indicted by a grand jury at the same time that the defendant is charged. This process is referred to as an *in personam* (against the person) action. If the jury finds the property forfeitable, the court issues an order of forfeiture.

Federal law requires that criminal and civil forfeiture procedures be used in cases when the proceeds to be seized (other than monetary instruments such as cash, stocks, bonds, etc.) exceed US$500,000, or the seizure involves real estate where a possible claim could be made by a prospective owner.

Administrative Forfeiture

This is the most common form of forfeiture used by government agencies, particularly when the proceeds of a crime do not involve real estate, non-monetary assets do not exceed $500,000, or a bond or claim for the property has not been made. Frequently, property that is administratively forfeited is put into official use by the agency. For example, a computer purchased using a stolen credit card number could be put into official use by the law enforcement agency that seized it. The computer must then be held by the agency for a minimum of two years, after which it can be sold. Placing property into official use is only one example of how administrative forfeiture may benefit a law enforcement or investigative agency. Other examples include the following:

- *Law Enforcement Training*—conducting courses in asset forfeiture procedures, ethics for asset forfeiture proceedings, case management, etc.
- *Equipment and Operations*—securing new equipment such as computers, cellular telephones, surveillance equipment, travel, uniforms, and office space for task force operations.
- *Detention Facilities*—expenses related to the construction, maintenance, or upgrade of incarceration or holding facilities managed by a participating agency.

Funding obtained through administrative asset forfeiture proceedings may also be used for tracking asset forfeiture expenditures, purchasing associated accounting systems, supporting drug awareness and education activities, and providing limited funding for officers and agents assigned to short-term task force projects. As described in the *Guide to Equitable Sharing of Federally Forfeited Property for State and Local Law Enforcement Agencies*,[40] forfeited proceeds can also be divided among a host of federal, state, and local law enforcement agencies. This is where the controversy begins.

Although police departments and investigative entities are discouraged from relying on funds derived from equitable sharing as a means to supplement their operational budgets, many do just that. Indeed, during one of your author's own tenure as a Criminal Research Specialist with the U.S. Secret Service (he also served in a collateral role as the asset forfeiture specialist for his field office), he witnessed firsthand the tremendous power of asset forfeiture in supporting training, travel and funding of new equipment purchases.

In our opinion, there is also an inherent contradiction within the National Code of Professional Conduct for Asset Forfeiture espoused by the U.S. Department of Justice's (DOJ) Asset Forfeiture and Money Laundering Division. The code states that "law enforcement is the principal objective of forfeiture. Potential revenue must not be allowed to jeopardize the effective investigation and prosecution of criminal offenses."[41] However, a conflict becomes apparent when we consider the minimum threshold levels that the DOJ has established for forfeiture action ($2,500 for vehicles, $10,000 for real estate, and $1,000 for monetary instruments and other assets). In fact, what the Department of Justice is stating is that for offenses below these threshold levels, forfeiture is not recommended. So, if no funds are to be garnered, what value is there for the lead agency or equitable sharing partners to take action?

What if a group of offenders committed 35 separate violations over a ten-month period, each in the amount of $900? Since the first case was not prosecuted, would follow-up investigative work necessarily ensue? If the tragic events of 9/11 have revealed nothing else, they have stressed the importance of collaborative efforts among law enforcement and intelligence agencies. Present-day forfeiture policies appear to oppose this cooperative spirit.

Equally importantly, asset forfeiture regulations, particularly non-criminal proceedings such as 18 USC 981[42] or administrative forfeiture, are generally less stringent than the rules for lawful search and seizure found in the Fourth Amendment. While parties who have a compelling legal interest in the property should be informed by the seizing agency prior to completing the forfeiture transfer process, notices published in local newspapers are rarely adequate; nor, as we can attest from our own experiences handling asset forfeiture cases, do all government agencies aggressively seek to locate possible property stakeholders. In short, the burden of proof regarding property ownership resides with the proprietor.

Examples of such cases include Nashville landscaper Willie Jones, the owners of the Red Carpet Motel, and pizzeria owner Anthony Lombardo. These individuals were not involved in crimes; however, their property was initially seized pursuant to asset forfeiture regulations. After enduring the lengthy, expensive processes of judicial action, their property was returned to them.

Accordingly, civil rights groups such as the Mackinac (Michigan) Center for Public Policy (1998) have recommended the following reforms to existing asset forfeiture laws:[43]

- Remove incentives for law enforcement agencies to employ asset forfeiture;
- Shift the burden of proof from property owners to government;
- Establish nexus and proportionality requirements for forfeiture;
- Eliminate legal hurdles to citizens' ability to challenge forfeiture;
- Require law enforcement agents to publicly justify forfeiture proceedings;
- Enact protections against forfeiture for innocent owners of property;
- Allow third-party creditors the opportunity to recover seized property.

It is through adequate training in Constitutional law and civil rights that the United States can ensure the protection of our freedoms so carefully outlined in the Fourth, Fifth, and Sixth Amendments of the Bill of Rights. This preparation will also ensure that the American judicial process will remain a model of fair and equal justice around the world.

Agencies Responsible for Prosecuting White-Collar Offenders

The Office of the United States Attorney

While investigators and agents develop white-collar crime cases, their ultimate disposition rests with the office of the United States Attorney. This entity determines whether enough evidence exists to merit adjudication. From aiding investigators in the completion of the search warrant application to prosecuting cases, the role of the U.S. attorneys—and assistant U.S. attorneys who serve them—cannot be overstated.

A function of the Criminal Division of the United States Department of Justice's Office of the Attorney General, assistant U.S. attorneys (AUSAs) provide prosecutorial oversight for more than 900 federal statutes and related civil matters. From alien smuggling and trafficking in endangered species to terrorism and violent crime, AUSAs provide investigators with legal guidance in conducting searches, collecting evidence, obtaining testimony, and counseling witnesses and victims of crimes through the Federal Victim/Witness program.

With respect to white-collar crime, AUSAs play a critical role in coordinating multi-agency participation in cases involving asset forfeiture and money laundering, computer crime, fraud, organized crime and racketeering, and public integrity. The role of prosecuting attorney is often performed by the most seasoned AUSA located within a respective district or section. However, junior AUSAs are equally important, as they are often the link between their office and the field investigators assigned to a case. For additional information on the role of the U.S. Department of Justice's Criminal Division, refer to the Department's website located at URL: http://www.usdoj.gov/criminal/

Chapter Summary

For more than seven years, America's response to the horrific events of September 11, 2001 in Washington, D.C. and New York City has continued to unfold. The emphasis on tracking money laundering as a means to thwart acts of terrorism is the cornerstone of this response. With an estimated $500 billion to $1.5 trillion (US) in illicit financial transactions occurring each year, the importance of the white-collar crime investigator's appreciation for—and awareness of—offenses such as mail fraud, wire fraud, embezzlement, access device fraud, fraud in connection with the use of computers, and conspiracy cannot be overemphasized.

Understanding the key elements of these statutes is not enough. As a future investigator, you must also become familiar with the U.S. Constitution's Bill of Rights, specifically the Fourth, Fifth, and Sixth Amendments. Without proper respect for the search, seizure, and arrest process, the conviction of suspects will rarely be realized, and the entire judicial process will be sullied. Lastly, the use of asset forfeiture can be an effective tool when applied properly; however, great care must be taken to ensure that is not utilized inappropriately.

ADAPTED READINGS

Reading 8–1: Lawrence Malkin and Yuval Elizur, *Terrorism's Money Trail*

> *One of the earliest themes offered in this book is the connection between white-collar crime and funding terrorism. Now that you are armed with a fundamental understanding of the legal process, especially as it pertains to money laundering, this reading will afford you the opportunity to better understand this relationship.*

"Follow the money" is a classic technique for chasing criminals. It can be used as a sharp instrument to pry evidence from a bank account or a blunt one to seize assets on the orders of a prosecutor. Al Capone was put away for paying no income taxes because nothing worse could be proven against him. Evidence of disguising the profits of crime by laundering them into legally held bank accounts, businesses, and real estate has helped corroborate the testimony of turncoats that destroyed most of the mafia's muscle. Can tough money-laundering laws take down terrorists? They will probably help, in the same way that less stringent laws have slowed the drug trade by making it less profitable —though they certainly have not stopped it.

Congress and the Bush administration bought a comprehensive toolkit against money laundering in last October's hurried passage of the USA Patriot Act. At least in intent, it is probably the least objectionable part of the law permitting expanded wiretapping, detention, listening in on lawyers, and other license to law enforcement hidden in the deceptively cute acronym for the "Uniting and Strengthening America by Providing Appropriate Tools Required to Intercept and Obstruct Terrorism Act of 2001." The authorities now have five years to find out whether their enhanced financial tools actually work to obstruct terrorists instead of merely finding them after they strike. But the law must be used seriously because it has a sunset provision. It expires unless renewed halfway into the next presidential term.

Privacy advocates, libertarians, and especially the financial institutions now charged with onerous duties they have long resisted are among those who will keep the money-laundering provisions under close scrutiny as the shock of last September 11 recedes. Democrats in Congress have already begun worrying that the Bush administration will use its new tools against terrorists but not against white-collar money launderers. The only thing certain is that no law, even one with a trajectory as long as this one, is a magic bullet. It is more like a blunt instrument and must be used in conjunction with meticulous counterintelligence. That includes the penetration of terrorist cells, or at least their close surveillance, of which the financial sleuthing that proved so woefully inadequate before September 11 can only be a part.

Like so many other things after last summer's terrible events, passage of the law was a paradox. Its provisions were ready because they had been drafted by the Clinton Treasury but left on the shelf because of fierce opposition by conservative Republicans, especially Phil Gramm of Texas, then chairman of the Senate Banking Committee. The proposals were designed to facilitate tracing the untaxed money of Americans in foreign banks and to seal off the American financial system from the profits of crime, including the wealth of foreign kleptocrats. Too much of that had already reached American banks or their subsidiaries abroad.(1)

The new law also was meant to continue raising the barriers against drug money, which the first Bush administration began erecting at the Economic Summit of 1989. This initiative had grown into an international campaign to stanch the flow of dirty money by exposing offshore havens, especially in the Caribbean and the South Pacific. These banks are little more than cash registers passing on dirty money from places like Russia and Colombia for deposit in the safe financial centers of America and Europe.

Because of the terrorist threat, comparing the approaches of the Clinton and the second Bush administrations is like comparing apples and oranges. The Clinton people treated money laundering as a problem to be solved by bureaucrats because there was little hope of help from Congress. Officials came at it as a weapon to defend human rights by taking down corrupt dictators. As Democrats, they were also more sympathetic toward deploying money-laundering laws against tax evaders. That was one reason that Republicans refused to strengthen the laws.

The current Bush administration treats money laundering strictly as a law enforcement matter backed by diplomacy and is able to do so precisely because it was handed the legal authority by Congress. Money laundering now comes under the Treasury's Enforcement Division, headed by Jimmy Gurule, a former narcotics prosecutor and Notre Dame law professor. The Treasury's chief counsel, David D. Aufhauser, happened to be at a money-laundering conference in Oxford on September 11. He was immediately flown home from England by military transport to help organize a high-level financial task force against terrorists. He later recalled that under Oxford's dreaming spires, "it was as if we were looking at the world through the wrong end of the telescope."(2)

Since the international campaign began in the 1980s, Gian Trepp, a Swiss writer on money laundering and a critic of his own country's secretive banks, reckons that not one criminal case anywhere has been brought to court solely on the basis of information gathered through money-laundering investigations.(3) However, Jonathan Winer, former chief of enforcement for the State Department and now a Washington lawyer with a banking practice, argues that the campaign itself has ratcheted up the banks' defenses.

Months before September 11, Citicorp, one of the international banks most notorious for looking the other way when dictators deposited corrupt millions was so rattled by public exposure that it hired away the Federal Reserve Board's money-laundering specialist, Richard Small, to raise its own barriers. But the Bush administration, as in so many other multilateral engagements, initially kept the international campaign at such a distance that a number of the Treasury's money-laundering specialists left in disgust.

Then flying terrorists financed by Osama bin Laden's organization slammed into the World Trade Center and the Pentagon. In the rush to do something, Congress enacted almost all the Clinton proposals, but not without a very difficult passage. House Republicans at first stripped out the money-laundering sections of the proposed USA Patriot Act so they could be put in a separate bill, which could then be weakened with the none-too-discreet assistance of lobbyists for American banks, securities houses, and insurance companies, which had been heavy contributors to Republican causes.

Inside the White House, a battle raged between national security officials and deregulation advocates, the latter led by Lawrence Lindsey, director of the president's National Economic Council. His legislative supporters included many of the same Texas Republicans who fought the federalization of airport security with the same ideological bias against all government. Senate Democrats, realizing that the money-laundering provisions would never reach the statute books in any effective form unless they were put aboard the legislative express train carrying the anti-terrorism law, held it hostage with their one-vote majority. The previous year, Gramm, then Senate Banking chairman, had asserted that tighter rules against money laundering would be enacted over his dead body; in a shameless turnaround, he now endorsed passage of the same provisions to protect "democracy and capitalism . . . the crowning achievements of mankind on earth." (4)

Bankers in the Front Lines

The institutions of democratic capitalism soon found themselves drafted to serve reluctantly in the front lines of the nation's security. In the past, their clients had been able to hide, like the Wizard of Oz, in offshore banks behind curtains of lawyers and financial front men. Now bankers are supposed to know enough about how their clients not only make but spend their money to help ensure that funds in their custody will not end up financing another terrorist attack. And they must follow an old principle called know-your-customer: don't accept money from people who can't explain how they made it. This is turning out to be more difficult than it might seem.

For the first time, the rules were extended to stockbrokers, who first attempted to obtain an exemption, then argued that they could not identify all their clients, even though government regulations have long stipulated that every brokerage house not only must know its clients but their personal investment goals. But offshore, ten major U.S. brokerage firms surveyed by the Senate Permanent Investigations Subcommittee after the passage of the USA Patriot Act reported a total of 45,000 accounts holding $140 billion for companies and trusts, many of them untraceable. (5) Trepp says that when he told U.S. Treasury enforcement officials in 1997 that serious amounts of drug money were being laundered through the stock market, they simply refused to believe him, fixating on the drug dealer's stereotypical suitcase of $100 bills laundered through banks.

The new law prohibits anonymous accounts and bars American banks and brokerage houses from accepting money from "shell banks." These brass-plate banks are established on offshore islands for the express purpose of escaping official scrutiny by maintaining no connection with any regulated bank. The law also bars U.S. banks from accepting deposits that have been bundled together from a number of customers in a way that makes it impossible to distinguish dirty money from clean.

In another important but little noted shift in law enforcement policy, the cash reporting provisions of the tax code were inserted in banking laws at the insistence of Michael Oxley, chairman of the House Financial Services Committee and a former FBI agent. When high-end businesses ranging from Mercedes dealers to Tiffany's report cash transactions of more than $10,000, the information on tax evasion can no longer be withheld by the Internal Revenue Service from other agencies fighting money laundering and terrorism.(6)

But the principal reporting tool remains a Treasury form called the Suspicious Activity Report, which even its proponents admit is more useful in proving a case afterward than in preventing crime beforehand. Banks and brokers must report any transaction that "has no business or apparent lawful purpose or is not the sort in which the particular customer would normally be expected to engage." Since this is essentially a judgment call, financial bureaucrats have a habit of inundating the authorities with paper to protect themselves, and there is just not enough manpower to monitor the SARs that pile up for weeks in the Detroit office of the IRS, where operatives of that famously inefficient and underfinanced organization enter them into a computer. One obvious solution is a form of profiling that subjects Arab money and banks to the meticulous scrutiny now lavished on Arab airline passengers.

But in the globalized economy, an airline gate can be made far more strait than a foreign bank account.

Trepp says, "The methods used by professional launderers are the same in all these markets, and smelling the difference between a tax-evading dentist in Stuttgart, a drug dealer in Milan, and a terrorist in London is something that has to be done case by case." While this Swiss expert finds little difficulty in spotting the difference between various shades of money—black (terror, drugs, corruption, arms), dark gray (tax fraud), and gray (tax evasion), assembling information on suspicious bank transfers is a tedious operation during which prosecutors must obtain the cooperation of many turf-protective agencies in the United States and other countries.

Looking for the Terrorist Needle

It is theoretically possible to computerize and cross-reference records to match the usual suspects with their financial crimes, so that reporting systems can be reversed to ferret out terrorists by asking where a client's money is going as well as where it is coming from. Larry Ellison, the founder of Oracle Corporation, has offered free software to the U.S. government to establish a national security system that would, for example, link airline reservation systems to a database of arrest warrants. If it had been in operation on September 11, it might have stopped at least one of the September 11 terrorists.(7)

Banks have massive piles of data but do not know where to look for the terrorist's needle; they are pleading for detailed government information, which intelligence agencies have always been reluctant to disclose, lest it be leaked. At Citicorp, the task of monitoring the data has fallen to the department enforcing sanctions because its computers scan thousands of transactions a minute. They also come up with hundreds of false positives. Most are quickly eliminated, but not always. One fairly common Arabic name on the first presidential list of terrorist suspects happened to hit on the bank account of a respectable doctor in California. He had to spend months fighting a federal order freezing his assets.

When the names of suspects extend to accounts abroad, as so many do, the banks run into a wall. They call it the problem of the customer's customer. While the American banks can easily trail a money transfer to their own customers from, let's say, the German banker for the Hamburg-based Al Qaeda Import Corp., privacy laws or just plain competitive practice can and often do stop the inquiry when it reaches Germany. "You can't expect Deutsche Bank or Barclays to give its American competitors a list of all its customers," explained one banking lawyer. In some European countries, banks unwillingly tip off suspects because local laws require them to warn customers that they are providing information to a foreign country.

Sovereignty is therefore likely to slow, if not stop, international database links, while the plague of stateless terrorism is by definition not only international but leaves financial traces as diffuse as smoke. Technological difficulties aside, there simply is no politically possible way to organize a system through which an official agent could hack into a supercomputer, obtain reliable information about international money movements, and compile anything resembling a master list, as Congress seems to hope. But potential for mischief in quick decisions, especially by nervous, inexperienced, or xenophobic officers, has already been demonstrated by the mistakes coming to light in mass arrests of young men with Arabic names last autumn. They are already familiar to airline passengers and a fact of life to the authors of this article, one a lifetime resident of Israel, the other formerly resident for years in England, France, and Spain, the European countries with the longest experience of domestic terrorism. Suffice it to say that striking a balance between civil liberties and protection from terrorists is a delicate matter for law enforcement anywhere; more to the point, following the money to find terrorists is a more appropriate task for intelligence agencies than bank supervisors and the border police.

Ineffective Tools for Catching Terrorists

Israeli operatives monitoring Arab money are always amazed at how much they learn about where to look from reading newspaper reports of commercial investments. What had fallen into disuse with the CIA until September 11 was a classic espionage technique of pressuring, bribing, and otherwise suborning officials of commercial and central banks. It is not hard to obtain information about clients and suspects from a bank in Nairobi or Madrid by quite legally promising the manager to steer him some deposits by American companies. The agency surely has or at least had the capability to locate such managers. To give an example personally known to one of the authors: for some 30 years, an operations officer at a major American bank, born in the Middle East and fluent in French and Arabic, has popped up in places like the Paris office of the Bank for Credit and Commerce International when it was taken over after its collapse in 1994, in Saudi Arabia when the kingdom found itself in financial trouble, and in Beirut when that city reopened to commerce after a generation of civil war.

Those who actually chase terrorists argue that however helpful money-laundering tools may be, they are too slow and insufficient to prevent acts of terrorism. John Moscow, the lead financial investigator for the District Attorney of New York, applauds the new laws for undermining terrorists' financial supports and slowing down their transfers. "But on the one-off times when they fund a suicide run, there is nothing we can do to catch them. If you are talking about 20 people coming to New York on vacation with lots of extra money, we can't do it. We can't stop a couple of thousands of dollars coming in at one time."(8)

While laundered money usually can be detected in something close to broad daylight, information about terrorist money usually has to be sought in darkness. Money-laundering authorities follow the trail to a legal account from dirty money earned by drugs, prostitution, extortion, payoffs, or corruption on a grand scale. They then use the paper trail to prosecute the account holder. He can be a dictator or a drug baron, as long as the money can be traced back to him, just as it was to Manuel Noriega of Panama, who now sits in jail.

If the process were really symmetrical, it ought to work in reverse to catch terrorists by targeting an ostensibly clean charity or business whose resources are diverted to buying weapons and training foot soldiers. But catching a common criminal or a political kleptocrat after the fact with evidence of money laundering that can be used in court is just fine; catching a terrorist after the fact can be a catastrophe, as it was on September 11.

This was a principal failing of the Federal Bureau of Investigation, whose procedures are geared toward collecting evidence for prosecutors, which it fears will be tainted by sharing with other agencies. The Central Intelligence Agency's culture (if not its present bureaucracy, with many more lawyers than espionage agents) is geared toward prevention. The new law and the Bush administration's policies are supposed to force them to work in tandem. The director of central intelligence and the head of the FBI now attend the same morning briefing with George W. Bush. Whether his orders to them to cooperate will end their traditional turf war will only be known over time.

Moreover, terrorist money does not necessarily move through banks. Money sent by bin Laden's Al Qaeda organization flew under the radar via Western Union, storefront money transfer businesses, and hawalas. The sums passed through this last exchange mechanism by terrorists are often so minute as to be indistinguishable from those sent by its usual customers, workers from the Indian subcontinent in the Middle East, and more recently, in Europe and America. Anyone who wants to send money home—or to a terrorist confederate in another country—takes cash to the hawala office and receives a receipt in return. The manager faxes a code word to a trusted partner abroad, and the office there pays when the recipient shows up with the code word. The Rothschild family banks operated much the same way in the nineteenth century and, like the hawalas, settled their accounts at the end of the year. Although any faxed evidence of individual transfers is quickly destroyed, it would not even have been noticed when Al Qaeda was preparing a rubber raft with explosives for two suicide bombers that blew a hole in the side of the U.S. destroyer *Cole* in the port of Yemen. Papers found in Al Qaeda's Kabul offices after the Taliban were chased from the Afghan capital indicate that the out-of-pocket expenses for the *Cole* attack, which killed 17 American sailors on Oct. 12, 2000, were only $10,000.(9)

Since September 11, unimaginably ingenious ways of moving money and goods have emerged. Al Qaeda is said to run a sizable share of the large and profitable Middle Eastern trade in honey, which not only provides a business front to transfer money but to hide weapons and drugs in sticky containers that customs officers would rather not open for inspection.(10) The organization is also believed to own perhaps a dozen tramp steamers. Diamonds from the failed states of Central Africa are reported to have been stolen or dumped into the hands of the continent's traditional business class—Lebanese traders who sell them for huge profits that finance the Hezbollah terrorists in Lebanon, and Al Qaeda as well.(11)

And of course there is the drug trade, which has proven notoriously resistant to the money-laundering strategy originally designed for the express purpose of stopping it, a measure of the task facing American forces in the fastness of Central Asia's hidden valleys. Afghanistan was Europe's principal heroin supplier until the Taliban bowed to international pressure and banned poppy farming. But the end of their brutal rule may yield the perverse revival of opium cultivation for its huge cash flow to the country's warlords. Could Al Qaeda quietly resume its role as their bankers?

Where to Look for Terrorists

Drugs aside, investigations by the *New York Times* and the *Financial Times* of London differ on the profitability of Al Qaeda's various front companies. But both newspapers describe them as divisions of a sort of shadow multinational that move money to inconspicuous terrorist subsidiaries.(12) That gives investigators a window into its operations, but only if they know where and how to look. The Secretary of the Treasury, Paul O'Neill, says that once the September 11 hijackers were identified it was possible to recreate "a spider web of all their financial connections."(13) It still took several months for FBI and Treasury officials to track the operation's estimated $500,000 bankroll, mainly through U.S. channels; the investigation continues abroad. The Treasury's task force is now concentrating on using its new powers to starve out terrorists by dismantling their finances, and O'Neill declared in January that Al Qaeda was "having trouble paying [its] people."(14) One can only wish the T-men good luck, but most of all more sophistication and sharper instincts.

Even after terrorist sleepers are identified, money may sit just as quietly in their bank accounts as they do in society. If a suspect does not know he is being shadowed, his transfers may provide leads. If he knows he is being shadowed, he has two choices, neither of them good. He can do nothing, which in effect freezes his financial resources. Or he can move some or all of the money, which leaves a trail for investigators to follow. Thereafter, his funds can remain under surveillance for years.

Roger Kubarych, a New York banking consultant and former fellow at the Council on Foreign Relations, stresses the importance for money-laundering specialists to build up such reserves of information, in law enforcement or bank databases. Funds transferred to a flight school or a uranium wholesaler from suspect charities or front companies would set off an alarm. Nevertheless, police need to be only half as imaginative as terrorists, although they must be more alert. If the anti-terrorist network tracking Al Qaeda had been better organized and equipped with legal authority, it probably would have spotted the movement of money to flight schools and their Arab students well before September 11. In order to cripple its ingenious plot, investigators would not have had to imagine it in all its horrible detail, only to be alive to the familiar threat of airline hijackings.

Even some of the flight schools were more alert than the authorities. The FBI was warned of the bizarre behavior of Zacarias Moussaoui, the man later accused of being the twentieth hijacker, by a Minnesota flight school which found it alarming that his principal interest was training on flight simulators and communicating with the control tower. Even after Moussaoui was arrested last August 16, the FBI was constrained by the wall between domestic and foreign intelligence—demolished in part by the new law—from obtaining a warrant to examine the information on his laptop computer. (Moussaoui was to have been flown to France with his laptop for investigation free of U.S. legal constraints and was to have arrived September 17.)(15)

Also too late, FBI agents developed the detailed money trail in his indictment that cites a cash deposit of $32,000 to open a bank account in Norman, Oklahoma, on February 26, 2001. Another $69,985 was wired on September 18, 2000, a year before the attack, from Abu Dhabi to the Florida SunTrust account of the hijack leader Mohammed Atta and a confederate. The two banks filed

Suspicious Activity Reports. These were not followed up because the transfers fit profiles of the way Middle Eastern students finance their studies. So much for mere profiling.

The Reluctant Banks

Banks and securities houses long resisted a role in screening out dirty money. Until September 11, their ostensible reason was an insistence on protecting their customers' privacy. A minority of shady banks, mainly in Florida and Texas, made money by laundering drug profits but were protected when Senator Gramm demonized money-laundering laws as an anti-libertarian attack on individual privacy. But the really big deposits do not remain in small border banks or Caribbean havens, which have to forward them to money center banks or major securities houses. That is where the real laundering—or at least the essential rinsing and spin drying—takes place, by making the money available for transfer or reinvestment.

The principal concern of the financial heavyweights was not really protecting their clients' privacy but protecting their own profits. What the banks really objected to was the cost. Now they are being forced to install the tracking software and hire more oversight officers to ensure that their deposit and lending officers comply with the new law, even if they have to turn away suspicious customers and cut their credit lines. Bankers' bonuses may suffer from dropping dubious accounts, but few dare complain, lest they be accused of giving aid and comfort to the enemy. Officials of Western Union, who before the attacks were unaware they were transferring Al Qaeda money, objected afterward in a meeting with New York State regulators that more stringent rules to identify customers would cost the company too much money. One of the regulators pointed out of his downtown office window toward the hole punched in the sky on September 11, and angrily asked, "How much value do you want to put on a human life?"(16)

Meanwhile many large American banks have already decided not to risk their reputations by accepting such deposits from shell banks. They say they now are finding money squirreled away in anonymous or merely suspicious accounts, which they promptly shut down so as not to be accused of keeping terrorist money. Bankers, regulators, customs officers, and policemen whose files held bits and pieces of information are putting them together to make connections they never thought about before—and that includes the Persian Gulf, the loosely regulated headquarters of many of the wildcat banks of the modern world. As much as $100,000 is said to have been sent to one of the September 11 hijackers, Marwan al-Shehhi, through a money exchange in Abu Dhabi, capital of the United Arab Emirates; this year the UAE adopted its first comprehensive money-laundering law.(17)

A year ago, who would have given a second thought about a connection between an Abu Dhabi bank account and a front company in the Philippines? Once the Americans told the Arab bankers what to look for, they made the connection; it turned out to be a conduit for Al Qaeda money. Successes like this energize the bureaucracy. Before September 11, a customs officer or a bank examiner with an unproven suspicion would most likely hesitate to start a bothersome investigation that might dead-end itself and his career along with it. Since September 11, the career rewards are exactly the reverse. For more than two years, a federal financial enforcement agent had been building a case against the al-Barakat hawala network in Somalia. After September 11, she finally got the high-level support and interagency cooperation she needed to curtail its operations and stop it from using U.S. banks to handle its cash.

"Shards of information that lay separate and untouched in the files are being pulled out and put together. No bank wants to be touched by a terrorist in the uncertain future," says Jonathan Winer. "Middle East governments certainly knew about Arab fighters in Chechnya and Kosovo, but even though we tried to tell them back in 1998, it wasn't until September 11 that they began to realize how they had been used."

A Real War Against Money Laundering

While the principal motive for such coordination by law enforcement may be self-preservation, the principal direction is political, and that remains the principal imponderable. To maintain foreign confidence and cooperation in its fight against terrorism, the Bush administration will have to persevere against money laundering, since the tools for both are interdependent. Traditionally, the U.S. Treasury has welcomed foreign money from any source to fill the gap in the country's balance of payments. Only in the last years of the Clinton administration did the Treasury begin to draw the line at laundered money, and even then it was tentative, lest it impede global money flows into Wall Street. After George W. Bush took office, that line of defense soon disappeared entirely, lest it discomfit American business and its bankers, only to return after September 11 like a line drawn in the dirt.

Will foreign governments continue helping the Bush administration convert that line into a protective wall? Europeans and Israelis, after all, have been living with terrorism for years, generally accommodating themselves to it with civil courage and allowing only occasional lapses in civil liberties. They live without the illusion of invulnerability that has sustained Americans for too long and formed the fragile underpinning for George W. Bush's unilateralism, until that, too, collapsed in the rubble of the World Trade Center.

In Germany, the governing Social Democrats had to engage in a serious debate over strengthening the country's laws because the excesses of the secret police under Nazi and then Communist rule had sensitized society to violations of privacy. The presence of Al Qaeda hijackers on German soil, which also stoked anti-immigrant feelings elsewhere in Europe, helped tilt the balance a few notches away from freedom toward security. The German Finance Ministry now will permit banks and the antiterrorist police to cross-reference their databases, although decentralization among law enforcement authorities and Germany's ill-connected and inefficient banking system makes such cooperation minimally helpful.(18)

But as the immediate terrorist threat recedes, this could upend the continuing transatlantic debate on the privacy of computerized data, in which Europe has been far more strict than Washington. When a letter inspired by George W. Bush arrives asking for information, an official of the Swiss Bankers Association says it now is readily supplied by his member banks. But he wonders how cooperative the Swiss and others will be when the request arrives from a prosecutor on a fishing expedition.

The Swedish government has demanded to see the information that led the U.N. Security Council to freeze the accounts of three Somali-born Swedish citizens, one a candidate for parliament. Sweden does not have a seat on the Security Council, which acted on undisclosed U.S. intelligence linking the three to the al-Barakat network, but France is a permanent member and has asked to review all the sanctions cases.(19) The British, so ably equipped to supply troops trained to combat terror in Northern Ireland, have always fought shy of regulation that might frighten depositors away from doing business in the City of London. They stand ready to pick up Wall Street business fleeing excessive regulation.

Most resistance has come from the Middle East. Throughout the autumn, the U.S. government had to send senior diplomats to plead with Saudi royalty to close the bank accounts of suspected terrorist financiers; one of them, a Jeddah businessman whose accounts were frozen by Britain and the United States, filed suit in London, which means that evidence will have to be produced in court. Early this year, Saudi Arabia finally began to yield, announcing a law against money laundering and freezing 150 bank accounts of those suspected of terrorist connections, although the Saudi Arabian Monetary Authority gave no details.(20)

No country has longer or more decisive experience with terrorism than Israel. When Arab petrodollar reserves piled up during the 1970s, the security services stayed on watch against any attempt by their enemies to buy into Western corporations or otherwise use their money to turn Western commerce or diplomacy against Israel. Nothing like that happened, and alarm yielded to complacency. Money launderers appeared on the scene in a serious way only after Russian-Jewish mobsters started using Israel as an escape hatch when the Soviet regime collapsed.

Israel presents an ironic parallel with Saudi Arabia. Increasingly powerful Russian-born politicians run charities to which mobsters contribute, and this cash nexus has not made it easier for the Israeli police to prosecute some of the suspect donors. Moreover, Israel depends more on foreign capital than the United States and is reluctant to frighten off investors. Another reason that Israel's financial defenses against Arab terrorists do not match its aggressive military stance is that it cannot touch accounts controlled by Yasser Arafat's Palestinian Authority. Under international and especially American pressure by the Clinton administration, Israel passed a stringent money-laundering law, and under further prodding from the Bush administration, enforcement is being strengthened.

The Bush Treasury, which was forced by events to impose tighter money-laundering regulations, has been no less diligent than the Pentagon in pursuing bin Laden's men. But it will be no easy task for the administration to merge an all-out war against terrorists with the previously phony war against money launderers. If the Bush administration operates by effectively profiling banks mainly in Islamic countries, it risks alienating Middle Eastern governments whose intelligence it badly needs. And the Bush Treasury probably can abandon hope of cooperation from European financial regulators if it deals only perfunctorily with money launderers and, let's say, energy companies with offshore subsidiaries accused of misusing corporate assets for political payoffs (no, not Enron but Elf-Aquitaine, the object of France's latest financial-political scandal, with secret accounts in Luxembourg and Liechtenstein instead of the Caymans). Unless the U.S. government resolves this dilemma, its agents may be reduced to trading information with their foreign counterparts on a case-by-case basis, as both have always done.

On January 29, at the first congressional oversight hearing on the new money-laundering laws, Democrats made it clear that they will be watching the Treasury as it issues new regulations under the Patriot Act. Paul Sarbanes, the Senate Banking Committee chairman, first complimented Treasury undersecretary Kenneth Dam on "the most intense financial investigation in the history of the world." Then he made two observations on the Treasury's new rules, although he did not press Dam further. First, he noted that a new foreign customer could literally investigate himself merely by signing a certificate that he was not a fronting for a shell bank. Second, the Treasury rules permit American banks to accept deposits from an offshore bank if as few as one-quarter of its shares are in the hands of a real bank and not an unidentified shell, a loophole, Senator Sarbanes noted, big enough to permit entire companies, or at least their offshore subsidiaries, to pass through. No one was so coarse as to mention the hundreds of offshore companies set up in the Cayman Islands by the Enron Corporation to help disguise its cash position and limit its tax payments.

Long after the troops come home from Afghanistan, financial officials will have to continue their less glamorous but essential detective work. There is little doubt that the detectives themselves will be as eager to pursue their quarry as the Special Forces in the bleak Afghan hills; among other things, tracking and labeling potential terrorists will make the investigators' lives easier in the long run. But what will their bosses do when they suddenly find a friendly dictator or a rich, Republican tax evader in their crosshairs?

Notes

(1) See Lawrence Malkin and Yuval Elizur, "The Dilemma of Dirty Money," *World Policy Journal*, vol. 18 (spring 2001).

(2) Speech at a seminar on the USA Patriot Act, sponsored by Glasser LegalWorks, New York City, February 11, 2002.

(3) Unless noted otherwise, quotations in the text are drawn from interviews conducted by the authors.

(4) "Senators Target Terrorists' Cash Flow," *International Herald Tribune*, October 6, 2001.

(5) Statement of Sen. Carl Levin (D-Michigan) before the Senate Banking Committee, January 29, 2002.

(6) Money Laundering Alert (Miami), January 2002. This is the principal newsletter in the field. Its website is www.moneylaundering.com.

(7) Larry Ellison, "A Single National Security Database," *International Herald Tribune*, January 31, 2002.

(8) Speech at a seminar on the USA Patriot Act, February 11, 2002.

(9) Thomas Fuller, "Driving Al Qaeda: Religious Decrees; Terrorism Expert Lays Out Evidence," *International Herald Tribune*, January 31, 2002. The expert is Roland Jacquard, a Lebanese-born French author and terrorism adviser to the U.N. Security Council, who has obtained a trove of such documents. An unpublished memoir about the U.S.S. *Cole* is attributed to Rifai Ahmed Taha, an Egyptian wanted for killing tourists in Luxor in 1997. Testimony from Ahmed Ibrahim al-Said al-Najar, a former Egyptian military officer arrested in Albania and executed in Egypt, reports that Arab recruits in Al Qaeda's Afghan camps were paid $300 a month, and Afghans considerably less.

(10) Judith Miller and Jeff Gerth, "Qaida Suspected of Using Honey Trade as Cover," *International Herald Tribune*, December 10, 2001.

(11) Douglas Fara, "Al Qaeda Cash Tied to Diamond Trade: Sale of Gems from Sierra Leone Rebels Raised Millions, Sources Say" and "Digging Up Congo's Dirty Gems: Officials Say Diamond Trade Funds Radical Islamic Groups," *Washington Post*, November 2 and December 30, 2001, respectively.

(12) Mark Huband, "Inside Al-Qaeda: Bank-rolling bin-Laden," *Financial Times*, November 29, 2001; Kurt Eichenwald, "Terror Money Hard to Block, Officials Find," *New York Times*, December 10, 2001.

(13) Dan Eggen and Kathleen Day, "U.S. Probe of September 11 Financing Wraps Up: Terror Money Traced Via ATM, Credit Card Usage," *Washington Post*, January 7, 2002.

(14) Interview of Paul O'Neill, Charlie Rose, Public Broadcasting System, January 15, 2002.

(15) David Johnston and Philip Shenon, "Man Held Since August Is Charged with a Role in September 11 Terror Plot," *New York Times*, December 12, 2001; Dan Egger, "Suspect's Silence Baffled Agents Before September 11," *International Herald Tribune*, February 1, 2002.

(16) Paul Beckett and Carrick Mollenkamp, "In Wake of September 11, Regulators Crack Down on Money-Transfer Industry," *Wall Street Journal*, December 28, 2001.

(17)   Associated Press, "Emirates to Curb Banks," *New York Times*, January 24, 2002.

(18)   "Geldwasche: Finanzielle Rasterfandung" (Money laundering: The financial cross-roster), *Der Spiegel*, no. 41, 2001.

(19)   Serge Schmemann, "Swedes Take Up the Cause of 3 on U.S. Terror List," *New York Times*, January 26, 2002.

(20)   Charles M. Sennott, "Financial Regulators Seize Momentum of War on Terror," *International Herald Tribune*, February 2, 2002.

Source: *World Policy Journal*, © 2002 World Policy Institute.

Reading 8–2: Joseph T. Wells, *An Unholy Trinity: The Three Ways Employees Embezzle Cash*

Author Joseph Wells is frequently regarded as one of the founding fathers of fraud detection. This article presents his insights on the crime of embezzlement, using the legal concepts presented in this chapter. In addition, you will likely find yourself drawing connections to the research of Cressey and Yeager presented earlier in Chapter 7 of this text.

In the U.S. alone, occupational fraud and abuse may carry a price tag of more than $400 billion. Such crimes include embezzlements of cash that aren't necessarily complicated—just covert, insidious, and potentially devastating.

On his third day as chief internal auditor for *Reader's Digest*, Terence McGrane stepped into a hornet's nest. It all happened innocently enough. While learning the ropes on his new job, McGrane met with one of the vice presidents to learn more about the company's accounts payable system. McGrane brought a stack of sample invoices to the meeting.

The vice president, routinely reviewing the documents, stopped suddenly. The invoice in front of him bore his name. "That is not my signature," the vice president said. He and McGrane quickly found four other invoices supposedly authorized by the vice president. All were forgeries. The vice president was baffled, but McGrane recognized the signs of a fraudulent billing scheme.

McGrane soon confirmed his suspicions. The financial jolt registered $1,057,000 in losses attributable to one Albert Miano. A supervisor in the painting department, Miano had worked for the company for more than 10 years. He was married and outwardly very stable; but the facts were irrefutable. Miano had created phony invoices for painting contractors who didn't exist, forged the approval of a vice president, and deposited the proceeds into his own bank account. Only about $400,000 was traced to tangible purchases, which included boats, automobiles, and homes; he was earning about $30,000 a year. Mysteriously, the other $700,000 in cash was never located. Miano served two years in prison.

The Cost of Crime

According to the 1996 Report to the Nation on Occupational Fraud and Abuse, a study conducted by the Association of Certified Fraud Examiners, embezzlement schemes such as Miano's are both prevalent and incredibly costly. Also known as The Wells Report, the study concludes that the average company loses about six percent of its gross revenues to all forms of occupational fraud and abuse. That staggering sum, if multiplied by the gross domestic product of the U.S., would mean an annual cost of more than $400 billion. Embezzlement, along with fraudulent statements and other corrupt acts such as bribery and bid rigging, represent the principal ways employees defraud their organizations.

The term "occupational fraud and abuse" is broadly defined in the report as "the use of one's occupation for personal enrichment through the deliberate misuse or misapplication of the employing organization's resources or assets." More than 2,608 fraud examiners participated in the study, which sought to estimate the probable cost of occupational fraud and abuse in the U.S.; determine characteristics of perpetrators of these offenses; profile data from victim organizations; and establish a uniform classification system for occupational fraud and abuse cases.

The three costliest embezzlement schemes, which include larceny of cash, skimming, and fraudulent disbursements, are illustrated in the following scenarios. Although in some instances names have been changed to protect identities, the stories are true; and other versions of them are constantly being played out in organizations around the world.

1 *Larceny of Cash Median Loss $22,000*

Some people would argue that auditors have no sense of humor. But Bill Guardo knows better. Guardo worked as a branch manager of a consumer loan finance company in New Orleans. For reasons that aren't exactly clear, he began stealing money from the finance company's bank deposits.

One day Barry Ecker, the company internal auditor, decided on a whim to test Guardo's sense of humor. With a straight face, Ecker told Guardo, "Well, I'll see you Monday. We're going to pull an audit on your branch." With that, the internal auditor, who had no idea about Guardo's thefts, turned on his heels and left.

Over the weekend, Guardo was left to stew in his own juices. He knew that his fraud would be easy to spot, since he had been stealing money from the deposits he took to the bank on a daily basis. On Sunday night, Guardo called the company president at home and confessed. He was immediately fired but returned the several thousand dollars he took. As a result, the company decided not to prosecute him.

The moral of this story? The ol' fake audit gets them every time.

The Guardo fraud represents one type of cash larceny: thefts from deposits. The other principal type is register theft. Larceny, according to *Black's Law Dictionary*, is "felonious stealing, taking and carrying, leading, riding, or driving away with another person's property, with the intent to convert it or to deprive the owner thereof."

The key element in a larceny scheme is the fact that there is no effort to cover up the theft. Unlike the skimming schemes defined below, the cash has already been recorded on the books. In general, cash larceny schemes are not a high risk area for businesses. Presumably because adequate physical controls exist over the custody of cash in most organizations, these schemes accounted for only one percent of the total losses identified in the study.

2 *Skimming Median Loss $50,000*

Brian Lee excelled as a top-notch plastic surgeon. Exuding a serious yet gentle manner, the 42-year-old bachelor took quiet pride in his beautification efforts, which included nose jobs, liposuction, face lifts, and breast enhancements. Lee worked for a large physician-owned clinic in the southwestern U.S. In a bad year he took in $300,000 in salary and bonuses; a good year would net him $800,000.

Somehow, that magnificent salary was not enough for Brian Lee. During one four-year stretch, the physician also skimmed several hundred thousand dollars from the clinic. When the issue came to light, the clinic contacted its law firm, who in turn contacted Doug Leclaire, a Certified Fraud Examiner, to conduct an independent investigation. Leclaire's interviews with the clinic staff turned up serious operational and control problems. It seemed that Dr. Lee would simply tell certain patients to pay him directly, bypassing the clinic's billing system altogether.

Dr. Lee's fraud—like so many others—was detected entirely by accident. One of his patients, Rita Mae Givens, had paid him personally by check for a rhinoplasty procedure. She later decided to see if her insurance company would reimburse her for the operation, so she called the clinic for a copy of her bill. There was none.

Doug Leclaire, following standard fraud examination procedures, saved the interview of Dr. Lee for last. Lee immediately confessed that he had a number of patients pay him directly. He was apologetic and even helped Leclaire piece together the evidence proving that Lee had embezzled several hundred thousand dollars from his professional colleagues.

Dr. Lee furnished a motive for his misdeeds: simple greed. He was a driven man, much like his father and brother. Since Lee's schedule didn't permit much recreation, playing financial one-upmanship on his family became his hobby. It was important for him to have more money than his relatives.

In the end, the greed of the clinic itself overcame reason. Lee was their top revenue producer, so the doctor was allowed simply to pay back the money he stole. No termination. No prosecution. No notoriety. But the clinic decided not to put Lee back into the arms of temptation, and they instituted controls to prevent future incidents. It's a good thing, apparently. The good doctor told Leclaire that, given the chance, "I would probably do it again."

"Skimming" is the embezzlement of cash from an entity prior to its being recorded on the books. The cash skimmed can include sales, receivables, and refunds. Sales skimming can take the form of unrecorded sales, as in the case of Dr. Lee, or they can be understated, where an amount less than the full sale is reported to the company. In receivables skimming, the thefts are often those that are simply unrecorded on the books. When funds are diverted from accounts receivable, the amount owed can be reduced on the books by write-off schemes.

Skimming schemes account for about a quarter of the losses in cash misappropriations, while fraudulent disbursements make up about three-fourths of the losses. It's possible that skimming schemes make up a smaller percentage because of their inherent nature: when someone purchases a product or service, or pays a bill, concealment of the transaction is absolutely necessary to avoid detection by the customer.

3 Fraudulent Disbursements Median Loss $75,000

Bruce Livingstone actually started the problem by taking his girlfriend on a trip at the company's expense. To disguise the disbursement, he unwisely named a senior female auditor as his traveling partner.

The situation came to light when the bogus travel expense voucher landed on the desk of that very same senior female auditor for approval. Obviously, the voucher set off warning bells and buzzers, and the matter was referred to Harold Dore, Director of Internal Audit at the large medical college where this incident occurred. Dore wondered if he was looking at the tip of an iceberg and decided to interview Livingstone's assistant, Cheryl Brown, to see what she knew. Mysteriously, Cheryl canceled the interview at the last minute because her uncle had supposedly been shot in California. Brown left in such haste that she didn't even bother to pick up her paycheck. Dore smelled a rat.

Livingstone's office was sealed to prevent any tampering of evidence, and Dore began a search of its contents. He found that Livingstone had been selling the school's dental tools to students from the back door and keeping the money for himself. When Dore began to inspect the accounting records—specifically the list of vendors in Livingstone's office—the investigation took a surprising turn.

Dore trimmed the vendor list to those with only a post office box and selected 50 of those invoices for examination. It didn't take long to focus in on one particular vendor, Armstrong Supply Company. The invoices supporting the disbursements to Armstrong ostensibly were for office supplies, but the invoices themselves looked fishy. They had all been produced on plain bond paper with a simple typewriter. The descriptions for the supplies purchased were vague. Then Dore found the smoking gun: blank invoices for Armstrong Supply Company under Cheryl's desk pad.

Cheryl Brown confessed to her bogus invoice scheme, documenting some $63,000 in loot. Her thefts began only five months after she was hired. Cheryl claimed she and her husband were both addicted to drugs, which prompted their embezzlement scheme. Brown struck a plea bargain with the prosecutors, agreeing to pay the money back, serve a probated sentence, and serve a six-month term of house arrest.

Fraudulent disbursements can take one of five principal forms. Brown chose the costliest type—the billing scheme. The other categories of fraudulent disbursements include payroll schemes, expense reimbursement schemes, check tampering, and register disbursement schemes.

Fraudulent disbursement schemes provide a unique opportunity for the fraudster. The company is essentially "tricked" into making a legitimate-appearing disbursement. Unlike larceny or skimming schemes, the employee is not even physically required to take custody of the funds; the money can be converted indirectly by the employee through a third source, such as a shell company or an accomplice vendor.

Managing the Risks

The Report to the Nation on Occupational Fraud and Abuse offers two lessons for the fight against fraud. First, the ways employees embezzle money aren't necessarily complicated; they invariably employ larceny, skimming, or fraudulent disbursement methods to conduct their schemes. Second, the study discloses trends that can guide internal auditors in their detection and deterrence efforts. Fraudulent disbursements account for three-quarters of the losses, and the most expensive tend to be fraudulent disbursements through billing schemes. Therefore, internal auditors seeking to get the biggest bang for their investigative bucks should begin by making sure company vendors are for real.

Since stealth is a key element in the *modus operandi* of occupational fraud and abuse, estimates about its prevalence and cost will probably never be completely known. The $400 billion figure may, therefore, be a gross understatement. The certainty is that, whether by skimming, larceny, or fraudulent disbursements, embezzlement is out there; and companies are paying the costs.

Source: *Internal Auditor*, © 1998 Institute of Internal Auditors.

Thinking Activities

1. Review each of the specific, individual white-collar criminal statutes and the elements that comprise them in this chapter. Prepare a short hypothetical scenario that either meets, or does not meet the elements for each individual offense. Share these with your fellow classmates and discuss them in small groups.

2. Are there comparable state laws to the federal statutes that you examined in the previous question? If "yes," where might these violations be found and what are the maximum penalties?

3. Using the Internet, download a sample search warrant application, and prepare a hypothetical search warrant for one of the scenarios you presented in question #1. What are some of the specific details you would want to include in your warrant application and why are they important?

4. How might money laundering be tied to both white-collar crimes and violent crimes? What are some actions that you might take to build an effective investigative partnership with other agencies interested in working on money laundering cases from different angles?

5. During a raid on a restaurant involved in access device fraud, you discover a storage room filled with computers, cash, and deeds to commercial real estate located in a nearby city. Provided these items are proceeds of the access device fraud case you have been investigating, what method or methods of forfeiture would you pursue (i.e., civil judicial, criminal, administrative) and why? What specifically would you do with this property (if anything)?

9 White-Collar Crime Analysis and Trends

If the number of white-collar criminal incidents since the year 2000 is any indication of the future, you, as a white-collar crime investigator, will be truly embarking upon a career in a growing field during an exciting time in history. From Enron and WorldCom to Martha Stewart and Lewis "Scooter" Libby, the past nine years have revealed that offenses such as fraud, embezzlement, and misuse of office are very much on the minds of both the media and the American public. Yet it is the concept of white-collar crime as the nexus to other forms of *mala in se* criminal activity, namely terrorism, that has prompted the enactment of broad, sweeping legislation which may ultimately change this nation's entire system of justice from the American *due process* model of the past 230 years to a more centralized *crime control* model, such as the one employed in the former Soviet Union.

For example, the *USA Patriot Act of 2001* (HR 3162), which was further revised in 2007, relaxes many of the government's existing rules and procedures for the electronic interception of information gleaned from cellular telephones, fax machines, pagers, and e-mail. This is especially true if suspicions exist that these devices are being used for fraudulent purposes linked to acts of terrorism[1] (refer to HR 3162, sections 201–2). Bank records and other financial institution data are now more readily accessible to police than at any time in the past two centuries. Investigative personnel at the law enforcement field office level, such as an assistant special agent in charge (as opposed to senior headquarters personnel at the deputy director or agency administrator levels), now have the ability to obtain "books, papers, documents and other items for an investigation to protect against international terrorism or clandestine intelligence activities, provided that such investigation of a United States person is not conducted solely upon the basis of activities protected by the first amendment to the Constitution[2]" (HR 3162, section 501 (a)(1)).

Similarly, in the wake of the September 11, 2001 attacks, a U.S. Defense Department's effort to develop a Total Information Awareness (TIA) project was conceived allowing law enforcement personnel to simultaneously query numerous public and private databases.[3] With just a few clicks of a mouse, a target's criminal history, medical records, financial statements, employment file, tax information, driver's license and vehicle registration data would be available to the investigator or intelligence analyst. Although much of this project was subsequently de-funded by Congress, elements of the original plan exist today in the Information Awareness Office.

While the line between possible links to terrorism and protection of our rights established in the First and Fourth Amendments to the U.S. Constitution is difficult to define, what has become obvious is that, in the name of combating global terrorism, the United States government is willing to allocate far more resources, with far broader powers, towards white-collar criminal investigations than it has in the past.

Boston Globe reporter Michael Kranish notes, "to investigators, there may be no more effective way of tracking terrorists than the adage of 'follow the money.' "[4] With respect to such investigations, the government's most important resource is ultimately not found in a myriad of databases, electronic wire intercepts or even financial statements available to the criminal investigator; but rather, it is embodied in the skills, talents, and tenacity of one person to synthesize, process, and effectively disseminate this information. This critical resource is known as the *intelligence analyst*.

Intelligence Analysts: Who Are They?

As discussed in his comprehensive text entitled *Intelligence 2000: Revising the Basic Elements*, editors Peterson, Morehouse, and Wright refer to criminal intelligence as "a process involving the collection, evaluation, collation, analysis, dissemination, and re-evaluation of information on suspected criminals and/or organizations."[5] Thus, the intelligence analyst, often referred to by a variety of other titles such as law enforcement intelligence analyst, crime analyst, intelligence research specialist, or criminal research specialist, is responsible for critically examining data and employing a wide range of quantitative, qualitative, and data visualization techniques in an effort to answer questions or provide recommendations to supervisory personnel.

Most analysts have a minimum of two years of college education, while many possess four-year baccalaureate degrees or even graduate degrees.[6] Proficiency with information technology systems and a wide range of software applications, ranging from basic word processing and spreadsheet programs (e.g., Microsoft Word, Excel, etc.) to advanced statistical compilers and link analysis programs such as SPSS (Statistical Package for the Social Sciences), Analyst's Notebook and Crime Workbench, are also required for many of these positions. A background in accounting, business management, and financial statement analysis may also prove useful.

Frequently, senior-level intelligence analysts within the United States have prior experience within a law enforcement setting as either a sworn (i.e., gun carrying) or non-sworn (civilian) employee, as opposed to being recruited directly from academic institutions or private research entities.[7]

Most intelligence analysts are affiliated with one of the three major professional associations prevalent in the field. These are the International Association of Law Enforcement Intelligence Analysts (IALEIA), the Alpha Group Center (ACG), or the International Association of Crime Analysts (IACA).

Established in 1980, IALEIA's mission "is to bring excellence and professionalism to intelligence analysis worldwide."[8] As the oldest and largest of the professional law enforcement intelligence associations, IALEIA's ranks include nearly 2,000 members in 48 countries. Through its affiliated organization, the Society of Certified Criminal Analysts (SCCA), the working intelligence analyst can obtain an important certification, which can prove vital in ensuring his or her professional credibility when testifying in court.

Unlike the not-for-profit IALEIA, the Alpha Group Center (ACG) is a privately-held commercial organization with a permanent staff of four instructors and an administrative assistant. ACG is tasked with providing training and research in the area of crime analysis.[9] Among ACG's largest clients are the federal, state, and local law enforcement agencies located within the State of California. Through a partnership with the California Department of Justice and the state university system, ACG offers instruction leading to the Certified Crime and Intelligence Analyst (CCIA) credential.

Lastly, the newest of the professional analytical entities is the International Association of Crime Analysts (IACA). Formed in 1990, IACA membership holds constant at about 1,000 dues-paying associates. In sharp contrast to IALEIA's broad international membership (i.e., about 28 percent of its members live and work outside of North America), nearly 90 percent of IACA's membership is located within the United States.

There is considerable controversy within the law enforcement intelligence community as to what represents the optimal combination of education and prior professional experience.[10] However, what is not in dispute is the need for strict adherence to ethical codes of conduct for those personnel who possess access to sensitive information systems such as the FBI's National Crime Information Center (NCIC), National Law Enforcement Telecommunications System (NLETS), Treasury Enforcement Communications System (TECS-II) or the United States Secret Service's Master Central Index (MCI). Each of these systems allows the analyst to query restricted access datasets to obtain information such as arrest records, travelers' flight histories and border-crossings, as well as a variety of financial transactions. Armed with such sensitive information, it is essential that analysts employed in the field are worthy of the highest trust and confidence.

The Integrity of the Analyst

As we discussed earlier in this book, mathematical explanations such as the Nash equilibrium demonstrate that corrupt government officials can be linked with the very criminal organizations they are expected to investigate and ultimately destroy. Accordingly, in order to ensure the integrity of the analyst, most candidates undergo a thorough background investigation prior to being hired, which often includes the following: a comprehensive credit check, illegal drug screening, neighborhood and known associates canvas to explore the candidate's personal character and ties to his or her community, criminal background check, and driver's license history review. Some agencies employ more stringent assessment practices such as successful completion of a polygraph examination and a psychological evaluation. Even after the candidate has been hired, many agencies perform updates to the employee's background investigation at five and ten year intervals.

Employing the all encompassing perspective of corruption control which you learned about in Chapter 5, nearly all law enforcement-sensitive information systems record the user's access identification code and the specific reason for the query; thus allowing periodic audits to be performed. In 1996, Title 18 of the United States Code, Section 1030 was revised[11] to ensure that government employees with lawful access to critical information systems could be held criminally responsible for intentionally destroying system records or disseminating sensitive data to unauthorized parties (see 18 USC 1030(a)(5)). The code of ethics for the Association of Certified Fraud Examiners (ACFE) highlights nine key areas that are typically found in agency guidelines governing the conduct of the intelligence analyst. These are as follows:[12]

1. Demonstrate a commitment to professionalism and diligence in the performance of his or her duties.
2. Shall not engage in any illegal or unethical conduct or any activity which would constitute a conflict of interest.
3. Exhibit the highest level of integrity in the performance of all professional assignments.
4. Comply with lawful orders of the courts.
5. Testify to matters truthfully and without bias or prejudice.
6. Obtain evidence or other documentation to establish a reasonable basis for any opinion rendered.
7. Shall not reveal any confidential information ... without proper authorization.
8. Will reveal all material matters—which, if omitted, could cause a distortion of the facts.

9. Shall continually strive to increase the competence and effectiveness of professional services performed.

Types of Law Enforcement Intelligence

Australian Intelligence Officer Joe Illardi of the Victoria Police notes that the purpose of all intelligence is "to provide foreknowledge and warning; as such, it is intended to be an integral part of the government decision-making process."[13] With respect to law enforcement operations, intelligence may be used in a variety of ways. For example, a credit card fraud squad at a small police department might use intelligence to plan a raid on a business engaged in skimming. A state investigative agency might use long-range intelligence forecasts in an effort to more effectively allocate personnel and equipment over a five-year period. In both of these examples, the value of the intelligence rests not only in the quality of the information gathered, but also in the ability of the analyst to employ the appropriate methodology to make this information useful to those who have requested it.

Accordingly, this section describes some of the more commonly-employed approaches utilized by law enforcement intelligence analysts in their efforts to provide agency decision-makers with timely and pertinent information.

Tactical Intelligence

One of the most common uses of intelligence is for tactical purposes. Defined by the U.S. Drug Enforcement Administration as "information on which immediate enforcement action—arrests, seizures, and interdictions— can be based,"[14] this approach is extensively employed at the federal, state, and local levels. Tactical intelligence provides "immediate targets providing direct action opportunity."[15] Most short-term surveillance operations, coupled with patrol officer observations and descriptions provided by witnesses and informants, produce information that can be analyzed tactically by exploring the who, what, why, when, and where of a particular incident (e.g., suspect, victim, and witness names, addresses, etc.). The use of information obtained through witnesses, patrol officers, victims, and other parties is commonly referred to as *human intelligence* or *HUMINT*.

There is a strong relationship between *HUMINT* and the technology used to gather data that will later be analyzed. For example, the Seal Beach Police Department in California uses live video feeds acquired through a secure Internet Protocol (IP) surveillance system to assess conditions at crime scenes prior to officers arriving on scene.[16] By visually scanning a warehouse for suspects during a breaking and entering call *before* officers enter the building, the Department is able to determine if the call is simply a false

Exhibit 9.1 The Information Awareness Office is based upon the Department of Defense's 2002 initiative known as Total Information Awareness (TIA). The purpose of TIA, which has never been approved by Congress, is to provide military and law enforcement personnel with the ability to electronically monitor and analyze seemingly disparate databases such as health, finance, and transportation to detect possible acts of terrorism.

alarm, or if there are armed criminals inside. This manner of tactical intelligence (using video surveillance) could just as readily be applied to a white-collar crime investigation. For example, agents could use this equipment to determine the best time of day to conduct an electronic benefit transaction (EBT) card fraud raid at a local grocery store. From a tactical perspective, these data work best when they are combined with information obtained from informants and patrol officer observations (i.e., *HUMINT*).

Despite technological innovations such as those being utilized by the Seal Beach Police Department, tactical intelligence most often employs a *deductive* analytical methodology. In other words, a known suspect or target is identified based on an investigator's guess or a witness's statement. The investigator then sets up a surveillance operation to obtain facts that will hopefully support this guess. Lastly, the analyst interprets these data to determine if the investigator's guess (which analysts refer to as a hypothesis) can be readily confirmed. Thus, tactical intelligence is dependent upon effective collection of facts "in a compiled and analyzed form."[17] The ultimate purpose of this analysis is to develop a case for investigation and prosecution. This intelligence process is also sometimes referred to by analysts as a *daisy chain*.

The accuracy of the daisy chain is dependent upon the quality of information provided to the analyst. If data are inaccurate, evidence obtained through subpoenas and search warrants may be suppressed at trial, allowing a conviction to be overturned or a known criminal to be acquitted (see Chapter 8). To minimize the potential hazards to a case posed by the daisy chain, analysts use a process known as *triangulation*.

Triangulation allows the intelligence analyst to substantiate the quality of the information provided by witnesses, suspects, patrol officers, and surveillance equipment. By verifying the accuracy of the data from its origin with secondary sources, analysts can establish a *confidence level* for the intelligence data. This affords senior managers the opportunity to make informed decisions about how to best proceed in the execution of warrants, conducting raids, effecting arrests, etc.

It is important for you to know that the process of determining the confidence level is neither arbitrary nor inherently simple. The analyst must

Exhibit 9.2 Military analysts use a variety of tools including signals intelligence and communications intelligence to identify trends and patterns in terrorist activity.

adhere to strict agency guidelines that place a quantitative value on information obtained through surveillance operations, reliable informants, or witness statements. Moreover, the analyst must consider the validity of the data from both external and internal perspectives. External validity of evidence refers to the authenticity of the article itself (i.e., has the evidence been altered or otherwise tampered with), whereas internal validity is the process of examining the content of a document, witness statement, or surveillance photo to better understand its meaning and its overall value to the case.[18]

Tactical intelligence analysis proves useful in apprehending the individual white-collar criminal, such as the casual counterfeiter or embezzler. However, its real value emerges as the building block for strategic intelligence.[19] Using tactical intelligence as a means to reach strategic conclusions may prove essential in apprehending a large-scale, organized criminal entity engaged in racketeering, money laundering, or conspiracy. It may also aid in establishing investigative priorities or effectively allocating departmental resources.

Interviewing Witnesses and Suspects

In Chapter 8 of this book, we referred to search and arrest warrants as the "workhorses of white-collar crime investigations." Indeed, lawfully obtaining evidence such as financial records, counterfeit currency, forged checks, and fictitious identification cards is critical to the successful prosecution of criminals. Equally important, however, is your ability as an investigator to obtain statements from prospective witnesses and confessions from suspects. To be effective in this area, you must have a thorough understanding of *proxemics* (i.e., the use of space and distance to create an atmosphere of openness or control), as well as the ability read the body language and facial expressions of suspects, victims, and witnesses. This is critical because non-verbal communications accounts for roughly 55 percent of all information exchanged between the two parties.

Basically, there are five types of questions that are used by investigators to obtain additional information on an incident, or gain a confession from a suspect. Each of these question types and appropriate examples appears below:

- *Narrative Question* (also referred to as an open-ended question): "Tell me about the roles and responsibilities of the employees who work at your business, EZ Credit Money Exchange, Inc."
- *Comparison Question*: "The man who you saw pass the counterfeit

hundred dollar bill . . . was he tall like Michael Jordan, or short like me?"

- *Leading Question*: "After you used the credit card you stole from your mother's purse to buy the sneakers on line, did you feel guilty or scared?"
- *Reaching-Back Question* (often used towards the end of the interview process): "Earlier in our conversation, you mentioned that you saw the teller that you work with at the bank hastily get into a car with someone during her lunch break. Can you describe the car and the person driving it?"
- *Direct Question* (sometimes referred to as a fixed-choice or logical question): "Did you hack into the U.S. Navy's automated personnel system?"

Employing these five question types in a systematic manner, especially when combined with a thorough knowledge of proxemics and your ability to assess body language and other non-verbal communications clues, you can obtain a wealth of information that can be used in the tactical analysis process. However, you must always remain steadfast in your adherence to agency policies and guidelines governing questioning of suspects, victims, and witnesses. This is especially important when questioning is conducted in a custodial environment and the individual being queried is the target of the investigation. Given its direct and specific nature, this form of questioning is often referred to as interrogation rather than interviewing.

Strategic Intelligence

Unlike the immediate returns that are evident from the use of tactical intelligence (e.g., quickly placing a suspect in custody, executing a raid with little or no injury to the officers involved), strategic intelligence can require weeks, months, or even years of careful data collection and analysis to identify trends and patterns. For example, the Financial Crimes Enforcement Network[20] (FinCEN) employs a strategic approach to identify possible money laundering trends occurring within the United States and abroad. By utilizing an *inductive* approach (i.e., gathering a wide range of data such as bank account numbers, subscriber names, telephone numbers, and physical addresses, and allowing intelligent information systems to graphically depict connections between these transactions), analysts are able to draw connections between individuals and entities that would never have become known using a basic tactical, *deductive* approach.

Exhibit 9.3 Military and law enforcement intelligence analysts use inductive soft-ware tools such as Pen-Link and Analyst's Notebook to link people, places, and events. Together they may be related to terrorism or other serious threats to national security.

While it may seem contrary to what you were taught in criminal justice courses like police patrol, the most effective way to use strategic intelligence is as a *reactive* (inductive) rather than a *proactive* (deductive) tool. This is because proactive analysis would require the analyst to primarily begin with a guess (hypothesis), such as an assumed target of the investigation, and attempt to find evidence to support or refute that hypothesis. In doing so, huge chunks of data seemingly unrelated to the suspect might be discarded because they do not "fit" the theoretical model that the analyst has constructed.

Exhibit 9.4 depicts the deductive process traditionally used in law enforcement investigations.

Comparatively, if the analyst does not begin the process with a hypothesis, but instead allows an intelligent information system to employ an inductive approach such as case-based reasoning (CBR), which can retrieve "cases from its memory, assesses their similarity, uses that measure to find a good or bad match and then uses that case to suggest a solution."[21] the analyst may uncover complex criminal networks that would have been missed using the deductive method. Relying on an ever-expanding case base that unites multiple databases links what might otherwise appear to be unconnected data (e.g., financial transactions, frequent telephone calls of

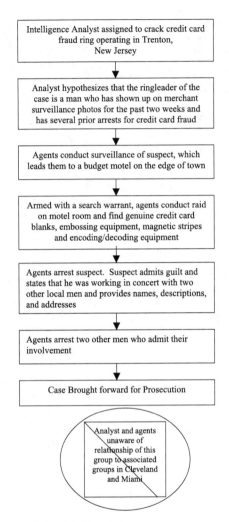

Exhibit 9.4 The deductive process in analysis.

short duration to/from a subscriber and a residence or business, and multiple vehicles registered to a common business address). Additionally, this method may yield a much broader perspective of a large criminal enterprise than could have been realized using the deductive, proactive approach to intelligence analysis.

This form of inductive link analysis, also referred to as *data visualization*, has the added advantage of being able to graphically depict relationships between quantitative and qualitative datasets—something that cannot be accomplished using traditional quantitative and qualitative statistical techniques. There are several manufacturers or intelligent software applications

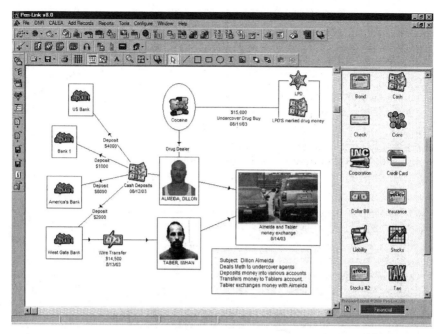

Exhibit 9.5 Pen-Link money laundering chart.

utilizing this inductive, link analysis approach, the most prominent of which are i2's Analyst Notebook, Memex's Crime Workbench, and Pen-Link. An example of a link analysis chart for a money laundering investigation appears in Exhibit 9.5.

Using Intelligence Analysis for Threat Assessment

In the challenging arena of white-collar crime investigation, the ability to connect individual suspects and groups of interest to larger criminal networks is essential. The legal framework for prosecuting crime syndicates has existed since the Racketeer Influenced and Corrupt Organizations Act[22] (18 USC 96) was first created in 1961. Designed to curtail the illegal activities of organized crime groups that had infiltrated labor unions in the 1950s, *18 USC 96*, also referred to as *RICO*, assigns felony penalties to groups engaged in both violent (e.g., murder, kidnapping, robbery) and non-violent offenses such as mail fraud, access device fraud, and forgery. Similarly, as you learned earlier in this book, since the passage of the Comprehensive Crime Control Act of 1984, the federal government can seize property found to be the proceeds of organized crime.[23] More recently, the creation of the USA Patriot Act of 2001 (HR 3162) has further broadened the authority of law enforcement officials to investigate entities believed to be associated with acts of terrorism.[24]

While each of these laws may prove useful at the prosecutorial stage, most cases would never reach this point without an effective mechanism for analyzing and assessing the threats and activities of organized crime groups. Threat assessment is normally considered when gauging the risk that an individual or group poses to a dignitary or public facility (e.g., the U.S. Secret Service uses a comparable classification system in order to protect the president from physical harm and safeguard the White House from nuclear, biological, or chemical attack). However, its application within the area of white-collar crime is less understood. By assessing the economic impact that an organized criminal group may pose to society as a whole, and by comparing one entity to another in terms of scope, expertise, size, strategy, and links to other criminal enterprises, law enforcement agencies are able to more effectively and efficiently allocate their resources and investigative assets than in the past.

One of the best tools currently being utilized in this area is referred to as *Project SLEIPNIR: The Long Matrix for Organized Crime*. A product of the Royal Canadian Mounted Police (RCMP), SLEIPNIR is named for the Old Norse Mythology legend of Slepnir, the horse belonging

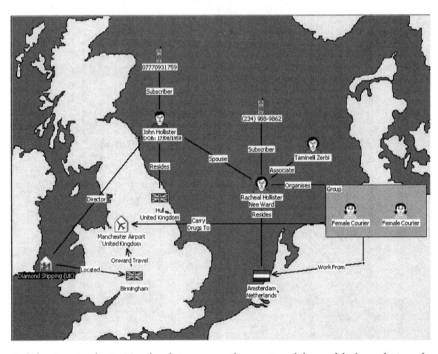

Exhibit 9.6 Analyst's Notebook is among the most widely-used link analysis software applications within the Intelligence Community today.

to Odin; however, the selection of this name is simply a random project assignment technique used by RCMP's Headquarters Unit, and has no symbolic significance. According to the Royal Canadian Mounted Police (RCMP), "the purpose of project SLEIPNIR is to provide threat measurement techniques that allow intelligence analysts to rank-order groups of organized criminals in an objective, comprehensive, and systematic way."[25]

Each of the elements included in the SLEIPNIR assessment matrix has been standardized through the use of the Delphi technique. The Delphi technique requires the formation of a panel of experts from diverse backgrounds, who come to a common consensus on the definition of key terms, establish categories, and quantitatively prioritize them in rank order. By utilizing the Delphi approach in the SLEIPNIR assessment process, the Royal Canadian Mounted Police are able to minimize subjectivity in the evaluation process. Moreover, the RCMP has reduced the likelihood of encountering three commonly encountered types of errors in intelligence research. These are *reliability* (measuring the same thing in the same way each time); *validity* (the extent to which the instrument measures what it purports to measure), and *generalizability* (applying the findings of a small sample population to the larger world around us).

SLEIPNIR consists of a matrix comprised of a listing of nineteen attributes of criminal groups, each of which was standardized using the previously mentioned Delphi technique. They are as follows:[26]

1. Corruption
2. Violence
3. Infiltration
4. Expertise
5. Sophistication
6. Subversion
7. Strategy
8. Discipline
9. Insulation
10. Intelligence use
11. Multiple enterprises
12. Mobility
13. Stability
14. Scope
15. Monopoly
16. Group cohesiveness
17. Continuity
18. Links to other organized crime groups
19. Links to criminal extremist groups

These nineteen attributes are placed along the vertical axis. For each of these nineteen attributes there are five possible values, which are numerically rank-ordered and are color-coded (i.e., high/red, medium/orange, low/yellow, white/green, or unknown/blue). In order to protect the names of the suspect groups from unauthorized dissemination, a name-to-letter coding system has been developed. The coded letter on the horizontal axis represents the names of each organized crime group. By applying this standardized tool, the crime analyst is able to depict the organized crime activity occurring within Canada's provinces.

While the United States had not adopted the SLEIPNIR matrix for assessing the economic risks posed by organized criminal groups, there are several similar models being used within the United States. Among the most progressive is the *Continuum of Money Management Sophistication* designed by Marilyn B. Peterson.[27]

A pioneer in the field of intelligence analysis and the former President of the International Association of Law Enforcement Intelligence Analysts (IALEIA), Marilyn Peterson has developed a truly inductive approach to white-collar crime research. Rather than establish targets and attempt to ascertain their assets and financial holdings, she believes that the analyst should focus on the money laundering process, and should work concentrically outwards to connect assets to individual criminals, corrupt businesses, and crooked government officials. She argues that "receiving profits from criminal undertakings is step one; being able to use them can become a much more complex series of steps."[28] Thus, the importance of financial techniques including bank record analysis, net worth analysis, and business record analysis for white-collar crime investigations cannot be overstated.

While it is beyond the scope of this book to discuss systems such as forensic accounting or internal auditing, Peterson's *Continuum* does an excellent job highlighting the broad range of uses for criminal enterprise profits from supporting one's basic needs to deviance.[29] A summary of this continuum and examples at each level are found in Exhibits 9.7 and 9.8.

In addition to Peterson's emphasis on "following the money" as a means to effectively investigate white-collar criminal cases, she has also successfully applied this approach repeatedly to narcotics trafficking cases and terrorist incidents during her nearly three decades of service to the New Jersey Division of Criminal Justice. It is her research into money laundering and its correlation with terrorist activities that has yielded a variety of new threat assessment models that effectively evaluate both physical threats and economic risk. As former IALEIA Executive Director Robert Fahlman and *Transnational Organized Crime* Editor Phil Williams state:

> Computer-assisted crime, sophisticated fraud, arms trafficking are all part of the organized crime repertoire and forms a threat to sovereignty,

1. Criminal profits used to obtain criminal products for self

In this scenario, the criminal may be a drug user who supports his or her habit by selling drugs to others. There is no long-term financial strategy employed here—merely survival on a day-to-day or week-to-week basis. The profits made by this level of criminal are seldom high due to the addiction present. This type of individual might be found as an associate to a non-traditional organized crime group, gang, or narcotics network.

2. Criminal profits spent on luxury items and living expenses

At this stage, the criminal may be someone who makes a moderate amount of profits from his or her criminal activity, but not so much that there is money left after it is applied to general living expenses and luxury items. This individual may be "living large" in the vernacular. There may be gang, network or group involvement by the individual. These profits could result from any number of types of criminal activity, ranging from narcotics sales to fraud. Lower-level drug dealers were seen to be spending their profits on automobiles, jewelry, clothing, gambling, and the repayment of drug debts (Washington-Baltimore HIDTA, 1998).

3. Criminal profits saved in currency—hidden by criminal

This level of profit making provides for money in excess of expenses being garnered. The excess money is not banked or invested, but rather is kept in its currency form and secreted where the criminal can access it easily. This is seen in narcotics networks and small-level crime groups. A few decades ago, this was a common occurrence in traditional organized crime groups (refer to Section IIA of this article, previously cited comment by *Frattiano* in 1986 testimony before President's Commission on Organized Crime).

4. Criminal profits moved through non-bank financial institutions for use off shore

In this scenario, profits are transferred through commercial transmitters or moved through *bureaux de change* (money changing businesses) to other countries for the purpose of either obtaining more criminal product (such as narcotics) or to provide profit shares to network members off shore. This can involve major money movements. As earlier mentioned, the U.S. Department of Treasury instituted a "geographic targeting order" against money remitters in the New York City area after $1.5 billion was seen moving from New York to Colombia in 1995 (FinCEN, 1996). Check-cashing companies have also been used to launder illegal profits.

5. Criminal profits placed into traditional banking system through multiple accounts

The most vulnerable step in the money laundering process is the "placement" of funds into the traditional banking system. Most of the federal legislation surrounding money laundering has focused on this step, with Currency Transaction Reports (CTRs) and Currency or Monetary Instrument Reports (CMIRs). The response to the $10,000 threshold on these reports has been breaking down the profits and the deposits into multiple transactions. "Smurfs" are used to make multiple deposits into accounts here so that the profits are then available for use here. All types of networks—entrepreneurial crime and organized criminal groups, use this approach. In one case, "smurfs" purchased postal and bank money orders, which were then deposited into an account to hide the source of the funds.

6. Criminal profits invested locally in real estate through nominees

This is a common use of illicit funds that has been occurring throughout the past few decades. In this scenario, the criminal profiteer purchases real property but places it in the hands of a spouse, relative, or close friend. These people act on behalf of the criminal to provide him or her with income (or a living arrangement) that does not directly connect back to the criminal. In another example, "Accounting practices that defy explanation are commonplace at organized crime-controlled corporations whose principals know that a paper trail can lead to prison...[For example] he [mob boss Scarfo's accountant] acquired his Northfield home from one Louis Russo...and assumed Russo's remaining $92,000 mortgage...without a written contract and at a cost of $1..." (New Jersey State Commission of Investigation, 1987, p. 15).

Steps One through Six of the Continuum of Money Management Sophistication
Source *IALEIA Journal*, Vol. 15, No. 2, p. 137

Exhibit 9.7 Steps One through Six of the Continuum of Money Management Sophistication.

7. Criminal profits used to purchase stocks, financial instruments and business interests
Stocks, bonds, and other monetary instruments can be purchased to invest criminal profits and gain a longer-term return. The appearance of criminals as owners or partners in businesses is not unusual. Sometimes, these business shares are bought directly, in other cases, the business interest is acquired through "influence." In one instance, Michele Sindona was alleged to be controlling 40 percent of the stocks traded on the Milan Stock Market (Sterling, 1990).

8. Criminal profits moved to other geographic locations and used to invest or make purchases of property there
Foreign nationals may view the United States or other industrialized countries as opportunities for them to make a lot of money which they can then send back to their native lands, living a wealthy lifestyle for some time to come. Since a number of these countries do not have money-laundering regulations, those governments may indirectly sanction such practices. The list of countries carrying "primary concern" regarding money laundering vulnerability includes—but is not limited to—Israel, Pakistan, Jordan, Kenya, Republic of Korea, Lithuania, Liechtenstein, Luxemburg, Mexico, and Nigeria (U.S. Department of State, 1997, pp. 77-95).

9. Financial professionals, attorneys, or others used as intermediary facilitators to acquire property with profits
As was earlier mentioned, a group of individuals known as Money Laundering Facilitators (MLFs) has arisen. These professionals know how and where to put money and how to avoid transaction reporting requirements and other items as earlier referenced by Savona. This can be an extremely lucrative business; rates for laundering money have been seen up to 25 percent.

10. Criminal profits are integrated into 'legitimate' investments and businesses and criminal becomes 'legitimate'
For some criminals, profits may be used to legitimize themselves and their families. Starting with illegal gains, they invest or make business partnerships that will allow them to live in the 'right' neighborhoods and send their children to the best schools. Moore (1994) notes that the offsprings of organized crime members are now getting Ivy League business degrees.

11. Criminal profits used to invest in financial institutions that can be manipulated to hide or invest other funds
Michele Sindona was reported to control several hundred companies and also banks which he manipulated to garner him even more profits (Sterling, 1990). Eastern European criminals control banks in Russia and elsewhere. Some banks in Miami (Florida) are believed to be in the hands of drug syndicates. According to Sterling (1990), the inspector-general of Colombia's Central Bank, Carlos Rodrigue Polonia-Camargo, was also the Cali cartel's financial *consigliere*.

12. Criminal profits used to manipulate governments
The use of narco-dollars to influence countries in South and Central America has been extensively documented. Likewise, the influence of illicit monies on the economic health of entire nations is currently being seen in Eastern Europe. The U.S. Department of State commented that "The increasing concentrations of wealth among criminal groups in several parts of the world is a concern...but also because these organizations have immense campaign coffers available to them and to candidates who covertly do their bidding" (1995, p. 79).

Table 9.2: Steps Seven through Twelve of the Continuum of Money Management Sophistication
(Source: *IALEIA Journal*, Vol. 15, No. 2, p. 138)

Exhibit 9.8 Steps Seven through Twelve of the Continuum of Money Management Sophistication.

societies, individuals, national stability, democratic values, national economics, financial institutions . . . and global codes of conduct. It will be through the effective use of intelligence and analysis that anti-organized crime efforts will become more successful[30]

The use of intelligence analysis as the proverbial bridge between investigating white-collar crimes and acts of global terror will only hasten its use

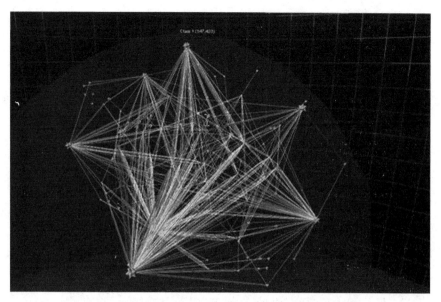

Exhibit 9.9 Data visualization technology allows military and law enforcement intelligence analysts to identify trends and patterns in bank account transactions, foreign travel, telephone calls, and other activities.

among law enforcement professionals at all levels of government, from the Federal Bureau of Investigation and Department of Homeland Security, to state police, county sheriffs, and local public safety and emergency management agencies.

We have no doubt that those of you who are trained in areas such as common computer applications (e.g., word processing, spreadsheet use, and database design), quantitative and qualitative statistics, data visualization, accounting, and financial statement analysis will prove to be the most competitive candidates for positions in the field of criminal intelligence, and will ultimately serve as America's most valuable criminal justice resource on the front lines of the Global War on Terrorism.

In summary, while the thought of working a "desk job" may not appear as glamorous as performing surveillance in the field or kicking in doors, the hard work and due diligence of our analysts contribute tremendously to all facets of the criminal justice arena, ranging from combating drug smuggling and human trafficking, to intercepting illegal firearms and identifying violent offenders. Nearly all of these analysts employ a myriad of financial examination tools and often discover that fraud, identity theft, and money laundering are precursors to the *mala in se* activities their agencies are tasked with combating.

Chaper Summary

In Chapter 9 of this book, you were exposed to the basics of intelligence analysis. The chapter highlighted the differences between deductive and inductive analysis, and how both are used to combat white-collar crime.

ADAPTED READINGS

Reading 9–1: Tim Weiner, *How to Make a Spy*

> As we forge ahead in the Global War on Terrorism, now referred to among some law enforcement, military, and intelligence analysts as "the long war," it has become readily apparent that we are ill-equipped to adequately handle these challenges. As this reading will illustrate, only by reinvigorating America's human intelligence collection capabilities will we be able to adequately address these threats.

War is the ultimate intelligence failure. When intelligence fails, the consequence is the Korean War in 1950. The consequence is the Vietnam War in 1965. The consequence is 9/11. The consequence is Iraq today. The long war in which we are now engaged is an intelligence war, and we will win it or lose it by virtue of our intelligence.

A decade ago, the CIA's problems included dwindling money, haywire technology, dispirited personnel, revolving-door leadership, and a drifting sense of mission. Taken together, they were devastating. In his recent memoir, George J. Tenet, director of central intelligence for seven years under Presidents Bill Clinton and George W. Bush, described the CIA he inherited in 1997 as a "burning platform"—an oil rig on fire in a stormy sea.

Today, six years after 9/11, money is no object at the CIA. The agency is working hard to fix its information technologies. Gen. Michael V. Hayden is perhaps the most capable director since Robert Gates, now secretary of defense, who led the country's espionage service more than 14 years ago. And everyone knows what the mission is: to know the enemy, to prevent the next Pearl Harbor, and to provide the president with the information he needs to construct a strategy for the United States—not for tomorrow, but for five years beyond the horizon. These are the same reasons the CIA was created 60 years ago this past summer.

But General Hayden must carry out that mission with the least experienced workforce in the history of the CIA. Half his analysts, and a roughly equal fraction of his clandestine service officers, have been hired since 9/11. As youngsters in their 20s have replaced people in their 40s and 50s, the result has been an abridgment of intelligence. "For every 10 analysts with fewer than four years' service," General Hayden has testified, "we only have one experienced analyst [with] between 10 and 14 years of service." By the CIA's own standards, these are trainees.

The crucial problem for the CIA is recruiting and training Americans willing to devote their lives to spying. It is, in a word, talent. It has been a problem for six decades.

The annals of the CIA are filled with lamentations by spy chiefs bemoaning the agency's lack of expertise. At a headquarters meeting on June 23, 1958, Allen W. Dulles, one of the CIA's early directors, complained that he was "at a loss as to what component of the Agency he can turn to when he desires specific information on the USSR." The agency had none to speak of. Its reporting on the Soviets was pure wind. Richard Bissell, chief of the clandestine service and architect of the 1961 Bay of Pigs invasion, described the CIA as fundamentally incompetent: "By the late 60s, the Agency already had, I thought, a rather lamentable record," said Bissell. The CIA lacked basic skills in military affairs, political analysis, and economic analysis, according to Bissell. The agency had become nothing more than a secret bureaucracy—and a "very sloppy" one at that.

A generation later, early in the Reagan years, a young Robert Gates won promotion to the CIA'S chief of intelligence analysis with an attention-grabbing memo to Director of Central Intelligence William J. Casey. "CIA is slowly turning into the Department of Agriculture," Gates wrote. Gates said that the agency was filled with amateurs "pretending to be experts." Their work was "irrelevant, uninteresting, too late to be of value, too narrow, too unimaginative, and too often just flat out wrong." They had missed or misinterpreted almost every important development in the Soviet Union and its advances into the Third World over the past decade.

The CIA has never had a golden age. It is a myth of the CIA's own making, the product of the publicity and political propaganda of the agency's early days. It held that the agency could change the world, and it helps explain why the CIA is so impervious to change. But, in truth, the agency has suffered from the same persistent weakness since the beginning—a lack of skilled, well-trained spies. As early as Oct. 27, 1952, Gen. Walter Bedell Smith, the director of central intelligence during the Korean War, convened his 26 most senior officers at headquarters. He said that "until CIA could build a reserve of well-trained people, it would have to hold its activities to the limited number of operations that it could do well, rather than attempt to cover a broad field with poor performance" by "inferior personnel." "We can't get qualified people," he lamented. "They just simply don't exist."

General Smith was right. Espionage is not America's strong suit. The United States has struggled and failed for 60 years to create a first-rate secret intelligence service—in part because of what makes Americans who they are. Americans want foreigners to think like us, to speak like us, to be like us. The oceans that protected the United States for so long also served as a gulf that kept it from knowing the world.

The number of people at the CIA who can haggle in a bazaar in Tajikistan or hope to understand a rapid-fire conversation in Arabic remains vanishingly small. Gates himself once said the agency has long been incapable of dispatching "an Asian-American into North Korea without him being identified as some kid who just walked out of Kansas." The CIA's traditions are a large part of the problem. Its fears for its own security long prohibited hiring first-generation Americans with close relatives living overseas. They have weeded out people with unusual backgrounds rather than welcoming them into the fold. As director of central intelligence, Gates once wanted to hire an Americans citizen raised in Azerbaijan. The recruit was rejected because he failed to score high enough on the written English test. Gates was furious. "I've got thousands of people here who can write English," he fumed, "but I don't have anyone here who can speak Azeri."

To succeed, the CIA will need a new cadre of highly skilled analysts and daring officers—men and women with the discipline and self-sacrifice of the nation's best military officers, the cultural awareness and historical knowledge of the nation's best diplomats, and the sense of curiosity and adventure possessed by the nation's best foreign correspondents.

It is no longer enough for the CIA's recruiters to promise to find this talent. They have searched for decades and have yet to fill the agency's ranks with the officers and analysts the job requires. It may be simply too hard to find the proper skills among the present generation of young Americans. But it would not be impossible to create them. Herewith, a modest proposal:

* Invest $20 billion in the Boren Scholarships in the next five years.

Part of the National Security Education Program, the Boren Scholarships, named after former Sen. David L. Boren of Oklahoma, were established in 1991 under the aegis of the Institute for International Education to train a new generation of national security officers. The annual budget today is $2 million for undergraduates and $2 million for graduate students—a ridiculously low investment.

* Use the money to teach 100,000 native-born Americans to speak Arabic, Chinese, Farsi, Korean, Pashto, and Urdu.

Twenty billion dollars is a sum roughly equal to the combined costs of one Stealth bomber ($2 billion), one new Navy submarine ($3 billion), and one brigade's worth of Army Future Combat System technology ($15 billion).

* Start the program with high school seniors.

They would commit to five years of language training upon turning 18. The clock starts running when they graduate from high school. They must continue their studies throughout their summers in college. They must also take college courses in the history and culture of the nations where the language they are studying is spoken. If they graduate from college with a B-plus average or better, pass a basic fluency test, and meet other high standards, they have first crack at $100,000-a-year jobs waiting for them in the military, the State Department, or the CIA.

    * Require them to serve a minimum of two years in those jobs, before or after embarking on graduate studies.

Perhaps 1 in 10 of the 100,000 high school seniors would stick it out. But the United States would then have 10,000 more language-qualified Americans than it does today.

    Perhaps 1 in 10 among the 10,000 would have what it takes to serve the nation by spying overseas instead of sitting in the pastel-colored offices of American government. That crucial work is not running coups, overthrowing foreign leaders, selling political propaganda, buying elections, or any of the other traditional missions of the CIA's clandestine service. That work is espionage. The United States can continue to build all the billion-dollar spy satellites it wants. But satellites cannot tell us what we need to know. In the end, the only way to know the mind of the enemy is to talk to him.

    For decades, tens of thousands of clandestine service officers have gathered only the barest threads of truly important intelligence—and that is the CIA's deepest secret. Their mission is extraordinarily hard. But the United States still does not understand the people and the political forces it seeks to contain and control. The CIA has yet to become what its creators hoped it would be.

    Espionage is, as President Eisenhower once said, a distasteful but vital necessity. The United States had better get good at it. Language, history, and culture are where Americans need to begin.

Want to Know More?

Tim Weiner's history of the CIA, *Legacy of Ashes* (New York: Doubleday, 2007) offers an unsparing look at the agency's blunders, infirmities, and resistance to change during the past six decades. Amy B. Zegart examines how and why the United States's counterterrorism efforts failed in the run-up to 9/11 in *Spying Blind* (Princeton: Princeton University Press, 2007).

    In *A Look Over My Shoulder* (New York: Presidio Press, 2003), former Director of Central Intelligence Richard Helms argues that the United States has failed to establish a first-rate espionage service. Thomas Powers's *The Man Who Kept the Secrets: Richard Helms and the CIA* (New York: Alfred A. Knopf, 1979) looks at the operations of the CIA during the Cold War. Milt Bearden and James Risen offer the compelling story of how the KGB's counterterrorism agents compromised CIA spies in the Soviet Union in *The Main Enemy: The*

Inside Story of the CIA's Final Showdown with the KGB (New York: Presidio Press, 2004).

The Web site of the CIA's Center for the Study of Intelligence offers a searchable index of declassified articles from the CIA's in-house quarterly, Studies in Intelligence. In "Spies Unlike Us" (FOREIGN POLICY, March/April 2005), former CIA operative Robert Baer argues the agency must reform its hiring practices to permit the employment of American citizens with foreign ties.

For links to relevant Web sites, access to the FP Archive, and a comprehensive index of related FOREIGN POLICY articles, go to ww2.ForeignPolicy.com.

Source: *Foreign Policy,* © 2007, Carnegie Endowment for International Peace.

Reading 9–2: Marilyn B. Peterson, *Applying Heuer's Analysis of Competing Hypotheses (ACH) in the Law Enforcement Intelligence Environment*

> *Scholar Richard Heuer's Analysis of Competing Hypotheses (ACH) is among the most important methodological advances to the intelligence community in the past 30 years. In this article, author Marilyn Peterson expertly summarizes the key elements of this method, which will undoubtedly find its way into your toolkit should you pursue a carrer in the area of intelligence analysis.*

I. Introduction

In 1999, Richard J. Heuer Jr., published *The Psychology of Intelligence Analysis* through his former agency, the U.S. Central Intelligence Agency.(1) Both the intelligence and law enforcement communities embraced this book because it focused on the mind of the analyst. More specifically, the analyst's ability to function and operate in a manner that directly coincides with conducting any relevant tasks related to his or her assignment.

One of the most intriguing concepts in Heuer's book is found in Chapter 8, accordingly entitled, "The Analysis of Competing Hypotheses" (ACH). Heuer (1999) defines the analysis of competing hypotheses as "a tool to aid judgment on important issues requiring careful weighing of alternative explanations or conclusions." (p. 95). In other words, ACH gives analysts a framework to evaluate what may happen in the future, or may have already happened in past occurrences. Since most analysis is done in an environment lacking a sense of certainty, such framework as proposed by Heuer is evidently necessary.

Throughout the various stages of the intelligence process, data are collected, evaluated, compiled, analyzed, and also utilized as a basis for conclusions and recommendations. The purpose of this article is to explore the use of the ACH process to the conclusion-drawing phase of law enforcement investigations.

II. Heuer's Analysis of Competing Hypotheses

Heuer's process is shown in Figure 1.1. He notes that there are three elements that differentiate ACH from conventional analysis: (a) the thorough examination of alternatives; (b) the identification of the key bits of data that carry the most diagnostic weight; and (c) the painstaking attention to refuting hypotheses (p. 108).(2)

The first step, identifying hypotheses, is an accepted but essential phase within the context of the analysis itself. However, it should be noted that the methods by which analysts identify hypotheses may not be sufficient enough, because the alternatives that they choose to explore are often not explored as adequately and thoroughly as one might expect them to be. Heuer suggests using a group of analysts to essentially "brainstorm" the possible hypotheses. He further notes that five decision-making techniques limit the thorough consideration of all possibilities: (a) satisficing,(3) (b) incrementalism, (c) consensus, (d) reasoning by analogy, and (e) relying on a set of "good" versus "bad" principles to distinguish between them (Heuer, 1999, p. 43). Such a rush to judgment to preclude hypotheses can result in tremendous failures in the area of intelligence. In this step, Heuer notes that even the weakest hypothesis should be retained, rather than simply discarded. In this manner, data made available at a later date may strengthen the use of that particular hypothesis, or any others involved in the process.

Heuer suggests that—if the conclusion is to have a significant political impact, or there is a broad range of possibilities—more alternatives should definitely be considered. He notes, however, that most people cannot consider more than seven possible alternatives at one specific time; hence, the suggested maximum number to engaged during this process at any one given time is seven (1999, p. 98).

Throughout the duration of step two, significant evidence or arguments may include not only the "facts" known, but also the opinions and points of view from the lead analyst on the case and other experts. This type of evidence may result in further critical questioning about what one might expect to be seeing if, in fact, the evidence or opinion presented is indeed true. Heuer notes that it is important to look beyond the obvious, and attempt to discover what is actually missing (1999, p. 99). Figure 1.2, demonstrates this concept by exploring the issue of the War in Iraqi. According to Heuer, if the Iraqi embassies had not been instructed to take extra security precautions, this could be a strong indication that they did not intend to retaliate.

In step three, what essentially occurs is the preparation of a matrix and viewing the "diagnosticity" of each piece of evidence. Then, after this process occurs, the hypotheses are compared to each specific piece of evidence to determine which provide the best fit. "Diagnosticity," as per Heuer (1999), is the "relative likelihood" of a particular hypothesis based on the piece of evidence (p. 102). The matrix notations may be positives (+) or negatives (−), or may be expressed as percentages of probability such as consistent (C), inconsistent (I), or not applicable (NA) or even text in some cases.

Step four allows the analyst to refine the matrix by adding new hypotheses or pieces of evidence, combining some or deleting those that no longer appear to be valid. Heuer notes that even the deleted hypotheses should be kept, in a separate place to make sure what has been considered and can be recalled (Heuer, 1999. p. 103).

In step five the matrix is thoroughly reviewed to determine which particular hypothesis the evidence best supported. Approaching this review by attempting to disprove a hypothesis (i.e., looking for evidence that allows you to reject hypotheses or determine that they are unlikely) is extremely beneficial in the end of the process. The most important factor in this entire stage is the role played by the analyst, not the matrix. This is because it is the analyst who ultimately determines what hypothesis is most likely to be employed. However, it is important to remember that the hypothesis that renders the most support is the one that is a continuation of one's previous thinking. Performing the ACH model makes it likely that more of the alternatives will be considered.

In the Heuer model, step six allows the analyst to identify the evidence that is most responsible for the chosen hypothesis. It also allows for the identification of information that may be incorrect, such as disinformation or deception (Heuer, 1999, p. 105). Accordingly, step seven calls for reporting the conclusion that has been reached. It is also where the analyst is given the opportunity to present the probability of the accuracy of his or her conclusion. Heuer (1999) notes "analytical judgments are never certain." (p. 106).

The final step is to remain vigilant in the acquisition and analysis of additional information that could change the outcome of analysis. The analyst must be prepared to update the analysis whenever necessary.

Figure 1.1 summarizes the eight critical steps in the Heuer's Analysis of Competing Hypotheses.

In Figure 1.2, three hypotheses have been developed and five pieces of evidence have been gathered in response to the question, "will Iraq retaliate for U.S. bombing of its intelligence headquarters?" The matrix in Figure 1.3 shows that most evidence supports the hypothesis that Iraq will sponsor minor terrorist acts against the United States in retaliation. It also suggests that the most unlikely hypothesis is that no retaliation would occur, since this would be an unacceptable loss of face for former leader Saddam Hussein and "face" was believed to be an important component of his psyche and of his top commanders. In the matrix, Figure 1.3, the fact that Hussein indicates that he would not attack, is seen by Heuer to support all outcomes.

III. Applying Heuer's ACH in a Law Enforcement Environment

Heuer presents his "Analysis of Competing Hypotheses" to be used in a predictive manner; that is, to compare possible future activities in an international intelligence context. Within the field of law enforcement, analysts arrive at

1. "Identify the possible hypotheses to be considered. Use a group of analysts with different perspectives to brainstorm the possibilities.
2. Make a list of significant evidence and arguments for and against each hypothesis.
3. Prepare a matrix with hypotheses across the top and evidence down the side. Analyze the 'diagnosticity' of the evidence and argument—that is, identify which items are most helpful in judging the relative likelihood of the hypotheses.
4. Refine the matrix. Reconsider the hypotheses and delete evidence and arguments that have no diagnostic value.
5. Draw tentative conclusions about the relative likelihood of each hypothesis. Proceed by trying to disprove the hypotheses rather than prove them.
6. Analyze how sensitive your conclusion is to a few critical items of evidence. Consider the consequences for your analysis if that evidence were wrong, misleading, or subject to a different interpretation.
7. Report conclusions. Discuss the relative likelihood of all the hypotheses, not just the most likely one.
8. Identify milestones for future observation that may indicate events are taking a different course than expected."

Figure 1.1 Steps for Analyzing Competing Hypotheses.

(Source: Heuer, 1999, p. 97)

Question: Will Iraq retaliate for U.S. bombing of its intelligence headquarters?

Alternative Hypotheses:

> H1: Iraq will not retaliate.
> H2: Iraq will sponsor some minor terrorist action.
> H3: Iraq is planning a major terrorist attack, perhaps against one or more CIA installations.

Evidence:

> E1: Saddam public statement of intent not to retaliate.
> E2: Absence of terrorist offensive during the 1991 Gulf War.
> E3: Assumption that Iraq would not want to provide another US attack.
> E4: Increase in frequency/length of monitored Iraqi agent radio broadcasts.
> E5: Iraq embassies instructed to take increased security precautions.
> E6: Assumption that failure to retaliate would be unacceptable loss of face for Saddam.

Figure 1.2 Heuer's Example of ACH.

(Source: Heuer, 1999, p. 101)

	H1	H2	H3
E1	+[4]	+	+
E2	+	+	−
E3	+	+	−
E4	−	+	+
E5	−	+	+
E6	−	+	+

Figure 1.3 Heuer's ACH Matrix: Will Iraq Retaliate?

(Source: Heuer, 1999, p. 102)

hypotheses or conclusions in every investigation and analytic study—covering past events and future activities. Thus, the possibilities for using ACH in law enforcement setting are indeed varied.

However, some modifications of the original ACH model should be made when applying it within the law enforcement environment because in the law enforcement intelligence process, data evaluation for reliability and validity often occur prior to analysis of the data—usually in the collection or collation stage. In contrast, it is not until step three of the original ACH model that the possibility of deception or disinformation is taken into account. By performing up-front evaluation of the data, and bringing forward that evaluation along with these data, law enforcement analysts can better determine which pieces of evidence may have the most weight in step three. This will afford the analyst the opportunity to predict or postdict what may occur or has occurred. The law enforcement examples used in this article show the evaluation data assigned to each piece of evidence.

Law enforcement analysis uses a "4 × 4" or "5 × 5" model of evaluation.(5) Data are evaluated for the reliability of their sources, as well as for their own internal validity. Source evaluation scales range from 1 to 4 or A through D (sometimes 1 to 5 or A to E). Reliability scales generally go from Reliable, (Usually Reliable is also periodically used), Sometimes Reliable, Unreliable, to Reliability Unknown. A reliable source is one that has been unquestioned or well tested in the past. Usually reliable information is from a source that has provided reliable information in the past most of the time (Peterson (2000), in Morehouse, & Wright, Eds., 2001, p. 92). A police source, for example, might be viewed as reliable, while information from a confidential informant might be viewed as usually or sometimes reliable, depending upon the history of the information provided by the source. Similarly, the validity of the data can be judged from Confirmed, (Probably True), Possibly True, Untrue, to Factuality Unknown. Confirmed data may be corroborated by two or more sources or be known to be a fact. Probable data refers to information that is consistent with past accounts, while doubtful data is inconsistent with past accounts (Peterson (2000) in Peterson, Morehouse, & Wright, Eds., 2001, p. 92). Heuer's (1999) suggestion that doubtful hypotheses be given complete consideration along with those that appear more likely would make analysts more apt to use data that were of unknown reliability and validity, rather than information known to be unreliable or untrue.

IV. Potential Uses of ACH in Law Enforcement

There are a variety of criminal activities in which ACH could be used as an analytical methodology. In the post-9/11 world, one use of the ACH technique would be forecasting the future actions of terrorist organizations. An ACH matrix on predicting terrorism is seen in Figure 1.4. In this example, the question, "Will al-Qaeda attack in the Continental United States (CONUS) in the

Question: Will Al-Qaeda attack the United States in the near future?
Alternative Hypotheses:

  A. Al-Qaeda will mount a large-scale attack on United States soil in the near future.
  B. Al-Qaeda will mount a large-scale attack on United States interests outside the U.S. in the near future.
  C. Al-Qaeda will mount a series of small-scale attacks on U.S. soil.
  D. Al-Qaeda will mount a series of small-scale attacks on U.S. interests outside the U.S. in the near future.
  E. Al-Qaeda will mount attacks on U.S. allies in the near future.
  F. Al-Qaeda will not mount an attack on U.S. soil in the near future.
  G. Al-Qaeda will not mount an attack on any U.S. interests in the near future.

Evidence:
  1. Increase in communications among al-Qaeda contacts. (A/1)
  2. Presence of "sleeper cells" in the United States. (A/1)
  3. Continued influence of Osama bin Laden/inability of U.S. to find and kill bin Laden. (A/2)
  4. Increases in security within the United States. (A/1)
  5. Capture, by U.S. and allies, of varied al-Qaeda operatives have provided U.S. law enforcement with greater knowledge and understanding of al-Qaeda methods of operation. (A/1)
  6. U.S. involvement in Iraq war lessens focus of U.S. on al-Qaeda—causing less focus on securing U.S.(B/2)
  7. Two "anniversaries" of September 11 attacks have passed without another attack on U.S. soil, possibly because bin Laden is waiting for the U.S. to relax its readiness. (B/2)
  8. There has been an increase in frequency of al-Qaeda linked bombings and attacks on western interests in other countries. (A/1)
  9. Impact of U.S./Iraq war on Islamic terrorism elsewhere—causes more possible support for terrorist activities due to their dislike of U.S. involvement in Iraq. (B/2)
  10. bin Laden has made statements that major attacks against the U.S. will occur again soon. (A/3)
  11. The high porosity of U.S. borders with Canada and Mexico and their potential for use by terrorists to enter the U.S. and attack. (A/1)

Figure 1.4 Example of ACH Used in Law Enforcement: Anti-Terrorism.

near future?" is asked. The potential hypotheses shown range from a major attack in CONUS carried out by al-Qaeda, to no attack on the United States, its allies, or points of interests. While additional hypotheses are certainly possible, the suggested limit of seven is followed. A listing of twelve pieces of evidence is then shown, compared, and contrasted against open-source media information.(6) In step four, one previously-held piece of evidence was combined with another to form evidence 5. Evidence 12 was also added to the list in step 4.

In the evaluation of these data, they are seen to be generally corroborated and generally true, partly as a result of using only information generally known, and not having confidential informant or inside information available. The pieces rated "B" are scored accordingly because they are more within the context of an opinion than of a particular fact, and are therefore less factual. The "3" rating on evidence 11 is reflective of Osama bin Laden's claims over the past two years that the U.S. will be attacked indirectly (i.e., without direct attacks on CONUS).

The completed matrix in Figure 1.5 tallies the evidence in comparison to the hypotheses. Hypotheses F and G (no attacks), with eight inconsistent each, are least likely to occur. Hypotheses A and B, pointing to a large-scale attacks on U.S. soil or American interests, has four inconsistents, and appears less likely. This evidence points to the greatest likelihood that smaller-scale attacks in the U.S., or against U.S. interests outside the United States, or against U.S. allies will occur in the near future. These hypotheses have only three inconsistencies and should thus be forwarded to management as the analysts' preferred hypotheses. The two hypotheses suggesting no attacks will occur in or outside the U.S. have the least support in the evidence.

Looking further into the area of predictive protective analysis, ACH could also be applied to information on incidents including executive visits, special events (e.g., the Olympics, Pan Am Games, other sporting events, etc.), and timed activities (threat assessments covering particular periods of time such as holiday seasons, anniversaries of previous attacks, etc.).

A second example of applying the ACH method to law enforcement investigations is in predicting where the next series of crimes might occur. Typically, crime analysts look at temporal analysis, geographic distributions, and crime patterns in trying to predict the next in a series of crimes. All of these are valid methods, but they can be enhanced by the use of the ACH method. Figure 1.6 shows a listing of hypotheses and evidence regarding a series of bank robberies in the fictitious town of New City.

Again, a series of six hypotheses are under consideration. Nine pieces of evidence were listed, along with their evaluation codes. In this example, a few items might be considered critical pieces of information. The lack of enhanced security (evidence 2) and the delivery of a sum much larger than previously available (evidence 7) might support either hypothesis B (First National) or hypothesis C (Fidelity) as the most likely. Evidence 4 indicates that C/Fidelity

	H-A	H-B	H-C	H-D	H-E	H-F	H-G
Evidence 1	C	C	C	C	C	I	I
Evidence 2	C	I	C	I	I	I	I
Evidence 3	C	C	C	C	C	I	I
Evidence 4	I	C	I	C	C	C	C
Evidence 5	I	C	I	C	C	I	I
Evidence 6	C	C	C	C	C	I	I
Evidence 7	I	I	C	I	I	C	C
Evidence 8	C	C	C	C	C	I	I
Evidence 9	I	I	C	C	C	C	C
Evidence 10	C	C	C	C	C	I	I
Evidence 11	C	I	C	I	I	I	I

Figure 1.5 ACH Example Matrix—Al-Qaeda's Future Actions.

Question: What bank (if any) will be targeted by bank robbers in New City the next month?

Alternative Hypotheses:

  A. No banks will be robbed in New City during the next month.
  B. An attempt to rob First National will be made.
  C. An attempt to rob Fidelity Bank will be made.
  D. An attempt to rob Suncoast Federal Bank will be made.
  E. An attempt to rob Third Federal Bank will be made.
  F. An attempt to rob Community Bank will be made.

Evidence:
1. Eight bank robberies have occurred in New City over the past five months, with an average of two banks being robbed per month. The last of the eight occurred two weeks ago. (A/1)
2. New City Police have concluded that the bank robbers have collected information on their targets to maximize their activities and that some inside information may have been available to them. (A/2)
3. Only two of the eight bank robberies that have occurred have resulted in the arrest of the alleged robbers; robberies continued after the arrest of these two individuals. (A/1)
4. Fidelity Bank is in the general area in which three of the previous robberies have occurred. (A/1)
5. Suncoast Federal was one of the first banks robbed four months ago. (A/1)
6. According to crime analysts, two of the banks, Community Bank and First National, fit the geographic profile of where the next robbery might occur. (A/2)
7. First National and Fidelity are both scheduled to receive deliveries from the local Federal Reserve Bank of over $250,000 in the next ten days. (B/2)
8. The eight robberies that have occurred netted between $18,000 and $45,000 each. (A/1)
9. Due to the recent robberies, Suncoast, Third Federal and Community have updated their security procedures and protocols, hiring additional security personnel. (B/2)

Figure 1.6 Example of ACH in Law Enforcement—Bank Robberies.

might be less apt to be chosen since it is close to sites previously robbed (conversely, some might judge that it is more likely to be robbed since it is in the targeted geographic region; analytic judgment is subjective and may differ). Also, evidence 6 indicates that hypothesis B (First National) and hypothesis F (Community) fit the geographic profile of the next target.

The matrix in Figure 1.7 then shows that hypothesis B, First National, is most likely to be robbed, based on the evidence given, while Suncoast Federal (D) seems the least likely.

A third example of a law enforcement use of the ACH method is to view past activities to determine which is the most likely to have occurred ("postdicting"). For example, an investigation into the activities of local motorcycle gang members might uncover various possible legal and illegal activities of the gang's members as suggested in Figure 1.8.

Figure 1.9 is a matrix containing the above hypotheses and evidence. Reviewing it, one can see that the least likely hypothesis is D, that The Wheeler's is not

	H-A	H-B	H-C	H-D	H-E	H-F
Evidence 1	II	C	C	C	C	C
Evidence 2	I	n/a	n/a	n/a	n/a	n/a
Evidence 3	n/a	C	I	C	C	C
Evidence 4	n/a	C	C	I	C	C
Evidence 5	I	C	I	I	I	C
Evidence 6	n/a	C	C	I	I	I
Evidence 7	n/a	n/a	n/a	n/a	n/a	n/a
Evidence 8	C	C	C	C	I	I
Evidence 9	I	C	C	C	C	C

Figure 1.7 ACH Matrix Example—Potential Bank Robbery.

Question: Is the Wheeler's Motorcycle Gang a Criminal Network?
Alternative Hypotheses:

- A. The Wheeler's is a criminal network.
- B. The Wheeler's includes particular members who engage in criminal activity.
- C. The Wheeler's is associated with a known OMG that is engaged in criminal activity but is not known to engage in criminal activity itself.
- D. The Wheeler's is not a criminal network.

Evidence:
1. The Wheeler's has been organized for five years and includes about 45 members. Its leadership includes several individuals who have criminal records. (A/1)
2. The Wheeler's is alleged to be involved in the sale of methamphetamine across Southern Illinois. (B/2)
3. Several past members of the Wheeler's have "graduated" on to being members of the Hell's Angels local chapter; the Hell's Angels is an acknowledged outlaw motorcycle gang. (A/1)
4. Members of the Wheeler's include individuals who work in local government offices and local retail outlets. (A/1)
5. Some Wheeler's members have women associates who work in topless bars in nearby towns. These associates may also receive money in return for sexual favors. (B/2)
6. Wheeler's members have been seen at OMG "runs" associating with members of OMG members. (B/3)

Figure 1.8 Example of ACH in Law Enforcement—Potential Illegal Activity by Motorcycle Gang Members.

	H-A	H-B	H-C	H-D
Evidence 1	C	C	I	I
Evidence 2	C	C	I	I
Evidence 3	C	C	C	I
Evidence 4	I	n/a	C	C
Evidence 5	C	C	I	I
Evidence 6	C	C	C	I

Figure 1.9 ACH Matrix: Outlaw Motorcycle Gang.

a criminal network. The most likely hypothesis is B, that some Wheeler's members are involved in criminal activity, with one "not applicable" and no "inconsistents".

One final example of attempting to apply ACH in a law enforcement environment is in a homicide investigation. In Figures 1.10 and 1.11, respectively, the hypotheses and evidence in a homicide case are listed.

In this example, the evidence accumulated-to-date appears to be somewhat inconclusive, except to suggest that one of the six targets may be the perpetrator. Among them, targets B, D and F show more inconsistency among the evidence, with targets A, C, and E having capability and motive.

It should also be noted that the information being reviewed here may or may not be true, and thus cannot be relied upon to provide conclusive data.

Question: Who is the most likely suspect in the Victim X homicide?
Hypotheses:

1. Target A is the most likely perpetrator.
2. Target B is the most likely perpetrator.
3. Target C is the most likely perpetrator.
4. Target D is the most likely perpetrator.
5. Target E is the most likely perpetrator.
6. Target F is the most likely perpetrator.
7. None of the above is the most likely perpetrator.

Evidence:
1. Target A was seen near the scene of the murder of Victim X and had a motive to kill Victim X. (B2)
2. Target B told witnesses that he wanted to kill Victim X because he had stolen narcotics from him. (B2)
3. Targets C and D are members of an opposing gang to Victim X. (A2)
4. According to Target E, Victim X had participated in a drive-by killing of his cousin. (D4)
5. Target F was the last person to see Victim X alive; while Target B was on a trip to California at the time. (B2)
6. Targets A, C and E have 45 automatics, which was the type of gun used to kill Victim X. (A1)

Figure 1.10 Example of ACH in Law Enforcement—A Homicide Investigation.

	H-A	H-B	H-C	H-D	H-E	H-F	H-G
Evidence 1	C	I	I	I	I	I	I
Evidence 2	I	C	I	I	I	I	I
Evidence 3	I	I	C	C	I	I	I
Evidence 4	I	I	I	I	C	I	I
Evidence 5	I	I	I	I	I	C	I
Evidence 6	C	I	C	I	C	I	I

Figure 1.11 ACH Matrix: Homicide of Victim X.

V. Possible Use of ACH in Strategic Planning and Forming Recommendations

Another potential use of the ACH process involves considering alternative recommendations. Typically, analysts develop recommendations as an off-shoot of their conclusions. The recommendations are chosen based on a number of criteria, such as legal and resource constraints, possible consequences, the agency's mission, the political environment, attempts in the past, the probability of success, etc. (Fahlman & Peterson, 1997, p. 29). There are often multiple recommendations developed, with the possibility that managers will chose to implement some rather than others.

For example, in the bank robbery hypothesis above, it was determined that the most likely outcome was that the First National Bank would be the next target. The recommendations that might be made to follow this hypothesis might include in the following:

A. Increased patrol of the First National Bank area bysquad cars

B. Placing undercover operatives within the First National Bank to intervene in any robbery attempt

C. Educating First National Bank personnel about the proper response to a robbery attempt

D. Placement of surveillance personnel and snipers on the perimeter of the First National Bank area, to apprehend the robbers during their attempt

E. Limiting access to the First National Bank to individuals screened by security personnel

F. Closing the bank down during the crucial period when they are to receive the Federal Reserve transfer

G. Changing the scheduled Federal Reserve transfer

H. Investigating bank personnel to determine who might be providing inside information to others

Using a similar methodology, an analyst could take these eight possibilities and place them on top of a matrix. Criteria affecting decisions like those shown in Figure 1.12 could be listed along the left side of the matrix.

In this example, the recommendations are on the top and the constraints/decision criteria are on the left. It is observed that recommendations F and G are the least workable (i.e., closing down the bank and changing the schedule of federal reserve deposits) while recommendations B, D and H are the most likely options to be successful (i.e., employing undercover operatives, surveillance personnel and bank personnel for investigations). However, B is outside the department's expertise, D is outside its financial resources, and H is too lengthy to be effective. It might then be suggested that the department borrow outside expertise to put in an undercover operative, or that a special funding source be quickly found to support surveillance activities. The fact that the

1. **Departmental resources:** budget constraints would not allow day-long surveillance; other measures may be affordable.
2. **Agency mission:** city department is responsible for patrol and crime solving.
3. **Bank Cooperation:** The bank does not want any program enacted that will constrain customers and negatively impact business.
4. **Expertise:** There are no undercover operatives available that could pass as a bank employee
5. **Time Constraints:** next robbery due to occur soon.
6. **Possibility of Success:** most likely with surveillance, undercover, or finding informant.

Criteria	A	B	C	D	E	F	G	H
1. Resources	C	C	C	I	C	NA	NA	C
2. Mission	C	C	C	C	C	C	C	C
3. Bank Coop.	NA	C	C	C	I	I	I	C
4. Expertise	C	I	C	C	C	NA	NA	C
5. Time	C	C	C	C	C	NA	NA	I
6. Success	I	C	I	C	I	I	I	C

Figure 1.12 Example of Recommendations v. Criteria/ ACH-Type Matrix.

robberies have occurred at opening and closing periods should cut down on some of the surveillance time, and thus reduce costs.

VI. Conclusions

Heuer's Analysis of Competing Hypotheses (1999) is a methodology designed to assist CIA analysts in developing predictive hypotheses used to guide international policy. Through his writing, we can begin to understand this process. Building upon this foundation—and testing its application within law enforcement analysis—allows us to see how it can be utilized more broadly in crime analysis, investigative operations, and strategic planning.

Because of its efficacy, this methodology should be incorporated into both basic and advanced analytic courses. The application of this paradigm across the spectrum of law enforcement analysis should be further explored and documented.

Notes

(1) This volume is available through the Government Printing Office (email orders at *orders@gpo.gov* ISBN 1 929667–00–0) or through download at *www.odci.gov/csi*. It is permitted to be copied in whole or in part by non-governmental organizations for educational purposes.
(2) The refuting of hypotheses is key to solving logical puzzles. In typical puzzles, the material is often presented in the negative ("John did not visit Paris.") to eliminate possible answers, leaving the puzzle worker with the correct answer after the negatives have been eliminated.

(3) Heuer defines "satisficing" as choosing the first hypothesis that seems correct, rather than exploring all possibilities.

(4) In the matrix, a positive or plus sign means the hypothesis is likely based on that piece of evidence, while a negative or minus sign means it is less likely based on that evidence. A double minus indicates a very strong argument against this hypothesis; likewise, a double plus sign would indicate a very strong argument for a hypothesis. (Heuer, 1999, p. 102).

(5) The primary difference between the four level and the five level evaluation matrices is that in both reliability and validity scales, steps two and three are combined in the four level matrix.

(6) This example, while containing some actual data, is fictitious, being based on general knowledge gleaned through news reports and does not reflect any agency's known/actual hypotheses or evidence.

References

Fahlman, R. & Peterson, M.B. (1997). *International Association of Law Enforcement Intelligence Analysts Journal* (Volume 10). Lawrenceville, NJ: IALEIA, Inc.

Heuer, R.J. (1999). *The Psychology of Intelligence Analysis*. Washington, DC: U.S. Government Printing Office

Peterson, M.B., Morehouse, B., Wright, R., Eds. (2000). *Intelligence 2000: Revising the basic elements*. Lawrenceville, NJ: Law Enforcement Intelligence Unit

Source: *IALEIA*, 1 (2), 2003, 126–144, International Association of Law Enforcement Intelligence Analysts, Inc.

Thinking Activities

1. What role might you envision for yourself with respect to the field of white-collar crime research and investigation? In other words, would you prefer to serve as an academic researcher, intelligence analyst, investigator, prosecutor, or defense attorney? Why?

2. If given the option of performing tactical intelligence or strategic intelligence which option would you prefer? Why?

3. Practice conducting mock interviews using the questioning techniques discussed in this chapter. Be sure to use a variety of question types (i.e., narrative, comparison, leading, reaching back, and direct) and to observe each other's non-verbal communications as well as their verbal responses.

4. After learning about the skills and abilities required to execute the responsibilities of an intelligence analyst, describe why you would (or would not) succeed in this position. Which of your qualities could be assets to this type of job? Which qualities would be liabilities? For example, do you focus exclusively on the existence of one solution to a

problem, or can you be persuaded to consider alternate viewpoints? Are you able to challenge assumptions that you've acquired through your education, experience, family and culture? If so, how would you approach this task? Are you able to explore alternate interpretations of an issue or event? Why or why not?

10 Where Do We Go from Here?

The Future of White-Collar Crime

In the previous nine chapters that comprise the core of this text, you have been exposed to the concept of white-collar crime from a variety of perspectives. From the history of offenses such as forestalling, forgery, and fraud to the sophisticated techniques of modern-day hackers, crackers, and counterfeiters, much of the emphasis was placed on connecting the theories and typologies of white-collar crime. Yet this book also progressed beyond theory by providing students with a legal framework for white-collar offenses. Because of the pervasiveness of corruption within American society and its inextricable links to other forms of criminal behavior, a substantial portion of this work also focused on corruption control strategies within the United States. Lastly, we provided you with a foundation in investigative and analytical techniques germane to the field.

The book began with our assertion that white-collar crime is not simply a crime of the wealthy perpetrated by large, faceless corporations on an unknowing or uncaring public. Nor are such offenses restricted to the highest echelons of government. Indeed, while high-profile cases such as Enron and the S&L scandals of the 1980s attract the interest of media outlets, advocacy groups, and elected officials, it is the individual acts of identity theft, credit card fraud, and Internet phishing that we, as individuals, feel most personally when our bank accounts are depleted or our credit ratings are damaged. Former Speaker of the House Thomas "Tip" O'Neil once remarked that "all politics is local." Without question, the same can be said for white-collar crime.

You have also learned that white-collar offenses such as credit card fraud, computer hacking, and even cigarette tax stamp counterfeiting are not the seemingly insignificant crimes that many people believe them to be. Terrorist entities across the globe rely on financial crimes as a mechanism to fund their actions. For example, at the time of his December 2001 arrest in Illinois in connection with the September 11th attacks, suspected terrorist Ali al-Marri had more than 1,000 credit card numbers in his possession.[1] Similarly, Imam Samudra, who masterminded the 2002 Bali bombings, wrote an entire chapter in his autobiography entitled "Hacking, Why Not?" and urged his fellow jihadists to extend their Holy War to the Internet and to attack Western computer systems.[2] Lastly, William Billingslea, Senior Intelligence Analyst for the Bureau of Alcohol, Tobacco, and Firearms, estimates that millions of dollars have been funneled to terrorist organizations through cigarette tax stamp fraud.[3]

Whether we are examining corporate wrongdoing, large-scale incidents of public corruption, or individual illicit acts of fraud, forgery, and embezzlement, what actions should America's justice system and policymakers take to combat these activities? In order to provide appropriate recommendations for addressing these concerns, we must first discuss the future trends with respect to white-collar crime.

Trends and Patterns in White-Collar Crime

While the United States and other Western nations appear to have made progress in countering some forms of crime in the past twenty years, white-collar crime scholar Jay Albanese (1995) asserts that such forms of crime are cyclical. Indeed, we introduced this idea in the first chapter of this book. Thus, the important question that we should be asking is not, how do we curtail criminal activity, but rather, based on trends analysis, when is it likely to increase again? And, when it does increase, how can we best prepare to meet this challenge?

Even the most ardent positivist criminologist would have to concede that there appears to be a correlation between dramatic changes in socio-economic policy and changes in offense rates. These changes occur regardless of whether the tendency of the government leans towards increasing social spending (such as during the L.B. Johnson Administration and the "War on Poverty") or favors cutting public programs, as was the case during the Reagan era. In short, those periods in American history in which the most pronounced impacts on social and economic policies are implemented may also experience the greatest increases in criminal activity.

For example, despite former President Clinton's enthusiasm for social reform, his earliest efforts to pass comprehensive legislation were thwarted by Congress (e.g., his position on gays in the military and his stance on universal health care), and led to a gradual reduction in his efforts to implement socioeconomic policy reform. During this same period, the following trends were reported:

• According to the U.S. Department of Justice report, *Homicide Trends in the United States: 2000*, homicide levels during the Clinton presidency

Exhibit 10.1   President George W. Bush addresses corporate leaders on Wall Street in New York on the formation of the Corporate Fraud Task Force (CFTF) in July 2002. Designed to enhance Securities and Exchange Commission capabilities in combating corporate fraud, the CFTF has been widely criticized in rulings by the Second and Fifth Appellate Circuits for being overly aggressive in their zeal to prosecute potential white-collar criminals, and denying Constitutional protections to several defendants.

dropped to their lowest levels since prior to the L.B. Johnson Administration era in the 1960s.[4]

- The U.S. government's *Indicators of School Crime and Safety* (2002) report noted that "the total nonfatal victimization rate for students ages 12 through 18 generally declined between 1992 and 2000, from 144 per 1,000 students in 1992 to 72 per 1,000 in 2002."[5]
- The juvenile violent crime index dropped dramatically during the second half of Clinton's first presidency (i.e., post realization that significant efforts at social policy reform would be thwarted by the Republican-controlled congress)
- Despite a redesign of the National Crime Victimization Survey in 1992, which makes prior year comparisons more difficult, property crime rates continued to decline from 1993 through 2000.[6]

Based upon our analysis of the past eight years of the Bush Administration, it appears that President George W. Bush will not follow his father's

Exhibit 10.2 *The inextricable links between the energy sector, public officials, and alleged acts of corruption and fraud have led the authors of this book to call for a pre- and post-federal service moratorium on switching to and from public service to oil, gas, and power companies.*

legacy with respect to the lull in social and economic policy formulation that was reflective of the former George H.W. Bush Administration. For better or worse, the second President Bush has taken a consistently activist stance on issues ranging from national security (e.g., the USA Patriot Act of 2001 and the Homeland Security Act of 2002) to increased defense spending and diverting federal funds from public programs towards private faith-based initiatives. Thus, President Bush has set an agenda for social and economic reform. Based on the cyclical nature of criminality, it is anticipated that increased crime rates will accompany these broad, sweeping changes in policy. It is unknown whether these increases will manifest themselves through increased levels of violent crime, an upsurge in less reported, less sensationalized illegal acts such as financial crimes, or both.

To provide a simple historical modeling example, if we examine just the first few years of the twenty-first century, it appears that both incidents of violent and while-collar criminality are rising, as evidenced by the 2.1 percent increase in the National Crime Index from 2000 to 2001.[7] Incidents of total crimes reported to police also increased (i.e., murder rates rose 2.5 percent in 2001, and property crime rose 2.3 percent). More applicable to this text, Internet fraud complaints more than tripled during 2002, along with increases in identity theft since 2001. Internet hacker activity increased dramatically beginning in 2001, with computer crime losses costing businesses and individuals $78 million more in 2001 than in 2000.

Aside from the proliferation of information technology based crimes, incidents of corporate crime have also increased sharply since the beginning of the 21st century. From the collapse of Enron and ImClone in December of 2001 to the WorldCom and Adelphia scandals in March 2002, the direct and indirect consequences resulting from billion dollar losses on Wall Street and in professional investors' and retirees' accounts is only beginning to be realized.

Lastly, with respect to elite deviance, the two terms of the George W. Bush Administration have yielded resignations from several senior level officials

Exhibit 10.3 Law enforcement officials in Canada conduct a raid on a business in which money laundering was suspected. Fraud, forgery, and identity theft, and their connections to money laundering are also used as funding conduits for terrorism.

who were mired in controversy and indicted for federal crimes. For example, Harvey Pitt, former Chairman of the Securities and Exchange Commission who had been tasked with "cleaning up" corporate accounting and fraud, resigned in June of 2002 after it was determined that he had withheld important information that did not reflect favorably on the ethics of his preferred candidate for the lead position of the new Accounting Oversight Board. In December of 2002, Treasury Secretary Paul O'Neill stepped down amidst criticism that his "performance as treasury secretary had not inspired confidence."[8] O'Neill and White House Economic Advisor Lawrence Lindsey (who also resigned about the same time) both had ties to failed energy giant Enron. In March of 2003, Richard Perle, one of former Defense Secretary Donald Rumsfeld's key advisors, resigned from his post amidst questions about accepting a six-figure fee to advise the telecommunications company Global Crossing on a Defense Department matter.[9]

Questions have continued to surface about the seemingly overwhelming role that Halliburton has played in the U.S. occupation of Iraq. Vice President Dick Cheney previously served as CEO of Halliburton. In addition, Ray Hunt, Chairman of Hunt Oil who is currently partnering with Halliburton on a $1.45 billion (US) natural gas development project in Peru strongly endorsed by the Bush Administration, is a longtime friend and political campaign financial supporter of President Bush.

The Bush Administration's official announcement in April 2003 that the Defense Department would establish an advisory board of former U.S. oil industry executives to control the Iraqi oil industry followed months of closed-door collective government and corporate strategic group planning events held even prior to the U.N. Weapons Inspectors official reports on Iraqi disarmament or the official start of the war. These statements contradict former White House Press Secretary Ari Fleisher's comments in which he remarked that "the only interest that the United States has in the region is furthering the cause of peace and stability, not [Iraq's] ability to generate oil."[10] Philip Carroll, former CEO of Shell Oil Company, was selected to serve as the head of the new Iraqi oil board. Carroll previously ran Fluor Construction Corporation, the Pasadena, California-based company whose shares rose 15 percent when it was announced that his firm would play a significant role in the rebuilding of Iraq at the close of the war.

These incidents, coupled with the criminal convictions of "Scooter" Libby, Larry Franklin, David Safavian, and Jack Abramoff—all of whom were close associates of the president—suggest that the Bush Administration will be recorded for posterity as substantially challenged in addressing the issue of elite deviance.

Recommendations for Social Change

Based on this chapter's earlier discussion on the cyclical nature of criminality, it appears that America is confronting another surge in incidents of white-collar crime. The George W. Bush Administration is clearly one that advocates activism with respect to the formulation of social and economic policy. Reported property crime has continued to rise and the use of information technology to engage in acts fraud and identity theft has soared. Corporate scandal has amassed financial harm on the American economy rivaled perhaps only by savings and loan scandals of the 1980s. Issues of elite deviance also continue to doggedly pursue public officials at all levels of government, and in both major political parties.

Now that we have identified that we are at the pinnacle of the cycle, is there anything we can do to stop it? Or, must we simply wait for the pattern to reverse itself? Unfortunately, the latter is not a viable option given the pronounced links between white-collar crime and acts of international terrorism discussed throughout this text. If America fails to take action, the lives of innocent people around the world may be endangered. However, we must also guard against an overly all-encompassing approach to investigation and prosecution in order to preserve and maintain our freedom.

While there is no panacea with respect to curtailing today's white-collar crime, we do believe it is possible to reduce its impact, at least until the crime cycle changes direction. Our suggestions, which we refer to as the five *recommendations for social change* are as follows:

1. *Take white-collar crime seriously:* For years, the United States, including its media, government officials, academicians, and citizenry have practically ignored the inherent value in studying white-collar criminality, investigating crimes such as access device fraud and check forgery, and prosecuting persons engaged in embezzlement, counterfeiting, and other consumption-oriented offenses. The tragic events of September 11, 2001, coupled with marked increases in identity theft and computer crimes, clearly indicate how seemingly "insignificant" financial crimes may be related to funding terrorist activities or other *mala in se* activities. While there is always a need to conduct additional research on topics such as serial murder profiling, the academic and popular literature base in this area is far more extensive than it is for white-collar crime research. Only through scholarship will the field continue to expand, thus allowing incidents to be studied in greater depth. In the face of multi-billion dollar big pharma fraud, the sub-prime real estate crisis, and the next yet-to-be-identified scandal, the financial health of America may be inextricably linked to our ability to investigate with-collar crime from both practical and academic perspectives.

2. *Break the corporate–state corruption paradigm:* Unholy alliances between big businesses and corrupt government officials have permeated the American political system since at least the era of the Teapot Dome Scandal. Major corporations such as Halliburton have enjoyed extraordinarily lucrative deals in both Democratic (e.g., L.B. Johnson) and Republican (e.g., G.W. Bush) presidential administrations for nearly half a century. Far too many cabinet officials have extensive ties to the energy (e.g., natural gas, oil, electric, nuclear, and hydroelectric power) and telecommunications sectors. In an effort to combat such relationships, prospective senior level employees of the executive branch should be required to undergo a two-year separation period from the energy or telecommunications sectors prior to their tenure in public service, and should not be permitted to work directly or indirectly for these organizations, or their lobbying interests, for at least five years following their departure from public office.

Spouses and close relatives of these public officials should not be permitted to hold positions in any energy or telecommunications sector corporation or their lobbying interests during the incumbent's term of office, and for at least five years thereafter. Lastly, neither the public official nor any member of his or her family should be allowed to hold any financial interests in any energy or telecommunications-related entity during the incumbent's term of office or for at least five years thereafter.

Financial and personal interest disclosure statements attesting to each of these conditions should be completed prior to assuming office, and updated each year for the five years following the employee's departure from government service. With respect to the relationship between the legislative branch and the energy and telecommunications sectors, it is anticipated that recent revisions to campaign financing laws, coupled with public awareness of high-profile cases such as Enron and World-Com, may ultimately improve perceived and actual improprieties in this area.

3. *Remember Strain Theory:* As discussed in Chapter 6 of this book, Merton's Theory of Social Strain (1938) bears out most appropriately for individual white-collar offenders (e.g., embezzlers, forgers, counterfeiters, etc.) who might engage in such acts as a means to obtain goods and services that cannot be obtained legitimately. Given the increase in casual currency counterfeiting and individual Internet-related crimes, significant public pressure should be placed on the supply side of the American economy to curtail hard-target marketing, particularly in demographics unlikely to possess legitimate means to purchase them, such as children and areas of low-socioeconomic status. Sending out pre-approved credit card offers to communities with substantial rates of unemployment, or marketing expensive products to juveniles and young

adults who do not have the requisite level of income necessary to purchase such commodities should be avoided, lest we see the unintended consequence of increasing rates of property crime.

4. *Employ non-traditional analytical techniques:* While a deductive methodology may prove useful in investigating a homicide, starting with a hypothesis on a money laundering case will, at best, likely result in nabbing only one small element of a large, organized, criminal network. Far too often, the investigator selects the "target" long before much of the essential data are available for analysis. By avoiding the deductive approach in favor of an inductive methodology, seemingly unrelated events may form the basis for an effective and cohesive investigative strategy. Moreover, by using information technology-based link analysis and data visualization tools such as those mentioned earlier in this book, the analyst may uncover new relationships that warrant additional investigative attention. Lastly, applying mathematical concepts, such as Nash's Equilibrium or other forms of participatory game theory to law enforcement integrity testing may result in the formulation of new policies and procedures to prevent collusion on the part of government employees and the criminal element they have sworn to apprehend.

5. *Beware of the all encompassing vision of crime control:* As a free and open society committed to the preservation of individual liberties, America must ensure that due process remains the cornerstone of its legal system. Legislation such as the *USA Patriot Act of 2001* must be thoroughly examined to ensure such laws do not present grave risks to our Fourth Amendment protections against unreasonable search and seizure. In addition, broad interpretations of asset forfeiture, particularly when related to the seizure of property in matters related to financial crimes possibly committed as a conduit for funding terrorist activities, should be heavily scrutinized for Constitutionality. Under no circumstances should investigative agencies focus on seizing funds or equipment for possible agency use as a pretext for conducting investigative operations. The rights of Americans afforded through the U.S. Constitution, especially the inalienable right of due process of law, must be upheld at all costs even if in doing so safety and security are diminished, or white-collar crime investigations remain unclosed. Moreover, execution of criminal sanctions for white-collar offenses may prove limited at best; as evidenced by the lack of prosecutions-to-date under section 802 of the Sarbanes-Oxley Act.

While the five recommendations for social change contained in this chapter will not eliminate white-collar crime, they will likely cushion the impact of such incidents during those times when we are at the top of the pattern. Moreover, these suggestions will also have the benefit of expanding the scholarly literature in the field, something that is essential if we are to understand why white-collar crime occurs, and what may be done to curtail such acts. Criminologist Edwin Sutherland, the "father" of white-collar crime theory, remarked that "the sentimental reaction toward a particular white-collar crime is certainly different from that toward some other crimes."[11] Only through thoughtful and scholarly research, serious investigative efforts, and a steadfast commitment to change public opinion with respect to the adverse impact of white-collar crimes on American society can we truly hope to reduce the impact of "Today's White-Collar Crime" for ourselves and our future generations.

Chapter Summary

Chapter 10, the final chapter of this text, identified the cyclical nature of crime and likely present day and future trends in white-collar criminality. The chapter also offered five recommendations for slowing the flow of white-collar crime in America, including placing a critical value on white-collar crime research and investigations; implementing stringent regulations on transitioning to and from senior executive branch positions into the energy sector and telecommunications-related positions or allied occupations; limiting hard-target marketing whenever possible; utilizing inductive research methodologies, data visualization techniques, and participatory game theories in white-collar crime intelligence work; and lastly, upholding the rule of law.

ADAPTED READINGS

Reading 10–1: William Billingslea, *Illicit Cigarette Trafficking and the Funding of Terrorism* (Bureau of Alcohol, Tobacco, Firearms, and Explosives, Washington D.C.)

> *Although the study of white-collar crime is certainly worthy of study in its own right, the nexus between illicit forms of activity such as fraud, forgery, counterfeiting, money laundering and terrorism has validated its criticality in 21st Century Criminology. In this article, author William Billingslea expertly connects the social and legal themes presented in Chapters 7 and 8 of this book via the issue of illicit cigarette trafficking and its relationship to funding terrorism.*

Since the dawn of terrorism, procuring finances sufficient to sustain terror operations has been a priority for terrorists. The illicit sale of cigarettes and other commodities by terrorist groups and their supporters has become a crucial part of their funding activities.

Raising the tax on cigarettes widens the difference between the wholesale price and the retail price of the product and inadvertently creates opportunity for traffickers, who evade the tax and gain the profits. Today cigarette traffickers can make as much as $60 per carton of cigarettes sold illicitly.

Because of the immense profits in the illicit cigarette trade, as well as the potentially low penalties for getting caught, illicit cigarette trafficking now rivals drug trafficking as the method of choice to fill the bank accounts of terrorists and terrorist groups. Investigators have discovered that traffickers in the United States and the United Kingdom are providing material support to the Hezbollah and the Real IRA (RIRA), among other terrorist groups. In addition, law enforcement research indicates that groups tied to al Qaeda, Hamas, PKK (the Kurdish Workers Party), and Islamic Jihad (both Egyptian and Palestinian) are involved in the illicit trafficking of cigarettes.

Background and History

The trafficking of cigarettes by terrorists and their sympathizers has been going on worldwide since the mid-1990s, and the last four years have seen a sudden increase in trafficking. The trafficking schemes provide the terrorist groups with millions of dollars annually, which fund the purchasing of firearms and explosives to use against the United States, its allies, and other targets.

Investigations have revealed that the terrorist groups work with organized crime groups as well as with the international drug trafficking organizations. Organized crime and drug trafficking organizations already have established trafficking routes, as well as business contacts for the transfer of the commodity for profit. The Bureau of Alcohol, Tobacco, Firearms, and Explosives (ATF) have found that Russian, Armenian, Ukrainian, Chinese, Taiwanese, and Middle Eastern (mainly Pakistani, Lebanese, and Syrian) organized crime groups are highly involved in the trafficking of contraband and counterfeit cigarettes and counterfeit tax stamps for profit.

Known and suspected Hezbollah and Hamas members have established front companies and legitimate businesses in the cigarette trade in Central and South America. Indications from law enforcement sources are that these companies traffic in contraband and counterfeit cigarettes and tax stamps for profit and then use the proceeds to purchase arms and ammunition.

Using consumables, specifically cigarettes and gasoline, groups that are funding terrorism not only place a legal commodity into an illegal market system but also commit money laundering, fraud (both consumer and business), and tax evasion. The key is that these traffickers are not using the illicitly obtained funds for personal gain but are actually providing the funds as direct support to specific groups that espouse their political or ideological agenda.

Terrorist Group Involvement

The involvement of terrorist groups and their support personnel in the illicit movement of consumables began in the 1980s. The activities of the business people in the Middle East and Asia became a model in how to succeed in making money when most normal government or civil operations in these regions had become impotent or nonexistent. Terrorist groups and terrorist support networks observed how in uncertain or extreme times business people were still making money and had adapted to the cultural changes and hardships.

This was evident in the gold souks in Beirut, Lebanon, and the ad hoc gasoline service stations established along major lines of communication by entrepreneurs. These ad hoc businesses operated out of the back of vehicles and houses, and these business people were flourishing and expanding their hastily established operations. The primary reason they were so successful was that they were providing needed and luxury items to the average consumer after the economic system in the region had basically collapsed due to conflict or natural disaster. These business people were so resourceful it has been reported they were actually tunneling under the Israeli defense lines into the Gaza Strip bringing in gold and cigarettes from Egypt.(1)

Selling their goods, these businessmen were evading import duties and sales and use taxes. In addition to the tax evasion, the business people were committing fraud by offering counterfeit products and providing products that had been obtained illegally for sale at cheaper prices, as well as doctoring products.

This type of system was easily adaptable to most regions of the world. It became a more important method of obtaining funds as countries began to raise the taxes levied on consumables to overcome budget deficits of the late 1980s and early 1990s. At the same time, governments in Europe and North America raised the taxes levied against tobacco products and alcohol in hopes of reducing their use. Although initially this did lower the demand for these items, it also made illicit trafficking more profitable. Entrepreneurs began to establish front companies and offshore businesses in Cyprus, Gibraltar, the Isle of Man and the Isle of Wight in the United Kingdom, and Bermuda and the Bahamas in the Caribbean. These businesses were established for the sole purpose of moving normally legal commodities (cigarettes, alcohol, and gasoline) through illicit channels to avoid the taxes and import duties associated with them.

Illicit Cigarette Trafficking around the World

In Europe: The IRA was one of the first groups to begin using cigarettes to fund their activities. Investigations by the Gardaí (Irish National Police), the Royal Ulster Constabulary (RUC), Scotland Yard, and U.K. Customs have led to seizures of cigarettes worth millions of dollars, as well as arms and explosives associated with the cigarette trafficking schemes. The IRA involvement in the illicit cigarette trade was due to the rise in taxes on cigarettes in the United Kingdom, Ireland, and most of northern Europe. By illicitly trafficking in cigarettes, and thereby avoiding the taxes and import duties, the IRA would be able to make an enormous profit. Current estimates place the amount of money made from the trafficking of illicit cigarettes by the three primary factions of the IRA, the Provisional IRA, Real IRA, and the Continuity IRA, at more than $100 million in just the past five years. According to police figures, the Provisional IRA is the biggest fundraiser generating $8.3 million to $13.2 million annually. This is compared to the Real IRA, which raises $8.3 million annually, as well as the Loyalist Volunteer Force, which raises $3.3 million and the Ulster Volunteer Force (UVF), which raises $2.5 million annually. A senior police officer in Northern Ireland stated that the Real IRA now resembles a criminal organization that sometimes carries out acts of terrorism rather than a terrorist group that has to dabble in crime.(2)

In keeping with a current trend in terrorist financing, dissident Irish republicans have joined forces with criminals in Britain to raise millions of dollars through cigarette trafficking and the sale of illegal fuel. According to British police information, the Real IRA has crossed the Irish Sea to Great Britain to expand their illicit operations. A report from a British House of Commons select committee stated that approximately $30 million was raised annually by paramilitaries on both sides of the sectarian violence in Northern Ireland.

A British Minister of Parliament was reported as claiming that an Irish charity worker, employed to distribute aid in war-ravaged Croatia, was secretly setting up contacts with weapons smugglers in the Balkans.(3) The charity worker had been known to Garda intelligence for 10 years prior to his post with the charity Irish Aid. The Minister of Parliament went on to state that the charity worker's employment in the Balkans occurred some 10 years after Garda intelligence had identified him as the leader of the Continuity IRA. The deals established in Croatia were an exchange of funds acquired from trafficking in illicit cigarettes for arms and ammunition.

In the Middle East: The Kurdish Workers Party (PKK) is involved in the trafficking of contraband cigarettes and tax stamps. In one particular instance in 2000, the Turkish military and Turkish federal police conducted a raid at a PKK safe house, which was suspected of actually being one of the PKK headquarters for eastern Turkey. Initially, the Turkish authorities were expecting to find caches of arms, ammunition, and explosives. But the authorities actually found a gravure printing press for producing counterfeit tax stamps and other forged documentation.

The European Union commission on cigarette smuggling named the PKK as a "Kurdish Terror Network" regarding the group's involvement in the illicit trafficking of cigarettes.(4) The EU Commission report states the PKK made large sums of money marketing smuggled U.S. cigarettes into Iraq across the Turkish border. The EU also alleges that the PKK has been smuggling American brand cigarettes into Iraq, where Saddam Hussein's son Uday would then control the cigarettes. Reports indicate that Saddam Hussein made as much as $2.7 billion annually after 1991 on the cigarette and oil smuggling business.

Other terrorist organizations that have turned to illicit cigarette trafficking to provide funding are Hezbollah, Hamas, Islamic Jihad, and al Qaeda. Law enforcement research indicates that people connected to al Qaeda are involved in moving contraband cigarettes and counterfeit tax stamps throughout the United States and Europe. Al Qaeda sleeper cells establish legitimate businesses and move the illicit product through the normal domestic market, effectively hiding their operations in plain sight.

In the United States: An ATF investigation initiated in 1996 with the Iredell Sheriff's Department in North Carolina illustrates the illicit cigarette trafficking in the United States. This case involved a cigarette trafficking scheme in North Carolina, a low tax state, from which millions of dollars' worth of cigarettes were smuggled to Michigan, a high tax state. The defendants, 25 in all, were moving cigarettes by rental vehicles from Charlotte to Detroit to sell on the streets. Proceeds were then transferred by wire and by courier to bank accounts in Beirut, Lebanon. Portions of the proceeds were used to provide material support to the Hezbollah international terrorist organization in Lebanon. In 2001, a federal grand jury in Charlotte indicted the 25 persons for money laundering, cigarette trafficking, conspiracy, and immigration violations. To date, 20 defendants have been convicted for violations of the Contraband Cigarette Trafficking Act (CCTA), conspiracy, money laundering, and immigration violations. In addition, three of those defendants were found guilty of providing material support to a terrorist organization (Hezbollah). Five defendants remain fugitives. This investigation resulted in seizures of cigarettes, real property, and currency worth close to $2 million dollars.

In another investigation into the trafficking of contraband cigarettes prior to the traumatic events of September 11, 2001, ATF discovered that a convicted cigarette trafficker was tied directly to Hamas. During the execution of search and arrest warrants, the suspect stated, when asked about the identity of a person in his residence, that the man was his cousin and that he was in Hamas, and that he had come to the United States to escape from the Israelis.

On the Internet: In addition to the interstate and international trafficking of illicit cigarettes for profit, research indicates that the terrorist groups are beginning to get involved in the Internet sales of cigarettes. The Internet is a busy marketplace, and operating an Internet site doesn't require sellers to establish a business within the United States or Europe. People or groups that operate Internet-based cigarette sales can set up operations in places such as Gibraltar or the Colon Free Trade Zone and sell their contraband cigarettes in any state within the United States or any country in the world without actually having to be present in the state or country. Internet sales of cigarettes are robbing states of millions of dollars annually. Current laws are not designed specifically to regulate the Internet sales of cigarettes. The violation of the current law (known as the Jenkins Act) is a misdemeanor and is difficult to prosecute in a federal court when other criminal charges are not viable.

Economics of Illicit Cigarette Trafficking

Just what are the economics associated with terrorist involvement in the trafficking of illicit cigarettes? First, of course, are the funds that are lost by the states and the federal government due to the trafficking. It is estimated by state and federal tax authorities that by the year 2005, the combined state losses due to illicit cigarette trafficking could reach into the billions of dollars. This is critical in today's economy, when the majority of states are experiencing record deficits and are looking to raise the taxes on cigarettes to supplement their budget shortfalls.

Second, the monetary support gained by the terrorist groups from the trafficking can cause much more than fiscal harm to the United States and its allies. With the funds received from the trafficking of illicit cigarettes, terrorist groups can purchase more arms, ammunition and explosives and use them against the United States and its interests, putting U.S. citizens at risk, as well as providing for a climate of fear around the world. Law enforcement intelligence, as well as credible open source information points to a definite benefit to terrorist groups from the illicit sale of tobacco.

To fully understand how terrorist funding is being supported by illicit cigarette trafficking it is necessary to fully understand the methodologies involved, as well as the various schemes used to traffic the illicit cigarettes. In addition, to fully combat the growing problem of illicit cigarette trafficking, law enforcement must be proactive in its investigations, including recognizing the current and future trends regarding illicit cigarette trafficking.

Methodology

A key to the current methodology of the terrorist groups and people that provide them with material support is provided in the earlier reported statement by a senior police officer from Northern Ireland. He said the Real IRA is "looking more and more like an organized crime group that also conducts terrorist acts, rather than a terrorist group that conducts criminal acts." This statement is key because it reveals the new face of terrorism.

Terrorist groups, on the whole, have changed their face within the past decade. With the integration of world markets and the push for a more equal global trading system, terrorist groups have also shifted their focus to infiltrate the ever expanding global trade and world markets. The new face of terrorism does not include the traditional organizations or enterprises of the past. The new face is totally different. It is more goal-oriented, and it has no problem integrating perfectly legal enterprises with criminal or illicit enterprises.

T. R. Young stated that organized crime is a growth industry in the United States. His view is that organized crime constitutes between 10 percent and 25 percent of the gross national product. (5) With these figures, it is easy to understand why terrorist groups are beginning to act and operate in ways that are strikingly similar to organized crime. Organized crime's influence in world politics, world trade, and arms proliferation has grown tenfold since the opening up of Eastern Europe. It is no wonder many terrorist groups are working practically hand-in-hand with organized crime in order to obtain material and financial support for their organizations.

In many aspects the material support to terrorist organizations is based upon ethnic or cultural connections. With this in mind, both Europe and North America have seen a rise in immigrant involvement in criminal acts, including money laundering and fraud. Europe is having an extremely difficult time combating the amount of crime perpetrated by Albanian, Asian, and Russian organized criminal groups. The United States, although experiencing a decline in traditional organized crime groups such as the La Cosa Nostra, has seen a large rise in the amount of organized criminal groups ethnically tied to the Middle East and North Africa.

Establishment of Illicit Operations

How then do these "businesspersons" establish themselves in the United States? What allows them not only to succeed but also to expand their operations?

The general order of establishment is for the "family" to emigrate from their homeland singly but as part of a line of emigrants. They eventually become immigrants in Europe and North America and establish themselves and their family in retail and wholesale business ventures. In order to establish the business operations in the United States, the head of the family will usually immigrate to establish a retail sales or import-export trade business. The one uncompromising rule in the initial establishment is that it must be a male, which is the cultural norm for populations residing in southeast and southwest Asia and the Middle East. While there may be members who are not directly tied to the family, the norm is for family members to actually operate the business. In the case of the Middle Eastern criminal enterprises, the family will generally include fathers, sons, male cousins, uncles, and brothers.

The Schemes

There are various schemes used to traffic in illicit cigarettes. Some of the more obvious or most common schemes are trafficking from a low-tax state to a high-tax state, Internet and mail order sales, theft and hijacking, import-export operations, and counterfeiting cigarettes and tax stamps. Many of these schemes are used domestically and internationally and are often used in conjunction with other schemes. It's also not unusual for criminals to switch back and forth among schemes in an attempt to evade law enforcement scrutiny.

These are the trafficking schemes of choice among terrorist groups and the people that support them. The groups know it is important to be flexible. More than one scheme can be used depending on several factors including market forces and law enforcement scrutiny. Under pressure or scrutiny, it is common for the groups to turn to other crime or go underground. Once they come under scrutiny for cigarette trafficking, they will change to something else, such as gasoline fraud, food stamp fraud, and psuedoephedrine trafficking.

The sources of the illicit cigarettes come from several areas. They come from low-tax states, from a foreign free trade zone, from a customs bonded warehouse, from certain Native American reservations, from stolen or hijacked shipments, and from manufacturers of counterfeit cigarettes overseas.

Trends

Estimates from the various state tax officials show a decline of approximately $1.4 billion in revenue collection due to illicit cigarette trafficking. This figure, which is a 2001 estimate, shows just how lucrative cigarettes have become. Many states are reporting revenue losses; in 2001 nine states' combined loss was approximately $850 million. An IRS study has shown that, combined, states show over $1 billion in losses to non-taxed sales of cigarettes. To compound the problem, states continue to raise cigarette taxes as an easy way to raise needed revenue.

Just as with the organized crime groups of the past, terrorist organizations are drawn to illicit cigarette trafficking due to the possibility of large profits for little work. With the variations in state taxes levied on a pack of cigarettes nationwide, the illicit trafficker can make millions of dollars a year.

Indications are that terrorist involvement in illicit cigarette trafficking will grow. Each state that raises its cigarette taxes is a new prospect for illicit profits gained by trafficking in cigarettes.

In addition, the current relationship between terrorist groups and criminal groups will continue to grow. With the amount of profits obtained through illicit cigarette trafficking both types of organizations can benefit. This problem will not simply go away. The organizations and support mechanisms are fully entrenched in illicit cigarette trafficking operations. In some instances, the trafficking of illicit cigarettes are their only known means of support.

Notes

(1) Stephen Farrell, "Smugglers' Tunnels Undermine the Israeli Security Cordon," *The Times* (London), May 20, 2002.

(2) "Ulster Cigarette Smuggling Shock," *Belfast Telegraph* (Belfast, Northern Ireland), December 21, 2000.

(3) Donna Carton, "*Aid Worker Used Balkan UP Weapons Pipeline for Mercy Mission to Set Rebel IRA Terrorists,*" *Sunday Mirror* (London), December 17, 2000.

(4) "The PKK Is a Terrorist Organization," *Turkish Press Summary*, March 27, 2002.

(5) T. R. Young, Socgrad Mini-lectures, The Red Feather Institute, September 1999, http://www.rf-institute.com/lectures/047techcrm3.htm.

Source: *The Police Chief*, vol. 71, no. 2, February 2004. Copyright held by the International Association of Chiefs of Police, 515 North Washington Street, Alexandria, VA 22314 USA.

Reading 10–2: Abbe David Lowell and Kathryn C. Arnold, *Corporate Crime after 2000: A New Law Enforcement Challenge or Déjà vu?*

One of the major themes of this text has been the cyclical nature of white-collar crime. In other words, there are identifiable trends and patterns with respect to offenders and offenses that appear to emerge, regardless of the legal strategy used to combat fraud, embezzlement, and other non-violent illicit activities. In this final reading in your text, author Kathryn Arnold addresses the various legal strategies used by lawmakers and the courts in an effort to address the challenge of white-collar crime in twenty-first-century America. Will these new tactics work, or are they simply part of a pattern of criminal behavior that ebbs and flows with the tide of human history?

White-collar crime is in vogue. Although there are investigations and prosecutions throughout the country at any given time in which individuals and businesses are charged with corporate wrongdoing, 2002 and 2003 will likely be high-water marks for such cases. The reasons for the increase are obvious. Police and prosecutors respond most quickly when there are victims of criminal wrongdoing—the greater the harm and the greater the number of victims, the greater the priority given by law enforcement. When businesses flourish, profits are high, unemployment is low, and bankruptcies are sporadic, the conduct of businesses (including misconduct) is masked by economic success. Conversely, when companies fail, markets drop, layoffs are widespread, and Chapter 11 becomes common, the conduct which caused or contributed to such failures are examined closely under the law enforcement microscope. This is such an era. Corporate crime has become a central topic on the business pages, cable channels, in periodicals, and throughout the media.

Two-thousand two was the year Americans became versed in the failures that surrounded companies such as Enron Corporation, WorldCom, Inc., Adelphia Communications Corporation, Imclone Systems Inc., and Tyco International, Ltd. In 2003, the trend has continued as there are investigations concerning the financial dealings of AOL-Time Warner, Healthsouth Corp. and Tenet Healthcare, to name just a few.

It may seem as if 2002 was the most prolific era for investigations following business failures, but that is not the case. About a decade ago, there was a flurry of legislative and judicial activity concerning the failures of banks and savings and loans institutions throughout the nation. There are a number of similarities between the financial institutions crisis of a decade past and the current phenomenon of corporate failures. In both eras, regulators and law enforcement officials were criticized for being too lax before the events occurred. Then and now, elected officials incorporated the events into a dominant theme in the political landscape. Once the respective failures occurred, the law enforcement responses in both the financial institutions era and the current onslaught of corporate scandals has been massive, with some criticism that the response is an attempt to compensate for pre-failure neglect.

With respect to law enforcement's efforts now as during the Savings and Loan crisis, the question should be asked: Has the law enforcement response been effective or excessive in addressing the problem de jour? In considering that question, there is one large difference in the two different eras of business scandal and failure—the possibility of recovery for the victims of wrongdoing. Many of those adversely affected by bank and savings and loan failures enjoyed government-insured accounts and had the chance to recover the sums lost. With respect to business failures and market collapses today, there is no such insurance; the return to investors and others damaged by the business failures may be pennies on the dollar, if anything. This potential for unreimbursed loss has caused a great call for action by this era's victims, and perhaps an even greater response by law enforcement.

The impact of the current era of business failures has motivated all branches of government to react. Congress, which feels the pulse of public opinion most quickly, jumped into the fray with a new omnibus securities law containing a variety of new laws to address business crime. In addition, courts have been retooling the definition of "intent," perhaps the most essential ingredient in white collar crime charges, at the urging of prosecutors seeking a means to compel officials to answer for the actions of their businesses. Finally, agency regulators, prosecutors, and even private attorneys once again found creative avenues in all legal forums—administrative agencies, the courts, and licensing procedures—to seek redress from alleged wrongs and, in so doing, breathed new life into the law and practice of "parallel proceedings." This essay will focus on these three phenomena of the law enforcement reaction to the most recent explosion of business crime.

I. Congress Provides New Tools and Penalties for Business Crimes: Were They Necessary?

Before 2002 began, business crime was prosecuted under a number of statutes and theories, including conspiracy, Securities Exchange Act violations, fraud, mail fraud, wire fraud, and RICO. Alone or in combination, these statutes provided for penalties that could send wrongdoers to prison for over twenty years and could fine offenders millions of dollars. Nevertheless, because of the high profile nature of the business crisis and the political response, Congress legislated to specifically address such wrongdoing and to demonstrate its responsiveness to the "new" problem. To understand how quickly the pendulum in Congress can swing, consider the fact that in April 2002 the House of Representatives, supported by the Administration, rejected increasing prison sentences for mail and wire fraud from five-to ten-year maximums.(1) Only a few months later, when the Senate and President Bush sought an increase to ten-year maximums, the House of Representatives doubled the suggestion to pass a maximum penalty of twenty years.

This was precisely the reaction in the 1980s when the financial institutions crisis led to, among other things, enactment of the Financial Institutions Reform, Recovery and Enforcement Act of 1989 (FIRREA).(2) Before banks and S&Ls failed, similar statutes allowed prosecutors to bring indictments with charges ranging from conspiracy to provision of false information to lending institutions.(3) FIRREA made a number of changes to the law enforcement scheme which had the effect of treating alleged crimes associated with the financial institution as more egregious than many other federal alternatives. In this last era of greater attention to corporate (in that case financial institutions) crime, Congress reacted in a number of areas. It enacted new provisions to lengthen the statute of limitations to ten years for bringing numerous charges under FIRREA, including a mail and wire fraud offense that "affects a financial institution" when the statute of limitations remained five years for most other federal cases.(4) Similarly, the maximum penalty for certain bank offenses (i.e., wire fraud affecting a financial institution) was increased to thirty years(5) when a person charged with an equally serious federal offense (i.e., wire fraud affecting a health care provider) could receive a maximum of only five.(6) Furthermore, FIRREA made it a crime, in certain circumstances, for an officer of a financial institution to notify a customer that a grand jury subpoena for records had been served(7) although officials at other institutions (e.g., insurance companies, health care providers, brokerage houses) could notify the same customer of a subpoena with no penalty. The legislative response to the perceived need for additional law enforcement measures in the savings and loan crisis left a number of these anomalies.

Consequently, before Congress acted again in the midst of another corporate crime crisis, one question that should have been studied seems to have been neglected: was there any wrongdoing brought after FIRREA that could not have been charged or punished as severely before? The answer could have instructed Congress in 2002 of whether any changes in criminal law were actually necessary and what those changes might be. Nevertheless, the congressional reaction to the business crisis proceeded quickly, making more changes than a decade ago. No sooner than the first announcements of Enron's bankruptcy occurred and the WorldCom scandal developed, a public official declared the need for tougher and increased regulations and penalties. (8) Then, as before, the news media added their voices to the debate on editorial pages endorsing the concept of the need for more and stronger laws. (9)

A. *The Sarbanes-Oxley Act of 2002*

As a result of this call for tougher regulation and penalties, Congress passed the Sarbanes-Oxley Act of 2002 ("SOA"), (10) the securities equivalent to FIR-REA. There are numerous provisions in the SOA that will change the landscape of securities transactions throughout the country. New regulatory oversight entities, requirements of corporate disclosures, and parameters for accounting procedures all modified existing securities rules and regulations. Among the statute's provisions, however, are a number of modifications that specifically concern criminal law and procedure. Title VIII of SOA is separately titled the "Corporate and Criminal Fraud Accountability Act of 2002" and Title IX of SOA is entitled "White Collar Crimes Penalty Enhancement Act of 2002." (11)

As FIRREA did a decade ago, the new provisions at times incorporate changes to existing statutes or rules that apply in any investigative context, while other provisions have been drafted to apply only in securities cases, again resulting in a congressional "pronouncement" that securities law violations (like financial institutions violations a decade ago) will be treated as more "serious" than other federal crimes. As the SOA's new criminal provisions are applied in cases, the results will help determine whether these provisions were really needed or whether they were a cosmetic change to existing law enforcement capabilities. While there are more than a half-dozen changes to the criminal law in the SOA, they can generally be divided into those which: (i) create a new substantive offense for securities offenses; (ii) address the issue of obstruction of justice; or (iii) increase maximum penalties for existing and new offenses.

1. *New Substantive Offense for Securities Offenses*

From an initial reading of the new law, what might appear to be the most significant change is the creation of a new general securities fraud statute. This new provision, 18 U.S.C. § 1348, entitled "Securities Fraud", tracks the language of the general bank fraud statute that was passed after the financial institutions crisis a decade ago. (12) Just as banking crimes had been prosecuted before the passage of FIRREA, so too securities fraud cases had been addressed by the laws that existed before the SOA. Securities fraud, for example, was punishable under the Securities Exchange Act of 1934 (13) for decades. The new law, on its face, eliminates some of the older statute's requirements for some of the elements of a crime, with the intent of making it easier for prosecutors to obtain convictions. Specifically, SOA's provision for "securities fraud" does not require that the violation be "willful" or that a violation be "in connection with the purchase or sale" of a security. Instead of having to show that a defendant's actions were "willful," § 1348 requires only that a defendant "knowingly" execute or attempt to execute the alleged scheme to defraud.

Relieving a prosecutor of the requirement to prove "willfulness" in white collar cases is a significant reduction of proof. "Willfulness" in a criminal statute requires that the government prove (beyond a reasonable doubt) that the defendant took action knowing that it violated a legal duty, a specific rule, regulation or law. (14) A "knowing" and "intentional" violation, on the other hand, requires a prosecutor to show only that a defendant knew that he was acting; the prosecutor does not have to prove that the person charged knew that his conduct violated a legal duty, rule or law. (15)

While it appears that this change effectively lowers the bar for proof of a securities violation, it may not be significant in cases actually brought to trial. For the type of individuals usually charged with securities offenses, it is not hard for a prosecutor to show that the person is aware of the securities regulatory framework. A defendant in this category has probably had interactions with the Securities & Exchange Commission ("SEC") or stock market associations— at a minimum with respect to annual or quarterly filings. Defenses in these actions tend to focus on the defendant's lack of requisite intent; defense counsel will therefore argue that the defendant was acting in good faith, under mistaken belief of the factual wrongdoing (e.g., the falsity of the entries) or non-involvement, (16) rather than the lack of knowledge of a law or legal duty to undercut the charge of "willfulness." In other words, a business defendant hardly would claim that she purposely misstated the value of a company's earnings knowing that people would rely on the misstatement but was, nevertheless, not guilty because she did not know there was some law or rule which prohibited making misstatements to investors.

Similarly, while it appears that removing the requirement that a defendant's action be in "connection with the purchase or sale" of a security allows for broader prosecutions (now simply "in connection with any security"), that change too may be more cosmetic than real. Courts applying the old language gave it very broad definitions and allowed for instructions to juries that encompassed most of what a prosecutor would have wanted to bring in any event. (17) In total, these changes do, however, send a signal to prosecutors to utilize new provisions under the SOA even if, in practical effect, they do not change what courts require or prosecutors chose to prove about defendants on trial. It will take some time to determine whether the new laws actually make it easier for the government to win securities cases.

2. Obstruction of Justice

The second group of SOA criminal law changes and additions—those addressing obstruction of justice—may prove to add real weapons to a prosecutor's arsenal. One new provision, 18 U.S.C. § 1519, allows prosecutors to bring charges against someone who "knowingly alters, destroys, mutilates, conceals, covers up, falsifies, or makes false entries in any record . . . with the intent to impede, obstruct, or influence the investigation or proper administration of any matter within the jurisdiction of any departments or agency of the United States. . . ."(18) Existing law required the pendency of an action and the intent of an individual to impede or obstruct its direction.(19) The new law, which carries up to a twenty-year criminal penalty, was conceived to be intentionally broad. It does not require an actual investigation to be on-going; it captures an attempt by a person whether successful or not. It is so broad, in fact, that it arguably could be applied to a company's destruction of documents years before even a civil inquiry by an agency begins as long as that company's activities were "administered" by that agency and the company's intent was to cover its wrongdoing or hamper a then-only potential future investigation. Most significantly is that, as written, the statute does not require a "willful" or corrupt state of mind, again allowing the statute to cover activities which were not done with a knowledge of a law or legal duty.(20) A related provision expands the obstruction statute, 18 U.S.C. § 1512(21) to reach not only the individual who directs or persuades an obstruction (i.e., the destruction of evidence) to occur but also to reach the individual (even a support staff person) who carries out that instruction.(22) The defendant to be charged does not have to know (and the government does not have to prove) that a federal proceeding existed or was likely to occur. This is a true expansion of existing law.

As occurred with changes inspired by the financial institutions crisis of the 1980s, the new provision of the SOA applies beyond the area that caused its creation. So, while the new "obstruction" provisions are clearly directed at what was charged as the offenses in the case brought against Arthur Andersen, the new law could also be used by DOJ in any setting where an agency has jurisdiction over some business (i.e., government contracts). One of the SOA's obstruction provisions was written with the specifics of the securities fraud scandals in mind. In 18 U.S.C. § 1520, Congress enacted a requirement that records related to the audit function be preserved for five years and then made it a criminal offense to violate this record-keeping requirement.(23) Clearly such a violation in the past—failing to keep adequate records—would have been addressed by a regulatory agency and/or a civil case. Now, it has been elevated to a possible felony. All of these "obstruction" statutory changes and additions were brought about in response to the allegations and news articles that occurred at the outset of the Wall Street scandals, especially those concerning document destruction at Arthur Andersen. Ironically, the very conduct sought to be addressed was successfully charged and convicted by DOJ under the laws that were on the books before the SOA was passed.(24) Again, an important question is whether the new SOA provisions were necessary and if Congress, in the process of legislating, criminalized conduct that it did not intend to punish.

3. *Increase in Maximum Penalties for Existing and New Offenses*

In addition to drafting legislation that substantively changed what conduct violates the law, Congress increased the maximum penalties for new SOA violations and existing laws.

Table II.A.3.i. Increase in Maximum Penalties for Existing and New Offenses

15 U.S.C. § 78ff(a) Exchange Act Violations	5 to 20 years
18 U.S.C. § 1348 Securities Fraud (new)	25 years
18 U.S.C. § 1341, 1343 Mail and Wire	5 to 20 years
18 U.S.C. § 1349 Attempts/Conspiracy (new)	5 years to maximum of underlying crime
18 U.S.C. § 1350 False Audit Certification (new)	20 years
18 U.S.C. §§ 1519, 1520 Obstruction of Justice (new)	20 years
18 U.S.C. § 1512 Document Tampering	10 to 20 years

By singling out this group of statutes for increased maximum sentences, Congress created a patchwork of penalties (as it had done in FIRREA) different from the historic penalty of five year maximums for white collar offenses. As an example, the following federal felonies, which many would argue are as serious as the white collar offenses listed above, have the following maximum sentences:

Table II.A.3.ii. Increase in Maximum Penalties for Existing and New Offenses

18 U.S.C. § 1001 False Statements to Congress and Federal Agencies	5 years
18 U.S.C. § 924 Various Firearm Violations	5 years
18 U.S.C. § 371 General Conspiracy	5 years
18 U.S.C. 960 Various Narcotics Violations	10 years

In spite of the fact that the SOA dramatically increases maximum penalties for offenses, maximum penalties will only apply in rare cases and could have been achieved before the SOA was enacted. Regardless of what the SOA lists as the maximum penalty, all federal crimes are now determined under the United States Sentencing Guidelines ("Guidelines").(25) Under the Guidelines, the SOA offenses, like other statutes, will be assigned a basic offense level that may then be enhanced (i.e., amount of loss, victim impact, etc.) or reduced by other factors (i.e., acceptance of responsibility). In the end, the actual sentence will not likely be dramatically increased under the SOA.(26) In addition, the courts may sentence defendants to more than the maximum of any one charge by a prosecutor's request that sentences under different charges run consecutively and/or that a sentencing judge upwardly depart for egregious conduct.(27) In other words, if a prosecutor sought a ten- or twenty-year sentence in a case that was brought before the SOA, a prosecutor could use the existing law to achieve that result. New laws with theoretically higher maximum sentences filtered through the sentencing guidelines will operate that same way. Nevertheless, Congress clearly intended to send a message to the law enforcement community to be tougher on violators of business laws and regulations. Further, Congress's message will echo to prosecutors(28) and sentencing judges who will avail themselves of the new SOA maximums or use previously available means to enhance maximum penalties.

Indeed, SOA exerted a great deal of effort in setting out, defining, and prescribing very severe penalties for securities and business crimes. After the SOA's new provisions are put into practice, the legal community must evaluate the efficacy and impact of the new provisions.

II. Going After Corporate Leaders: "Lowering the Bar" for Proving Knowledge or Intent

Law enforcement officials often face a dilemma in addressing the leaders of companies in which there appears to be wrongdoing. These are the most visible figures, and they often have incurred the greatest benefits and rewards for the activities that prosecutors will allege violated the law. As high-level corporate officials, however, they often are not the business directors or officers involved in the actual conduct under scrutiny.

Clearly, if a corporate official herself orders a false entry, diverts a corporate asset, or engages in an inside security trade, that official can be prosecuted under normal statutes with their general requirements for knowledge, intent, and conduct. However, the suspicion is often that these officials may have stood by, aware of (or even tacitly encouraging) the wrongdoing, while employees lower on the totem pole carried out the bad acts. Law enforcement officials want high-level individuals to answer for the company's illegal activity, arguing this will have the largest impact on corporate wrongdoing and create the deepest deterrent against future conduct. Even with the removal of the requirement that an offense be proven to have been "willful,"(29) it is still often difficult for a prosecutor to prove that the highest corporate officials were involved if they sat on the corporate sidelines.

Even before SOA made changes in the law of intent, prosecutors had been seeking and courts had been crafting rulings to develop theories under which high-level corporate officials could be charged with serious corporate offenses, even if they only stood by in ignorance of the company's actions. Prosecutors have used the theory of "conscious avoidance," known alternatively as "willful blindness," or "deliberate ignorance," as a primary tool for combating corporate crime. This theory further expands prosecutors' ability to criminalize corporate conduct.

A. Conscious Avoidance

Generally speaking, criminal culpability requires a showing that one acted purposely, knowingly, recklessly, or negligently, as the law may require, with respect to each material element of the charged offense. Employing a securities example, a corporation (or its officials) has to "know" that a fraud is being perpetrated on investors. However, under the theory of conscious avoidance, a prosecutor can establish the defendant's knowledge of the existence of a particular fact without establishing positive (or actual) knowledge, if the prosecutor can establish that the defendant was aware of some probability of that conduct's existence.

The most influential discussion regarding conscious avoidance was set forth in United States v. Jewell,(30) in which the defendant drove someone else's car into the United States for a fee and claimed not to know that there were concealed drugs in the car. The prosecutors alleged that the defendant deliberately avoided positive knowledge of the presence of the contraband to avoid responsibility in the event of discovery. In offering the conviction, the appeals court emphasized that the concept of "conscious avoidance" does not reduce the *mens rea* (guilty knowledge) requirement of criminal offenses. The court held that the "substantive justification for the rule is that deliberate ignorance and positive knowledge are equally culpable."(31) The Jewell court adopted as its standard the Model Penal Code definition of knowledge: one knows a particular fact when one is aware of a high probability of its existence, unless he actually believes that it does not exist.(32)

Prosecutors have increasingly expanded the doctrine established in Jewell to assert criminal liability against corporations. For example, in United States v. Hiland,(33) a company and several individuals were convicted of introducing a new and misbranded drug into interstate commerce with the intent to defraud or mislead. The case was based on the contention that the company deliberately avoided the truth about the drug. The company argued on appeal that the trial court erred in giving a conscious avoidance instruction. In upholding the conviction, the court held that "the purpose of the willful blindness theory is to impose criminal liability on people who, recognizing the likelihood of wrongdoing, nonetheless consciously refuse to take basic investigatory steps."(34)

B. *Conscious Avoidance as a Tool*

The conscious avoidance doctrine is an attractive tool to address the new corporate law enforcement crisis. During recent months, senior officials representing companies being investigated for questionable accounting methods and other corporate wrongdoing have commonly asserted that they were not aware of the details of the allegedly improper transfers, entries, or other transactions set up by the company. In testimony before Congress, a senior official of Enron stated that his was such a very large corporation, that it would be impossible to know everything that was going on.(35) Using the case law established for the latest wave of alleged business crimes, prosecutors may use the conscious avoidance doctrine to argue that such executives were aware of a high probability of the conduct's existence and can be prosecuted for this level of involvement.

For example, prosecutors could introduce evidence that before the questionable accounting practice, a company's profits (and the corporate official's salary and bonus) were dramatically lower and with no real change in products or services (and only a change in accounting methods) the profits, salaries and bonuses soared. A company memorandum written before the business's failure and made available to that company's senior management indicating that certain business transactions were improperly structured or booked may also be used as evidence against the corporation. Prosecutors can further substantiate claims with other corporate documents or even casual observations by individuals along the corporate ladder.(36)

In some instances, Congress has adopted the concept and incorporated the theory or even the words of conscious avoidance law into legislation. For example, multinational corporations and companies that do business overseas should be particularly aware of the conscious avoidance doctrine as it relates to the Foreign Corrupt Practices Act ("FCPA").(37)

Defense counsel may make a number of arguments to avoid introduction of the conscious avoidance doctrine in their cases. One of the most basic responses to a prosecutor's request to argue for a jury instruction defining conscious avoidance is to assert that a prosecutor improperly wants to argue in the alternative that the defendant was aware of wrongdoing and that she avoided knowing about it. Part of the government's case will be based upon proof that a defendant had actual knowledge. Then, when there is a gap in proof, the prosecutor will jump to the idea that the defendant "avoided" the truth. Courts have often forced prosecutors to choose under which theory they want to proceed.(38)

In addition, most circuits have held that while the government may urge a conscious avoidance theory to support a finding of guilty knowledge, it may not advance that theory in support of a finding of "intent" to join a conspiracy or a finding of "specific intent" necessary to sustain a substantive charge for which specific intent is required. A defense counsel will argue that this is common sense because if a person does not know something (i.e., the object of a conspiracy) and is said only to be willfully blind about it, that person hardly can be said to have intentionally agreed to something about which she was literally unaware.(39) This means that a conscious avoidance instruction can be a double-edged sword to a prosecutor—it giveth (by allowing a prosecutor to fill in the knowledge gap in the case) and it taketh away (by specifically preventing a jury from finding or inferring intent from a lack of knowledge).

A third line of attack by defense counsel is similar to other arguments made by defendants to prevent jury instructions—the proof at trial simply does not support the charge. Since the conscious avoidance charge is based on inference, this line of opposition is often successful. A conscious avoidance instruction is only proper where the "surrounding circumstances are such that reasonable persons can conclude that the circumstances alone should have apprised defendants of the unlawful nature of their conduct."(40) Some cases have held that the instruction should rarely be given because there is difficulty in maintaining a clear distinction between behavior that constitutes conscious ignorance and that which is merely reckless and thus implies negligence.(41)

As business crime continues to be both a high priority and difficult to prove, Congress, prosecutors, and the courts will be confronted with proposals to make charging and proving offenses easier. Those operating in the business world today are wise to keep aware of how even the current law on "conscious avoidance" might bring them into the law enforcement net when they thought they had stayed out of the water altogether.

III. The Resurrection of Parallel Proceedings: Piling on by Agencies and Lawyers

A. Introduction to Parallel Proceedings

In conjunction with the creation of new crimes, increased penalties and a wider application of the doctrine of conscious avoidance, a final phenomenon of these eras of increased attention to corporate crime is the "parallel proceeding." Parallel proceedings are simultaneous or successive investigations, prosecutions, or other actions brought against a person, a corporation, or some other entity by federal and state governmental departments or agencies, or by a governmental entity and a private party.(42) Thus, parallel proceedings result when various offices in the federal, state or even the local law enforcement community (or sometimes private counsel in damage suits) decide to bring actions in the same case or matter at or about the same time. Parallel proceedings again give prosecutors another weapon in their arsenal with which to combat corporate crime.

In the financial institutions crisis, for example, it was not unusual for the failure of a savings and loan to lead to simultaneous federal criminal charges, state criminal charges, a Federal Deposit Insurance Corporation or Federal Savings & Loan Insurance Corporation action, and a handful of private lawsuits fueled by class action attorneys. There is no hard evidence that these multiple proceeding netted greater penalties for the individuals that were held account-able or that they facilitated greater recovery for victims. With respect to restitu-tion, for example, there was only so much money left to be simultaneously sought by all of the prosecutors and plaintiffs.

Observing current court dockets, one will witness the same phenomenon. The various Wall Street scandals have caused federal prosecutors, state Attor-neys General, various regulatory agencies, and private plaintiffs to simul-taneously respond to their respective constituencies and demand action—all of which aims at the same individuals and the same pocket of funds. Still, in some sense, these proceedings do not run parallel at all, but are concurrent and intersect in different ways. For example, Enron Corporation, Tyco Inter-national, Ltd. and WorldCom, Inc. are corporate examples of multiple pending actions including: federal grand jury investigations (and charges) in the state(s) of their corporate headquarters and/or financial filings, Securities and Exchange Commission inquiries or actions for injunctive relief and damages filed in federal court, oversight hearings by one/both houses of Congress in which corporate officials have been subpoenaed to testify, state Attorneys Gen-eral investigations or actions on behalf of the state's citizens, charges brought by state prosecutors, and private class action suits of thousands of investors seeking damages in state or federal courts.

Parallel proceedings change everything about the planning and strategy of a case. Whether to allow a client to testify in a civil deposition or before a con-gressional committee, for example, is a much different question when there is a grand jury just waiting to review a copy of that testimony. The decision of what affirmative actions to file or seek by way of counterclaim are also decided differently if regulatory agencies would use a client's pleadings as admissions in their own actions.

B. The Impact of Parallel Proceedings

Any investigation, lawsuit, or agency action involving a corporation, officer, or public official is a serious and disruptive matter. Parallel proceedings are par-ticularly difficult for industries that must meet strict regulatory compliance. The time and resources required for confronting multiple prosecutors and/or investigators can cripple a company and its officials. The "business" of the company, in effect, changes from its product or service to tackling costly litiga-tion. The resources and morale of a corporation will also deplete as various agencies require production of the same data or employees for questioning. In turn, legal costs will increase, particularly if a company decides to utilize differ-ent counsel for different proceedings. Such costs will also increase if the com-pany elects to pay for its employees' attorney fees.

In addition, various actions in the parallel proceedings call for different strategies that often do not work well together. Non-cooperation with a grand jury, for example, which might be appropriate in a single proceeding, may be counter-productive in the context of another parallel proceeding, in which an entity has to cooperate with a regulatory agency in order to receive or maintain a license or other benefit. Cooperating by supplying documents or testimony to the licensing agency may make them available to prosecutors and other investigating agencies. Similarly, documents and other information disclosed in one investigation may become discoverable by parties who otherwise would not have had access to them; or, they may be used in a different criminal or civil proceeding. The assertion of a privilege or defense may have unexpected results in another proceeding. For example, assertion of the Fifth Amendment privilege may result in civil liability due to its permissible adverse inference.

A corporation or its individuals do not even have assurances that fighting against any one of the parallel proceedings will terminate any of the others. To begin with, an adverse decision in one proceeding can be binding in another. For example, a criminal conviction may be *res judicata* in a civil suit, meaning that there can be no re-adjudication of a claim rendered unfavorably against a party. (43) On the other hand, a favorable resolution in one proceeding may not end the matter. A decision by a grand jury not to indict usually will not end civil suits for contract disbarment or a separate agency inquiry on non-criminal charges. Because the first proceeding brought by the government requires a higher burden of proof (i.e., beyond reasonable doubt) there is no "reverse collateral estoppel." In other words, the government can proceed on a second civil or administrative proceeding even if it fails in its criminal case. (44) Thus, where companies today face criminal investigations (let alone charges) while other proceedings are pending, there is usually no end to the potential problems.

C. Problems and Issues of Parallel Proceedings

1. National Information Infrastructure Protection Act of 1996

If companies or individuals who are a target of parallel proceedings think there is relief from various proceedings by claiming "double jeopardy", they are mistaken. There is little relief provided by the law to those that are being investigated, charged, or sued by federal and state authorities, two different state authorities, or by those proceeding on criminal and then civil bases. Neither the Constitution nor any statutory or common law rule prevents different federal agencies or different sovereigns from prosecuting a corporation and its officers simultaneously or successively in separate criminal and/or civil actions arising from the same transaction. (45) Although the Double Jeopardy Clause may preclude successive prosecutions by two entities (i.e., municipalities within a state), (46) a federal prosecution is not precluded by a prior state prosecution and the opposite also is also true. (47)

Similarly, the Supreme Court ruled in Heath v. Alabama, that the Double Jeopardy Clause does not prohibit two states from each bringing a criminal prosecution against an individual or entity premised upon the same conduct.(48) This is not a remote possibility given the interstate nature of most corporations. The cases growing out of the Enron Corporation collapse illustrate that charges have been filed in both Texas and New York. Corporations which operate in a number of states could therefore also be prosecuted and/or sued by successive states if allegations of wrongdoing can be alleged in the different locales.

2. Parallel Proceedings Wreak Havoc on Internal Compliance

One result of this heightened scrutiny of corporate practices is for attorneys to assist companies with internal reviews and to help them devise corporate compliance programs to prevent government investigations. In fact, corporate compliance programs can provide companies with a defense, or at least an argument, for reduced charges or sentences when a criminal investigation is commenced or a criminal conviction is obtained. DOJ's new guidelines for charging corporations with criminal offenses puts a premium on such compliance.(49) If the very efforts for creating a compliance program—an internal review or an inside counsel's investigation—can be obtained by government investigators, a company may be reluctant to undertake the very effort that the government has stated it wants to promote.

From a legal perspective, the first issue is whether the fruits of these reviews are protected, or if provided to one agency, are available to others. An attorney must evaluate whether communications between counsel and corporate officials and a counsel's work are covered by privilege.(50)

It is readily apparent how parallel proceedings create a field of landmines to corporations and their officials. A business which would otherwise want to share the results of its internal review to an administrative agency such as the SEC, in order to stay in business or keep its stock trading, can be found to have "waived" its privilege with respect to any other agency, investigation or lawsuit.(51) A company can even be found to have waived its privilege if it discloses its attorney-client material to too many of its corporate advisors.(52) It is difficult to imagine an effective compliance program in which the company involved cannot share its concerns with its outside auditors and accountants, but such a company can be handcuffed for this very type of cooperation.

Even if a company or individual can protect its privileges, the non-privileged information provided to one entity can readily find its way to other branches of government that are similarly conducting investigations based on the same or similar conduct. Agencies—federal to federal, state to state, or even federal to state—often share their information. Sometimes this occurs formally, pursuant to law or rule, and sometimes it results from practice or courtesy. Various federal regulatory agencies have agreements, rules, or policies to forward information that they deem to reveal wrongdoing to a law enforcement agency like DOJ.

Information provided to the SEC as part of disclosure obligations of a public corporation or in the context of an enforcement proceeding often will be disseminated or made available to prosecuting and other regulatory agencies.(53)

The federal rules permit the disclosure of grand jury materials to appropriate state or municipal officials for the purpose of enforcement of state criminal statutes "when permitted by a court at the request of an attorney for the government, upon a showing that such matters may disclose a violation of state criminal law." (54) To make matters even more complicated, DOJ often refers matters it decides not to prosecute to regulatory agencies with jurisdiction to take other than criminal action or even to other bodies like congressional committees. So, the target of parallel proceedings must consider when some of these "parallel" actions can be eliminated or stayed.

D. Eliminating Some of the Proceedings

Those trying to keep their jobs and stay in business, continue to raise business capital, manufacture or distribute their product, and also resolve any legal difficulties have a daunting task when the "move" made in one forum can be catastrophic in another. One goal for defendants is to limit the number of proceedings or at least to compel those with the greatest impact to proceed first. Achieving this result is not easy and it is especially the case when little prevents one agency from coordinating with or collaborating with another, even for the precise purpose of avoiding a defendant's or subject of an investigation's attempt to derail one or the other.(55) By now the law is fairly settled that any agency may proceed with its portion of the parallel proceeding as long as it has the authority to act and has not overreached in its specific action.(56) However, there are occasions where two proceedings can get too close.(57) In that rare occasion when courts have found this to occur, a corporation still faces the tactical question of whether it is worse to go to court in an offensive move to stop an agency with oversight over its business from proceeding.

In view of the problems caused by and enormous expenditures resulting from parallel proceedings, defense attorneys often consider whether to seek a stay of one proceeding in order to be better able to address and defend another ongoing proceeding. While courts, in the exercise of their discretion, may stay an action pending the resolution of another, it is the exception rather than the rule. The Supreme Court has ruled that if there is a possibility that a stay will damage someone, the movant for the stay "must make out a clear case of hardship or inequity in being required to go forward."(58)

Therefore, a balancing test generally will be applied by courts in considering the propriety of a stay in order to weigh the benefits to the movant against possible harm to others. The interests weighed generally include: (i) the interest of the plaintiff in proceeding expeditiously with the civil action and the prejudice to the plaintiff in delay; (ii) the burden on the defendants; (iii) the convenience of the courts; (iv) the interests of persons not parties to the civil litigation; and (v) the public interest.(59)

In practical terms, it is very difficult for an entity to stop law enforcement proceedings from going forward when there are regulatory or civil proceedings pending at the same time. The general rules that criminal proceedings get priority will prevail. Yet, that same private entity which is the subject of the criminal investigation is usually no more successful in seeking a stay of civil proceedings during the pendency of the criminal action. (60) This is true despite the fact that invariably government requests for stays of the very same civil proceedings are granted on the ground that a grand jury investigation is pending. (61)

In the face of an inability to actually prevent parallel proceedings, companies and individuals have attempted to curtail the manner that the information provided in one of the forums can be used in another. This tactic too has proven ineffective because it has been held that protective orders cannot be used to protect against self-incrimination, putting defendants to the choice of testifying in the civil actions or taking the Fifth Amendment, with the likely result of an adverse inference or default judgment. (62)

The one area where subjects of parallel proceedings have been somewhat successful in reducing the matters that they have to defend is not an enviable position. When a person or business finds itself actually charged and already a defendant in a criminal prosecution at the same time that there are civil or administrative proceedings pending against it, stays of civil discovery or of the administrative proceedings have been granted based on a showing of likely injury. (63) What constitutes recognizable injury will vary but a common situation can be avoided.

For example, where employees of a corporation are named as co-defendants to the entity in a criminal prosecution, a stay of a civil proceeding against the corporation might be sought until the criminal case has been concluded. This would prevent the employees from being called as witnesses in the civil case while the criminal charges against them remain undecided. Such employees undoubtedly would assert their Fifth Amendment privilege if called in the civil case and it could be argued that a stay would permit them to later testify in the civil action once the criminal charges had been resolved. The stay would prevent the corporation's opponent from taking advantage of the employee's silence and from gaining an adverse inference against the corporation in the civil action.

Considering that there are only so many penalties and that can be assessed against a business or its officials who have violated the law, it is a wonder that so many actions are brought against the same entities. Yet, in some instances different agencies have dissimilar reasons for acting and different authority to seek redress against corporate wrongdoing (money damages versus injunctive relief). In other instances, simultaneous actions are brought because each agency or plaintiff feels that there will not be any funds available if it does not mark its place in line as soon as possible. On still other occasions, parallel proceedings are brought because each movant feels it has to respond politically to public pressure or the criticism that it did not act quickly or forcefully enough in the past. Despite these better and worse reasons, a series of parallel proceedings make it nearly impossible for any business to continue once it has become a target. In both the financial institutions crisis and the current Wall Street scandals, parallel proceedings provide the government with another method of enhancing penalties for corporate wrongdoing.

IV. Conclusion

Ten years ago the impetus for new law enforcement initiative was the savings and loan crises and today it is the Wall Street scandal and tomorrow it will be something else. At these irregular intervals, it is as though the courts, legislators and law enforcement rediscover white collar crime—or at least are re-energized in addressing it. With each crisis over business-related crimes, there is a formula for the events that occur—blame for past neglect, a fury of legislative and agency activity to compensate for the past, and then defendants, their counsel, and the courts sorting through the changes for many years after the headlines subside. Whether this phenomenon is ultimately an effective process for reshaping the law to address changed business practices should be debated. This much, however, is clear—actions by Congress to create new crimes and increase penalties, efforts by prosecutors to influence courts to make it easier to achieve convictions, and the piling on of numerous proceedings by successive regulatory agencies provides the government with additional methods for attacking and punishing corporate crime, the defense bar with new challenges in representing clients, and commentators with a great deal to review.

Notes

(1) Susan Milligan, House OK's Tough Action Against Fraud Public Anger Fuels a Fast Response on Corporate Crime, *BOSTON GLOBE*, Jul. 17, 2002, at A1 (indicating that the House of Representatives failed to consider increasing prison sentences for corporate crime when it previously approved a package of accounting standards reforms in April of 2002).

(2) Pub. L. No. 107–73, 103 Stat. 183, (1989).

(3) 18 U.S.C. §§ 371, 1341, 1005.

(4) 18 U.S.C. § 3293; 18 U.S.C. §§ 215, 656, 657, 1005, 1006, 1007, 1008, 1014, 1344; 18 U.S.C. §§ 1341 & 1343; see also John K. Villa, Defending Bank & Thrift Directors and Counsel in the 90's, *Fraud, Money Laundering and Embezzlement* 1993, at 357, 64–65 (PLI Litig. & Admin. Practice Course, Handbook Series No. 482, 1993).

(5) 18 U.S.C. § 1343.

(6) Id.

(7) 18 U.S.C. § 1510(b)(1).

(8) Barrie McKenna, The WorldCom Debacle, *THE GLOBE AND MAIL*, Jun.

27, 2002, at B5 (noting Representative Billy Tauzin, Republication Chair of the House Energy and Commerce Committee, called for "tough new laws" to restore confidence in America).

(9) See Editorial, A Law That Protects Small Investors *WASH. POST*, Feb. 2, 2002 (indicating collapse of Enron should prompt legislators to reexamine securities and accounting laws).

(10) The Sarbanes-Oxley Act of 2002, Pub. L. No. 107–204, 116 Stat. 745 (2002).

(11) Id. at §§ 801 et seq., 901 et seq.

(12) New 18 U.S.C. § 1348 provides that:

> Whoever knowingly executes, or attempts to execute, a scheme or artifice—(1) to defraud any person in connection with any security of an issuer with a class of securities registered under section 12 of the Securities and Exchange Act of 1934 (15 U.S.C. 78l) or that is required to file reports under section 15(d) of the Securities and Exchange Act of 1934 (15 U.S.C. 78o(d)); or (2) to obtain, by means of false or fraudulent pretenses, representations, or promises, any money or property in connection with the purchase or sale of any security of an issuer with a class of securities registered under section 12 of the Securities Exchange Act of 1934 (15 U.S.C. 78l) or that is required to file reports under section 15(d) of the Securities and Exchange Act of 1934 (15 U.S.C. 78o(d)); shall be fined under this title, or imprisoned not more than 25 years, or both.

(13) Securities Exchange Act, 15 U.S.C. § 78a (2002).

(14) Kevin F. O'Mally *et al.*, Federal Jury Practice and Instructions § 17.05 (2002 Supp.)

(15) Id. at § 17.04.

(16) See infra, Section III.A., Conscious Avoidance, of this article.

(17) See McClure v. First Nat'l Bank of Lubbock Texas, 352 F. Supp. 454, 457 (N.D. Texas 1973) ("Thus the Act is designed to deal with substance over form and to regulate and prohibit fraud involved in the sale of promissory notes where such notes are sold or traded for purposes of speculation or investment in the same way that stock, bonds, or debentures might be traded, sold, or exchanged. Such an interpretation of the 'any note' provision of the statute is consistent with the 'dominating general purpose' of the Act . . .").

(18) 18 U.S.C. § 1519 provides that:

> Whoever knowingly alters, destroys, mutilates, conceals, covers up, falsifies, or makes a false entry in any record, document, or tangible object with the intent to impede, obstruct, or influence the investigation or proper administration of any matter within the jurisdiction of any department or agency of the United States or any case filed under title 11, or in relation to or contemplation of any such matter or case,

shall be fined under this title, imprisoned not more than 20 years, or both.

(19) E.g., 18 U.S.C. § 1505.

(20) 18 U.S.C. § 1519.

(21) Present 18 U.S.C. § 1512(b)(2)(B) states that:

> (b) Whoever knowingly uses intimidation, threatens, or corruptly persuades another person, or attempts to do so, or engages in misleading conduct towards another person, with intent to—(2) cause or induce any person to—(B) alter, destroy, mutilate, or conceal an object with intent to impair the object's integrity or availability for use in an official proceeding . . . shall be fined under this title or imprisoned not more than ten years, or both.

(22) The new provision of 18 U.S.C. § 1512 provides:

> (1) by redesigning subsections (e) through (i) as subsections (d) through (j), respectively; and (2) by inserting after subsection (b) the following subsection; (c) Whoever corruptly—(1) alters, destroys, mutilates, or conceals a record, document, or other object, or attempts to do so, with the intent to impair the object's integrity or availability for use in an official proceeding; or (2) otherwise obstructs, influences, or impedes any official proceeding, or attempts to do so, shall be fined under this title or imprisoned not more than 20 years or both.

(23) New 18 U.S.C. § 1520 provides that:

> (a)(1) Any accountant who conducts an audit of an issuer of securities to which section 10A(a) of the Securities Exchange Act of 1934 (15 U.S.C. 78j-1 (a)) applies, shall maintain all audit or review workpapers for a period of 5 years from the end of the fiscal period in which the audit or review was concluded. (2) The Securities and Exchange Commission shall promulgate within 180 days, after adequate notice and an opportunity for comment such rules and regulations, as are reasonably necessary, relating to the retention of relevant records such as workpapers, documents that form the basis of an audit or review, memoranda, correspondence, communications, other documents, and records (including electronic records) which are created, sent, or received in connection with an audit or review and contain conclusions, opinions, analyses, or financial data relating to such an audit or review, which is conducted by any accountant who conducts an audit of an issuer of securities to which section 10A(a) of the Securities and Exchange Act of 1934 (15 U.S.C. 78j-1 (a) applies . . . (b) Whoever knowingly and willfully violates subsection (a)(1), or any rule or regulation promulgated by the Securities and Exchange Commission under subsection (a)(2), shall be fined under this title, imprisoned not more than 10 years, or both, (c) Nothing in this section shall be deemed to diminish or relive any person of any other duty or obligation imposed

by Federal or State law or regulation to maintain, or refrain from destroying, any document.

(24) See Hous. CHRON. The Fall of Enron, Oct. 20, 2002, at 1 (noting the conviction of Arthur Andersen and various Andersen executives for obstruction of justice).

(25) In 1984, Congress ended the Sentencing Reform Act citing sentencing guidelines. See Pub. L. 98–473, 98 stat. 1837. The SOA does in fact mandate that the Sentencing Commission address the issues and make changes to increase penalties that reflect the great priority being given to this area of criminal law. See 18 U.S.C. § 3551. So, the net effect of SOA will be increased penalties, but these will come about more from increases in the sentencing guidelines than in increasing the theoretical maximum penalties under an offense itself.

(26) In addition to increased sentences, this Administration has also made changes to reflect the greater concern it is giving to this type of white collar crime by changing the rules for how and where convicted persons are incarcerated. Responding to the Attorney General, the Bureau of Prisons announced that it was ending the availability of facilities other than prison for white collar offenders. See Todd A. Bussert, NACDL Helps Members Fight Change In BOP Policy, *CHAMPION MAGAZINE* (NACLD NEWS) (March, 2003) available at http://www.nacdl.org (last visited March 20, 2003).

(27) See *U.S. SENTENCING GUIDELINES MANUAL* [hereinafter U.S.S.G. MANUAL] Adjustments, Part B § 3B1.1 (2002).

(28) Another example of the Department of Justice both hearing the message of Congress and also seeking that such a message be sent itself was the February 7, 2003 announcement adjusting the policy and criteria under which the Department of Justice would prosecute corporations or business entities. During the last administration, the Department published what has been called the "Holder Memorandum" which illustrated the factors that prosecutors should weigh in considering whether to charge corporations. See U.S. Department of Justice, Fraud Section, available at http://www.usdoj.gov/criminal/fraud/policy-.chargingcorps.html. This administration has set out the "Thompson Memorandum" which highlights similar factors as the Holder Memorandum such as the pervasiveness of wrongdoing within the corporation, the corporation's history of similar conduct, and the existence and adequacy of the corporations compliance program. See U.S. Department of Justice, Fraud Section, Corporate Fraud, available at http://www.usdoj.gov/dag/cftf/corporate_guidelines. htm; see also Carrie Johnson, U.S. Refines Criteria For Prosecuting Firms, *WASH. POST*, Feb. 7, 2003, at E1.

(29) See supra, Section I.A.1, New Substantive Offenses for Securities Offenses, of this article.

(30) 532 F.2d 697 (9th Cir. 1976).

(31) Id. at 700.

(32) Id. at 701.

(33) 909 F.2d 1114 (8th Cir. 1990).

(34) Id. at 1130 (citing United States v. Rothrock, 806 F.2d. 318, 323 (1st Cir. 1986)).

(35) Stephen Labator & Richard A. Oppel Jr., Ex-Enron CEO Contradicted-Witnesses Say He Received Warnings, *SAN DIEGO UNION TRIBUNE*, February 8, 2002 at A8.

(36) Various jury instructions describe the range of inferences. One states:

> In determining whether the defendant acted knowingly, you may consider whether the defendant deliberately closed his eyes to what would otherwise have been obvious to him. If you find beyond a reasonable doubt that the defendant acted with a conscious purpose to avoid learning the truth, then this element may be satisfied. However, guilty knowledge may not be established by demonstrating that the defendant was merely negligent, foolish, or mistaken.
>
> If you find that the defendant was aware of a high probability that (e.g., the statement was false) and that the defendant acted with deliberate disregard of the facts, you may find that the defendant acted knowingly. However, if you find that the defendant actually believed that (e.g., the statement was true), he may not be convicted.
>
> It is entirely up to you whether you find that the defendant deliberately closed his eyes and any inferences to be drawn from the evidence on this issue.
>
> Leonard B. Sand *et al.*, *Modern Federal Jury Instructions* at 3A–2 (2002).

(37) Foreign Corrupt Practices Act of 1977, Pub. L. No. 95–23, 91 Stat. 1494 (codified as amended at 15 U.S.C. §§ 78m(b), (d)(1), (g)–(h), 78dd–2, 78ff (1994) (amended by International Anti-Bribery and Fair Competition Act of 1998, 15 U.S.C. §§ 78dd–1 to 78ff (West Supp. 1999).

(38) See United States v. Ferrarini, 219 F.3d 145, 157 (2d Cir. 2000) (finding fact that a jury can—on the evidence—find actual knowledge does not mean that it can also find conscious avoidance, and thus government cannot have both actual knowledge and conscious avoidance instruction go to jury).

(39) See United States v. Tropeano, 252 F.3d 653, 660 (2d Cir. 2001) (citing Ferrarini, 219 F.3d at 155).

(40) United States v. Guzman, 754 F.2d 482, 489 (2d Cir. 1985).

(41) See United States v. McAllister, 747 F.2d 1273, 1275 (9th Cir. 1984) (citing U.S. v. Murietta-Bejarano, 552 F.2d 1323, 1325 (9th Cir. 1977)). When defense counsel are unsuccessful in preventing a conscious avoidance

theory in the case, they propose a jury instruction that informs the jury that, while knowledge is one component of intent, there are several other components and a finding of conscious avoidance alone cannot provide the basis for finding intent as a whole. See generally United States v. Beech-Nut Nutrition Corp., 871 F.2d 1181, 1195–96 (2d Cir. 1989). One example of a jury instruction on "conscious avoidance" is as follows:

> With respect to each of the counts in this case, you are required to determine whether the defendants acted with the requisite knowledge and intent, as I have already explained those elements to you. In determining whether defendants acted knowingly, you may consider whether either defendant deliberately closed his eyes, or consciously avoided what otherwise would have been obvious. I caution you, however, and I will explain in more detail below, that you may not consider this fact in determining whether the defendants acted with the requisite intent, that I have told you is necessary to sustain each of the individual charges.
>
> Let me point out the necessary knowledge cannot be established by showing that a defendant was careless, negligent or foolish. One may not, however, willfully and intentionally remain ignorant of a fact material and important to his conduct in order to escape the consequences of criminal law. If you find beyond a reasonable doubt that either was, as alleged by the Government, aware that there was a high probability that the alleged illegal act was not occurring but that the defendants deliberately and consciously avoided confirming these facts, then you may treat this deliberate avoidance of positive knowledge as the equivalent of knowledge, unless you find that the defendants actually believed that the alleged illegal act was not occurring.

(42) See Sec. Exch. Comm'n v. Dresser Indus., Inc., 628 F.2d 1368, 1374 (D.C. Cir. 1980) (en banc) (detailing meaning of parallel proceedings).

(43) See Brown v. Felsen, 442 U.S. 127, 131 (1979) (stating res judicata prevents litigation of all grounds for, or defenses to, recovery that were previously available to the parties, regardless of whether they were asserted or determined in the prior proceeding).

(44) See One Lot Emerald Cut Stones v. United States, 409 U.S. 232, 235 (1972) (finding the difference in the burden of proof in criminal and civil cases precludes application of the doctrine of collateral estoppel since the acquittal of the criminal charges may have only represented "an adjudication that the proof was not sufficient to overcome all reasonable doubt of the guilt of the accused.").

(45) See United States v. Wheeler, 435 U.S. 313, 316–17 (1978) (finding well-established principle that federal prosecution does not bar subsequent state prosecution of same person for same acts, and state prosecution

does not bar a federal one. Prosecutions under the laws of separate sovereigns do not, in the language of the Fifth Amendment, "subject [the defendant] for the same offence to be twice put in jeopardy").

(46) See Brown v. Ohio, 432 U.S. 161, 167–68 (1977); Waller v. Florida, 397 U.S. 387, 393–94 (1970).

(47) See Rinaldi v. United States, 434 U.S. 22, 28 (1977) (stating that the Constitution does not deny the State and Federal Governments the power to prosecute for the same act and that in our federal system the State and Federal Governments have legitimate, but not necessarily identical, interests in the prosecution of a person for acts made criminal under the laws of both (citing Bartkus v. Illinois, 359 U.S. 121 (1959))).

(48) 474 U.S. 82 (1985).

(49) See Johnson, supra, note 29 at E1.

(50) The classic formulation of the attorney-client privilege applies when the following elements are met:

(i) [w]hen legal advice of any kind is sought (ii) from a professional legal advisor in his or her capacity as such, (iii) the communications relating to that purpose, (iv) made in confidence (v) by the client, (vi) are, at the client's instance, permanently protected (vii) from disclosure by the client or by the legal adviser (viii) unless the protected be waived.

See United States v. Martin, 278 F.3d 988, 999 (9th Cir. 2002).

The work product doctrine stands on a different, and in some regards, broader footing. It "shelters the mental processes of the attorney, providing a privileged area within which he can analyze and prepare his client's case." Literally, the rules provide that the work product doctrine protects documents and tangible things prepared by the attorney in anticipation of litigation. See Fed. R. Civ. P. 26(b)(3);United States v. Adelman, 134 F.3d 1194, 1197 (2d Cir. 1998) (explaining that documents indicating litigation position "are discoverable only upon a showing of substantial need of the materials and inability, without undue hardship, to obtain their substantial equivalent elsewhere" and even if there was a need, "the Rule provides that the court shall protect against disclosure of the mental impressions, conclusions, opinions, or legal theories of an attorney or other representative of a party concerning litigation").

(51) See In re Sealed Case, 676 F.2d 793, 809 (D.C. Cir. 1982) (finding any voluntary disclosure by the client to a third party breaches the confidentiality of the attorney-client relationship and therefore waives the privilege, not only as to the specific communication disclosed but often as to all other communications relating to the same subject matter).

(52) See United States v. Newell, 315 F.3d 510, 525 (5th Cir. 2002) (holding defendant waived attorney-client privilege by disclosing communication made with in-house accountant while no civil or criminal action was imminent); In re John Doe Corp., 675 F.2d 482, 488 (2d Cir. 1982)

(noting that the release of attorney's report to accountant waived privilege).

(53) See, e.g., In re Columbia/HCA Healthcare Corp. Billing Practices Litig., 293 F.3d 289, 304–05 (6th Cir. 2002) (holding plaintiffs waived attorney-client privilege by releasing otherwise privileged documents to government agencies during investigation even though they continued to assert privilege as to other parties); Permian Corp. v. United States, 665 F.2d 1214, 1221–22 (D.C. Cir. 1981) (stating where the SEC has obtained sworn statements during an investigation, they may be utilized in parallel proceedings).

(54) Fed. R. Crim. P. 6(e)(3)(C)(iv).

(55) See United States v. Aero Mayflower Transit Co., 831 F.2d 1142, 1146 (D.C. Cir. 1987) (stating agency is not prohibited from seeking information merely because it is working cooperatively with the Department of Justice).

(56) See United States v. LaSalle Nat'l Bank, 437 U.S. 298, 313–14 (1978) (stating IRS "must show that the investigation will be conducted pursuant to a legitimate purpose, that the inquiry may be relevant to the purpose, that the information sought is not already within the Commissioner's possession, and that the administrative steps required by the [IRS] Code have been followed"); Dresser, 628 F.2d at 1380 (D.C. Cir. 1980) ("[T]he securities laws offer no suggestion that the scope of the SEC's investigative authority shrinks when a grand jury begins to investigate the same matters.").

(57) In United States v. Parrott, 248 F. Supp. 196, 202 (D.D.C. 1965), an indictment was dismissed where defendants were called to testify in an administrative proceeding and were unaware of criminal referral to the DOJ. Unknown to defendants, the AUSA conducting the grand jury investigation was an observer in this administrative proceeding. The district judge ruled that "the Government may not bring a parallel civil proceeding and avail itself of civil discovery devices to obtain evidence for subsequent criminal prosecution." Id. at 202.

(58) Landis v. N. Am. Co., 299 U.S. 248, 255 (1936) (stating the suppliant for a slay must make out a clear case of hardship or inequity in being required to go forward, if there is even a fair possibility that the stay for which he prays will work damage to some one else).

(59) In re Mid-Atlantic Toyota Antitrust Litig., 92 F.R.D. 358, 359 (D. Md. 1981).

(60) Where the same agency or related agencies are involved, courts are not inclined to grant a stay against the agency with civil power because such a stay would obstruct the enforcement of federal law and would require federal agencies "invariably to choose either to forego recommendation of criminal prosecution once [they sought] civil relief or to defer civil proceedings pending ultimate outcome of a criminal trial." United States v. Kordel, 397 U.S. 1, 11 (1970). Also, courts do not want to require even private plaintiff alleged victims to wait for the end of what could be

long criminal cases since doing so could make any relief too late or less valuable to those seeking redress now.

(61) See, e.g., Paine, Webber, Jackson & Curtis, Inc. v. Malon Andrus, Inc., 486 F. Supp. 1118, 1119 (S.D.N.Y. 1980) (reasoning that a policy of freely granting stays solely because a litigant is defending simultaneous multiple suits would threaten to become a constant source of delay and an interference with judicial administration); United States v. One 1964 Cadillac Coupe De Ville, 41 F.R.D. 352, 355 (S.D.N.Y. 1966) (granting government's motion for a stay of all discovery proceedings in the action until disposition of the criminal actions presently pending).

(62) In In re: Grand Jury Subpoena, 836 F.2d 1468 (4th Cir. 1988), an insurance company filed notice of its intention to depose four former officers and directors of a savings & loan company whose actions were being investigated by a Baltimore grand jury. The deponents moved to stay discovery until the investigation was completed, but the U.S. District Court in Alexandria, Virginia refused to grant the stay, and instead granted a request for a protective order sealing the depositions. Id. The grand jury disregarded the order and subpoenaed the depositions. The Fourth Circuit however, affirmed a denial of the deponents' motion to quash the subpoena, ruling that a protective order cannot substitute for invoking the privilege against self-incrimination, and should not be afforded the same status. Id. at 1475; see also Cooper, The Grand Jury Given Access to Civil Depositions, *NAT'L L. J.* (1988).

(63) See, e.g., Clark v. United States, 481 F. Supp. 1086, 1100 (S.D.N.Y. 1979), appeal dismissed, 624 F.2d 3 (2d Cir. 1980) (finding that a denial of the stays would severely strain defendants' resources both financial and otherwise and would unnecessarily complicate the proceedings here by creating the likelihood that the defendants might invoke the Fifth Amendment privilege).

Source: *The American Criminal Law Review,* © 2003

Thinking Activities

1. Now that you have read all ten chapters of this book, how has your perspective on white-collar crime changed since you first began your research?

2. Has this text lead you to desire to research a specific aspect of white-collar crime in more detail? What specific topics may prove worthy of additional study?

3. After reading the five *recommendations for social change* listed in this chapter, explain why you agree/disagree with these suggestions. If you were to propose your own recommendations, what would they include?

4. Based on the information presented in this text, are you now more or less willing to pursue a career in the area of white-collar crime research or investigation? Why? Or why not?

Notes

1 Today's White-Collar Crime

1 Aubert (1952).
2 Sutherland (1940).
3 Sutherland (1944).
4 Edelhertz (1970).
5 Bayley and Garofalo (1989).
6 Gordon and Curtis (2000).
7 Federal Bureau of Investigation (n.d.).
8 Heath (2007).
9 Quoted in Serwer (2000: 1).
10 Edelhertz (1970).
11 United States Department of Justice (n.d.c).

2 Information Technology and White-Collar Crime

1 Flory (1990).
2 Leiner *et al.* (1999).
3 McCollum (1999)
4 Plunkett Research, Ltd. (n.d.).
5 United States Secret Service (n.d.a).
6 United States Secret Service (n.d.b).
7 Brightman (2000).
8 Department of the Treasury (2006).
9 Telecomworldwire (1999).
10 Business Wire (2000).
11 Microsoft, Inc. (2000).
12 *Wall's Hacker and Cracker Links* (n.d.).
13 Festa (1998).
14 United States Department of Justice (n.d.b).
15 Press Trust of India (2008).
16 National White Collar Crime Center (2008).
17 United States Department of Justice (2002).
18 Messner (2007).
19 United States General Accounting Office (2002).
20 Andrews (2006).

3 The Corporate-State Corruption Connection

1 Glasner (2001).
2 Boyd (2001).
3 Pope (2002).
4 Berke (2002).
5 Center for Responsive Politics (2002).
6 Kadlec (2002).
7 Heath (2002).
8 Milbank and Kessler (2002).
9 Ibid.
10 Kurtz (1991).
11 Fenn (2002).
12 Tanner (2000).
13 Barrera (2005).
14 Sampson (2003).
15 Sampson (2003).
16 Chen (2000).
17 Schlegel and Weisburd (1994, p. 41).
18 Maddux (2002).
19 Farquhar (2002).
20 Terrell (2001).
21 Gerth (1992).
22 Hedges (1992, p. 61).
23 United States Government Accountability Office (n.d.).
24 Office of Management and Budget (2002).
25 Ibid.
26 Ibid., p. 1.
27 Albanese (1995, p. 6).
28 Patten (2007).
29 Bergstrom (2002, p. 1).
30 Holland (2002, p. 2).

4 The Origins of Public Corruption Control in the United States

1 Plato (1951).
2 Brightman (2004), p. 216.
3 Lloyd (1998).
4 Bedi (2002).
5 Johns (2002), p. 1.
6 Ibid., p. 2.
7 Brightman (2004).
8 Kramer (2002), p. 23.
9 United States Government Accountability Office (2007).
10 Lehr and O'Neill (2007).
11 Anechiarico and Jacobs (1996), p. 4.
12 Wells (2004), p. 43.
13 Plato (1951).
14 Quoted in Patton (1996), p. 10.
15 Anechiarico and Jacobs (1996), p. 19.
16 Ibid., p. 32.

17 Sinclair (1904).
18 Anechiarico and Jacobs (1996).
19 Roosevelt (1910).
20 United States Food and Drug Administration (1981).
21 Bishop (2004), p. 257.
22 Padover (2007), p. 56.
23 White House (n.d.).
24 Markowitz (1998).
25 Applewhite *et al.* (2003).
26 Nobel Foundation (n.d.).
27 Woolley and Peters (n.d.), para. 6.
28 Goedeken (2007).
29 Roosevelt (1927), quote on p. 472.
30 National Archives and Records Administration (n.d.), para. 2.
31 Ibid.
32 Ibid.
33 James Madison Center (n.d.).
34 Ibid.
35 Anechiarico and Jacobs (1996).
36 Lipset and Marks (2001).
37 Dreyfus (2001), p. 1.
38 Aberbach and Rockman (2000), p. 28.
39 Elwell (1996), p. 1.
40 Anechiarico and Jacobs (1996), p. 22.
41 Ibiblio.org. (n.d.).
42 Marjit and Shi (1998), p. 171.
43 Moore (2003), p. 29.
44 Patton (1996), pp. 10–11.

5 The "Modern Era" of Public Corruption Control

1   Rosoff *et al.* (2006), p. 332.
2   Schissel (2000), p. 2.
3   Sparrow (1998).
4   Aberbach and Rockman (2000), p. 32.
5   Ibid.
6   Bentham (1787).
7   Anechiarico and Jacobs (1996).
8   Ibid., p. 24.
9   Simon and Hagan (1998), p. 2.
10 Shestack (1998).
11 Aberbach and Rockman (2000).
12 Ibid., p. 12.
13 United States Office of Personnel Management (2002), p. 13.
14 United States Code (n.d.).
15 The Inspectors General (n.d.), para 1.
16 United States Office of Special Counsel (n.d.), para 1.
17 Anechiarico and Jacobs (1996), p. 27.
18 Simon and Hagan (1998).
19 Mayer *et al.* (1980), p. 14.
20 Ibid., p. 15.

21   Simon and Hagan (1998), p. 70.
22   Rosoff *et al.* (2006), p. 96.
23   United States Department of Justice (n.d.).
24   Ibid.
25   Aberbach and Rockman (2000).
26   Ibid.
27   Schlegel and Weisburd (1994), p. 221.
28   Conason (2001).
29   Aberbach and Rockman (2000).
30   Gerth (1992).
31   Ibid.
32   Hedges (1992).
33   Potter (2002), p. 145.
34   Aberbach and Rockman (2000), p. 140.
35   Anechiarico and Jacobs (1996).
36   White House (1996).
37   Aberbach and Rockman (2000), p. 180.
38   Electronic Privacy Information Center (2001).
39   Congressional Budget Office (2002).

6 White-Collar Crime Theory

 1   Merton (1938).
 2   Sutherland (1947).
 3   Sutherland (1949).
 4   Cressey (1953).
 5   Clinard (1952).
 6   Edelhertz (1970).
 7   Ermann and Lundman (1982).
 8   Vaughn (1982).
 9   Hagan (1990).
10   Simon (2002).
11   Weisburd *et al.* (2001).
12   Geis *et al.* (1995).
13   Magnuson (1992).
14   Geis *et al.* (1995).
15   Veblen ([1912] 1994).
16   Ibid., p. 60.
17   West (1967), p. 88.
18   Merton (1938).
19   Ibid.
20   Vold *et al.* (1998).
21   West (1967), p. 124.
22   Ibid., p. 84.
23   Vold *et al.* (1998).
24   Geis (1982), p. 38.
25   Vold *et al.* (1998), pp. 184–5.
26   Sutherland (1983).
27   Ibid., p. 7.
28   Cloward and Ohlin (1960).
29   Schlegel and Weisburd (1992), p. 115.

30 Tunnell (2000).
31 Mills (1956).
32 Geis *et al.* (1995), p. 53.
33 Ibid.
34 Messner and Rosenfeld (1994).
35 Vold *et al.* (1998).
36 Benson (1990).
37 Geis *et al.* (1995), p. 326.
38 Cressey (1953).
39 Schlegel and Weisburd (1992).
40 Ibid., pp. 56–7.
41 Wells (1992), p. 31.
42 Brown *et al.* (2001).
43 Clinard (1952).
44 Hartung (1950).
45 Burgess (1950).
46 Newman (1958).
47 Quinney (1964).
48 Schlegel and Weisburd (1992), p. 36.
49 Ibid., p. 37.
50 Newman (1958).
51 Quinney (1964).
52 Green (1990), p. 12.
53 Geis *et al.* (1995).
54 Schlegel and Weisburd (1992).
55 Geis (1982).
56 Clinard (1952).
57 Cressey (1953).
58 Friedrichs (2006).
59 Adler (1975).
60 Chesney-Lind (2006).
61 Daly (1989).
62 Ibid.
63 Naffine (1987).
64 Zietz (1981).
65 Chapman (1980).
66 Albanese (1995), p. 102.

7 Organizational Crime and Corporate Criminal Liabilities

1 Waters (2001).
2 McLean and Elkind (2004).
3 Schlegel and Weisburd (1992), p. 38.
4 Simon and Hagan (1998), p. 28.
5 Blakey (1980), p. 2.
6 Simon and Hagan (1998), p. 27.
7 Geis *et al.* (1995), p. 152.
8 Schlegel and Weisburd (1992).
9 Shapiro (1985), p. 45.
10 Letkemann (1973), p. 2.
11 Douglas *et al.* (1997).

12 United States Secret Service (n.d.c).
13 United States Department of Justice (n.d.e).
14 Green (1990).
15 Ibid., Chapter 8.
16 Ibid.
17 Schlegel and Weisburd (1992), p. 45.
18 Ermann and Lundman (1982).
19 Clinard and Quinney (1973).
20 Schlegel and Weisburd (1992), Chapter 2.
21 Wells (1992), p. 36.
22 Clinard and Yeager (1980).
23 Wells (1992).
24 Brown *et al.* (2001).
25 Wells (1992), p. 35.
26 Mills (1956).
27 Simon (2002).
28 Simon and Hagan (1998).
29 Simon (2002).
30 Ibid., p. 214.
31 Environmental Protection Agency (n.d.c).
32 Environmental Protection Agency (n.d.e).
33 Simon (2002).
34 Braithwaite (1982).
35 Wells (1992).
36 Friedrichs (2006), p. 298.
37 Green (1990), p. 255.
38 Friedrichs (2006).
39 Wells (1992), p. 36.
40 *Journal of Accountancy* Online, February (2004).
41 Bruderlin-Nelson (2008).
42 Lauer (2007).
43 Bryce (2005).
44 Hasslberger (2003).
45 United States Department of Justice (2001).
46 Bryce (2005).
47 Schlegel and Weisburd (1992), p. 80.
48 Braithwaite (1982), p. 81.
49 Ibid.
50 Friedrichs (2006), p. 336.
51 Geis *et al.* (1995), pp. 325–6.
52 Grose and Groves (1988).
53 Greenberg. (1993), p. 86.
54 Merton (1938).
55 Grose and Groves (1988).
56 Gordon (1996), p. 147.
57 Vaughn (1982).
58 FBI (2007).

8 White-Collar Crime: A Legalistic Perspective

1 Potter (2002), p. 13.
2 Friedrichs (2006).
3 *Magna Carta and American Law* (n.d.).
4 Murrell and Dwyer (1992), p. 18.
5 Ibid.
6 Wong Sun v. United States, 371 U.S. 471 (1963).
7 United States Constitution (1791).
8 Draper v. United States, 358 U.S. 307 (1959)
9 Murrell and Dwyer (1992).
10 Besselman (n.d.).
11 Lamelayer.com (n.d.).
12 Carroll v. United States, 267 U.S. 132 (1925).
13 Schneckloth v. Bustamonte, 412 U.S. 218 (1973).
14 Chimel v. California, 395 U.S. 752 (1969).
15 Burdeau v. McDowell, 256 U.S. 465 (1921).
16 California v. Greenwood, 486 U.S. 35 (1988).
17 Grosso (1994), p. 6.
18 Miranda v. Arizona, 384 U.S. 436 (1966).
19 King (n.d.).
20 Electronic Frontier Foundation (2001).
21 Albanese (1995), p. 13.
22 United States Postal Inspection Service (n.d.).
23 Cornell University Law School (n.d.h).
24 Cornell University Law School (n.d.f).
25 Cornell University Law School (n.d.g).
26 Friedrichs (2006).
27 Ibid., p. 115.
28 Cornell University Law School (n.d.i).
29 Cornell University Law School (n.d.c).
30 Cornell University Law School (n.d.e).
31 Ross (2001).
32 Levin (2001).
33 Hughes (2001), p. 1.
34 Cornell University Law School (n.d.j).
35 Petzinger *et al.* (1991).
36 Madsen (2001).
37 Kranish (2001), p. 2.
38 Cornell University Law School (n.d.k).
39 United States Department of Justice (1994).
40 Ibid., p. 37.
41 Cornell University Law School (n.d.d).
42 Kochan (1998).

9 White-Collar Crime Analysis and Trends

1 Electronic Privacy Information Center (2001).
2 Ibid.
3 Electronic Privacy Information Center (n.d.).
4 Kranish (2001).

5   Peterson *et al.* (2000), p. 1.
6   Schultz (2003).
7   Peterson *et al.* (2000).
8   Schultz (2003), p. 146.
9   Ibid.
10 Ibid.
11 Cornell University Law School (n.d.g).
12 Association of Certified Fraud Examiners (2003), p. 1.
13 Ilardi (2001), p. 7.
14 United States Drug Enforcement Administration (2003), p. 1.
15 Peterson *et al.* (2000), p. 9.
16 Cisco Systems. Innovative wireless ip video surveillance
17 Peterson *et al.* (2000), p. 10.
18 Leedy and Ormond (2001).
19 Peterson *et al.* (2000).
20 Financial Crimes Enforcement Network (FinCEN) (2007).
21 Toland (2003), p. 115.
22 Cornell University Law School (n.d.b).
23 O'Bryant and Seghetti (2002).
24 Electronic Privacy Information Center (2001).
25 Strang (2000), p. 1.
26 Ibid., pp. 3–4.
27 Peterson (2003).
28 Ibid.
29 Ibid., p. 132.
30 Peterson *et al.* (2000), p. 23.

10 Where Do We Go From Here?

1   United States of America v. Ali Saleh Hahlah Al-Marri.
2   BBC News (2004).
3   Billingslea (n.d.).
4   Fox and Zawitz (2003).
5   National Center for Education Statistics (2002), p. 1.
6   Klaus (2002).
7   Federal Bureau of Investigation (2002).
8   BBC News (2002).
9   McIntyre (2003).
10 Iritani and Daniszewski (2002).
11 Geis *et al.* (1995), p. 48

Credits

Text

Kathryn C. Arnold, 'Corporate crime after 2000: A new law enforcement challenge or deja vu?' from *The American Criminal Law Review* (April 1, 2003). Copyright © 2003. Reprinted with permission.

William Billingslea, 'Illicit Cigarette Trafficking and the Funding of Terrorism' from *The Police Chief* 71 (February 2004). Copyright held by the International Association of Chiefs of Police, 515 N. Washington Street, Alexandria, VA 22314. Further reproduction without the express permission from IACP is strictly prohibited.

Peter Carbonara, 'The scam that will not die: Nigerian advance-fee scams have fooled Americans for decades. Thanks to the Internet, they're now staging a disturbing resurgence.' from *Money* (July 1, 2002). Copyright © 2002 by Time, Inc. All rights reserved.

D. P. Champlin and J. T. Knoedler, 'Corporations, workers, and the public interest' from *Journal of Economic Issues* 37 (2003): 305–314. Reprinted by special permission of the copyright holder, the Association for Evolutionary Economics.

Charlie Cray, 'Disaster Profiteering: The flood of crony contracting following hurricane Katrina' from *Multinational Monitor* (September/October 2005): 19–25. Copyright © 2005 Essential Information, Inc. Reprinted with permission.

Charlie Cray, 'Meet the war profiteers' from *Multinational Monitor* (November/December 2006): 27–34. Copyright © 2006 Essential Information, Inc. Reprinted with permission.

Amber Ennis, 'A look at crime in the age of technology' from *The Forensic Examiner* 16, no. 4 (Winter 2007): 14–16. Copyright © 2007 by the American College of Forensic Examiners International. Reprinted with permission of American College of Forensic Examiners International via Copyright Clearance Center.

D.S. Glasberg and D. Skidmore, 'The dialectics of white–collar crime: the anatomy of the savings and loan crisis and the case of Silverado Banking, Savings and Loan Association' from *The American Journal of Economics and Sociology* 57 (1998): 423–425. Copyright © 1998 American Journal of Economics and Sociology, Inc. Reprinted by permission of Blackwell Publishing Ltd.

Brad Heath, 'Katrina fraud swamps system' from *USA Today* (July 6, 2007): 1A. Copyright © 2007 USA Today. Reprinted with permission.

Donald E. deKieffer, 'Terrorist links to commercial fraud in the United States' from

Figures

Bibliography

Aberbach, J. and Rockman, B. (2000) *In the Web of Politics: Three Decades of the U.S. Federal Executive.* Washington, DC: Brookings Institution Press.

Adler, F. (1975) *Sisters in Crime: The Rise of the New Female Criminal.* New York: McGraw-Hill.

Agency for Toxic Substances and Disease Registry (n.d.a) *ToxFAQs for Polychlorinated Biphenyls (PCBs).* Retrieved January 21, 2006 from http://www.astdr.cdc.gov/tfacts17.html.

—— (n.d.b) *Toxicological Profile for Polychlorinated Biphenyls (PCBs).* Retrieved January 21, 2006 from http://www.atsdr.cdc.gov/toxprofiles/tp17.html.

Albanese, J. S. (1995) *White Collar Crime in America.* Upper Saddle River, NJ: Prentice Hall.

Allen, J., Alberts, C., Behrens, S., Laswell, B., and Wilson, W. (2000) "Improving the security of networked systems." *Cross Talk*, October. Retrieved August 5, 2008 from http://www.stsc.hill.af.mil/crosstalk/2000/10/allen.html.

Andrews, R. (2006) "Baiters teach scammers a lesson." *Wired*, August 4. Retrieved August 5, 2008, from http://www.wired.com/techbiz/it/news/2006/08/71387

Anechiarico, F. and Jacobs, J. B. (1996) *The Pursuit of Absolute Integrity: How Corruption Control Makes Government Ineffective.* Chicago: The University of Chicago Press.

Applewhite, A., Evans, T., and Frothingham, A. (2003) *And I Quote.* New York: Thomas Dunne Books.

Associated Press (2006) "New details emerge in Los Alamos case." *CBS News*, October 25. Retrieved August 30, 2007, from http://www.cbsnews.com/stories/2006/10/24/national/main2122004.shtml

Association of Certified Fraud Examiners (2003) *CFE Rules and Regulations, Code of Ethics.* Retrieved August 11, 2008, from http://www.acfe.com/about/cfe-rules.asp?copy = ethics.

Aubert, V. (1952) "White-collar crime and social structure." *The American Journal of Sociology*, 58(3): 263–71.

Barrera, E. (2005) "Key figure in S.B. County scandal get probation." *Inland Valley Daily Bulletin*, November 29. Retrieved August 7, 2008, from Lexis-Nexis database.

Bayley, D. H. and Garofalo, J. (1989) "The management of violence by police patrol officers." *Criminology*, 27(1): 1–25.

BBC News (2002) "Bush to announce new economic team," December 8. Retrieved August 11, 2008, from http://news.bbc.co.uk/2/hi/business/2550603.stm.

—— (2004) "Bali bomber writes autobiography," September 7. Retrieved August 11, 2008, from http://news.bbc.co.uk/2/hi/asia-pacific/3634264.stm.

Bedi, R. (2002) "New fraud threatening bribery in India." *Dawn: The Internet Edition*. Retrieved August 8, 2008, from http://www.dawn.com/2002/04/05/int17.htm.

Benson, M. L. (1990) "Emotions and adjudication: Status degradation among white-collar criminals." *Justice Quarterly*, 7: 515–28.

Bentham, J. (1787) *The Panoptican Writings*. Retrieved August 8, 2008, from http://cartome.org/panopticon2.htm.

Bergstrom, B. (2002) "Last House member ejected was Philadelphia contractor." *Associated Press Online*. July 18. Retrieved August 7, 2008, from Lexis-Nexis database.

Berke, R. L. (2002) "Enron's collapse: The strategist; Associates of Bush aide say he helped strategist win an Enron contract." *The New York Times*, January 25, C1.

Besselman, J. P. (n.d.) "The knock and announce rule: 'Knock, knock, knocking on the suspect's door'." *Federal Law Enforcement Training Center*. Retrieved August 10, 2008, from http://www.fletc.gov/training/programs/legal-division/the-informer/research-by-subject/4th-amendment/knockandannounce.pdf/view.

Billingslea, W. (n.d.) "Illicit cigarette trafficking and the funding of terrorism." Bureau of Alcohol, Tobacco, Firearms, and Explosives. Washington, D. C.

Bishop, J. B. (2004) *Theodore Roosevelt and his Time Shown in his Own Letters*, Part two. Whitefish, MT: Kessinger Publishing, LLC.

Blakey, G. R. (1980) *Materials on RICO (Racketeer Influenced and Corrupt Organizations)—Criminal Overview* (NCJ—78839). Washington, D.C.: National Criminal Justice Reference Service.

Boyd, J. (2001) "Life after Enrononline: E-market's demise roils energy industry, but repeat unlikely in other sectors," December 10. *InternetWeek*, p. 1. Retrieved August 7, 2008, from Lexis-Nexis database.

Braithwaite, J. (1982) "Enforced self-regulation: A new strategy for corporate crime control." *Michigan Law Review*, 80(7): 1466–507.

Brightman, H. J. (2000) "The four c's of education: A study of the relationship between New Jersey's children, curricula, computers, and consumptive-criminality." Doctoral Dissertation, Seton Hall University.

—— (2004) "Corruption." In L. M. Salinger (ed.), *The Encyclopedia of White-Collar Crime and Corporate Crime*. Thousand Oaks, CA: Sage Publications, pp. 216–22.

Brown, S. E., Esbensen, F., and Geis, G. (2001) *Criminology: Explaining Crime and its Context*, 4th edn. Cincinnati, OH: Anderson Publishing Co.

Bruderlin-Nelson, C. (n.d.) "BMS pays $500M on fraud suits." Retrieved August 11, 2008 from http://www.fiercepharma.com/story/bristol-myers-squibb-pays-half-billion-dollars/2008–0. . . .

Bryce, R. (2005) "Texas goes after big pharma." Retrieved August 14, 2008 from http://www.texasobserver.org/article.php?aid = 1890.

Burgess, E. W. (1950) "Comment, and concluding comment." *American Journal of Sociology*, 56: 32–4.

Business Wire. (2000) "Adaptec seizes more than $1 million in counterfeit products," October 25. Retrieved August 7, 2008, from http://findarticles.com/p/articles/mi_m0EIN/is_2000_Oct_25/ai_66359960.

Carter, D. L. (1995) "Computer crime categories: How techno-criminals operate," July. Retrieved August 26, 2007, from http://nsi.org/Library/Compsec/crimecom.html.

Center for Responsive Politics (2002) "Enron's campaign contributions, 1989–2001" —Senate and House," January. Retrieved August 7, 2008, from http://www.freerepublic.com/focus/fr/606252/posts.

Chapman, J. R. (1980) *Economic Realities and the Female Offender*. Lexington, MA: Lexington Books.

Chen, D. W. (2000) "Dutchess County Republican official admits corruption," *The New York Times*, B5, February 19. Retrieved August 7, 2008, from Lexis-Nexis database.

Chesney-Lind, M. (2006) "Patriarchy, crime and justice: Feminist criminology." *Feminist Criminology*, 1(1): 6–26.

Cisco Systems (2005) "Innovative wireless IP video surveillance: City of Seal Beach police department," *The Print*, 18(2): 6. Retrieved August 11, 2008, from http://www.scafo.org/The_Print/THE_PRINT_VOL_18_ISSUE_02.pdf.

Clinard, M. B. (1952) *Black Market: A Study of White Collar Crime*. New York: Rinehart & Company.

Clinard, M. B. and Quinney, R. (1973) *Criminal Behavior Systems: A Typology*, 2nd edn. New York: Holt Rinehart & Winston.

Clinard, M. B. and Yeager, P. C. (1980) *Corporate Crime*. New York: Free Press.

Cloward, R. and Ohlin, L. (1960) *Delinquency and Opportunity*. New York: Free Press.

Computer Crime Research Center (2005) "Computer crime case: Former manager pleads guilty," July 11. Retrieved August 26, 2007, from http://www.crime-research.org/news/21.07.2005/1375

Conason, J. (2001) "The Bush pardons." *Salon.com.*, February 27. Retrieved August 9, 2008, from http://archive.salon.com/news/col/cona/2001/02/27/pardons/.

Congressional Budget Office (2002) *H.R. 2356: Bipartisan Campaign Reform Act of 2002*. Retrieved August 9, 2008, from http://www.cbo.gov/ftpdocs/33xx/doc3334/hr2356omb.pdf.

Cornell University Law School. (n.d.a) *Subpoena duces tecum*. Retrieved August 10, 2008, from http://topics.law.cornell.edu/wex/subpoena_duces_tecum.

—— (n.d.b) *U.S. Code Collection: Chapter 96, Racketeer Influenced and Corrupt Organizations (18 USC 96)*. Retrieved August 10, 2008, http://www4.law.cornell.edu/uscode/18/usc_sup_01_18_10_I_20_96.html.

—— (n.d.c) *U.S. Code Collection: Section 510, Forging Endorsements on Treasury Checks or Bonds or Securities of the United States (18 USC 510)*. Retrieved August 10, 2008, http://www.law.cornell.edu/uscode/18/510.html.

—— (n.d.d) *U.S. Code Collection: Section 981, Civil Forfeiture (18 USC 981)*. Retrieved August 10, 2008, http://www4.law.cornell.edu/uscode/18/981.html.

—— (n.d.e) *U.S. Code Collection: Section 1001, Statements or Entries Generally (18 USC 1001)*. Retrieved August 10, 2008, http://www.law.cornell.edu/uscode/18/1001%20.html.

—— (n.d.f) *U.S. Code Collection: Section 1029, Fraud and Related Activity in Connection With Access Devices (18 USC 1029).* Retrieved August 10, 2008, from http://www4.law.cornell.edu/uscode/uscode18/usc_sec_18_00001029 – 000-.html.

—— (n.d.g) *U.S. Code Collection: Section 1030, Fraud and Related Activity in Connection with Computers (18 USC 1030).* Retrieved August 10, 2008, from http://www4.law.cornell.edu/uscode/18/1030.html.

—— (n.d.h) *U.S. Code Collection: Section 1343, Fraud by Wire, Radio, or Television (18 USC 1343).* Retrieved August 10, 2008, from http://www4.law.cornell.edu/uscode/18/1343.html.

—— (n.d.i) *U.S. Code Collection: Section 1344, Bank Fraud (18 USC 1344).* Retrieved August 10, 2008, from http://www.law.cornell.edu/uscode/18/1344.shtml.

—— (n.d.j) *U.S. Code Collection: Section 1956, Laundering of Monetary Instruments (18 USC 1956).* Retrieved August 10, 2008, from http://www4.law.cornell.edu/uscode/18/1956.html.

—— (n.d.k) *U.S. Code Collection: Section 1963, Criminal Penalties (18 USC 1963).* Retrieved August 10, 2008, from http://uscode.law.cornell.edu/uscode/html/uscode18/usc_sec_18_00001963 – 000-.html.

Cressey, D. (1953) *Other People's Money: A Study in the Social Psychology of Embezzlement.* New York: Free Press.

Daly, K. (1989) "Gender and varieties of white-collar crime." *Criminology,* 27(4): 769–94.

Department of the Treasury (2006) "The use and counterfeiting of United States currency abroad, part 3. The final report to the Congress by the Secretary of the Treasury, in consultation with the Advanced Counterfeit Deterrence Steering Committee, pursuant to Section 807 of PL 104–132," September. Retrieved August 6, 2008, from http://www.ustreas.gov/press/releases/reports/the%20use%20and%20counterfeiting%20of%20u.s.%20currency%20abroad%20%20part%203%20september2006.pdf.

Douglas, J., Burgess, A. W., Burgess, A. G., and Ressler, R. K. (1997) *Crime Classification Manual: A Standard System for Investigating and Classifying Violent Crimes.* Hoboken, NJ: Jossey-Bass.

Dreyfuss, R. (2001) "Specters of socialism. [Review of the book *It didn't happen here: Why socialism failed in the United States*]." *The American Prospect.* Retrieved August 8, 2008, from http://www.accessmylibrary.com/coms2/summary_0286-11463998_ITM.

Edelhertz, H. (1970) *The Nature, Impact, and Prosecution of White-Collar Crime* (ICR 70–71). Washington, D.C.: U. S. Department of Justice.

Electronic Frontier Foundation (2001) "EFF analysis of the provisions of the USA Patriot Act," October 31. Retrieved August 10, 2008, from http://w2.eff.org/Privacy/Surveillance/Terrorism/20011031_eff_usa_patriot_analysis.php.

Electronic Privacy Information Center (2001) *H.R. 3162: USA Patriot Act.* Retrieved August 9, 2008, from http://epic.org/privacy/terrorism/hr3162.html

—— (n.d.) *"Terrorism" Information Awareness (TIA).* Retrieved August 10, 2008, from http://epic.org/privacy/profiling/tia/.

Elwell, F. (1996) "The sociology of Max Weber." Retrieved August 8, 2008, from http://www.faculty.rsu.edu/~felwell/Theorists/Weber/Whome.htm.

Environmental Protection Agency (n.d.a) *Hudson River PCBs*. Retrieved January 22m 2006 from http://www.epa.gov/region02/superfund/npl/0202229c.htm.

—— (n.d.b) *Consumer Factsheet on: POLYCHLORINATED BIPHENYLS*. Retrieved January 21, 2006 from http://www.epa.gov/safewater/contaminants/dw_contamfs/pcbs.html.

—— (n.d.c) *Comprehensive Environmental Response, Compensation, and Liability Act* (CERCLA). Retrieved August 10, 2008, from http://www.epa.gov/oecaagct/lcla.html.

—— (n.d.d) *Superfund Amendments and Reauthorization Act* (SARA). Retrieved August 10, 2008, from http://www.epa.gov/superfund/policy/sara.htm.

Ermann, M. D. and Lundman, R. J. (1982) *Corporate Deviance*. New York: Holt, Rinehart and Winston.

—— (2001) *Corporate and Governmental Deviance: Problems of Organizational Behavior in Contemporary Society*. New York: Oxford University Press.

Farquhar, M. (2002) "Capitol Offenses: D.C.'s long, unhappy history of sin." *The Washington Post*, L27, June 5. Retrieved August 7, 2008, from Lexis-Nexis database.

Federal Bureau of Investigation (2002) *Crime in the United States, 2001* (Press Release). Retrieved August 11, 2008, from http://www.fbi.gov/pressrel/press-rel02/cius2001.htm.

—— (n.d.) *Financial Report to the Public, Fiscal Year 2007*. Retrieved August 3, 2008, from http://www.fbi.gov/publications/financial/fcs_report2007/financial_crime_2007.htm.

Fenn, J. (2002) "Swift says she will focus on her family." *Lowell Sun*, December 27. Retrieved August 7, 2008, from Lexis-Nexis database.

Festa, P. (1998) "Windows 'back door' raises flags." *CNET News*, August 12. Retrieved August 6, 2008, from http://news.cnet.com/2100-1001-214387.html.

Financial Crimes Enforcement Network (FinCEN) (2007) "National Money Laundering Strategy". Retrieved August 11, 2008, from http://www.fincen.gov/news_room/rp/files/nmls_2007.pdf.

Flory, D. (1990) "The great blue box phone frauds." *IEEE Spectrum*, 27(11): 117–19.

Fox River Watch (n.d.) *The GE cancer study was flawed*. Retrieved January 22, 2006 from http://www.foxriverwatch.com/general_electric_PCB-health_study.html.

Fox, J. A. and Zawitz, M. W. (2003) "Homicide trends in the United States: 2000," (NCJ 197471). Washington, DC: United States Department of Justice.

Fox River Watch (n.d.) "The history of PCBs: When were health problems detected?" Retrieved January 21, 2006 from http://www.foxriverwatch.com/monsanto2a_pcb_pcbs.html.

Friedrichs, D. O. (2006) *Trusted Criminals: White Collar Crime in Contemporary Society*. Belmont, CA: Thompson-Wadsworth.

Geis, G. (1982) *On White-Collar Crime*. Lanham, MD: Lexington Books.

Geis, G., Meier, R. F., and Salinger, L. M. (eds.) (1995) *White Collar Crime: Classic And Contemporary Views*. New York: The Free Press.

Gerth, Jeff. (1992, April 19) The 1992 campaign; The business dealings of the President's relatives: What the record shows. *The New York Times*, 14. Retrieved August 7, 2008, from Lexis-Nexis database.

Glasner, J. (2001) "Enron: A bandwith bloodbath." *Wired*, November 30. Retrieved August 7, 2008, from http://www.wired.com/techbiz/media/news/2001/11/48732

Goedeken, E. (2007) "Charles G. Dawes establishes the bureau of the budget, 1921–22." *Historian*, 50(1): 40–53.

Gordon, D. M. (1996) *Fat and Mean: The Corporate Squeeze Of Working Americans And The Myth Of Managerial Downsizing*. New York: Free Press.

Gordon, G.R. and Curtis, G.E. (2000) "The growing global threat of economic cyber crime." National Fraud Center, Inc. Retrieved from http://www.utica.edu/academic/institutes/ecii/publications/media/global_threat_crime.pdf.

Green, G. S. (1990) *Occupational Crime*. Belmont, CA: Thompson-Wadsworth.

Greenberg, D. F. (1993) *Crime and Capitalism: Readings in Marxist Criminology*. Philadelphia, PA: Temple University Press.

Grose, G. and Groves, W. B. (1988) "Crime and human nature: A Marxist perspective." *Contemporary Crises*, 12: 145–71.

Grosso, A. (1994) "Search Warrant Applications." *The FBI Law Enforcement Bulletin*, December. Retrieved August 10, 2008, from http://findarticles.com/p/articles/mi_m2194/is_n12_v63/ai_16548134/pg_6.

Hahn, P. (1998) *Emerging Criminal Justice: Three Pillars for a Proactive Criminal Justice System*. Thousand Oaks, CA: Sage Publications.

Hartung, F. E. (1950) "White-collar offenses in the wholesale meat industry in Detroit." *American Journal of Sociology*, 65, 25–34.

Hasslberger, S. (n.d.) "Health supreme: California uncovers pharma fraud." Retrieved August 8, 2008 from http://www.newsmediaexplorer.org/sepp/2003/10/12/california_uncovers_pharma_fraud.htm.

Heath, B. (2007) "Katrina fraud swamps system." *USA Today*, July 601A.

Heath, J. (2002) "Enron chairman Lay a chum of both Bushes." *The Atlanta Journal-Constitution*, January 23, p. 4D.

Hedges, S. J. (1992) The color of money. *U.S. News & World Report*, 112(10): 57–61.

Heitmeyer, W. and Hagan, F. (2003) *The International Handbook of Violence Research*. London: Kluwer.

Holland, J. (2002) House panel votes to expel convicted congressman. *Amarillo Globe News*, July 19, p. 2.

Hudson River Sloop Clearwater (n.d.) "Clearwater presents the Hudson River PCB story." Retrieved January 22, 2006 from http://www.clearwater.org/pcbs/.

Hughes, J. E. (2001) "Elusive terror money slips through government traps." *USA Today*, Op-Ed, November 27. Retrieved August 10, 2008, from http://www.usatoday.com/news/opinion/2001-11-28-ncguest2.htm.

Ibiblio.org (n.d.) "Internet pioneers: Vannevar Bush." Retrieved August 8, 2008, from http://www.ibiblio.org/pioneers/bush.html.

Ilardi, G. J. (2001) "Terrorism and intelligence research: Parallel journeys in search of influence and utility?" *IALEIA Journal*, 15(1).

Iritani, E. and Daniszewski, J. (2002) "Iraqi oil lies below surface of U.N. talks." *Los Angeles Times*, November 5, p. A8.

James Madison Center (n.d.) *US History Curriculum: Chapter XI. The Great Depression*. James Madison University. Retrieved August 8, 2008, from http://www.jmu.edu/madison/center/main_pages/teacher/curriculum/chap11.htm.

Johns, C. (2002) "The mordida: Mexico and corruption." Retrieved August 8, 2008, from http://www.cjjohns.com/lawpowerandjustice/commentaries/mordida.html.

Kadlec, D. (2002) "Enron: Who's accountable?" *Time*, January 13. Retrieved

August 7, 2008, from http://www.time.com/time/business/article/0,8599,193520,00.html.

King, J. E. (n.d.) "Pleading the fifth and Miranda warnings: separating fact from fiction." *Lawyers.com*. Retrieved August 10, 2008, from http://research.lawyers.com/Pleading-the-Fifth-and-Miranda-Warnings.html.

Klaus, P. A. (2002) Crime and the nation's households, 2000 (NCJ 194107). Washington, D.C.: United States Department of Justice, Bureau of Justice Statistics.

Kochan, D. J. (1998) "Reforming property forfeiture laws to protect citizens' rights." Mackinac Center for Public Policy. Retrieved August 10, 2008, from http://www.mackinac.org/archives/1998/s1998–03.pdf.

Kramer, W. (2002) "Corruption and fraud stunt third-world growth," part two. *Fraud Magazine*, 16(4): 23.

Kranish, M. (2001) "Focus turns to money laundering in terrorism war." *Boston Globe*, September 15, p. A2.

Kurtz, H. (1991) "Scandal." *The Washington Post*, September 22, p. W10. Retrieved August 7, 2008, from Lexis-Nexis database.

Lamelayer.com. (n.d.) "Search and seizure: A guide to rules, exceptions, requirements, tests, doctrines, and exceptions." Retrieved August 10, 2008, from http://www.lamelawyer.com/files/sasg.pdf.

Lauer, K.A. (2007) "Defending government pharmaceutical fraud investigations: Assessing strategic options.! American Bar Association. Retrieved August 14, 2008 from http://www.lw.com/upload/pubContent/_pdf/pub1864_1.pdf.

Leedy, P. D. and Ormond, J. E. (2001) *Practical Research: Planning and Design*, 7th edn. Upper Saddle River, NJ: Merill/Prentice Hall.

Lehr, D. and O'Neill, P. (2007) *Black Mass: The True Story Of An Unholy Alliance Between The FBI And The Irish Mob*. New York: HarperCollins.

Leiner, B. M., Cerf, V. G., Clark, D. D., Kahn, R. E., Kleinrock, L., Lynch, D. C., Postel, J., Roberts, L. G., and Wolf, S. (1999) *A Brief History of the Internet*. Retrieved August 6, 2008, from Cornell University, Library website: http://arxiv.org/html/cs/9901011v1.

Letkemann, P. (1973) *Crime as Work*. Upper Saddle River, NJ: Prentice-Hall.

Levin, C. (2001) "Prepared testimony of the honorable Carl Levin (D-MI) United States Senator." Retrieved August 10, 2008, from http://www.fas.org/irp/congress/2001_hr/092601_levin.html.

Lipset, S. M. and Marks, G. W. (2001) *It Didn't Happen Here: Why Socialism Failed In The United States*. New York: W. W. Norton & Company.

Lloyd, M. D. (1998) "Polybius and the founding fathers: The separation of powers." Retrieved August 8, 2008, from http://www.mlloyd.org/mdl-indx/polybius/intro.htm.

Maddux, M. (2002) "Barnes guilty; Former Paterson mayor admits corruption." *The Record (Bergen County, NJ)*, July 2, p. A1. Retrieved August 7, 2008, from Lexis-Nexis database.

Madsen, W. (2001) "Questionable ties: Tracking bin Laden's money flow leads back to Midland, Texas." *In These Times*. Retrieved August 10, 2008, from http://www.globalresearch.ca/articles/MAD202B.html.

Magna Carta and American Law (n.d.). Retrieved August 10, 2008, from http://www.magnacharta.com/articles/article04.htm

Magnuson, R. J. (1992) *The White-Collar Crime Explosion: How to Protect Yourself and Your Company from Prosecution*. Columbus, OH: McGraw-Hill.

Marjit, S. and Shi, H. (1998) "On controlling crime with corrupt officials." *Journal of Economic Behavior and Organization*, 34(1): 163–72.

Markowitz, N. (1998) "Sex scandals and U.S. history." *History News Service*. Retrieved August 8, 2008 from http://h-net.msu.edu/cgi-bin/logbrowse.pl?trx = vx&list = h-announce&month = 9811&week = c&msg = tMkUSI%2b7fPjpFiI-ijjxfjQ&user = &pw =.

Martin, J. P. (2005) "Janiszewski asks judge to trim 41-month term." *The Star-Ledger* (Newark, New Jersey), April 6, p. 26. Retrieved August 7, 2008, from Lexis-Nexis database.

Mayer, A. J., Clift, E., Shannon, E., Borger, G., Willenson, K., Morris, H., and Smith, V. E. (1980) "A storm over Billy Carter." *Newsweek* August 4, p. 14.

McCollum, K. (1999) "Oregon student is convicted of providing pirated music." *The Chronicle of Higher Education*, September 3, p. A48.

McIntyre, J. (2003) "Top Pentagon advisor resigns under fire." *CNN.com*. March 28. Retrieved August 11, 2008, from http://www.cnn.com/2003/US/03/27/perle.resigns/index.html.

McLean, B. and Elkind, P. (2004) *The Smartest Guys in the Room*. New York: Portfolio.

Merton, R. K. (1938) "Social structure and anomie." *American Sociological Review*, 3 (Oct.): 672–82.

Messner, E. (2007) "TJX data theft called largest ever: 47.5m credit card numbers." *Network World*, March 29. Retrieved August 7, 2008, from http://www.networkworld.com/news/2007/032907-tjx-data-theft-largest.html.

Messner, S. F. and Rosenfeld, R. (1994) *Crime and the American Dream*. Belmont, CA: Wadsworth Publishing Co.

Microsoft, Inc. (2000) "U.S. customs cracks down on software counterfeiting in Georgia." Retrieved August 7, 2008, from http://www.microsoft.com/presspass/press/2000/Aug00/GeorgiaPR.mspx.

Milbank, D. and Kessler, G. (2002) "Enron's influence reached deep into administration." *Washington Post*, January 18, p. A01.

Mills, C. W. (1956) *The Power Elite*. Oxford: Oxford University Press.

Moore, E. (2003) "Network Security: Safeguarding systems against the latest threats." Regional Organized Crime Information Center. Retrieved August 8, 2008, from http://www.douglasmapolice.com/Downloads/network_security.pdf.

Murrell, D. S. and Dwyer, W. O. (1992) *Constitutional Law and Liability for Public-Sector Police*. Durham, NC: Carolina Academic Press.

Naffine, N. (1987) *Female Crime: The Construction of Women in Criminology*. Chicago: Allen & Unwin.

National Archives and Records Administration (n.d.) "Biographical Sketch of Herbert Hoover." Retrieved August 8, 2008, from http://www.ecommcode.com/hoover/hooveronline/hoover_bio/comm.htm.

National Center for Education Statistics (2002) "Indicators of school crime and safety, 2002" (NCES 2003–9; NCJ 196753). Washington, D.C.: United States Department of Justice, Bureau of Justice Statistics.

National White Collar Crime Center (2008) *2007 Internet Crime Report*. Bureau of Justice Assistance, Federal Bureau of Investigation. Retrieved August 7, 2008, from http://www.nw3c.org/research/site_files.cfm?mode = r.

NBC News (2003) "ATM fraud: Banking on your money." December 11. Retrieved August 29, 2007, from http://www.msnbc.msn.com/id/3607110/.

Newman, D. J. (1958) "White-collar crime: An overview and analysis." *Law and Contemporary Problems*, 23: 737.

Nobel Foundation (n.d.) "Charles Gates Dawes." Retrieved August 8, 2008, from http://www.nobelpeacelaureates.org/pdf/Charles_Gates_Dawes.pdf.

O'Bryant, J. and Seghetti, L. (2002) "Crime control: The federal response." *Almanac of Policy Issues*. September 12. Retrieved August 11, 2008, from http://www.policyalmanac.org/crime/archive/crs_federal_crime_policy.shtml.

Office of Management and Budget (2002) "Memorandum for the heads of departments and agencies: Use of government purchase and travel cards (M-02-05)." Retrieved August 7, 2008, from http://www.whitehouse.gov/omb/memoranda/m02–05.html.

Padover, S. K. (2007) *Wilson's Ideals*. Whitefish, MT: Kessinger Publishing, LLC.

Patten, J. N. (2007) "Congressional ethics: The fox and the henhouse." *Politics & Policy*, 35(2): 192–220.

Patton, M. Q. (1996) *Utilization-Focused Evaluation: The New Century Text.* Thousand Oaks, CA: Sage Publications.

Peterson, M. (2003) "Assessing criminal organization through their management of profits." *IALEIA Journal*, 15(2): 126–44.

Peterson, M. B., Morehouse, B., and Wright, R. (eds.) (2000) *Intelligence 2000: Revising The Basic Elements*. Washington, D.C.: International Association of Law Enforcement Intelligence Analysts.

Petzinger Jr., T., Truell, P., and Abramson, J. (1991) Family ties. *The Wall Street Journal*, December 6, A1.

Plato. (1951) *The Republic*. (F. M. Cornford, trans). Oxford: Oxford University Press.

Plunkett Research, Ltd (n.d.) *Introduction to the E-Commerce internet industry.* Retrieved August 5, 2008, from http://www.plunkettresearch.com/Industries/ECommerceInternet/ECommerceInternetTrends/tabid/168/Default.aspx.

Pope, C. (2002) "White professes innocence at Enron; incredulous senators say his answers only raise more questions." *Seattle Post-Intelligencer*, July 19, p. 1. Retrieved August 7, 2008, from Lexis-Nexis database.

Potter, G. W. (2002) *Controversies in White-Collar Crime*. Cincinnati, OH: Anderson.

Press Trust of India (2008) "Defacement of Indian website on rise." *Business Standard*. April 27. Retrieved August 5, 2008, from http://www.business-standard.com/india/storypage.php?tp = on&autono = 36392.

Quinney, R. (1964) "The study of white collar crime: Toward a reorientation in theory and research." *Journal of Criminology, Criminal Law, and Police Science*, 55: 208–14.

Roosevelt, A. E. (1927) "Why Democrats favor Smith: as a practical idealist." *North American Review*, 224(4): 472–75.

Roosevelt, T. (1910) "The new nationalism." Speech presented in Osawatamie, Kansas. Retrieved August 8, 2008, from http://academic.regis.edu/jriley/414%20new_nationalism.htm.

Rosoff, S., Pontell, H., and Tillman, R. (2006) *Profit Without Honor: White Collar Crime and the Looting of America (4th Edition)*. Upper Saddle River, NJ: Prentice Hall.

Ross, W. S. (2001) "U.S. to use every resource to defeat global terror network, Bush says." September 20. *GlobalSecurity.org*. Retrieved August 10, 2008, from http://www.globalsecurity.org/military/library/news/2001/09/mil-010920-usia05.htm.

Sampson, P. J. (2003) "North Bergen waits for more shoes to drop; Corruption probes likely to expand." January 5. *The Record (Bergen County, NJ)*. Retrieved August 7, 2008, from Lexis-Nexis database.

Sarbanes-Oxley Summary (2003) "A guide to the Sarbanes-Oxley Act." Retrieved August 11, 2008 from http://www.soxlaw.com.

Schissel, M. J. (2000) "Replacing Medicaid." *Free Market Medicine*. Retrieved August 8, 2008, from http://www.marketmed.org/medicaid.asp?fmmfont = fontsml.

Schlegel, K. and Weisburd, D. (eds.) (1992) *White-Collar Crime Reconsidered* Boston, MA: Northeastern University Press.

Schultz, L. (2003) "Crime and intelligence analysis certification." *IALEIA Journal*, 15(2).

Serwer, A. (2000) "Guys you wouldn't want as your broker." *Fortune*, March 20, p. 1.

Shapiro, S. P. (1985) "The road not taken: The elusive path to criminal prosecution for white-collar offenders." *Law and Society Review*, 19: 179–217.

Shestack, J. J. (1998) "Foreword: The independent counsel act revisited." *Georgetown Law Journal*, 86(6): 2011–26.

Shover, N. and Wright, J. P. (eds) (2000) *Crimes of Privilege: Readings in White-Collar Crime*. New York: Oxford University Press.

Simon, D. R. and Hagan, F. E. (1998) *White-Collar Deviance*. Boston, MA: Allyn & Bacon.

Simon, D. R. (1996) *Elite Deviance*, 5th edn. Upper Saddle River, NJ: Allyn & Bacon.

——— (2002) *Tony Soprano's America*. Boulder, CO: Westview Press.

Sinclair, U. (1904) *The Jungle*. New York: Doubleday, Page & Co.

Sonderby, C. P. (2005) "Guilty plea in international software piracy and financial crime prosecution: Case involves extradition for intellectual property crimes." U.S. Department of Justice. Retrieved August 29, 2007, from http://www.usdoj.gov/criminal/cybercrime/vysochanskyyPlea.htm.

Sparrow, M. K. (1998) "Fraud control in the healthcare industry: Assessing the state of the art." *National Institute of Justice, Research in Brief*. December. Retrieved August 8, 2008, from http://www.ncjrs.gov/txtfiles1/172841.txt.

Strang, S. J. (2000) *Project SLEIPNIR: An analytical technique for operational priority setting*. Royal Canadian Mounted Police. Retrieved August 11, 2008, from https://analysis.mitre.org/proceedings/Final_Papers_Files/135_Camera_Ready_Paper.pdf.

Sutherland, E. H. (1940) "White-collar criminality." *American Sociological Review*, 5(1): 1–12.

——— (1944) " 'Is white-collar crime' crime?" *American Sociological Review*, 10(2): 132–9.

——— (1947) *Principles of Criminology*, 4th edn. Philadelphia, PA: J.B. Lippincott.

——— (1949) *White Collar Crime*. New York: Dryden Press.

——— (1983) *White Collar Crime: The Uncut Version*. New Haven, CT: Yale University Press.

Tanner, R. (2000) "Pa. lawmakers in trouble with law." *Associated Press Online*, April 2. Retrieved August 7, 2008, from Lexis-Nexis database.

Telecomworldwire (1999) "Lucent's Chinese anti-counterfeit operations successful." July 15Retrieved August 7, 2008, from http://findarticles.com/p/articles/mi_m0ECZ/is_1999_July_15/ai_55157739.

Terrell, S. (2001) "New Mexico congress members get wired." *Santa Fe New Mexican*, May 6, p. A1. Retrieved August 7, 2008, from Lexis-Nexis database.

The Inspectors General (n.d.) "What is the Inspector General's (IG) mission?" IGNet.gov. Retrieved August 8, 2008, from http://www.ignet.gov/igs/faq1.html

Toland, J. (2003) "Applying case-based reasoning to law enforcement." *IALEIA Journal*, 15(1): 106–25.

Tunnell, K. D. (2000) *Living Off Crime*, 2nd edn. Lahnam, MD: Rowman & Littlefield Publishers, Inc.

United States Code (n.d.) *Inspector General Act of 1978*. Retrieved August 8, 2008, from http://www.access.gpo.gov/uscode/title5a/5a_2_.html.

United States Constitution (1791) *Amendment IV*. Retrieved from http://www.law.cornell.edu/constitution/constitution.billofrights.html#ndmentiv

United States Department of Justice (1994) *A Guide to Equitable Sharing of Federally Forfeited Property for State and Local Law Enforcement Agencies*. March. Retrieved August 10, 2008, from http://www.usdoj.gov/criminal/afmls/publications/guidetoeq.pdf

—— (2001) "Bayer to pay $14 million to settle claims for causing providers to submit fraudulent claims to 45 state Medicaid programs." Retrieved August 8, 2008 from http://www.usdoj.gov/opa/pr/2001/January/039civ.htm

—— (2002) "U.S. Announces What Is Believed the Largest Identity Theft Case in American History; Losses Are in the Millions." November 25. Retrieved August 7, 2008, from http://www.usdoj.gov/criminal/cybercrime/cummingsIndict.htm

—— (n.d.a) *False claims act cases: Government intervention in qui tam (whistleblower) suits*. Retrieved August 8, 2008, from http://www.usdoj.gov/usao/pae/Documents/fcaprocess2.pdf.

—— (n.d.b) *Identity theft and identity fraud*. Retrieved August 5, 2008, from http://www.usdoj.gov/criminal/fraud/websites/idtheft.html.

——. (n.d.c) *The Al Qaeda Manual*. Retrieved August 3, 2008, from http://www.usdoj.gov/ag/manualpart1_1.pdf.

United States Drug Enforcement Administration (2003) *"Intelligence"*. Retrieved August 11, 2008, from http://www.usdoj.gov/dea/programs/intelligence.htm.

United States Food and Drug Administration (1981) "The long struggle for the 1906 law." Retrieved August 8, 2008, from http://www.foodsafety.gov/~lrd/history2.html.

United States General Accounting Office (2002) "Identity theft: Prevalence and cost appear to be growing," GA0-02-363, March. Washington, D.C.

United States Government Accountability Office (2007) "Securing, stabilizing, and rebuilding Iraq," (GAO-07-122OT). Retrieved August 8, 2008, from http://www.gao.gov/new.items/d071220t.pdf.

—— Office (n.d.) "Antideficiency Act background." Retrieved August 7, 2008, from http://www.gao.gov/ada/antideficiency.htm.

United States Government Printing Office (n.d.) *Code of Federal Regulations*. National Archives and Records Administration. Retrieved August 7, 2008, from http://edocket.access.gpo.gov/cfr_2002/janqtr/pdf/5cfr310.101.pdf.

United States Office of Personnel Management (2002) *About the Senior Executive*

Service. Retrieved August 8, 2008, from http://www.opm.gov/ses/about_ses/index.asp.

United States Office of Special Counsel (n.d.) *Introduction to the OSC*. Retrieved August 8, 2008, from http://www.osc.gov/intro.htm.

United States Postal Inspection Service (n.d.) "Mail fraud and misrepresentation." Title 18, United States Code (19 USC 1341). Retrieved August 10, 2008, from http://www.usps.com/websites/depart/inspect/usc18/mailfr.htm.

United States Public Interest Research Group (n.d.) "PIRG make Pplluters pay!" Retrieved January 22, 2006 from http://www.pirg.org/reports/enviro/super25/page3.htm.

United States Secret Service (n.d.a) *History of Counterfeiting*. Department of the United States Treasury. Retrieved August 6, 2008, from http://www.ustreas.gov/usss/counterfeit.shtml.

—— (n.d.b) "Know your money." Department of the United States Treasury. Retrieved August 6, 2008, from http://www.ustreas.gov/usss/know_your_money.shtml.

—— (n.d.c) "National threat assessment center: Exceptional case study project." Department of the United States Treasury. Retrieved August 10, 2008, from http://www.ustreas.gov/usss/ntac.shtml.

Vaughn, D. (1982a) "Towards understanding unlawful organizational behavior." *Michigan Law Review*, 80: 201–26.

—— (1982b) "Transaction systems and unlawful organizational behavior." *Social Problems*, 29: 372–9.

Veblen, T. ([1912] 1994) *The Theory of the Leisure Class: An Economic Study of Institutions*. London: Macmillan & Co., Ltd.

Vold, G. B., Bernard, T. J., and Snipes, J. B. (1998) *Theoretical Criminology*. New York: Oxford University Press.

Wall's Hacker and Cracker Links (n.d.) Retrieved August 5, 2008, from http://www.geocities.com/SiliconValley/Lab/7378/hacker2.htm

Waters, J. (2001) "Enron flees to bankruptcy protection." *CBS Market Watch*. December 2. Retrieved August 10, 2008, from http://www.marketwatch.com/News/Story/Story.aspx?guid=%7B722A8401–8577B-4264-B72D-5249111B2A58%7D&siteid=mktw.

Weisburd, D., Warin, E., and Chayet, E. (2001) *White-Collar Crime and Criminal Careers*. New York: Cambridge University Press.

Wells, J. T. (1992) *Fraud Examination: Investigative and Audit Procedures*. Westport, CT: Quorum Books.

Wells, J. T. (2004) "Small business, big losses." *Journal of Accountancy*, 198(6): 42–48.

West, D. J. (1967) *The Young Offender*. Madison, CT: International Universities Press.

White House (1996) "Executive order 12993: Administrative allegations against Inspectors General." Office of the Press Secretary. Retrieved August 9, 2008, from http://www.thecre.com/fedlaw/legal15/eo12993.htm.

—— (n.d.) *Warren G. Harding*. Retrieved August 8, 2008, from http://www.whitehouse.gov/history/presidents/wh29.html.

Winters, B.I. (2004) "Choose the right tools for internal control reporting." *Journal of Accountancy Online*. Retrieved August 11, 2008 from http://www.aicpa.org/pubs/jofa/feb2004/winters.htm.

Woolley, J. and Peters, G. (n.d.) "Herbert Hoover statement on emergency relief and construction legislation." The American Presidency Project. Retrieved August 8, 2008, from http://www.presidency.ucsb.edu/ws/print.php?pid = 23152.

Yang, D. W. (2004) "Mission Viejo teen guilty in Internet auction fraud; defendant also admits $400,000 bank fraud." March 1, U.S. Department of Justice. Retrieved August 26, 2007, from http://www.cybercrime.gov/bartiromoPlea.htm.

Zietz, D. (1981) *Women Who Embezzle or Defraud: A Study of Convicted Felons.* Westport, CT: Praeger Publishers.

Index